THE AMERICAN EXPERIMENT

VOLUME I: TO 1877

THE AMERICAN EXPERIMENT

A HISTORY OF THE UNITED STATES

Steven M. Gillon ★ **Cathy D. Matson**

University of Oklahoma *University of Delaware*

HOUGHTON MIFFLIN COMPANY ★ BOSTON NEW YORK

Editor-in-Chief: Jean Woy
Sponsoring Editor: Jeffrey Greene
Senior Development Editor: Jennifer E. Sutherland
Editorial Associate: Michael A. Kerns
Senior Project Editor: Rosemary R. Jaffe
Senior Production/Design Coordinator: Jill Haber
Senior Manufacturing Coordinator: Marie Barnes
Senior Marketing Manager: Sandra McGuire

Cover design: Martin Yeeles
Cover image: *Trial by Jury,* by A. Wighe, 1849. (Museum of Art, Rhode Island School of Design. Gift of Edith Jackson Green and Ellis Jackson. Photography by Erik Gould.)

Printed in the U.S.A.

Library of Congress Catalog Card Number: 00-133862

ISBN: 0-395-67752-1

2 3 4 5 6 7 8 9-DOC-05 04 03 02 01

Brief Contents

Contents

Maps and Graphs

Preface

America's written history began more than five hundred years ago with the encounters of Native Americans, Europeans, and Africans who struggled to bend nature to their needs and understand or overwhelm each other in countless ways. As this richly textured history unfolded, scholars also created many twists and turns in our understanding of this past. During the last quarter of the nineteenth century, historians in the United States emphasized the roles of political and intellectual leaders, elections and diplomacy, and national institutions. "History is past politics and politics are present history," declared Henry B. Adams, a founding member of the American Historical Association (AHA), in 1884.

Challenges to this perspective arose by the turn of the twentieth century, as when Carl Becker, in his own presidential address to the AHA, referred to "everyman" in the widest possible terms as "his own historian." But not until the 1960s did scholars pioneer fresh methods in writing a more democratic history. The "New History" emphasized telling history "from the bottom up;" it found "patterns of intimate personal behavior" that revealed the lives of people who had remained hidden from our understanding of the past. The New History represented a dramatic turn away from the traditional ways of representing our political and cultural past. It forced scholars to expand and deepen our understanding of what is political and what is cultural for far greater numbers of people over time.

Recent work in political and cultural history extends these boundaries even farther by seeking common ground between traditional approaches and the pathbreaking ones of the New History. This work expands the definitions of politics beyond the realm of elite actors and powerful institutions to include the far wider arenas of public and private culture, and it incorporates an appreciation of how race, class, and gender have shaped our past. Recent work also recognizes the need for synthesis in historical writing, but without neglecting the threads of individual experiences in the larger fabric of American history.

Approach

Drawing on the best of these new directions in political and cultural history, this book narrates the broad contours of change at the imperial or national level, and, at the same time, explains the lives of people in diverse communities who lived sometimes ordinary, sometimes extraordinary, lives. We believe that it is equally important to study how institutions emerged, rulers ruled, and economies developed, as it is to explain everyday work, family life, and different customs.

We have chosen the title, *The American Experiment,* to underscore our belief that North America's past can be best understood as an ongoing struggle of various competing ideals regarding individuals, communities, and nations. These ideals were contested and continually reshaped for almost two centuries in the crucibles of Native American villages, European settlements, and African-American communities. The American Revolution tested and extended these ideals during struggles for what was perceived to be liberty and equality. But in those years, as well as in the subsequent decades of the early republic, ideals coexisted uneasily with social realities. For most of their history, Americans have struggled to reconcile their broad belief in individual liberty and equality with the reality of racism, class conflict, and gender inequality. This book uses the prism of politics and culture to explore this unfolding American experiment.

Themes

This book's four central themes highlight these ideals and realities on many levels. The first theme focuses on competing views of the proper role of government. For generations, colonists, then independent Americans, debated just what degree of control a central government should have over their everyday lives, what kinds of powers should be given to the government, and what kinds of leaders should rule. But when scholars recount this story, too often they focus primarily on charting the growth in the size and scope of the national government and the achievements of its political and intellectual leaders. This kind of narrative cannot fully explain the dynamics of American politics. We believe that American politics has been characterized by competing views of the proper role of government, including but not limited to the persistence of conservative attitudes about limited government, self-help, and individualism in the face of the growth of national government.

A second theme addresses issues of identity. What qualities do Americans believe define them best? The answers, we believe, change over time. Our history has been defined by the shifting struggles among ethnic, religious, regional, class, and racial groups to shape both a multiplicity of particular identities and a sequence of unifying images about being "American." Being "colonists" suggested to thousands of settlers that they were politically subordinate, as well as culturally and economically dependent, on the imperial center. But settlers often paid more attention to religious backgrounds, local social status, or their identity as residents of one locale. Post-Revolutionary Americans embarked on an intense struggle to make—or make over—their identity. They often spoke and wrote about "the nation," but the term meant different things to different parts of the population. For most of our history, American identity has been defined in racial terms, as African-Americans underwent the unsettling transformations of slavery, fought for emancipation, and later demanded the rights of citizenship. But especially in recent years, it has included the attempts of other disenfranchised groups—Hispanics, Asians, women, and homosexuals—to challenge the dominant structure and force a reluctant acceptance of their unique identities and their contributions to American society.

Third, the book explores the evolution of culture, both national mass culture and the variety of regional, ethnic, religious, and racial subcultures. From the start, colonists sometimes willingly, sometimes unwittingly blended characteristics of European and African cultures with the Indian cultures and natural environments in which they settled. Long before the American Revolution, the continent's amazingly heterogeneous population was undergoing rapid changes, continually negotiating accommodation of its internal cultural differences, and sometimes facing bloody conflicts over them. By the beginning of the twentieth century, new instruments of mass culture produced intense conflict between local cultures and a dominant national culture. Through this cultural evolution, we ask, has a distinctive *American* culture emerged? If so, when and how? If not, how shall we understand a plurality of cultures under the umbrella of a nation called America?

Finally, our book examines America's ambivalent attitude toward the outside world. Enormous changes in the structure of relations among world nations have occurred as we evolved from a knot of English colonies into a world superpower. But as with our attitude toward government and our resistance to cultural change, Americans have not completely abandoned the isolationist streak that has been so much a part of our past. Indeed, even during the period of America's rise to world power, our leaders were driven more by a desire to remake the world in our image than by a need to join the international community of nations. In the pages that follow, we have asked how Americans explained their place in this world of nations at various turning points in their own national evolution.

Features

The focus on themes and the use of "experiment" as a motif for understanding the American past structure our narrative and give students an organizing framework. We make the narrative accessible to students with generous use of revealing quotes and anecdotes. The book also contains a number of special features to enhance the narrative and to reinforce the themes.

Each chapter begins with a colorful vignette that highlights one or more of its central themes and provides focus questions to guide reading of its chapter. In addition to a chronology and a brief conclusion, every chapter contains a primary-source feature, "Competing Voices." This feature provides students with the opportunity to examine primary sources. It includes two sources that represent differing viewpoints about a common issue along with headnotes that place the sources in context for the student. Students are introduced to the tools of working historians and the enduring evidence of ongoing tensions in American life.

Study and Teaching Aids

The American Experiment is supported by an extensive supplements package including print, online, and CD-ROM resources.

@history, Houghton Mifflin's CD-ROM that features nearly one thousand primary sources, including video, audio, illustrations, and text, is available in a version specifically keyed to the chapters in *The American Experiment.* Available in

both instructor and student versions, *@history* is an interactive multimedia tool that can improve the analytical skills of students and introduce them to historical sources.

GeoQuest: United States is a CD-ROM designed to improve students' geographical literacy. The program consists of thirty interactive historical maps, each of which provides background information and a series of self-correcting quizzes so that students can master the information on their own.

The American Experiment web site has resources for both instructors and students. The instructor site includes the online *Instructor's Resource Manual*, primary sources with teaching hints, full-color maps, outline maps, and annotated links to other history sites. The student site includes ACE practice tests, primary sources, an annotated guide to the top historical research web sites, and research activities that can be used by instructors for assignments.

The online *Study Guide*, prepared by D. Antonio Cantu of Ball State University, includes learning objectives, chapter outlines with web links, identification terms, journal questions with Internet links, ACE practice tests, a multimedia scrapbook (an electronic exhibit of multimedia primary and secondary sources), and map activities. This *Study Guide* is free to students and may be found at www.college.hmco.com/history.

An online *Instructor's Resource Manual*, written by J. Kent McGaughy of Houston Community College–Northwest, is downloadable from Houghton Mifflin's U.S. history web site. It contains learning objectives, chapter summaries, chapter outlines, lecture strategies, topics for class discussion, historical perspectives, comparative chronologies, and map activities.

A printed *Test Bank*, also prepared by D. Antonio Cantu, provides over 1,200 multiple choice questions, and over 200 essay questions. These questions are also available in a *Computerized Test Bank* for both Windows and Macintosh platforms.

A set of *American History Map Transparencies* is also available to instructors upon adoption of the text.

Acknowledgments

At Houghton Mifflin, we would like to thank Sean Wakely and Beth Welch who skillfully guided the book through its early years, and Jan Fitter and Jennifer Sutherland who led us across the finish line. Most of all, we want to thank Jeff Greene, a patient but demanding editor who lifted our spirits at a difficult time, and Jean Woy who supervised the project from beginning to end. Finally, we appreciate all the hard work of Rosemary Jaffe, senior project editor; Jill Haber, senior production/design coordinator; Michael Kerns, editorial associate; Charlotte Miller, art editor; Pembroke Herbert and Sandi Rygiel, photo researchers; Cia Boynton, designer; Kathryn Daniel, copyeditor; Mary Dalton Hoffman, permissions editor; and Marie Barnes, senior manufacturing coordinator, who pulled it all together.

Steve Gillon also thanks his research assistants, Holly Furr and Heather Clemmer for all their help.

Writing a new textbook for U.S. history is an enormous task and one that couldn't have been done without the invaluable help of our colleagues who reviewed the manuscript at every stage. We thank

Kathryn Abbott, *Western Kentucky University*

Timothy Allen, *Trocaire College*

Michael Barnhart, *SUNY, Stony Brook*

Lori Bogle, *University of Arkansas*

Kevin Boyle, *University of Massachusetts, Amherst*

John Buenker, *University of Wisconsin, Parkside*

William Byrd, *Chattahoochee Valley Community College*

D. Antonio Cantu, *Ball State University*

William Cario, *Concordia University, Wisconsin*

Victor Chen, *Chabot College*

Peter Coclanis, *University of North Carolina, Chapel Hill*

Bill Corbett, *Northeastern State University*

Dallas Cothrum, *University of Texas, Tyler*

Robert Cottrell, *California State University at Chico*

Bruce Dierenfield, *Canisius College*

William Dionisio, *Sacramento City College*

Richard Ellis, *SUNY, Buffalo*

James Farmer, *University of South Carolina, Aiken*

Mark Fernandez, *Loyola University of Louisiana*

Mark Grandstaff, *Brigham Young University*

L. Edward Hicks, *Faulkner University*

Christopher Kimball, *Augsburg College*

Kenneth L. Kitchen, *Trident Technological College*

Kevin Kragenbrink, *California State University, San Bernardino*

Alan Lehmann, *Blinn College*

Kenneth Marcus, *California State Polytechnic University at Pomona*

Robert Mathis, *Stephen F. Austin State University*

Carl Moneyhon, *University of Arkansas, Little Rock*

Benjamin Newcomb, *Texas Tech University*

Sherry Smith, *University of Texas, El Paso*

June Sochen, *Northeastern Illinois University*

David Stebenne, *The Ohio State University*

Richard Straw, *Radford University*

Tyrone Tillery, *University of Houston*

William Wagnon, *Washburn University*

Patricia Wallace, *Baylor University*

James Woods, *Georgia Southern University*

Steven M. Gillon
Cathy D. Matson

THE AMERICAN EXPERIMENT

1

Out of Old Worlds, New Worlds

"The earth," according to the Cherokee myth of creation, "is a great island floating in a sea of water, and suspended at each of the four [main compass] points by a cord hanging down from the sky vault, which is of solid rock." The earth's creation began when little Water Beetle, tired of being crowded in the sky with all the other animals, dove below the water to find a new place to live. Water Beetle "came up with some soft mud, which began to grow and spread on every side until it became the island which we call the earth." As the mud was drying, Great Buzzard flew about, and "wherever his wings struck the earth there was a valley, and where they turned up again there was a mountain." And so the Cherokee country was full of mountains and valleys.

Eventually other animals arrived, carried by the streams that flowed out of the mountains, and they commanded a sun to cross the sky each day. The animals were divided according to their needs and abilities, and "plants and people were made, we do not know by whom." "At first there were only a brother and sister until he struck her with a fish and told her to multiply, and so it was. In seven days a child was born to her, and thereafter every seven days another, and they increased very fast until there was danger that the world could not keep them. Then it was made that a woman should have only one child in a year, and it has been so ever since." But all Cherokee know, and fear, that "when the world grows old and worn out, the people will die and the cords will break and let the earth sink down into the ocean, and all will be water again." The Cherokee were afraid of this.

People everywhere tell stories to explain their origins. Sometimes the stories seem fantastical or heretical. Often, as in the Cherokee myth of creation, certain themes sound familiar to listeners or readers because different cultures share certain views of the world. Most of these myths are not historical accounts of migrations, lives of kings, or daily affairs. But they are more than mere fictions intended to entertain people, for each myth contains core beliefs and values of the people who create it. Over the centuries the Cherokee retold and reshaped the details of their creation myth, putting in order the component parts of the world and giving words to physical and psychological phenomena as they understood them. The evolving myth gave names and causes to what they experienced in their everyday lives and collective expression to what each person might imagine as his or her reason for existence.

For centuries before roughly A.D. 1400, the Western Hemisphere was populated by hundreds of different Native American cultures. Their myths of creation varied from one region to another, just as their environments, family lives, religions, and political structures also varied. But incredible transformations—political, social, economic, and cultural—were taking place in Europe and Africa at that time, too, that would put these populations on a collision course. Soon many North American Indians would experience the arrival of Europeans and Africans, whose cultures thrust additional distinctions into the mix.

African slaves who were forcibly introduced into North America brought new ways of farming and cooking, new family and religious traditions, and much more that set them apart from Indians. Europeans experienced even sharper cultural contrasts with North American Indians. Frequently, they dismissed Indian myths as fireside stories or, worse, the false legends of "uncivilized savages." Europeans tended to hold the rise of printing and books in privileged esteem, even though very few Europeans were themselves literate at the time they came to the Americas, and strong oral traditions still prevailed on every continent. In addition, the early Spanish, French, English, and Dutch colonizers found remarkable, and sometimes objectionable, contrasts among African, Indian, and European values and customs. Not only did most Indians not share the Biblical narration of creation, they also cared little for European Christian values. Furthermore, Europeans readily noted the natives' peculiar ways of working, structuring families, reckoning property, telling time, recognizing political authority, and many other cultural givens. Africans brought to North America were also placed (usually at the bottom) in this cultural and political hierarchy that Europeans developed in their minds, laws, and social behavior. Differences in appearance and behavior quickly became a basis for social and legal distinctions governing use of the land and its resources. The juncture in history of these cultures—indigenous American, African, and European—could be nothing other than transformative for all three.

- What were the cultural backgrounds and historical experiences of the many different peoples who lived in the Americas and who came from other continents to this part of the world?

Chronology

30,000–10,000 B.C.	Ancient peoples cross Beringia
7000 B.C.	Cultivation of crops begins in the Mexican plains
3000–2000 B.C.	Cultivation of crops begins north of the Rio Grande
1000 B.C.–A.D. 500	Adena and Hopewell societies flourish in the Ohio Valley
500–1200	Anasazi flourish in southwest North America
600–1600	Rise of West African states
1000	Pueblo culture emerges in the Southwest
	Vikings reach North America
1400–1500	Maturing of the African kingdoms of Ghana, Mali, and Songhai
1420s	Portuguese explore west coast of Africa
1450	Iroquois form the Great League of Peace
1492	Columbus reaches the Caribbean
	Spain expels Moors and Jews
1515–1521	Spanish explore Florida
	Cortés conquers Aztecs
	Epidemics of smallpox ravage Caribbean and South American Indians
1517	Protestant Reformation begins
1533	Pizarro conquers the Inca
1534–1542	Cartier, De Soto, and Coronado explore areas of North America

- How did their first contacts affect these peoples from fundamentally different cultures? In what ways did they cooperate, and in what ways did they clash?
- What was the role of each culture in the destructive wars and devastating diseases that altered life for everyone? How did varieties of Indians, Europeans, and Africans share aspects of their cultures and blend their backgrounds into new cultures?

This chapter will address these questions.

The First Americans, to 1500

Indian creation myths often asserted that their particular people *always* lived in North America. Some myths also privileged one language group or tribe over its surrounding environment or elevated one group to a higher level of cultural accomplishment than neighboring groups. Scholars can show, however, that such claims could not have been true. Long migrations and numerous environmental adaptations marked the earliest known rising civilizations. Over centuries, hundreds of Indian cultures and languages developed (see map). A handful of great civilizations emerged and dominated different regions in the Western Hemisphere long before European and African presence.

Earliest North Americans

Migrations of people from other parts of the world into the Western Hemisphere probably began about 30,000 years ago. Many of the earliest migrants to North and South America shared their ancestry with Asians, and probably crossed a land bridge at the Bering Strait—also called Beringia—during the final Ice Age, which lasted from about 50,000 years ago until about 10,000 years ago. Enduring bitter cold, the earliest migrants into North America probably came in small hunting groups that followed large mammals such as the mastodon, bison, woolly rhinoceros, and a kind of antelope over long distances. Small hunter-gather bands of Paleo-Indians thrived on these animals as rich sources of meat for sustenance, dung for fuel, and bones for tools. Their populations grew rapidly and, by about 12,500 years ago, had spread overland from Montana to the southern tip of South America, called Tierra del Fuego, and throughout the eastern and southeastern portions of North America.

Another stream of migrants lived not on large animals as hunters, but rather on fish and small plants along the Pacific coastline of both continents. Ancient sites from about 12,000 years ago in Chile and Peru predate most of the earliest North American hunters, showing a possible second source of migration from some other part of the world than across Beringia. These South American populations were probably established by peoples who were semisedentary, or settled in camps only part of the year, and who migrated northward along the coast of South America from the southern tip of the continent.

Then about 10,000 years ago, the hemispheric climate warmed, and the large animals either became extinct or drifted far from human populations. In North America, Indian ancestors were forced to hunt smaller and scarcer supplies of game, and harsher conditions resulted in a decline in their numbers. Over time, dispersed populations adapted their societies to the deserts of the Great Basin, or turned to the resources of the forests around the Great Lakes, or pressed south and southeast to woodlands and plateaus.

As they became more sedentary, or more settled in semipermanent villages, these ancestors of modern Indians also began to cultivate certain plants. In central Mexico, the most important innovation was the cultivation of maize, or corn, along with beans, squash, sunflowers, and herbal grasses. The requirements of attending to these crops, and their abundant yields, stimulated a more highly organized polit-

North American Culture Areas Before European Contact This map shows both the large regions of Native American populations across the continent and names many of the cultures living within those regions in about 1500. In all, there were as many as 800 language groups in North America at that time.

ical system and village culture, which permitted populations to grow in size and complexity beginning about 3,000 to 2,500 years ago. From place to place, gender divisions of labor became more clearly differentiated, with men and women performing more specialized and defined tasks. They developed political systems that elevated some community members to positions of leisure or prestige. By about 500 B.C., several regions showed significant distinctions between powerful centers of population and the tributary villages surrounding them.

North American Cultures

We can understand aspects of long dispersed or dead Native American peoples, not only from the knowledge locked in their myths, but also from their stone tools and carvings, architectural remains, fragments of textiles, shards of pottery, and their alterations to the land itself. Assembling this archaeological evidence has not given us a complete portrait of the Western Hemisphere over time, but it does allow us to reconstruct snapshots of a remarkably diverse number of peoples, whose many cultures and systems of government underwent constant changes well before a European presence overwhelmed them. Estimates of Indian population vary widely, mainly because scholars will never be able to judge accurately how many people could be supported in ancient ecosystems and technologies. But many agree that by about 1450, or shortly before the first European wave, as many as 80 to 100 million people could have been living in the Western Hemisphere (compared with about 70 million people in Europe at that time); between 4 and 10 million lived north of the Rio Grande, the river that today forms part of the border between Texas and Mexico. Up to 25 million lived in the complex societies of Mexico and Peru. Between six and eight hundred different languages were spoken throughout the Americas (see map), pointing to more extensive cultural diversity than Europeans had ever experienced or could anticipate. Remarkably diverse cultural groups arose in different North American regions.

The eastern interior regions around the Ohio and Mississippi Rivers supported great peoples known as the Woodland cultures. From at least three thousand years ago, hunting and gathering peoples began cultivating certain crops—tobacco and maize among them—along with their regular foraging activities. Along the upper banks of the Ohio River, the Adena culture flourished until at least the second century A.D. The Adena were probably the first of the sedentary and complex societies of mound builders in North America, named for the great burial mounds that survive as a testament to this society's sophisticated organization of labor and hierarchical culture.

As Adena reached its peak and then began to decline, the Hopewell culture rose throughout the Mississippi–Ohio Valley, where its people also built enormous mounds presumably for burials and other ceremonies. Artifacts discovered in and near the mounds suggest a trade network that brought these mound builders into contact with peoples far away in the Rocky Mountains, along the Gulf and Atlantic coastlines, and around Lake Superior in the first centuries A.D.

Some time later, between 950 and 1400 A.D., another mound-building culture arose along the Mississippi River near present-day St. Louis, Missouri. The main center of this culture, Cahokia, supported an urban center of perhaps forty thousand people, more than any North American city contained until well after the American Revolution. Such density of population was probably possible because these early Indians adopted prolific varieties of maize from sedentary populations to their south, used relatively sturdy planting tools such as the flint hoe, developed a vast trade network, and subjugated subsidiary peoples. It is possible that Cahokia served as a ceremonial and distribution center for population sites around it and that a centralized political authority emerged by sustained warfare over generations. Certainly Cahokia supported pottery, metalworking, and tool making. At its center stood a ceremonial earthen temple that rose nearly one hundred feet high and covered a base of about fifteen acres, from the heights of which a commanding elite could issue decrees and receive tribute. Cahokia collapsed suddenly in the early 1400s, perhaps because its concentrated population strained available natural and cultivated resources. It is also possible that diseases introduced by European explorers who landed briefly on shorelines hundreds of miles away had devastating effects far to the interior of the continent where Cahokia lay. To the south of Cahokia, the Natchez people preserved Mississippian culture for many more generations.

In the semiarid southwest of North America, the Hohokam, the Anasazi, and the Pueblo cultures also attained great complexity. The Hohokam (of present-day Arizona) built hundreds of miles of irrigation canals before 100 A.D., which enabled them to produce two yields of grains and cotton a year. They cultivated crops with hoes, and their use of combs and looms allowed them to wear woven cotton clothing instead of animal skins, as many Indians of forested areas did. Their intricately designed pottery was traded extensively deep into the central plains of Mexico.

The Anasazi of the Chaco Canyon in New Mexico built spacious apartments and recessed religious meeting halls, and developed seasonal calendars, sophisticated pottery, roadways, and extensive irrigation systems. Overcome by extensive drought and the onslaught of enemy peoples, the Anasazi were reduced greatly in number during the late 1200s. During the 1300s, Athapaskans, seminomadic migrants from much colder climates to the north, began to raid the farmlands of Anasazi and forced them to flee south.

The Pueblo, descended from the Anasazi in subsequent centuries, settled along the Rio Grande in present-day New Mexico. Theirs was a rich culture of several languages, elaborate matrilineal clans, and religious societies. Pueblo agricultural techniques permitted the cultivation of plentiful crops in extremely arid conditions.

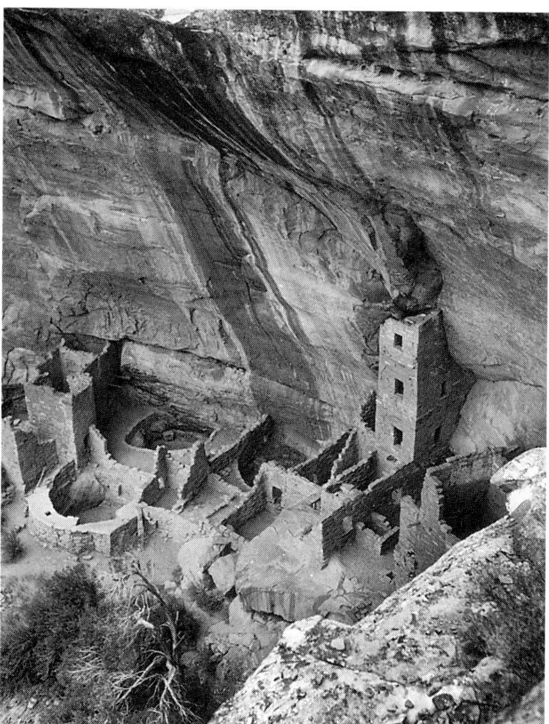

Cliff Palace, Mesa Verde
The Anasazi constructed elaborate communities in the faces of dramatically steep mountainsides in the Southwest. Cliff Palace, in modern-day Arizona, had over 220 rooms and 23 ceremonial kivas. *(Photo Researchers. Photo by Werner Foreman.)*

They were living in over fifty large settlements when the Spanish came to that area in the 1500s. Some of the Pueblo towns contain the oldest continuously used dwellings in America. These "cliff dwellers" also built underground chambers called kivas for men's political and religious meetings. Some Athapaskan people gradually settled down around the Pueblo towns and turned to the farming methods Pueblos taught them. These became known as the Navajo.

Far to the east, descendants of the Adena–Hopewell peoples settled in the temperate and relatively wet climates stretching from the Great Lakes and Appalachian Mountains to the Atlantic coastline. Mainly comprised of small villages, clustered as tribes, and based on shared kinship, rising cultures extended from today's Florida through New England, across the southern piedmont and tidewater regions, and up into the valleys of the Hudson and Connecticut Rivers.

After the 1300s, the Chesapeake region proved to be hospitable for migrating Algonquian peoples, and by the late 1500s, about twenty thousand had settled in the area. Many of them formed a confederacy under the powerful leader, Powhatan. Toward the interior, the confederacies of Creek, Catawba, Choctaw, Chickasaw, and Cherokee also took shape. These Eastern Woodland cultures were very different from the highly structured and centralized peoples of the Southwest and Ohio Valley. Eastern peoples shared a combination of clan-based kinship lineage and villages sustained by pragmatic concerns about work, defense, integrating captives, and marriage alliances. They changed leaders frequently and allowed tribal members widespread participation in decision making. They also had minimal bureaucracies, little specialization of jobs and services, and frequent travel and game playing among clans.

The agriculture of these southeastern cultures would amaze Europeans. Although they were settled in villages most of the time, they did not till the soil in ways familiar to Europeans. Having chosen a section of forest to cultivate, young Indian men and women burned off the underbrush, and then mixed the ashes with decaying leaves to make a rich soil for planting. Often men and women also "girdled" trees by slashing off a swath of bark and wood around the circumference of the trunk; in subsequent seasons, the tree trunks remained standing but in the absence of shady leaf cover, Indians cultivated plants in the nutritious forest soil. Eastern peoples also kept their soil rich in nutrients, and increased their crop yields, by interplanting crops of maize and beans together. Sometimes they added dead fish to the soil as fertilizer. All of these practices were startlingly new to Europeans.

Native Americans of the eastern coastal plain rarely wasted any products that could be derived from trees. Houses were made of sapling poles, covered with layers of bark or leafy branches. Skilled Indian craftsmen devised needles for sewing clothing and household goods, eating utensils and bowls, weapons, baskets, even boats. In 1590 the English artist-turned-explorer Thomas Harriot would remark of the Algonquian in the southeastern woodlands, "the manner of makinge their boates . . . is verye wonderfull. For whereas they want [i.e., lack] Instruments of yron, yet they knowe howe to make them as handsomlye . . . as ours." Indeed, Native American cultures did not mine mineral ores such as copper, tin, lead, and iron—which might have led to the production of kettles, knives, axes, and plows.

Europeans frequently identified this shortcoming as the source of Native American inferiority. However, what Europeans presumed to be "advances," or evidence of their own superiority, also had at least one critical advantage for Native American cultures: by not mining ores, it had not become necessary to devastate their forests for fuel to run forges and mills, or to change the contours of the land to extract ores, or to reorganize their families and villages to provide labor for dramatically different kinds of labor in metal work. Native American alterations of the landscape were of a slower pace and a different quality than in the European experience.

Along the eastern coastline and north of the St. Lawrence River, Algonquian-speaking peoples of over fifty different cultures formed semisedentary or nomadic bands that hunted and fished on seasonal territories. The Cree, Micmac, Chippewa, Montagnais, and others of northerly climates remained thinly populated and spread out over expansive hunting grounds. A chain of Algonquian-speaking peoples also inhabited virtually the entire Atlantic coastline, where they adopted agriculture in their seasonal productive cycles; the hoe and fishing spear became important tools for the Narragansett, Pequot, Delaware, and others.

Between these two Algonquian-speaking regions lay the territory of the other large language group of the Northeast, the Iroquoian-speaking peoples who had settled into sedentary cultivation beginning about 4,500 years previously. As elsewhere in the Western Hemisphere, success in growing corn, beans, and other edible plants led to rapid population growth. So dense were the various Iroquois settlements by the 1400s that fifty to sixty "longhouses," often sheltering dozens of families each, spread out along the rivers of present-day western New York. By the 1570s, the five great "nations" of the Iroquois centered in what would become western New York—the Mohawk, Onondaga, Oneida, Cayuga, and Seneca—created a confederacy called the "Great League of Peace" for commercial and religious reasons, and probably to subdue enemy tribes around them. According to legend, the great orator Hiawatha carried the invitation to join the League from village to village, promising that even as all five nations claimed common descent from the same maternal line and spoke the same Iroquoian language, each nation could also continue to enjoy its separate clan identity. Their goal, professed Hiawatha, was peace within the League and unified war against enemies such as the Erie and Huron.

Mesoamerican and South American Cultures

In Mesoamerica and South America, a variety of cultures of varying sophistication—including the Olmec, Maya, Toltec, Aztec, Inca, and others—combined under powerful leaders. Unlike in North America, bands of hunter-gatherers (seminomadic groups who combined hunting and agriculture) and sedentary peoples organized into chiefdoms tended to come under the domination of imperial heads of elaborate state societies that grew into mighty empires. As in North America, the cultivation of new food crops supported much larger populations, which in turn required more complicated social structures. By about 2000 B.C., great temples and pyramids, bureaucracies dedicated to sustaining both living rulers and demanding gods, and religious castes that enjoyed tremendous luxury existed in Mesoamerica.

Each successive rising empire developed vast processing and craft enterprises that made tools, textiles, pottery, and weapons. And in order to sustain such unparalleled prosperity and extend their societies, each empire engaged in diplomacy and waged regular warfare that brought great areas of the countryside under centralized urban control in order to feed thousands of people at a time.

The primary culture in central Mexico to attain such cultural sophistication was the Olmec people, who settled a dense population on the highlands of what would become Mexico City between 1000 B.C. and about A.D. 650. The powerful Olmec religious and political elite dominated the production of thousands of weavers, stone masons, potters, and other craftsmen, and they gathered tribute from a great trading region that extended across the dry lands to the north into present-day Arizona. The majestic Pyramids of the Sun and the Moon stand even today as evidence of the masses of laborers subjugated by the Olmec Empire for temple building.

Around 900 A.D., the Toltec swept down from present-day Mexico City to conquer regions around the central places of Monte Albán and Teotihuacán—which may have grown to over 250,000 by then—and to overwhelm the Maya people of the Yucatan peninsula. Since about 300 A.D., the Maya had enjoyed a sophisticated agricultural culture, which supported a leisured class, jewelry of gold and silver, hieroglyphic writing, a mathematical system with the number zero, and calendars more accurate than anything Europeans would know for centuries.

Then, around 1200 A.D., the Toltec mysteriously retreated from the edges of their empire and drew in around the central highlands. Over the next century, the Aztec people migrated into this area from drier northern climes, consolidating their control over central Mexico. By 1325, they had founded Tenochtitlán (now Mexico City). By the time the Spanish approached this capital city in 1519, its population was about 300,000, making it one of the largest concentrations of people in the world. (London contained only 75,000 people in 1500.) Tenochtitlán supported thousands of craftsmen engaged in producing both necessary and luxury goods. Massive pyramids to the sun and moon gods stood at the center of the metropolis; there, high priests regularly sacrificed captives of war and virgins to their sun god. They constructed wide and deep causeways from outlying regions into the heart of the city, which carried resources and tribute from conquered peoples in outlying regions. An irrigation system brought fresh drinking water to the city; skilled craftsmen and important bureaucrats filled the streets, and everywhere markets filled with foods and household wares provisioned townspeople and traders. The Aztec rulers had subjugated well over 5 million people, from whom they collected not only agricultural tribute but also unfortunate captives who were regularly offered in sacrifice to the sun god, Huitzilopochtli, at bloody public rituals.

Stretching along the Andes Mountains in present-day Peru, another agricultural culture flourished between 900 and 200 B.C. At amazing heights of over ten thousand feet, Andean peoples irrigated their rich soil and produced yields of potatoes that the most modern farming techniques cannot match. Like the Aztecs, this Chavín mountain culture built great temples and developed a sophisticated bureaucracy until a prolonged drought decimated them around 300 A.D. In the next centuries, two new

The Great Temple at Tenochtitlán At the height of Aztec-Toltec civilization in central Mexico, which coincided with the arrival of Cortés and his Spanish soldiers in 1519, this capital city—built on marshy lowlands and linked to the mainland by broad causeways—had a dense population of over 300,000, more than any European city. Its great public works and Pyramids to the Sun and Moon were connected by an elaborate irrigation system. From this metropolis, priests, warriors, and rulers held absolute authority over hundreds of thousands of people in the countryside. *(American Museum of Natural History #32659.)*

empires arose in Peru: the Mochicans of the north developed fine pottery and fabulous pyramids, and the Tiwanaku farther to the south adapted crops such as cotton, potatoes, and the ever-present maize to elaborate terracing and irrigation systems. Both cultures, however, failed to survive the return of drought conditions.

Between roughly 1200 and 1400 A.D., the Inca (Quechua) peoples rose out of many warring farm populations to take control of the southern Andean highlands. In an epic battle in 1438, a young warrior leader who took the name Pachakuti subdued enemies to the north and reorganized the surrounding dense population into a centralized state. In their myth of creation, Andean peoples explained that their ancestors had come from nature and, upon death, had returned to the rocks, lakes, and trees. It was fitting, then, to honor and respect the land with many rituals, to take from nature only what was necessary. At the same time, Inca rulers aggressively extended the empire's influence over two thousand miles to the north and south of their Peruvian capital, Cuzco, a city of 250,000 people by the end of the 1400s. The trained warrior class was even fiercer than that of the Aztec, and a refined system of roads communicated edicts and routed massive tribute of grain from far-flung peoples. Imperial leaders also drove their subjects relentlessly to mine silver and gold in tremendous quantities. Whereas North Americans had no large domesticated animals, the Andean people used the llama extensively for heavy hauling, their wool for textile production, their dung for fuel, and their meat for protein. Neither the Aztec nor the Inca used wheels, but an elaborate accounting system that used knotted colored cords, or *quipu,* aided Inca couriers who spread news throughout the great expanse of the empire. By 1500 A.D., the Inca Empire embraced between 8 and 12 million people.

Old World Peoples in Africa and Europe, 1400–1600

Across the Atlantic Ocean, other diverse societies developed on the west coast of Africa and in western Europe from roughly 500 B.C. to A.D. 1500. As Native American societies in the Western Hemisphere became dense and complicated settlements, many African cultures likewise rose to powerful stature or fell to the domination of neighboring peoples. African systems of hunting, fishing, and agriculture became highly productive by the time of the Inca Empire in the 1400s, and the population of sub-Saharan Africa reached as many as 20 million by then. Many African nations interacted with Muslim Arab traders crossing the Sahara, and soon West African peoples would also encounter Portuguese captains landing along the Ivory and Gold Coasts from yet another rapidly changing region of the world.

West African Cultures and Kingdoms

West Africa was peopled by many cultures speaking many languages, linked by various kinship structures, and following assorted economic systems. But from Cape Verde to Angola, most groups shared a few fundamental qualities (see map). Before 3000 B.C., people of the savanna, an open grassland straddling the equator between the Sahara Desert and the tropical rainforest, developed productive agricultural and herding practices that changed very little until the modern era. Rice, millet, sorghum, root crops, and various vegetables were grown by the same slash-and-burn technique used by North American coastal Indians. After clearing the land by burning away the brush, men and women worked the ash into the ground, cultivated small fields until they depleted the land of its nutrients, and then moved on to clear new lands.

Extended families were the basic source of individual and community identity for most West African societies. Families were often matrilineal, or structured along the female kinship line, so that property and political authority over others descended through a person's mother and aunts. Most West African cultures also based important decisions on complex family relationships: what crops to produce, how to distribute goods and services, and how to punish lawbreakers. Most of these cultures also believed, as North American Indians did, that spirits dwelt in all of nature, that a transcendent continuity linked human beings with the natural environment , and that ancestors of the living regularly intervened in worldly affairs. Consequently, a woman should cultivate the soil with respect and a man thank a hunted beast for the meat and hide it provided a village. Doing so honored departed ancestors and invited their guardianship of the harvest and hunt. Like some advancing societies on every continent at that time, certain African peoples organized themselves hierarchically, conferring different rights and obligations on individuals of different stature and at times creating mighty states.

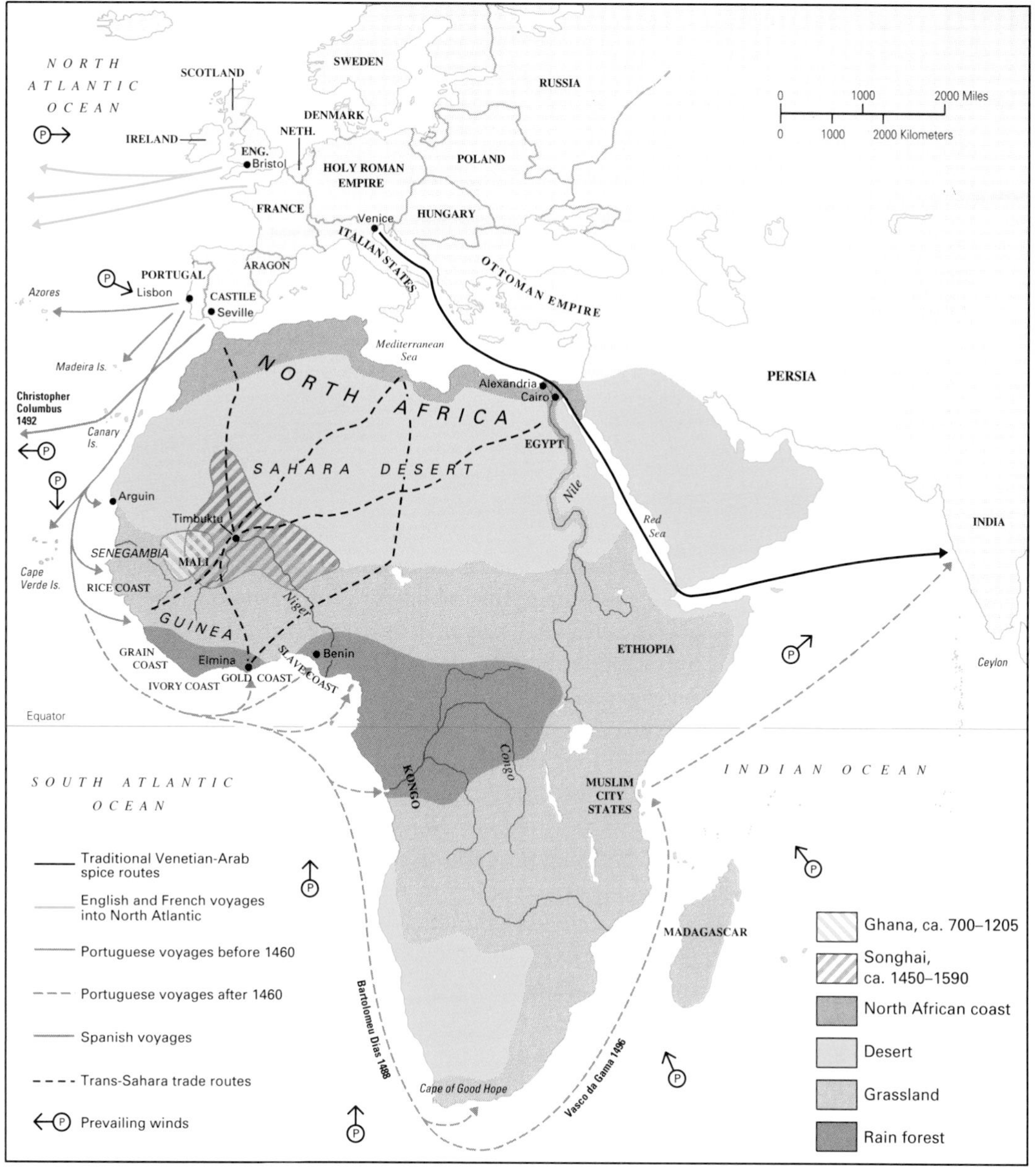

Africa in 1500 The great nation-states of Songhai and Ghana covered much of the western African territory soon to be in regular contact with European traders and slavers. Many cultures of western Africa were already familiar with the slave trade to their own interiors; after 1500 Europeans would also discover that the area was rich in resources.

From the sixth to the eleventh centuries, the powerful kingdom of Ghana developed on these agricultural and kinship foundations. Spanning the Sahara, to the Gulf of Guinea and the Atlantic Ocean, to the Niger River of the interior, Ghanaian rulers orchestrated the building of trading towns, training of skilled craftsmen, and caravan trading with far-flung Arab peoples. Ghanaians extended their influence over neighboring peoples by developing superior pottery and household crafts, iron tools, trade in salt and gold, and hierarchical social structures marked by tribute-gathering elites and great armies.

Invading northern African peoples, primarily Muslims, defeated the Ghana Empire after protracted struggles. In Ghana's place, the kingdom of Songhai (Mali) rose and prospered until the fifteenth century. Its religious and trading center, Timbuktu, attracted visitors from all over northern and western Africa, and even from Mediterranean nations. South of Songhai, in the sophisticated city-states of Congo and Benin, large communities of artisans, legal experts, and religious leaders congregated in thriving urban centers. Europeans noted with awe that strong elites were able to vanquish numerous agricultural villages within a large area. As Columbus sailed toward the Caribbean in 1492, Songhai was enjoying its greatest prosperity and power over subordinate populations.

Traditional European Societies

During the first centuries of the Middle Ages, from about 500 to 1100, most people in Europe lived in changeless poverty farming the land and raising livestock. Depending on where they lived and their relationship to the nobility or gentry, who owned most European lands, people might be called serfs, peasants, or tenants. Together, the overwhelming majority of the population experienced regular droughts, steep taxes, low crop yields, and the insular social relations of people who traveled and traded very short distances from their birthplaces.

Most peasant families labored long and hard merely to survive on land they could never expect to own. They worked with fragile wooden plows, only occasionally aided by draft animals, to break resisting soil. Neighbors shared the sickles they used to cut grain stalks by hand. Farming was task-oriented: men, women, and children performed their arduous duties according to the seasonal rhythms of the weather and the Catholic Church calendar, punctuated by occasional great fires sweeping across forests and fields, or overly long, wet winters that could tip a family's marginal existence toward starvation. The seasons were even related to the numbers of Europeans born, for greater numbers of babies entered the world in the early spring and early fall months than at other times of the year. Similarly, greater numbers of medieval Europeans died in the bitter months of January and February, and in disease-ridden August, than in other months. Infants and childbearing mothers lived a bit more precariously than most people did, but no one was spared undernourishment, disease, unemployment, and violence. Life was, as Thomas Hobbes put it in the early seventeenth century, "nasty, brutish, and short."

Across western Europe one-third of all children died before their fifth birthday, and only half of the young survivors endured the hardships of life until their twenty-second year. By the 1300s, regular crop failures resulted in famines that spread across the central and northern European countryside in swaths of starvation. The devastation reached unimaginable depths when the Black Death, or bubonic plague, wiped out one-third of Europe's population in the few years between 1347 and 1353.

Europeans developed a dramatically different relationship to the land than the Native Americans of the Western Hemisphere. They cleared the land of trees and other "encumbrances." They burned trees for fuel, chopped up logs for house construction, and overhunted their woodlands. They cultivated acreage by turning over the same soil year after year, or alternating tillage with fallow—or vacant—portions.

They planted in rows, marked their lands with fences, and valued attachment to the land over migration to new places. They herded livestock, which they kept in shelters and prized highly for the labor, manure, and food they yielded a farm family. And they worked long days and months in the same small fields to scratch out a subsistence, and maybe a little extra. The requirements of wood for housing, fuel, and mining and smelting industries led to widespread deforestation. In all of these ways, Europeans were dramatically different from Native Americans.

Moreover, European lands were owned exclusively by the sovereign, the church, or the nobility. Local peasants worked the land and craftsmen provided goods and services. Wealthy households also kept many retainers to attend to the needs of noble families. Their walled estates, castles, and monasteries created a stark reminder of wealth and power in contrast to the countryside's impoverished peasants and few scattered freehold farmers.

European laws and social customs often ensured that only men owned and inherited property, that women remained subordinate, and that children learned strict obedience and hard work under disciplining eyes—practices that stood in sharp distinction to Native American and African cultures. Boys of seven or eight years old were regularly sent to learn a trade and girls "farmed out" to learn housekeeping and perhaps supplement the family income. Such situations were not always happy ones; many children became lonely or suffered abuse in their adopted households, and anxious young adults often expressed an unfulfilled desire for personal independence. Among both the middling and well-to-do, marriage was not a matter of love and choice, but an arrangement by the parents to preserve lands and cement family relationships. In England, the oldest son might not marry until he was about thirty years old because he needed to wait until he could inherit a portion of his father's land or trade.

European Peasants at Work This contemporary drawing shows peasants using a shared community draught horse to harrow their field in the spring. They also would have used hand flails to thresh grain in the early fall. Following the rhythms of the sun and the seasons, they worked hardest in the fields from March to August, but the chores of repairing wooden tools, threshing and grinding grain into flour, and attending to numerous other farm tasks by hand occupied peasants year round. *(By permission of the British Library.)*

Peasants rarely had the opportunity to plan their children's work and marriages. Indeed, more often than not, they lived on the edge of survival. During the late Middle Ages, after 1100, some regions began to benefit from using more oxen and horses to cultivate fields, experimenting with crop rotation, introducing iron plows, improving milling, and taming wastelands and bogs for new fields. However, even though peasants enjoyed increased amounts of food, there was little improvement in general nutrition or longer lives. For one thing, most of the increase in food came from expanding cereal crops. Vegetables were still seasonal and scarce, and most peasants consumed fish or meat only occasionally. For another thing, increased agricultural production was often not enough to feed a family or village, especially when landlords or marauders took much of a crop by law or treachery. Then, too, many peasants faced dispossession—being thrown off the land by its owners—usually a sentence of early death. Roving bands of the landless became thieves and beggars along rural roads everywhere in Europe during the 1200s and 1300s.

While millions of peasants endured wrenching poverty, their rulers, the nobility, and church leaders led lives of comfort and privilege. The church and state levied endless taxes on their struggling peasant populations. Compounding the misery of the poor were the wars that broke out repeatedly among European princes and nobles. Eventually, the combination of tensions erupted into open peasant revolts in many parts of England and Europe. For example, Flemish peasants in northern Europe rose up against an oppressive Church and merciless landlords in the 1320s, demanding food and lower rents. Over the next seventy years, rebellion spread to other areas. By 1381, a peasant revolt spread over much of England's countryside in the largest lower-class rebellion in that island's history.

It also took many centuries for England and Europe to emerge as commercial powers on the high seas. For much of the Middle Ages, Viking warriors from northern Europe terrorized the coastal peoples of the British Isles and France. Eventually their streamlined boats mastered the forceful currents of the northern Atlantic; they first occupied Iceland to the west in the late 800s, and in the late 900s Erik the Red, an outlaw on the run, moved his bands of Norsemen on to Greenland. There Erik established contact with the Inuit (Eskimo) Indians, while his son, Leif, sailed along the coast of North America just after the year 1000 A.D. Although Leif Erikson left a few sailors at the short-lived colony called Vinland (in what is now Newfoundland), the Norsemen visited the area of present-day Maine only occasionally, to gather wood for fuel and to trade with Native Americans. Further voyages in later centuries by fishing vessels continued to whet the appetites of Europeans for dominion and resources in the Western Hemisphere. But the process of fanning out commercially and imperially was slow. Begun when Columbus arrived in the Caribbean, European expansion was still in its infancy when English settlers decided to stay permanently along the North American coast over one hundred years later.

One important catalyst of this commercial transformation was the growing number of merchants in England and Europe who had been expanding their trade and fortunes for some time. The Catholic Church and western European states sponsored two centuries of crusades (1095–1270) against Muslim "infidels" in the eastern Mediterranean countries. Despite the horrors of medieval warfare, contact with Muslim and other merchants throughout the Arab world promoted European trade with new lands, and consequently introduced nobles, professionals, and merchants to exotic material comforts.

Gradually, Italian merchants took control of the spice and silk trades. They led European efforts to bring back from China implements to measure earthquakes and locate direction (the compass), chairs, gunpowder, and skilled craft techniques. The introduction of these goods and ideas into Europe prompted more sophisticated merchant connections in banking and transportation routes, and more regularized fairs and marketplaces to trade. The young Venetian trader, Marco Polo (1254?–1324?) is the best known of these travelers to far eastern Asian kingdoms. By 1477, his journals had been published on European presses that owed much to the invention of moveable type in China, and his impressions of the Far East sparked great expectations about the benefits to Europeans of trade with China.

Europe's Internal Transformation, 1400–1600

From about 1050 to 1250, as faraway Cahokia and Ghana were achieving their greatest accomplishments, Europe entered a phase of dynamic internal transformation that would culminate in aggressive external expansion and colonization. On the land, powerful forces of change altered traditional agriculture and the population rose quickly. Across the seas, although China and the Islamic world would continue to be commercial giants, peoples of the eastern Mediterranean, Middle East, and northern Africa gradually yielded their dominant positions in trade and culture to Europeans.

Agriculture and Commerce

By the 1400s, England and Europe were undergoing profound transformations. In England, for example, until the 1400s cottagers, peasants, and laborers made up about three-fourths of the population. They typically lived in very small dwellings, kept vegetable gardens, and supplemented their needs with fish from local streams and game from nearby forests. Most of this population counted on having rights to use plots, or long strips of land, from the landlord's large open fields beyond their villages, on which they grew rye, wheat, barley, or oats. Together, villagers shared access to these plots, agreeing on communal rights and obligations in using and maintaining them.

During the 1400s, these traditions were noticeably giving way in England and on the Continent to new social relations in the countryside. New economic forces bound together farmers, merchants, and distant buyers to an extent never known before in Europe. Also during the 1400s, plagues, grinding scarcities of food, and peasant revolts seemed to ebb. Although half of the world's children still died before reaching the age of five, farmers were producing more to eat and the population began to grow slowly in fortunate regions of Europe. The terrible cycles of mass death subsided, and by the early 1500s, people began to comment on the rise of local populations, longer life spans, and more work to go around. For decades, even with more people available to produce food and clothing, old farming strategies could not keep up with growing needs. In northern Europe and England, inefficient strip farming kept crop yields very low. To make matters worse, more people were squeezed onto the same meager plots that had been used for centuries. The pastures and forests of many commons, which were used collectively by eligible members of the village, became crowded with livestock and depleted of game and timber.

Two other developments accelerated these changes. Once ships began to cross the Atlantic Ocean to search for land and wealth, the lifestyles of Europeans became tied to discoveries in their distant colonies. Most important, the great influx of New World silver into Europe and England led to inflation that drove up the price of consumer goods, and drove down the price of farmers' grain. Everywhere, it cost much more of a family's income to buy necessities. Even well-to-do yeomen—independent landowners—sometimes could not afford to hire necessary labor at harvest time. Second, England's prosperity was tightly bound up with the foreign markets for its raw wool and woolen cloth. Great amounts of merchants' capital and skilled labor supported this enterprise, which was in turn linked to the Dutch businesses in Antwerp that sent English woolens into markets of northern and eastern Europe. But when the Antwerp firms announced they had more wool than they could sell, and changes in the currency standards hurt merchants with outstanding foreign debts, England's economy entered a downturn. England's merchants and manufacturers argued that the country had to have new markets. Landlords in the countryside, wanting to take advantage of expanding urban and foreign markets, grew increasingly impatient with the inefficiencies of patchwork quilt strips farmed by dozens of peasants. Especially in England, landlords who wished to increase yields teamed up with woolen manufacturers who wished to take over land for sheep grazing. Powerful landowners turned to England's national government, Parliament, to secure laws for "enclosing" the open fields of traditional village communities. Under Parliament's Enclosure Acts, written titles were required in order to retain control over landed property; not surprisingly, these titles were issued to powerful individuals who consolidated holdings for cultivation or put up fences for sheep pastures.

Relations in the countryside underwent dramatic changes as a consequence of the Enclosure Acts. Among the winners were landlords in the English gentry who now owned enclosed lands. Yeomen sometimes hung on to their lands and benefited from the inflation during the 1500s by selling their surpluses to city consumers at rising prices. But the nobles who collected fixed rents from their tenants received payments declining in value. Shrinking income, combined with steeply rising prices for luxuries, crimped their aristocratic lifestyles and political prestige. And for the three-quarters of the population who were nontenant peasants and hired field laborers, enclosures created a tenuous existence, indeed. Peasants without titles to the land they worked were thrown off the soil.

A new set of social and legal arrangements, based on private access to the land and protection of contracts that gave title to landholdings, began to displace centuries of collective land use on the commons. Without a commons, the landless peasant had no place to graze a cow, gather firewood, or net a fish. Thousands of families lost their status as relatively autonomous farmers and became wage earners for new landlords or cottage spinners of wool. By 1600, sheep outnumbered people three to one in England, and malnourishment was rampant. As Sir Thomas More pointed out in his famous plaint, *Utopia* (1516), the loss of farm lands had destroyed a way of life, so that "your sheep . . . eat up men."

Eventually, thousands upon thousands of dispossessed farmers, servants, and craftspeople looked elsewhere in England for scarce employment. Many of them migrated to London from their now-enclosed lands or came as farmers' children seeking jobs as laborers, servants, and apprentices. Manufacturers and master artisans set up shops in cities because they knew the labor supply would be cheap and plentiful, and that workers would also be consumers of foods and finished goods. Ambitious professionals and merchants found that their fortunes were tied to the resources of cities, too.

But the influx of people from the countryside also created tremendous suffering in the cities. Migrating rural people competed for limited housing and jobs, and the prices of daily necessities skyrocketed. Huge numbers of destitute souls in the port towns and London plummeted into squalor. Urban society and culture also shocked newcomers to the cities. In London—as in Amsterdam, Lisbon, or Paris—the customary relations of rural villages, where people knew the rules of social decorum and where prices and rhythms of agricultural life hardly changed over a lifetime, were breaking down. Instead of weighing justice between buyers and sellers in village markets, or preserving the relatively unchanging values of goods and services, people seemed to be driven by the unabashed pursuit of private profit. Instead of changeless levels of rural poverty or maybe modest comfort, cities offered prospects for personal improvement—although they just as often produced bewildering amounts of failure.

Commerce changed in England, too. For centuries, most merchants had formed intimate partnerships with family and trusted personal friends in order to protect their investments from unscrupulous competitors and shelter themselves from excessive risks. Some merchants won specific government privileges as monopolied trading companies. But during the late 1400s, the view already circulating in thousands of small workshops and food stalls that profit seeking was acceptable—even good—permeated groups of merchant investors who sank their capital into urban projects, war expeditions, and "ventures" to foreign lands. Perhaps, many writers reasoned, it would be good for business and of great benefit to the nation to do away with these monopolies and their protected privileges. Then, individuals would be freer to bargain among themselves for the best prices, and to dispatch ships to richer markets, without regard for stultifying government restrictions.

Most English merchants did not adopt this way of thinking until production of commodities increased sufficiently for export to foreign buyers. But some of the most prominent merchants became champions of the Enclosure Acts when they discovered that landless country folk could be mobilized to receive raw materials from merchants and, in their homes, manufacture textiles, shoes, and small implements. In this "putting out" system, merchants focused on the production of woolen cloth; they directed women and children to wash and comb wool, which was then spun into yarn, which men in turn wove into cloth. Merchant dealers collected the cloth in the countryside for fulling and dying at city manufacturers' establishments. Of course, a strong market existed not far from producers' doorsteps, for every English

Merchants of Luxury Wares In contrast to rural peasants, wealthy urban merchants in the 1400s and 1500s dealt with manufactured goods from a variety of regions and nations and, as this image shows, provided city dwellers with loans and credit to stretch their abilities to buy necessary and luxury wares. *(Giraudon/Art Resource, NY.)*

household needed to replenish its woolen cloth and clothing from time to time, and few households could produce enough on their own. But merchants concentrated on exporting a steady supply of cloth to distant lands, and the government aided them with bounties, or cash incentives, to subsidize this exporting. Slowly, then, evolving rural and urban relations gave rise to interlocking dependencies among rural producers, merchants, and the government. Soon some of the people disaffected by these new social relations would make daring voyages across thousands of miles of ocean in order to make a fresh start in North America.

The Nation-State and the Renaissance, 1400–1600

The system of local lords constantly warring against their nominal rulers, and one another, came to a gradual end in the 1400s. First in Portugal, then in France, Spain, and England, new monarchs asserted their control over splintered factions and regions. Rising monarchs professed to be above the petty quarrels of fiefdoms, estates, or factions, and promised to unify feuding regions into nations, not unlike the imperial rulers of centralized states in the Americas might have promised. To do this, European monarchs raised great armies and created royal bureaucracies, paying for them with loans from wealthy merchants who benefited from crown protection of their interests on the seas and in foreign countries, and with taxes on the citizens who were promised protection from preying local lords.

This process of forming unified nation-states began in Portugal when John I consolidated fractured nobilities in the 1380s. In Spain, Ferdinand of Aragon married Isabella of Castile in 1469, uniting the two most important Spanish kingdoms. In order to create the social unity they needed for absolute rule, Ferdinand and Isabella then proceeded to crush the nobles of many regions of Spain, to support the Church's Inquisition, whose torture chambers tested the wills of all subjects suspected of disloyalty, and to expel Muslims (called Moors) from Grenada and then the entire country in 1492. Unconverted Jews were given six months to become Christians or be expelled, too, which prompted many Jews to migrate to more tolerant countries such as Holland and Ottoman-ruled Bosnia.

In France, Louis XI began to unite noble armies under his crown in the 1460s, which permitted general peace to return after nearly one hundred years of persistent warfare. In England, long-feuding noble households clashed in the War of the Roses in 1455. For the next thirty years, the Yorks and Lancasters battered each other, and only when Henry VII defeated the last Yorkist king in 1485 did peace return. For the next hundred years or so, English kings would rely, not on the nobles, but on the representative institution of Parliament to bolster their power.

The interests of merchants and monarchs often corresponded. For example, merchants used the new royal navies to protect their commerce from marauding pirates on the open seas. A few companies of merchants also enjoyed royal contracts, or monopolies, for exclusive commercial privileges. Groups of protected merchants in Constantinople, Genoa, or Antioch, for example, took the surpluses of small farmers living throughout the interior of foreign lands to markets at unimaginable distances. The same merchants returned to their homelands with ships full of exotic wares: salt and pepper, wines, spices, silk and tapestries, gunpowder, drawings and descriptions of technical inventions, and new books. Merchants promised to fill royal coffers with part of their commercial profits—especially the silver and gold they sought in foreign lands. In time, this alliance of politics and commerce, of crown and merchants, became indispensable for the migration of great numbers of European people to the Western Hemisphere.

These efforts during the 1400s to unify many different peoples into nation-states and to support the prosperity of merchants in international trade coincided with a sweeping cultural revival: the Renaissance. Across Europe beginning in the 1300s, many wealthy commercial families began to invest portions of their fortunes in an unparalleled burst of building, painting, mapping, printing, and traveling. Together, merchants, statesmen, and intellectuals renewed their interest in the Greek and Roman classics, in secular learning, and in nature and scientific inquiry. The leaders of countries, armies, churches, universities, and municipalities sought to validate or elevate their authority by enlisting the aid of inventors and artists in creating great public works. Painters sought to reconcile the intense Christianity of the era with both ancient philosophy and secular discoveries about nature and the heavens. Michelangelo (1475–1564) turned his artistic focus from mystical representation of divine subjects to studying the human body.

The Renaissance also spurred change in science, literature, law, and politics. Merchants hired Renaissance astronomers and cartographers to explore and map unknown lands to the south and east of Europe, and they promoted more efficient shipbuilding techniques. Entrepreneurs experimented with new navigational instruments such as the compass, the Arab astrolabe, which permitted accurate calculation of north–south distances (latitude), and the sextant, which measured the degree of altitude of celestial bodies. Galileo Galilei (1564–1642) challenged the teachings of the Roman Church when he turned his telescope from contemplating the "perfect" movement of heavenly bodies toward the craters and other imperfections of the Moon's surface. William Shakespeare (1564–1616) warned theatergoers about the disruption caused by corrupt heads of state, famines, and plagues; only wise rulers, a stolid social hierarchy, and satisfaction of people's essential needs could guarantee the security of the nation. Legal experts examined the sources of stability and order in societies. Niccolo Machiavelli (1469–1527), who wrote *The Prince* in 1513, rejected the tradition of investing politics with religious themes; instead, he wrote more personal, realistic, and sometimes scathing portraits of political rulers and their lust for power.

The Reformation, 1517–1563

The great religious revolt that developed alongside the agricultural, commercial, cultural, and political transformations shaking Europe is known as the Reformation. For centuries, the Catholic Church vied with traditional folk beliefs for spiritual power over European people. By the 1400s, it claimed the authority to sell "indulgences," or dispensations from punishments still due in earthly life and in purgatory (a station after life before the soul advances to heaven) even after sins were sacramentally absolved. Although indulgences had been granted in the 1000s to encourage men to fight in the crusades, by the 1400s, popes sold them to raise much-needed funds for building cathedrals and hospitals. Anxious masses of heaven-hungry people readily adopted the innovation, and dug deep into their pockets to help make the Church wealthy.

The German monk Martin Luther (1483–1546) recoiled from this practice of selling spiritual benefits. Even more, he rejected what he saw as the Catholic Church's teaching of a "theology of works." Since the 1100s, followers of church leader St. Thomas Aquinas believed that priests could help sinners improve their chances of salvation by administering the sacraments and forgiving sins. Luther wanted a return to the teachings of St. Augustine of Hippo who, around A.D. 400, professed the doctrine of predestination, or the belief that God alone determined who was saved and who was damned for eternity, without any regard to the conduct of people in this life. But Luther went a step further in the early 1500s, rejecting the idea of a vengeful God who dispensed justice and salvation capriciously and embracing the Biblical principle that sinful mortals could be sanctified through faith. Luther emphasized that eternal salvation was a gift from God, ensured only by faith in Christ and not something sinners, repentant or otherwise, could win by good works.

In 1517 Luther posted ninety-five theses on the door of the castle church in Wittenberg that criticized many practices of the Catholic Church. He encouraged lay people to turn to the Bible for authority and to query the wisdom of ordained priests. Although he did not set out to start a revolution, Luther's actions ignited smoldering discontents into a dissenting movement that would shake the foundations of European society. A church investigation of Luther's beliefs led to his excommunication, or expulsion, in 1521. But his teachings spread widely and an organized rival church emerged in the German states over the coming years. The emerging Lutheran Church retained only two of the seven sacraments (baptism and holy communion); discarded the practices of fasts, pilgrimages, and veneration of relics; and abolished the requirement of celibacy for priests.

What had begun as an internal church matter soon became a catalyst for political change. In his own country, Luther attracted the support of German princes who wished for greater autonomy from Rome. In the much larger Holy Roman Empire, Lutherans confronted the mighty opposition of the grandson of Ferdinand and Isabella, Charles V. The printing press, invented shortly before Luther was born, became a powerful instrument for the movement to spread its arguments against the Catholic Church, as well as Holy Scripture. Soon Lutheranism attracted massive numbers of European people willing to fight great religious wars that overlapped with the process of nation making over the next century.

In France, the state harshly persecuted the "Protestants" who embraced Luther's teachings. One such Protestant, the lawyer John Calvin (1509–1564), fled to Geneva, Switzerland, where he created a model Protestant community with even stricter rules than Lutherans advocated. Calvin extended the doctrines of Luther to include "predestination," or the belief that God had chosen a few "elect" citizens for salvation and had relegated the great majority to eternal damnation. Calvinists became vigilant of their every public and private action, watchful for the signs that they might be among the elect. Moreover, they tried to enhance their standing in the community and their personal material success in a "calling" so as to highlight the signs of election if they were present. As a result, Calvinists believed that thrift, hard work, sobriety, and providing strong role models to all citizens would join material success and spiritual commitment. Even if the appropriate moral behavior were not itself proof of election, an immoral life would surely indicate one's place among the "unregenerate," or the unsaved.

Calvinists energetically cultivated their beliefs beyond Geneva. Dutch and German Reformed churches grew quickly, and in Scotland, John Knox set up the Presbyterian Church. French Calvinists drew strength from merchants, rising middle classes, and nobles who tried unsuccessfully in 1560 to seize power and then suffered forty years of persecution by the French Catholic state. In the St. Bartholomew's Day Massacre of August 24, 1572, royal armies slaughtered thousands of believers, and only when Henry IV, who had been raised as a Protestant, ascended to the throne in 1589 did dissenters regain hope. Henry issued the Edict of Nantes in 1598, granting freedom of worship, but the majority of the population remained Catholic and Henry himself converted to Catholicism. Many French Protestants, called Huguenots, migrated out of the country, as many Lutherans had left Germany earlier, and soon the Catholic Church initiated a Counter-Reformation that promoted the teaching and missionary movement of Jesuits, who revitalized Catholicism in Europe and aided later efforts to expand abroad.

The Reformation followed a different path in England. Shortly after the Tudor family took the throne, King Henry VIII (ruled 1509–1547) asked the pope to annul his marriage to Catharine of Aragon, daughter of Ferdinand and Isabella, because she failed to bear a son to inherit the crown. When the pope denied Henry's request in 1531, the latter forced the annulment by co-opting the church's power in England and forcing a convocation of the clergy to recognize Henry as the supreme head of a new Church of England, which was also called the Anglican Church. Henry hand-picked a new Archbishop of Canterbury, Thomas Cranmer, who readily approved the king's annulment. Further, Henry took steps toward enhancing the prestige of his Anglican Church by selling extensive monastic landholdings to his political favorites.

But in the view of many English people influenced by the strong tide of reform ideas on the continent, the new church retained far too many Catholic beliefs and rituals. Henry's daughter Mary (ruled 1553–1558) briefly restored Catholicism, but the definitive settlement of the Anglican faith came during the reign of Henry's second daughter, Elizabeth I (ruled 1558–1603). By the time Elizabeth ascended the throne, a great number of English people were willing to embrace the Reformation, but not everyone agreed about just what that meant. On the one hand, the monarch emphasized the importance of English-language Bibles and an English-language liturgy, although she retained many of the ceremonies of the Anglican Church and its episcopal hierarchy. On the other hand, Calvinists demanded a wholesale "purification" of all traces of Catholicism and denounced the rituals of Mass; many withdrew from public worship and promoted private reading of the Bible.

These Puritans included aristocrats, gentry, intellectuals, some clergymen, and merchants, as well as middling artisans and farmers. In addition to Puritan experiences of religious repression, a brewing economic crisis during the late 1500s caused some of England's great Puritan gentlemen to lose their lands. Monopolied trading companies prevented many rising Puritan merchants from entering new routes of commerce. Chronic underemployment drove many impoverished artisans, especially in the textile trades, into the Puritan fold, along with hundreds of dispossessed farmers.

In England and in Europe, the Reformation also gave rise to smaller groups who criticized the "worldliness" of Calvinists. The Anabaptists, for example, appealed strongly to women and poor people who had been excluded from playing a role in the new dissenting churches and favored a stricter separation of church and state. Anabaptists were persecuted by traditional churches and Calvinists alike, as were other dissenting denominations that arose out of the era's religious fervor, including the Mennonites, Amish, Baptists, and Quakers (see Chapter 3). In time, many dissenters would join the large numbers of Puritans who exited England to share in the transformation of North America.

Taking to the Seas, 1420–1600

The transformations in Europe during the 1400s did not immediately spur the "discovery" of lands and peoples in the Western Hemisphere. Decades of consolidating innovations and institutions in Europe, of false starts and failures getting out of Europe, and of disappointing encounters with new peoples and new lands, preceded the permanent settlements that we often identify with European success.

In addition, not all European nations explored the "New World" at the same time or the same pace. Just as important, the various cultures of Africa and North America were at different stages of their own internal developments at the time scholars often associate with the encounters of Europeans with the New World. During the 1400s, Portugal dominated European exploration and was relatively unchallenged in the African slave trade. But in the next century, Portuguese influence over new lands and peoples was eclipsed by Spanish colonization.

Portuguese Exploration and African Slavery

African people were not strangers to the condition of slavery. Indeed, through human history slavery has existed in a bewildering number of societies for many different purposes. Slavery has been known in vast ancient empires and small agricultural kingdoms; Mediterranean, Chinese, Russian lands; warring and peaceful peoples. The reasons why people have been forced into slavery have also varied, from the need for labor to a desire for specialized craftsmen, warriors, concubines, artists, or victims for sacrifice. As Ghana rose in power, slavery grew in Europe and England; Slavs (from which peoples the term *slavery* is derived) taken in repeated wars were sold in large numbers to English masters, and in parts of Europe it was perfectly acceptable for parents to sell their children into slavery. When European attention turned to exploration of West Africa after 1400, slavery was already well known there. Arab traders and powerful coastal kingdoms frequently held African individuals in bondage for payment of debts or as an exchange for food during famines. Muslim caravans sold Africans as "chattel"—a kind of human property—to remote places.

The Slave Trade in Africa Slavery was widespread in Africa long before Portuguese traders starting landing along the continent's western coastline. But for centuries, African slaves were primarily debtors, criminals, or captives of wars, and often slavery was a temporary condition. Once Europeans came, slaves were removed from Africa, permanently, and almost always for lifelong slavery. Europeans who landed at the Gold Coast, or what became known as the "Slave Coast," reached farther and farther into the interior to take larger numbers of Africans into bondage. *(Paris, Bibliothèque nationale de France, photo © B.n.F.)*

By the early 1400s, the Portuguese became the first European nation systematically to explore West Africa and exploit its people and resources. Although the small country had never distinguished itself as a wealthy or a commercial nation, it was located strategically at the intersection of the coveted Mediterranean Sea and the mysterious Atlantic Ocean. Adventurers already knew about coastal Guinea's vast stores of gold, as well as Benin's renowned iron craftsmen. But it was not until the 1420s that Portugal's Prince Henry "the Navigator" (1394–1460) contributed church revenues to numerous expeditions that attempted to map and explore Atlantic islands and Africa's west coast. At home, Portuguese scholars promoted new sailing and shipbuilding techniques that they had learned from Ottomans and Arabs.

In short order the Portuguese set out to break the hold of Moorish (North African) and Turkish traders on the long-distance trade in goods and slaves. Establishing valuable connections to Madeira after 1418, and the Azores after 1427, where forced labor produced sugar and wine for ready European markets, Portuguese traders extended their reach. Crews of Portuguese sailors seized dozens of Africans in the 1440s and returned with them to Lisbon. In the following decade, the raiders paid Africans to capture neighboring people in exchange for coconuts, citrus fruit, swine, and small trinkets. Soon, the Portuguese built offshore "factories" on islands near Cape Blanco and Cape Verde, and from there conducted a lucrative slave trade. Although the Portuguese failed to subdue powerful African kingdoms to the interior, they exploited rivalries among the weaker small states and built outposts such as Elmina, on the Gold Coast of West Africa, in the 1480s. There, Africans of many languages and cultures could trade slaves for European goods, or the Portuguese could trade slaves for African gold. By 1487, Bartholomeu Dias had extended Portuguese influence in Africa below the Sahara all the way to the Cape of Good Hope. In 1497 Vasco da Gama rounded the Cape of Good Hope and journeyed up to India. Along the way he took slaves, spices, and valuable handicrafts that whet the appetites of the Portuguese elite for more of this trade.

Europeans had long associated slavery with the production of sugar. During the 1300s, Italians had taken sugar cane out of West Asia and set up plantations on Mediterranean islands that used slave labor. The Portuguese slave trade expanded rapidly once planters started sugar production on the island of Madeira in the 1470s, where their constant need for new supplies of West Africans was fueled by their policy of working slaves to death. Soon, Portuguese merchants extended slavery to the Canary Islands, and although Columbus failed to enslave native people of the Caribbean, voyagers who followed in his footsteps to Hispaniola carried African slaves to work the sugar mills constructed there in about 1510. To ensure a steady supply of African labor, Spain granted Portugal a monopoly of the carrying trade in 1518. They then teamed up with Dutch bankers to begin vast sugar enterprises in northeastern Brazil that were supported through the 1500s with shipload after shipload of African slaves.

The slavery Europeans developed after 1400 was quite different from their previous experiences of the institution. Although slavery was already well-entrenched in Africa, the forms known by most tribes were neither permanent nor heritable. Moreover, most African slaves in Africa became slaves as captives of war or intertribal conflict rather than based on race, and even in bondage they retained certain personal rights. When Europeans became involved in African slavery, however, they systematically exploited dense populations, removed native peoples from their soil to distant places, and put them and their descendents in permanent bondage.

Christopher Columbus

After Ferdinand and Isabella united Spain, they shifted their focus toward circumventing the Muslim traders who dominated the Mediterranean and northern African land routes to China and India. By the late 1400s, sailors, geographers, and merchants had long accepted that the world was round, but they mistakenly believed that Europe, Africa, and Asia covered more than half the world's surface and that the Atlantic Ocean was but a narrow ribbon of water. So, few people thought about how long a ship's voyage across the Atlantic might be. Of course, word spread quickly that Portuguese ships were already claiming the riches and power to be gained from finding a new route to the East. The Spanish monarchs also knew that the king of Portugal had refused to support the bold proposal of a young Genoese sea captain, Christopher Columbus (1451–1506), to find this route by sailing west. Heads of state in France and England had been even quicker to dismiss the preposterous bid. At first too concerned about national unification to pay much attention to Columbus, Isabella was later convinced by his persistence, as well as by Spain's desire to consolidate an empire of its own, to outfit a westward voyage.

Columbus set out from Palos, Spain, on August 3, 1492 with some ninety eager but mostly inexperienced young mariners on three small vessels. He had little formal education himself, but years of practical experience on the high seas. Nevertheless, the sailors' confidence in Columbus's dream of sailing west soon turned to fear and near mutiny. About three thousand miles out to sea, the crews demanded to go home. Columbus managed to quell this discontent for two more days, when on October 12 the island he would name San Salvador (now Samana Cay) appeared on the horizon. Believing that the Caribbean islands were a gateway to a vast stretch of China that lay just beyond their sight, he named his "discoveries" the West Indies and called the Arawak people of the island "Indians."

In a short time, Columbus and his crews sailed on to Cuba (which he mistook for Cipangu, or Japan), and then to Hispaniola. There, he encountered the great numbers of Taino living on the region's islands. Columbus was at first amazed at the physical perfection of the Taino, who were "very well built, with very handsome bodies and very good faces." Yet he also presumed Taino inferiority: "It appeared to me that these people were very poor in everything. . . . They bear no arms, nor are they acquainted with them, for I showed them swords and they grasped them by the blade and cut themselves through ignorance." Shortly, Columbus and others would conclude that differences of dress and physical appearance that were judged to be "uncivilized" suited Native Americans "to be good servants" of the Spanish (see Competing Voices, page 37).

In December 1492, Columbus, a number of Taino Indians, and a portion of his crews caught the westerly trade winds and sailed home. They arrived to the acclaim of the Spanish crown and publicists alike, and in the next years Columbus, now dubbed the Admiral of the Ocean Sea, received funding for three more expeditions. Although Columbus announced to his benefactors that "all the inhabitants" of the islands he had explored "could be made slaves," his political and financial backers kept their eyes on the material, not the human, riches he claimed to have found. Based on the gold jewelry he saw native people wearing, Columbus had left about forty of his mariners behind on the north coast of Hispaniola with orders to locate the gold mines he was certain were there.

Before they discovered how badly mistaken Columbus was about the gold, the Spanish monarchs appealed to the pope for support in declaring their right to rule over the places in which Columbus had staked their flag. Ferdinand and Isabella asked for nothing less than a division between Portugal and Spain of all as-yet-undiscovered lands to the west. In 1494 Spain and Portugal negotiated the Treaty of Tordesillas, drawing a line from north to south about 1,100 miles west of the Cape Verde Islands. All undiscovered lands to the west of the line would belong to Spain; to the east, to Portugal. The terms of this treaty made two matters clearer than ever: Portugal's preeminent imperial position would henceforth be challenged, and Spain's imperial authorities would be determined to conquer what Caribbean islands they could, and all lands that lay beyond them.

In late 1493, the Spanish crown had dispatched a convoy of seventeen ships laden with more than twelve hundred to colonize the Caribbean. However, when the fleet arrived at Hispaniola, nothing was left of the Spanish fort or the men planted there earlier, for their raids against Taino villages had brought retaliation that laid waste the Spanish settlement. In months to come, Columbus's failure to find gold and his brutal treatment of native peoples alienated him from both settlers on the islands and the Spanish monarchs at home. When on his third voyage in 1498 Columbus continued to exaggerate about his own leadership, and to mistreat Spanish sailors and Native Americans alike, the crown ordered him home in leg irons.

On a fourth, and final, voyage to the Caribbean from 1502 to 1504, Columbus engaged in now-familiar disregard of native peoples and their lands, this time along the coast of Central America. Everywhere Columbus had landed, disease, destruction of fields and settlements, and the introduction of slavery had transformed Indian ways of life. Even on his deathbed in debtor's prison in 1506, Columbus misguidedly insisted that the lands he discovered lay in the Far East. By then the Treaty of Tordesillas was a mere parchment pact, for France, Holland, and England would soon enter the contest for settlements in the Western Hemisphere despite Spain's imperial claims. As a final irony, it was not Columbus's name that was assigned to the two continents of the "New World," but that of Amerigo Vespucci (1451–1512), a Florentine merchant who sailed for Spain in 1499 near the South American coastline. By the early 1500s, a few Europeans had begun to understand that the large area of land across the Atlantic was not connected to Asia at all. Then in 1507 the German cartographer Martin Waldseemüller produced a world map that showed large land masses, "the new lands" of the Western Hemisphere, as a separate continent. He named it "America," in honor of Vespucci, and the name endured.

The Spanish Century

Spain's ascendancy among the European empire builders held firm during most of the 1500s. Its growing army of *conquistadors* accepted the invasion of the Western Hemisphere as a new crusade. Fame, personal wealth, and glory for their nation motivated scores of adventurers to undertake conquering missions, first in the Caribbean, and then into the North American interior. Spanish raids through the islands were especially cruel because the populations of native peoples lacked the means to fend off European attackers and succumbed quickly to the fiery weapons and devastating germs of their invaders. Spanish marauders subjugated the populations in the Bahamas, Hispaniola, Puerto Rico, Jamaica, and Cuba, forcing native islanders to work as slaves in intensive agriculture or brutal mining camps. As native populations declined rapidly in the early 1500s from disease and harsh labor conditions, Europeans were already clearing Caribbean land and importing African slaves to work the plantation estates that transformed life on the islands.

In 1511 Spaniards began making plans to explore the mainland to the west. Within two years, Vasco Nuñez de Balboa crossed the narrow Isthmus of Panama to the Pacific Ocean, and by 1519, Hernán Cortés (1485–1547) and his army of about four hundred men, a dozen horses, and some cannon, landed at the site of Vera Cruz. In the next months they marched two hundred miles to Tenochtitlán at the heart of the mighty Aztec empire of the Mexican interior (see page 11). Cortés's troops marveled at the splendors of this magnificent city, and at the works of the Aztec master-engineers whose thousands of drafted laborers put up the massive pyramids and numerous public buildings that dominated the city's life.

The thirty-four-year-old Cortés advanced quickly against local populations with superior arms made of steel, dogs trained to kill on command, and a steady supply of Spanish horses whose presence alone stunned thousands of native peoples into submission. He also had at his side an Aztec woman named Ala Malinche, who translated the Nahuatl language for Cortés as the conquest proceeded. The Spaniards also exploited discontent among portions of the subjugated countryside against the imperial Aztec rulers in a "divide-and-conquer" strategy; tribute-poor villages were willing to join in a revolt against their mighty overlord Moctezuma. Some of the peoples living on agricultural sites between the coast and Tenochtitlán may have believed that Cortés was the Toltec god Quetzalcoatl, returning to free them from the Aztec. Locals who chose not to fight alongside Cortés fled the central plains to remote mountains or the arid north, inadvertently hastening the conquest of Tenochtitlán and its surrounding area.

Once they invaded Tenochtitlán, Spanish *conquistadors* easily plundered the mountainous coffers of tribute lying in public storehouses, no small amount of which made its way back to the Spanish crown. Cortés and his relatively small entourage captured Moctezuma, the Aztec ruler, which further weakened the heart of the Aztec empire. Although the dwindling numbers of Aztec rallied to drive out the Spanish in 1520, smallpox continued to weaken them, and a reconquest of the capital city in 1521 ended Aztec resistance. Indeed, European diseases, primarily smallpox, reduced the Aztec Empire from nearly 25 million inhabitants to about 2.5 million in fifty years.

For some time to come, the Spanish faced serious difficulties sustaining permanent settlements in Mexico and ruling them effectively. But the lure of gold and glory outweighed the risks of failure, and *conquistadors* continued to answer its call in large numbers. In the 1520s, Francisco Pizarro (1470–1541) began a bloody march through the expansive Inca Empire with fewer than two hundred soldiers. He seized Cuzco, the capital city, in 1533 and mercilessly executed Inca chief Atahualpa. European diseases had reached the Inca long before they laid eyes on the foreigners, and by the time of Pizarro's arrival, virtually half the Inca population had already perished from his assault. Pizarro declared Spanish sovereignty over all the Inca with very little Indian resistance. In the next decades, Spanish explorers' discovery of rich silver mines through the Americas ensured that their monarchs would continue to support devastating invasion strategies.

Spanish *conquistadors* had less success conquering and settling the Gulf Coast region and the interior to the southwest. Juan Ponce de León (1460–1521) landed on the southern Atlantic coast in 1513, naming it after the Easter holiday, *pascua florida*, or Florida. Over the next years, Ponce de León made several unsuccessful attempts to take slaves from the nearby Indian villages, but in 1521 his efforts resulted in his own death at the hands of hostile warriors. In 1528 Panfilo de Narvaez and a small group of Spanish mariners began wandering along the Gulf Coast and into the dry Southwest. The significant legacy of this expedition was the amazing journal of Alvar Nuñez Cabeza de Vaca (1490–1557?), whose sometimes fantastical stories included an account of an opulent empire he called Cibola. There, Cabeza de Vaca had seen "cities of gold"—possibly misinterpreting vistas of the yellow sand and rock in the brilliant sun. Illusory or not, his claims prompted other Spaniards to trek into the North American interior, across what would one day become Texas.

Hernando de Soto (1496?–1542) landed in Florida in 1539 with an army of over seven hundred men and over three thousand hogs and cattle. De Soto pressed into the interior, forced Mississippian Indians into labor, and plundered food from villages as needed. As he despaired of finding an empire to conquer, preferably one mightier than the Aztec, De Soto was attacked first by the powerful Alibamu of present-day Alabama, and then by the enraged ancestors of the Chickasaw. His forces depleted, De Soto marched farther west across the Mississippi River, but died shortly after turning back in 1542. The next year his surviving soldiers reached other Spaniards in Mexico, where they reported the fierceness of the Indians they had encountered. What they could not report, however, was how severely the diseases they had carried with them on their exploits had reduced mighty chiefdoms to small, interdependent tribal groups.

In 1540 the Spanish officials in Mexico launched another attempt to find Cibola. Francisco Vasquez de Coronado (1510–1554) took three hundred men and horses, and over seven hundred Indian carters, along ancient Indian trading paths into North America. On the way, they passed the Pima settlements, and then the Pueblo Indians along the Rio Grande, whom Coronado attacked without apparent reason and scorned for what he thought was the rude simplicity of their culture. His expedition pressed into the western Great Plains and there spied great herds of buffalo. But there was no Cibola, no gold, and no glory for Coronado. He returned to Mexico in disappointment.

Spaniards concluded from these efforts that the great riches they had pillaged from the Aztec and Inca Empires were not duplicated in the lands north of the Mexican plains. Nevertheless, during the 1500s *conquistadors* and the settlers who followed them made an indelible imprint on the Western Hemisphere. For an entire century, the Spanish model gave other European nations a powerful example of how—and how not—to conquer regions of the New World.

The Effects of Contact

Overlapping the economic, religious, and political transformations occurring among the cultures that collided in the Western Hemisphere in the 1500s was a profound transfer of goods, foods, ideas, social organization, and diseases. Called the "Columbian Exchange," this transfer eradicated the centuries of separation between the hemispheres and started the process of regular communication among many different cultures. Few Europeans knew what to expect from their first encounters with Africans or Indians, but peoples of all three world regions continually adjusted to one another. Some of these adjustments were incremental and only slowly affected daily activities; others were jarring, violent, or even devastating.

Peoples who had developed very different ways of exploiting their environments and meeting their material needs shared the excitement of exchanging new items of comfort or necessity. Animals and plants were part of this trading phenomenon. Livestock came on the earliest ships to newly conquered cultures. Even on Columbus's first voyage, cargoes of cattle and horses ensured not only a supply of meat for Spanish consumption, but also animal power for cartage and construction. For Indians who had no experience of such animals, the scale of work and ease of transport made possible with European cattle and horses changed village life immeasurably. Grazing cattle, as well as foraging goats and swine, changed the ecology of many Caribbean islands. In Mexico, the cattle brought from Spain provided raw hides for export. Horses escaped from Mexico and migrated northward, where they made a tremendous impact on the lives of Pueblo, Yaqui, and other large populations of the Southwest. In time, the Arapaho, Sioux, and other peoples of the Great Plains also adopted horses. Besides livestock, the Spanish introduced barley, wheat, oats, rice, rye, melons, dandelions, olives, coffee, and other foods. Europeans also brought firearms and cannons, the "great fire trumpets" that terrified Mexican emperors and subjects alike.

Sugar was also among the items introduced from the Old World to the New. Already in the 1400s, Portuguese traders knew about the value of sugar grown in the Azores, and during the 1500s, the cultivation and consumption of sugar quickly surpassed animal hides to become the second-greatest export from the New World (next to silver). When the Portuguese took Brazil in the early 1500s, they relocated Native American populations to lands hundreds of miles away from familiar rivers and fields, and introduced African slaves to produce sugar for European markets. Dozens of merchants scurried to invest in growing Brazilian and Caribbean sugar, which became popular immediately in Europe and England despite its doubtful nutritional and medicinal worth. Quickly following the merchants were thousands of Spanish, Dutch, and French colonizers who aspired to make fortunes on this increasingly fashionable commodity.

In order to satisfy the constant demand for killing work in the cane fields, the now-entrenched slave trade provided the answer. By the end of the 1500s, over 90 percent of the Africans forcibly removed from their homelands to become slaves in the Western Hemisphere went to the West Indies, Brazil, and the Spanish borderlands. During the 1500s, about 250,000 African people came on slave ships to the New World. Another 200,000 were brought in chains in the brief period from 1600 to 1621. Such a massive scale of transplanting people for their labor had never been known in Africa or Europe. Moreover, the atrocious treatment slaves experienced on the "midpassage" across the ocean and the ruthless requirements of plantation labor were nothing like the predominantly domestic servitude of ancient and medieval slavery in Europe. Finally, in contrast with the many different ethnic and national peoples of Europe subjected to slavery as war captives or orphans during earlier centuries, slavery in the Western Hemisphere after 1500 became based almost entirely on race.

Europeans adopted many new foods found in the New World, including maize from Mexico, which was adopted as a staple of families everywhere, especially in the Mediterranean, and used as a food crop for livestock in other places. About three generations after maize had been cultivated in France, the Englishman John Locke marveled that it "serves poor people for bread . . . [and] is good nourishment for their cattle." Beans, squash, and various root crops also were transported back to Europe, where their ease of cultivation and high calorie content made them welcome dietary additions. Peru contributed the potato to northern European populations, and tomatoes entered the southern European diet. Tobacco, a New World crop at first believed to be a valuable medicine, was grown widely in Europe after 1550 because of the rage for chewing and smoking it. Vanilla, cotton, peanuts, and chocolate became standard fare in Europe by 1600, too.

The most important commodity that European people extracted from the New World was silver. Once they had subjected tens of thousands of Native Americans to forced labor in the mines, conquerors of the Inca and Aztec Empires helped themselves to vast quantities of gold and silver. Skilled craftsmen turned much of this wealth into jewelry and statuary, while merchants introduced great quantities of ingots and bullion into European trade. Between 1520 and 1600 shipload after shipload of silver returned to Spain. After the crown skimmed its Royal Fifth of the value of each delivery, merchant families spent other portions of it on lavish luxuries. In a short time, New World silver began to trickle into commerce with Spain's trading partners. With so much new wealth circulating in Europe, wars became more costly and more deadly, prices of daily necessities rose due to an inflationary spiral, and the standard of living for most Europeans declined dramatically. The wages craftsmen received for their work stayed the same, but the money bought less because of inflation. And the rents collected by aristocrats from their tenants were worth less in real value once inflation penetrated the countryside.

But the Indians of the New World experienced a far greater disaster: the rapid dying of great numbers of Indians from European diseases. When Columbus came to the Caribbean, the Taino probably numbered hundreds of thousands in Hispaniola, but by the 1520s, no more than a few hundred remained, and soon almost every trace of that culture had vanished. At about the time the Taino almost disappeared,

"Indio con Virguelas" [Indian with Smallpox] Smallpox was the greatest killer of Native Americans in the Western Hemisphere following the arrival of Europeans. In only two years, an epidemic that began with the Spanish invasion had swept through the plains of Mexico and ravaged the Aztec population; the grim scenario would be repeated among other peoples in generations to come. Not until the 1720s was inoculation against smallpox possible. *(*Trujillo Del Peru, *v.2 by Martinez Camanon.)*

the Aztec of the Mexican highlands also were declining rapidly. Warfare, starvation, relocation and the resulting decline of Indian family life, and demoralization that reportedly led to widespread infanticide and suicide, claimed huge numbers of peoples who came under Spanish influence. European diseases claimed the most lives in these waves of decimation. Smallpox, influenza, typhus, malaria, measles, and pneumonia were the major causes of the worst demographic disaster in world history. By about 1520, one Indian reported from Peru that the smallpox "spread over the people as great destruction. . . . Very many died of it, they could not stir; they could not change position, nor lie down on one side, nor face down, nor on their backs. And if they stirred, much did they cry out."

How could the devastation of most Native American peoples have occurred so quickly? The answer lies in how diseases spread. Europeans had developed immunities to these invisible viruses, having been exposed to them repeatedly, but the New World populations had never before experienced them. The viruses brought by Europeans were even more mysterious when epidemics spread to Indian villages ahead of European contact, as it did in the American Southeast. And the fact that so many Indians died while few Europeans seemed to be affected confirmed some Native Americans' beliefs that arriving ships carried either great gods or invincible new human rulers. Much evidence also shows that Native Americans, in a kind of perverse revenge, gave syphilis to their European conquerors, probably beginning with Columbus's voyages, although it is also possible that milder strains of syphilis existed in Europe earlier.

CONCLUSION

The spread of agriculture over many centuries wrought profound changes in ancient Indian cultures. By the time Europeans encountered them, most peoples of the Caribbean and the coastal mainland lived in sedentary villages or semi-permanent encampments. They had organized themselves into clusters of families and hierarchical communities that were recognizable to Europeans, and they identified among themselves leaders, servants, and specialists of many kinds. With the notable exceptions of the Aztec and Inca, the Native American cultures that experienced the most contact with first Europeans were sometimes closer to the strangers from across the Atlantic Ocean than they were to nomads or hunter-gatherers who lived in high northern latitudes or remote regions of their own North American interior.

When the Portuguese and Spanish explorers pushed aside Islamic supremacy in commerce with a burst of energy in the 1400s, and went on to conquer islands and empires stretching over thousands of miles in the New World, they did not simply introduce new cultures to Africans and Native Americans, who then willingly adopted them. As we have seen, by 1450 the pace of change reached incredible heights in all three world areas. Some medieval technological, agricultural, and commercial innovations changed living conditions dramatically within Europe, while religious and political turmoil uprooted huge numbers of Europeans; together, these upheavals were preconditions for explorations and contact in the generations to come. Surely some of the fluctuating fortunes of city-states and villages in the Americas also set the terms of Indian responses to Europeans. And the rich and fluctuating heritages of African peoples not only affected the patterns of their forcible removal from that continent, but also set certain parameters for their mixing with other cultures in the New World.

Initial dreams of glory and gold gave way quickly to the reality of difference, disappointment, and sharpening tensions among strangers. The first toeholds of Europeans in the Americas contrasted sharply with the extinct and existing great Native American city-states of Mound Builders, Aztec, Inca, and southwestern peoples. And yet, within only a short period of time, the demographic tables reversed. While life was no doubt difficult for European colonizers, who experienced starvation, death, and disease in the first years of each settlement, millions of Indians and Africans throughout the Americas perished by the steel weapons, harsh work regimens, oppressive political authority, and especially the diseases of migrating European strangers. As Spain extracted shiploads of hides and precious metals from new lands, smallpox, cholera, measles, and other deadly diseases took a greater toll on Native Americans than Europeans had ever experienced in the bloodiest of wars. At the same time, Spanish explorers and settlers required greater and greater replenishment of slaves from Africa who, by the early 1500s, performed an array of tasks as forced labor.

The Cherokee myth of creation does not disclose what happened when the pressure of European and other Indian encroachments became unbearable. However, it does reveal much about the Cherokee respect for—and awe of—nature and the place of humans in a spectrum of living things. It is intriguing to wonder whether the myth's familiar explanations of creation eased introductions between the Cherokee and new Europeans, or whether its starkly different view of Cherokee homelands and social order contributed to alienation between the two cultures.

For thousands of years the Americas were separated from Europe and Africa. Long before peoples of different continents mixed, thousands of different North American cultures rose, flourished, and profoundly changed—sometimes repeatedly—in dynamic interaction with each other. Peoples of Africa and Europe, too, underwent significant changes that laid the foundations for both cultural sharing and cultural conflicts when they did finally meet.

SUGGESTED READINGS

Brian M. Fagan's *The Great Journey: The Peopling of Ancient America* (1987) is one of the most authoritative interpretations of early human history in the Western Hemisphere. Among the best work on North America before European contact, see the collection of essays in Thomas E. Emerson and R. Barry Lewis, eds., *Cahokia and the Hinterlands: Middle Mississippian Cultures of the Midwest* (1991); Bruce Smith, *The Mississippian Emergence* (1990); Frederich Katz, *The Ancient American Civilizations* (1972); William F. Keegan, ed., *Emergent Horticultural Economies of the Eastern Woodlands* (1987); and Philip Kopper, *The Smithsonian Book of North American Indians Before the Coming of the Europeans* (1986). Alvin M. Josephy, Jr., ed., *America in 1492* (1992), contains important essays by key scholars of many North American areas on the eve of European contact.

Studies that focus on Indian culture in interaction with Europeans in North America are numerous, but see James Axtell, ed., *The Indian Peoples of Eastern America: A Documentary History of the Sexes* (1981). For the Eastern Woodlands peoples, see Alfred Goldsworthy Bailey, *The Conflict of European and Eastern Algonquian Cultures, 1504–1700* (1969); and the fascinating and readable ecological study by William Cronon, *Changes in the Land: Indians, Colonists, and the Ecology of New England* (1983). Also, D. W. Meinig, *The Shaping of America*, Vol. 1: *Atlantic America, 1492–1800* (1986), is the best cultural view of European settlement in relation to the Indians; and Neal Salisbury, *Manitou and Providence: Indians, Europeans and the Making of New England, 1500–1643* (1982), is a signal contribution to the ethnohistory of the Northeast with a strong cultural emphasis. For the Southeast, see Charles Hudson, *The Southeastern Indians* (1976).

The indispensable and path-breaking work of Alfred Crosby, Jr., shows in detail how Indian and European cultures influenced each other extensively; see his *The Columbian Exchange: Biological and Cultural Consequences of 1492* (1972) and *Ecological Imperialism: The Biological Expansion of Europe, 900–1900* (1986).

For demographic patterns, see Russell Thornton, *American Indian Holocaust and Survival: A Population History Since 1492* (1987). For a wide variety of maps showing the locations and migrations of many Native American groups, and a comprehensive bibliography, see Carl Waldman, *Atlas of the North American Indian* (1985).

Three studies are excellent starting points for the African background: Paul Bohanan and Philip Curtin, *Africa and the Africans* (2nd ed., 1971); Basil Davidson, *The African Genius* (1969); and J. D. Fage, *A History of West Africa* (4th ed., 1969). Also see Richard Olaniyan, *African History and Culture* (1982). Recently, the magisterial study by John Thornton, *Africa and Africans in the Making of the Modern World, 1400–1680* (1992), makes fascinating connections between African life and slave trading patterns. A valuable look at how the slave trade affected Africans is in Paul E. Lovejoy, "The Impact of the African Slave Trade on Africa: A Review of the Literature," *Journal of African History,* 30 (1989): 365–94.

For overviews of the great changes overtaking European people and western European nation states, see Ralph Davis, *The Rise of Atlantic Economies* (1973); J. H. Parry, *The Establishment of the European Hegemony: Trade and Expansion in the Age of the Renaissance* (1966); Kenneth R. Andrews, *Trade, Plunder, and Settlement: Maritime Enterprise and the Genesis of the British Empire, 1480–1630* (1984); and David B. Quinn, *England and the Discovery of America, 1481–1620* (1974).

For work on European exploration and conquest before Columbus, see the detailed overview by Samuel Eliot Morison, *The European Discovery of America: The Northern Voyages, A.D. 500–1600* (1971); and for changes within Europe, Carlo M. Cipolla's *Guns, Sails, and Empire: Technological Innovation and the Early Phases of European Expansion 1400–1700* (1975) contains fascinating detail and important analysis. Kirkpatrick Sale, *The Conquest of Paradise: Christopher Columbus and the Columbian Legacy* (1990), though one of the most critical appraisals of Columbus, also offers a provocative perspective for discussions.

For the Portuguese, see Charles Boxer, *The Portuguese Seaborne Empire: 1415–1825* (1969) and *The Dutch Seaborne Empire, 1600–1800* (1965). For the earliest French settlement in the New World, see Olive P. Dickason, *The Myth of the Savage and the Beginnings of French Colonization in the Americas* (1982).

For Spain's long century of imperial domination in the Western Hemisphere, start with Charles Gibson, *Spain in America* (1966). Also see James Lang, *Conquest and Commerce: Spain and England in the Americas* (1975), and Hugh Thomas, *Conquest: Montezuma, Cortés, and the Fall of Old Mexico* (1993). For the French presence, see Marcel Trudel, *The Beginnings of New France, 1524–1663* (1973).

Important perspectives on European motives and influences during the early phases of colonization are offered by Simon Schama, *The Embarrassment of Riches: An Interpretation of Dutch Culture in the Golden Age* (1987), and Eric Wolf, *Europe and the People Without History* (1983).

Interpreting the Cultures of Strangers

Competing Voices

Columbus Describes the Taino

In letters to the Spanish monarchs, Christopher Columbus offered some of the first written impressions of the New World made by a European. Although he was perplexed about the Taino Indians' political organization and ways of working, Columbus was clearly astonished at the natural bounty of the islands and physical beauty of the people. The following passage is dated February 15, 1493.

I found very many islands peopled with inhabitants beyond number. And, of them all, I have taken possession for their Highnesses, with proclamation and the royal standard displayed; and I was not gainsaid . . . I followed [the] coast [of the island Juana] westwardly and found it so large that I thought it might be the mainland province of Cathay. And as I did not thus find any towns and villages on the sea-coast, save small hamlets with the people whereof I could not get speech, because they all fled away forthwith, I went on further in the same direction, thinking I should not miss of great cities of towns. . . . I sent two men into the country to learn if there were a king, or any great cities. They traveled for three days, and found interminable small villages and a numberless population, but nought of ruling authority; . . . The lands thereof are high, and in it are very many ranges of hills, and most lofty mountains incomparably beyond the Island of [Tenerife]; all most beautiful in a thousand shapes, and all accessible, and full of trees of a thousand kinds, so lofty that they seem to reach the sky. And I am assured that they never lose their foliage; as may be imagined, since I saw them as green and as beautiful as they are in Spain. . . . And the nightingale was singing, and other birds of a thousand sorts. . . . There are palm trees of six or eight species, wondrous to see for their beautiful variety; but so are the other trees, and fruits, and plants therein . . . there is honey, and . . . in the earth there are many mines of metals; and there is a population of incalculable number. . . . In [La Spanola], there are many spiceries, and great mines of gold and other metals. The people of this island, and of all the others that I have found and seen, or not seen, all go naked, men and women, just as their mothers bring them forth; . . . and of fair stature, but that they are most wondrously timorous. . . . It is true that since they have become more assured, and are losing that terror, they are artless and generous with what they have, to such a degree as no one would believe but him who had seen it. Of anything they have, if it be asked for, they never say no, but do rather invite the person to accept it, and show as much lovingness as though they would give their hearts. And whether it be a thing of value, or one of little worth, they are straightways content with whatsoever trifle of whatsoever kind may be given them in return for it . . . they all believe that power and goodness are in the sky, and they believed very firmly that I, with these ships and crew, came from the sky; and in such opinion, they received me at every place where I landed, after they had lost their terror. And this comes not because they are ignorant; on the contrary, they are men of very subtle wit, who navigate all those seas, and who give a marvelously good account of everything . . . they never saw men wearing clothes nor the like of our ships. . . . It seems to me that in all those islands, the men are all content with a single wife; and to their chief or king they give as many as twenty. The women, it appears to me, do more work than the men. Nor have I been able to learn whether they held personal property, for it seemed to me that whatever one had, they all took share of, especially of eatable things. Down to the present, I have not found in those islands any monstrous men, as many expected, but on the contrary all the people are very comely. . . . Since thus our Redeemer has given to our most illustrious King and Queen, and to their famous kingdoms, this victory in so high a matter, Christendom should take gladness therein and make great festivals, and give solemn thanks to the Holy Trinity for the great exaltation they shall have by the conversion of so many peoples to our holy faith; and next for the temporal benefit which will bring hither refreshment and profit, not only to Spain, but to all Christians.

Las Casas Reveals the "Villainies of the Spanish"

Opponents of the *conquistadors* and Spanish crown policies gave voice to their concerns starting very early in the conquests. One of them was Bartolomé de Las Casas (1474–1566), a Spanish Catholic friar and later bishop of the Indies. Las Casas protested that Indians were not granted equal legal status under Spanish law. In 1540, the churchman brought together a mountain of chilling evidence about Spanish violations of Indian rights in *Brevisima relación de la destrucción de las Indias,* which he sent as a report to King Charles V.

There were ten kingdoms as large as the kingdom of Spain. . . . Of all this the inhumane and abominable villainies of the Spanish have made a wilderness, for though it was formerly occupied by vast and infinite numbers of men, it has been stripped of all people . . . over twelve million souls innocently perished, women and children being included in the sad and fatal list. . . .

As for those that came out of Spain, boasting themselves to be Christians, they had two ways of extirpating the Indian nation from the face of the earth: the first was by making bloody, unjust, and cruel wars against them; and the second was by killing all those that so much as sought to recover their liberty, as some of the braver sort did. And as for the women and children that were left alive, the Spaniards let so heavy and grievous a yoke of servitude upon them that the condition of beasts was much more tolerable. . . .

What led the Spanish to these unsanctified impieties was the desire for gold to make themselves suddenly rich, in order to obtain dignities and honors that were in no way fit for them. . . . The Spanish so despised the Indians . . . that they used them not like beasts, for that would have been tolerable, but looked upon them as if they had been the dung and filth of the earth, and so little did they regard the health of their souls that they permitted the great multitude to die without the least light of religion. . . .

From which time forward the Indians began to think of ways that they might take to expel the Spaniards from their country. And when the Spanish saw this they came with their horsemen well armed with swords and lances, making a cruel havoc and slaughter among them, overrunning cities and towns and sparing neither sex nor age. Nor did their cruelty take pity on women with children, whose bellies they ripped up, taking out the infants to hew them to pieces. They would often lay wagers as to who could cleave or cut a man through the middle with the most dexterity, or who could cut off his head at one blow. The children they would take by the feet and dash their innocent heads against the rocks.... They erected a kind of gallows broad and low enough so that the tormented creatures might touch the ground with their feet, and upon each one of these they strung thirteen persons, blasphemously affirming that they did it in honor of our Redeemer and his apostles. ■

These contrasting views existed side by side for generations of European conquest in the Western Hemisphere. Flattering accounts of beautiful Indian physical features and material generosity persisted until they became codified into a "noble savage" perspective and inspired thousands of enthusiastic colonizers to join in the migrations to the "new world." This view almost always anticipated that Europeans' "civilized" religion and culture would prevail over cultures that seemed to be less mature, less endowed with prosperity and comfort, or more vulnerable to the environment and human enemies. Some views proposed—or assumed—that Indians could provide valuable sources of forced labor.

Critical accounts by writers such as Las Casas were intended to arouse public outrage and promote crown reforms of newly conquered areas. Las Casas wished to end the harsh system of Spanish tribute-taking begun by the *encomenderos,* or great landlords, of South America. But the rulers who rose to power in the New World refused to abide by reforms passed in distant Spain, and it was not until the 1570s that the depredations against Indians diminished somewhat.

In the hands of rival European nations, which were becoming increasingly Protestant and intent on creating empires of their own, Las Casas's writings were useful as scandal sheets that brought shame to Spanish colonizers. A Dutch artist named Theodore de Bry, who had never been to the colonies, depicted Spaniards wantonly exterminating defenseless Indians. To the semiliterate populations of Europe who saw De Bry's illustrations, Las Casas seemed to offer definitive proof of Catholic depravity and to support a somehow superior Protestant view of New World peoples. This *Leyenda Negra,* or Black Legend, fueled the propaganda machines of northern European states, although in light of modern studies that show unparalleled demographic disaster wherever Spain claimed dominion, the legend carried a ring of truth.

Questions for Analysis

1. What human and natural characteristics of the Taino does Columbus find amazing? Why?
2. What assumptions does Columbus make about the future of the Taino?
3. What major indictments does Las Casas bring against Spanish colonizers?
4. Reading historical documents involves distinguishing between verifiable facts and individual perceptions; facts are reliably true, whereas perceptions might be distorted. What is probably true in each of these accounts, and what is open to question? Which statements are observations, and which are judgments?
5. Are there any similarities between Columbus's and Las Casas's views?

2

The First Experiments, 1540–1680

"Be pleased to bring me home, with all due haste," wrote Mary, a young servant in Maryland, to a relative in London. "For I have been ill used in this country, worked at all manner of tasks both inside the house and out, and made the object of ridicule for each and sundry small error in keeping this wretched house." "The fire went out today," she wrote on March 3, 1668, "which brought wrath from master's oldest [son], and master used [beat] me sorely when he found the cider gone sour, though it be Amos [the master's slave] who left it in the sun." On another occasion, Mary pleaded for money to pay for a return trip to England, noting her frequent hunger and persistent headaches. Although she had been tempted to run away, Mary chose instead to deceive her master by stretching out her household chores so they took up most of the day, "else I must get to the [tobacco] field and bend my back til it ache."

Mary was thirteen years old when she came from London to the marshy shore of Maryland to be an indentured servant. Her ship captain noted that she was "good at house keeping and numbers" and that her new master had cleared land somewhere "in the tobacco country." Her story is typical of the experiences of many, many thousands of young men and women who came to Virginia, Maryland, Antigua, and Barbados during the early 1600s. Roughly 85 percent of the British who migrated to the colonies in the early seventeenth century came as indentured servants, or bound laborers, to masters who needed their labor to clear land, keep house, plant and tend tobacco fields, market goods, or care for motherless children.

Mary's new life must have been lonely: she was almost completely cut off from communication to England and, because her master did not live in a village, had only infrequent connections to other households scattered about the countryside. In addition, Mary's field and house labor was very different from traditional European women's work. For one thing, her tasks overlapped with men's chores, and for another, the household was often comprised of both kin and non-kin. Although Mary probably had been accustomed to poor living conditions in England, the ones she encountered in her master's home were even worse. A single-room house with a dirt or plank floor, almost no furniture, straw pallets for sleeping, and a stifling dimly lit interior without windows—these were Mary's daily surroundings. She had "one set of coarse linen clothing" to wear most of the year and a few articles of outerwear for the colder months. Most servants were glad to acquire shoes and elated to eat a meal of more than corn and a piece of meat, dried or in a soup. Mary was quite aware that the shortage of women in Maryland made it possible for her to have her pick of unmarried men. But she lamented that "not one of them be young as I, and none a likely father of my babes, most being advanced in years and disagreeable in manners." Yet it was unthinkable for a young woman to remain single in Mary's world, so she would have to choose one of the eligible, if less-than-satisfactory, men to provide her with the tentative securities of marriage and a roof over her head.

Mary's story ends abruptly in the historical record, but the few details we have about her experiences conform to the sketchy lives of many other early settlers in North America. Thousands of servants accepted harsh conditions because they hoped to rise above the poverty that was their lot in Britain or Europe. Few, however, expected the rough treatment and poor health they encountered, or the cultural adjustments they were forced to make. Thousands of others would come to North America in the early 1600s in families, with tools for farming or skills for making necessary goods. People of diverse national, religious, ethnic, and racial backgrounds struggled in numerous wilderness locations to begin their lives over again in dramatically different surroundings than they had ever known. Some early settlements failed, and some flourished. Like Mary's, their collective experiences raise important questions.

- What was the range of experiences of colonists coming from Spain, France, Holland, and England?
- Given the hardships they faced, why did so many thousands of settlers come to North America year after year?
- What did the early colonists hope to accomplish by starting life over on the other side of an ocean, and what immediate obstacles did they have to overcome?
- What political and cultural differences emerged as the earliest North American colonies took hold?

This chapter will address these questions.

Struggles for New World Dominion, 1540–1680

During the 1500s, Portugal and Spain sent out tens of thousands of adventurers, farmers, and servants to colonize its vast claims. Spain's conquest of the Western Hemisphere remained relatively unrivaled until the early 1600s. France, Holland, and England had a variety of plans for transplanting people during the 1500s, and a variety of motivations spurred small groups of individuals to migrate, but the great waves of migration from those nations came decades later. Dutch colonists in North America experienced frustrations, disasters, and near failure at their small settlements, while French migrants were sparsely dispersed across northern territories for generations. Although England's rising imperial power eventually would replace Spain's, the island nation established only a few small villages that hugged the North American coastline until the early 1600s. Moreover, European peoples' adaptations to new environments, conflicts with Native Americans, encounters with people from other European nations or ethnic origins, and growing reliance on the labor of African and Caribbean slaves introduced numerous unresolved cultural tensions.

Governing Spain's Empire

By the mid-1500s, many of Spain's missionaries and government officials in Florida and New Mexico viewed the Native Americans around them as potential allies in creating a buffer zone against Dutch, English, and French settlers. St. Augustine, established in 1565, served first as a Spanish outpost to spy on enemy ships sailing nearby, as well as a beacon to potential colonists of Spain's intentions to stay in North America (see map).

The Spanish Empire was officially the private property of monarchs in the home country, who tried to impose uniform control over their colonies by appointing *viceroys* to rule over new territories and hear local disputes. However, because Spain's American empire was vast and discontinuous—a collection of islands in the Caribbean, the Mexican highlands, and portions of South America—it was not the viceroys but the *conquistadors* and petty Spanish officials who lived in the scattered colonies amid Native Americans who held the empire together. *Conquistadors* and local officials organized the *encomienda* system, under which the Spanish forced local populations to work in mines and fields. Spaniards who became lords over large populations lived in high style on the tribute in goods and specie (gold and silver) they extracted from native residents.

At the New World's greatest mine at Potosí (meaning "to thunder," or "to burst") in Bolivia, thousands of Indian workers extracted silver in fourteen-hour shifts at altitudes Europeans could not endure. Starting in 1545, merchants sent its rich stores of silver on galleons to Spain, where runaway inflation resulted from introducing huge quantities of the precious metal (see page 18). By the 1570s, Potosí's population was over 120,000, making it larger than Seville, Madrid, Rome, or Paris.

Whether Europeans praised or scorned the Spanish conquest, few doubted that the lives of native peoples were changed dramatically by the encounter. Once the devastation of disease and warfare somewhat subsided, remnants of Native American populations came together to form new societies that melded attributes of

Chronology

1560s–1580s	England overruns Ireland
1565	Spanish found St. Augustine, Florida
1578	Gilbert receives patent for "Newe Founde Land"
	Drake reaches California
1584–1587	Roanoke settlement
1588	England defeats Spanish Armada
1603	Champlain begins colonization of New France
1607	Jamestown founded
1609	Hudson explores North America for Holland
1610	Santa Fe founded
1619	First Africans brought to Virginia
1620	Plymouth founded
1626	Dutch buy Manhattan Island
1630	Massachusetts Bay founded
1634	Maryland founded
1635–1637	Pequot War
1636	Williams founds Rhode Island
	Harvard College founded
1637	Hutchinson banished from Massachusetts
1643	New Sweden founded
1662	Halfway Covenant
1675–1676	Bacon's Rebellion
1675–1677	Metacomet's (King Philip's) War
1680	Pueblo Revolt in New Mexico

many peoples. Migrants from Spain constructed the cities of Quito, Mexico City, Havana, San Juan, and Santo Domingo on the ruins of Native American cities and temples. By the 1590s, over 200,000 Europeans, mostly Spanish, had crossed the Atlantic, and over 125,000 Africans had been forcibly brought to Brazil and Caribbean islands to work for Portuguese and Spanish plantation lords. Few European women came on the colonizing ships (10 percent of the total at most), but in time communities of mixed *mestizo* (Indian-European) and *mulatto* (African-European) peoples populated Spain's extensive empire.

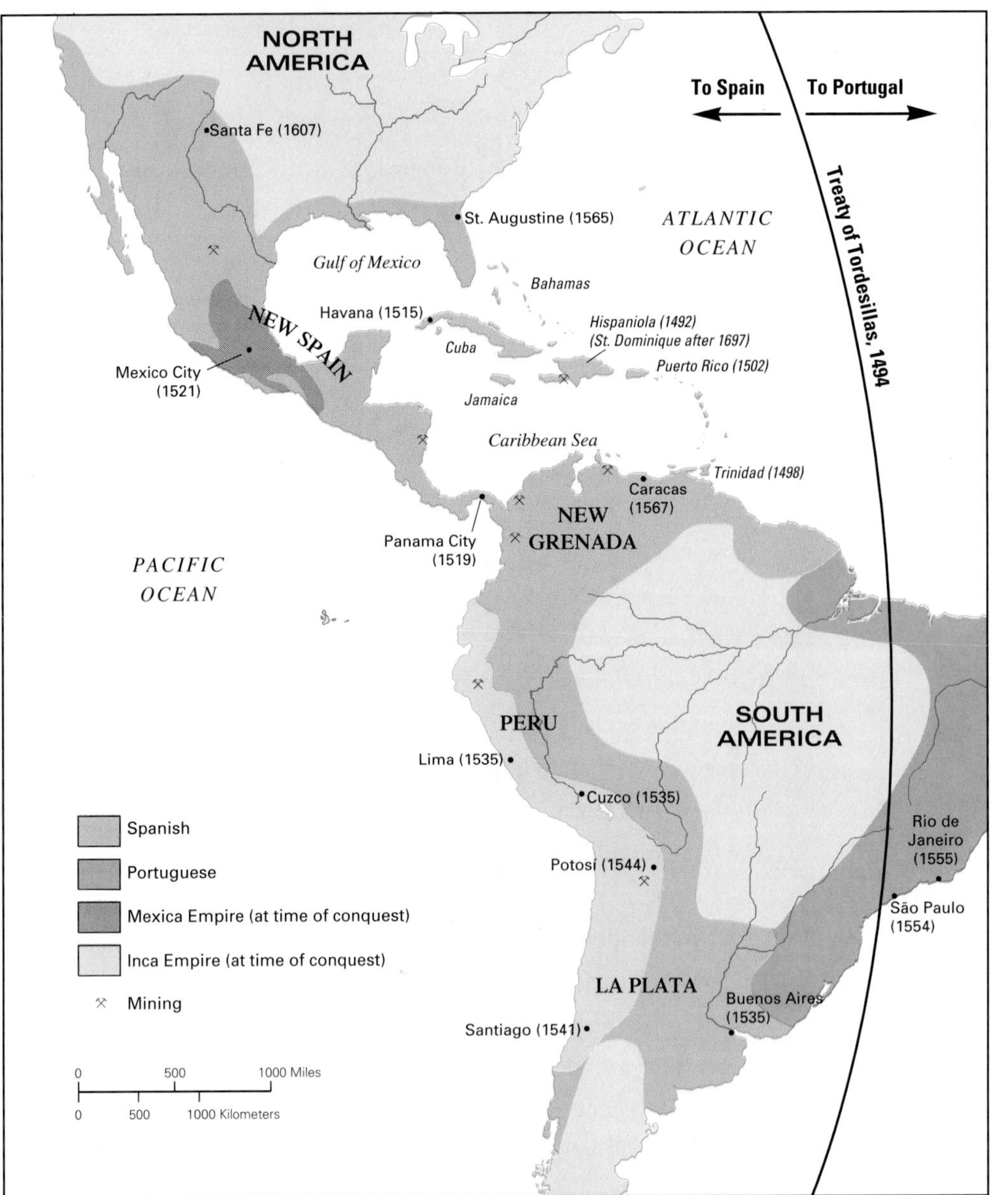

Extent of the Spanish Empire in the 1500s Spanish authorities governed vast amounts of the Western Hemisphere within a very short period of time after the first conquests. The Aztec and Inca empires, and numerous cultures through the Caribbean, Central America, and South America strenuously opposed the advance of Spanish troops and then settlers, but eventually succumbed. For over a century, no other European power claimed so much dominion outside its own nation-state, or held it for so long, as Spain in the Western Hemisphere.

Spain's religious objectives in its foreign colonies also led to policies that had unintended consequences. In 1573 Philip II decreed it illegal to enslave Indians or extract tribute from them forcibly. Thereafter, Spain's goal would be to convert Native Americans to Catholicism and create a *creole,* or mixed Spanish and Indian, culture that incorporated Spanish customs. The king's ban on Indian slavery was never effectively enforced, but his promotion of Native American conversion spurred renewed interest in mission activity abroad. Franciscan monks claimed to have converted thousands of Florida's Indians north of Mexico by about 1650, but few monks learned Indian languages, and few Indians mastered Spanish. Both cultures retained their clothing styles, food preparation methods, and sexual mores. The monks established over thirty missions in Florida, but once diseases ravaged surrounding populations, local farmers, weavers, cooks, and others refused to provide the labor that missions needed to survive.

Spanish soldiers and Franciscan missionaries also fanned out to Santa Fe, New Mexico (founded in 1610), 1,500 miles north of Mexico City. There they encountered the village complexes and irrigated farms of the Pueblo. The Franciscans took Native American wives and, together, built missions to protect and educate the new converts among the Pueblo villages. The first governor of New Mexico, captain-general Juan de Oñate, joined them with his wife Isabel Tolosa Cortés, the granddaughter of Mexico's conqueror and great-granddaughter of Moctezuma. Oñate's goal was to establish the five hundred Spanish who had accompanied him out of Mexico, including ten Franciscan monks, on a series of *encomiendas* in New Mexico. However, the Indians defiantly resisted. In 1598 at Acoma, numerous Pueblo villages banded together to oust the Spanish forces but lost about eight hundred men, women, and children to the weapons and brutal tactics of the Spanish. In years to come, Oñate's excessively cruel behavior drove many of the Spanish settlers off the *encomiendas* and into Santa Fe, and stiffened the resistance of Apache and Navajo people in the countryside to conversion efforts.

Spanish authorities in Mexico recalled Oñate in 1606, but tensions in New Mexico continued. By about 1630, almost 100,000 Pueblo, Apache, and Navajo people had been baptized, a much higher number of converts than New England Puritans could claim in years to come. But few Indians chose to live in the diminished *encomiendas,* and when a long period of drought set in, the Pueblo began to blame the Spanish for their troubles.

Finally, in August 1680, Pueblo villages revolted against the Spanish missionaries. Instigated by orders of Hopi chiefs, especially the charismatic leader Popé, Native Americans burned priests at the stake, and whole villages rose up against Spanish-speaking colonists who lived north of Santa Fe. Over 400 lay dead in the countryside, and some 2,000 took refuge in government buildings, while Pueblo warriors demanded that the Spanish release their peoples from forced labor, contrived intermarriages, and Christian practices. After a five-day siege, everyone affiliated with the Spanish missionaries fled to the south. Leaders of Pueblo villages then formed a strong confederacy dedicated to wiping out all trace of the Spanish, who retreated to El Paso.

A certain portion of the Pueblo population did not hold the Spanish in such contempt. After all, the Spanish had introduced sheep, wheat, fruit trees, and horses. And they had protected the Pueblo from the nomadic Apache and Navajo who routinely attacked their villages. Moreover, many villagers did not accept the new Pueblo confederacy leadership any more than they wished for a Spanish reconquest of New Mexico. The long-term solution, only slowly adopted, was a mixture of Pueblo and Catholic cultures after 1692.

French Toeholds

France's territories in North America remained far more sparcely settled than Spain's. One deterrent to settlement was manpower: France's perpetual need to send armies elsewhere in Europe skimmed off the poor, restless, and young male population that might have gone to the New World. In 1562 the Huguenot Jean Ribault helped bring nearly 150 religious dissenters to Parris Island (later Beaufort, South Carolina), where he left them to build a fort and shelters while he returned to France for supplies. But religious wars at home consumed Ribault, and the starving colonists resorted to cannibalism until a passing English pirate ship helped them escape their desperate situation. Two years later, another French expedition established a toehold on St. Johns River (later Jacksonville, Florida), where colonists put up Fort Caroline. They were at first well received by the Timucua Indians nearby, who in return for food and clothing asked for French help in warding off the Spanish. But in 1565 the Spanish captain-general, Don Pedro Menéndez de Avilés built a rival fort at St. Augustine, Florida, and marched his troops north through the swamps to Fort Caroline to slaughter over five hundred French colonists.

Far to the north along the coastlines of Newfoundland, Labrador, and Nova Scotia, fishermen and trappers established a tenuous presence. By 1500, the cod-rich Grand Banks was a regular stopping place for English, Dutch, Flemish, and Portuguese fishermen. When King Francis I sent out Giovanni da Verrazzano in 1524 to explore the region stretching from the Carolinas to Nova Scotia, he relied on fishermen to show him the way. Between 1534 and 1543, Jacques Cartier made three voyages along the St. Lawrence River in hopes of securing great wealth for the French king, each time accompanied by skilled fishermen. Cartier also looked for a route to the East Indies through the terrain that Waldseemüller's map (see page 28) now called America. Although he failed to find such an avenue to riches, Cartier did explore the maritime areas that Iroquoian-language Indians called Canada (probably meaning "village").

The fur trade quickly came to define the French presence in North America. In contrast to the great state systems of South American Indians, Canada's Micmac and Montagnais Indians were hunter-gatherers who lived in small family-based groups and had no permanent cities (see map of North American culture areas, p. 5). Nevertheless, enthusiastic about trading their furs for European iron wares, cloth, and glass trinkets, they welcomed Cartier's first trading post in 1541. By the late 1500s, the French government sponsored more aggressive exploration in Canada. Starting in 1604, Samuel de Champlain, a French cartographer and gentleman, began a series of eleven voyages to Canada. The Montagnais and Algonquian soon learned that Champlain was a fair dealer and readily agreed to trading terms. In addition, Champlain wanted to create a religious haven for Catholics and Huguenots who were beleaguered by the religious wars in France. Between 1604 and 1606, he was instrumental in planting Acadia (Nova Scotia) with mainly Huguenots, most of them impoverished refugees from their homeland. In 1608 he settled more of his countrymen in Quebec City, which would soon be a continental crossroads for the fur trade.

But amicable relations among cultures and religions deteriorated quickly in the next years. If the fur trade introduced welcome new technologies (such as guns) and tools (such as knives) to Indians, it also stimulated wars and long migrations of peoples in quest of precious peltry. By the early 1600s, members of the Micmac, Huron, Erie, and other cultures killed one another more efficiently and neglected the hunting and agricultural activities that had sustained their way of life. Champlain aided Algonquian raids against Mohawk villages on Lake Champlain, which initiated a long era of tensions. By 1615, the French traders reached Huronia, an area of dense settlements that wished to trade directly with the French and thereby undermine agreements with intermediate tribes to the east. European diseases also brought familiar demographic devastation, and weakened Indian communities became prey for their traditional enemies who now wished to corner the fur trade.

In addition, Huguenots and Catholics in Acadia argued fiercely over theology and civic responsibilities. In 1625 the French government declared Catholicism to be the religion of its territory in North America and in 1627 banned Protestants from New France, thereby deepening disagreements among French colonists. On the frontiers, Jesuit missionaries who lived among the Huron and Montagnais, attempting to convert natives to Catholicism, raised suspicions about their true intensions: when a smallpox epidemic broke out in 1644, the Huron believed it was part of missionaries' efforts to sabotage Indian control of the fur trade. Nevertheless, the fur trade continued to attract trappers known as *coureurs des bois* (forest runners) who extracted

A Northern Indian's Knife, 1600s
As the fur trade developed, Indians acquired many luxury and necessary goods from Europeans, including knives such as this one, which was decorated with a tracery of beads that showed the personal or tribal name of the owner. Knives were used not only in hunting but in many different household chores as well and became important articles of exchange. *(Musée de l'Homme.)*

valuable pelts and introduced European goods and economic ways. Far from the restraining laws of government or traditional institutions, these fur traders also married and lived with Algonquians of New France. To the scorn of Jesuit missionaries, trappers adopted many Indian customs and declined to teach Indians "civilized" French ways.

In all, no more than two thousand French settlers came to New France before 1663. But thereafter, the French government took over direct control of New France, planted a military-style leadership in the major cities of Montreal, Quebec, and Three Rivers, and then made arrangements to transport hundreds of women, most of them orphans and widows of European warfare, into the colony to become wives and servants of landowning farmers. By the 1690s, *seigneurs,* or landed gentry, accumulated vast stretches of land along the St. Lawrence River and imposed various taxes on local settlers, although they never consolidated political power enough in the colony to act like true aristocrats.

Meanwhile, some intrepid souls migrated down the Mississippi River, naming new settlements after renowned trappers such as Louis Jolliet or missionaries such as Jacques Marquette, and transplanting their wheat-based economies to the fertile valleys near the former Cahokia. René-Robert Cavelier, Sieur de La Salle, took parties of settlers to the Gulf of Mexico, seeking the elusive "northwest passage" to the Pacific Ocean. In 1682 La Salle claimed for France virtually all of the interior of North America, calling it Louisiana in honor of his king, Louis XIV. However, two years later La Salle returned by sea to the mouth of the Gulf of Mexico with about 280 soldiers and colonists, intending to use thousands of Natchez and Creek allies to raid Spanish forts and silver mines to the south. Instead he ended up in Texas, where he was murdered by his own recruits in 1685. For decades to come, French Louisiana was little more than a dumping ground for undesirable criminals and desperately poor Frenchmen, cross-hatched by fur trading trails and a few wretched forts, while most French migrants went to the warm and prosperous Caribbean islands of Martinique, Guadaloupe, and St. Dominique (taken from Spain in 1697).

Dutch Republican Colonies

During the late 1500s, the Netherlands, consisting of present-day Holland in the north and Belgium in the south, became the most prosperous country in Europe, and Amsterdam, the commercial capital of the Atlantic world. In 1602 city merchants, known as *burghers,* established the Dutch East India Company, which used the advanced shipping and financial services of their country to take over Portugal's role in Asian and African trade. In 1609 the different political districts of the Netherlands were united into the Dutch Republic, further boosting the efforts of Dutch planters to finance large Caribbean sugar plantations, search for exotic spices in Indonesia, secure grain and timber from Baltic peoples, and enter the New World fur trade.

North America was never a major target of conquest and colonization for the Netherlands, but its trappers and fishermen competed with French adventurers to find a passage to the East Indies. In 1609 the East India Company hired sea captain Henry Hudson to find this route; instead, he found the abundant river valley that was named for him and encountered the Iroquois who would become European trading partners. Once a few intrepid Dutch adventurers founded Fort Nassau near present-day Albany in 1614, Amsterdam merchants grew hopeful that the settlers could trade with Native Americans for huge amounts of beaver, martin, deer, otter, and other furs. The enterprising merchants funded a new Dutch West India Company (WIC) and secured a government charter for its business in 1621. This charter set up a joint stock company, an enterprise that sold shares of stock to investors in order to underwrite expensive ventures abroad while spreading the risk of investment. It also authorized Pierre Minuit to purchase the island of Manhattan from Native Americans for the equivalent of a dozen beaver hides in 1626. Minuit assumed leadership of the struggling settlement and began to recruit refugee Protestant families to the town of New Amsterdam.

But the fledgling colony of New Netherland got off to a slow start. Minuit complained that the Company's "servants" did not work enough and that "scrapings of all sorts of nationalities" coming to the island—including Germans, Scots, Scandinavians, French, free and slave Angolans, and Brazilians—harmed rather than helped settlement of the colony. Directors in Amsterdam were also dismayed about reports of Jewish families arriving, as well as "Papists, Mennonites and Lutherans . . . many Puritans . . . atheists and various other servants of Baal."

To make matters worse, trappers spent their time north of the settlement, and few people wanted to leave commerce for farming in New Netherland during these early years. Even when the Company began to grant *patronen*—or important landholders—huge tracts of land on which they were expected to settle at least fifty immigrant families as tenants within four years, the landscape seemed to remain empty. Only Kiliaen van Rensselaer set up a thriving patroonship upriver. Most immigrants chose instead to claim *bouweries*—small grants of free land to heads of households—in New Amsterdam or nearby on Staten Island and Long Island.

New Amsterdam was situated in the center of dense Algonquian village life. Following Minuit's rule, Governor Willem Kieft promised to protect Algonquians fleeing their Indian enemies in return for a close trading relationship. But overcome with greed for Algonquian land, Kieft instead launched a war against the vulnerable Indian settlements. From 1639 to 1645, attack followed attack, with Algonquians fleeing west across the Hudson River away from the "unnatural, barbarous, unnecessary, unjust, and disgraceful" assaults of the Dutch. Hundreds of Dutch settlers fearful of retaliation relocated to Caribbean islands. Over two hundred Europeans perished in the bloody massacres of those years; a thousand Indians may have died. To the interior, Dutch efforts to ally with their Iroquois fur trading partners heightened tensions with the French and Huron. As beaver hunting grounds receded from Dutch settlements, all sides used European guns to engage in bloody conflicts over furs. Almost constantly at war, the Iroquois became ever more dependent on imported Dutch goods that they previously made among themselves. By 1650, New Netherland had grown to only 1,500 souls.

In the meantime, Minuit returned to North America and in 1638 initiated a settlement of about four hundred Swedish Protestants around Fort Christina (near today's Wilmington, Delaware). The population at the fort and its surrounding farms,

Early New Amsterdam Compared to its parent city, Amsterdam, this small colonial port had only a few homes crowding the tip of the island during the early 1600s. However, New Amsterdam became an important strategic location for Dutch trading. A few of the mother country's largest ships brought colonists much-needed goods each year, while colonial merchants waited anxiously to exchange furs and timber. *(Library of Congress.)*

called New Sweden, was small; nevertheless, its settlers put up sturdy log cabins and traded successfully in the interior for furs the WIC wanted. In 1651 the Company and the ambitious governor at New Amsterdam, Pieter Stuyvesant (governed 1647–1664) agreed to lead a military expedition against New Sweden, which surrendered peacefully and accepted the WIC's authority. Soon, however, greater threats to New Netherland would come from English colonists in the Chesapeake and New England, as well as from "Yankee" English settlers moving onto farmland east of the Hudson River and on Long Island.

Early English Exploration and Settlement

Numerous English fishing and trapping parties made efforts to establish profitable stations in the North Atlantic during the 1400s, but it was not until 1497 that England established extensive claims over this territory. That year, Henry VII hired a young Genoese sailor named John Cabot to cross the ocean. Fishing crews guided Cabot to what might have been "newe founde lande" (Newfoundland) or Cape Breton Island, which he claimed for England. For the next half-century, English leaders did little to advance Cabot's slim inroad into North America. But while a few Englishmen voyaged each year to fish the Grand Banks, momentum gathered in England for colonization abroad. As people displaced by enclosures in the countryside (see page 18) surged into London, the population exploded from 55,000 in 1550 to 200,000 in 1600. Overwhelmed by the crime, health hazards, and demands on institutions to accommodate such huge numbers, public officials yearned to rid the city of its unwanted. When a sustained internal economic crisis added to England's difficulties, manufacturers and merchants also aggressively sought markets abroad.

Queen Elizabeth's rivalries with foreign powers, combined with her support for the Reformation, provided sparks for England's initial efforts at exploring the Western Hemisphere. The so-called Sea Dogs—Sir Francis Drake, Sir John Hawkins, Sir Humphrey Gilbert, and Sir Walter Ralegh—convinced Elizabeth to support their ambitions to build an overseas empire based on conquest, raiding for slaves, and piracy. In turn, Elizabeth relied on these brazen adventurers to provide her with aid to Protestant allies in the Netherlands and to groups of French Huguenots. Secretly, she encouraged English merchants to pool their capital for North American ventures.

In 1577 Drake set out from England with four tiny ships—one of them his famous *Golden Hind*—and 164 crew members on what was publicly billed as a voyage of trade and exploration. Unofficially, however, the queen had given Drake permission to prey on Spanish Caribbean ports and to sail to the Isthmus of Panama to capture Spanish gold and silver mined from Peru and Mexico. Drake's stupendously successful privateering richly rewarded his backers and whetted English appetites for dominion abroad. Elizabeth dubbed Drake a knight.

Meanwhile, English troops under the command of Drake and Gilbert relentlessly drove Irish Catholic clansmen out of their towns and fields in a kind of guerrilla warfare for decades in the 1500s, inflicting starvation and razing homes. English publicists contributed to the brutality with propaganda; Irish "savages," they wrote, deserved to be utterly wiped out because they resisted advancing English "civilization." The victors established a "plantation" system by granting Irish lands to English and Protestant Scottish freeholders. Having set a precedent for conquest over, and intolerance of, different cultures, Gilbert convinced Elizabeth in 1578 to grant him a charter to take settlers to lands previously claimed by Cabot. Although in 1583 he finally took three shiploads of settlers across the Atlantic to Newfoundland, most of them returned to their homelands. On the third voyage out to stock new settlements, Gilbert and his ship were lost at sea.

After Gilbert's disappearance, his half-brother, Sir Walter Ralegh, eagerly assumed the rights of the royal charter for exploring North America. Assured by a fisherman that "very handsome and goodly people" lived to the south, Ralegh began to recruit investors and colonists. In 1584 the gentry promoter Richard Hakluyt wrote *Discourse of Western Planting*, which professed that on American lands "great numbers [of English poor] may be set to work," "to the unburdening of the realm . . . at home." American settlements would stimulate the languishing English shipbuilding industry and put an end to Spanish domination of heathen peoples. Merchants also hoped that successful colonies abroad would provide them with markets for English manufactures.

Ralegh's first commissioned ship of settlers sailed in late 1584, past the West Indies, and to the Outer Banks of present-day North Carolina, where Roanoke Island lay. After a dire winter of scarcities and deaths, the few remaining settlers seemed to have made a beginning for themselves. Their chosen site lay where numerous Algonquian villages quarreled among themselves. Those closest to the coast, under the leadership of Wingina, hoped that Ralegh's people would ally with them against enemy Indians. But soon these Indian villages grew suspicious that the English had come only to steal from them and eventually overpower them.

Indian fears were justified, for no sooner had Ralegh named the region Virginia (after the virgin queen, Elizabeth I) than he ordered soldiers to force Indians to trap furs for export and turn over food to the English colonists. If they resisted, instructed Ralegh, "bring them all in subjection to civility." Settlers quarreled with the Indians, stopped farming their small clearings, and attacked Roanoke Indian villages in early 1586. When the pirate Francis Drake stopped at the settlement briefly and warned of possible Spanish raids along their coastline, many Virginians returned to England. The Indians slaughtered a second, small party of new settlers, and when the commander of a third ship arrived, only to find a vacant settlement, he left a few soldiers to garrison the meager fort while he returned to England for reinforcements.

Ralegh attempted to settle Roanoke and "civilize the heathens" again in 1587 on a fourth venture of 117 colonizers. This time the settlers included a more mixed group of women and children, craftsmen and farmers, and a governor and talented artist named John White. It was White's daughter, Virginia Dare, who may have been the first English child born in the Western Hemisphere. But their collective fate was firmly tied to events back in England in 1588, and success at Roanoke eluded this group, too.

Secoton, A Village in [North] Carolina in about 1585
John White, who accompanied the Roanoke settlers, created an extensive visual record of life among the villages of the Powhatan confederacy. In this picture of daily life, people gather around sacred fires to pray (lower left) and dance around a circle of posts (lower right), while women in the central aisle prepare food. Well-ordered fields of corn add to the sense of harmony and give a settled feel to the village. Well-thatched roofs over houses were intended to convey the "civilized"—as opposed to "savage" or nomadic—lifestyles of the Indians around Roanoke. *(Miriam and Ira D. Wallach Division of Art, Prints and Photographs, New York Public Library. Astor, Lenox and Tilden Foundations.)*

When John White returned to England for supplies, Elizabeth detained his ship for her navy. King Philip II of Spain had grown angry about Elizabeth's support for the Dutch Protestants who sought to dethrone him, and was furious at the success of Drake's Sea Dogs against his Spanish treasure fleet. With Mary Stuart, Queen of Scots, Philip conspired to overthrow the English government. When Elizabeth had Mary beheaded in 1587, an undaunted Philip stepped up plans to crush the Netherlands and invade England with his great Armada, a fleet of 130 ships, 2,400 pieces of artillery, and over 30,000 men. Under the command of Drake, however, English ships battled the Armada in the English Channel for nine days in 1588. Drake's small fire ships raged against Philip's impressive fleet and finally drove it away with the help of a strong "Protestant Wind."

Elizabeth was now able to proclaim England's naval supremacy, but for the suffering settlers in Roanoke, this was hardly inspiring news. When White returned to Roanoke in 1590, he found a "Lost Colony," empty of inhabitants. The houses had been "taken down" and household goods "spoiled and scattered about." White believed that hostile Indians attacked and killed the English soldiers and settlers. Modern scholars have also proposed that perhaps Spain struck a fatal blow from the south, and a third possibility is that the settlers, in order to survive, assimilated into the Indian villages nearby or to the north in the Chesapeake Bay. Whatever their fate, the only trace of the former colony was a single word carved into a doorpost—"Croatoan," the name of an Indian tribe near present-day Ocracoke that had befriended English settlers.

England's Southern Plantings, 1607–1680

Elizabeth's successor, King James I, renewed crown interest in colonizing North America at the opening of the new century, and the economic crisis in his kingdom spurred groups of adventurers and settlers to begin anew across the Atlantic. Seeking riches, resources, and trading opportunities, hundreds of people came to Virginia and Maryland. These settlements quickly departed from the customs and cultures that people knew in their homelands, and distinctive communities arose in frontier conditions. In time, many Chesapeake settlers would achieve relative stability, and some would enjoy phenomenal economic success. In the early years, however, numerous Indian wars, widespread servitude and slavery, and increasingly unequal land ownership strained the small societies forming in that region.

Virginia's Beginnings

Disappointed with his Roanoke failure, Ralegh transferred his rights to settle in North America to a group of London merchants, who recruited additional investors and in 1606 accepted a charter from King James I (reigned 1603–1625) for the Virginia Company. Two groups were set up within the Company. One of them, the Virginia Company of Plymouth, attempted a settlement of about a hundred men on the Kennebec River at Sagadahoc in present-day Maine. But disease, Indian attacks, and a bitterly cold winter without sufficient supplies convinced the settlers to abandon their camps.

The other group, the Virginia Company of London, settled much farther south. Three ships left England in late 1606 with 144 men who were expected to find riches in the New World quickly. A midwinter Atlantic crossing made the expedition arduous, but 105 hardy colonists survived. The next April they reached the mouth of the James River in present-day Virginia, where they set about putting up meager thatched huts and a protective fort.

Over the next three years, about four-fifths of the colonizers died from starvation and disease. The river was a perpetual source of typhus and dysentery, and few of the earliest migrants knew how to fish and farm. They might have completely perished if the Indians nearby had not helped by bringing food. Powhatan, recognized as a chief over about twenty-two area tribes, quickly grew wary of the Englishmen but hoped that, in return for food, colonists would help him subdue enemy villages beyond his current area of influence.

Food was not the only problem; the settlers also failed to find rich stores of silver and gold to send their investors back home. In 1609 the Company formed a joint stock company, which drew in life-saving funds for the colony, established a plan for granting land to would-be settlers, and appointed a resident governing council. They honored their king by naming the permanent settlement James Town.

Still, colonists quarreled incessantly—about sharing work and supplies, about allotments of land for houses and fields, about access to arms and ammunition, and just about everything else. In 1608 John Smith, an experienced military commander, joined James Town's governing council and gradually imposed his authority over the settlement and set colonists to work. "He that will not work," he declared, "shall not eat." With the blessings of Company directors in England, Smith negotiated with the Indians for peace and food and set up land surveys to determine boundaries of private and government holdings.

Troubles were not over, however. In early 1609 an interim governor, Sir Thomas Gates, set out from England with about five hundred additional settlers. Although the ships were blown off course and spent some weeks in Bermuda (a journey immortalized in Shakespeare's *The Tempest*), many settlers arrived in James Town eventually. Of these newcomers, many could not, and others would not, work the mosquito-infested fields around the fort. Some of them preferred to steal corn and other necessities from Powhatan's tribes. Powhatan lamented the cruelties of the English: "Why will you take by force what you may obtain by love? Why will you destroy us who supply you with food? What can you get by war?" In the midst of natural bounty, colonists destroyed Indian resources and chose to starve; they burned their shelters for fuel, they ate every last animal, and sent home alarming reports of cannibalism. When the horrid winter of 1609–1610 was over, only about sixty of the five hundred residents were still alive.

Just when the remaining few had decided to leave, a new fleet of three hundred men, including Gates's replacement Governor Thomas West, Baron De la Warr, arrived and ordered the starving Virginians to stay, share the supplies his ships brought, and reset land boundaries. In 1612, a legal code of *Laws, Divine, Morall, and Martiall* stipulated the requirements of work for every inhabitant, on both common and private projects, as well as their duties of military defense. The struggling band of settlers began to send a few commodities back to the English investors by 1614, including furs, timber products, silk grass, a crude kind of iron, and local herbs.

But De la Warr also inherited ongoing tensions between settlers and Indians of the region. For many months, Powhatan's warriors had been killing individuals who wandered from James Town, to which the English responded by slaughtering whole villages. By 1614, Powhatan, whose villages were worn out by disease and warfare, sent his English-speaking daughter Pocahontas to James Town for peace negotiations. Pocahontas did more than negotiate: she stayed, converted to Christianity, and married John Rolfe.

Desperate to turn a profit for their English investors, the Company directors in London resorted to three measures. First, they permitted Rolfe to introduce "oronoco," or West Indian tobacco, into English markets in 1614. Until then, King James I and much English public sentiment protested the cultivation and use of the commodity. Smoking, said James, was "a custom loathsome to the eye, hateful to the nose, harmful to the brain, dangerous to the lungs, and in the black stinking fumes thereof, the nearest resembling the horrible smoke of the pit that is bottomless." But even James had to admit that import duties imposed on the popular "weed" brought the crown much-needed revenue. By 1618, Virginians were sending regular shipments of tobacco to eager London buyers; by 1620, the colony turned almost exclusively to producing tobacco. Until 1629, prices soared to undreamed-of heights.

Second, in order to lure able workers to Virginia's tobacco fields, the Company put Edwyn Sandys in charge of the colony in 1618. Two years before that, the Company introduced a new system for distributing land, known as the headright system: each head of household would receive 50 acres of land for himself and 50 acres more for each immediate family member and servant he brought to the colony. The Company was at first hopeful that this plan would stimulate migration. But in the process of making claims, unforeseen distortions in the headright system began to develop. Surveying and patenting land was so complicated and costly that many newcomers to Virginia sold their claims to land brokers who could survey or dispose of individuals' lands at profit. In addition, some colonists consolidated large holdings by pooling family claims or by buying those of newcomers. Soon, "plantations" (a term that at first meant simply a farm but in the Virginia context came to imply a great estate) filled the fertile river ways around James Town, although most large land claims remained uncultivated for some time.

Third, in 1619 the Virginia Company granted settlers the first representative assembly in North America, called the House of Burgesses. The governor and councilors, who were chosen based on their land claims, swore to make and interpret laws "as the home Parliament doe." But the new government system had barely begun when disaster struck in 1622. Long-suffering local Indians had been deprived of their lands, forced into labor, and nearly starved themselves by feeding their crops to Englishmen. In March, Powhatan's brother, Opechancanough, sent warriors to attack several defenseless farms along the James River. They killed at least 347 settlers and prompted many others to flee from the countryside and demand to return to England. The shocked and besieged colonists became demoralized and nearly starved that winter.

A royal investigation of the troubles resulted in King James revoking the Company's charter and declaring Virginia a royal colony in 1624. The king now appointed the governors, and although the burgesses still initiated colonial laws, the crown rather than the Company now approved them in England. In addition, the crown extended the right to vote for burgesses from certain landed men in the colony to all free adult men.

Tobacco exports, rising immigration, and more stable government in Virginia provided settlers with a formula for becoming a permanent colony. But these measures did not bring immediate calm. By the mid-1620s, the nearly 6,000 colonizers who came to Virginia under the Sandys government had been reduced to less than 1,200. For the next ten years, colonists fought with Opechancanough and the villages he controlled, and they still lacked sufficient farming tools, ate meagerly, and witnessed an appalling number of their infants die. When the population did begin to rise by the 1630s, tensions grew again with the Indian villages adjacent to their frontier plantations. In 1644 Opechancanough led a last desperate attack, slaying over five hundred colonists. The English settlers struck back with a vengeance, crushing whole villages and killing Opechancanough. Finally in late 1646 the remaining Powhatan confederacy members recognized their dependence on the crown of England, and both sides agreed on territorial boundaries.

Meanwhile, Virginia's government assumed the structure it would keep for the rest of the colonial era. In 1634 the assembly created counties, each with a justice of the peace presiding over local affairs. Each county also had a court, usually comprised of the most prestigious landowners. Each county also overlapped as an Anglican parish, with a church and a vestry—often the justices—who chose ministers. By the 1640s, justices also served frequently in the legislature, so that prosperous planters could hope to attain high status and serve in important offices. Almost all key leaders in Virginia's county and provincial governments were appointed by the governor, and political positions quickly became a means to acquire land or commercial privileges. Through shrewd marriage arrangements, council and assembly members created interlocking kinship networks that inherited wealth and power for generations to come.

Founding Maryland

George Calvert, Lord Baltimore, did not sponsor colonization in order to make profits in the New World, but rather to provide persecuted English and Irish Catholics a new start. In 1632 King Charles I gave Baltimore a charter for a proprietary colony, one that conferred great powers—not unlike a medieval lord's—to organize use of the land and defend it against outsiders. Soon known as Maryland, its proprietor Lord Baltimore was tantamount to king over the 6.5 million acres given to him. But he died before he could assume such honors, and his son Cecilius succeeded him both as Lord Baltimore and proprietor of Maryland.

The first migrants to Maryland in 1634 founded the tiny settlement of St. Mary's City. But the colony grew very slowly. Baltimore's plan assumed that Catholic gentlemen would claim titles to vast estates in the colony, just as manor lords of a bygone

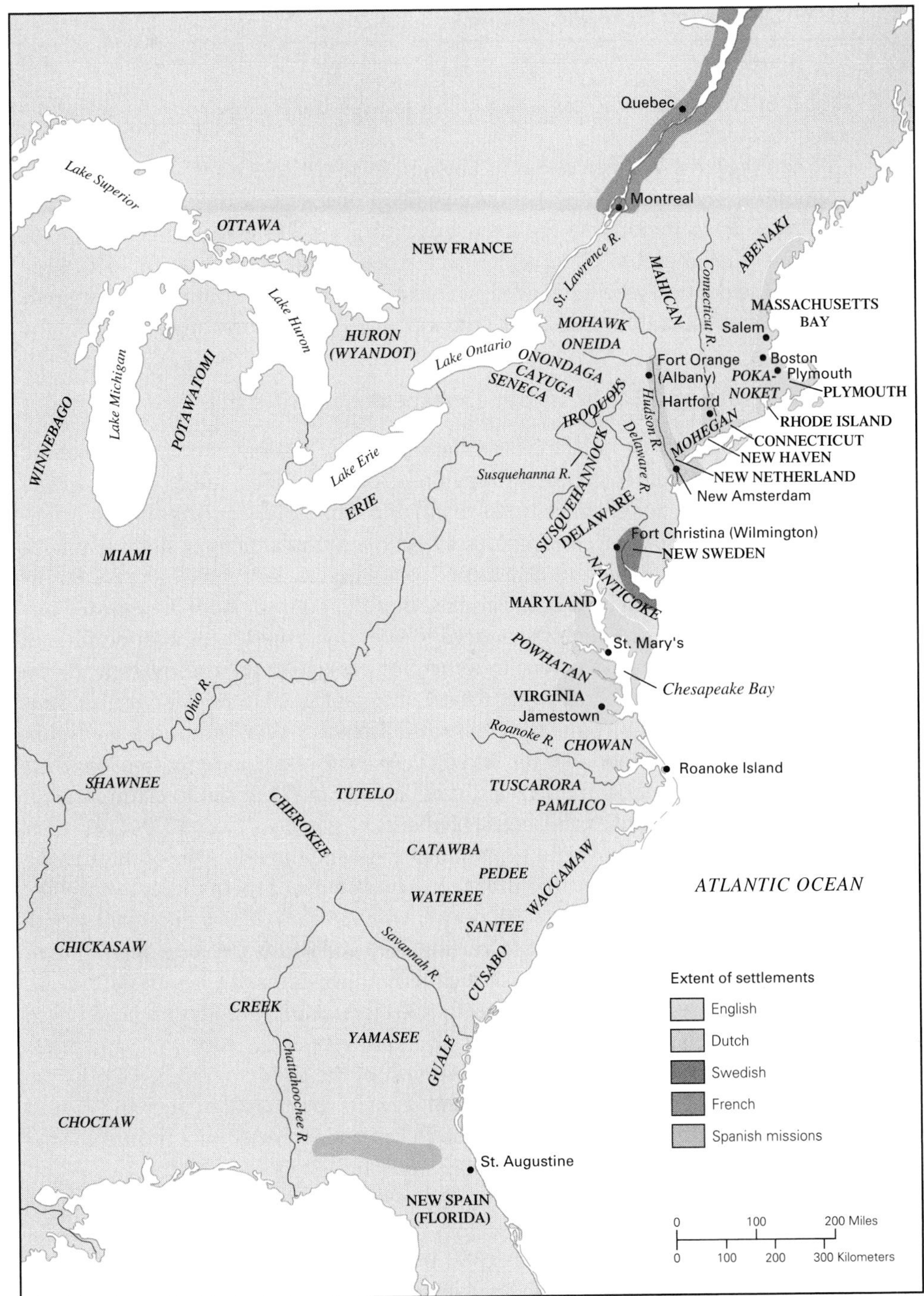

European Settlement and Indian Cultures of Eastern North America, 1650 Numerous towns and settlements dotted the Atlantic coastline by midcentury, while Indian populations disappeared or dispersed toward the interior of the continent.

English era, and on these estates they would settle Protestant servants who were expected to honor the authority of quasi-feudal courts. But few Catholics migrated to Maryland during Charles I's relatively tolerant reign (1625–1649), while the large number of Protestants who came as servants to work the colony's tobacco fields built a majority quickly.

When the Civil War broke out in England in 1642, Protestants overthrew Lord Baltimore. To regain his colony, Baltimore had to concede a bicameral legislature that gave Protestants a majority in the elective assembly. He also granted toleration to all Christians (though not to the small Jewish community) in the colony. By 1660, when religious and political rebellion ended, Maryland had a system of courts like Virginia's and an Assembly capable of thwarting the will of any remaining Catholic lords.

Life and Labor in the Chesapeake, 1640–1680

Once they overcame the worst of their "starving times," Chesapeake settlers set about stabilizing their fragile societies. Although religion remained a major difference between white Virginians (primarily Anglican) and white Marylanders (mixed Anglican, Catholic, and Puritan), both colonies developed similar labor systems and family structures. Both colonies quickly turned to tobacco as their most lucrative export crop, and both turned to their homeland's young and poor for labor. Indentured servants, migrants such as Mary, who agreed to work for a master for a set number of years (usually from four to seven) in return for passage to the colony, came to the Chesapeake in large numbers by the 1620s. Contracts signed in England usually stipulated that servants to Virginia were to receive "freedom dues"—a modest amount of clothing, and some food—at the end of their terms. In Maryland, freedom dues usually consisted of a hoe or an ax, a suit of clothes, and the right to claim 50 acres of their own land beyond established settlements.

Many servants brought useful agricultural skills, and three-fourths of the arriving servants during the seventeenth century were men, most of them under twenty-five years old. But the opportunity to start life over with freedom dues at the end of service was more often a dream than reality. Grueling work and abusive masters often spurred servants to run away before the end of their terms. Two-fifths of Chesapeake's seventeenth-century servants died before they fulfilled their contracts. Those who survived years of servitude watched tobacco prices fall and stay low after 1630, while land prices rose and a few great planters accumulated most of the good riverbank sites. By the 1660s, many planters simply refused to grant servants their freedom dues and instead rented land to them as tenants. Remigration to England increased, and frontier life became dangerous and uncertain for runaways and landless poor ex-servants.

Family life in the Chesapeake before the 1680s departed dramatically from patterns in the home country. Life expectancy remained below the English average: at age twenty, a man in Virginia could expect to live to forty-five, with 70 percent dead by age fifty. Although women who lived to age eighteen in England could expect to live to about age forty-five, the same women in the Chesapeake were likely to die in their thirties from complications of childbirth and lowered resistance to typhus and dysentery during pregnancy. In the first years, Chesapeake men outnumbered women five to one, and even when live births finally began to outnumber deaths in the colony, this stark imbalance of genders persisted. As a result, beginning a family was difficult, and about 70 percent of men never married or produced heirs. Since women had to finish their terms of service before marrying, many of them bore their first child well into their twenties. One-fifth of women in the seventeenth-century Chesapeake had illegitimate children, and about one-third were pregnant at their weddings. Men who married in their thirties or later often left widows and hungry children behind. Although many widows remarried quickly, half the children in parts of the Chesapeake had lost at least one parent by age twelve; one-third of the children could expect to lose both parents before they reached adulthood.

Family loyalties, patterns of inheritance, and emotional bonds were seriously affected by these developments. Servants were at first little more than strangers to most masters, yet they had to live in his household or on his property. Orphans became a financial burden for the county courts or were divided among distant relatives, who were obliged to care for them and make important life decisions for them. Stepparents and stepsiblings made claims on property that deprived children of their anticipated inheritances. When fathers died young, traditions of hierarchical household roles began to break down. Many English customs and laws about paternal authority gave way to colonial innovations. For example, because men anticipated the possible early death of their sons, many Chesapeake husbands named a wife as the executrix of their wills, thereby increasing the authority of women over family land. Other husbands left land to their widows in order to enhance their chances of remarriage.

Creating a farm in the Chesapeake wilderness was arduous work for both men and women. While new settlers broke ground to plant food crops and tobacco, they often lived in lean-to huts because felling trees and planing boards was very time-consuming. Even when time permitted building a sturdy dwelling, planters tended to build modest one-room houses averaging 18 by 22 feet so they could put more labor into tending their tobacco fields and gardens. Since there were few gristmills in the countryside, farm women and girls pounded corn for two or three hours a day to produce the family's regular subsistence. Women were constantly busy tending garden vegetables, making cider or beer, preserving meat, baking, plucking chickens, or laboring at some other endless daily chore. In addition, women turned sheep's wool and flax into fiber for spinning, weaving, and fulling cloth, which was then cut, sewn, and mended until it wore out. Straw mattresses, hand-made wooden tools and bowls, perhaps a rough-hewn table and sitting bench, and a cherished carving knife were among the most important household items in the early years. Visitors rarely saw chairs, curtains, eating utensils, or storage chests. Even at the end of the 1600s, most Chesapeake farmers washed their few articles of clothing very infrequently and stood around the table to eat. The most well-to-do Chesapeake planters had not yet begun to acquire the clocks, wine glasses, or imported silks that elite English families enjoyed.

Sugar and Slavery in the Caribbean

By 1600, hundreds of thousands of people from four continents had transformed the Caribbean islands into profitable plantations based on slave labor (see page 29). Seventeen tiny English settlements were founded between 1624 and 1641. Although many of them did not survive, after the 1620s Barbados, St. Kitts, Antigua, Nevis, and Montserrat attracted large numbers of settlers from England who purchased tracts of fertile land. For a while, tobacco cultivation guaranteed prosperity; when its price plummeted after 1630, planters in Antigua and Barbados turned to a new staple export: sugar.

Dutch traders, who seized Brazil in 1630, began a marketing campaign to turn sugar and its byproducts, molasses and rum, from luxury commodities into items of mass consumption in Europe. They introduced Brazilian methods of growing and processing sugar cane to English planters at Barbados and transported sugar to Europe for the fledgling English colony. Barbadian and Antiguan planters were readily attracted to the higher profits from sugar production than from tobacco, but only a few of them could afford the equipment needed to cut, boil, refine, and package sugar. Those few consolidated huge estates, relegating the majority of farmers to tiny holdings. With England's acquisition of Jamaica in the 1650s, another island began to produce "white gold."

Planting, harvesting, and processing sugar cane was unrelenting work and required a reliable and constantly replenished labor supply. The blistering tropical climate, miserable food quality, and inadequate clothing dissuaded many potential indentured servants from coming to the islands. By the early 1660s, planters complained regularly that unruly servants "knew not their place in the order" of social relations or ran away. So when Dutch merchants offered to bring slaves from Africa to Barbados, planters rejoiced. Already they had enslaved Indians since 1627, but their population was declining rapidly. Soon planters discovered that African slaves were genetically protected from the deadly malaria that afflicted New World settlements in recurring waves, and that the Dutch could bring a steady supply of slaves.

A Female Negro Slave, with a Weight chained to her Ankle.

A Female Caribbean Slave
Although this image of a woman weighted down by slavery was created in 1795, the conditions of endless toil, the shame of being deprived of clothing and personal modesty, and the cruelty of being chained like a criminal to the plantation system were all present in the early 1600s Caribbean plantations. *(Tozzer Library, Harvard University.)*

Caribbean laws tell the tale of the rapid rise of slavery. By 1636, every black person brought to Barbados became a slave for life, and over the next years, additional laws gave masters extensive rights to their slaves' labor and leisure time. By the 1660s, these slave codes excluded slaves from testifying against free people in courts of law and mandated brutal physical punishments for food theft or practice of African religious rituals. Other Caribbean islands adopted slavery and slave codes similar to the Barbadian example.

By the 1660s, unfree blacks in the Caribbean outnumbered whites, despite an astoundingly high mortality rate on sugar plantations. By the 1670s, when slavery was just beginning to gain a foothold in the Chesapeake, some 30,000 slaves toiled on Barbados alone. At least half of all children born into Caribbean slavery died before the age of five, and adults brought from Africa to the islands rarely survived more than ten years of incessant plantation work. Most Caribbean landlords and masters chose to live a leisured lifestyle in London, while their hired overseers managed the cultivation of crops and disciplining of slaves on the islands.

Tobacco and Slavery in the Chesapeake

Planters in both the Caribbean and the Chesapeake regions grew dependent on international markets, and together they experienced withering tobacco prices in glutted foreign markets after 1630, which forced them to find new economic strategies. But unlike Caribbean growers, Chesapeake planters continued to grow tobacco as their primary export.Typically, they cultivated a smaller tract of land than in the Caribbean and worked as many hours as their indentured servants did each day. And although the Chesapeake adopted slavery, its rise differed from Caribbean slavery.

In 1619 John Rolfe purchased Virginia's first blacks from a Dutch shipper. More Africans soon followed, but for decades Africans and black Caribbeans introduced into Virginia and Maryland had an ambiguous status. Through the 1650s, it was unclear how the Virginia courts should treat slave or mulatto women who sued white men for abuse. Nor did the courts have a consistent stance toward white men who defended the black "servants" of other white men (the word *slave* was not yet regularly applied to African-Americans) against charges of running away. England's repression of the Irish had demonstrated clearly that language, customs, and religion were sufficient reasons for sustained acts of violent prejudice. But in the Chesapeake, early official documents did not automatically associate people of dark skin color with the status of servant or slave. Indeed, a few Africans owned land and worked alongside their white servants. Anthony Johnson, for example, came to Virginia as an indentured servant in 1621 but eventually achieved his freedom and owned a tract of 250 acres on the eastern shore. Johnson employed not only white servants but also a black man whom he claimed was his "Negro for his life."

Only gradually did planters begin to describe people of African origins as slaves and declare their offspring to be slaves. They were aided in this transformation by a few important factors. First, European settlers came from cultures that accepted degrees of freedom and unfreedom in every layer of society. Force and violence, absolute rights to a person's contracted labor, and harsh legal punishments for infractions of laws were familiar to settlers. Further, physical differences and "heathen" religions were long held in scorn by most Europeans.

Second, indentured servants became a less reliable source of labor over time. Third, by the 1650s, the Caribbean example of slave plantations provided a legal model for creating a permanent supply of human labor, a supply that steadily increased. Beginning in the 1640s, legislators of Virginia and Maryland began to institutionalize slavery, passing a series of laws forbidding Africans to own guns, join the militia, make labor contracts with servants, or travel without permission. In 1661 a Maryland statute defined black people as slaves for life; Virginia laws did the same in 1670.

Over the next thirty years, Chesapeake lawmakers stipulated that a slave's Christianity would not qualify the person for manumission. They defined the status of black laborers as "chattel slaves," or human property, and denied them most of the civic and legal privileges of white society. In a radical departure from the historical examples of slavery in the Mediterranean and Africa, Chesapeake planters declared that the children of female slaves would be born into lifelong slavery. In 1705 the Virginia Assembly declared that no master could whip a white servant without his or her permission, but the law was silent about how masters might punish slaves. Courts affirmed that white servants could bring suits about property, but slaves could not acquire land or contest its ownership.

Even so, the number of slaves in the Chesapeake rose only gradually. In 1640 only 150 blacks were reported in Virginia, not all of them slaves. In 1680 the number had climbed to only about 4,000 slaves, but shortly thereafter the demand for labor on maturing mainland plantations grew significantly and the price of slaves began to fall noticeably, initiating a period of much greater slave importations.

The New England Colonies, 1620–1680

Starting two hundred miles north of the Chesapeake, climate and geography made it impossible to produce staple crops for export. The earliest settlers to that region extracted furs and timber and established a mixed economy that included livestock grazing, diverse craft production, and trades-related commerce. The first English migrants into the northern colonies were a relatively diverse people, often coming as families, and they agreed that they should live in tightly knit villages centered around strong civic and religious institutions. Many came as Protestant religious dissenters who were committed to establishing utopias in the wilderness. A steady and substantial flow of migrants each year, as well as the large families they produced, visibly reinforced the prosperity of Plymouth, Massachusetts Bay, Connecticut, and Rhode Island—the northern English colonies founded by 1660 and known as New England.

Separatists at Plymouth

After the Virginia Company of Plymouth failed to establish an outpost at Sagadahoc (see page 53), the directors decided to renew exploration in this northern part of their patent a few years later. In 1614 they hired Captain John Smith, who had helped stabilize Virginia, to explore the area. Smith gave "this most excellent place" the name New England in 1616, and the site of his encampment in the Company patent—a former Pawtuxet village—he called Plymouth. A horrendous epidemic wiped out many coastal Indian villages that year, convincing Smith that "Providence" had created a "vacant lande" for English settlement. In 1620 the Company directors in London created a separate Council for New England and announced that they would make grants of land in Plymouth.

However, some of the English investors in the Virginia Company rejected the Council for New England. Instead, they approved the plan of a London merchant named Thomas Weston to form a joint stock company and deliver a group of colonizers to the northern patent. In return for passage and supplies, settlers agreed to send back fish, furs, and timber products for seven years, after which time their debt to the Company would be cleared. Weston signed up 102 colonists—35 from Leyden, Netherlands, and the others from around London—who crammed themselves into a tiny wine carrier called the *Mayflower.*

The Leyden migrants were Separatists, a subgroup of Protestant Puritans who had fled Scrooby, England, in 1609. As Puritans, they denounced vestiges of Catholicism in the Church of England and rejected modernization, including the corrupting influences of troubled commercial cities and the armies of poor people displaced by enclosures. They supported the stern poor laws and labor guilds that regulated social and economic behavior. Eventually their beliefs compelled these Separatists to leave the Church of England, and since denunciation of the state church could result in a death penalty, they left England. But in the Netherlands they again encountered materialism that interfered with their religious zeal, so they appointed William Bradford to arrange with Weston for passage to America.

The Separatists who embarked on the *Mayflower* in September 1620 became known as the Pilgrims. From the beginning, these "saints" were a minority among "strangers" outside their religion. Moreover, when the settlers realized that their crowded and leaky vessel had come ashore outside of their Company grant, forty-one Separatists agreed "to covenant and combine together into a civil body politic" that had only nominal attachment to the sovereignty of King James I. On November 21 they asked all adult male Separatists and "strangers" alike to sign this document, the Mayflower Compact.

The Mayflower Compact would remain only a parchment commitment until settlers could assure their survival. During their first winter, women and children, along with seriously weakened men, slept aboard the *Mayflower.* Disease, compounded by bitter cold and few supplies, carried away half of the settlers during this initial "starving time." Had it not been for the Wampanoag Indians, more would have perished. Massasoit, the Wampanoag leader, offered food and taught the newcomers how to plant maize; in return, the Pilgrims promised to protect the Indians if they were attacked by the Narragansett. Squanto, a Wampanoag who already spoke both Spanish and English, became a valued agricultural adviser to the Pilgrims. An Abenaki from Maine named Samoset also befriended the newcomers.

Despite a good first harvest and the famous first Thanksgiving feast in the fall of 1621, settlers' relations with the Indians around them grew strained. The first governor, William Bradford, believed the Indians were "savage and brutish men," little more than "wild beasts." When word of the Virginia massacre of 1622 reached Plymouth, Miles Standish, a Non-Separatist professional soldier, insisted on arming men in the settlement and barring Indians from entering Plymouth—behavior unbecoming an ally. Meanwhile, Pilgrim cattle were ranging freely on Wampanoag hunting grounds, and settlers took over homes in Indian villages that had been abandoned in the wake of European diseases. When Standish ferociously raided Indian enemies, and then put the head of a Narragansett Indian on a stake at the village entrance, Massasoit realized that the settlers wanted more than to extract furs peacefully and defend the region together against external enemies.

When new ships came, carrying scores of non-Separatists, the original Pilgrim goals of living compactly in mutually dependent relations rapidly broke down. Hard work, shared resources, a community granary, and equally shared land became utopian dreams as colonists turned to other activities. For example, settlers at Mount Wollaston (renamed Merry Mount in 1628) cavorted around a maypole and enticed Indians into their camp with a promise of alcohol and guns. Bradford sent Miles Standish to arrest and remove the instigator, Thomas Morton. Also, in 1624 Bradford and his closest advisers gave up their communal goals and made each family responsible for a private holding. Settlement became decentralized, and many colonists turned from securing furs and timber products for the Company to herding cattle and planting fields for themselves. By the 1650s, the colony comprised eleven town centers surrounded by individual family farms and grazing tracts.

These social problems were aggravated by the absence of a crown charter in Plymouth that could have stipulated government structure and procedures. Instead, the religious goals of the settlement became tied closely to the activities of government. To be a "freeman" with the right to hold land and serve in the representative assembly (established in 1639) required membership in a Separatist church. However, the Non-Separatist majority resented having to pay taxes while being excluded from the political life of the colony. Numerous challenges to the colony's laws arose by the 1660s. In addition, few Plymouth colonists wanted to conform to English trade regulations during the 1600s; instead, they exchanged their surpluses of food and hides with Protestant neighbors in the Massachusetts Bay colony to the north and quarreled with English investors about what returns they should send back to the mother country. By 1692, Plymouth was far surpassed in strength and prosperity by its neighbor Massachusetts Bay.

The City upon a Hill

Most of the first settlers at Massachusetts Bay were also Puritans from England. But unlike the Pilgrims, Massachusetts Puritans did not separate from the Church of England, but rather wished to reform it from within. In addition, these Puritans did not reject the modernizing processes in England outright, but sought to shape social change by altering the corruptions of government and making individuals accountable through hard work and moral virtue. From hundreds of pulpits and many seats in Parliament, Puritans challenged the monarch's claim to rule by divine right and denounced the Church of England's similarities with the Catholic Church. When Charles I adjourned Parliament in 1629 and set loose the Bishop of London, William Laud, to persecute Puritans, they began to plan their migration to a safe haven abroad. This decision was made urgent by the economic depression that threw numerous Puritan spinners and weavers out of work in the English midlands.

Under the formidable leadership of John Winthrop, a member of the English gentry who had attended Cambridge and practiced law, a group of Puritans obtained a land patent from the Virginia Company's Council for New England, as well as a joint stock company charter from Charles I. Within a short time, the directors and most stockholders of the Massachusetts Bay Company were Puritans. At a meeting in Cambridge, England, they secretly elected Winthrop their governor in North America and pledged to take the charter with them, leaving them free to govern themselves.

Aboard the ship *Arbella* in 1630, Winthrop implored the first colonists to remember that "we shall be as a City upon a Hill." Success of the first generation would ensure that others would follow, for "the eyes of all people are upon us." The first step toward that success was the large number of Puritans who came to Massachusetts. The first four hundred settlers established Salem, and a few months later nearly seven hundred more migrants—about half of them Puritans—left England on eleven ships and came to the Boston area.

Predictably, however, the first winter was difficult. "We built us our wigwam, or house," wrote one settler. "It had no frame, but was without form or fashion, only a few poles set together, and covered with our boat's sails." Others burrowed into caves and hillsides. Over 200 died of exposure, undernourishment, and disease, while some 100 gave up and returned to England. But by the end of spring, six new towns had been "planted"; by the fall, another 1,500 settlers arrived. Nearly 18,000 more colonists came to Massachusetts Bay in the next twelve years in this "Great Migration," thus ensuring the colony's survival.

Additional reasons accounted for early success in Massachusetts. The first generation of Puritan Massachusetts came not as soldiers of fortune, or single young male servants, but largely as families with skills as artisans, farmers, and household producers. Most heads of households had been freeholders, or landowners and taxpayers, in England. They came to the New World not primarily to seek personal fortune—though many hoped to prosper in their callings—but to establish communities in which distinctions between the rich and poor were smaller than in English society. Massachusetts colonists also had well-educated leaders, many of them clergymen, who were experienced in local government.

Although many settlers did not come to Massachusetts out of religious zeal, Puritans held Calvinist beliefs in predestination and the election of "saints" to salvation (see page 63), which had a powerful impact on the colony's development. The Puritan conversion experience—an intensely individual moment of realizing one's own unworthiness and receiving God's redeeming grace that came only at the end of prolonged self-examination, self-doubt, and self-discipline aimed at an impeccable moral record—helped give intellectual and spiritual coherence to the colony. So did the training of an erudite ministry, which was able to attend Harvard College after its founding in 1636 and to lead congregations of Puritans for generations in Massachusetts.

Puritans also set a high standard of diligence and justice in their daily living with non-Puritans through the doctrine of the "calling," or work at some employment or public service endeavor that contributed to secular and spiritual improvement. Work for survival and worldly gain thus became dignified as a moral contribution to society. Learning to read, too, was a means to recognize God's grace in the writings of the Bible, as well as an invaluable aid in business.

Decentralized self-governance, through local churches and town meetings, also strengthened rather than fragmented their experiment in its early years. Minister John Cotton insisted that each congregation, or local group of worshipers, have control over its own membership and sit as one enclave in church. Only those presumed to be male saints would choose ministers for each congregation, keep the church finances, and admit other saints to their group, and only saints would enjoy the sacraments of baptism and communion.

Soon Winthrop and a close group of supporters institutionalized these political trends by transforming the colony's charter into the Massachusetts General Court, a body that combined the governor and a unicameral legislature of Assistants chosen by the "freemen," or the small portion of all males in the colony who were both shareholders in the Company and members of the Puritan Church. The General Court enjoyed extensive governing powers over both freemen and all other residents of the colony. Its laws, for example, limited the right to vote and hold office to adult male members of Puritan congregations, even though they were never a majority. By 1634, Assistants also sought more authority to tax the entire population of colonial residents.

But Assistants also expanded the political and legal powers of the towns, which somewhat dispersed authority outward from the colonial leadership. Over Winthrop's objections, the Assistants decreed that each town would elect two deputies to represent townspeople in the legislature. In 1641 Assistants passed a "Body of Liberties" that defined crimes against property and citizens; rights to vote and hold office would be based on sainthood rather than property, which included much of the population in the first generations. In England, where landholding was the basis of the franchise, few adult men could vote. Also, Massachusetts freemen elected their local officials and determined their duties; in England, crown appointees held considerable powers over local citizens.

The Massachusetts government further refined itself when, in 1644, Goody Sherman sued a wealthy merchant named Robert Keayne for the return of one of her sows, which she claimed the merchant had taken and penned on his land. Although the Assistants sided with Keayne, representatives of the towns and general public opinion favored Goody Sherman and ruled in her favor. The decision stood, but just to make sure that the town representatives would not override them in the future, the Assistants separated the two wings of the General Court and required that both houses approve all legislative measures with a majority vote. Thus was created a bicameral legislature intended to balance the rights of local townspeople and the emerging colonial elite.

Dissent and Compromise

In Winthrop's utopia, mutual dependencies were supposed to knit colonists together. The rich would help provide for the needy, and the middling and poor would work hard and respect the authority of their betters. Distinctions of class and status would not tear the colony apart because Puritans' faith united them in a higher truth. But the same Puritans who had been a dissenting, partly underground movement in England refused to tolerate religious and intellectual differences in New England. For example, when Roger Williams, minister of the church in Salem, Massachusetts, protested that spiritual matters had been unjustly blended with the duties of government, leaders around Winthrop grew alarmed. When Williams opposed the government's policy of seizing Indian lands without payment, he further infuriated the General Court, which banished Williams from the colony in 1635. Williams took a number of followers to a spot they named Providence and, true to his beliefs about Indian lands, bought a tract from the Narragansett. Portsmouth and Newport rose quickly, and in 1644 the towns acquired a charter from Parliament to set up self-rule as the colony of Rhode Island.

Differences also arose in Massachusetts over the activities of Anne Hutchinson, a mother of seven living children and a well-respected, skilled midwife. Hutchinson was an intellectual and social leader in Boston, a woman "of a nimble wit and active spirit," who held weekly prayer meetings in her home primarily for women

The Trial of Mrs. Hutchinson Despite her long ordeal of being questioned by Massachusetts clergy and political leaders, Anne Hutchinson showed stamina, wit, and almost perfect consistency in her stated beliefs throughout her trial. *(Miriam and Ira D. Wallach Division of Art, Prints and Photographs, New York Public Library. Astor, Lenox and Tilden Foundations.)*

of the neighborhood. Salvation, Hutchinson reminded her listeners week after week, came through the "covenant of grace" and direct revelation by God of one's election. In order for Puritans to discover their election, they needed to reject all worldly interference and to submit only to the saintliest and most inspired ministers. Perhaps, some colonists whispered, their ministers in Massachusetts were not saints at all.

Hutchinson was a threat to Puritan clergymen not only because of what she said, but also because she was a woman. Just as women did not vote in their communities or hold church and political offices, they were not supposed to preach to congregants. In addition, Hutchinson was popular. Her devoutness drew a wide following of merchants who scorned commercial regulations imposed by the General Court, craftsmen who resented restrictions on their wages, young people who tired of firm control by their elders, and women who attended Hutchinson's meetings.

Hutchinson was brought to trial in 1637 for the heresy of *antinomianism,* or asserting that inner grace was sufficient to achieve salvation and that church rules and ministers were unnecessary for that goal. She stood for three days before Winthrop and an array of other powerful men, explaining that her meetings were merely open discussions and that her beliefs accorded with Calvinism and Scripture. But she was found guilty of eighty-two offenses against the church and government, especially her claim to have a direct relationship with God. Banished, she and her children followed Roger Williams into Rhode Island. She moved later to Westchester County, New York, where she was killed in an Indian attack.

Other dissenters also appeared in Massachusetts. Baptists, who insisted that not infants but only adults who had been properly instructed and lived a godly life should be baptized, were run out of the colony. Quakers, who abolished baptism and communion entirely and taught that everyone could find salvation through an Inner Light, were denounced as Antinomians. Four Quakers, including Hutchinson's disciple Mary Dyer, were hanged for their views. Even within the Puritan fold, baptized infants growing up in holy households were not experiencing conversion. Such "declension," or sliding away from the Puritan mission, had serious consequences for the future of the colony, since those unconverted inhabitants would not be able to present children for baptism and church membership in the future.

The hunger for land and the steady increase in population led to further "hiving off" of settlers in new directions away from the original core of settlements. For example, Thomas Hooker migrated out of the colony in 1630 because he feared leaders were too restrictive about landholdings. His group settled the town of Hartford, and other groups of land-seekers founded Windsor and Wethersfield; together these settlements became a self-governing colony in 1639 called Connecticut. In time they accepted the protection of a single charter over the entire province, which mostly replicated Massachusetts Bay's charter but also gave most male property owners—not just church members—the right to vote. Families in the fishing and fur trades settled additional towns, including the prosperous and rigorously Puritan ones in the colony of New Haven, founded in 1643, and the frontier communities of Maine and New Hampshire.

Rising religious dissent, fewer conversions, and the scattering of settlers, gave Massachusetts ministers strong reasons for concern that the non-Puritan majority would destroy their experiment utterly. Events in England intensified these concerns when in 1642 thousands of Puritans joined Scots Presbyterians in a civil war against Charles I. Puritans in Parliament and in peoples' armies were finally victorious in 1646. Under Oliver Cromwell, God's rule on earth seemed assured, for in 1649 Parliament executed Charles and installed a republican commonwealth. Encouraged by rising Puritan power in England, Massachusetts ministers met in 1648 and formulated a reply to quell their own internal discord. Their Cambridge Platform decreed that each church would have additional local powers: to choose its ministers and dismiss them, refine matters of doctrine, and examine its own applicants for membership.

But then in the 1650s spirits sank in New England as Cromwell's government turned dictatorial. Charles II, son of the recent king, restored monarchical government in 1660 and dashed Puritan expectations of the millennium. Moreover, in New England the intense zeal of the first generation continued to wane among children of the next generation. In 1662 ministers adopted the Halfway Covenant in an effort to regenerate their congregations. All baptized parents could henceforth present their children for baptism, even though they themselves claimed no conversion experience. Baptism, and not conversion, became the route to a "halfway" membership in the church, a step that drew in thousands of new members.

Daily Life in New England

The first institution established in every Massachusetts locale was the congregation and its meetinghouse, the site of both church services and local government affairs. But the formation of "townships," or systems of land owning and use, rapidly followed. In Massachusetts Bay and Connecticut, provincial leaders made township grants of roughly 36 to 50 square miles to certain heads of households known as "proprietors." These men parceled out some of the land among themselves and dispensed other plots to arriving heads of households in "fee simple," or free of obligations to landlords or the government. These freeholders were able to use the land as they chose, to rent or sell it as they pleased—the antithesis of the manorial system that England had known for centuries, and of the obligations of tenancy and social hierarchies of plantations in the Chesapeake.

In practice, the tight-knit communities envisioned by the first immigrants were hard to create and harder to sustain. In the towns, all male heads of households could attend town meetings at which they chose "selectmen" to govern them and passed a host of legal ordinances to see that fences were maintained, wolves run off town lands, petty disputes among inhabitants settled, and affairs among townspeople regulated. But many town meetings became raucous occasions for airing all manner of personal quarrels. In addition, many early Massachusetts towns tried to reproduce an open-field system of agriculture that emphasized clustering around a town center and sharing common fields for grazing, cutting timber, or orchards. But colonists soon divided their open fields into permanently owned family lots, and the tradition of sharing land faded quickly as settlers turned all the land in their grants into private holdings.

Landholdings became more unequal, too. As townships multiplied rapidly, proprietors granted themselves parcels of land repeatedly while newcomers got smaller single tracts (see diagram). Large landholdings reinforced social status and political authority of some proprietors in the towns. Further, the practice of "partible inheritance," by which fathers bequeathed their estate in portions to all of their male children, or all male and female children, accentuated differences among colonists. By the end of the third generation, the holdings of some family heirs were too small to support a sizeable family or to be handed down to the even more numerous next generation.

Yields of crops in New England did not rise as quickly as many farmers hoped they would because of rocky soil and limiting traditional technology. But many farmers prospered by diversifying their activities. Inhabitants processed agricultural goods and manufactured small crafts at home that could be sold in villages or distant towns. Cheese, feathers, tar, straw hats, and other items that even children could be set to making, filled up the corners of wagons going to coastal towns loaded with grain and vegetables. Timber provided containers, tools, vessels for inland and transatlantic trade, houses and barns, fences, and cider presses. Diligent farm families used potash produced from burning underbrush and worn wooden objects to make soap and finish homemade cloth; many supplemented agricultural activities with fishing or cattle herding. By the 1640s, when migration slowed, colonists were exporting small surpluses of agricultural products to the West Indies and Chesapeake settlements; by the 1660s, many families hired out their children occasionally to neighbors who needed extra hands for harvests, plantings, weaving, smithing, or pressing cider. By the end of the 1600s, over one-fifth of New Englanders made a primary living from lumbering, fishing, or producing crafts.

In the midst of this emerging prosperity, traditions of social and family structure altered noticeably. Compared with the Chesapeake, New Englanders saw less disease and enjoyed better diets. As a result, New Englanders lived longer, bore healthier babies, and raised more children to adulthood than their neighbors to the south. Life expectancy for men was sixty-five, and for women sixty-two. Most children not only survived infancy, but thanks to the relatively even gender ratio, they also married young and reared large families. It was not at all unusual for families to boast eight to thirteen children, though five or six living into their teenage years was the norm. Such relatively large New England families did not often require many indentured servants or slaves to perform fieldwork. The male head of household ensured that fields were planted and livestock tended, while his wife took care of the vegetable garden, swine and chickens, supply of wood fuel, dairy house, and local exchanges. Growing daughters watched the youngest children and helped with tedious chores. Some children were sent to work as apprentices in nearby towns or seasonal laborers on neighbors' farms. But most stayed at home where they were needed for planting, hoeing, harvesting, mending, washing, cooking, chopping, and all manner of other tasks. Nobody should

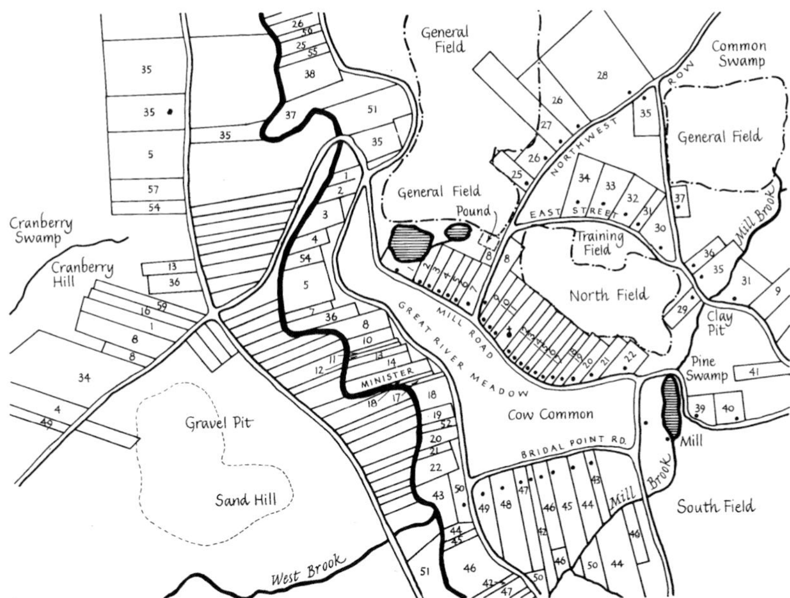

Sudbury, Massachusetts, c. 1650 Although many English towns had been laid out with large areas that were shared by inhabitants and preserved for generations as common land, most New England settlers experienced rapid development of townships based on private landholding. The buying and selling of land led to clusters of "home lots" for original settlers at the center of town with many additional plots added to family holdings over time. ("Figure 9: Sudbury, Massachusetts: The Village Center" from Sumner Chilton Powell's *Puritan Village: The Formation of a New England Town* © 1963 by Wesleyan University, by permission of University Press of New England.)

live alone, intoned Puritan leaders; individuals needed to be members of families, congregations, and towns, in which rights and obligations were clearly known, and survival could be ensured.

Gradually, this productive family unit underwent further change. Numerous individuals—some of them merchants and fishermen, some widows or sons who left home—did not belong to congregations or participate regularly in town affairs by the third generation. In addition, quarreling between neighbors and within families was on the rise. For example, children and young servants, who were expected to be obedient and cheerful, were being disciplined by New England courts more frequently by the mid-1660s. Violence between fathers and sons, and between men and their female servants, was another reason for legal intervention. Sometimes wives who failed to "keepe the household tranquilitye," or servants who talked back once too often, became subjects of official rebuke or discipline. But overall, wives were legally handicapped in the same ways their female English forebears had been. Common law traditions did not allow a woman to own property independently of her husband, unless he wrote a will or marriage agreement entitling her to a share. A law in England, duplicated in most New England colonies, reserved for the wife a "widow's third," or use of a third of her husband's property when he died.

Colonists and Indians: Coexistence and Conflict, 1630–1680

Colonists struggled to establish families and farms in their first coastal settlements. In addition to this challenge, every new colony in North America faced the difficulties of maintaining peaceful trade and diplomacy with Native Americans throughout the frontier. Often, peace gave way to conflict. By the late 1600s, cultural, political, and economic differences between Europeans and Native Americans could not be negotiated effectively. Open warfare marked both northern and southern frontiers in 1675.

Cultural Contrasts

Europeans, having come from countries where forests had been reduced dramatically, game animals hunted to near extinction, and wild fruits and nuts endangered, marveled at the natural abundance of North America. They had never seen such sizes and varieties of trees, for example. "The soil is most fruitful," wrote the first James Town settlers, "laden with good Oake, Ashe, Walnut trees, Poplar, Pine, sweet woods, Cedar, and others yet without names." It seemed incredible to Europeans that Native Americans did not exploit the forests for profit.

Further, Indian forms of worship and spiritual beliefs scandalized many Europeans because they seemed similar to the horrors of the Catholic Inquisition or even witchcraft. Although many Native American tribes organized their religions around deities and priest-like leaders, and practiced regular rituals and feasts, Europeans failed to see any similarities to Christian practices. English, French, and Spanish writers could not understand why Indians believed in a continuity of kinship between humans and animals, as well as polytheism—the belief in many gods or spirits. It did not take long for Europeans to begin using the labels of "savage," "heathen," and "barbarian" to characterize Indian religions.

Most Woodlands Indians had a keen attachment to the land around them, but they neither owned land nor formulated laws about inheriting it, and buying and selling land was unheard of. In contrast, Europeans believed that the Old Testament had enjoined them to take dominion over the earth, to transform nature for their use, and to observe a strict separation between humankind and the environment. Private possession of land for a man's profit and his heirs' enjoyment seemed fitting. So did fences, protective legal codes, and rules of family inheritance. When Indians failed to tame the wilderness with fields and fences, argued settlers, they lost their rights over it.

Few Native Americans strove to own goods the way Europeans did. Most eastern Indians stressed the community's access to important resources; they shared food, shelter, medicine, and fuel roughly equally during times of need. Although most Indians welcomed the opportunity to trade, they prized strength, bravery, and sound judgment more than items of private wealth. As one European observer noted, "They love not to bee encumbered with many utensils." Most eastern Indians traded goods because it brought prestige to individuals and peace to communities. Scholars use the word *reciprocity* to explain how many Woodlands peoples sustained a network of interdependent villagers and clansmen who shared goods in ongoing exchanges as a way to soften differences between rich and poor, or to redistribute the bounty of fortunate families among those whose resources ran low. Europeans accumulated goods for quite different reasons, including advancing personal comfort or enhancing individual reputation.

Few Native American rulers inherited their positions or held their authority over villages or clans permanently. Men or women earned a temporary right to lead in battle or make important community decisions based on their prowess or generosity. Through the European lens of understanding, however, Indian politics was "primitive" because it typically lacked supreme rulers with permanent, absolute authority over all members of a geographical nation.

Europeans admired the way Native American families nurtured and educated children for many years in tight kinship and village groups. But they puzzled over the weakness of marriage ties and the strong voice of Indian wives in important matters. French, Spanish, and English settlers all noted with horror the frequency of premarital sex and the practice among some Indian men of taking more than one wife. In addition, Europeans often regarded Indian men as lazy because they rested at home for long periods between hunting and warring expeditions, whereas women appeared to work harder because they daily tended both fields and households.

Europeans often thought that Native Americans did not know how to keep records and, some said, even lacked a recorded history. In fact, most Indian cultures recorded information with beads, paintings, or pictograms, and they recounted their histories orally. Although few Europeans could write, and even fewer owned books, they were surrounded by written records such as economic accounts, land deeds, legal agreements, letters, and diaries that affirmed relations between people. For generations, treaties signed between Indians and Europeans carried various meanings for the different parties, sometimes leading to deep misunderstandings.

Early Tensions in the North

Cultural differences between Europeans and Native Americans underlay many of the tensions that persisted after the first years of contact. Tensions arising from conflicting perceptions about the land erupted in 1637 when Pequot warriors attacked Puritan farmsteads in the Connecticut River valley that were impinging on their hunting grounds. The Massachusetts General Court called out militiamen from the townships to lead assaults on the Pequot. In short order, Puritans had leveled a central village of some five hundred Pequot, tracked down survivors, and sold some into Caribbean slavery. Native Americans' "sinful" and socially alien ways, declared Cotton Mather and other Puritan ministers, had been the "the Devil's owne work."

In 1643 leaders of Massachusetts Bay, Plymouth, New Haven, and Connecticut formed a New England Confederation to defend themselves against the threat of further Indian attack and to deflect Indians' anger against them by setting the tribes against one another. Other colonists attempted to Christianize friendly Native Americans by setting up special mission towns for "praying Indians" and introducing John Eliot's translation of the Bible into Algonquian. But their successes were few; the spread of the gospel was often dampened by the spread of disease into

Indian villages. Moreover, Algonquian villagers acquired alcohol and guns, which drastically altered their customs of ritual and war.

English colonizers greedily sought the animal hides they knew would be valuable for hats, coat and glove linings, and home furnishings. Indians in turn were pleased to acquire strouds (large pieces of rough cloth), iron implements and pots, and small household amenities. But the effects of this trade far surpassed anyone's expectations. Native Americans quickly became dependent on Europeans for tools and clothing, hunting their western reserves more intensely in order to satisfy European demand for furs. In the uncontrolled search for beaver and deer, Native Americans exhausted the sources of their own nourishment and shelter, which unbalanced their ecology in numerous unforeseen ways. Once beaver were hunted to depletion in an area, their dams no longer controlled the flow of creeks; with deer and other small game gone, valuable clearing of underbrush ceased. When the supply of game sank so low that it did not reproduce itself enough to feed Micmac, Algonquian, and other tribes, they believed their entire religious cosmology was in crisis. "We have displeased the spirits of the beaver," noted one village elder, and "the beaver will now displease us" by bringing deep hunger, long winters, and internal quarreling.

European settlers knew that without peaceful diplomacy, the fur trade would deteriorate and frontier settlers would be endangered. But it was difficult to determine how, and with which tribes, to form agreements. By the 1660s, intense competition among Iroquois villages was exacerbated by increased warfare against the Huron and Erie villages near the Great Lakes and by the persistent migration of Europeans from the east. The French averted serious warfare in their advance south along the Mississippi River by negotiating trading terms with the Natchez, Choctaw, Chickasaw, Illinois, and other tribes. In the northeast, Dutch and English settlers along the Hudson River invited Iroquois hunters to bring pelts to their forts to conduct trade. Although this policy introduced inconveniences between trading parties, it avoided the terrible open conflicts that would erupt elsewhere when some English settlers insisted on pressing relentlessly into the interior for land and resources.

New England Erupts

The white population of New England grew to about 55,000 by the 1670s, while the Indian population steadily declined from over 100,000 on the eve of European settlement to a few thousand inhabitants in the 1670s. Hungry for land, colonists in Plymouth and Rhode Island encroached on Wampanoag and Narragansett hunting grounds. For years Metacomet, the son of Wampanoag chief Massasoit, had listened to appeals from his people to stop the Europeans. In 1671 the Wampanoag were forced to surrender their guns and agree to be ruled by Plymouth's English law. Tensions grew over the next years, and Indians murdered a number of English settlers in western towns, for which Massachusetts authorities ordered the hanging of three Wampanoags. In July Metacomet (or, as the English named him, King Philip) led large bands of warriors against the English towns on the western fringe. By the fall, Narragansett and Nipmuck had joined Metacomet's men, and raids against the English spread to the Connecticut River valley.

Portrait of Metacomet, or King Philip
This ennobling portrait of the New England Wampanoag leader shows a mixture of adaptations to English trappings—note his gun, powder horn, regal cape, and bejeweled crown—along with traditional Indian attire. Metacomet tried repeatedly to accommodate the wishes of New England settlers but, in the end, fought to preserve his authority among his confederacy and to prevent excessive settler claims on Indian land by driving the newcomers "into the Sea." Metacomet's people lost, and their leader's head was displayed on a post. *(Courtesy of the Haffenreffer Museum of Anthropology, Brown University.)*

Colonists at first thought they would win a quick victory. But Metacomet's men had secreted away hundreds of guns over years of trading and had learned how to repair them. His warriors ambushed Europeans trampling noisily through the woods. In early 1676, they attacked Plymouth and Providence. One-tenth of all the men in Massachusetts were killed or taken captive, and at least eighteen New England towns were flattened. Almost 1,200 homes were ruined and 8,000 cattle—critical to Plymouth's economy—were slaughtered. King Philip's warriors got within twenty miles of Boston, and on the frontier they held shivering captives in their tents. Mary Rowlandson, a minister's wife from a small western town, spent over eleven weeks in 1675 as a captive assigned to work as a servant of a warrior and his three wives. Although Rowlandson was released unharmed, others were less fortunate. Atrocities were reported on both sides.

In the summer of 1676, Massachusetts settlers rallied to the common defense and began to retaliate in what became New England's bloodiest war against Native Americans. New Englanders asked Mohawk from New York to stage ambushes against the Narragansett and persuaded the converted "praying Indians" to spy on Narragansett villages. With the murder of King Philip, and subsequent food shortages, the Native American alliance fell apart. King Philip's head was displayed on a stake in Plymouth, and New Englanders sold dozens of war captives into slavery in the West Indies. Metacomet's War exacted enormous casualties on both sides, and it took years to replant colonists' fields and replenish the brush that harbored Indians' game. Fear reached even into New York, where Iroquois leaders and colonists met at Albany in 1677 to form an alliance called the Covenant Chain, which sought to protect the fur trade for everyone and insulate the Iroquois against their enemies to the east and west. But for generations, colonists recounted the horrors of frontier conditions and retold Mary Rowlandson's captivity story.

Southern Conflicts

By the second generation of settlement, Virginia had become a colony of remarkable contrasts. While a few great planters consolidated estates in the coastal region stretching from Delaware to Albemarle Sound and prospered from tobacco production there, many colonists failed to attain the benefits of good land, marriage and family, and marketable surplus crops. By then, planters were exploiting the labor of many indentured servants, some of whom were denied the freedom dues stipulated in their contracts. Though servants continued to come to the Chesapeake, slavery also took hold. And with each new ship came a few optimistic planters who disembarked hoping to attain a great plantation and gentry status.

Nathaniel Bacon, one of these would-be great planters, acquired considerable grants of land and political privileges through his kinship with Governor William Berkeley. Bacon arrived in Virginia in 1674, just as western settlers had begun turning selective acts of violence into full scale raids against the Doeg and Susquehannock (see "Competing Voices" page 79). Berkeley implored "poor, indebted, discontented, and armed" settlers to cease their hostilities. But some of the Virginia militia, led by an ancestor of George Washington, ignored Berkeley's urgings and joined with forces from Maryland to attack Susquehannock encampments. Before Virginians could claim any decisive victory, Doeg and Susquehannock Indians slaughtered over thirty settlers in January 1676, sending the entire colony into panic demanding immediate retaliation.

Governor Berkeley responded with orders to construct forts above the Virginia fall line, a natural divide between eastern settlements and frontier Indian villages. Further, he restricted the fur trade to a few carefully licensed colonists. Both measures angered frontiersmen, who demanded freedom to hunt as they chose. In addition, growing numbers of ex-servants, migrating new settlers, and runaway slaves grew land-hungry and, frustrated with Berkeley's cautious land-granting policies, joined in the protests. In Maryland, small planters agreed to ride with Bacon into the frontier and issued their own stern protests against their colony's high taxes, low tobacco prices, and seemingly arbitrary government.

Bacon, whose plantation lay east of the fall line near brewing troubles, believed he had been denied the political privileges due to a man of his inherited status. Seeing his chance to gain preferment, he organized disgruntled frontiersmen against Doeg villages with demands on the governor to push Native Americans farther back from expanding planters, ex-servants, and squatters. At first Bacon convinced the colonial assembly to confer authority on his ragged band of malcontents to overrun the frontier and turn Indians into slaves. But in the early summer of 1676, Berkeley expressed opposition to this policy, dismissed Bacon from the council, and denounced the militia's depredations on the frontier. Bacon in turn won election to the House of Burgesses and, from the frontier, marched scores of agitators against James Town. There, the rebels tried to burn the capital to the ground while Bacon exhorted slaves to leave their masters. Although Berkeley fled the city, and the county militia refused to fire against their hero Bacon, he never effectively took over government. By the fall, Bacon had died in jail of swamp fever, and the rebellion soon wound down.

Although Bacon's Rebellion was the largest internal colonial uprising before Lexington and Concord in 1774, poor and discontented southern frontiersmen joined in protests elsewhere during the 1670s. For example, in the more sparsely settled Carolina region, mutinous small planters under the leadership of John Culpepper and George Durant demanded lower duties on tobacco exports and better tracts of interior land. Piggy-backing on Virginia events, they ran the governor out of office at Albemarle and briefly controlled the provincial government. Near still-tiny Charles Town (later, Charleston), planters encouraged Cherokee, Yamasee, Creek, and Chickasaw warriors to capture their Indian enemies and sell them as slaves to both English planters and Spanish missions to the south. Intermittent warfare sparked by fur traders and exporting merchants intensified tensions on the Carolina frontier and put government elites on notice about the region's instability.

CONCLUSION

For over a century, Spain was the primary European power in the New World, holding dominion over Mexico and the Caribbean, and expanding into the Floridas and New Mexico. While *conquistadors* marched across the lands, pillaging and extracting great riches from the conquered lands, English propagandists struggled to arouse interest in exploration in their country, and the Dutch and French added a small presence to the mixture of peoples in North America.

In the early 1600s, England's colonists established two regions of settlement, reflecting two ways of life. Lagging behind the Caribbean colonies, Virginians slowly overcame their starving times when they turned to growing staple crops for export and adopted servants and slaves to perform the work on their plantations. The first New Englanders often brought dissenting religious convictions and usually came as families able to develop a diversified economy. Within both regions, a few hardy settlements included a bewildering array of people from European backgrounds who went through a daily grind of chores, adapting to local conditions, prior inhabitants, labor needs, and religious impulses in particular ways.

From the beginning cultural strains complicated the colonizing process, and most European settlements soon reached a point of intense competition with Indians and other Europeans for furs, fish, or some other resources. Cloth, metal weapons, and cooking pots transformed the lifestyles of Iroquois, Catawba, Cherokee, Creek, and other tribes, as well as the Algonquian peoples along the coast who survived early wars and epidemics, and then endured the introduction of guns and alcohol. By the 1670s, northern and southern regions erupted into large-scale warfare that transformed relations among all cultures on the landscape.

By 1680, there was much success to celebrate and many obstacles yet to confront. Although some colonists gained a degree of material prosperity, religious toleration, and political liberty, not everyone in the colonies shared a good life. Three times more people, including thousands of servants such as Mary who pleaded to go home at the opening of this chapter, migrated into the Chesapeake during the seventeenth century than into the northern colonies. Yet the Chesapeake population remained smaller than New England's for years. The gap between rich and poor, skilled and unskilled, protected and vulnerable, entitled and oppressed, grew wider in each colony over the years. Slavery also became more institutionalized, putting a stain on colonists' belief that their settlements might revitalize or liberate human potential. Despite these mixed results, a few North American colonies had been planted and would endure.

SUGGESTED READINGS

For the Spanish presence, David Weber's *The Spanish Frontier in North America* (1992) is a model of comprehensive coverage and judicious argument, covering Spanish settlement and governance from Florida to California. For French colonization of Canada, the best work is W. J. Eccles, *The Canadian Frontier, 1534–1760* (rev. 1983). The background to English colonization is treated best in Nicholas P. Canny, *Kingdom and Colony: Ireland in the Atlantic World, 1560–1800* (1988), and David B. Quinn, *Raleigh and the British Empire* (1947). Karen Ordahl Kupperman, *Roanoke: The Abandoned Colony* (1984), is a fascinating account of the "Lost Colony."

Peter Wood et al., eds., *Powhatan's Mantle: Indians in the Colonial Southeast* (1989), is the best collection of essays about early European and Indian contact in the Southeast. For the development of the Chesapeake during the 1600s, see T. H. Breen and Stephen Innes, *"Myne Owne Ground": Race and Freedom on Virginia's Eastern Shore, 1640–1676* (1980); Lois Green Carr, Russell R. Menard, and Lorena S. Walsh, *Robert Cole's World: Agriculture and Society in Early Maryland* (1991); Wesley Frank Craven, *White, Red, and Black: The Seventeenth Century Virginian* (1971); James Horn, *Adapting to a New World: English Society in the Seventeenth Century Chesapeake* (1994); and Gloria L. Main, *Tobacco Colony: Life in Early Maryland, 1650–1720* (1982).

For Caribbean sugar and slavery, Richard Dunn's *Sugar and Slaves: The Rise of the Planter Class in the English West Indies, 1624–1713* (1972) is the most authoritative account. Philip D. Curtin, *Africa Remembered: Narratives of West Africans from the Era of the Slave Trade* (1967), offers valuable first hand accounts, while Winthrop D. Jordan, *White over Black: American Attitudes Toward the Negro, 1550–1812* (1968) offers the best and most comprehensive interpretation of attitudes and values about race. Daniel P. Mannix and Malcolm Cowley, *Black Cargoes: A History of the Atlantic Slave Trade* (1962) focuses on the capture and transport of African slaves; see also James A. Rawley, *The Transatlantic Slave Trade* (1981).

Edmund Morgan makes two short but influential contributions to understanding Puritan settlement in *The Puritan Dilemma: The Story of John Winthrop* (1958) and *The Puritan Family* (1966). For the Separatists, see John Demos, *A Little Commonwealth* (1970). For understanding why settlers came to New England, what ideas and institutions they transported with them, and the cultural ways they developed in the 1600s, see David Grayson Allen, *In English Ways: The Movement of Societies and the Transferal of English Local Law and Custom* (1981); David Cressy, *Coming Over: Migration and Communication Between England and New England in the Seventeenth Century* (1987); and David Hall, *Worlds of Wonder, Days of Judgment* (1989). Hall's study makes the argument that popular religious beliefs endured alongside stabilizing Puritan ones. Neal Salisbury, *Manitou and Providence: Indians, Europeans, and the Making of New England, 1500–1643* (1982), explains cultural encounters in the first years.

The best starting point for understanding Metacomet's War is Russell Bourne, *The Red King's Rebellion: Racial Politics in New England, 1675–1678* (1991). Two opposing views of the governor and Nathaniel Bacon are offered in Wilcomb E. Washburn, *The Governor and the Rebel: A History of Bacon's Rebellion in Virginia* (1957), and Thomas Jefferson Wertenbaker, *Torchbearer of the Revolution: The Story of Bacon's Rebellion and Its Leader* (1940).

Race, Land, and Political Rights on the Frontier

Competing Voices

"Manifesto Concerning the Troubles in Virginia"

By autumn 1675, Doeg and Susquehannock Indians in western Virginia had begun to ambush and murder settlers who refused to stop fencing in frontier land for their private use. Friction erupted into the warfare of Bacon's Rebellion that brought poor servants, runaway slaves, recent immigrants, and land-hungry planters together against the Indians. Nathaniel Bacon rallied supporters to arms and defended their actions with a stirring rationale for revolt.

If virtue be a sin, if Piety be guilt, all the Principles of morality goodness and Justice be perverted, We must confess That those who are now called Rebels may be in danger of those high imputations, Those loud and several Bulls would affright Innocents and render the defence of our Brethren and the enquiry into our sad and heavy opressions, Treason. But if there be as sure there is, a just God to appeal to, if Religion and Justice be a sanctuary here, If to plead the cause of the oppressed, . . . If after the loss of a great part of his Majesty's Colony deserted and dispeopled, freely with our lives and estates to endeavor to save the remainders, be Treason, God Almighty Judge and let guilty die . . . but let us trace these men in Authority and Favour to whose hands the dispensation of the Countries' wealth has been committed; let us observe the sudden Rise of their Estates compared with the Quality in which they first entered this Country . . . let us consider their sudden advancement and let us also consider whither any Public work for our safety and defence or for the Advancement and propagation of Trade, liberal Arts or sciences is here . . . adequate to our vast charge, . . . and see what sponges have sucked up the Public Treasure and . . . juggling Parasites whose tottering Fortunes have been repaired and supported at the Public charge. . . .

Another main article of our Guilt is our Design not only to ruin and extirpate all Indians in General but all Manner of Trade and Commerce with them, . . . [but] Although Plantations be deserted, the blood of our dear Brethren Spilt, on all Sides our complaints, continually Murder upon Murder renewed upon us, [there are the Governor's licensed traders] at the Heads of the Rivers . . . [who] buy and sell our blood, and do still notwithstanding the late Act made to the contrary, admit Indians painted [for warfare] and continue to Commerce, although these things can be proved yet who dare be so guilty as to do it.

Another Article of our Guilt is To Assert all those neighbour Indians . . . to be outlawed, wholly unqualified for the benefit and Protection of the law. . . . [For] since the Indians cannot according to the tenure and form of any law to us known be prosecuted, Seized or Complained against, Their Persons being difficulty distinguished or known, Their many nations' languages, and their subterfuges such as makes them incapable to make us Restitution or satisfaction would it not be very guilty to say They have been unjustly defended and protected these many years.

"Virginia's Deplored Condition"

Many eastern planters sympathized with the grievances raised by frontier settlers, but few endorsed the methods used by Bacon and his followers. Bacon not only defied the governor's orders respecting arms and violence, but attacked the central authority of a fragile and self-conscious elite. At stake was the law of the frontier and the social hierarchy white Virginians had inherited from English tradition. William Sherwood, an eastern planter, voiced the establishment's condemnation of Bacon. It's original subtitle—An Impartial Narrative of the Murders Committed by the Indians There, and of the Sufferings of His Majesty's Loyal Subjects Under the Rebellious Outrages of Mr. Nathaniel Bacon—was anything but impartial.

... [E]very one endeavours to get great tracts of Land, and many turn Land lopers, some take up 2000 acres, some 3000 Acres, others ten thousand Acres ... and never cultivate any part of it, only set up a hog house to ... prevent others seating, so that too many rather than to be Tenants, seat upon the remote barren Land, whereby contentions arise between them and the Indians ... turning their Cattle and hogs on [the Indians' lands] and if by Vermin or otherwise any be lost, then they exclaim against the Indians, beat & abuse them ... for it is the opinion of too many there, (and especially of their General Mr. Bacon) that faith is not to be kept with the heathens....

[Bacon, not content with the Governor's pardon of his initial depredations on the frontier] gets the discontented rabble together, and with them resolved to put himself, once more on the stage, and on the 21st day of June [1676] he entered James Towne, with 400 foot, & 120 horse, set guards at the state house, kept the Governour, Council and Burgesses prisoners, and would suffer none to pass in or out of Town, and having drawn up all his forces to the very door & windows of the state house, he demanded a Commission to be General of all the forces that should be raised during the Indian War, he and all his soldiers crying out No Levies, No Levies. The Assembly acquainted him they had taken all possible care for carrying on the Indian War at the easiest charge that could be, that they had redressed all their Complaints, and desired that for satisfaction of the people, what they had done might be publicly read, Mr. Bacon answered there should be no Laws read there, that he would not admit of any delays, that he came for a Commission, and would immediately have it, thereupon sending his soldiers into the State house, where the Governour, Council & Burgesses were sitting and threatening them with fire and sword if it was not granted, his soldiers mounting their Guns ready to fire ... so that Order was given for such a Commission as Mr. Bacon would have himself.... The next morning ... now Mr. Bacon having a Commission, shows himself in his colours, and hangs out his flag of defiance (that is) Imprisoning several loyal Gentlemen and his rabble used reproachful words of the Governour ... it was imagined he & his soldiers would march out of Town, yet they continued drinking and domineering, the frontier Counties being left with very little force, and the next day came the sad news that the Indians had that morning killed Eight people within thirty Miles of town, in the families of some of them that were with Mr. Bacon, yet they hastened not away, but the next day having forced an Act of Indemnity, and the Assembly being at the Burgesses' request dissolved, Mr. Bacon after four days' stay, marched out of Town....

During Mr. Bacon's thus Lording it, and seizing the estates of such as he terms Traitors to the Commonality . . . The Indians taking advantage of these civil commotions, have committed may horrid murders, . . . not only in the frontier Counties, but in the inward Counties. . . .

Thus is that Country by the rashness of a perverse man exposed to ruin, and is in a most calamitous & confused condition, lying open to the cruelty of the savage Indians. . . . God in mercy divert the Issues of War which much threateneth the Country, by the Indians & the rabbles killing up, & destroying the stocks of Cattle, pulling down the Corn field fences, turning their horses in, and such like Outrages, so that unless his sacred Majesty do speedily send a considerable supply of men, Arms, Ammunition, & provision, there is great cause to fear the loss of that once hopeful Country, which is not able long to resist the cruelty of the Indians or rebellion of the Vulgar. ■

Although Bacon's rebels marched into Jamestown, they could not hold the capital for long. Nor did they take over the frontier. Indeed, on Governor Berkeley's orders, soldiers hanged twenty-three rebels after Bacon died in jail. But the rebellion was widespread, and it showed how frustrated many indentured servants and poor farmers had become, and the extent to which Indians had become a scapegoat for white settlers' land hunger. Colonists needed land to grow crops, create an inheritance for their children, and claim many civil rights in Virginia. That need was now overlaid with perceptions about the nature of the frontier and racial tensions among different peoples. Frontier settlers' fear and loathing of Indians rarely abated but only grew in the years to come. Moreover, the great eastern planters and royal officials who deplored the violence on the western frontier had no abiding concern for the welfare of the Indian peoples. Rather, they feared the threats to their own elite rule and property that arose during the prolonged violence of Bacon's Rebellion.

Questions for Analysis

1. What were Bacon's grievances with regard to the frontier and political authority in Virginia?
2. What defense did Berkeley's supporters make of their efforts to suppress Bacon? Which reasons for opposing Bacon are vitally important, and which are secondary?
3. What racial attitudes are expressed in these passages?
4. Are there any areas of agreement between the disputants?
5. Do Bacon and Sherwood exaggerate the truth? If so, for what purpose?

3 Imperial Connections, 1660–1748

Late in 1731, Parliament's House of Commons summoned retired ship captain Fayer Hall to testify before the members about his years of experience living and trading in the West Indies. For months, the politicians had been conducting hearings on the state of the Caribbean trade. Angry planters and merchants from the islands were demanding that Parliament "end the wretched habits of the illicit trade" between French, Spanish, and Dutch foreigners in the islands and the British North American colonists. Foreigners, they lamented, paid well for colonial goods and sold their sugar, molasses, and rum at far lower prices than the British did, so colonists were attracted to the foreign islands for trade. It was foreign sugar, they insisted, that ended up on the tables of British citizens, which not only diminished planters' and merchants' profits but, worse, undermined the moral fiber of the British Empire.

This "sugar interest" of absentee landowners, slave traders, Jamaica and Barbados merchants, and London sugar refiners blamed colonists for trading more between "the bays of Boston to the bays of Spain's Havana" than within the British Empire. And they promoted sweeping legislation to keep North American colonists away from foreign islands. Now Fayer Hall, an inveterate smuggler hated by this "sugar interest," stood before some of the most prestigious men in the empire and delivered advice that Parliament did not want to hear.

"'Tis the best known secret," Hall reminded Parliament, "that our illicit trade to foreign parts does bring us a greater benefit than the legal runs of goods." Hall would know. He had hauled goods from one place to another in the Atlantic world for many years. He had traded in peace and war, to mainland and island colonies, legally and illegally. Widely respected for "fair dealing with goods of any nation," Hall insisted that whatever legislation Parliament passed to please planters and merchants of the "sugar interest" would be useless and possibly detrimental to Britain's interests.

In truth, said Hall, "our home ports [in England] will never take in much of the bounty rising from colonial soil," and "there is not sufficient trade in the English parts of the [Caribbean] to keep the New England merchants happy." Colonists who shipped their surpluses of farm and forest goods to the West Indies never found sufficient markets at the English islands, and so they traveled "around and about the foreign ports" to trade. "Colonials need the foreign stops," he insisted, in order to sell all of the goods they carry. In addition, it was the "illegal profits from the French and Dutch" trade that enabled colonists to pay English merchants for the cloth, tools, metal wares, and many household necessities they imported. As Hall put it, "The French and Netherlanders [in the Caribbean] want the colonial wheat, and will give a higher price than our own [English] islands will offer. In consequence, the risk of being caught running into foreign ports, though considerable, is generally thought to be productive of greater [profits] than the legal trade."

The island planters and merchants carried tremendous weight in British politics, more so than a retired captain who spoke for colonists on the other side of the Atlantic Ocean. The House of Commons listened respectfully to Hall's defense of colonial interests and his plea that Parliament "leave the trade of our empire free and clear" of restrictions "in all of its ports," and promptly disregarded his counsel. The Molasses Act of 1733 established higher duties on sugar, rum, and molasses, and detailed the principle of keeping Britain's trade in the British Empire. From a diplomatic point of view, Parliament argued, the empire had to protect itself from foreign competition and show the world its strength as a closed imperial system. In addition, the Molasses Act, if enforced properly, would force colonists to submit to the will of the mother country.

Colonial North American merchants greeted news of the Molasses Act's new taxes and crackdown on smuggling with anxiety. As Fayer Hall had reasoned before Parliament, it was "but natural and of practical Sense" for merchants to "follow their own Interest" by finding buyers and sellers wherever they were conveniently located. Parliament's new law seemed "selfish." And as Hall predicted, merchants systematically evaded the act, while royal officials seldom enforced its provisions.

These discussions about sugar—an immensely popular but nutritionally unnecessary commodity—symbolized two important developments in the English Empire. First, as the initial colonies took root, the political, economic, and cultural connections between colonists and the imperial center matured and deepened. Colonists had many reasons to be optimistic about opportunities for expanding onto their frontiers and trading across many national and geographical boundaries. But second, British subjects in both worlds became increasingly aware of the problems of ruling a large empire. As the empire matured, as its network of social relations became more complex, the different interests within the empire expressed uncertainty about how to cultivate, regulate, or restrict their particular interests. Even as North Americans became more aware of their Englishness, they also noted the differences between the home country and colonies, as well as the differences marking colonists from one region, religion, occupation, or race to another. The coexistence of both optimism and tensions raises important questions about British North America in the century after 1660.

- As the process of founding and developing colonies proceeded, what distinctive features characterized the new colonies in North America after 1660?
- How did English authorities try to organize the trade, politics, defense, and cultures of their colonies? How did colonists respond?
- How did colonists participate in developing their political, economic, and cultural opportunities in light of their positions both within North America and within the British Empire?
- How did the colonists reconcile their continuing expansion and maturing societies with the numerous wars and social tensions that persisted in North America?

This chapter will address these questions.

The Restoration Colonies, 1660–1685

The first settlements in North America had been grounded on the religious convictions of individuals and the initiatives of private companies. These experiments took root, flourished as agricultural communities or staple-exporting colonies, and began to expand onto new frontiers. Clusters of crown officials and local representative assemblies ran the settlements. After 1660, new streams of settlers from various countries began migrating to other parts of North America. In England, Charles II (reigned 1660–1685) restored the Stuart monarchy. The colonies' expanding populations and England's need to manage and defend its interests in the New World prompted Charles to take firm control of governing the empire.

Colonies formed during the Restoration would be different from the earlier ones (see table page 91). Charles II took an active interest in sponsoring two new regions of settlement. One, between New England and Virginia (see map page 86), became known as the mid-Atlantic region and included New York, New Jersey, Pennsylvania, and Delaware. The other, south of the James River to Spanish Florida, was known as "the Carolinas" (later divided into South and North Carolina). In each case, Charles chose proprietors from among his political inner circle, men who could be counted on to support the crown's commercial goals, the Anglican Church, and the divine right of kings. Detesting the rising power of the colonial assemblies in the original colonies, Charles appointed colonial governors who were committed to utter royal control and experienced in military, rather than civilian, affairs.

The Carolinas

Few Europeans had come ashore between Virginia and Spanish Florida before 1660. A handful of Puritans and West Indian planters had tested the land but failed to at-

Chronology

1642–1649	Civil War in England
1649–1660	Cromwellians rule England
1651	First Navigation Act
1660	Restoration of Charles II
1663	Carolina proprietorship established
1664	English conquer New Netherland
1681	Pennsylvania founded
1683	New York assembly established
1685	James II becomes King of England
1685–1689	Dominion of New England
1688	Glorious Revolution
1689	Leisler's Rebellion
	Andros ousted from Massachusetts
	Maryland rebellion
1689–1697	King William's War
1692	Salem witch trials
1702–1713	Queen Anne's War
1715	Yamasee War
1718	New Orleans founded
1720–1742	Walpole serves as prime minister in England
1720s–1740s	Land bank experiments
1728	Benjamin Franklin begins *Pennsylvania Gazette*
1733	Molasses Act
1740–1748	War of Jenkins's Ear (War of the Austrian Succession)

tract a large flow of colonizers. In 1663 Charles II gave a group of eight proprietors extensive personal rights over this region, known as "the Carolinas," permitting them to shape the destinies of their territories in North America. As aristocrats, most of them wished to establish strictly hierarchical societies, with inherited land ownership.

In 1669 one of the proprietors, Anthony Ashley Cooper, hired rising scholar and publicist John Locke to create a plan for settlement. In subsequent years, Locke would become associated with political upheavals that paved the way for propertied individualism and representative government. But during the founding of the Carolinas, he believed in a conventional, hierarchical form of social organization.

The Restoration Colonies
During the 1660s two large regions were added to England's empire in North America. One, which emerged following the conquest of the Dutch in 1664, was the mid-Atlantic area that became New York, East Jersey, West Jersey, Pennsylvania, and Delaware. The other, stretching from Virginia to Spain's claims at the Savannah River, was Carolina, or as colonists called it "the Carolinas."

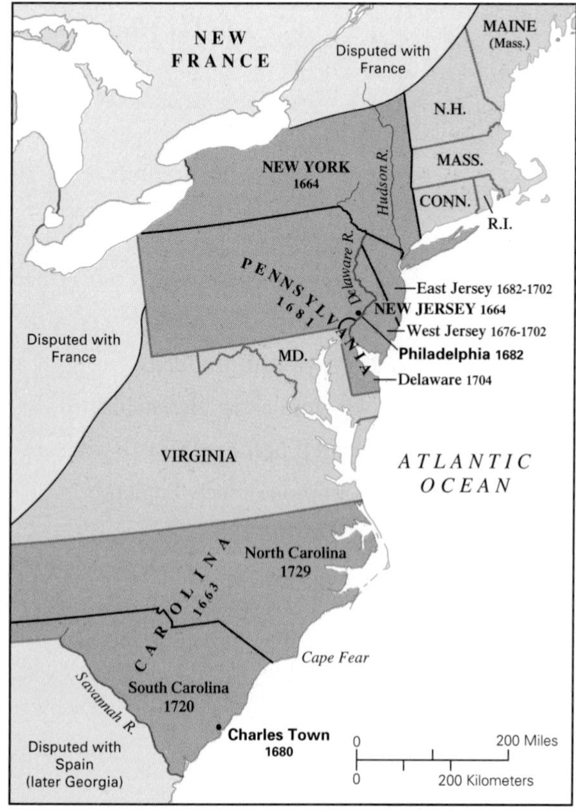

His *Fundamental Constitutions of Carolina* called for a nearly feudal form of landownership, complete with nobles, yeomen, and serfs. The plan was impressive on paper but impossible to implement in the New World environment, and little true government developed until the 1720s.

Instead, over two hundred planters from Barbados immediately staked out private plantations and introduced "seasoned," or acclimated, African slaves to herd cattle and do field labor. A few English servants and farmers, as well as some French Huguenot refugees, settled where the Ashley and Cooper Rivers met near what became Charles Town. Residents around the small trading post also ignored the proprietors' wishes when they started a thriving fur trade with Native Americans and began to capture slaves from enemy Indian camps. The quest for fur and slaves set planters and small farmers in the Carolinas on a course of prolonged frontier violence that lasted to the 1720s. In 1715 frontier tensions erupted into a devastating war of trappers, small farmers, and aspiring planters against the Yamasee people.

Meanwhile, planters sought a cash crop that could turn a profit as great, or greater, than the tobacco grown by Virginia planters to their north. By the early 1690s, Carolinians had found it: rice. Long a staple in the diet of West Africans, rice was brought to North America by slaves and slave traders. Slaves probably taught Carolina planters how to transform the marshy coastal lowlands into rice fields. Within the first generation of settlement, rice planters' profits far outstripped those of their Virginia neighbors. By 1720, the countryside around Charles Town supported a dense population of slaves growing and processing rice. The "rice belt" stretched from Cape Fear (now North Carolina) to the edge of Spanish dominion on the Savannah River.

Success depended on the steady importation of slaves. When seasoned Caribbean slaves proved insufficient in numbers, planters stepped up importation of African slaves, who had the advantage of resistance to malaria. This disease, transmitted from Africa by the same ships that brought slaves, was often deadly to Europeans but far less threatening to Africans. Just after 1700, within the lifetime of the first planters, the number of slaves surpassed the number of whites in the colony. By 1720, almost two-thirds of the colony's population was African slaves, subject to the severe slave code treatment that Barbadian planters had perfected (see page 61). And, with little toleration themselves for the mosquito-infested swamps, planters left cultivation to their slaves and overseers and lived in the comforts of Charles Town. In all these respects, Carolina differed from the Chesapeake colonies and resembled the Caribbean island societies.

In the northern parts of the Carolinas, a few settlers ventured into the Albemarle Sound region during the 1660s and 1670s. They were cut off from the Chesapeake planters to their north by the shallow inlets of the Dismal Swamp, which prevented even ships from approaching. Poor families came to the sound from Virginia, raising tobacco and corn, and ignoring the proprietors' demands for quit-rents. In 1664 William Drummond arrived from England to govern the settlers around the sound,

Mulberry Plantation In 1708 Thomas Broughton began to acquire hundreds of acres for his rice and indigo plantation near Charles Town on the Santee River. In the foreground of this painting stand the slave quarters, built in African style and housing multiple slaves. During the Yamasee War of 1715, the Broughton mansion in the background was fortified against assault from Indians. *(The Gibbes Museum of Art, Carolina Art Association.)*

but he, too, discovered the hostility of the independent farmers. In 1677 farmers seethed with discontent about the cost of rents and export taxes on their tobacco. John Culpepper, a leading Albemarle Sound planter, spearheaded the ouster of Drummond and frightened the proprietors into leaving settlers' land alone.

In 1704 the colonists around the sound finally established their first town, Bath. By then, the frontier was home not only to farmers, but to ranchers, miners, and lumbermen as well. Although the land was too dry for rice cultivation, it was heavily forested with pines, which provided sources of naval stores such as tar, pitch, turpentine, and ship masts. Subsidies from the English government after 1705 for producing naval stores failed to attract large numbers of migrants, however, and the Albemarle area remained sparsely settled in the 1700s. In 1719 royal authorities separated South Carolina from lands to its north and made it a royal colony. The proprietors' families retained North Carolina until 1729, when it too became a royal colony.

New York and New Jersey

Just before the Second Anglo–Dutch War (1665–1667), Dutch settlers at New Netherland surrendered peaceably to a small British fleet in its harbor in 1664. From the Dutch point of view, the colony had never been profitable; from the English point of view, it lay within the original Virginia charter of 1606 and had been wrongfully occupied by the Dutch. Charles II gave his brother James, duke of York and Albany, proprietary rights over a vast stretch of land north of the small port. Already lord high admiral and a leader in the African slave trade, James eagerly appointed his first governor, Colonel Richard Nicolls, and pledged religious toleration and property protection for all residents of New York.

Like the eight proprietors of the Carolinas, the duke of York held almost unlimited power over his colony. Although he never set foot in New York, he tried to rule personally from afar by appointing government officials, making laws regulating public affairs and commerce, and overseeing the courts. Often he appointed inept or corrupt royal governors; nevertheless, the colony gained stability from the influx of energetic farming peoples after the 1670s. English immigrants lived relatively quietly alongside Dutch residents, and the colony gained a reputation for toleration of diverse languages and religions. A few well-connected merchants built strong links to English commerce during the late 1600s, but commerce with Amsterdam continued as well. Although English residents followed their traditions of inheritance and social institutions, strong elements of Dutch custom and law prevailed among the original families. For example, though churches abounded in the colony, no Anglican parishes appeared until the 1690s.

Nicolls tried to rule New York without a representative assembly. For a while, he governed with the advice of a handpicked council, and colonists took legal disputes to an appointive court of assizes firmly under Nicolls's control. But this arrangement fell apart when in 1665 the duke of York gave a portion of his grant between the Hudson and Delaware Rivers to two friends, Sir George Carteret and Lord John Berkeley (brother of the Virginia governor), thus creating New Jersey. Carteret and Berkeley gave New Jerseyans the right to elect an assembly, which helped attract more immigrants to that colony than to New York. As unsettling as this was, James was even more unnerved when leading Dutch families failed to support his efforts to defend English settlers in the Delaware River Valley and on Manhattan or Long Island during the third Anglo–Dutch War (1672–1674). In New York City, former Dutch civic and political leaders, who were still the leading figures of the Dutch community, refused to aid English military efforts. In 1673, the port city became Dutch again for fifteen months. After the restoration of English rule, a few prominent Dutch merchants refused to swear allegiance to England, giving in only after the new governor, Edmund Andros, threatened to confiscate their property. Other wealthy Dutch families coped with shifting political alignments by marrying into, or socializing with, English families.

With the coming of peace, many Dutch settlers resented their wealthy countrymen, who "became more English by the day." For their part, English colonists began to resent Andros's accommodation to Dutch trade. Especially irksome were his refusal to curtail trade with Amsterdam and his decision not to renew commercial revenue laws that favored their trade through England. When Andros returned to England in 1680, English leaders in the colony refused to pay import duties until the colony was guaranteed a representative assembly. In 1683 the duke of York finally yielded to this demand.

Nearby, the two proprietors of New Jersey soon found out that a number of Puritans and Dutch Protestants had settled in their dominion already. Resisting rule and taxation by Restorationists, these religious dissenters created a dilemma for the proprietors. In 1674 Berkeley decided to sell his lands to two Quakers, but they soon fell to quarreling over the management of the colony. In the next decade they turned the grant over to three trustees, one of whom was the influential Quaker William Penn (see below).

In 1676 the province was divided into West and East Jersey, the latter going to Carteret, who in turn sold his share in 1682 to yet another group of proprietors, one of whom was Penn. In order to attract capital and make the colony solvent, Penn brought in even more proprietors over the next years, until twenty-four owner–rulers headed the divided colony. Here and there in the east and west portions of the colony, settlers of diverse backgrounds clustered into towns. An influential population of Quakers emerged in many towns and farms along the Delaware River. By 1702, however, proprietors and citizens alike grew weary of their constant fragmentation. They agreed to unite the two portions and become one royal colony of New Jersey.

Pennsylvania and Penn's Delaware

Pennsylvania also began as a gift from the crown to a proprietor. In 1681 Charles II awarded a great tract of land to William Penn, primarily to pay off a debt the crown owed to Penn's father. The northern boundary stretched far into the unknown west. To the south, Penn's grant overlapped Maryland claims, which were finally settled in 1767 when Charles Mason and Jeremiah Dixon surveyed a line between the two colonies.

In his early twenties, Penn had left behind a life of privilege and wealth to join the relatively new dissenting Protestants in the Society of Friends, or Quakers. By his mid-thirties, Penn had published fifty books and pamphlets about Quaker beliefs. His grant of land, which he named Pennsylvania, became a refuge for fellow Friends. Quakers were a radical sect within the Protestant fold, but they were not Calvinists. As their founders George Fox and Margaret Fell taught, salvation was available to all believers because each person carried an "inner light" of grace. This idea was not much different from the notion of individual reason that liberal philosophers were beginning to popularize in the broad movement called the Enlightenment (see page 111). Quakers gathered in weekly meetings, but unlike Puritan services, their worship was not led by a pastor or centered on a sermon. Rather, anyone could speak out at meetings about their experiences of inner light. Pious and principled, Quakers were nevertheless persecuted because they refused to fight in the army, pay taxes to support the Church of England, or conform to gestures of cultural deference such as tipping one's hat to "betters."

Penn's colony also differed from established ones in secular matters. Colonists did not have to fight for the creation of an assembly because Penn's charter required him to convene one. His Frame of Government of 1681 provided that Christians of all denominations could vote and hold office and that no taxes could be used to support a church. In the legislature, both upper and lower houses were to be elected by the enfranchised male property holders. The governor was to have no veto, and there was to be no established church. Penn insisted, however, that the structure of government was less important than the men who ran it. "Governments rather depend upon men than men upon governments. Let men be good, and the government can't be bad."

Such toleration of personal and religious beliefs encouraged rapid settlement in Pennsylvania. In the early years, great numbers of Quaker immigrants from England, Ireland, and Wales flocked to the new colony, outdone only by Puritan New England immigration in its first generation. Although this population was diverse in its skills, material endowments, and origins, Pennsylvania nevertheless bore a strong imprint of Quaker ideals. Elsewhere in North America, Quakers' antipathy to prevailing social hierarchies, wars, and conventional dress brought ridicule and persecution. The Quaker belief that women in their churches were as capable as men of leading their followers stirred up much opposition outside Quaker communities in Pennsylvania.

Land, declared Penn, would not be free, but neither could any person accumulate vast estates. Instead, it would be available at a low cost and widely distributed. In just over a decade, thousands of people came from northern England and Germany, settling the fertile lands close to good waterways and the carefully planned port city of Philadelphia, meaning "brotherly love." As Quakers spread away from the coastline, relations with Indians remained peaceful thanks to the settlers' religious convictions about generosity and love, and Penn's firm policy of friendliness and purchasing titles for Indian lands. The Lenni Lenape (or Delaware) Indians were especially open to forming an alliance with Penn's settlers because it implied protection against their long-time enemy, the Iroquois.

ENGLISH COLONIES IN NORTH AMERICA

Name	Founded by	Founded	Charter	Made Royal	Type of Colony in 1775
Virginia	London Co.	1607	1606 1609 1612	1624	Royal (under the Crown)
Plymouth	Separatists	1620	None		(Merged with Mass., 1691)
Maine	F. Gorges	1623	1639		(Bought by Mass., 1677)
New Hampshire	John Mason and others	1623	1679	1679	Royal (absorbed by Mass., 1641–1679)
Massachusetts	Puritans	c. 1628	1629	1691	Royal
Maryland	Lord Baltimore	1634	1632	——	Proprietary
Connecticut	Mass. emigrants	1635	1662	——	Self-governing
Rhode Island	R. Williams	1636	1644 1663	——	Self-governing
New Haven	Mass. emigrants	1638	None		(Merged with Conn., 1662)
N. Carolina	Virginians	1653	1663	1729	Royal (separated informally from S.C., 1691)
New York	Dutch	c. 1613			
	Duke of York	1664	1664	1685	Royal
New Jersey	Berkeley and Carteret	1664	None	1702	Royal
Carolina	Eight nobles	1670	1663	1729	Royal (separated formally from N.C., 1712)
Pennsylvania	William Penn	1681	1681	——	Proprietary
Delaware	Swedes	1638	None	——	Proprietary (merged with Pa., 1682; same governor, but separate assembly, granted 1704)
Georgia	Oglethorpe and others	1733	1732	1752	Royal

Penn also held that government should enforce religious morality. At first Quakers affirmed their determination that "lying, profane talking, drunkenness, drink of healths [toasts], obscene words, incest, sodomy, rapes, whoredom, fornication, and other uncleanness . . . all prizes, stage plays, cards, dice, May games, gamesters, masques, revels, bull-baitings, cock-fightings, bear-baitings, and the like . . . [and all] rudeness, cruelty, looseness, and irreligion, shall be . . . discouraged and severely punished." Although the frequent restatement of these and other Quaker guidelines for orderly lives set a lasting tone for Philadelphia society, the increasing size of the city and its densely settled surroundings made enforcement of such laws very difficult.

In 1682 Penn inherited the mixed Swedish and Dutch settlement of Delaware (see page 49), which had become English at the time of the conquest of New Netherland in 1664. Unwilling to rule the small colony, James, the duke of York, handed it over to Penn, who in turn called it the Lower Three Counties because it was perceived as merely an appendage of Pennsylvania. However, the strategic and commercial significance of Delaware, whose entire eastern shore lay along a bay and river way leading to Philadelphia, was not lost on future generations. In 1701 Delawareans were granted their own representative assembly, though they continued to share Pennsylvania's governor. That same year, Pennsylvanians got a new Charter of Privileges that increased the assembly's powers to make laws, especially those concerning taxes, by effectively abolishing the upper house and creating a single, or unicameral, legislature—the first one in any English colony. In 1704 Penn granted Delawareans status as a separate government.

Shaping Imperial Commerce

As European nations began to spread their influence throughout the Western Hemisphere, they developed policies to organize and govern their colonies. Some policies addressed the interests of manufacturers, shipbuilders, and merchants; some aided conquering armies; and some defined the ways colonists were to develop the economies and political life of their new environments. Underlying those policies were fundamental ideas about how people throughout the empire should live together and prosper.

Mercantilism and the Colonies

Spain, the preeminent colonial power in the 1500s, set the model for imperial economic policy that other nations would follow. Spanish rulers actively protected shipbuilding and the transport of goods and people. One group of investors, the Casa de Contratación, held a monopoly of ships, merchants, and goods crossing the Atlantic Ocean, including the navy convoys that escorted merchant vessels through dangerous waters. Dutch and English merchants and manufacturers pressured their governments to create monopolies as well. Directors in the Dutch East India Company (1602) and the Dutch West India Company (1621) obtained exclusive privileges to transport goods and people to the vast areas of the Far East and the Western Hemisphere. The English East India Company (1600) and the Royal African Company (1672) enjoyed immense power as the sole legal carriers of British goods and people among many continents.

Support for monopolies began to decline, however, when new manufacturing and colonizing interests rose in these countries. In England, the government nurtured new economic and political interests that opposed the old commercial monopolies. Monopolies, they reasoned, privileged only a few traders and prevented competition or expansion of trade. If England wished to take its place alongside powerful nations, the new interests argued, it would have to encourage home production, export goods of greater value than it imported, and protect the moral character of its inhabitants by prohibiting the importation of certain "superfluities," or luxury goods. English traders would also have to defeat the formidable commerce of the Netherlands, whose power monopolies were giving way to open competition among shippers. But whereas Dutch merchants enjoyed benefits from the commercial principle that "free ships make free goods," English merchants sought extensive government intervention in the economy to protect now one, and now another, rising economic interest. Their thinking and policies later became known (and criticized) as *mercantilism,* the term used in 1776 by the famous Scottish political economist, Adam Smith.

In the 1600s, most mercantilists believed that, given the chance, people would serve their own self-interests and compete for personal gain. They also believed that the world contained only a finite amount of wealth and that wars against competing nations were the primary way to increase their own nation's share. As the philosopher and scientist Francis Bacon put it in the mid-1600s, in order to prosper you had to "beggar thy neighbour." Within the nation, mercantilists said, inhabitants needed a wise government to harness production, to curb the greedy and destructive tendencies of competition, and to promote and channel the exchange of goods through regulation.

By the late 1600s, many mercantilists believed that wealth was not necessarily finite, but that expanding commerce with far-flung peoples helped create strong empires. A commercial empire, they wrote, should have one center from which flowed finished goods and many widely distributed satellites that consumed the center's manufactures and sent back raw materials for additional production in the "home country." Eventually, argued optimists, the English Empire would become independent of all foreign ports of call. And since, shipload for shipload, finished goods cost more than raw materials, the home country would benefit the most.

In the early 1600s, the tobacco and sugar plantations in the West Indies were the primary basis for England's rise to world power. But through the century, the North American colonies became increasingly important suppliers to the West Indies of food, work horses, lumber products, and agricultural surpluses. In payment for these goods, West Indies merchants and planters provided North Americans with credit notes and specie, or silver and gold, which were then sent to England and Europe to pay bills for manufactured goods.

This pattern of dependencies stayed in place for generations to come. But in these early years, England did not fully appreciate their West Indies colonies, and the Dutch took over much of the Caribbean and North American carrying trade. In 1651 one observer noted that "nine of ten shippes that doe departe from our island possessions [in the West Indies] land at Amsterdam" with tobacco and sugar. That year, Cromwell's Commonwealth Parliament passed the first extensive code of mercantile regulations, called Acts of Trade and Navigation, which established England's right to all of its colonies' trade. All goods were to be carried on English or colonial ships, manned by crews that were at least half English or colonial, and return to England before touching at any foreign ports. English sailors were forbidden from serving on Dutch ships, and foreign ships were barred from trading between colonial English ports.

With little enforcement machinery in place to ensure compliance, colonists largely ignored the first Navigation Act. Sugar and tobacco merchants who used Dutch carriers protested against the Navigation Act. In the northern colonies, some leading Protestants were also dismayed that Cromwell's government would pass such regulations. And from the southern colonies, planters wrote to London demanding to "continue our free trade with the Netherlanders" and other nations.

The Restoration government of Charles II (1660–1685) ignored colonial protests. In 1660 Parliament increased the proportion of English crewmen to three-fourths on every ship. It also "enumerated," or listed, colonial products that could be traded only within the empire and had to be shipped first to England to pay duties. All of the critical staple goods—tobacco, sugar, indigo, molasses, dyewoods (used to color fabric), cotton, furs, pitch, tar, masts, resin—were listed, along with a few products New Englanders exported. The duties on enumerated commodities would add revenues to English coffers, while the channeling of all colonial goods to England would undermine Holland's commercial supremacy.

Future navigation acts elaborated on the principles of protection, raising revenue, and self-sufficiency in the empire. The Staple Act of 1663 required merchants to carry all tobacco, sugar, and indigo to England, pay duties there, and only then have the freedom to re-export the goods to other ports. All European goods intended for colonists also had to stop in England first and pay duties. A Duty Act of 1673 required captains of colonial ships to post bond that guaranteed they would deliver all enumerated goods to England or else pay a "plantation duty" before sailing.

Other acts implemented the mercantilist principle that colonies should not manufacture goods that competed with English products. The Wool Act of 1699 prohibited colonial exportation of finished woolens and imposed duties on English woolen imports. A bevy of customs collectors was sent to the colonies to enforce the act in the vain hope that smuggling would cease. In 1696 Parliament established a system of admiralty courts to hear maritime cases and mete out justice without juries. London also created a Board of Trade to watch over governors and customs officials. Comprised of merchants, politicians, and economic writers, the board became a powerful advisory bureaucracy.

The Maturing Atlantic System

The three Anglo–Dutch imperial wars that ended in 1674 officially broke the Dutch hold over New Netherland, the Delaware River, and much of the African slave trade. The peace that followed, along with the Acts of Trade, gave English and colonial merchants more freedom to develop their own commerce. In 1600 English exports consisted almost entirely of woolen cloth. By 1690, English merchants were exporting ships, textiles, and many necessary goods to colonial ports, and re-exporting great quantities of sugar and tobacco to European ports. England's most important markets were now in the New World. Mercantile policies stimulated productivity, brought rising incomes to many English people who found employment in commercial trades, made the seas safer for commerce, and raised revenue for the government's treasury.

The defeat of the Dutch and their monopoly of the African slave trade brought important benefits to England and its North American colonies. The slave trade and slave labor allowed many English merchants and island planters to amass huge fortunes. By the late 1600s, commodities produced by slaves in the Western Hemisphere accounted for the overwhelming value of goods sent to England. In addition, many North American colonists benefited from providing insurance, wharfage, and storage services; sailors, clerks, and carpenters found their services in demand; and retailers stocked their stores with goods from distant places. Consumers throughout the colonies became accustomed to such goods as sugar, tea, wine, and numerous household amenities.

By the early 1700s, islands and continents were linked by numerous interdependent relationships. Some arose and survived because particular mercantile regulations protected and promoted them. For example, sugar, coffee, and rum were shipped to England, and in return the West Indies planters received credit or gold and silver from London merchants. Planters and island merchants paid out the credit or cash to slave traders from Africa and northern merchants who supplied foodstuffs and timber products. Northern colonists used profits from this West Indies trade to purchase English manufactured goods.

Other dependencies developed between the northern colonies and West Indies islands. By the 1690s, nearly half of Boston's entering goods came from the West Indies. In the next decades, Boston captains regularly stopped on their return trips for Carolina rice or Chesapeake tobacco, both of which were re-exported out of northern colonial ports to Europe. The West Indies trade permitted colonists to earn the specie and credit to pay for goods coming from England. But planters needed North American colonists, too, because of their strong focus on slavery and staples production. Up and down the coastline colonists gristed grain into flour, salted fish and packed it into barrels, and fashioned timber into containers. The West Indies trade promoted more shipbuilding and shipping services, as well as the employment of hundreds of fishermen, millers, and craftsmen in cities such as Boston, New York, Philadelphia, Baltimore, Salem, and Newport. Some colonists processed Caribbean goods for local use. Household consumers snapped up refined sugar, and their demand for rum made from West Indies molasses rose rapidly after 1690. A few venturesome manufacturers turned cocoa beans into chocolate that some felt was superior to the best Dutch chocolate.

It is impossible to know whether these activities expanded because of England's commercial regulations, or in spite of them. No doubt, certain markets developed because English laws made them a better risk than other available options. A rising merchant in Connecticut, for example, told his partner in London that he "would

London's Docks By the 1690s, the West Indies trade had become a vital part of England's overseas commerce. At this time, more than a dozen oceangoing ships were likely to be docked in London, unloading their cargoes of sugar, tobacco, and other Caribbean products. Within a few years, an entire section of the London docks sheltered scores of Caribbean-bound vessels at one time. *(West India Committee Archives.)*

just as soon get potash from a hundred farmers here, and have a ready sale in the home country, as venture with some other product of great value but no bounties [cash incentives paid from England]." But it is also true that some exports never covered by mercantile laws became a vital part of colonial commerce. Among these were grain and flour, fish, lumber, livestock, dairy products, and small agricultural surpluses from all the northern colonies.

As Captain Hall's testimony to Parliament revealed, another portion of colonists' trade also fell outside of mercantile laws: the smuggling network. Colonial merchants regularly visited foreign ports in the West Indies, illegally trading food and shoes for French sugar, or flour and barrel staves for Spanish molasses. For over a century, smuggling had steadily risen throughout the English Empire. Port officials could be bribed to falsify customs papers and allow goods to enter the colonies duty-free. Petty colonial traders helped the great transatlantic merchants by stashing away containers of forbidden items that eventually made it into retail shops throughout the country.

By the 1720s, sugar, rum, and tea were high on the list of desirable illicit goods. Smugglers themselves were popular heroes in colonial ports because they brought welcome foreign goods and sold them cheaply. The same smugglers often were legal traders, too, for they carried colonial wheat and flour, cheese and butter, and other untaxed necessities to consumers throughout the Atlantic world.

Rulers in England and the colonies worried constantly about the growth of illegal trade. No matter whether it was Dutch, French, Spanish, or English, an empire required unifying policies to channel people and goods, give institutional character to imperial goals abroad, protect and support its colonizers, and shape the beliefs and behaviors of its inhabitants. Imperial writers incessantly reminded colonists that their interests were subordinate to those of the home country. But officials were helpless to halt most illegal trade, and their complaints became empty pleas against what they saw as serious dangers to the orderly rise of the empire.

In all, despite colonists' complaints that the Acts of Trade inhibited their commercial growth, much of their economy was left unregulated and much of their trade went through illegal channels that imperial authorities did not—or could not—block. The colonists prospered both because some mercantile laws existed, and because some potential restrictions did not exist. Indeed, colonists enjoyed exclusive control over a wide range of economic activities. Before long they would associate these expansive productive activities with the political rights associated with self-government.

Crises at Home and Abroad, 1685–1700

Mercantile regulations and Restoration politics annoyed many colonists who wanted to secure opportunities for commercial advancement or political preferment. Designing men at the center of the empire, men who knew little about the practical side of colonial life, seemed to be snatching away those opportunities. Economic restrictions interfered with "the natural course of our traffic," complained New Englanders, and the stipulations of the Massachusetts charter conflicted with the many new mercantile laws. Charles II's hopes for aristocratic rule and domination of the Church of England in religious affairs in the Carolinas and New Jersey also sent alarming signals to Protestants. Thus, when Charles's Catholic successor, James II, assaulted long-held liberties, the colonists resisted, sometimes with violence.

The Dominion of New England, 1686–1689

In 1684, incensed that Massachusetts had systematically violated the Acts of Trade and denied Anglicans the right to vote, the crown revoked the colony's charter, a cornerstone of Puritan claims to legitimacy since the 1630s. On Charles II's death in 1685, his brother and successor James II set plans in motion to ensure that other colonies did not expand their assemblies' privileges. Most colonial assemblies, or lower houses of bicameral legislatures, had been increasing their powers over governors, crown-appointed judges, and royal officials. Assemblies had begun to realize the value of having representative government, in which trusted local leaders served as counterweights to imperial authority.

In 1686 James II abolished New York's assembly and turned over the government to a royal governor. James then appointed Sir Edmund Andros, a former governor of New York, to the now-royal Massachusetts government, which had been renamed the Dominion of New England. Next, James canceled the founding charters of New York and New Jersey and the corporate charters of Connecticut and Rhode Island, and combined all of the charterless colonies, along with New Hampshire and Plymouth, into the Dominion. Finally, the king attacked many colonial rights in Massachusetts: he abolished the assembly, declared the Church of England the only legitimate religion in the colony, vowed stringent enforcement of the Acts of Trade and Navigation, and revoked many privileges to which township and county governments had become accustomed.

In addition to this political restructuring, James and Andros favored a handful of loyal merchants with Royal Navy protection of their commerce in return for cooperation with royal measures. Merchants outside this charmed circle were outraged when Andros consistently waived port regulations for his favorites. Andros also raised taxes in the Dominion and challenged all existing titles to land granted under the original colonial charter of Massachusetts—a step that naturally infuriated town leaders. As Puritan minister Cotton Mather wrote, "The fox has been made master of the hen house." Soon Andros would find that he had gone too far in destroying the liberties and institutions that had evolved for three generations.

The Glorious Revolution, 1688–1689

James II converted to Catholicism in 1676 and during the next decade made many efforts to bring Catholics into high political offices in England. He favored closer trade and diplomatic relations with predominantly Catholic France, where Protestant Huguenots were still persecuted (see page 46). Fearing that irreversible trends had been initiated, Parliament plotted to replace James with his Protestant daughter Mary, who had married the Dutch head of state and a Protestant, William of Orange. In 1688, at the head of a small army and with widespread popular support, William and Mary assumed the crown from a fleeing James in what became known as the Glorious Revolution.

The new monarchs agreed to accept a Bill of Rights, which set limits on their authority, as well as on the powers of the judiciary. No longer could the crown make or suspend laws, levy taxes, or keep standing armies without the consent of Parliament. Moreover, Parliament gained the right to control the expenditure of tax money. In turn, Parliament was to have frequent meetings, free elections, and open debate of issues. In law courts, every person was guaranteed trial by jury. William and Mary promised to restore traditional civil liberties and to act as "limited monarchs" who could no longer claim to rule by "divine right."

The Glorious Revolution spurred a reexamination of many central political beliefs. Long hoping to enhance the authority of Parliament at the expense of the monarchy, a dissenting group of politicians known as Whigs—including the earl of Shaftesbury and his secretary John Locke, who had been instrumental in the founding of Carolina—put themselves in the service of the new regime. In his *Two Treatises on Government,* published in 1689–1690, Locke eloquently justified the Glorious Revolution. He began by stating that each individual has inalienable rights, including life, liberty, and property. Governments are necessary because inequalities naturally develop over time and the strong prey on the weak. But governments are voluntary agreements between the people and their rulers, and governments derive their rights from the consent of the people. This radical notion became a cornerstone of representative government. Governments have the responsibility to protect their citizens, and the only just taxes are those that the people—either directly or through their elected representatives—agree to grant the government. James II had so systematically violated the contract between rulers and ruled that the Glorious Revolution had been right and necessary.

Locke's political writings were read widely in North America. Consent of the governed and the right to be represented in government were ideas that gave legitimacy to colonists' assemblies, or "little parliaments," and inspired direct action against the governors James II had appointed.

Colonial Political Revolts, 1689–1691

In Boston, news of the Glorious Revolution turned frustrated and angry colonists against hated magistrates and port officials. In April 1689, the local militia overthrew Andros's regime. Although he tried to flee dressed as a woman, one wary colonist noticed a man's heavy boots under his skirts. Andros was arrested and deported to England. Ministers, intellectuals, artisans, and the poor dismantled the existing government. For three years the colony was run outside of the Dominion of New England framework, without a charter, but with a form of representative self-government.

For a time, the colony's elite feared that great numbers of disgruntled people might rise up against duly constituted authority. However, nothing came of lower-class disorder in the streets, and the elite were consoled when William and Mary refused to grant Massachusetts voters the right to elect their own governor in the new royal charter of 1691. In other respects, the elite and average Massachusetts citizens grew disappointed together. This happened most notably when the crown insisted that voting rights be based on property ownership rather than church membership, and that Anglicans be granted full citizenship with Puritans. These political changes were applied not only to Massachusetts, but also to Plymouth, too, which was united with Massachusetts in 1692.

In New York, word that Andros had been deposed in Boston set off long-smoldering tensions in that colony, where about 60 percent of the inhabitants still claimed Dutch heritage. When news arrived that William and Mary had assumed the throne in England, the New York City militia overran Fort James and renamed it Fort William. When the governor fled to England, rebellious colonists took over the colony. The core of the rebellion was made up of Dutch settlers; their leader was the German-born Jacob Leisler, who traded extensively with Dutch merchants. The movement that emerged in New York was comprised mainly of "a middling sort" of Dutch, German, and French citizens and "the rising traders of this fair city." Long Islanders, farmers along the Hudson River, and middling residents in New York City may have defined themselves differently, but they were united in their loathing of the "papist" governor and James II.

In the next thirteen months, Leisler focused the attention of the insurrectionists on two goals. One was to defend the colony from hostile French and English actions. This required constant pleading with small landowners, Albany fur traders, and working people in the port city for revenue to buy military supplies. Leisler's second goal was to keep order within the colony. After freeing debtors from jail and admitting artisans and petty traders into city government, Leisler turned toward repressing his enemies. He denied many English colonists legal and social rights and imprisoned many merchant opponents for months without a trial. He even sent the representative assembly home when its actions displeased him.

At first city merchants and wealthy landowners hoped to benefit from Leisler's takeover. But when his government struck down legislation that had protected city privileges, including its monopoly on sifting and grading the colony's grain and flour exports, defections mounted. In 1690 King William sent English troops and a new governor to restore calm, and royal authority, to the colony. The governor appointed anti-Leislerians to his council and called for the coup leader's arrest. In 1691 Leisler and his son-in-law, Jacob Milbourne, were hanged and decapitated for high treason. But Leisler was so popular that few New Yorkers attended the hanging, even though in England hangings were among the most popular public entertainments. For years to come, New York's artisans and housewives told stories about their briefly popular leader.

In Maryland, a Protestant rural protest against the Catholic Lord Baltimore erupted in 1681. Tensions remained high for years. When word reached the colony in 1689 that William and Mary had replaced James, John Coode and Josias Fendall led a Protestant Association to depose Baltimore. Coode and Fendall were seasoned rebels, for both had supported Nathaniel Bacon in Virginia fourteen years earlier. The Association seized control of the government in July 1689 and pledged to cut taxes and fees paid by planters, reform the customs agencies that annoyed exporters, and expand the rights of the largely Protestant Assembly. The new Maryland rulers implemented most of these measures, and in 1691 William and Mary made the colony royal. The crown also established the Church of England and deprived Catholics of the right to vote and worship publicly. When the fourth Lord Baltimore converted to the Church of England in 1715, the colony became a proprietary holding once again.

Little Parliaments

In the wake of the Glorious Revolution, much remained the same about how colonists were governed. They were, after all, inheritors of English political ideas and institutions, lived under English charters and appointed governors, and abided by English common law traditions. But much would change, too. During the 1690s, the crown took firm control over the appointment of governors and granted them extensive powers. Governors decided when the assemblies sat in session, exercised veto power over the assemblies' choices of speaker, commanded their handpicked councils (upper houses of legislature) to initiate desirable legislation, and appointed justices to virtually all colonial courts. Governors also had tremendous economic power because of their ability to grant landholdings and dispense provincial revenue. Most governors saw their position as a stepping stone to higher office in England; some were corrupt or contemptuous of the people they ruled.

Other, and eventually far more significant, changes occurred beneath the level of governors' authority. For example, the Glorious Revolution inspired the colonial assemblies to be vigilant for signs of imperial encroachments or arbitrary royal rule in the colonies, as republican theory had taught. The seething discontent of certain religious, ethnic, and occupational groups added to challenges against repressive royal officials, and many interest groups developed a political distance from the governing elite. The assemblies became important vehicles for colonists to develop a political identity separate from their imperial one. The 1689–1691 rebellions made it possible for assembly representatives to claim a much greater degree of self-government in provincial affairs than they enjoyed just a generation earlier. Although they had not yet read John Locke's treatise about individual liberties and consent of the governed, many colonists were expressing disagreement with the crown's claim to have absolute authority over subjects who lived a thousand miles from the mother country. (See Competing Voices, page 118.)

Colonial assemblies nurtured both political innovations that stemmed from the Glorious Revolution and republican ideas about balanced government, liberty, and corruption. Citizens demanded, and got, annual elections in many colonies after 1689. Assemblies wrested control from governors of certain revenues. Although they were not permitted to print money without Parliament's approval, some assemblymen led efforts to gain a greater hold over assessing and collecting taxes and spending the revenue they raised. This power of the purse gave assemblymen important leverage in negotiating with governors, as when they withheld revenue for military expeditions or governors' salaries, or attached provisions to new tax bills that favored the interests of their rural or middling urban constituents. Assemblies also began to experiment with printing their own paper money as a way to promote economic development and help rural people and debtors meet their obligations.

As the assemblies grew stronger, especially relative to the governors, many colonists also began to think about the qualities that should be required of good rulers. Elites in most colonies were still politically and culturally weak. They lacked the uncontestable stature of high birth, landed inheritance, and continuous cultural recognition that distinguished the English gentry. After the Glorious Revolution, however, individuals in the emerging elites had to negotiate carefully their authority over colonists. Although "great citizens" of many colonies feared that the colonial assemblies would become parochial discussion clubs concerned only with mundane local duties, they dared not dismiss the growing authority of the assemblies to strip "high-standing families" of their customary privileges.

These fears diminished as colonial elites became more stable. Provincial leaders made powerful family alliances through shrewd marriages or networks of commercial and professional ties in New England, Virginia, and New York. These families in turn sought and won many provincial political positions. In Virginia, the Lees, Byrds, Randolphs, and Carters headed most important committees. In New Jersey, a small coterie of families ran the assembly year after year. The Lees, Carters, Adamses, Livingstons, DeLanceys, and other families used their influence and official positions to protect their interests against imperial trade and tax policies. For example, elite assemblymen frequently responded to popular outcries against imperial prohibitions on certain exports by nullifying specific trade laws. Or they might refuse to authorize higher taxes to support imperial military campaigns.

In order for colonial elites to succeed, they needed the support of middling colonists. Because events surrounding the Glorious Revolution created greater sensitivity about the rights of individual citizens in the political process, colonial representatives listened more carefully to the demands of ordinary people. For example, after Bacon's Rebellion, the Virginia elite knew that yeomen farmers would not hesitate to rise again if the burdens of taxes and debt became too great. The assembly therefore lowered poll taxes and property taxes in Virginia during the eighteenth century and minimized the property requirement for voting despite royal wishes to raise it. Some of the northern colonies also lowered their property requirements for voting. Almost universally, colonists accepted the premise that land should define the electoral process, although sometimes they added the requirement of membership in the established churches. In seven colonies a man had to be at least sixteen years old and own a "freehold" of roughly fifty acres, or show proof of working a farmstead, in order to vote. Given the wide availability of land in the early generations, the electorate expanded to nearly 60 percent of colonial free white adult men during the 1700s. The remaining 40 percent were single sons living at home, indentured servants, or landless individuals.

Comparatively few men could hold provincial office, however, since colonies typically required ownership of a thousand acres or more for officeholding. Even freeholders who owned enough land or property to vote often faced obstacles to the ballot. Generally, when voting took place at county seats or coastal cities, participation diminished as distance from the polling place grew. In New York, Virginia, or New Jersey, where colonists often cast their votes *viva voce* (by stating a preference out loud), the fear of reprisals for publicly choosing the "wrong" candidate kept many voters away from the polls. Furthermore, some towns or regions were reluctant to send representatives to distant government halls because they would lose their services in the local community. In addition, the free choice of candidates was diminished when candidates plied voters with liberal servings of alcohol in a practice known as "passing the sack" or "swilling the bumbo." Very few colonists objected to this kind of personal appeal for votes, and the practice underscored expectations that members of the elite would hold all significant colonial offices because they were the "natural betters" of the people and would rule in everyone's best interests.

Witches

While the crises involving the Dominion of New England and responses to the Glorious Revolution brewed, the conditions leading to the greatest outbreak of witchcraft in colonial America also unfolded. Belief in supernatural causes for everyday events had remained strong in the colonies, as in Europe, and colonists were periodically accused of being possessed by Satan or witches. Even the most educated and devout Puritans believed God sent them signs of his pleasure and wrath through nature. Newborn infants were searched for deformities that might indicate a mother's or baby's corruption by the forces of evil. Astrological charts were a common means of determining when to plant crops.

Although many New England colonists, especially leading merchants and ministers, no longer held these traditional beliefs, a significant portion of all local populations did. Some of them joined other vigilant colonists in ferreting out supposed witches for public trials, often recalling the biblical passage, "Thou shalt not suffer a witch to live." Occasionally, civil authorities in Massachusetts or Connecticut agreed to hang people, primarily outspoken older women, single women, or town gossips and nuisances. In addition, colonists harbored suspicions about women who were not able to have healthy children, widows who wished to be economically independent, and the elderly.

The causes of the events in Salem Village and Town during 1691 and 1692 may never be entirely clear. Certainly, some factors can be traced to the revocation of Massachusetts's charter in 1684 and the subsequent overthrow of Andros. Over a longer period of time, rivalries among local families over landholding, jealousies over farming success, and a contentious new minister's arrival also created tensions in the community. Poor farmers of Salem Village resented the rising status of the commercial and trading families of Salem Town. Some of the young women of the Village worked as servants in the homes of mature women who may have made no secret of these resentments. The servants may in turn have felt anxious about their potential for successful marriage and homemaking. When the epidemic of accusations began, some of the targets of witchcraft accusations were married women who had ordered the "afflicted" girls to perform "endless" chores.

At first, the daughter and niece of Village minister Samuel Parris simply played at voodoo and dancing they had learned from the household's West Indies slave, Tituba. When the girls extended their play to having fits, gesturing wildly, and "speaking in tongues," the village elders stepped in to extract a confession from Tituba. To rid themselves of suspicion, the girls further accused an elderly pauper woman and a homeless village widow of tormenting them. As events unfolded,

The Salem Witch Trials
These images of punishments of witches portray events in early England. The Massachusetts hangings during the summer of 1692 probably resembled the top drawing. *(Folger Shakespeare Library, Washington, D.C.)*

other girls from the Village accused certain wealthier church members from Salem Town of witchcraft. Afflicted, supposedly tormented accusers turned on members of their community with charges of having used "cunning," conjuring, spells, and consorting with the Devil to win over the young girls to witchcraft.

Within a few weeks, not just peripheral elderly women but some of the most respected successful "good wives" of the community were accused and sent to jail to await trial. Over a hundred suspected witches, including a four-year-old child who was kept in chains for nine months, filled the jails. But without a charter or royal governor, trials could not proceed. Finally, in May 1692, when Governor William Phips arrived, a special court was set up to hear testimony. Dozens of community folk who had been caught up in the vortex of accusation, deceit, and doubtful evidence set neighbors against one another. Of the twenty-seven people who came to trial, nineteen were condemned and hanged; when Giles Cory refused to enter a plea, he was pressed under stones until he died.

Events in Salem highlighted tensions that had been smoldering for decades. Similar conditions could be found in many other places, sometimes giving rise to fears of impending social chaos. But the episode in Salem was not repeated elsewhere, possibly because nowhere else were the particular combination of personal and social tensions duplicated. Within a few months of the executions, word had spread about the hysteria, and a popular outcry against the Salem excesses helped quell its spread. Moreover, some colonial leaders, including prominent Boston ministers, scoffed at the pagan heritage that explained unforeseen events as the workings of the devil or witches.

Politics and Culture in the New Century, 1700–1748

By 1700, colonists had made a number of painful political and cultural adjustments, but their settlements had matured and begun to prosper noticeably. As the new century began, however, colonists entered a prolonged period of reassessing their place in the empire, in both war and peace. As colonists expanded onto new frontiers of North America and traded more widely with distant peoples, they became more aware of their own independent opportunities to prosper. Moreover, they were increasingly "refined" and "improved," they said, by the new goods and new intellectual trends they encountered by mingling with people in numerous places outside the imperial settlements. At the same time, British rulers were redefining the political, cultural, and economic interests of the whole empire, and involving colonists in struggles to secure and defend those interests. Thus wars, too, became transforming experiences.

Renewed Imperial Warfare

The Protestant monarchs, William and Mary, initiated a new era of warfare. After a generation of warring against Europe's commercial titan, the Netherlands, English rulers, merchants, and soldiers turned against rising imperial France after the Glorious Revolution. In 1689 war broke out with France over James II's claim to the English crown. King William's War (known in Europe as the War of the League of Augsburg) sparked conflicts along the frontiers with New France for eight years. Following a flurry of skirmishes against fur trading forts around Montreal and New York's northern waterways, Iroquois and English forces attacked French, Huron, and Erie forces, eventually taking Port Royal in Acadia (later known as Nova Scotia). The French repeatedly attacked frontier settlers in Maine, New Hampshire, and New York, destroying Schenectady in 1690. In the Caribbean, French troops took over the sugar island of Santo Domingo in 1697 and renamed it St. Dominique. Overall, however, neither nation won much territory, and colonial militiamen came home to New York and New England resentful of their treatment by British officers, the near-starvation rations they endured, and the devastating effects of smallpox on their troops.

The greatest losers in this war were the Iroquois. Their fur trade lay in shambles as hostilities had drawn every warrior, young and old, into battle. Hundreds of women, children, and aging Mohawk and Oneida people fled to French forts seeking shelter from Indian enemies in the Ohio Valley. Even after the Treaty of Ryswick in 1697, France's Indian allies kept attacking Iroquois villages, until finally in 1701 the Iroquois agreed to remain neutral in future European conflicts and forgo future raids and blood feuding against the pro-French Indians. Long into the eighteenth century, the Iroquois remained wary of both English and French traders and diplomats, fine-tuning their own methods of negotiation and defending the land between French Canada and English America for the remnants of their confederacy.

European powers were at peace only briefly. By 1702, England was at war again, this time fighting both France and Spain in Queen Anne's War (called the War of the Spanish Succession in Europe). French troops and their Abenaki allies burned several frontier settlements in Maine. In 1704 Abenaki and Mohawk Indians attacked settlers in Deerfield, Massachusetts, burning fields, looting homes and stores, and killing 48 residents; another 112 were taken captive. English soldiers were able to hold Newfoundland and, in 1710, recapture Port Royal in the northern periphery, partly because the Iroquois did not want to fight in this war and chose to protect their fur trade instead. But when the British tried to take the city of Quebec in 1711, they suffered a costly defeat.

Because Spain and France were allies, Queen Anne's War also drew in southern planters and Indians. Very early in the war, English forces burned much of the Spanish settlement of St. Augustine. Then in 1704 Carolinians mobilized thousands of Creek warriors to march into Florida, where they razed Pensacola and Apalachee villages near Spanish fields. In response, Spanish soldiers invaded from the south, crossing into the vulnerable plantations around Charles Town and nearly overrunning the city in 1706.

Queen Anne's War was a contest among Europe's empire builders for territory and peoples around the world. By the Treaty of Utrecht in 1713, which brought it to a close, England gained all of Newfoundland, Acadia, and the icy lands of Hudson Bay. It also acquired Gibraltar and negotiated trading rights with portions of Spanish South America. In anticipation of renewed hostilities, the three imperial powers fortified North American frontiers adjacent to their older settlements, as well as the major cities of St. Augustine, Havana, and Louisiana. Spain, fearing English expansion into the Floridas and the land around its valuable silver mines, put up permanent settlements in Texas starting in 1718. Over the next few years, hundreds of Spanish soldiers, missionaries, and ranchers moved into the region. The Caddo people fought in vain to ward off Spanish and Mexican efforts to settle in their "Kingdom of Téjas." In the years to come, Caddo villages were able to trade goods with both French missionaries and Spanish farmers. Nevertheless, the Caddo people were gradually edged farther into the interior. All that would remain of their legacy was the name Texas.

Postwar tensions also developed between English frontier settlements and their Indian neighbors. Sparsely settled Carolinians lived in fear of Indian attacks from remnants of the Yamasee villages that Europeans had tried to devastate during the early years of the fur trade and Queen Anne's War. In New York, the Iroquois had developed a refined diplomacy before the war that gave them a great deal of control over the fur trade. By negotiating arrangements to trade with both the French and English, they also built a Covenant Chain of many treaties that held their Huron and other western Indian enemies at bay. After Queen Anne's War, the Iroquois resumed these trade and diplomatic relations. But English colonists did not recover as easily: the war had strained resources and exacted a death toll that left a tragic imprint on their farming communities.

Colonists also learned important lessons about their ability to sustain long and costly wars. The colonial militia was difficult to mobilize and move quickly to points of conflict. Colonists were consistently stingy about supplying food and blankets, and loathed paying their taxes. Merchants, retailers, and women consumers throughtout the colonies had been made painfully aware of the crushing difficulties inflicted by war on their commercial economy. The few fortunes made by privateers hardly compensated for the misery coastal towns faced long after treaties were signed. Dependent on the crown for commercial protection and military defense, and impoverished by wars that had lasted nearly twenty years, colonists were sorely ready for peace.

Challenging Imperial Arrangements

During the reign of George I (1714–1727) and the early years of George II (1727–1760), England was mostly at peace. Its statesmen focused less attention on internal colonial activities than in the period between 1685 and 1713, and more attention on strengthening the political and economic life of the mother country. The leading politician for many of these years was Sir Robert Walpole, the king's closest minister and adviser from 1720 to 1742. Walpole enjoyed the support of Whig manufacturers and merchants who favored aggressive economic expansion, and he developed a new style of politics based on patronage and favoritism. In addition, Walpoleans expanded the government bureaucracy and promoted more widespread banking and financial services.

The rise of this "court" party—so named because of its identification with urban, commercial, and banking interests—alarmed many Britons. The Glorious Revolution had helped "true born Englishmen" become suspicious of powerful central government. Now, Walpole had initiated a practice of doling out important government and military positions to men who promised to support particular crown measures. Appointments to important posts, inside information about business deals, and outright bribery were all in Walpole's arsenal of favoritism. His critics in England—known as the "country" faction—feared that Walpolean bureaucracy and patronage would destroy Parliament's hard-won independence from the crown. Corruption of political leaders would ensue, they charged, with the inevitable result of harming the very character of the English people. Critics believed that unstable new groups of merchants, investors, bankers, and office seekers in the court faction had replaced the proper leadership of the country faction, or landed gentlemen. Walpole's administration had created a permanent national debt and a standing army, both of which were additional perils to the English people.

The "country" arguments offered colonists strong reasons to be suspicious of incompetent or malicious government officials who might rule against the wider interests of the colonists, just at the time that the colonial assemblies began asserting new powers. Governors, wrote some colonists in their budding newspapers, too often had gained their posts by marrying daughters of influential politicians. Once in office, they asked the assemblies to allocate precious colonial tax revenues for their exorbitant salaries or unnecessary military fortifications. Some crown appointees tried to curb the powers of the assemblies, but usually to their regret after 1730. Others simply neglected to direct colonial affairs firmly, thereby creating habits of "assembly governance." For example, when Governor George Clinton of New York quietly decided not to impose certain crown directives on the colonists in 1744, including new taxes on goods they consumed, assembly representatives debated how to raise revenues and conduct internal trade according to their own perceptions of the colony's welfare.

In other colonies, assembly representatives defied imperial wisdom and printed colonial paper money. For decades, colonists complained that their merchants shipped most coin and paper credits to England to pay for imported goods, leaving scant amounts of money in the colonies for use in daily transactions. Some assemblies had approved modest printings of paper money to help fund military expeditions or ease the burdens of rising taxes. Now, during years of relative peace in the 1720s to 1740s, eleven colonies printed paper money that would circulate in domestic exchanges and would be drawn out of circulation regularly by making the money valid for paying colonial taxes. Some colonies also issued paper money widely to internal settlements and based repayment of the paper notes on the mortgages of farmers' land. By most colonial reports, these "land banks" helped ease payments of local debts and stretched the buying power of thousands of colonists. Opposition came, however, from merchants on both sides of the Atlantic when some colonies kept printing more and more paper money without providing for its withdrawal through taxation. In Rhode Island and Massachusetts, paper money had so depreciated by the 1740s that storekeepers began to grumble that their debtors were offering "worthless scraps of paper."

International traders who needed silver, gold, or bills of exchange for their business abroad also protested against paper money. Parliament responded to their complaints of "a deteriorating medium of exchange" by passing a Currency Act in

1751 that disallowed the New England colonies from creating land banks or accepting paper money as legal tender. The crown advisers on the Board of Trade also bristled against the colonial currency practices. Colonists, argued board member Charles Townshend, had grossly violated the "natural order" of colonial subordination to crown authority by printing their own money.

Walpolean Whig policies on economic development and international commerce also irritated colonists. Numerous Acts of Trade passed in the late 1600s affirmed the mercantilist belief that colonists should not be manufacturing goods that competed with production in the home country, and that they should conduct their trade only within the empire. Through Queen Anne's War, additional legislation restated the theoretical limitations of colonial economies. But few of these laws entirely suppressed colonial production or exchange of the goods they regulated. Indeed, growing trade with the West Indies islands—British and foreign—proved to be the linchpin of colonial growth. Shortly after Queen Anne's War, colonists noted that the British sugar islands were unable to buy all the flour, grain, fish, and timber products of the mainland colonies. American ships began to call at French, Dutch, and eventually Spanish islands, where merchants paid in cash.

British observers grew alarmed that this trade would undermine the power of the empire, especially when it became illegal smuggling during wars. For one thing, colonists preferred French over English molasses, which was used to distill rum (especially in New England). This trade deprived English merchants of carrying the raw material in their ships to English rum manufacturers, whose business also declined. For another, colonists sent larger and larger portions of their grain, flour, and timber products to the French islands, and then carried away French sugar to mainland colonists or to European ports. Indeed, when a serious international recession hit world trade during the 1720s, many English sugar planters feared the collapse of their island enterprises.

In the wake of a heated public and Parliamentary discussion about the future of the British West Indies and role of northern American colonies, island planters won the Molasses Act of 1733. In order to make English prices for sugar and molasses more competitive, colonists were henceforth expected to pay a relatively high duty (6 pence per gallon) on French molasses purchased for their colonial distilling enterprises. In addition, it was hoped that by making prices of English island goods acceptable, colonists would take more of their provisions to them.

Colonists disagreed with both the reasoning and the tax. All of the West Indies islands, and not just a few English ones, were the "sinew and blood" of colonial trade, argued northern merchants. Without open markets for their goods at any islands they chose, farmers would suffer and captains would fail to bring back the cash and credit that was vital for paying colonial debts for English manufactured imports. The whole triangle of dependent commercial relations would vanish. Parliament, however, turned its back on colonial pleas. And even when sugar prices rose in England and Europe by the mid-1730s, colonists persisted in smuggling, bribing port officials, and collecting foreign coin to "grease the trade of our humble [colonial] peoples."

Once again, however, mercantile legislation was powerless to hold back colonial production or trade with the West Indies. Colonial merchants' ships, although smaller than the oceangoing vessels of England, were becoming so numerous that

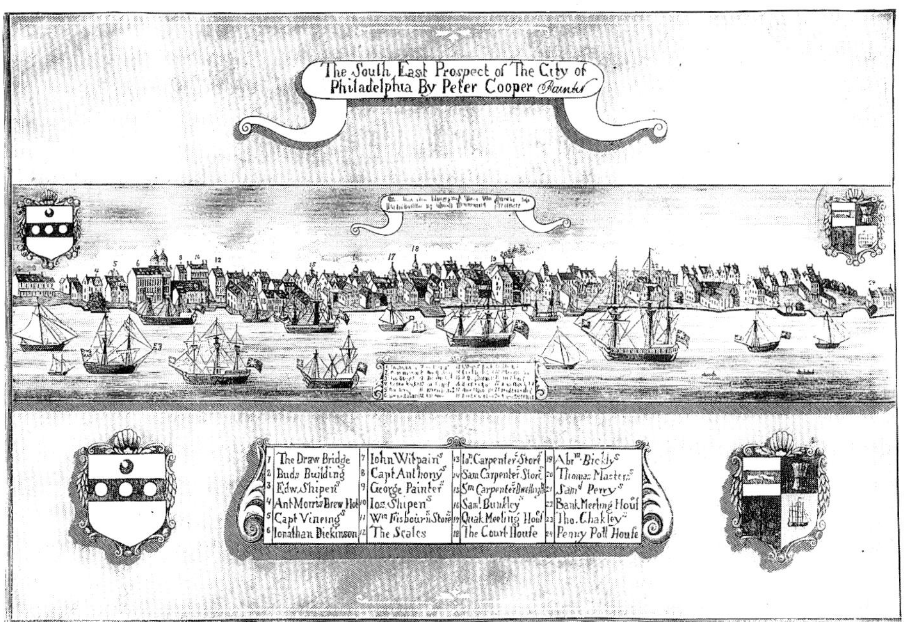

Southeast Prospect of the City of Philadelphia, 1720 Although settled much later than Boston, Jamestown, and New York, Philadelphia became the premier city of North America by midcentury. The scale of ships, warehouses, and brick homes is dwarfed by any view of a great European port at this time, but the artist is clearly trying to show the rising prosperity of this colonial port. *(Library Company of Philadelphia.)*

by 1750 captains from Boston, Philadelphia, and New York City brought over 80 percent of colonists' exportable goods to the West Indies. By then, colonial merchants also handled and shipped well over half of the imports North Americans purchased from England. In addition, colonial production of textiles multiplied despite the Wool Act of 1699; their production and exchange of fur hats continued despite the Hat Act of 1732; and their manufacture of raw iron and iron goods grew rapidly despite the Iron Act of 1750.

Midcentury Warfare

The end of Queen Anne's War in 1713 initiated a generation of peaceful commerce—though not continuous prosperity—that was interrupted with renewed warfare in 1738 when the War of Jenkins's Ear began (in Europe, the War of the Austrian Succession, 1740–1748). Robert Jenkins, a popular English smuggler who was trading illegally at Spanish Caribbean islands, drew colonists abruptly into war when Spanish *guarda costas* captured Jenkins and tortured him. The incident gave George II sufficient pretext to order England into war.

At first, an expedition against Porto Bello in Panama went very badly for the thousands of southern colonists who volunteered to fight the Spanish; hundreds died in battle and of yellow fever. In addition to Virginia and Carolina troops, the new colony of Georgia became a buffer against the mainland Spanish settlements, and General James Oglethorpe raised Georgia troops to raid St. Augustine on behalf of British interests. By 1744, France had entered the war to aid Spain, and border raids began along the northern colonial frontier. Governors mustered troops from Massachusetts and Maine, first to hold Port Royal in Nova Scotia, and then in 1745 to seize French Louisbourg on Cape Breton Island and raise the British flag over this French stronghold in North America.

Although southern British settlements seemed to be secure, and much northern French territory under British control, the war began to take a terrible toll on mainland colonists. Massachusetts soldiers began to die of diseases in Canadian camps, Indians and French attacked many spots on the northern English frontier, taxes in New England rose to unbearable levels, and naval press gangs yanked young New England men out of their homes and job sites to serve in the Royal Navy. In 1748 the war ended in relative stalemate, for in the Treaty of Aix-la-Chapelle England exchanged Louisbourg for Madras in India, which had fallen to the French during the European phase of the war.

Colonial Americans greeted news of the peace treaty with dismay. The return of hard-won Louisbourg proved especially disappointing. Suddenly, too, the impulses to expand onto the frontier seemed stymied. Fur traders from Pennsylvania, New York, and Virginia who had extended British influence into the Ohio Valley looked forward to dominating the trade around the Great Lakes and to the Mississippi River. But the French still stood in their way.

Thousands of French migrants had settled in the lower Mississippi River basin early in the 1700s, especially at Biloxi and Mobile, despite violent opposition from the Natchez Indians. After a devastating war between the French and Indians in 1729, remaining colonizers congregated around the budding port of New Orleans. With aid from the Choctaw and the introduction of slavery, the French began producing indigo and rice. Aggressively pursuing trade with Indian tribes around them, the French drew great quantities of deer skins, tobacco, and grains into New Orleans. The small French settlements thrived and grew—to the consternation of English colonial planters who wished to expand westward.

British colonial land speculators also formed companies to occupy the Ohio Valley and beyond. Aided by ambiguous wording in their original charters, which stipulated no definite western boundaries, some southern colonial governments backed the grand plans of the land companies. For example, the Virginia legislature created the Ohio Company of speculators in 1749, and the crown promised 500,000 acres of land north of the Ohio River. Naturally, news of the company's plans for expansion, and rumors about the formation of even more land companies, was met with alarm in French settlements. Along with their Indian allies around the Great Lakes, French authorities expressed grave fears about the encroachments of trappers and speculators in the disputed Ohio Valley.

Fears grew, too, in the frontier British settlements, where hundreds of unprotected colonists were staking new claims and building towns. And along the coastline, townspeople also became dismayed to learn that English merchants regularly traded at Spanish and French ports in the Caribbean. While not technically illegal during times of peace, such open business relations with long-standing foreign rivals flew in the face of efforts by English policymakers to subordinate colonial

Many Peoples in Louisiana By the early 1700s, French missionaries and traders had encountered many different Indian peoples near the mouth of the Mississippi River. The Illinois people (on the left) became important fur trade partners with the French and Spanish; here they display a hunting bow, fishing spear, various plants, and cured skins. Some Indians, including the man standing at the far right, became slaves on European farms and worked alongside the African slaves introduced by Europeans to the region by the early 1700s. *(Peabody Museum, Harvard University.)*

interests to those of the imperial center with new commercial regulations during the 1730s and 1740s. Together, territorial and commercial issues at midcentury caused many colonists to become anxious about relations with their own colonial elites, as well as rulers in the mother country.

Transatlantic Cultural Influences

By the late 1600s, the rise of mercantilism and the new emphasis on representative governments were producing profound cultural changes throughout Britain's empire. Throughout England and the Continent, a "scientific revolution" had been challenging folk, pagan, and traditional views about the natural and intellectual world. Simultaneously, a "commercial revolution" embodied the efforts of emerging European empires to take over foreign lands, make ships and shipping more competitive, and increase the wealth of nation-states by expansive trade. As these two revolutions continued, an intellectual movement known as the Enlightenment extended and deepened the cultural refinement and interconnectedness of European peoples throughout the transatlantic empires.

Enlightenment writers questioned cherished traditions or invited experimentation in daring new realms of science and nature, religion, civil law, and even universal truths. In 1687 English mathematician and astronomer Sir Isaac Newton published

Principia, or Mathematical Principles of Natural Philosophy. In it, Newton explained that all physical objects obeyed not God's particular commands, but unchanging scientific laws, such as gravity and the laws of motion. God, according to this Newtonian view of the world, did not have to intervene in every little event but could stand back and watch his creations operate as designed. In turn, human beings could measure, predict, and even manipulate nature to their needs and wants. Indeed, any right-reasoning individual could discover the underlying causes and effects of all natural phenomena.

John Locke's *Essay Concerning Human Understanding,* printed in 1690, rejected the long-standing belief that individuals are born with innate traits and are prefabricated to think and act in given ways. The mind at birth is, in his famous phrase, a *tabula rasa,* a blank slate, on which the person's senses and his or her ongoing experiences write the stuff of life. According to Locke, reason, environment, and experience shape character; education, actions guided with regard for others in the community, and the exercise of universal natural rights in the political arena are the proper focus of human efforts.

These Enlightenment ideas, which gradually diminished the direct role of God in everyday events, emphasized individual reasoning and the limitless potential for human intervention in shaping the forces of nature. But Puritan leaders and northern governors often embraced ideas from the Enlightenment without abandoning their religious convictions. John Winthrop, Jr., the governor of Connecticut for many years, owned a telescope and corresponded with members of the Royal Society of London, the most renowned group of English philosophers and scientists. Microscopes made minutia accessible for detailed study, and telescopes brought the heavens close to Earth. Detailed reports, attention to methodologies, claims to having found proofs, dissemination of findings to broad audiences, and critical debates that demanded even more investigation—all marked a burgeoning interest in making science a field of study with regular laws and accessible to people across national and language barriers. In commerce, too, writers claimed to be finding the "laws of trade" that might render human behavior in markets more predictable. Harvard, an early training ground for colonial ministers, soon added astronomy, chemistry, geology, and other "lawful sciences" to its curriculum.

By the early 1700s Enlightenment writers tended to undermine beliefs in witches, supernatural events, and philosophies based on the world's essentially chaotic character. The world, they insisted, had been created in an orderly fashion, and human beings, through reasoning, had the capacity to investigate and understand it. Each person had the power to comprehend the natural laws of the universe by careful study. Some colonists, convinced by Enlightenment notions, became deists who looked for God's plan in nature rather than in the Bible, and who tended to blend science and reason with God's laws for human action. And many Enlightenment writers used provocative and alluring language to convince many people of their correctness. They were aided by the growing number of printing presses in major cities that disseminated new ideas through public print.

Nobody epitomized the Enlightenment's impact in the colonies as fully as Benjamin Franklin (1706–1790). As the son of a Boston soap- and candle-maker, he came from a humble background. But when at age seventeen he ran away from his brother's shop, where he was apprenticed to learn printing, Franklin began a rapid rise in Philadelphia. At age twenty-three he owned his own print shop, where he edited and published the *Pennsylvania Gazette,* a journal he printed continuously until his death. At age twenty-seven he finished the first *Poor Richard's Almanac,* a periodic publication that offered advice, reflected on the weather, reported new inventions, and reminded readers about the best routes to personal happiness and success. By age forty-two, Franklin stood at the center of Philadelphia's educated and scientific community. He had founded the Library Company; established a fire company; began the academy from which the University of Pennsylvania would emerge; and organized a "semblance of the Royal Society of London," which soon became the American Philosophical Society. Then Franklin retired from business and devoted himself to scientific inventions such as the Franklin stove, the lightning rod, treatises on geology and astronomy, experiments in surgery and medicine, and improvements in ship designs. Just as significant, by the 1740s, Franklin had entered politics. His views on immigration, paper money, land speculation, and colonists' role in the empire made him a national figure. Franklin repeatedly served as a representative to pan-colonial meetings, as a colonial agent in London, and as the American ambassador to France after the Revolution. Franklin served as the oldest member of the Constitutional Convention as well.

Benjamin Franklin This Charles Willson Peale portrait of the famous colonial politician, philosopher, scientist, and cultural leader was done late in Franklin's life, but it shows him at the height of refined American dress and stately composure. Paper, ink, and pen convey Franklin's extensive participation in the intellectual life of the empire, and the bolt of lightning in the background is grounded by a rod, invented by Franklin. *(Historical Society of Pennsylvania.)*

It is hard to evaluate the precise effect of the intellectual elite's labors on a semiliterate public accustomed to speaking and listening in a much different way. But certain Enlightenment influences permeated the colonies by the early 1700s. For example, here and there, planter and merchant families began to shift their strategies of child rearing. Some backed away from traditional wisdom that held that infants were born with evil wills that had to be broken, and proposed instead that children were "but blanks or voids upon whom the kind glances and firm direction" of the parent could inscribe wisdom conducive to social good.

Some leading urban colonists also initiated new societies that brought middling and elite people together, including debate clubs to discuss philosophical issues; "improvement societies" to promote literacy, sobriety, and civic-mindedness; and "invention societies" to "promote useful knowledge." Presumably, great numbers of colonists could afford the time and money these learning and leisure organizations entailed. Judging by the membership lists, however, it was clusters of gentlemen and rising merchants in the major cities who sustained the Subscription Library Society and the Moot Club of New York, or Franklin's Union Fire Company and American Philosophical Society of Philadelphia.

Wealthy Quaker and Anglican merchants also undertook a variety of social reform efforts. The Hospital for the Sick Poor was built in Philadelphia in 1751 and the Bettering House for the elderly and feeble in 1767. The able-bodied poor, widows, and orphans were housed in "spinning schools," where they were required to produce goods that the institutions' merchant–owners could sell, thereby reducing taxes the wealthy paid for poor relief and reimbursing the owners for their investment. Critics charged that the wealthy were attempting to control the lives of colonists who preferred to live and work independently. Indeed, hospitals and poorhouses looked like imposing jails.

Enlightenment thinking also changed the way colonists thought about doctors and lawyers, and paved the way for acceptance of both professions. Before the 1720s, colonial lawyers were trained in England, some to be Anglican clergymen, and some to be philosophers. As a result, many colonial lawyers could recite the works of Locke and other political philosophers but knew little about the great legal theorists of their era. Southern lawyers in particular were prone to write poetry and editorials while they practiced law, in part because their services were infrequently needed, and in part because their education had neglected training in the law. To many colonists, lawyers simply awaited opportunities to accept cases in which they argued pretentiously and "fooled the entire courtroom into some desired outcome." In addition, lawyers seemed to charge outlandish fees for their services. But the Enlightenment's emphasis on reason and empirical knowledge encouraged literate colonists to read widely, and many of the books available for them to import were legal treatises. Harvard and Yale began to offer courses in the law, although a training period with a practicing lawyer was of greater help in learning practical aspects of the profession.

Physicians, especially those trained in Edinburgh's medical school, drew public criticism as well. For generations colonists had believed in treating injuries and diseases with a minimum of intervention; most colonists had never met a person who had experienced surgery. Dissecting human cadavers and lecturing on anatomy and chemistry were considered to be intolerable breaks with the course of nature. Eventually, however, enlightened medicine gained respectability. Some New England ministers, for example, found room within their spiritual teachings to support new wisdom about halting the spread of certain diseases. In the early 1720s, a few Massachusetts preachers were in the forefront of those who supported inoculating Bostonians against smallpox with injections of a less virulent strain of the virus.

Boston boasted a printing house as early as 1674; William Bradford printed works in Philadelphia in the 1680s, and then moved on to New York in 1693. Their minor print-runs of religious texts, however, reached small audiences. But in 1704, the *Boston News-Letter* began to appear, and by the 1720s, New York City and Philadelphia had weekly publications as well. Charles Town residents could read the *South Carolina Gazette* by 1732, and even Williamsburg printed the *Virginia Gazette* after 1735. In New York, John Peter Zenger's *New York Weekly Journal,* launched in 1733, became a mouthpiece for criticizing the governor. Zenger was tried for sedition—spreading antigovernment sentiments—in 1735 and won a significant victory for freedom of the press when the jury acquitted him. Most of the newspapers changed hands frequently (Franklin's *Pennsylvania Gazette* was an exception) and reprinted stories about European and English events. But some papers also lifted excerpts or printed wholesale the essays of English publicists who were close to the Enlightenment. Richard Steele's *The Spectator* and Joseph Addison's *The Tatler* delighted readers in Boston during the 1720s. Week after week, readers could find reprints of John Trenchard and Thomas Gordon's polemical essays against religious bigotry and financial corruption in government, published under the pseudonym Cato during 1720–1723 and compiled as *Cato's Letters.* Caustic, humorous, and always up-to-date about political intrigues and scandals, these essays helped colonists understand and adopt messages of the Enlightenment as they were filtered through the oppositionist political discussions of England.

The ideas and cultural experiments that began in elite circles had two profound effects on ordinary citizens during later colonial decades. First, formal education had the intended result of reinforcing distinctions among different social layers of colonial society. Few poor or middling colonists took courses in geometry, cartography, astronomy, anatomy, or fine arts at college. Second, it had the unforeseen result of popularizing notions about the duty of rulers to conform to the public will, as John Locke had espoused in his *Second Treatise of Government,* and about the capacity of individuals to overcome the adversities of birth and station through hard work, Benjamin Franklin's theme.On the one hand, the Enlightenment seemed to separate the elite from the majority of colonists; on the other hand, it seemed to promote a greater degree of social equality and natural ability among all white males.

CONCLUSION

Migrants who built farms and cities in the Restoration colonies after 1660 did not have to struggle for a toehold in North America as hard or long as the earlier waves of migrants did. And by the 1680s, they enjoyed unmistakable signs of stability and prosperity. Expanding commerce and colonial settlement spurred colonists' optimism about attaining ever-higher levels of material comfort, institutional maturity, and cultural refinement. To a great extent, policymakers in England aided these colonial developments by creating commercial bureaucracies, trade and manufacturing regulations, and laws against foreign connections. Together, mercantile policies imposed a rudimentary system of governance and commerce over the colonies.

However, it was one thing for policymakers to design an empire in London, and quite another for colonists to live by that design. The crown exercised greater control over its dominion after the Restoration, and carefully picked governors to enforce royal authority. But the Glorious Revolution reinforced colonists' habits of expecting certain political "rights" through their representative assemblies. And decades of practicing local lawmaking and community building taught colonists to cherish self-government.

Similar tensions arose concerning colonists' commerce. If trade was, on the one hand, the sinews connecting all parts of the empire into a great power to compete against foreign empires, it was also, on the other hand, the means by which colonists pursued new opportunities to grow—often outside the watchful gaze of imperial officials, or blatantly defying that gaze. And the new imported commodities, which made life a little better for great numbers of middling white colonists, also set apart and helped consolidate the authority of a few elite officeholders, merchants, and planters.

The expanding theaters of international warfare, and the persistent possibility that it could erupt again, underscored the fragility of political leadership in the British colonies and the need to be watchful for commercial opportunities and setbacks. Wars proved to be long and costly affairs, and they failed to give one empire or another definitive claims over contested areas of North America. Moreover, war proved to be a mixture of commercial or political opportunity for some colonists, and dire hardship for others.

As the eighteenth century progressed, colonists continued to appreciate the political, institutional, and cultural benefits of life in the English Empire. But where the empire's influence did not extend, or where imperial authority was easily ignored, opportunities for colonial distinctiveness arose and set the stage for rising tensions between the imperial center and its colonies in years to come.

SUGGESTED READINGS

For the rise of English commerce and mercantilism, good starting places are Kenneth R. Andrews, *Trade, Plunder, and Settlement: Maritime Enterprise and the Genesis of the British Empire* (1984); Thomas Barrow, *Trade and Empire* (1967); Ralph Davis, *The Rise of Atlantic Economies* (1973); and Michael Kammen, *Empire and Interest: The American Colonies and the Politics of Mercantilism* (1970). For opposition to mercantilism, see Joyce Appleby, *Economic Thought and Ideology in Seventeenth Century England* (1978). Ian K. Steele, *The Politics of Colonial Policy* (1968), is the most readable introduction to European imperial efforts at shaping Atlantic and frontier policies simultaneously.

For the impact of mercantilism on the colonies, see Paul G. E. Clemens, *The Atlantic Economy and Colonial Maryland's Eastern Shore: From Tobacco to Grain* (1980); Curtis Nettels, "British Mercantilism and the Economic Development of the Thirteen Colonies," *Journal of Economic History, XII* (1952): 105–14; Marcus Rediker, *Between the Devil and the Deep Blue Sea: Merchant Seamen, Pirates, and the Anglo-American Maritime World, 1700–1750*

(1987); and James F. Shepherd and Gary M. Walton, *The Economic Rise of Early America* (1979). The maturing Atlantic system of commerce is covered perceptively in Richard Pares, *Yankees and Creoles: The Trade Between North America and the West Indies Before the American Revolution* (1956), and important comparative perspectives on colonies, staple crops, and slavery are presented in Richard B. Sheridan, *Sugar and Slavery: An Economic History of the West Indies* (1973).

Development of the North American colonies established after 1660 may be followed in Kenneth Coleman, *Colonial Georgia* (1976); Thomas Condon, *New York Beginnings* (1968); Mary Maples Dunn, *William Penn: Politics and Conscience* (1967); H. T. Merrens, *Colonial North Carolina* (1964); Oliver Rink, *Holland on the Hudson: An Economic and Social History of Dutch New York* (1986); and Robert M. Weir, *Colonial South Carolina* (1983).

The most useful starting point for events in North America during the Glorious Revolution is David S. Lovejoy, *The Glorious Revolution in America* (1972). The impact of the Glorious Revolution on the colonies is also covered admirably in Richard R. Johnson, *Adjustment to Empire: The New England Colonies, 1675–1715* (1981); D. W. Jordan, *Maryland's Revolution of Government, 1689–1692* (1974); and Jack M. Sosin, *English America and the Restoration Monarchy of Charles II* (1982).

Witchcraft is one of the most popular topics of colonial scholarship. For the English background, see Keith Thomas, *Religion and the Decline of Magic: Studies in Popular Beliefs in Sixteenth- and Seventeenth-Century England* (1973). For a multilayered approach, turn to John Demos, *Entertaining Satan: Witchcraft and the Culture of Early New England* (1982). For the view that witchcraft arose out of tensions created by rapidly growing New England communities, see Paul Boyer and Stephen Nissenbaum, *Salem Possessed* (1974); and for a fascinating account of the gender and inheritance aspects of witchcraft, see Carol F. Karlsen, *The Devil in the Shape of a Woman: Witchcraft in Colonial New England* (1987).

Provincial political development, as it departed from English traditions of legislative process and state power, is the subject of Bernard Bailyn, *The Origins of American Politics* (1986). For a focus on the ideological differences between England and America, see Robert M. Calhoon, *Dominion and Liberty: Ideology in the Anglo-American World, 1660–1801* (1994); Edmund Morgan, *Inventing the People: The Rise of Popular Sovereignty in England and America* (1988); Jack M. Sosin, *English America and the Revolution of 1688: Royal Administration and the Structure of Provincial Government* (1982); and Kammen, *Empire and Interest*, cited above. The more local, and particularly American, aspects of political development may be followed in Bruce Daniels, *Town and Country: Essays on the Structure of Local Government in the American Colonies* (1978); Jack P. Greene, *Peripheries and Center: Constitutional Development in the Extended Politics of the British Empire and the United Sates, 1607–1788* (1986); and Kenneth Lockridge, *Settlement and Unsettlement in Early America: Political Legitimacy Before the Revolution* (1981). Alan Tully, *Forming American Politics* (1994), shows the connections between inherited ideas and rising political institutions in Pennsylvania and New York.

Colonial wars are admirably covered in Howard Peckham, *The Colonial Wars, 1689–1762* (1964). For aspects of cultural development, whether related to European Enlightenment or distinctive American developments, see Jean-Christophe Agnew, *Worlds Apart: The Market and the Theater in Anglo-American Thought, 1550–1750* (1986); Richard D. Brown, *Knowledge Is Power: The Diffusion of Information in Early America, 1700–1865* (1989); Charles E. Clark, *The Public Print: The Newspaper in Anglo-American Culture, 1665–1740* (1994); Ronald W. Clark, *Benjamin Franklin* (1983); David Conroy, *In Public Houses: Drink and the Revolution of Authority in Colonial Massachusetts* (1995); Richard Beale Davis, *Intellectual Life in the Colonial South* (2 vols., 1978); Brooke Hindle, *The Pursuit of Science in Revolutionary America, 1735–1789* (1956); Kenneth Lockridge, *Literacy in Colonial New England* (1974); Irving Lowens, *Music and Musicians in Early America* (1964); Hugh Rankin, *The Theatre in Colonial America* (1965); and A. G. Roeber, *Faithful Magistrates and Republican Lawyers: Creators of the Virginia Legal Culture, 1680–1810* (1981).

Competing Voices

Colonial and Imperial Views of the Assemblies

Charter of Privileges, October 28, 1701

Contests developed in many colonies over the proper balance of power between assemblies and governors. In Pennsylvania, founder William Penn was committed to the principle of political participation by the governed, and the colony's charter reflected that principle. Then, in 1692, just ten years after the colony's founding, Parliament placed Pennsylvania under the royal governor of New York. As the crown-appointed rulers tried to restrict the assembly's privileges, assemblymen responded by enlarging their powers and reducing those of the governor's council of advisers. In 1701 the assembly, under Penn's leadership, printed a plan of government that reinstated basic civic freedoms and the assembly's authority.

I the said William Penn do declare, grant and confirm, unto all the Freemen, Planters and Adventurers, and other Inhabitants of this Province and Territories, these following Liberties, Franchises and Privileges. . . .

First

Because no People can be truly happy, though under the greatest Enjoyment of Civil Liberties, if abridged of the freedom of their Consciences, as to their Religious Profession and Worship . . . I do hereby grant and declare, That no Person or Persons, inhabiting in this province or Territories, who shall confess and acknowledge *One* almighty God . . . shall be in any Case molested or prejudiced . . . nor be compelled to frequent or maintain any religious Worship, Place or Ministry, contrary to his or their Mind. . . .

And that all Persons who also profess to believe in *Jesus Christ,* the Saviour of the World, shall be capable . . . to serve this Government in any Capacity, both legislatively and executively. . . .

For the well government of this Province and Territories, there shall be an Assembly yearly chosen, by the Freemen thereof, to consist of Four Persons out of each County, of most Note for Virtue, Wisdom and Ability . . . Which Assembly shall have Power to chuse a Speaker and other their Officers; and shall be Judges of the Qualifications and Elections of their own Members; sit upon their own Adjournments; appoint Committees; prepare Bills in order to pass into Laws; impeach [indict] Criminals, and redress Grievances; and shall have all other Powers and Privileges of an Assembly, according to the Rights of the free-born Subjects of *England* and as is usual in any of the King's Plantations in *America.* . . .

That the Freemen in each respective County . . . may . . . chuse . . . sheriffs and Corners . . . And that the Justices of the respective Counties shall or may nominate and present to the Governor *Three* Persons, to serve for Clerk of the Peace for the said County. . . .

That the Laws of this Government shall be in the Stile, viz. *By the Governor, with the Consent and Approbation of the Freemen in General Assembly met.*

William Shirley to George Clinton, August 13, 1748

New York was a more tightly controlled royal colony than Pennsylvania. For nearly a century after the English conquest in 1664, its ruling families were tied closely to English affairs, and New York's governors maintained a powerful hold over lawmaking, the dispensation of justice, and revenue collection and spending. But by the 1740s, assemblymen had accumulated one small power after another. By the time Governor George Clinton took office, clearly defined political interests existed in the assembly and those interests often were at odds with the crown's instructions to Clinton. Clinton looked to William Shirley for guidance on how to stem the New York assembly's "usurpations" of power. Shirley had spent many years as a judge of the admiralty courts, governor of Massachusetts, commander of Anglo-American forces in imperial wars, and then governor of the Bahamas. His assessment of the situation and advice to Clinton show that he was deeply loyal to the crown and determined to enforce its authority in North America.

Sir, . . . I have informed myself of the state of His Majesty's government within this Colony [of New York] and find that several late innovations have been introduced by the Assembly into it, and incroachments made upon His Majesty's prerogative greatly tending to weaken his government. . . .

It appears by the Acts of Assembly that . . . for about twenty eight years past, . . . the [financial] support of His Majesty's Government were made for the term of five years, and no application of any part of the money . . . was made in these Acts; but there was only one general appropriation in them, vizt. *For the support of His Majesty's government* . . . all monies levied by Acts of Assembly were during that time drawn out of the Treasury by warrant from the Governor and Council.

And I find that during that time all publick warlike stores for the defence of the Colony were lodged in the King's Magazine with the Store Keeper and issued by order of the Governour in whose sole disposal they were.

And it does not appear that within this time the Assembly assumed to themselves the appointment of such officers, as it appertain'd to the Governour to appoint. . . .

BUT I find that in the year 1743 . . . the Assembly instead of making the . . . support of His Majesty's Government for the term of five years, pass'd an Act . . . [that stipulated] the granting salaries for the support of the governours and other officers from year to year only . . . tending to create an intire dependency of the Governour and other Officers upon the Assembly, and to weaken His Majesty's Government in this Colony . . . and in cast the Governour or any of those officers dye . . . there is no provision for the support [of government.]

It appears by the Minutes of the Assembly's proceedings that the Acts thus made for your Excellency's annual support are pass'd the last of the Sessions, and . . . that unless you pass the others which are lay'd before [by the Assembly] for your Consent, the Act [to pay your annual salary] will not be passed.

It appears likewise that since the year 1743 considerable advances have been made by the Assembly towards usurping the nomination of Officers which it appertains to the Governour to appoint, and the power of turning such as are actually appointed by him, our of their posts. . . .

The Assembly have likewise taken the custody and disposal of the gunpowder provided for the use of the King's garrison and defence of the Colony, out of your Excellency's hands into their own. . . .

And I find likewise they have taken from your Excellency the passing of the Muster Rolls of all the troops raised for the defence of the Colony . . . and issuing the pay for them and their officers. . . . I find also that since 1743, they have assumed the power of erecting, by Acts of Assembly, fortifications. . . .

The Assembly seems to have left scarcely any part of His Majesty's prerogative untouched, and they have gone great lengths towards getting the government, military as well as civil, into their hands. . . . I think no time should be lost for letting the Assembly know you expect that for the future they should provide for the support of His Majesty's government in the same manner which former Assemblies used to do it.

Neither Clinton nor his successors were able to reverse the New York assembly's gains during the coming years. Elsewhere in North America, other colonial assemblies were also expanding their authority over the daily lives of colonists and sometimes openly defying the crown's principle that colonies were always subordinate to the interests of the imperial center. But after the Glorious Revolution, colonial assemblies grew more vigilant about their "liberties," refining their definitions of them in the context of conflicts with imperial authorities. Although colonists often referred to these liberties as the freedoms of all "true born Englishmen," they were usually clear that this was not the same thing as "the English system of rule," in which liberty was reliant on deference, patronage, and elite privilege.

Questions for Analysis

1. What privileges does the Pennsylvania charter spell out? Why are they so important to colonists, and so likely to cause alarm in English government?
2. What are Shirley's main objections regarding the "incroachments" of colonial assemblies on royal power? Why does he believe these privileges are dangerous in the hands of colonial assemblymen?
3. What were the implications of colonial claims to greater self-government?
4. How might growing assembly powers in many colonies have contributed to the growing sense of a separate identity?

4

Colonial Maturation and Conflict, 1680–1754

As William Morison traveled north from Maryland in 1744, he gave some people the impression of being "a very rough spun, forward, clownish blade, much addicted to swearing." During his stay at "Curtis's [inn] at the sign of the Indian King" in New Castle, Delaware, Morison grew "much affronted with the landlady . . . who, seeing him in a greasy jacket and breeches and a dirty worsted cap . . . took him for some ploughman or carman and so presented him with some scraps of cold veal for breakfast." Agitated, Morison cried, " . . . if it wa'n't out of respect to the gentleman [sitting with me]," he would throw the food "out the window and break her table all to pieces should it cost him 100 pounds for dammages."

The gentleman who traveled northward with Morison that spring—and the recorder of these events—was the well-respected Maryland physician Alexander Hamilton. Hamilton was careful to write in his journal that Morison was not the ruffian he seemed to be, but a fun-loving man of the "middling sort." Morison did not have inherited status in the gentry or an important crown appointment. Next to Hamilton, debonair in green velvet coat and lace-trimmed shirt, Morison "seemed to be but a plain, homely fellow." "Yet," continued Hamilton, "he would have us know that he was able to afford better than many that went finer." At the conclusion of his outburst against the landlady, Morison took "off his worsted night cap, [and] pulled a linnen one out of his pocket and clapped it upon his head," declaring, "Now, . . . I'm upon the borders of Pensylvania and must look like a gentleman." As the men rode away, Morison also insisted that "he had good linnen in his bags, a pair of silver buckles, silver clasps, and gold sleeve buttons, two Holland shirts, and some neat night caps; and that his little woman at home drank tea twice a day."

These material possessions certainly did not put Morison close to the wealth of true gentlemen who displayed far more refined clothing, manners, and speech. But neither was he poor. Just days before meeting Morison, Hamilton had dined with the family of a Susquehanna ferryman, who ate their meal from "a dirty, deep, wooden dish which they evacuated with their hands, cramming down skins, scales, and all. They used neither knife, fork, spoon, plate, or napkin because, I suppose, they had none to use."

Morison was one of thousands of colonists who enjoyed modest prosperity from work on their landholdings and at small trades that produced household and personal goods. Life for most colonists by midcentury was better than it could have been in England or Europe. In addition, Morison, and so many others of this "middling" station who sought material comfort and public recognition, did not overtly challenge the authority of their "betters," at least not often. In their optimism, the "middling sort" praised the openness of colonial society, the many different geographical regions, cultural origins, high wages, and job opportunities for people willing to work. Indeed, by the 1750s free white inhabitants of the North American colonies enjoyed the fastest-rising living standards in the world.

Some colonists, however, were shocked at the rapid rise of this new wealth among their neighbors, and especially that it had begun to replace inheritance of property and family name in creating status. Left unchecked, they believed, the trend would cause the decline of colonial elites in the near future, while others predicted threats to imperial rule itself. Still other colonists pitted the relative security of middling colonists to the growing number of poor. In every region, the gap was widening between those who became successful or even privileged, and those who, despite struggle, experienced downturns, bad luck, devastating illness, and daily hunger. In Northern cities the extremes of rich and poor became distressingly evident by the 1720s. The frontier remained a questionable terrain for making a fortune. In the Chesapeake region, the stratified social organization was becoming more hierarchical, more uneven. And the South was witnessing the apparent paradox of opening up political institutions to more white citizens *and* tightening the reins of slavery. Some of these disparities foreshadowed the midcentury conflicts within the colonies that accompanied their maturation.

- What kinds of social and cultural distinctions developed among colonists during the 1700s?
- What groups of immigrants continued to stream into the colonies, why did they come, and where did they settle?
- How did the political and cultural maturation of rural settlements differ from those of cities and villages on the coast?
- What kinds of tensions marked the colonies during the 1700s, and why did some of them erupt into significant conflicts?

This chapter will address these questions.

Chronology

1689–1697	King William's War
1702–1713	Queen Anne's War
1705	Rice no longer enumerated
1711–1713	Tuscarora War in the Carolinas
1712	Slave uprising in New York City
1720s	Scots-Irish immigration increases
	Germans settle mid-Atlantic colonies
1730s	Virginia tobacco inspection laws
1732	Georgia colony chartered
1739	Stono Rebellion
1739	Great Awakening begins
1741	Second slave uprising in New York City
1740–1748	King George's War
1747	Ohio Company of land speculators formed
1754	Disputes with French and Indians in Ohio country grow

Growth and Diversity in the Colonies

Sooner or later, every colony overcame the initial scarcities of supplies, difficulties of defense, and losses due to illness and demoralization during the "starving times." Stable, then growing population developed in New England first, then the mid-Atlantic, and finally the South by the early 1700s. In each region, people in the white population began to marry younger and live longer. Then, the trickle of immigrants to North America in the later 1600s became a flood in the last colonial decades. Indeed, more people came per year from the Old World to the New in the last portion of the colonial era than in any other time of settlement. Some of these newcomers stayed near coastal settlements where they benefited from existing social networks, resources, and institutions. But most of them headed to the frontier.

New Immigrants

In 1700 about 250,000 people of European and African descent lived in the North American colonies. In the next generation that number more than doubled, and by the eve of the American Revolution, 2.5 million people resided in the thirteen colonies. Immigration accounted for a significant proportion of this rising population. Over 4,500 people arrived each year from 1700 to 1760; in the next fifteen years an amazing average of about 15,000 individuals arrived per year. Between

1700 and 1770, nearly 275,000 African slaves were brought into North America, and about 50,000 English convicts came, primarily to Maryland and Virginia, bound to many years' labor. In that same time, about 210,000 free whites came into the mainland colonies, including many more women and children than had come on the transatlantic ships during the founding decades of settlement. Whether white or black, colonists were surrounded by the very young and the aging. In 1775 half of the colonial population were under sixteen years old, and many children had the novel experience of getting to know their grandparents.

This unprecedented growth introduced cultural changes that colonists only began to grasp before the mid-1700s. White women in most settlements could marry early in their twenties and hope to raise a number of children to adulthood; a majority of them bore five to ten children. Most families in the north, and wealthy families in the south, lived in environments of greater abundance than in Europe, and they enjoyed a comparatively better diet than Europeans. This healthier and longer-lived population, said some observers, would make colonists ever-more powerful members of the empire. Benjamin Franklin noted in a 1751 pamphlet that England's overall population of nearly 7 million was greater than white North America's for the time being, but colonists were doubling their numbers every twenty-five years, a rate of growth much faster than England's. Soon, warned Franklin, the colonial population would overtake England's in size and tip the balance of cultural and political power toward the colonies.

Immigration also rose to new heights during the mid-1700s. Conditions of travel across the ocean remained difficult—over 15 percent of migrants died on the middle passage from Europe or shortly after their arrival—and even in the final colonial years, when would-be servants flocked into North America, traders bought and sold human labor "as they do their horses." Still, ships bringing scores of white indentured servants seeking land and employment came to the northern ports of Boston, New York, and Philadelphia more frequently than to the Chesapeake—where slavery increasingly replaced white labor.

Great numbers of people surged onto the far frontiers by the 1740s, searching for fertile land in the Appalachian foothills and along the river ways of the interior (see map). Unprecedented numbers of non-English people came in these late colonial years. One group, the Scots-Irish, descendants of Presbyterian Scots whom the British government had forced to settle in northern Ireland during the 1600s, flocked through Philadelphia to seek farm land and greater religious freedom. At least 100,000 and maybe 150,000 came before 1760, and another 55,000 came in the last fifteen colonial years. When they found that land was not simply there for the taking, hundreds of Scots-Irish became squatters on Native American lands on the western frontiers of Pennsylvania, Maryland, Virginia, and North Carolina. The Tuscarora and Yamasee had been weakened by disease, and during the 1730s the Cherokee and Catawba suffered from smallpox on the Carolina piedmont. While these reduced populations struggled to rebuild their strength or moved temporarily to new hunting locations, immigrating Europeans assumed the land was vacant. By the late 1730s, Scots-Irish had filled the Shenandoah Valley of Virginia; in the 1740s they headed over the piedmont plateau into North Carolina; by the end of the colonial period, they were streaming into the frontiers of South Carolina, where they raised grain, livestock, and tobacco without slaves.

Other groups of immigrants also arrived during the 1700s. About 80,000 Irish poured into the Delaware Valley over the century. A smaller number of Scots—probably about 40,000—came toward the end of the colonial period. Most of them were Jacobites, supporters of the Catholic Stuart monarchs, forced to migrate after the failure of rebellions in 1715 and 1745. In 1746 the defeated Jacobites were loaded onto departing vessels and put down in North Carolina, where a hard-scrabble life awaited them.

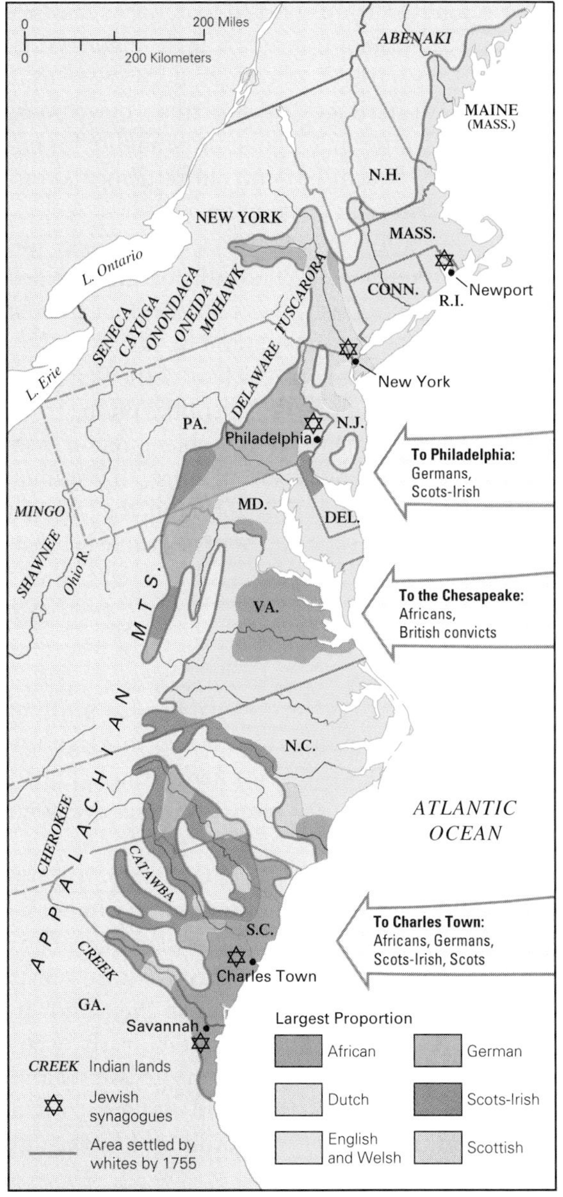

Immigration and Migration in the 1700s After 1720 both slave importation and European immigration increased dramatically in many colonies. At the same time, colonists were expanding onto western frontier lands 200 miles beyond the first ribbon of colonial settlement. Thousands of newcomers were German, Scots-Irish, and Scottish in the last colonial decades.

Over 90,000 Germans also arrived after 1720, most of them from the severely depressed Rhineland. Most, too, endured a grueling voyage of about fifteen weeks fraught with filth, hunger, disease, and harsh treatment by the crew. Germans who came to the mid-Atlantic region often became redemptioners, voluntary servants who stayed together as families and bound themselves to masters for a set period of time. Unlike indentured servants, redemptioners found their own masters. Following the pathways of earlier frontier migrants, these *Deutsche* (later, Pennsylvania Dutch) settled rich soil just beyond the fringe of settlement, twenty to one hundred miles west of the Delaware River. Later, they fanned out toward the foothills of the Appalachian Mountains in the Cumberland and Shenandoah Valleys. Lutherans, Moravians, Mennonites, and smaller religious groups tended to come as families and began with grave earnestness the difficult task of transforming the countryside. To the south, a sizeable group of Salzburgers settled in the new colony of Georgia (see page 144). To some colonists of British heritage, these German newcomers sometimes added a startling dimension to frontier life. Benjamin Franklin, for example, complained that German "aliens" had "swarm[ed] into our settlements" until they outnumbered colonists of English heritage in certain regions.

Small numbers of Huguenots fled persecution in France to Charles Town and New York City during the 1700s, where their French cultural identity became melded with the polyglot populations around them. In contrast, Jewish families that entered northern cities made distinctive contributions to commerce and handicrafts. Germans and Scots, far more numerous than either Huguenots or Jews, settled far from the "melting influences" of cities, preserving their culture and identities on the frontier. In the mid-Atlantic region, German immigrants were often able to retain their language and tradition by rejecting marriage to the English around them. In Virginia, where white planters and small farmers shared a fear of slave rebellion, the colony's elite cherished its Anglican background and English cultural heritage, while Scottish frontiersmen maintained their Presbyterian faith and distinctive cultural ways.

Families and Servants

The burgeoning birth rate had even more impact on the colonial headcount than rising immigration. Growth from natural increase accounted for two-thirds of the new population born after 1700 in North America. While women in England had about five live births and fifteen grandchildren, white colonial women averaged eight births and forty-two grandchildren.

Such phenomenal growth, which fundamentally altered traditional family ways, had two general causes. One was the healthier environment for parents and children. More plentiful foods, fewer seasons of scarcities, and less crowded living conditions permitted local populations to fight off diseases more effectively. Colonists were also marrying earlier. In England women typically married in their mid- to late-twenties; in the colonies many married and began families in their early twenties. Since pregnancy and childbirth happened regularly between age twenty and forty-five for many women, and was a dangerous ordeal, wives and mothers created elaborate networks of support in local communities, often coordinated by the talents and ceaseless energies of town midwives.

In European society the family had long been seen as "a little commonwealth," with clear roles prescribed for fathers, mothers, and children. Colonial families of European origin inherited this model and applied it to their settlements. The male head of the household represented the family in public affairs, voting in local elections and serving as an elder of the church. He also wielded nearly unqualified authority over his wife, children, servants, occasional laborers, and slaves.

On farms, men built homesteads, barns, and other outbuildings, planted and cultivated the fields, mended fences, and herded and butchered livestock. Harvests were especially difficult episodes for families short of children and servants. Daily toil was relieved briefly with trips to markets with surpluses of farm goods or to stores to buy sugar, tea, sewing notions, or nails. A visit to the miller brought with it welcome conversation and a drink with friends. Over 90 percent of colonial families organized their lives around farming, but men also regularly shared skills such as carpentry, blacksmithing, milling, and butchering with neighbors. Some of these activities afforded men more contact with people outside the family and immediate neighborhood than women had.

Throughout the colonies, white children were the subordinates of their fathers, who assigned their household tasks, meted out discipline, and decided whether they should be sent to a neighbor or town craftsman as a servant or apprentice. Parents frequently expected unquestioning obedience from their children, and because children's contributions were essential to the household economy, only elite parents—who had servants or slaves to perform the menial tasks typically assigned to children—could afford to indulge their sons and daughters.

Almost all colonists of European origin agreed that women were naturally subordinate to men. In the earliest New England settlements, the Puritan minister John Winthrop had declared that a woman's husband "is her lord, and she is subjected to him, yet in a way of liberty, not of bondage; and a true wife accounts her subjection her honor and freedom." Modesty, chastity, deference, and quiet diligence in household tasks were among the qualities expected in women. Most spent their lives under the firm rule of fathers, husbands, and perhaps male relatives. In many colonies, laws permitted husbands to "correct" their wives' behavior with verbal chastisement and physical punishment.

Most women accepted the limitations and demands of marriage, although slowly over the 1700s women gained modest privileges, such as the ability to help choose their husbands. Few widows stayed unmarried for long, for their homemaking skills and their children's labor were highly prized. Of course, not all marriages proved to be good ones. In New England it was possible, if difficult, to end a poor union; outside of New England, laws permitted only men to initiate divorce proceedings.

According to English law, widows and unmarried women could own property, run businesses, and be heard in court. But once married, a woman became subject to her husband under the law of *coverture* and could no longer make contracts to start a business, for example, or sail a ship, hire a servant, sell a farm, or write a will. Her property became that of her husband upon marriage, and her husband was entitled to all her wages. Only in the case of her husband's prolonged absence or sudden death could a woman act in her husband's name to handle business obligations.

Daily Life in the Colonies
Almost every young woman spent hours every week spinning wool or cotton yarn that went into making bed linens, garments, and fabrics used for sifting flour or making sails. Not every household had a spinning wheel, but one was always nearby at a neighbor's or relative's house. Once spun, yarn was woven into fabric by men in some areas, by women in others. *(American Textile History Museum.)*

Indentured servant women often were treated worse than women of middling families. Well into the 1700s, young female servants wrote to English relatives about "toiling almost day and night" with "scarce any thing but Indian corn and salt [pork] to eat" or little clothing against cold weather. Many were forbidden to marry during their contracts because masters feared they would run away or neglect their duties. Servants who became pregnant risked having their services lengthened if masters believed they took too much time off to have and nurture infants. At the end of her service, perhaps in poor health and well advanced into her child-bearing years, a female servant often had difficulty finding a man willing to marry her.

However, both servants and married free women could gain some recognition of their worth through their work. The relentless rhythms of gardening and laundering, procuring and processing foods, cooking and baking, consumed many hours each day. Intermittently, smoking meat, dairying, pressing cider, tending chickens, and transforming wool and flax into usable clothing occupied another large portion of time. Homemakers counted themselves fortunate when their daughters were old enough to help with chores or tend smaller children. Most farm wives also could break away—although only temporarily—from their prescribed domestic roles when they helped in the fields during planting and harvesting times, or when they made trips to local shops to exchange small surpluses or acquire imported goods. As a woman aged, she instructed younger people, gained expertise in managing complex household enterprises, and exercised significant moral influence on community decisions. And among women, the birthing of a child provided a forum not only for helping a neighbor but for sharing news and arranging community events that brought additional recognition to the vital roles women played in the colonial experience everywhere.

 Varieties of Life in the North

As the seventeenth century ended, many northern colonists hoped that the tribulations of the Glorious Revolution, witchcraft trials, frontier and international wars, and settling the wilderness would be put behind them. Well-ordered townships and families, many colonists agreed, should continue to provide a foundation for social order and future prosperity. A stratified society in which colonists understood their obligations to rulers, wives and children deferred to the will of their husbands and fathers, and servants and slaves labored obediently for their masters, continued to dominate thinking about proper social organization. However, these beliefs continued to be challenged in many ways after 1700.

The Atlantic Economy

The overwhelming majority of colonists farmed or engaged in activities related to farming. Still, many of them would have agreed with one New York farmer who regularly shipped flour to urban residents: "Commerce is the sinews that link us to each other, and all of us to the greater world of empires." The risks of trading goods in long-distance markets continued to perplex merchants everywhere in the 1700s, but most colonists welcomed the new imported goods that increased their daily comfort. English merchants continued to satisfy much of the colonial demand for clothing, agricultural implements, earthenware goods for households, medicines and seeds, glassware and paper products, and other "dry goods." In fact, colonists collectively were debtors to English firms for most of the 1700s. By the late colonial years, debts for imported goods from England had risen, said some American merchants, to "alarming heights."

But colonists continued to import more and more desired goods, such as manufactured tools and dish wares, and by the 1720s English goods were reaching even the remotest corners of the colonies. On the other side of the Atlantic Ocean, however, English firms did not increase their demand for northern colonial products. So, in order to pay what they owed English merchants and manufacturers, colonial businessmen aggressively sought other markets that might have goods to carry into England and Europe, or that would pay gold, silver, or bills of exchange for colonial products. By the late 1600s, merchants at southern European islands (the Canaries, Madeira, the Azores), plus those at Caribbean ports of call, received the salted fish, barrel staves, shingles, cheese, and work horses that New Englanders traded for slaves, molasses, dried fruit, and other tropical commodities colonists craved, or for cash that could be sent to English creditors. Most northern merchants agreed that without the West Indies markets, they "might have collapsed under the dual weight of debt to the mother country and too many goods from our own producers" which England would not buy. The West Indies markets, both English and foreign, became the nerve center of northern merchants' trade by the 1720s. Merchants in New England and the mid-Atlantic regions also increasingly carried southern tobacco, indigo, and rice directly to English markets. In fact, this coastal trade, which consisted of a series of linkages among colonial ports, grew by leaps and bounds during the 1700s—to nearly half of northern colonial cities' trade by 1750.

International trade involved more than the exchange of goods among far-flung nations. It also brought colonists into contact with one another across long distances and forged new kinds of social relations among them. Coastal cities and market towns became focal points for the exchange of goods and information among all layers of colonists. Craftsmen and manufacturers distributed goods such as shoes and straw hats through middlemen, while retailers collected many small supplies of cheese, feathers, beeswax, flaxseed, and other goods from rural households for later transport to urban exporters. In the larger towns, distillers turned West Indian molasses into rum and then marketed it throughout the north and via the African slave trade. Boston, New York, and Philadelphia merchants invested in enterprises to produce glassware and simple iron house wares, refine sugar and make chocolate, or process tobacco into snuff and timber waste into potash (used to make soap and glass). Ironworks dotted the countryside not far from New York and Philadelphia, and by the end of the colonial period, merchant-manufacturers operated some 80 furnaces and 175 forges near mines, timber, and employable townspeople, which in turn supplied colonists with kettles, implements, and gun parts.

International commerce also drew merchants, middlemen, sailors, workers, and clerks into new kinds of employment. Fishing and lumbering became more complicated enterprises that served worldwide demand. Young men whose family land had become unproductive turned to whaling. Shipbuilding and shipping services flourished in Boston; Newport, Rhode Island; and New Haven, Connecticut. Colonists there benefited from collecting fees from carrying goods, as well as sales of ships to merchants in distant ports, thereby helping to offset the ever-present debts to English merchants. By the 1730s, northern colonists built most of the vessels that carried goods into the West Indies and developed intricate webs of exchange with ports along the Atlantic and in the Caribbean. New England ships dominated this American traffic, though New York City and Philadelphia merchants aggressively competed in shipbuilding. Their city docks teemed with several hundred oceangoing vessels, many of them now produced and owned by colonists.

Ancient lore told of pirates roaming the Mediterranean Sea and Indian Ocean, looting and burning merchant ships. The Spanish discovery of great wealth in Mexico and Peru had attracted hundreds of pirates to the Western Hemisphere, and by the end of the seventeenth century they felt comfortable docking at Port Royal, New York City, and numerous Caribbean islands. During the 1690s, New York City became an especially hospitable New World rest stop for pirates fresh from harassing the sea lanes out of West African and Red Sea ports. Governors welcomed the money and loot enriching some city stores and homes. Only in 1699 did the new Whig governor, the earl of Bellomont, move to end the colony's piracy by arresting the notorious ringleader, Captain William Kidd, and sending him to England for a highly publicized trial. After Kidd was hanged in spring, 1701, Parliament issued a series of new laws to enable colonial governors and admiralty courts to round up pirates.

After this, piracy in North America declined. In its place, smuggling gained larger appeal at every colonial port. Despite certain protections and incentives that the Acts of Trade guaranteed, the acts for the most part irritated colonists, particularly when they forced goods into certain markets or required payment of port duties. By 1700, mercantilist policymakers in England knew very well that colonists systematically ignored the Acts of Trade provisions that limited their commercial opportunities. Merchants became outspoken critics of laws that channeled staples such as sugar and tobacco to England, foreclosing the possibility of seeking better markets elsewhere on their own. And numerous northern merchants simply resorted to lawbreaking: regularly entering ports "under cover of night," bribing port officials, and trading with the enemy during the many wars of the colonial era.

Cities and Market Towns

Coastal cities and towns were the vital connections between rural settlements and transatlantic peoples. As much as 25 percent of a city's jobs were in trades affiliated with commerce, including rope and sail making, shipbuilding, carting, insurance services, and warehousing. Colonial cities were also the primary centers of politics, culture, and material growth. Royal officials and key colonial authorities resided in cities and port towns. Changing fashions and cultural innovations filtered through cities from distant places.

These civic and cultural nerve centers were relatively small. Boston had peaked at about 16,500 inhabitants in the mid-1700s and was slowly declining. New York City rose to about 22,000 near the time of the Revolution; Philadelphia reached nearly 30,000 by then. Charles Town and Newport boasted about 10,000 souls each by 1750. Numbers such as these fell far short of the populations of London, Paris, or Amsterdam, but for the typical colonist the quality of life in colonial cities and towns was decidedly different from life in the countryside. People of many cultural backgrounds mingled in crowded public spaces during market or election days. City residents built homes close together, many at dockside where the coming and going of ships attracted finely dressed merchants, sailors from distant places, immigrants, and British port officials. Although city residents still depended on country producers for many foods, they enjoyed a wider range of available crafts and services than farm families did.

Although only 5 percent of colonists lived in cities during the 1700s, they shared an undisputed importance in linking all colonists to the outside world. The European Enlightenment had its most direct influence on urban people (see page 112). And the "traffick and mercantile business" of myriad shops and marketplaces in Philadelphia, Boston, and New York City supplied people with goods from unheard-of places. Boston was "furnished with many fair shops; their materials are brick, stone, lime, handsomely contrived . . . and a townhouse built upon pillars where the merchants may confer. . . . Their streets are many and large, paved with pebble stone, and the south-side adorned with gardens and orchards. The town is very rich and populous." In 1725 a writer complained in the *Boston News-Letter* that personal prosperity had reached such proportions that he "could hardly hear the minister's first prayer for the rustling of silk gowns and petticoats."

At the apex of the urban social structure were a small number of families, most of whom owed their status to royal appointments and commerce. Merchants who enjoyed the advantages of a family inheritance or a shrewd marriage could expect to sustain commercial success during their adult lives, and to do far better than middling colonists. In Philadelphia, well over half the trade of the city was controlled by about a hundred families, the very richest of whom were Quakers. In Boston and New York City, the wealthiest inhabitants owned ships that sailed beyond the West Indies and Europe to the Red Sea, West Africa, and Honduras.

In their public and private lives, the elite emulated the English gentry. Great brick mansions, with columned porticoes, lofty balconies, and rooftop gardens, were the pride of New York City's well-to-do. A number of rising citizens also boasted townhouses that colonists rarely saw in the northern countryside. Brightly colored wallpaper adorned the Walton, Beekman, Cruger, and Roosevelt homes in New York, and female gentility was hardly complete without expensive silver and china to host teas. Festive turtle barbecues drew important families together every spring. Coaches, great parlor clocks, and writing tables became signs of economic success, although most elite homes were still sparsely adorned compared with English gentry estates.

Daring commercial families who wished to expand their influence beyond shipping invested in real estate, rented properties to tenants, provided insurance and banking services to neighbors, and started small manufacturing enterprises. Their agents operated transportation into the interior to buy up farmers' surpluses for export. The "better sort" also filled top public offices and shared command of colonial troops with royal officers.

In all, though, elite families in the colonies were few. Urban communities contained a much larger number of middling families—many of them rising artisans and shopkeepers, or enterprising merchants. Artisans produced glassware, stoneware, paper, nails, guns, locks, cabinets and chests, and numerous other household and farm goods. Along with retailers and waged workers, they built shops, made goods in them, and tended to their sales and distribution throughout the city. They baked bread, butchered meat, constructed cabinets, built churches, tailored clothing, and hauled all manner of goods to and from the surrounding countryside. Even small crossroads towns such as Baltimore grew in the mid-1700s because its merchants and artisans exported great quantities of wheat and flour to the West Indies, which in turn gave employment to many coopers, blacksmiths, carters, and sailors.

Some of the "middling sort" prospered more than others. Men who had weathered the difficulties of establishing a business or setting up a successful shop after completing an apprenticeship could expect to acquire a few amenities—chairs might replace crude benches, knives and forks complement the spoons of earlier generations, wooden storage chests provide for clothing, extra tools aid householders, firkins hold cheese and pickles. Middling colonists who prevailed against debt and disease could expect to have windowpanes and bedspreads by the 1750s, and perhaps extra clothing for special occasions.

Still, even city producers who owned their houses, tools, and personal items were far less affluent than the great merchants. A hard-working artisan might become prosperous enough to pay his debts and expand his shop's business by hiring apprentices and occasional laborers. But most artisans were content to pass on the

Urban Craftsmen Coopers were one of the most common and necessary kinds of craftsmen in colonial America. They supplied merchants, storekeepers, and householders with all manner of containers for storage and shipment. This view of a cooper's shop shows the simple tools and unharried, close working conditions that these skilled men experienced. *(Courtesy, American Antiquarian Society.)*

"secrets of the trade" to their children and to earn a "competency," or a modest income that provided a few comforts for their families.

At the bottom of northern colonial society were domestic servants, day laborers, recent immigrants, cartmen, unemployed veterans, orphans, and sailors. The many unskilled laborers and recent immigrants who gravitated to the cities were likely to experience extended periods of poverty. Male laborers rarely secured enough weeks of work per year, or enough pay, to support a growing family. Wives and children often supplemented the family income as domestic servants, wood haulers, hemp combers, or washerwomen. Freed slaves and indentured servants filled about half of the laborers' jobs of Philadelphia during the later 1700s.

When wars or recessions disrupted international commerce, people near the bottom of the social ladder became even more vulnerable to hunger and poor health. Although this "lower sort" were less numerous than the middling, colonial cities did not always have sufficient essential resources, or have them at affordable prices, for their poor. Hundreds of people in the major coastal cities lived in crowded rented houses where they subsisted on a bare minimum of food and fuel.

Rarely could a family accumulate enough food and fuel to tide them over during the inevitable illnesses, accidents, confinements after childbirth, or fluctuating employment conditions.

Sometimes poverty struck a family or an individual for a short period of time, as when illness prevented a young man from working, or infirmities of old age forced a person to rely on the kindnesses of family and neighbors. Sometimes, too, a family overcame the temporary setbacks of migrating or going bankrupt and went on to live in greater security as the years passed. But more and more often, northern cities could not adequately provide for their homeless, unemployed, widowed, and orphaned. Rural women who had lost their husbands and had little prospect of remarrying in the countryside came to the cities in ever larger numbers after 1720, where some hoped to open a shop or help run a boarding house. Many of them resorted to domestic servitude or prostitution.

The primary means by which a city could act charitably toward the poor was by raising taxes. But the wealthy strenuously resisted this remedy, and payments to the needy remained woefully small. Poorhouses, workhouses, and orphans' asylums provided a little temporary help, but they were chronically overcrowded. As conditions worsened during King George's War (1740–1748), Bostonian rioters attacked several institutions and demanded that authorities remove the homeless, prostitutes, and infirm from the city altogether.

The Boston riots stemmed from deep concerns of many colonists about the growing number of destitute or helpless residents in the cities. Some feared that poverty would bring increased crime against property or higher taxes for prosecuting and punishing criminals. By the early 1700s, many families and small communities in the North were less willing, and often less able, to provide jobs and shelter individually for the poor. Instead, they began to argue that government officials—who were usually middling and wealthy colonists—ought to shoulder the responsibility.

These discussions about poverty were related to changing cultural attitudes about wealth. Many of the "better sort" and middling colonists were beginning to shed their anxieties about seeking profits and to praise rather than scorn those who prospered. Looking out for oneself began to replace the older rule of cooperating for the community's welfare and setting fair prices and wages. In previous times most colonists had expected merchants to provide for local needs first, before exporting foods. During the 1700s, merchants argued that selling goods abroad, where rapidly rising prices might bring great profits, would increase the wealth of the colonies overall.

Traditional beliefs about the community's welfare lingered on in colonial life, and sometimes erupted in anger when consumers and small producers thought principles of market fairness had been violated. Impoverished colonists with hungry families occasionally protested the departure of a ship full of colonial grain. And from time to time, poor and middling inhabitants of many towns and cities fiercely opposed higher prices for food and necessities. Often their efforts resulted in temporary local legislation to fix certain prices, but no overall remedies materialized.

Periodic wars left deep scars on colonial cities. By the end of Queen Anne's War in 1713, widows, orphans, and disabled veterans were an inescapable presence in all northern cities. After a generation of peace, King George's War gave a few merchants opportunities to make immense profits from contracts to supply troops and privateer against enemies, but average citizens felt the sting of soaring taxes and shortages of necessary goods. The expedition against Louisbourg in 1744 left unprecedented numbers of Boston widows and orphans reliant on public relief, while the end of the war in 1748 brought high unemployment in shipbuilding and provisioning trades. Almost 20 percent of the Boston population was deemed too poor to pay taxes, and the workhouse and almshouse overflowed. In New York, over six hundred widows and orphans depended on the city government for subsistence and the bottom half of taxable citizens owned only about 4 percent of urban wealth.

Since the North's temperate climate did not support sugar and rice agriculture, slavery was never as significant there as it was in the South. Still, slaves were present in every northern port. By the 1740s, Philadelphia's population was about 9 percent slave; New York City's, about 18 percent. New Jersey and Pennsylvania together had about 14,000 slaves by the end of the colonial period, Delaware about 2,000, and New England about 15,000. New Yorkers owned 19,000 slaves by the late colonial period, some 3,000 of whom worked in the homes, stables, and busy docks of New York City's elite. Newport, Rhode Island, merchants had the dubious distinction of being more involved in the slave trade than any other northern port, as they supplied interior settlements with much-needed labor. Northern slaves were widely dispersed, no more than a few in any given household or farm. Many served as liverymen who worked with horses or as boatmen who ferried goods between country estates and the city.

Urban slaves had more opportunities to learn skills and hire themselves out for wages than rural slaves. But racial tensions also flared more intensely in cities than on farms. In 1712 twenty-three slaves in New York City took an oath of secrecy and vowed to avenge the poor treatment they endured from their masters. Armed with hatchets, homemade knives, and pikes, they set fire to a barn and killed at least nine white colonists. During the subsequent investigation, dozens of slaves were questioned, some tortured, and twenty-one executed; some committed suicide when they learned they would be hanged for treason, and some were burned at the stake. In 1741 a more elaborate "conspiracy," probably involving dozens of slaves, free African-Americans, and white servants, came to light. An informer divulged to authorities that plans were underway to raze the city, set free its three thousand slaves, and flee to the countryside. A series of suspicious fires erupted around the waterfront, damaging merchants' warehouses, and the spreading blaze destroyed part of Fort George at the entrance to Manhattan. In the following months, testimony in the courts dragged on. A sixteen-year-old Irish servant woman was offered her freedom in exchange for fingering some free blacks and slaves in the city, while numerous free blacks gave contradictory and confusing statements about the alleged arson plot. By the early fall, fearing that the Spanish—whom they were then fighting in King George's War—would send spies into the city to conspire with the slaves against them, colonists hastened to judgment. Eighteen slaves and four whites were hanged, thirteen slaves burned at the stake, and about seventy banished to the West Indies.

A few colonists questioned the social and moral rightness of slavery. In 1754 Philadelphia Quaker writer John Woolman insisted that human beings had a single original source of creation, and that the inferior level of intelligence and moral

Urban Slavery Colonial cities were home to hundreds, or even thousands, of slaves by the mid-1700s. City slaves often learned specialized skills for serving in a master's business or household. But cities also became the ports of entry for new slaves put on auction. Slaves from many nations and languages, as well as different stages of "seasoning," mingled in northern colonial cities. *(Nantes, Musée du Château des ducs de Bretagne, photo © Ville de Nantes-A.G.)*

refinement attributed to slaves was not inborn but the result of degrading treatment by their masters. Since, reasoned Woolman, white labor had not undergone generations of treatment similar to that of African labor, "Should we, in that case, be less abject than they now are?" But overall, Woolman's view was an exception, and not until the Revolution did colonists question slavery more widely.

New England

By 1720, New England's population reached 100,000, most of it native born. This was far too many people to enjoy the earlier traditions of partible inheritance, by which fathers bequeathed a sizeable farmstead or lands to all or most of their offspring (see page 70). Already, lands had been divided repeatedly, and overpopulated towns pressed hard on the resources available for local subsistence. As a result, increasing numbers of men and women approached their late twenties or early thirties waiting for their fathers to bequeath a marginal tract to them. Buying a distant parcel was costly, especially because young people who had lived at home for years rarely had savings. Moving away from local, familiar relationships was also a daunting prospect for many colonists. Even when colonists could claim a landed inheritance, it was often too small or too "worn out" and infertile to yield a subsistence by the eighteenth century. As many New Englanders put it, their settlements had become "crowded."

Increasingly, young people in New England looked for ways to make a living while they waited for a landed inheritance, or uprooted themselves from kin and neighbors to make a life elsewhere. One solution to crowding on the land was for young people to leave the towns of their births and migrate to cities in search of jobs. Unfortunately, such efforts ended in adding rural migrants to the growing pool of underemployed and poor. Another solution was to resettle on the frontiers of western New York, Nova Scotia, the southern piedmont, or what eventually became New Hampshire and Maine.

A more promising solution was for young men from crowded farms and towns to hire themselves out to other farmers in the area in return for some cash payment, room, and board for a contracted period of time. Alternatively, rural men could apply themselves at part-time work in "by-employments," or trades related to farming such as carpentry, barrel making, trapping, fishing, beekeeping, cider pressing, and fence mending. By-employments helped bring in cash that could be set aside for purchasing land later on. Moreover, demand for these skills increased after 1700 because migration into New England slowed and fewer tools and household items arrived on in-coming ships. As a consequence, colonists had to produce more of these items themselves and find different ways to exchange their meager farm surpluses for manufactured imports. Fishing, whaling, shipbuilding, and carrying other colonies' goods provided a partial safety valve for some New Englanders. Many young people from Connecticut and Massachusetts turned away from farming entirely and tried their luck at blacksmithing, seafaring, carpentry, or storekeeping. Salem and Marblehead fishermen sold their plentiful catches of cod and mackerel to feed Caribbean slaves and southern Europeans. By the 1750s, over 4,500 men were employed in the coastal fishing industry.

After acquiring his own land, a farmer might continue enhancing his income with by-employments, especially in remote communities where land had to be cleared and shelters built. Men with special skills were valuable not only to their families, but to the community as a whole. After toiling at ceaseless rounds of daily chores, wives and daughters earned cash or "store-bought" goods by selling cheese, bags of feathers, garden vegetables, small pieces of fabric, and the like for trade with other households. A family of six or eight would not only struggle mightily to bring in agricultural crops, but also be consumed between seasons and in evenings improving or repairing the farm and equipment. Sometimes this work could be done by a farmer and his sons, but often it required the special skills of a neighbor who would expect a "payment" of cash, time, or equivalent skill in return. In all of these ways, many New Englanders in the countryside adjusted to the "crowding" that early prosperity brought.

Sometimes colonists were unable to adjust to adversity. For example, New Englanders faced a serious commercial downturn after Queen Anne's War ended in 1713. Large numbers of men had gone off to distant fronts in that war—in some New England locales, up to one-third of the adult male population—and many did not return. As a consequence, far fewer colonists engaged in farming, fishing, construction, and many small trades. When combined with the declining quality of eastern New England soil, merchants had much less fish, lumber, and flour to export between 1715 and 1727 than in prewar years. Coastal and West Indies traders were thus forced to import more grain and flour from the mid-Atlantic. To pay for it they carried more sugar, molasses, coffee, and slaves from West Indies ports. In addition to earning profits from these new arrangements, merchants stimulated colonial consumption of the goods they carried, as well as greater production of rum, especially in Massachusetts.

The Mid-Atlantic

New Jersey, Pennsylvania, Delaware, and parts of New York comprised another region. Farmers, artisans, and merchants in this mid-Atlantic area shared many social and cultural characteristics with New Englanders, but their opportunities to prosper were more widespread and sustained. Wartime expeditions did not require as many men and such high taxes as in New England. In southeastern Pennsylvania, a dense population of farmers blessed with rich soil, a long growing season, and intricate markets for surplus foodstuffs steadily increased the prosperity of commercial farm families. Farmers and merchants of New York, Pennsylvania, and New Jersey were poised by the 1730s not only to help feed Caribbean islanders and southern European people, but also to support growing populations of craftsmen and retailers in colonial towns. When King George's War struck, demand rose for the foodstuffs that mid-Atlantic colonists could supply, and few men were pulled away from rural production for military duties. After the war, poor harvests in eastern Europe forced England and southern Europe to import large amounts of grain and flour from Philadelphia and New York merchants, while West Indies demand also revived quickly. As the contrasts between the mid-Atlantic region and New England during the late 1730s and 1740s became widely known, ever more immigrants shunned Boston and Newport in favor of mid-Atlantic ports, especially Philadelphia.

By midcentury, the Hudson and Delaware River valleys had become colonial bread baskets. But the two areas developed differently. In New York, great estates had been granted to governors' favorites at the end of the seventeenth century, and the interior filled more slowly with fewer freeholders than the lands spreading west of Philadelphia. In New York, many tenants and small farmers rented farmland from the manor lords, who often imposed rules for what was grown, how tenants could market their goods, and what obligations they owed the landlords. These obligations probably did not thwart the ambitions of either landlords or tenants, both of whom wished to forward their agricultural exports to the growing port at the base of the Hudson River. But in time the perception of widening inequalities, and of missed opportunities for freeholders, grew into open conflict in the hinterlands of New York.

Although Pennsylvania was settled long after other northern areas already flourished, it developed quickly because it became a magnet for immigrants and the government readily granted freeholds to colonists. By midcentury, the land beyond Philadelphia was the fastest-growing region in North America. The maturing hinterlands produced beef and pork, wheat and flour, cheese and other farm surpluses for export, which in turn supported a coastal merchant community. Wheat produced in southeastern Pennsylvania and northern Delaware was renowned in the West Indies and southern Europe; and Philadelphia's construction of new ships surpassed New York's in quality and number by the 1750s. Merchants sent great quantities of English and European goods into the interior, while wagoners and boatmen traveled throughout the settled areas of Pennsylvania, Delaware, and eastern Maryland collecting bushels of wheat and barrels of flour. These activities spurred the production of conveyances and containers, employment at mills and taverns, and elaborate networks of buying and selling at small shops throughout the region. Farmers were often able to perfect craft skills alongside their rural enterprises or expand into shopkeeping. Western New Jersey and northern Delaware farmers were natural satellites in these maturing relationships between country and city, as were the rising numbers of itinerant or semiresident farm laborers throughout the entire mid-Atlantic region. Although many single men and families failed to become freeholders after the 1720s and were thus obliged to rent cottages and acreage as tenants, the generalized poverty of England's countryside was unknown in the colonial mid-Atlantic.

Varieties of Life in the South

From the eastern shore of Maryland, through Virginia, the Carolinas, Georgia, and down to the Spanish borderlands, the southern colonies shared characteristics that set them apart from their northern neighbors. It was not just the presence of slaves and reliance on agriculture that created southern distinctiveness. Rather the key difference was southern planters' deep dependence on the labor of slaves and the export of staples to prosper. The plantation system did not spur city development, for its people were more dispersed. The white population was also sharply divided between the few great planters and the majority of struggling tenants and small farmers. Together, the "slave colonies," as merchants referred to southern settlements, produced about 95 percent of the value in goods that England bought from its mainland colonies during the 1700s. Still, there was no single "South," but rather many distinctive regions, founded at different times by settlers with varied cultural backgrounds and political goals.

The Chesapeake Colonies

By 1700, the poverty of Virginia's and Maryland's early years had given way to relative prosperity of cleared farms and generally rising tobacco export levels, widespread use of slave labor, and defined social and political groups. Indentured servants continued to migrate into the upper Chesapeake, but fewer came to the region after 1700. Instead, planters imported slaves whose labor created greater profits and greater material comfort for increasing numbers of white settlers, and slaves produced by far the greatest value of goods that flowed into Britain. In addition, a middling population of farmers—maybe 30 percent of white families in the region—owned land and slaves. By clearing farms a few miles from inlets and swamps, these new settlers avoided the diseased conditions of coastal areas. As larger numbers of white women arrived, the gender ratio began to even out. Better health and the greater probability of marriage made stable families possible, including more living children, and eventually kinship networks extended over counties in tight webs of sharing, indebtedness, and inheritance.

As Chesapeake society continued to mature, social relations more closely resembled European traditions emphasizing men's authority over women. By 1700, the Chesapeake was home to fewer widows because both men and women lived longer and married at more nearly equal ages than they did in the early years. But simultaneously, women who did become widows lost power over their husbands' estates and their children's futures because patriarchal norms stipulated that collateral male kin—uncles, brothers-in-law, fathers-in-law—should control property and offspring. At all levels of Chesapeake society, men exercised ever-more power over younger kin, servants, and slaves as communities settled into familiar European family patterns.

Men's greater authority at home went hand in hand with the creation of more stable elites among the so-called first families of the Chesapeake. Whereas in the founding years, planter-businessmen busily invested in land, supervised their labor, and struggled to develop strong commercial ties, by the 1720s the elite boasted fortunes that bought luxury goods to adorn their home. A few Chesapeake planters had become wealthy tobacco plantation owners who used their economic stature to exert political and cultural control over other colonists.

The elite expected deference from lesser white property owners, just as they expected obedience from their slaves. Sometimes this deference took the form of coercing the "lesser sort" to conform to the elite's rules of behavior. But usually deference to the colonial elite took more subtle forms. For example, in the Virginia tidewater region, roads were so poor and the demands of farm work so continuous that social visiting was rare; only very special events such as weddings, court days, or funerals brought people together. Under these conditions, meetings among colonists took on pointed, sometimes ritualistic, significance. Court days, barn raisings, and holiday church services became the occasions for prolonged contact between the elite and small farmers of the Chesapeake, times when personal and economic business could be transacted. In the process, deference could be ratified by institutional rituals. Drinking, hunting, gambling, horseracing, and dancing together underscored that all white men observed common traditions and civil laws. At the same time, differences of dress, speech, kinship connection, or political office affirmed that elite men would best display and protect those traditions and laws. Public feast days, especially those honoring military victories or celebrating elections, brought colonists of all social levels together. Militia musters, for instance, required all men between sixteen and sixty of particular neighborhoods to gather in central locations. On these occasions, white colonists bonded across the social hierarchy, while the elite reinforced its superiority to poor white colonists. For the first families, public events became times for soliciting votes to public offices, which few begrudged them. Most colonists agreed that the great propertied planters would understand how to secure the political interests of small farmers and establish "natural government" controlled by society's "better sort."

Within a few years, the distance between the elite and the rest of Chesapeake society grew measurably. Wealthy planters focused ever more on emulating, or imitating the manners and lifestyles of the English gentry. They began to build larger houses, wear finer clothes, sponsor grand balls and election day parties, narrow the circle of intermarrying, and tout their educations in cultural refinement and classical scholarship. Expensive attire, important public offices, and cultivation of gentrified manners were important avenues for this elitism. For girls, music, dancing, and reading the Bible were often the extent of their formal educations. For boys, private tutoring in classical texts and languages, as well as accounting, could be a steppingstone to higher social status.

Slavery and the Chesapeake

By the 1690s in the Chesapeake, greater and greater numbers of slaves were becoming essential for the success of planters' agriculture. Southern gentry families and northern merchants alike benefited from the production and transport of staple crops, the slave trade, and the constant shipbuilding, barrel making, warehousing, insurance brokerage, and middlemen's enterprises required by Chesapeake (and other southern) agriculture.

Once the Dutch monopoly of slave transport ended in the 1690s, British merchants began to carry first thousands, then hundreds of thousands, of slaves from Africa and the Caribbean to southern plantations (see Competing Voices, page 158). About 6 million Africans were forced into slavery by the English and French during the 1700s, most of whom were carried to the West Indies and Brazil. By 1750, the

Eleanor Darnall (1704–1796) Though not yet a teenager in this painting, Darnall is dressed in the fine clothing of Chesapeake elite families and has the facial and body composure of a much older woman. Surrounded by the domestic comforts of a pet and flowers, and standing before a lavish estate she will one day inherit, Eleanor is an example of refinement and distinction that most colonial young women would never share. *(Maryland Historical Society.)*

single island of Jamaica had nearly seven hundred sugar plantations worked by over 100,000 slaves. Shippers brought between 260,000 and 320,000 slaves into the mainland colonies, 90 percent of them to the South, from 1700 to 1760.

The Chesapeake tobacco planters participated actively in this great forced migration. From 1700 to 1770, they acquired as many as 80,000 Africans, and by the 1730s, they could also count on steady natural increase of "country-born" slaves—those born in the colonies. In 1704 Virginia had a white population of 75,600 and roughly 10,000 slaves. Maryland's slave population was also about 10,000 by then.

The transition in the Chesapeake from a society in which many white farmers labored alongside indentured servants and a few black slaves to one in which slaves provided almost all the field labor in tobacco occurred at the end of the 1600s. Fewer indentured servants chose to migrate into the Chesapeake by then, for a variety of reasons. At the same time, planters turned more systematically to the labor of slaves and solidified the separation of races by strict slave codes (see page 61).

By the 1730s, tobacco prices had recovered and remained high for a number of years. Virginia legislators passed effective inspection laws in 1730, and Maryland followed with similar legislation in 1747, which regularized packaging and raised the quality of leaves sent to market. An agreement written in England to supply France with great amounts of southern tobacco also renewed planters' interest in producing "the weed." They responded quickly to both the higher prices and the additional French demand by working slaves harder, encouraging the birthing of more slaves, and cultivating more extensive plots of tobacco throughout the tidewater stretching from Delaware, through Maryland, Virginia, and North Carolina's Albemarle Sound. Since the Chesapeake's tobacco agriculture required regular, but not excessively demanding, attention from slaves, planters did not have to work their slaves with the reckless disregard for health and welfare shown in the Caribbean. Moreover, many colonial tobacco planters realized the importance of encouraging slaves to develop families and produce children. Many Virginia planters grew solicitous of slave children's health, and some permitted pregnant female slaves to reduce their work regimens. As a result of these "considerations," by the 1750s, American-born slaves outnumbered Africans in the Chesapeake.

During these same years, planters became better entrepreneurs as well. Growers extended tobacco planting into the region beyond the fall line, a sharp break in the landscape that marked the end of the tidewater and beginning of the piedmont. The most successful tobacco planters had become creditors or local bankers for less prosperous farmers. Elite planters became middlemen and marketers for their lesser neighbors' tobacco as well, and received substantial fees for their work.

This era of agricultural and commercial expansion, as well as uncontested business leadership in the Chesapeake, did not last. "Factors," or representatives, came from Scotland to buy tobacco directly from Chesapeake growers and transport it to Glasgow firms. At first, Scottish factors provided the large planters with valuable services and credit, and they helped small tobacco farmers wrest their economic independence from the local elite. In time, however, colonists would lament their loss of control over their commerce to foreigners.

In addition, environmental and commercial conditions spurred many planters in Maryland and northern Virginia to convert some of their investments from tobacco to wheat. By the late 1740s, when the price of grain and flour in Europe was rising rapidly, some planters began to reason that wheat would be a good crop to sell abroad, especially given tobacco prices' unnerving fluctuations. Moreover, wheat, unlike tobacco, gave rise to new jobs and more complicated markets. Middlemen gathered up small surpluses, millers set up impressive buildings to grist flour, coopers made waterproof barrels, and a host of shipbuilders and shipping firms welcomed wheat and flour exporting. Greater economic diversity in turn boosted the growth of towns such as Baltimore and Norfolk, which were as populous as many northern coastal cities by the 1770s, boasting nearly 10,000 people each and a host of new services and retail shops. Tobacco remained the most important export for Chesapeake farmers, but grain cultivation brought important changes to the region.

The Carolinas

For a half century after 1660, the Carolina region was more heavily populated by Native Americans than by European immigrants. Indeed, European settlers reported such frequent and hostile Indian raids against them that only a few daring cattle ranchers and fur traders came to stay at first. Seasoned Caribbean and West African slaves—present from the beginning of Carolina settlement—taught planters herding and trapping techniques. By the 1700s, North Carolinians extracted lumber products and processed tar and pitch—vital to shipbuilding—for sale to English merchants. South Carolina merchants sent deer hides to England and carried Caribbean sugar to many ports. By the 1740s, Eliza Lucas Pinckney, who had grown up on a South Carolina plantation, developed ways to grow and process indigo, a plant that thrived in dry soil unfit for other crops, and produced a dark blue dye used in textile manufacturing. An English bounty, or cash incentive, to produce more indigo also spurred production and export of that crop.

But one commodity above all others characterized the agriculture and labor of the colonial Carolinas: rice. Rice was not an obvious choice for production in the low country, for European peoples had rarely consumed rice before the 1700s. It was Africans who provided the labor, the field skills, and knowledge about tools, such as heavy mortars and pestles, used to separate the husks from the grain. Thus, even though the Chesapeake planters got an earlier start with their slaveholding and tobacco agriculture, Carolina planters surpassed them quickly in the value of their exports, numbers of their slaves, and profits lining their pockets by the 1730s. After 1705, rice was no longer enumerated by Parliament's Acts of Trade, and in 1730 the crown permitted planters to ship rice directly to southern Europe, where demand grew rapidly. Following King George's War, planters and merchants diverted supplies to additional markets in northern Europe. Slaves already made up about 70 percent of Carolina's population, and by the 1760s they represented about 80 percent of coastal people throughout the South. At the same time, thanks to the labor of thousands of slaves, a handful of rice planters were the richest men in North America.

In many respects, the Carolinas had more in common with Caribbean plantations than with Chesapeake settlements. In the Caribbean, a few absentee planters held immense wealth made from the slave trade and sugar production on the islands; Carolina planters also tended to leave their slaves and fields in the hands of overseers. Sugar and rice production both altered the ecologies in which they were produced and required such thorough transformations of the landscape that Native American societies were devastated. Slaves brought from Africa or the Caribbean islands—as opposed to those born on the plantations—continued to be a large proportion of South Carolina's and the Caribbean's laborers. For planters, the brutal toil of slaves on the sugar and rice plantations produced unimaginable wealth. Although Chesapeake tobacco would play a major role in filling the imperial treasury, sugar and rice became even more significant for England's shipbuilding, commercial employment, refining enterprises, and rapidly expanding personal wealth even at the end of the colonial era.

Georgia

Georgia, named for King George II (ruled 1727–1760), was founded in 1732. The colony was given three herculean tasks to accomplish for imperial rulers in England: provide an environment for England's poor to work as silk and wine farmers; defend the perimeter of the empire by regular militia drilling; and be a model of how a colony could grow and remain virtuous without alcohol or slavery. James Oglethorpe, John Percival (later, the earl of Egmont), and trustees who also held Parliamentary seats joined together to acquire a charter, at first raising capital for the enterprise from wealthy Anglicans. But when the Georgia promoters came forward with their lofty goals, Parliament for the first time invested funds in a colonial scheme.

The enlightened founders of Georgia sent out nearly three thousand settlers in the first two years, but the majority were not English and only a fraction of them stayed very long. Most early Georgians were Protestant dissenting Salzburgers who had been expelled from Germany, Moravians who wished to leave their homelands in Bohemia and Moravia, French Huguenots who had grown weary of intolerance, and Scottish Highlanders. Soon, pacifist Moravians left for North Carolina because they did not wish to fight Native Americans and Spaniards in Georgia. Then Scots who failed to secure decent landholdings left in disgust for South Carolina. Others complained that inspired leaders had foolishly laid out Savannah as an impracticable grid on a sandy and marshy topography, and that settlers received far too little land to support their families.

Between 1750 and 1752, trustees of Georgia recognized they were failing. Twenty years after the founding there were fewer people in the colony than at the time of the first ships. Colonial leaders dropped the ban on alcohol, allowed the importation of slaves, gave up on silk and wine production, and permitted enterprising rice and indigo growers to step in. Georgians surrendered their charter in 1752 and became a royal colony. Within a few years, the coastal settlements took on the distinctive characteristics that already marked South Carolina: a slave majority, a small resident planter elite, and staple crop agriculture.

Slave Work and Culture

Africans forcibly removed from their native villages and homelands were packed by the hundreds into the holds of cargo vessels for the "middle passage" to the Western Hemisphere. It is difficult to grasp the pain and despair Africans faced when they were captured and coerced onto ships that would remove them from homelands forever. Terrified by the appearance of white Europeans and dismayed at their inability to communicate, many Africans taken into bondage rebelled and were killed before they even boarded vessels. Others were branded and then faced horrors on board the hellish ships. Chained immobility, inadequate nutrition, fear, lice, dysentery, suicide, and contagious diseases claimed the lives of over 15 percent of Africans headed for Brazil, the West Indies, or North America.

On arrival in the West Indies or mainland low country, the crises of relocation did not abate. Completely severed from kin, local communities, familiar food and language, and adequate sleep, slaves were forced into a new life of relentless toil. Epidemics of yellow fever, smallpox, measles, and intestinal diseases took many more lives. But work itself was the most brutal killer.

In the British West Indies, the price of sugar remained high and the cost of slaves declined during the 1700s. As a result, masters worked slaves as hard as possible in the cane fields in order to satisfy the rapidly expanding demand for sugar. For example, Barbados planters imported over 80,000 slaves in the first three decades of the eighteenth century, but the black population rose only about 4,000. Moreover, because many more male slaves were brought to the Caribbean than females, and because poor nutrition and harsh treatment significantly reduced the number of children that women bore, the African population in the West Indies did not grow naturally until after emancipation in the 1800s.

North American slave communities differed from those of the Caribbean. Peoples of many nations mingled in the Carolinas and Chesapeake, constantly negotiating particular cultural and labor conditions. Country-born slaves did not always share cultural traits with recently arrived Africans. Among African arrivals, Angolans and Ibo had difficulty communicating with each other. "Seasoned," or acclimated, slaves from the West Indies had little in common with a Philadelphia

A Tobacco Plantation While a planter smokes a pipe and confers with his overseer, slaves on this Chesapeake plantation perform all of the tasks related to planting, cultivating, harvesting, sorting, packaging, and delivering the profitable tobacco. Slaves also fashioned the tools for coopering and made barrels for transporting hogsheads of "the weed." Ships in the background navigate right up to the edge of the plantation lands. *(Library of Congress.)*

house slave. Yet the condition of enslavement itself, and the preservation or compromising of cultural ways forged in the labor conditions imposed on slaves, resulted in distinctive slave communities.

In the Chesapeake, most farms remained relatively small or were parceled into a number of sections. But tobacco required constant attention. Slaves transplanted young seedlings; scoured the plants for bugs and worms; nurtured the leaves along; picked and hung the leaves at harvest; sorted and barreled them; and kept racks, hoes, and sheds in repair. Slaves in the Chesapeake generally worked in "gangs," which were supervised closely and devoted to repetitive field work from sunup to sundown. When slaves were concentrated in larger numbers on Chesapeake plantations, they had the opportunity to specialize in particular skills. Planters who wished to produce much of their necessary food, building materials, clothing, and tools encouraged slaves to learn the required skills. African-American midwives attended white and black women giving birth; African-American men made nails, fine cabinets, and riding gear. On the expansive Virginia plantation of George Mason, for example, slaves labored as coopers, sawyers, carpenters, tanners, cord-wainers, spinners and weavers, curriers and farriers, and all manner of food preservers.

In South Carolina the work regimen on rice plantations more closely resembled life in the West Indies than in the Chesapeake. Carolina planters imported slaves at a faster rate, and brought more of them directly from Africa, than their counterparts in colonies to their north. Most Carolina slaves worked in rice fields, where disease and relentless irrigating or planting in marshy areas took a heavy toll and made pregnancy and childbirth arduous. In rice country, mortality was high and, even with new shiploads of Africans, males outnumbered females significantly. During hot seasons in South Carolina, when malaria and yellow fever were nearly a certainty, planters fled to Charles Town. In their place, black overseers organized and disciplined working slaves into teams for the monotonous and isolated chores of rice cultivation. Although a large number of slaves might work together on a plantation, the close supervision of work and the swampy terrain of lowland Carolina made it difficult for slaves to create extended kinship networks or communicate with neighboring plantations.

Still, many South Carolina slaves acquired personal property under the region's "task system." Unlike the gang labor system of the Chesapeake, tasking involved completing a stipulated amount and kind of work. Once slaves finished their allotted task on a rice or indigo field, they were free to grow and sell vegetables, row boats for local white people, or raise chickens or fish for extra protein. Time away from tasking could amount to half a working day. The tiny bit of autonomy permitted by the task system did not mitigate the harshness at the core of slavery, but it helped slaves invent survival tactics and lent a modicum of dignity to their daily existence.

Whether in the Chesapeake or newer colonies to the south, most slaves lived in quarters, clusters of small cottages set apart from the master's house. In the Chesapeake, large tobacco estates were divided into a few quarters, each organized by an overseer or the planter himself. When the day's fieldwork was declared finished, slaves retreated to quarters, a community within a community, to build support networks, share food, and transmit valued medical advice. Although masters often did not recognize slave marriages and could sell individual slaves away from their plantations and partners at any time, slaves created parent and spouse roles within the extended black community. Existing families adopted children who had been sold away from their mothers on other plantations. And slaves in the quarters fostered both practical and emotional ties across family lines; for example, a shawl that provided a young woman's sole added adornment at weddings might be passed from one house to another for years. Members of the entire quarters drew comfort and resources from one another. African terms for *brother* or *sister, uncle* or *aunt,* were readily applied beyond the boundaries of kinship. Given the precariousness of slave life and nuclear families, extended kinship networks were far more important for slaves than for whites.

Slaves from Africa brought a great range of customs to the colonies and spoke a variety of languages. In South Carolina's lowlands, for example, a majority of African-born slaves understood a Gullah dialect that incorporated words from English and several African tongues. In the Chesapeake, where many slaves chose to adopt English as a common language, extended and nuclear families developed their own surnames and long-standing kinship traditions, which they passed on from one generation to the next. In both regions, slaves retained many of their customs and languages in work songs, agricultural technology, ceremonies, and religious practices. On quarters, they often built houses in familiar African styles and constituted families based on African marriage, coming-of-age, and funeral customs.

Despite pressures from masters to adopt Christian ways, many slaves preserved basic African religious traditions or combined African and Christian religious ways, especially in their music and dance. Planters often protested against slave adoption of Christianity, though, because they feared that preaching love, equality, and universal brotherhood might lead slaves to question their condition. But over time, and especially during the Great Awakening of the 1740s (see page 149), some slaves adopted and altered Christian messages about inner freedom and the value of community, reshaping them to suit the rhythms and regimens of their new lives.

Masters generally forbade or ignored slave marriages, and they always retained the power to break up families by sales of adults or children. But they could not stop the frequent informal weddings and baptisms in slave quarters. Further, masters who denied the connections of family and community in slave quarters risked the longer-term consequences of fewer slave children being born and poor work performance. Compared with the extremely harsh conditions of the West Indies, mainland masters better clothed, fed, and cared for the health of their slaves.

Although many slave families and communities were resilient and endured for generations, relationships in the slave system overall were, by definition, subordinate to the desires and laws of masters. For example, white male sexual exploitation of vulnerable female slaves created a sizeable mulatto population in South Carolina by the late 1700s, making it all the harder to constitute stable slave relationships. Slave women, of course, did not share even the most minimal personal and civil rights that free or servant white women enjoyed. The slave work regimen prevented accumulation of many worldly goods and sufficient leisure time for formal education and the arts. Endless work sapped energy and opportunity for the "refinement" that many white Europeans anticipated their own work would bring. Moreover, white European values and laws usually were hierarchical and violent. In the English culture, laws punished numerous petty crimes by death, riots occurred over personal insults, and nations went to war over religious beliefs. It was a small step for Britons to extend violent power over slaves in the colonial south. Southern planters often believed that branding, castration, tearing apart families, public whippings, and shameful disfigurement were extensions of white European values, reinforced by long-standing views about racial inferiority.

Maturity Brings Conflict, 1739–1754

Everywhere in British North America by 1750, maturing settlements showed unmistakable signs of having achieved many colonial and imperial goals. Yet along with their successful production and reproduction, colonists were beginning to note that cities and older coastal farmlands were growing "crowded." And they often tempered their exhilaration about taming the wilderness with fears about social conflicts on the frontiers. Cutting across both northern and southern coastal and frontier regions, colonists also began to understand that the blessings of rapid natural increase, great influx of immigrants, and established slavery also heightened class, family, and racial tensions.

Slave Resistance and Rebellion

Many masters reasoned that slaves had a barbarous, savage nature that had to be constantly checked. Indeed, slavery was premised on the use of force and the prevalence of fear among both masters and slaves. Yet slaves throughout the colonies developed ways to accommodate or resist daily degradation. Building separate cultural and economic spheres was one way to reinforce personal dignity and perhaps gain a small increment of food or clothing. Some slaves worked odd jobs for planters or hired themselves out during slow weeks of the agricultural seasons in order to acquire cooking utensils or shoes.

More daring slaves resisted work by slowing down, breaking tools, or stealing from their master's household bit by bit. Some took the incredible risk of poisoning a beloved pet in the master's household, sassing the overseer, or sneaking out at night to visit neighboring slaves. Brutal punishments awaited those who were caught running away.

Open rebellion by groups of slaves was rare in colonial North America because the likelihood of being caught was so great, and the consequences so severe. The widespread assumption that Africans and African-Americans were slaves based on skin color made hiding from white society almost impossible. Moreover, in every colony but South Carolina, the white population was sufficiently large and dispersed to deter slaves from forming independent runaway slave societies such as those that appeared in Brazil or the mountains of Jamaica. A few mainland slaves "took their freedom" and escaped to the homes of free blacks in Philadelphia, New

York, Newport, or Williamsburg during the colonial era. Even then, their safety was never assured.

The most violent colonial slave revolt occurred in late 1739 near Charleston, South Carolina. Since 1699, governors of Spanish Florida, who wished to set up a buffer zone between their settlements and the English, had been inviting Carolina slaves to run away to Spanish territory with promises of freedom and land. As a result, scores of runaway slaves formed small communities in the countryside around St. Augustine, the largest of which was America's first free black community at Gracia Real de Santa Teresa de Mose (Mose, for short), which was led by an educated former slave, Francisco Menéndez, in the 1730s.

Then, in September 1739, South Carolina newspapers rumored that nearly seventy slaves had run away recently to an area near Spanish St. Augustine. The trickle of runaways, feared planters, was turning into a flood that would sweep huge numbers of "rice slaves" out of South Carolina. When the opening conflicts of King George's War (called the War of Jenkins's Ear) broke out between Spanish and English people in the West Indies later that year, fears became reality. Near the Stono River, at least seventy-five newly arrived Africans and a few more seasoned slaves who spoke Gullah began a march toward Spanish Florida, hoping to convince hundreds more to join them. Along the way, the runaways broke into white storekeepers' shops and killed a number of whites who they feared would spread word of their location to plantation masters.

At first it seemed that a great number of Carolina slaves had successfully escaped their monotonous field routines and masters' random brutalities. In a clearing along the way, they chanted joyfully about their new "liberty." But the runaways stayed too long in the marshes and lit campfires that attracted the colonial militia, who caught and killed two-thirds of the runaways. Planters executed another sixty fugitives in the coming months. Despite this outcome, revolts took place the next year elsewhere in South Carolina and in Georgia, possibly inspired by the Stono Rebellion and almost certainly sustained by the great stream of African slaves brought into the southern colonies during the 1730s.

The Great Awakening

During the mid-1730s, clergymen and itinerant preachers began to remind colonists about the dangers of material success, rising incidence of both luxury and poverty, and the apparent waning of religious fervor. Concerned ministers blamed the "cold formality" of church services for declining membership in congregations, and they set out to inspire renewed piety and faith with preaching that appealed more to the heart than the head. A "Great Awakening," as scholars often call it, swept through settled North America, exhilarating people of all statuses, occupations, levels of education, and regions. Its leading ministers exhorted colonists to abandon their trust in reason to resolve the era's anxieties and to rely on the heart instead. Not through books and newspapers, but through the preached word—in dramatic, huge, public encounters—ministers counseled ordinary colonists to reject the emptiness of material goods. Revivalists insisted that listeners admit their utter personal depravity and prophesied the divine wrath to be unleashed on unrepentant populations. Waves of cholera, diphtheria, and influenza seemed to be signs of God's displeasure. Crop failures resulting from hail, locusts, and wheat rust provided sufficient warnings about impending greater doom should the masses not repent immediately.

Jonathan Edwards, a Congregationalist minister in Northampton, Massachusetts, preached stingingly to his flock in 1735: "The God that holds you over the pit of Hell, much as one holds a spider or other loathsome insect over the fire, abhors you. His wrath toward you burns like fire; He looks upon you as worth of nothing else but to be cast into the fire." In rural New Jersey and Pennsylvania Presbyterian minister William Tennent called on sinners to have a spiritual rebirth, claiming that his own son had been raised from the dead by God's wonderful powers. Dutch Reformed leaders such as Theodore Frelinghuysen also led large public prayer meetings during the mid-1730s.

Then, in 1739 an English Anglican clergyman named George Whitefield came to the colonies and inspired thousands upon thousands of colonists to listen to messages of sin and salvation even more fervently. Newspapers printed reports of his revival meetings in England and the colonies, spreading anticipation of his visits. Whitefield came to the American colonies seven times, and during the mid-1740s stayed for three years, enthralling thousands with his traditional biblical messages and appeals for renewal of faith. Whitefield walked and rode on horseback through the colonies, drawing out converts to the new waves of "enthusiasm." His message was simple: individuals had allowed intellectual influences to crowd out the purity of religious feeling that flowed from the heart, and established clergymen had used Enlightenment rationalism to justify their elite styles and to distance themselves from their congregations.

Thousands of young adults joined churches for the first time during the Great Awakening. Thousands more were "born again" and helped split off portions of their existing congregations in order to form new churches. William Tennent's son, Gilbert, denounced Boston Congregational clergymen and built a huge following among the poor and single females of the city. In Southold, New York, James Davenport led hundreds of converts out of Congregationalist churches to form "New Light" churches. By 1742, New Light ministers and followers existed up and down the coast.

Old Lights, or leaders of the original Presbyterian, Congregational, and Anglican churches, lashed out in protest. In the South, the rising number of converted slaves was especially disturbing to planters, who banned their slaves from joining white churches. Converted African-Americans along the Savannah River were even able to call black preachers before the end of the colonial period. Baptists, at first strong only in New England, continued to grow in number in Virginia through the 1750s and 1760s. Old Lights insisted that the "wildness," the "quakings and tremblings" of revival followers were little more than provocations by untrustworthy—and outsider—clergymen. But splits in the colonial Protestant denominations endured for years. Presbyterians did not agree to reunite until 1758, and then the criticisms of New Lights were incorporated into church procedures and liturgy. Anglicans lost

George Whitefield (1714–1770) A tireless itinerant through towns and rural crossroads from Georgia to Massachusetts, Whitefield came from England to the colonies to spread the Great Awakening message to thousands of listeners, who responded in droves and in turn questioned both spiritual and political authority. Whitefield and a few other dissenting preachers spearheaded a grassroots movement that led to new religious denominations, and revivals of the old, at midcentury. *(Trustees of the Boston Public Library.)*

untold numbers to the Presbyterians and Baptists—permanently. In Massachusetts and Connecticut, Old Lights tried to punish dissenters by forcing them to pay taxes to the original churches and banishing many New Lights from political office. But the swell of influence continued to grow until New Lights won control of the Connecticut assembly in 1759.

Indeed, although the Great Awakening reached a peak in 1742, it continued to have a strong impact on colonists' public and personal religious character. Quakers, who did not really participate in the revivals, waned in numbers thereafter. Anglican and Congregational churches declined as well, whereas Presbyterians and Baptists rose in influence over the coming years. Great Awakening leaders shuddered that humanistic Enlightenment teachings had permeated existing Old Light schools. In 1746 New Light Presbyterians, dissatisfied with Harvard, formed the College of New Jersey (later Princeton University). In 1754 the Baptists followed with the formation of the College of Rhode Island (later Brown University), the Dutch Reformed with Queen's College (later Rutgers University) in 1766, and the Congregationalists with Dartmouth in 1769. Even earlier, in the 1740s, a new denomination—the Methodists—was splitting from Anglican ranks as well. Although Methodists did not form a separate church until 1800, individuals believed that the Anglican ministers were preaching abstractions and appealing mostly to wealthy southerners for membership. Partly in response to criticisms of Methodists and others, Anglicans created new institutions in the 1750s to reinforce their heritage: the College of Philadelphia (later University of Pennsylvania) and King's College in New York City (later Columbia University).

Amid all the splintering of old denominations and the proliferation of new religious persuasions, most New Light preachers emphasized to their converted masses the importance of emotion over doctrine, and the need to seek an experience of God's grace rather than submit blindly to any particular clergyman. New Light ministers were receptive not only to the poor, young, and anxious white population. Free and slave blacks were accepted into many of the new Protestant churches, and at times encouraged to form their own meetinghouses. Furthermore, although New Lights never put forth an explicit political program for secular society, they did give colonists a vehicle for developing a critical posture toward figures and institutions of authority in politics, religion, and the law. This would be important by the final colonial decades, when critical religious sensibilities that had brewed for over twenty years helped give voice to the emerging American identity at the time of the Revolution.

Land in Trouble

Colonists often regarded their frontiers with fear, as places that harbored hostile Native Americans, strange ethnic groups, and runaway servants and slaves. Many frontiers bordered on the dominion of foreign nations, such as French territory along the Great Lakes or the southern Spanish borderlands. These areas often had permeable or uncertain boundaries across which people of different nations sought freedom from bondage, markets for goods, or perhaps just a plot of land for cultivation or herding.

In the British South, almost continuous settlement existed from the coastal plains to the Appalachian Mountains by about the 1740s. But in the piedmont and foothills, colonists sometimes were not certain about ownership of tracts, which in turn fueled clashes among different groups of Europeans and with Native Americans. For example, Virginia speculators, whom Indians called "long knives," organized the Ohio Company in 1747 and attempted to survey a large land claim near what later became Pittsburgh. While Native Americans sent war parties against the intruders, the young surveyor George Washington learned that his job measuring uncleared terrain required Indian-fighting skills as well. Further to the south, settlers were spreading westward out of South Carolina into Cherokee lands, provoking minor clashes that would soon erupt into warfare during 1760 (see Chapter 5).

The southern frontier also became contested terrain by the 1750s. The Great Awakening was still flourishing in the South's western regions, where new Baptist churches threw up serious challenges to the gentry's religious and cultural authority. At the same time, many frontier settlers began to grow weary of making peaceful appeals for political representation or lower taxes for frontier inhabitants, and to mobilize for more forceful changes. These frontier "Regulators" lived along the entire Carolina fringe of settlement. In South Carolina, backcountry farmers, mostly recent Scots-Irish immigrants, formed vigilante bands for local protection during the 1760s and condemned the eastern establishment for failing to enforce its own laws in the west. Further, threatened the Regulators, if frontiersmen did not gain representation in the colonial government, they would take responsibility themselves for the protection of their homes and fields from Indian raids, bandits, and speculators. In 1769 the colonial assembly granted six new courts in the west and reduced taxes, but they denied the western counties representation.

In North Carolina, Regulators demanded not more government but less. Taxes, they cried, were collected in the west but benefited only easterners. In any event, frontiersmen were unable to pay them. Farmers demanded paper money and an end to suits against them for debts, mortgages, and nonpayment of taxes. So deeply felt were the Regulators' grievances that in 1771 they fought bitterly against eastern militiamen at the Battle of Alamance. Governor William Tryon's 1,200 militiamen rode out to the heart of Regulator territory to defeat some 2,000 men in armed uprising. Only a few died on each side, but in months to come the uneasy eastern establishment forced frontier settlers to swear allegiance to the crown government.

In the northern colonies, western and rural conflicts tended to erupt not over political rights but over ownership of land. During the 1740s, for example, farmers in eastern New Jersey angrily defended land that had been granted to them by New York governors when the two colonies were connected imperial jurisdictions. Once New Jersey gained independent colonial status, its proprietors sent wealthy agents into the countryside to claim rights over some lands that the farmers held, provoking fierce rioting from 1745 to 1755.

Property rights also sparked tensions along New York's Hudson River, where tenants of the Livingston and other landed families refused for a number of years to pay their rents. In 1753 anti-rent riots broke out. Then during 1765 and 1766, the Hudson River valley was turned upside down. Three generations previously, the New York governor had awarded huge tracts of land to favored colonial families. Although much of the disputed land lay completely undeveloped, some heads of these families rented out hundreds of small parcels to poor immigrant tenants, many of them German or Dutch. By midcentury, New Englanders who were spreading west expected to take up portions of the great landlords' estates, either by buying them outright or simply squatting and tilling the soil. When the landlords attempted to evict the squatters with court orders, and then to forcibly remove them, riots broke out. For months squatters ranged through the countryside, burning buildings and threatening tenants who remained loyal to the landlords. They clashed openly with county jail keepers and sheriffs until royal officials ordered British troops sent from New York City to quell the riots.

Farther to the west in New York, speculators tried to take Mohawk lands that lay outside Albany after 1753, only to have Chief Hendrick announce to the governor that henceforth the Iroquois would not honor the Covenant Chain between them. In the early 1760s, farmers moving out of New England with titles from New Hampshire to settle new lands just to the west (which would become Vermont later), clashed with speculators who held titles from New York. By staunchly defending lands that were technically claimed by New York, Ethan Allen's "Green Mountain Boys" created a de facto state of Vermont by 1777.

Beyond the land settled by British subjects were vast areas inhabited by Native Americans and claimed by rival Spanish and French. The Spanish were making important strides toward colonizing the Floridas, the Southwest, and California through the final decades of British rule in North America (see Chapter 5). The French also extended their influence over North American Indians, squatters, and land companies. During the 1740s, the French began to refortify their positions along the St. Lawrence River and to establish a military presence in the Ohio River valley. Colonists, especially Pennsylvanians who had been sent out by their government to create habitable trading posts and farms, and the Virginians whose settlements lay closest to new French forts, bristled. In 1753 Virginia sent George Washington on another mission into the wilderness, this time to warn the French under Marquis Duquesne to leave the area. Washington, now a commander of the Virginia militia, was not willing to negotiate terms with the Delaware, Mingo, and Shawnee who lived in the territory. Furthermore, Duquesne rebuffed him. The French proceeded to take over the Virginia encampment and scatter the colonial militia. In the spring of 1754, Washington returned to the Ohio country. This time he simply ordered his men to open fire on the first French patrol they encountered, which happened about fifty miles from Great Meadows where the Allegheny and Monongahela Rivers meet. This attack started the bloodiest colonial war.

CONCLUSION

By the end of the colonial era, a steady line of settlement stretched from Georgia to Maine, from the Atlantic coastline to the Appalachian ridge. Tentacles of settlement reached from cosmopolitan cities where shops displayed fineries from Europe, into the wilderness where colonists lived with the barest of essential goods. Colonists were linked by commerce to foreign places that previous generations of settlers had never heard about, and the level of their material comfort was rising steadily. Great numbers of middling people were overcoming rude lifestyles, periodic unemployment, and political exclusion.

Although colonists typically still thought of themselves as inhabitants of separate provinces, or as "true born Englishmen," they were beginning to recognize a new identity: their shared Americanness. Expansion, immigration, and maturation contributed to new colonial thinking about being Americans. Communication among the colonies also drew people together as never before. The life-sustaining activities of commerce invited many colonists to think not so much about their immediate surroundings as about the fluctuations of international markets and effects of wars. South Carolina rice planters, for example, communicated more frequently with New York City merchants than with neighboring planters in Virginia. Rivalry with Native Americans, resistance of slaves, and continuing claims by France and Spain to both West Indies islands and North American borderlands also spurred colonists to think about their cultural distinctiveness from other peoples.

At the same time, distinctions among the social ranks of colonists grew more noticeable, and ethnic diversity, distinctive family patterns, different labor systems, and many cultural factors all made it hard to imagine how colonists might be united. Regional differences were also becoming pronounced, for in many respects New England culture and community ways were growing more remote than ever from Virginia's, and both were increasingly distinct from the West Indies or Mississippi frontier. Even at the end of the colonial era, there was no single American character, but rather a rich diversity of ethnic, religious, economic, and regional circumstances. To say that despite their differences, colonists were unified in their attachment to an empire defined as "English" stretches reality, for much of colonial life was not "English." South Carolina's slave majority was an obvious reminder to colonists that they were far from London. So was continuing contact between Native Americans and colonists, and the violence of huge, and advancing, frontiers. Colonists underscored their differences when they called Scottish frontiersmen "Jacobites" long after the English episode that had earned them the label as dangerous political dissenters. Quakers and Catholics were never welcome in colonial Massachusetts. Women of elite households often were as resentful of widows and orphans draining tax revenues for their upkeep as male politicians were. Farmers along the Hudson River scorned efforts by merchants in New York City to set the prices and terms of grain sales. Visitors from England mocked efforts by some of the southern gentry to emulate the lifestyles of gentlemen in London.

Indeed, colonists never shared a common condition, or a common set of aspirations for the future. Rather, they shared a willingness to criticize the heightened intervention of imperial authorities in their everyday lives. And eventually they shared general views about constitutional and political crises developing in the empire after 1763. These shared views enabled colonists to create a temporary political community in order to transcend other differences and separate from the empire during the Revolution.

SUGGESTED READINGS

Bernard Bailyn, *The Peopling of British North America* (1986), is a short but grand overview of immigration into the colonies. Exciting new scholarship has explored aspects of frontier change due to immigration and migration, with respect to ethnicity, religion, and race. See, for example, Donald Chipman, *Spanish Texas, 1519–1821* (1992); Gregory Evans Dowd, *A Spirited Resistance: The North American Indian Struggle for Unity, 1745–1815* (1992); Tom Hatley, *The Dividing Paths: Cherokees and South Carolinians Through the Era of Revolution* (1993); Rachel N. Klein, *Unification of a Slave State: The Lives of the Planters in the South Carolina Backcountry, 1760–1808* (1990); Robert D. Mitchell, *Appalachian Frontiers: Settlement, Society, and Development in the Preindustrial Era* (1991); Timothy Silver, *A New Face on the Countryside: Indians, Colonists, and Slaves in South Atlantic Forests, 1500–1800* (1987); Daniel B. Thorp, *The Moravian Community in Colonial North Carolina: Pluralism on the Southern Frontier* (1989); Albert H. Tillson, *Gentry and Common Folk: Political Culture on a Virginia Frontier, 1740–1789* (1991); and Daniel Usner, Jr., *Indians, Settlers, and Slaves in a Frontier Exchange Economy: The Lower Mississippi Valley before 1783* (1992).

For the cultural maturation see Richard Bushman, *The Refinement of America: People Houses, Cities* (1992); and for political and institutional maturation see Jack P. Greene, *Pursuits of Happiness* (1988). For work and home life, including material culture, see James A. Henretta and Gregory H. Nobles, *Evolution and Revolution: American Society, 1600–1820* (1987); Ronald Hoffman, Cary Carson, and Peter J. Albert, eds., *Of Consuming Interests: The Style of Life in the Eighteenth Century* (Charlottesville, 1994); Stephen Innes, ed., *Work and Labor in Early America* (1988); and Stephanie Grauman Wolf, *As Various as Their Land: The Everyday Lives of Eighteenth-Century Americans* (1993).

For family life in colonial America, see Karin Calvert, *Children in the House: The Material Culture of Early Childhood, 1600–1800* (1992); Philip Greven, *Four Generations* (1970); Edmund Morgan, *The Puritan Family* (1966); David Narrett, *Inheritance and Family Life in*

Colonial New York City (1992); Mary Beth Norton, "The Evolution of White Women's Experience in Early America," *American Historical Review, LXXXIX*, 593–619; Daniel Blake Smith, *Inside the Great House: Planter Family Life in Eighteenth-Century Chesapeake Society* (1980); Laurel T. Ulrich, *Good Wives: Image and Reality in the Lives of Women in Northern New England, 1650–1750* (1982); and Helena M. Wall, *Fierce Communion: Family and Community in Early America* (1990).

On the centrality of commerce, see Marc Egnal, "The Economic Development of the Thirteen Continental Colonies, 1720–1775," *William and Mary Quarterly, XXXII*, 1975, 191–218; Thomas M. Doerflinger, *A Vigorous Spirit of Enterprise: Merchants and Economic Development in Revolutionary Philadelphia* (1986); James H. Levitt, *For Want of Trade: Shipping and the New Jersey Ports, 1680–1783* (1981); Nancy F. Koehn, *The Power of Commerce: Economy and Government in the First British Empire* (1994); John McCusker and Russell Menard, *The Economy of British America, 1607–1789* (rev. ed., 1991); and Cathy Matson, *Merchants and Empire: Trading in Colonial New York* (1998). The most important contribution for northern cities is Gary Nash, *The Urban Crucible* (1979); but see also Billy Smith, *The "Lower Sort": Philadelphia's Laboring People, 1750–1800* (1990); and G. B. Warden, *Boston, 1689–1776* (1970). For slavery in the northern cities, see Thomas J. Davis, *A Rumor of Revolt: The "Great Negro Plot" in Colonial New York* (1985); and Jean R. Soderlund, *Quakers and Slavery: A Divided Spirit* (1985).

No single study has covered the North comprehensively, but regional aspects and comparative perspectives are offered in many important works. See, for example, Richard Bushman, *From Puritan to Yankee: Character and the Social Order in Connecticut, 1690–1765* (1967); Barry Levy, *Quakers and the American Family* (1988); James T. Lemon, *The Best Poor Man's Country* (1972); Kenneth Lockridge, *A New England Town: The First Hundred Years, Dedham, Massachusetts, 1636–1736* (1970); Paul R. Lucas, *Valley of Discord: Church and Society Along the Connecticut River, 1636–1725* (1976); Jackson T. Main, *Society and Economy in Colonial Connecticut* (1985); Peter C. Mancall, *Valley of Opportunity: Economic Culture Along the Upper Susquehanna, 1700–1800* (1991); and Stephanie Grauman Wolf, *Urban Village: Population, Community, and Family Structure in Germantown, Pennsylvania, 1683–1800* (1976). Sharon V. Salinger, *"To Serve Well and Faithfully": Labor and Indentured Servitude in Pennsylvania, 1682–1800* (1987), is the most meticulous analysis of indentured servants in the mid-Atlantic region.

Two important new works synthesize the extensive scholarship on slavery, plantations, commerce, and culture of the colonial south: Ira Berlin, *Many Thousands Gone: The First Two Centuries of Slavery in North America* (1998), and Philip D. Morgan, *Slave Counterpoint: Black Culture in the Eighteenth-Century Chesapeake and Lowcountry* (1998). Aspects of slavery and plantation life in the Chesapeake are also perceptively captured in T. H. Breen, *Tobacco Culture: The Mentality of the Great Tidewater Planters on the Eve of the Revolution* (1985); and Mechal Sobel, *The World They Made Together: Black and White Values in Eighteenth-Century Virginia* (1987). The classic study that explains slavery's origins and rise in the context of labor needs and the southern qualities of agriculture is Edmund Morgan, *American Slavery, American Freedom: The Ordeal of Colonial Virginia* (1975). For the low country, see Betty Wood, *Slavery in Colonial Georgia, 1730–1775* (1984), and Peter Wood, *Black Majority* (1974). An important comparative study is Philip Curtin, *The Rise and Fall of the Plantation Complex: Essays in Atlantic History* (1990). For work on the early development of slave communities within the southern agricultural system see Gwendolyn Midlo Hall, *Africans in Colonial Louisiana: The Development of Afro-Creole Culture in the Eighteenth Century* (1922), and A. Leon Higginbotham, Jr., *In the Matter of Color: Race and the American Legal Process in the Colonial Period* (1978).

Much work remains to be done on the life of small farmers in the Chesapeake and low country, but see the admirable study by Gregory A. Stiverson, *Poverty in a Land of Plenty: Tenancy in Eighteenth-Century Maryland* (1977). For smaller regions within the South, see Paul G. E. Clemens, *The Atlantic Economy and Colonial Maryland's Eastern Shore* (1980); E. Roger Ekirch, *Poor Carolina: Politics and Society in Colonial North Carolina, 1729–1776* (1981); Harry Roy Merrens, *Colonial North Carolina in the Eighteenth Century* (1964); and Robert Weir, *Colonial South Carolina: A History* (1983). For Georgia's emergence, see Kenneth Coleman, *Colonial Georgia* (1976), and Betty Wood, *Women's Work, Men's Work: The Informal Slave Economies of Lowcountry Georgia* (1995).

Two important works link the Great Awakening to the American Revolution: Patricia Bonomi, *Under the Cope of Heaven: Religion, Society, and Politics in Colonial America* (1986), and Alan Heimert, *Religion and the American Mind* (1966). A pathbreaking study that applied anthropological methodologies to master–slave relations and to the religious revivals of the era in Virginia is Rhys Isaac, *The Transformation of Virginia, 1740–1790* (1982). Outstanding biographies of leading New Light preachers include Frank Lambert, "*Pedlar of Divinity*"*: George Whitefield and the Transatlantic Revivals* (1994); Perry Miller, *Jonathan Edwards* (1949); and Patricia Tracy, *Jonathan Edwards, Pastor: Religion and Society in Eighteenth-Century Northampton* (1979).

Competing Voices

Two Views About Transatlantic Slave Trading

The Horrors of the Middle Passage

Every person transported from Africa to the Western Hemisphere as a slave experienced the wrenching terrors of the transatlantic voyage known as the "middle passage." Many did not survive, and nobody survived unscathed. Olaudah Equiano, whose recollections are excerpted below, was a slave in three places: Africa, Barbados, and Virginia. He bought his freedom after years of service to various masters and on the eve of the American Revolution fled to London. There, he published his memoirs in 1789.

> One day [in Africa], when all our people were gone out to their works as usual and only I and my dear sister were left to mind the house, two men and a woman got over our walls, and in a moment seized us both, and without giving us time to cry out or make resistance they stopped our mouths and ran off with us into the nearest wood. I was left in a state of distraction not to be described. I cried and grieved continually, and for several days I did not eat anything but what they forced into my mouth. At length, after many days' travelling, during which I had often changed masters, I got into the hands of a chieftain in a very pleasant country. This man had two wives and some children. . . . This first master of mine, as I may call him, was a smith, and my principal employment was working his bellows.
>
> I was again sold and carried through a number of places till . . . at the end of six or seven months after I had been kidnapped I arrived at the sea coast. The first object which saluted my eyes when I arrived on the coast was the sea, and a slave ship, which was then riding at anchor, and waiting for its cargo. These filled me with astonishment, which was soon converted into terror, when I was carried on board. I was immediately handled, and tossed up, to see if I were sound, by some of the crew; and I was now persuaded that I had got into a world of bad spirits, and that they were going to kill me. . . .
>
> When I looked round the ship too and saw a large furnace or copper boiling, and a multitude of black people of every description chained together, every one of their countenances expressing dejection and sorrow, I no longer doubted of my fate; and, quite overpowered with horror and anguish, I fell motionless on the deck and fainted. When I recovered a little I found some black people about me, who I believed were some of those who had brought me on board, and had been receiving their pay; they talked to me in order to cheer me, but all in vain. . . . I now saw myself deprived of all chance of returning to my native country, or even the least glimpse of hope of gaining the shore, which I now considered as friendly; and I even wished for my former slavery in preference to my present situation, which was filled with horrors of every kind, still heightened by my ignorance of what I was to undergo. I was not long suffered to indulge my grief; I was soon put down under the decks, and there I received such a salutation in my nostrils as I had never

experienced in my life; so that with the loathsomeness of the stench, and crying together, I became so sick and low that I was not able to eat.

. . . Two of the white men offered me eatables; and on my refusing to eat, one of them held me fast by the hands, and laid me across, I think the windlass, and tied my feet, while the other flogged me severely. I had never experienced any thing of this kind before; and, although not being used to the water, I naturally feared that element the first time I saw it, yet, nevertheless, could I have got over the nettings, I would have jumped over the side, but I could not; and besides, the crew used to watch us very closely. . . .

At last we came in sight of the island of Barbados; the white people got some old slaves from the land to pacify us. They told us we were not to be eaten but to work, and were soon to go on land where we should see many of our country people. This report eased us much; and sure enough soon after we were landed there came to us Africans of all languages. . . .

On a signal given (as the beat of a drum) the buyers rush at once into the yard where the slaves are confined, and make choice of that parcel they like best. The noise and clamour with which this is attended, and the eagerness visible in the countenances of the buyers, serve not a little to increase the apprehension of terrified Africans, who may well be supposed to consider them as the ministers of the destruction to which they think themselves devoted. In this manner, without scruple, are relations and friends separated, most of them never to see each other again.

Justifying the Slave Trade

By the mid-1700s planters did not have to prove the profitability of the slave trade to representatives in Parliament. Nevertheless, when English policymakers needed to promote a new war or planters wished to compete effectively with foreigners, they justified the slave trade anew with newspaper articles and pamphlets. The following passage was penned in 1745, by a British writer who tried to link the economic advantages with an intellectual rationale for the slave trade.

But is it not notorious to the whole World, that the Business of Planting in our British Colonies, as well as in the French, is carried on by the Labour of Negroes, imported thither from Africa? Are we not indebted to that valuable People, the Africans, for our Sugars, Tobaccoes, Rice, Rum, and all other Plantations Produce? And the greater the Number of Negroes imported into our Colonies, from Africa, will not the Exportation of British Manufactures among the Africans be in Proportion; they being paid for in such Commodities only? The more likewise our Plantations abound in Negroes, will not more Land become cultivated, and both better and greater Variety of Plantation Commodities be produced? As those Trades are subservient to the Well Being and Prosperity of each other; so the more either flourishes or declines, the other must be necessarily affected; and the general Trade and Navigation of their Mother Country will be proportionately benefited. . . .

. . . that the general NAVIGATION of Great Britain owes all its Encrease and Splendor to the commerce of its American and African Colonies; and that it cannot be maintained and enlarged otherwise than from the constant Prosperity of both those Branches, whose Interests are mutual and inseparable?

Whatever other Causes may have conspired to enable the French to beat us out of all the Markets in Europe in the Sugar and Indigo Trades, etc. the great and extraordinary Care they have taken to cherish and encourage their African Company, to the End that their Plantation might be cheaply and plentifully stocked with Negroe Husbandmen, is amply sufficient of itself to account for the Effect; for this Policy, they wisely judged, would enable them to produce those Commodities cheaper than we, who have suffered the British Interest to decline in Africa, as that of the French has advanced; and when they could produce the Commodities cheaper, is it at all to be admired that they have undersold us at all the foreign Markets in Europe, and hereby got that most beneficial Part of our Trade into their own Hands? . . .

As Negroe Labor hitherto has, so that only can support our British Colonies, as it has done those of other Nations. It is that also will keep them in due Subserviency to the Interest of their Mother Country; for while our Plantations depend only on Planting by Negroes, and that of such Produce as interferes only with the Interests of our Rivals not of their Mother-Country, our Colonies can never prove injurious to British Manufactures, never become independent of these Kingdoms, but remain a perpetual Support to our European Interest, by preserving to us a Superiority of Trade and Naval Power.

Masters and slaves existed together in a world of stark contrasts between them. Slaves struggled to prevail against conditions that stripped them of their heritage and dignity—or simply to survive the conditions of work—while British officials and colonial planters put the requirements of building an empire and personal fortunes above moral concerns. The slave trade occupied a prominent place in the British commercial system covering many continents and many peoples. Often the imperatives of competing with rival nations for the lands and resources of the New World gave the slave trade, and the labor of slaves on plantations, first priority in the minds of policymakers. Certainly, the profits to be made in the slave trade and in the products of slave labor were unsurpassed in all of imperial commerce. But the costs for the millions of people who were forcibly made a part of this profitable system were tremendous.

Questions for Analysis

1. Olaudah Equiano exemplifies many different reasons to condemn the slave trade. Find passages that address psychology, family, quality of life, and general physical conditions. Which complaints seem to be most compelling?
2. What criticisms of the slave trade are directed at conditions in the New World, and what ones stem from West African experiences? How are Equiano's two experiences different?
3. What specific points are made in defense of the slave trade? What general attitudes about race and slavery are revealed in the specific points?
4. Is there a tension between economic motivations for the slave trade and its moral justification? Can the two views be reconciled?
5. How might slave trading have differed in the many European nations involved in the practice?

Forging the American Experiment, 1754–1775

Toward the end of 1768, well-to-do southern planter William Drayton grew alarmed about the turn of events in South Carolina. The year before, Parliament had enacted the Townshend Duties, back-breaking taxes on a long list of colonial imports and an elaborate enforcement system. Now, men of "scant education" and "dearth of public service" had entered the political limelight in South Carolina to lead protests against the act. Small retailers, butchers, carpenters, shoemakers, and others "of modest means" had formed committees to cease importing goods from England, hoping to pressure English merchants into supporting colonists' pleas for repeal.

Drayton was not opposed to such a "nonimportation movement" in principle. Three years earlier, planters and merchants had led a similar boycott to win repeal of the Stamp Act. What annoyed Drayton was that "gentlemen of property and standing" were suddenly sharing public life with men of little political experience, men who might provoke riotous behavior. "Nature never intended that such men should be profound politicians or able statesmen," sneered Drayton. Traditionally, men with Drayton's high stature in the colonial assembly, secure wealth and family name, and close connections to English commerce and culture had assumed the leadership of political protests.

But by October 1769, "middling" men led South Carolina's nonimportation movement, declaring that they would no longer "stoically submit to all the illegal encroachments that may be made on [their] property, by an ill-designing and badly-informed ministry" in England. Nor would they wait for genteel leaders such as Mr. Drayton to formulate their political response to Parliament. They, the middling colonists, had been "in some degree useful to society"; their hard work earned "a decency suitable to their stations in life." Furthermore, these upstarts argued, they represented "ninety-nine out of every hundred . . . *of all North-America,*" and had "as equal a measure of *common sense* as any men." What did Drayton represent? Nothing, said the artisans, except an inherited fortune. He had never worked "by the labour of either his head or his hands."

Such bold challenges to authority—against both colonial and imperial leaders—arose more frequently after 1750. A prolonged war fought in North America from 1754 to 1763 raised anxieties about the character and future of the empire. Following the war, a parliamentary discussion about how the North American colonies should grow and prosper led to numerous laws to shape the empire's future. With each passing year, colonists formulated replies to real and imagined parliamentary aims. At the same time, colonists grew anxious about the future of their frontiers and commerce. They began rethinking both their place in the empire and their relationships to one another in North America. Along the way, they tested many kinds of responses to Parliament's offensive new laws. Some of their actions came from calm consideration of grievances; some came from frustration and growing habits of violence.

During the long process of thinking, writing, and rioting from 1764 to 1775, many colonists also changed their minds about their place in the empire and in the colonies. William Drayton was one of them. In 1775 he wrote that he had erred in his earlier disapproval of actions by "the people of my good province." Perhaps Drayton had cynically calculated that he could hold political office only if he followed popular opposition to Parliament, for he knew he was a "servant of the public." Perhaps he genuinely believed Parliament had overstepped its authority. In any event, Drayton joined thousands of colonists in the third and final nonimportation movement initiated by a Continental Congress of delegates from all the colonies.

- What kind of war did colonists fight in between 1754 and 1763, and how did that war affect the rising tensions in the English Empire?
- What kind of goals did colonists formulate for their own futures as they repeatedly protested the actions of Parliament?
- How did protests lead to new colonial political authority, extralegal committees, and outright mob actions?
- What shared cultural identity helped colonists forge unified actions? What differences hampered cooperation among them?

This chapter will address these questions.

Chronology

1754	Albany Congress
1755	Braddock defeated by French and Indians
	Acadian removal begins
1756	Seven Years' War begins in Europe
1760	George III takes the throne
1763	Treaty of Paris
	Pontiac's Rebellion
	Proclamation Line determined
	Massacre of the Paxton Boys
1764	Sugar (or Revenue) Act
	Currency Act
1765	Stamp Act
	Sons of Liberty formed
	First Quartering Act
	First nonimportation agreement
1766	Declaratory Act
1767	Townshend Duties
1768	Incident with Hancock's sloop, *Liberty*
	British troops arrive in Boston
1770	Boston Massacre
1771	Tryon defeats Regulators at Battle of Alamance
1772	First Committee of Correspondence
	Gaspée incident
1773	Tea Act and tea parties
1774	Coercive (or Intolerable) Acts
	First Continental Congress and Association Agreement
1775	Battle of Lexington and Concord

The Great War for Empire, 1754–1763

King George's War, which ended in 1748, had exacted a heavy toll on colonial lives and morale. In addition to the burdens of higher taxes, disrupted farming, and loss of lives, the British had handed back their main acquisition, Louisbourg. Worse, French expansion into the heart of North America continued to worry English colonists beginning to settle in the vast lands west of Virginia in the Ohio Valley. In 1754 French troops and the Virginia militia clashed near the Ohio River. One year later, the frontier erupted into the greatest war for empire in colonial experience. In a short time, the conflict spread throughout Europe. Its major theaters of action, though, lay in this vast expanse of contested land, still largely unknown to Europeans, but for centuries home to great numbers of Native Americans.

Onset of War, 1754–1760

The first clashes of what would become a global contest among European nations for the dominion of North America began in the forests of the Ohio Valley. In 1749 Parliament granted the Ohio Company of Virginia rights over land that was already settled by a mixture of many Native American groups, French trappers and squatters, and migrating British colonists. Raiding parties of Canadians and Ottawa Indians struck at both colonial settlers and the Miami, Shawnee, Seneca, and Delaware Indians of the region through 1753.

In early 1754, a young militia captain and surveyor named George Washington was sent into the contested area with a Virginia contingent to repel the French who had moved south from Canada. As tensions grew and skirmishes led to deaths in an undeclared war, Washington built Fort Necessity at a southern fork of the Ohio River. French soldiers attacked colonists and set up Fort Duquesne nearby. Washington responded in May with a retaliatory raid from his encampment up the Monongahela River, killing all but one of a French reconnaissance party. Responding in turn, the French attacked Washington and his troops at Fort Necessity on July 3. Washington, overmatched, surrendered at Great Meadows the next day, and as the Virginia militiamen retreated, French troops forged an alliance with nearby Delaware and Shawnee Indians.

Even before news of this defeat reached London, British officials had requested that colonists come together, along with members of the Iroquois Confederacy, to plan a common defense. At first, some colonists cheered this opportunity to conquer "popish slavery" in French Canada and defend "British libertie" in the Ohio Valley. Benjamin Franklin drew up the Plan of Union in early spring 1754. The plan proposed formation of a grand council of representatives from the colonial assemblies and a chief negotiator appointed by the crown. This council would discuss and settle on terms of mutual interest to Indians and colonists regarding frontier defense, trade, and land occupation. The masthead of Franklin's *Pennsylvania Gazette* carried a cartoon of a segmented snake, broken into pieces representing the British mainland colonies and bearing the injunction that colonists "Unite or Die."

In June 1754, representatives from the New England colonies, New York, Maryland, and Pennsylvania met in Albany, New York, to develop a plan for dealing with the threat of French troops on the frontier and to negotiate alliances with the Iroquois. However, the Albany Congress foundered and failed. For one thing, Iroquois chiefs had grown weary of repeated land grabs by New York colonists and angrily broke off relations. Instead of cooperating, the Iroquois villages north and northeast of English settlements threatened to redirect their fur trade and diplomacy to New France.

For another thing, colonial legislators were not willing to combine their militias, finances, and political authority. They jealously guarded their separate colonial identities as competitors for western land. Moreover, even as the official meetings were in session, land and fur trade agents from various colonies flocked to Albany to make secret deals with individual Iroquois leaders. The Iroquois delegates grew furious that individual colonists would try to undermine efforts of their official negotiators, who were presumably working for the mutual interests of everyone. In the face of such conflicting colonial actions, the Iroquois broke off talks and refused all proposed alliances with the British.

The Albany plan's failure and Washington's surrender to French troops at Virginia's back door were evidence to British policymakers that the colonists could not defend themselves or the interests of the empire. Focusing their concerns on the strategic Ohio Valley and fishing and whaling communities of Newfoundland, including the fortified outpost of Louisbourg, and on the farming families of Nova Scotia, the British government discussed ways to eliminate the French presence. French troops continued to live in Newfoundland after King George's War, and French fishermen harvested huge quantities of cod from the northern waters. Anticipating that hostilities would spread to this region, British officials ordered troops and settlers to found the city of Halifax, Nova Scotia, in 1749.

By mid-1754, tensions in both the Ohio Valley and Canada built to the breaking point. In 1755 Major General Edward Braddock, the British commander-in-chief in North America, met with governors from eight colonies to plan the eviction of the French from North America. They initiated a multipronged attack on the Ohio Valley, the Mohawk Valley, and French Acadia (see map). Braddock set out against France's Fort Duquesne in the Ohio Valley himself, where he encountered formidable opposition from enemy troops. Brushing off offers of aid from the western Delaware Indians, and hampered by lack of experience in the wilderness, Braddock ordered his troops to slice a road through the dense forests. His baggage train included luxuries suited to a gentlemanly lifestyle, a typical entourage in more formal English warfare. As Braddock swaggered to within ten miles of Fort Duquesne, 1,500 French foot soldiers and Indians surrounded and annihilated both the redcoats and Braddock. The disaster was the worst defeat of British forces in North America to that time.

The British had one important success in 1755: they were able to expel the French from Acadia. About a thousand French settlers had remained in Acadia (present-day Nova Scotia) when Britain assumed control of the area in 1713. By 1750, their numbers had grown to about ten thousand. When representatives of Acadian villages refused to swear oaths of allegiance to England, Nova Scotia's British governor ordered the expulsion of the entire Acadian community. In August 1755, British troops marched in and began the forcible removal of civilians, looting

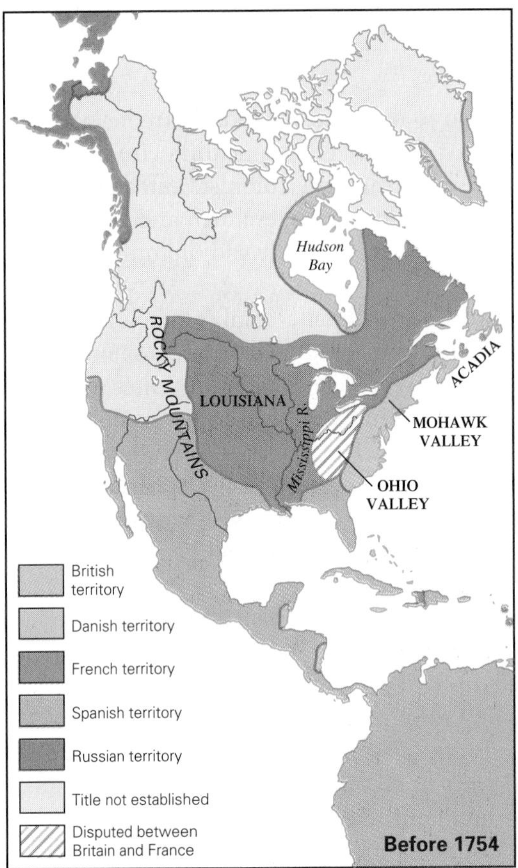

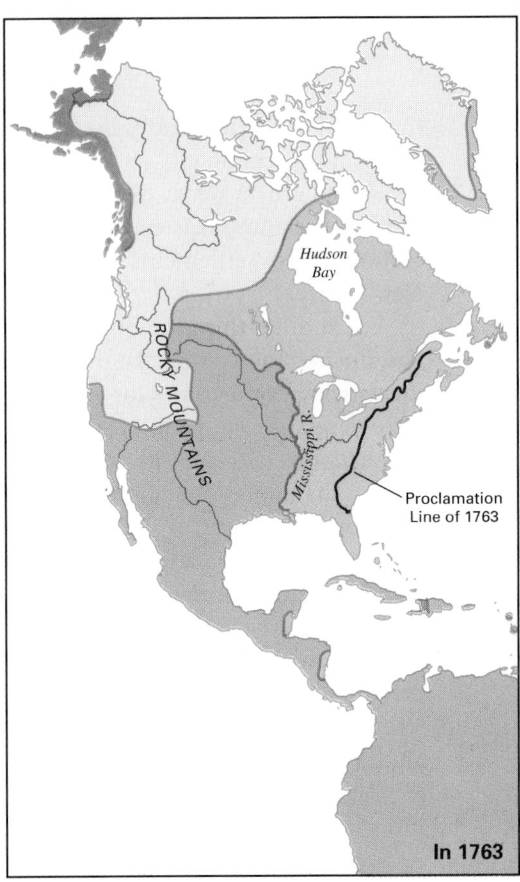

European Claims in North America, 1754 and 1763 The French and Indian War was truly a conflict for dominion of North America. By the Peace of Paris in 1763, the disputed Ohio Valley and northern fisheries had become British territory, as had the entire French claim throughout the continent and Spanish Florida.

and burning farms. Land-hungry New Englanders flocked into the area and bought farms at drastically reduced prices, while hundreds of Acadians dispersed into the countryside to the west and down the St. Lawrence River with few possessions and little to sustain themselves in hostile territories. Eventually, a few hundred out of the ten thousand Acadians settled near multiethnic New Orleans, where they contributed much, including the name "Cajun," to the local culture.

Global War

In 1756 France and Britain formally declared war on each other, and the conflicts that began in the North American forests spread to colonial possessions in the Caribbean, the Pacific, and India. As this French and Indian War widened and spread into Europe as well, it became known as the Seven Years' War, or the Great War for Empire. Braddock's replacement, Lord Loudoun, arrived in North America in 1756. Initially, he fared just as poorly as his predecessor. The French fought with guerilla war tactics in the dense forests, mustering a combination of poorly trained Canadian and European soldiers, Indian allies from the dispersed smaller tribes around the southern Great Lakes, and Irish conscripts who had fled British rule. Thousands of Americans fled from western Pennsylvania and New York to the safety of eastern settlements. To the southeast, Cherokees and Choctaws tried in vain to remain officially neutral. But in the confusion of frontier fighting and traditions of intertribal rivalries, many village leaders exploited British and French hostilities and made no consistent efforts to defend frontier settlers. Overall, colonists soon realized this war was broader than any previous encounter between European empires in North America. Its goals involved capturing complete dominion over North America and the costs to do this—human and financial—were immense.

British and colonial ways of fighting and attitudes toward warfare couldn't have been more different. Loudoun favored highly organized campaigns with soldiers trained to fight in formation, as well as to set up camp, build shelters, and perform numerous menial tasks on command. For even small infractions of discipline, soldiers in this "standing army" submitted to brutal floggings or reduced food rations. The colonists, in contrast, were accustomed to service in local or colonial militias, as volunteers for a single campaign or short stay. Few militiamen knew how to drill, and fewer still were accustomed to following orders unconditionally. Most had learned to find cover and aim from behind trees rather than to march in formation or advance in bayonet charges. Colonial militia usually served under captains whom they knew, and they resented the British officers who declared militia units to be "the dirtiest, most contemptible, cowardly dogs that you can conceive." Many colonial volunteers resisted British command altogether.

To make matters worse, civilians grew ambivalent about rising colonial taxes that their assemblies passed in order to support the war. Legislators themselves protested Loudoun's requisitions of supplies from coastal populations and the endless need for tax money to underwrite campaigns that butchered their citizens. The forests, they also charged, were no place for gentlemen's wardrobes and tea services. For his part, Loudoun grew increasingly disgusted with colonists whom he believed "have assumed to themselves, what they call Rights and Privileges, totally unknown in the Mother Country. . . . They will give you, not one Shilling, to carry on the War; they will give you not one thing, but for double the Money it ought to cost."

Loudoun's French counterpart was Marquis Louis-Joseph de Montcalm, a veteran of European warfare. In 1756 Montcalm initiated measures to professionalize the French forces in North America, including stringent drilling practice and attacking in formation. At first, the strategy proved successful when the French took Oswego, New York. But in 1757 Montcalm's European standards of conduct backfired tragically. When he took Fort William Henry, Montcalm offered the British soldiers and camp followers the opportunity to return home in return for their promise not to fight against the French again. But his Erie and Huron allies refused to conform to French rules of war. They proceeded to take prisoners, murder, and scalp New Englanders as they left the fort. In the days to come, they also indiscriminately massacred neutral Indians and New York citizens.

On the other side of the Atlantic, new parliamentary leaders and policies changed the course of the war. William Pitt became secretary of state in late 1757 and remained responsible for directing the war effort until its virtual end in 1761. Pitt understood the gravity of the colonists' claim that they bore huge financial burdens for a war over which they had little control. Pitt offered colonists a compromise they could not refuse: in return for colonial commitment and obedience in the field, he promised reimbursements to the assemblies in proportion to their contributions, more decentralized command of the colonial militia, and the removal of Loudoun. Colonial morale began to revive in early 1758, and Pitt further boosted provincial spirits by sending thousands of fresh British troops to serve alongside the militia.

In 1758 the British again took Louisbourg, the premier symbol of French military strength in North America. Shortly thereafter, George Washington happily commanded the lead battalion that captured Fort Duquesne, renaming it Fort Pitt (later, Pittsburgh). Then the last of the French outposts on the New York frontier fell to the British. Within months, Montcalm retreated to Quebec, where on September 13, 1759, he met the British forces under General James Wolfe at the Battle of Quebec on the Plains of Abraham. In a great European-style formal battle, both European commanders lost their lives, and each army lost over two thousand soldiers. But the British won the day. In the following year, the British cut off supply movements from southern France and moved against Montreal. By forging an alliance with the Iroquois and cornering a few last French forces at Montreal, the British finally forced the enemy's surrender on September 8, 1760.

Fighting raged on elsewhere in the world for another three years. In the Caribbean, most French possessions fell to the British, and in the Philippines, Manila surrendered to the British in late 1762. Finally, the Treaty of Paris brought the Great War for Empire to an end in early 1763 (see map page 166). Under its terms, France regained its precious sugar islands of Martinique and Guadaloupe in the Caribbean. But it lost all claim to land east of the Mississippi River and gave to Spain (its ally at the end of the war) all French lands to the west of the river, plus the city of New Orleans, the "gateway to North America." Spain also reclaimed the Philippines and Cuba, but it lost the Floridas to Britain in 1763. For decades, Spanish authorities had tried to consolidate their empire's rule in North America over native and migrating populations of Mexico, California, Texas, and New Mexico. The loss of St. Augustine in Florida and the lack of population growth in Louisiana would create serious setbacks to Spain's imperial goals.

Britain, however, gained dominion over vast lands stretching from Hudson Bay to the Caribbean Sea, and from the Atlantic Ocean westward to the Mississippi River. In England, raucous parades and public gatherings celebrated victory against the country's archenemies, Spain and France, both of which were financially crippled and almost completely expelled from North America. In the colonies, the lands stretching to the north and west of older settlements offered tremendous prospects for expansion. In addition, colonists anticipated rapid commercial recovery because their vital connections to West Indies islands and British ports could be resumed. It seemed like a joyous time to identify with the British Empire.

The Death of General Wolfe The British capture of Quebec in 1759 was a turning point in the Seven Years' War. The heroic death of Britain's leading commander, here surrounded by concerned officers and Native American allies on the Plains of Abraham, was elevated to mythic proportions by Benjamin West's painting years later. The painting rallied patriotic fervor in London just as Americans were recovering from the shock of the Boston Massacre. *(National Gallery of Canada, Ottawa.)*

Tensions on the Frontier

The Treaty of Paris gave the British Empire unparalleled claims over new land. But those claims spurred numerous disputes within North America. For example, New Yorkers and New Hampshire residents clashed over the soil that lay east of Lake Champlain. During the 1760s and 1770s Ethan Allen, his Green Mountain Boys, and a rising tide of migrants into this area endured years of conflict with outsiders until they became a new state, Vermont, in 1777. In the 1760s, Pittsburgh and Wheeling became small frontier villages surrounded by quarrelling speculators, officials, and farm families. And farther south, dozens of families settled in remote North Carolina along the Watauga River, where they jostled over land rights for years.

These disputes overlapped with the tensions between Europeans and Native Americans in the land negotiated by the peace treaty. For decades it had been clear that Native Americans did not have the same frontier objectives as Europeans. Throughout the war, alliances between Indians and Europeans also proved elusive and frustrating. For example, in late fall 1759, between three and four thousand Cherokee responded to the persistent wartime violence on their hunting grounds by renouncing their long-term trading alliance with South Carolinians and attacking backcountry colonists. Repeatedly assailed by the Cherokee and their allies, frontier settlers relocated closer to the coastline. When Cherokee bands continued the attacks, British regular troops retaliated by destroying Native American towns along the Appalachian foothills. In 1761 the Cherokee farther west also threatened to overrun Virginia until they, too, were subdued temporarily by British troops. However, for years to come, Cherokee villages sporadically raided backcountry settlers, who in turn demanded more protection from the South Carolina government.

The greatest Indian uprising of all came in the region around the Great Lakes, where Native American grievances had been building ever since the British took possession of the French forts there at the end of 1760. British traders had defrauded tribal members in sales of rum, blankets, and fishing tools, while British soldiers occupied forts on tribal lands, recklessly overhunting and overfishing the resources on which neutral villages depended. Worst of all, the British general Jeffery Amherst abandoned the conventional courtesy of giving "gifts" of kettles, gunpowder, and provisions to secure friendly relations with the Indians. Amherst declared that the midwestern tribes must learn to live "without our charity." As a consequence of this measure, the inhabitants of many villages that depended on British guns and ammunition for hunting nearly starved.

Spurred by these frustrations, a number of young tribal warriors and rising chiefs adopted the teachings of the Algonquian-speaking visionary Neolin. Convinced that Native Americans had been corrupted by European goods, Neolin called for a pan-Indian alliance to drive Europeans from their lands and return to traditional ways. As the alliance grew during 1760–1761, it elevated strong cultural leaders who could motivate large numbers of their people. One of these leaders, the Ottawa chief Pontiac, brought together tribes from Michigan to western New York in May 1763 and led them against the British garrisons west of Fort Niagara. Then thousands of Native Americans proceeded to attack Fort Michilimackinac in upper Michigan and to massacre over two thousand white settlers in the area.

An enraged General Amherst vowed revenge against Pontiac's Rebellion. In a flurry of letters to commanders at western forts reviling the Indians as "vermin" and "ignorant savages," Amherst proposed that the British should spread smallpox through the tribes by offering "gifts" of infected blankets from the Fort Pitt hospital. Captains at Fort Pitt were happy to comply. The resulting epidemic laid waste Delaware, Shawnee, southern Creek, Chickasaw, and Choctaw throughout the southeast.

Ultimately, Pontiac's Rebellion ended with the return of British prisoners, the surrender of some Indian leaders to British courts of justice, and acknowledgment of British political control over the region. Determined to prevent future conflicts, the British ministry also drew a line on maps of the frontier intended to define the limit of European expansion. The Proclamation Line of 1763 (see map page 166) extended from the farthest northern tip of Maine to the southernmost parts of Georgia. Land to the west of the line was off-limits to European settlement or speculation.

Indians along the Appalachian ridge expressed their satisfaction with the terms of the Proclamation Line, but colonists seethed. The war, they fumed, had been won by their long and costly sacrifices, and now the West should be cleared for their use. In Pennsylvania anger rose to a fever pitch, when in December 1763 a group of fifty-seven vigilantes known as the Paxton Boys—predominantly Scots-Irish Presbyterians—marched against Indians at Conestoga, in Lancaster County. Under the mistaken belief that these Indians had been part of Pontiac's Rebellion, the Paxton Boys massacred six of them. Two weeks later, they slaughtered another group of Conestoga Indians who had been offered protection in a public workhouse. In their boldest move, the Paxton Boys ignored their Quaker rulers' pleas that the violence cease and pursued the Moravian Indians near Bethlehem. When the Indians took refuge in Philadelphia, at least six hundred frontier rebels marched into the city, where only Benjamin Franklin's promise to defend frontier land claims against the Indians calmed the disturbance.

Meanwhile, thousands of colonists moved west, unaware that they approached—and then crossed—the Proclamation Line. New Englanders crossed into the northern Green Mountains; New Yorkers poured into Mohawk country; hunters and poor families reached the foothills of Appalachia in Virginia and North Carolina; and hundreds of immigrants began clearing the land that would become Tennessee and West Virginia. Streams of families and individuals looking for farms and grazing lands formed the front guard of this migration. Hard on their heels came the surveyors of influential land companies formed by ambitious speculators in groups such as the Ohio Company. Anticipating that this region would became a great heartland, these companies made claims on millions of acres they hoped to turn into huge profits.

Given the surge of settlement that violated the Proclamation Line's protection of Native Americans, British authorities adjusted their policies. Frontier negotiators began to press the Iroquois and Cherokee to cede lands permanently to the British. The Treaty of Hard Labor, signed in 1768, granted large numbers of European settlers the right to stay on Cherokee lands along the upper Tennessee River. The Treaty of Fort Stanwix later that year determined that the Iroquois would retreat from the Ohio Valley and remain on homelands farther northeast.

In the southern backcountry, formal treaties meant very little. Tensions throughout the 1760s encompassed not only enduring strife between colonists and Indians, but scuffles among colonists as well. In South Carolina, the French and Indian War and the Cherokee struggle left a legacy of violence. Planters and yeomen denounced the raids of highway bandits, runaway slaves, horse thieves, and angry Native Americans against their property. Lacking "proper sheriffs and law," frontier planters organized themselves in 1763 into groups known as the Regulators and took justice into their own hands. Claiming that they had lived for years without political representation, paying high taxes to an eastern establishment that ignored them, the Regulators periodically whipped or taunted outlaws on the fringes of South Carolina society whom they suspected of theft, arson, or simple "vagrancy." In 1769 the colonial legislature set up six new circuit courts in the backcountry. Assemblymen also lowered frontier taxes. But to the end of the colonial era, Regulators in the western counties argued that their representation in the Assembly was inadequate and their safety under constant threat.

North Carolinians asked not for more, but less, government (see Competing Voices, page 196). After 1740, their frontier was increasingly dotted with storekeepers who imported textiles, agricultural implements, and small household items for ambitious small farmers who offered hides, tobacco, corn, tallow, or feathers in exchange. Even so, economic security eluded many farmers. Hundreds of new families built up enough credit to buy slaves and establish tobacco plantations out west, but when tobacco prices plummeted after 1763, storekeepers began to dun farmers for unpaid debts, and eastern authorities raised property taxes to help pay war debts. For struggling and cash-poor farmers, these were frightening times. The situation worsened when sheriffs refused to take country goods as payment for taxes, the colonial government refused to issue sufficient paper money, and frontier farms were seized during 1768 for nonpayment of taxes.

In response, western North Carolinians organized their own Regulator movement and attempted repeatedly to close the county courts that heard cases against debtors. Taxes, argued Regulators, should be levied in proportion to what the land could grow, not according to number of acres a farmer owned. In addition, farmers should be allowed to pay taxes in the goods they produced from the forests and soil. After all, they had little else. In 1769 the North Carolina assembly passed the Johnston Bill, which declared such protests "unlawful rioting" and possibly treasonous against the crown. In 1770 Governor William Tryon raised a large company of eastern militia to march west against the Regulators. In early 1771, over 2,000 Regulators met Tryon and his men at the Battle of Alamance. When the smoke cleared, 29 men were dead and over 150 others wounded. One Regulator was executed on the spot; twelve others were tried later for treason—of whom eight eventually "swung from ropes." But as the treason trials proceeded in the east, violence continued to brew out west on the piedmont. Tryon's petty officials, trying to extract oaths of allegiance to the crown from the nearly seven thousand western North Carolinian families, reported miserable failures.

In the final colonial years, Shawnee Indians north of the Ohio River exerted claims over their historical lands, but Lord Dunmore, the last colonial Virginia governor, sent two expeditions against the Shawnee in 1774. In the melée that is now called Dunmore's War, the Shawnee surrendered their claims to Virginia. But very quickly, two neighboring colonies attempted to grab the Shawnee land now in Virginia's possession. Aggressive Pennsylvanians moved to, and rebuilt, abandoned Harrodsburg, while speculating North Carolinians organized the Transylvania Company in order to occupy land between the Cumberland and Kentucky Rivers. Meanwhile, a prominent planter-judge, Richard Henderson of North Carolina, hired the strapping Daniel Boone to oversee the construction of the first major western roadway, through the Cumberland Gap to the Kentucky River. This Wilderness Road cut a swath through valleys and forests from eastern settlements in North Carolina to the remote posts of Boonesborough and Harrodsburg. This road fueled speculators' efforts to organize a government for the proposed colony of Transylvania, which was to cover most of today's Kentucky. But by 1775, events in the East had taken a turn toward crisis, and colonists turned their attention across the Atlantic more intently than ever.

Rethinking Empire, 1763–1765

After the French and Indian War, the British Empire entered an unprecedented upswing of commercial development that put its people into successful competition with the Dutch, Spanish, and then the French for dominion and resources on four continents. The war also extended British influence across thousands of square miles of new terrain in North America. Soon, England would become the first western nation to enter the Industrial Revolution. This amazing confluence of rising commerce, new dominion, and early industrialization provoked a transatlantic discussion about the role of colonies in the empire: What benefits did colonists enjoy because they were in the empire, and how fully would they share in England's prosperity? To what extent should colonists help defray the costs of the French and Indian War, and help defend frontiers from Spanish and French interests in the future? Following 1763, inhabitants of the British Empire were propelled into an unforeseen, deeply consequential period of discussion about these issues, a period known as the Imperial Crisis.

Markets and Goods

The French and Indian War had a mixed impact on colonists. While some experienced economic opportunities, others encountered one difficulty after another. The war heightened demand in the colonies and England for iron, wood, and textiles, and brought new people into production of war supplies. Before the war's end, new

Iron Foundry of Peter Curtenius Despite Parliament's efforts to regulate colonial production of finished iron goods in 1750, mining and manufacturing developed at a rapid pace in the colonies. In 1767 Peter Curtenius took advantage of colonial demand and nearby sources of timber for fuel and iron ore to build a successful foundry outside New York City. At first, Curtenius's factory focused on making agricultural and household items; by 1775, the enterprise was poised to produce bayonets and small cannon balls for patriots. *(© Collection of the New-York Historical Society.)*

ways to harness water and steam power, new tools to fashion goods, and newly organized factories began to replace traditional small-shop production in England. These changes in turn encouraged new work and consumption habits throughout the empire. Innovative rules changed the ways colonists used their labor and leisure time and separated their workplaces more distinctly from home. New work arrangements in turn made possible the importation and production of more goods, and of higher quality.

After the war colonists imported more household goods—dishware, textiles, cabinets, notions, and the like—from abroad than ever before. By 1765, English merchants were sending about 20 percent of the country's exported manufactures to colonists, who enjoyed greater buying power and rising levels of comfort. Shopkeepers' inventories expanded, newspapers advertised imports from all over the world, and probate records of the deceased listed a startling array of fabrics, trinkets, tools, and furniture.

How did colonists pay for these wants and needs? The answer depends on the colonial region, and the strata of buyers and sellers. In most locales, agricultural exports provided the backbone of credits earned abroad. For a few years after the French and Indian War, western small farmers experienced a devastating decline of tobacco prices. By the final colonial years, tobacco prices recovered and production through the tidewater and frontier counties surged. Scottish investors subsidized the planting of new land in Virginia and Maryland, granted year-long credit to migrating small farmers, and set up stores that provided imported goods and accepted farmers' firkins of cheese, buckets of tar, and bags of feathers, which the storekeeper transported to the coast. Some South Carolina planters rose far above middling means to enjoy lavish lifestyles based on slave labor. Just as Parliament initiated a discussion that reshaped imperial policy toward the colonies, South Carolina planters aggressively marketed larger exports of indigo to England and rice to southern Europe.

The mid-Atlantic breadbasket benefited from a combination of rich soil, ambitious farmers, and a maturing infrastructure of crafts and local markets. Ship after ship departed the northern Chesapeake Bay or Delaware River laden with flour and wheat for the West Indies and southern Europe. After 1765, eastern European production of wheat fell, and England imported large amounts of flour and grain from Philadelphia and New York City. High demand abroad assured colonial farmers and merchants of rising prices, which in turn generated greater efforts to produce for export. The resulting prosperity of the Connecticut, Hudson, and Delaware valleys became obvious to foreign visitors, who marveled at the expansive cultivated fields and the comforts of commercial farming homes. Families pressing onto the frontier of Virginia and Maryland cleared lands to grow not only the ever-present tobacco but also wheat. "We are certain to find markets for our flour in the [Caribbean] islands, and to sell all but our wagon wheels to the merchants," boasted a Maryland miller.

New England producers were more diversified than mid-Atlantic colonists. The northern fisheries employed over four thousand men and over four hundred small craft in harvesting and drying cod and haddock for southern Europeans. New England merchants, sailors, and shipbuilders involved in the West Indies trade supplemented wheat and flour shipments with leather and shoes, shingles and wooden containers, and an array of crafts from Boston, Newport, Providence, Hartford, and Salem. Like New Yorkers, New Englanders invested portions of their fortunes in processing West Indies goods at sugar refineries, rum distilleries, and chocolate "manufactories." New Englanders also carried over half a million gallons of locally distilled rum to foreign buyers after the French and Indian War.

Indeed, colonists seemed to be recovering quickly from the French and Indian War and realizing unheard-of commercial and farming opportunities. Colonial and English writers noticed that items formerly treated as "luxuries," and accessible only to the wealthy, were becoming available to great numbers of middling consumers in America who had a "natural taste to refine their living" after the war. Together, accelerated production, falling prices, and aggressive marketing added up to what many scholars call the "consumer revolution" of the late 1700s.

Not all colonists experienced such rapid recovery after the French and Indian War. Indeed, large numbers of colonists felt the aftershocks of war for years. British troops stationed on the postwar frontier needed food and other necessities that colonists often withheld. Despite Pitt's promises to reimburse colonial war expenses, he authorized less than half of the standing army's continuing costs during the 1760s, which left soldiers with little means for paying their bills. In the cities, artisans and shopkeepers had struggled to fill orders for military goods, often on the promise of payment some time in the future. But after the war, some of them joined the "starving poor with naught but a will to live to sustain them" as they wandered from town to town. Thousands of young sailors lost their lives at sea on privateering vessels, and thousands of fathers and sons did not return home from western fronts. In New York City, Boston, and Philadelphia, the charity dispensed to widows and orphans depleted meager government resources. Small producers complained about shortages of raw materials—wood, leather, and farm by-products—which stymied their work. Consumers complained that wartime prices had soared and then not declined in the peace that followed. Colonists began to realize that although the French and Indian War opened up a huge western space for their future development, it also bequeathed a thick web of debts, unemployment, and uncertain commercial revival.

Individual merchants had made direct loans to colonial governments from their own fortunes, and by 1763, they clamored for repayment. And although some merchants had profited handsomely from raiding enemy ships or smuggling to Cuba, Martinique, or the coastline of Honduras, many had risked their ships and goods and lost everything. Among the merchants who tried to meet colonists' huge demand for imported goods after the war, many fell deeply into debt to English creditors. English creditors usually required silver, gold, or bills of exchange as forms of payment, but colonial merchants often did not have enough of these after the war and frequently failed to make their payments. In 1765 a few of the most reputable merchants of New York and Philadelphia went bankrupt, sending shivers through urban populations and calling forth renewed warnings against consuming "luxuries and superfluities."

Legislating Obedience

The Great War for Empire was a crushing burden to the English treasury. By 1763, the country's debt to soldiers who had been quartered in the colonies, and to creditors who had loaned the government huge sums, approached an unprecedented £130 million. How would such a debt be paid? British officials such as William Pitt, Charles Townshend, and Thomas Pownall—who rose in power along with the progress of the recent war—blamed the North American colonists for the problem. Colonists, they argued in Parliament, had refused to raise sufficient taxes for the war effort. Worse, they had systematically evaded the Acts of Trade and Navigation, elevating smuggling with French possessions to an art. Now, they continued, the empire's prosperity and power depended on enforcing colonial economic obedience and political subordination.

Parliament began to implement its harsher perspective in 1761. It urged colonial governors to clamp down on the illegal entry of foreign goods and end the widespread practice of bribing officials to overlook customs duties. Beginning in Massachusetts, the governor issued documents called Writs of Assistance, which permitted port collectors to inspect the holds of ships and merchants' warehouses for illegal goods. James Otis, a prominent lawyer from a highly reputable family, assailed the writs as an invasion of private property. In a famous argument before the Massachusetts Supreme Court in 1761, Otis insisted that protection of a citizen's private property must be held in higher regard than a parliamentary statute. The writs, Otis argued, violated "the [unwritten] English Constitution," which in turn guarded "customary practice" or "fundamental law"—that is, the basic natural rights of all citizens. But Otis lost his case. Most legal experts at that time did not share Otis's point of view. Instead, they still believed that parliamentary law and custom had equal weight. In addition, the Writs of Assistance case bore on merchants' business, but it did not touch most people's daily affairs directly and so did not attract widespread attention.

The British government continued to pass stringent legislation intended to make colonists subordinate to the interests of the crown and Parliament. In 1761 Lord Bute had been appointed secretary of state and first lord of the treasury by the young King George III (reigned 1760–1820). In 1762, as a step toward halting the illegal trade between colonists and the foreign Caribbean islands, Bute steered the Revenue Act through Parliament. The act prohibited crown-appointed customs officials from subcontracting their jobs to other men, who depended on bribes from merchants to pay the appointed officials for the privilege of holding such positions. The act also authorized royal navy ship captains to seize all British vessels trading at French islands. Bread, shoes, and timber had been "flowing in profitable channels to the popish merchants of the [French] islands," lamented a British soldier, "while our regulars starve in their naked feet" on the American frontier.

Bute resigned in 1763, and the task of shoring up British finances fell to George Grenville. Early in his short term, Grenville became widely unpopular in England because he attempted to arrest a popular parliamentary representative, John Wilkes, for seditious libel against the crown. Although the radical Wilkes fled safely to France, Grenville's actions led to rising public demands for freedom of the press. When Grenville attempted to raise land taxes, wealthy English landowners dug in their heels and refused additional taxes on their estates. In addition, a recession in England made it hard to squeeze middling and lower-rung consumers with higher excise and luxury taxes. The average English consumer or small producer sometimes paid as much as one-third of her or his income to sheriffs and county tax collectors.

By contrast, colonists paid very little, most no more than 5 percent of their incomes, on taxes to local and provincial government; and they seemed to be ordering huge quantities of goods from English merchants following pent-up wartime demand. Indeed, British policymakers believed that colonists were in a better position to help pay the debts of the French and Indian War than were the people of England. But Grenville knew that colonists would resist higher taxes and opposed Parliament's proposal to raise them. The legislation that Parliament passed ensured that colonists would not be asked to defray the British national debt, but only to help offset the cost of keeping ten thousand troops in North America.

But to colonists, Grenville's revenue proposals did not seem mild at all. They already associated him with enforcement of the Proclamation Line and vilification of popular colonial smugglers and privateers. Now, making colonists pay for regiments of the standing army during peacetime seemed authoritarian and unjust. Postwar ministries had vowed they would govern by persuasion and compromise, but Grenville was spouting hard-line mercantilist reasoning that reduced the colonies to minor satellites of the glorious imperial center in London.

In 1764 the Grenville ministry's Sugar Act extended the terms of the Revenue Act. It combined the battle against smuggling with the search for revenue. Crown officials in residence at colonial posts now had to extract huge amounts of paperwork from captains and merchants. Failure to have the proper papers made illicit traders more vulnerable to capture after 1764, and quick prosecution of naval laws in the crown's vice-admiralty courts kept violators away from "democraticall" colonial juries and assemblies.

Colonists loudly protested the Sugar Act's duty of three-pence per gallon on molasses. Since passage of the Molasses Act in 1733 (see page 108), foreign sugar, molasses, and rum had been taxed at higher levels than equivalent British goods in hopes of making British commodities more competitive. But crown officials barely enforced the Molasses Act, so New England merchants bought cheap French and Spanish molasses for their expanding rum distilling enterprises. In this trade, colonial merchants also sold large amounts of farm produce, timber, and flour. As payment, in addition to molasses and sugar, they received silver and paper credit that was used to offset debts to English merchants for the manufactured goods colonists imported. This web of trade was absolutely necessary for the survival of the empire, argued colonial merchants.

Nevertheless, the Sugar Act created conditions that had long-term repercussions for relations between the colonies and England. Unlike earlier mercantilist legislation, the Sugar Act combined explicit revenue-raising provisions with enforcement machinery. The act affirmed the right of royal government to tax the property of colonial merchants and exact their obedience.

Colonists reacted to the Sugar Act swiftly but moderately. The colonial assemblies petitioned for its repeal, but raised no serious challenge to the right of Parliament to regulate and tax them. Only a few voices insisted that "all Taxes ought to originate with the people." Some traders simply evaded the law and continued smuggling with impunity. Others corresponded with fellow merchants, expressing their irritation with the increased number of surprise searches. In New York and Boston, merchants called on urban artisans and shopkeepers to support a movement to halt imports from England until Parliament repealed the Sugar Act. This first attempt to organize a generalized boycott (see page 161) did not win widespread support, however, because the act had little direct impact on most colonists. In a short time, colonists resumed trade as usual.

Shortly thereafter, Parliament sent the Currency Act to the colonies. This measure prohibited colonists from printing any more paper money (see pages 107–108) and ordered the withdrawal of existing colonial currency from circulation by 1769. Merchants in London objected that colonial paper currency reduced the value of British goods when Americans converted their local monies for international exchange. Colonial paper money also violated a central maxim of that era: that all "artificial" currency had to be backed by sufficient "funds" of truly valuable gold and silver. Colonists simply let their currency "float on the crest of public trust," which could collapse at any time under the weight of public and private debt.

Grenville added the Quartering Act in early 1765, which authorized army commanders in the colonies to requisition supplies from assemblies and build barracks for troops or quarter them in public buildings and taverns. Although the act forbid the army from taking over private homes and warehouses—actions that had outraged many Americans when Lord Loudoun commanded French and Indian War forces—soldiers seemed to swarm through northern colonial cities. Already overcrowded and coping with great postwar poverty and joblessness, cities became quite unfriendly places to house redcoats, as we shall see.

Deepening Commitment, Rising Violence, 1765–1770

Until 1765, colonists believed that Parliament's new laws were misguided but justifiable attempts to create commercial and legal order for the mutual benefit of all imperial inhabitants. But subsequent laws seemed to betray different parliamentary intentions and different colonial consequences. Beginning in 1765, new policies disrupted widespread colonial habits of consumption, challenged cherished assembly privileges, and undermined the principle of reciprocal benefits throughout the empire by insisting on colonial subordination to the sovereignty of Parliament. As they experienced the Stamp Act, the Townshend Duties, the Boston Massacre, and the Tea Act, colonists began to see a deliberate design to deprive them of natural liberties.

The Stamp Act Crisis

To house and supply the British troops in the colonies in 1765, the Grenville ministry turned to a common English source of revenue: a stamp tax. Since 1694, fees collected from stamping certain documents or taxing particular commodities had been an important source of revenue in the home country. Even some of the colonies had experimented with stamp taxes from time to time. Why, then, did colonists raise a storm of protest when they received word of Parliament's Stamp Act, due to take effect in 1765?

In part, the sweep of the act was alarming to colonists. The measure levied taxes on court documents, contracts, playing cards, land titles, newspapers, and most other printed items. Even more important, Parliament had imposed a tax on "internal commerce," colonists' daily exchanges of necessary goods and services. Previously, colonists had legislated most of their own domestic tax needs, while Parliament had taxed external affairs, especially international commerce. The Stamp Act shattered this tradition.

Eight colonial assemblies discussed openly the extent of Parliament's authority over them. Although most assemblymen admitted Parliament's right to tax, they differed over whether that authority was absolute or limited. If limited with respect to taxation, then in what other ways might Parliament's power be limited? If absolute, then what was the nature of colonial assembly jurisdiction over revenue? Many voices insisted that although Parliament had sole authority to tax and regulate international commerce, only the provincial assemblies could levy taxes on colonists' internal business and property. For decades, colonists called internal taxes a "gift of the people," delegated to their duly elected representatives, by their free consent. Colonists had gradually conferred on their "little parliaments" in each colony sole authority to initiate money bills, allocate funds for public projects, and set levels of taxation. Even Grenville admitted that colonists should be taxed "only with their own Consent."

Colonists raised still another question: How could they give or withhold consent for parliamentary legislation when they did not have representatives in that body? British leaders countered that parliamentary legislators "virtually" represented everyone in the empire, but this argument did not convince many colonists. Benjamin Franklin proposed that "if you chuse to tax us, give us Members in your Legislature [Parliament], and let us be one People." But officials in England rejected Franklin's idea. Colonists lived too far away to be incorporated into Parliament. In any event, theory and policy held that colonists had to remain subordinate members of the empire.

In May 1765, young Patrick Henry rose in the Virginia assembly to give a radical interpretation of events. Virginians, he stated, enjoyed all the privileges of British citizens in the empire, including the right of self-taxation. No laws that originated outside their colony required Virginians' obedience. The Virginia assembly voted down the Henry plan, but newspapers published his *Virginia Resolves* widely, alongside the many newspaper protests appearing by mid-1765. By then, the Stamp Act had begun to touch the lives of colonists in all economic strata, from city to country, from New England to Georgia. Critics denounced not only the pocketbook effect that the act would have on average citizens, but also its unconstitutional nature.

The Sons of Liberty

Protests against the Stamp Act spread beyond representative assemblies, into the shops, inns, and streets of towns throughout the colonies. In August 1765, a group of merchants, artisans, and shopkeepers in Boston called the Loyal Nine organized

Patrick Henry The young Virginia lawyer and colonial assemblyman was one of the first, and most radical, southerners to become an ardent patriot. Beginning with his authorship of the Virginia Stamp Act Resolution in 1765, and continuing through the stormy final months of the Continental Congress in 1775, Henry never wavered in his zeal for individual rights and popular liberty. *(Colonial Williamsburg Foundation.)*

a mass demonstration of city inhabitants, which marched through the streets and hung an effigy of Andrew Oliver, the colony's stamp distributor. Through the night, bonfires lit up the city and protesters cried for Oliver's resignation. Although Oliver pledged not to enforce the Stamp Act, the crowd's actions continued until the night of August 26, when a mob pulled down the wealthy Lieutenant Governor Thomas Hutchinson's house.

Meanwhile, in New York City, merchants and tradesmen joined together to form the Sons of Liberty, a coalition of urban dissenters who sought to join citizens throughout North America together against the Stamp Act. Sons of Liberty groups formed quickly in every colonial city from Portsmouth, New Hampshire, to Charles Town, South Carolina. Middling colonists joined the Sons in order to play a greater role in politics "out of doors"; some members of the elite joined in hopes of controlling angry mobs. Even the most radical members of the elite, including Christopher Gadsden of Charles Town and Samuel Adams of Boston, worried that the Sons of Liberty would discredit the protest movement by engaging in excessive violence.

Hundreds of colonists joined leaders of the Sons of Liberty at a pan-colonial Stamp Act Congress in New York in October 1765. Delegates from nine colonies formulated a bold "Declaration of Rights and Grievances" that set forth their view of the proper limits of British rule in the colonies. Parliament, the declaration stated, did not have the right to tax colonists without their legislative consent. The delegates demanded repeal of the Stamp and Sugar Acts because they infringed on American "rights and liberties." Merchants, rising smaller traders, and artisan entrepreneurs at the Congress also protested the Stamp Act's undermining of regular trading relations. In October, about two hundred merchants in New York City and Albany called for a nonimportation movement. Several women called "she merchants" joined the protest, and hundreds of consumers in New York agreed that halting merchants' orders for goods would help bring Parliament to its knees. Shortly thereafter, their Boston and Philadelphia compatriots also agreed to suspend orders for English goods. Hundreds of urban merchants, artisans, and consumers signed agreements to boycott British imports and produce more of their own "necessities."

Even with this organized resistance underway, crowds continued more violent activities "out of doors" in 1765. Reports of tarring and feathering officials who supported the Stamp Act appeared up and down the coastline. Peter Oliver, a loyalist to British rule in America, described unruly colonists heating "Tar untill it is thin, & and pour[ing] it upon the naked Flesh . . . After which, sprinkl[ing] decently upon the Tar . . . as many Feathers as will stick to it, Then hold[ing] a lighted Candle to the Feathers."

"Respectable" colonists criticized these activities as the deeds of a "rabble" and a "reptilian mob" that could lead the colonies into "anarchy." But few colonists acted spontaneously or randomly, and most protest actions involved little more than ridicule and ostracism as means of punishing their enemies. Even at times of violence, the Sons of Liberty carefully chose their targets before crowds entered the streets, and the targets tended to be property, not persons. Andrew Oliver and Thomas Hutchinson went unharmed amid mob actions. Jared Ingersoll, a prominent resident of Connecticut, at first opposed the Stamp Act but then volunteered to collect provincial taxes under the law's auspices. Confronted by an angry mob that demanded his resignation, Ingersoll capitulated and returned home peacefully. In November 1765, about three thousand citizens raged through New York's streets crying "Liberty!" and advanced on the homes of British regimental officers; but no harm befell them. That same day, a large crowd threw bricks at New York's Fort George, where a humbled and unharmed Lieutenant Governor Cadwallader Colden agreed to hand over the tax stamps.

This kind of urban crowd behavior had a long tradition in England and its colonies. For generations, Britons had formed mob protests against Catholics and Jews, "usurious" merchants and greedy millers, or prostitutes and excisemen. Every November 5, zealous Protestants burned the pope in effigy and celebrated Catholic Guy Fawkes's failure to destroy English government in 1605. Fishermen, artisans, and laborers in every colonial port had, from time to time, rioted against being forced into the royal navy. In 1765 Stamp Act rioters drew on this varied tradition of joining poor and middling citizens together to protect economic self-interest, jobs, and businesses, and to voice deep-seated fears that crown authority could become overblown and tyrannical. Their arguments and the nature of their popular resistance were not new. However, they occurred more frequently than in the past and contributed to a generalized breakdown of deference toward crown authority.

The frequent cry of "Liberty!" during the Imperial Crisis also sounded familiar to most colonists, for it was the term used for centuries to invoke the individual's birthright to be shielded from governments that tried to usurp life and property. Liberty guaranteed personal rights to acquire and enjoy property, exercise civil responsibilities in society, and defend fellow citizens from internal and external threats to liberty.

Colonists were also familiar with writings that warned them to be vigilant over the delicate balance between good government and power-hungry interests that could corrupt the public good. These republican writings insisted that it was the duty of Parliament to check the crown's tendency to grasp at power, especially in the form of excessive taxes and expensive war chests. In order to detect infringements of liberty, republican representatives had to be selfless and public-spirited, "virtuous" to a fault. In 1765, when colonists raised the cry "Liberty and Property!" they believed Parliament was not protecting their liberties. To the contrary, Parliament had brushed aside colonial consent, denied them direct representation, and passed a series of unjust laws against colonists' property. They rushed into protests, invoking their republican heritage. But at that time, most colonists hoped for repeal of bad laws and a return to normal. Very few of them challenged the authority of Parliament and crown to govern.

By the time the Stamp Act Congress's declaration reached Parliament late in 1765, the king had replaced Grenville with Lord Rockingham, a "softer mind" who viewed America as a continent of vast productive potential and commercial markets for English manufactures. Rockingham agreed with London merchants that colonial nonimportation was seriously harming imperial commercial interests. Along with Old Whigs who favored compromise with colonists, he agreed to work for repeal of the Stamp Act. But hard-liners in Parliament held a majority, and they were incensed at reports of violence against port officials in America. In March 1766, Rockingham and the Old Whigs compromised with the hard-liners: Parliament repealed the Stamp Act but added the Declaratory Act, a strong restatement of its sovereign power to "bind the colonies and people of America in all cases whatsoever."

Colonists greeted news of the Stamp Act's repeal with a mixture of celebration and suspicion. Some believed that the nonimportation movement had forced Parliament to back off. Others pointed to measures that still irritated colonists. The New York assembly, for example, refused to comply with the 1765 Quartering Act. Only in 1767, when Parliament passed a Restraining Act suspending the assembly's activities until it supplied the resident army regiments, did New Yorkers reluctantly obey the law to quarter redcoats.

The Townshend Duties Crisis

Rockingham's ministry collapsed following the repeal of the Stamp Act, and the king appointed William Pitt, the hero of the French and Indian War, as prime minister. Pitt, chronically ill with gout, handed over the ministry to the Chancellor of the Exchequer, Charles Townshend, in 1767. Townshend had served for many years on the Board of Trade, the crown-appointed body that oversaw commercial affairs, and he supported parliamentary hard-liners who wished to tax colonists more. However, Townshend shifted the focus of colonial taxation in two ways. First, instead of using taxes to pay war debts and billet British soldiers in America, he proposed to use them to pay salaries of governors, customs officials, and judges, thereby freeing them from dependence on colonial legislatures. Colonial assemblies stood to lose their hard-won "power of the purse-strings" as political leverage against salaried crown appointees. Second, Townshend diverted revenue collection from internal to external trade, hoping to address colonial complaints about their rights and win their compliance.

However the duties passed by Parliament in 1767 aroused colonial resentments once again. The extensive list of items Townshend proposed to tax—imports such as paper, paint, lead, glass, and tea—would translate into huge financial sacrifices for colonists. Moreover, Parliament established a Board of Customs Commissioners to enforce the Townshend Duties and assigned a number of new customs officials to American ports. Four vice-admiralty courts were set up in Halifax, Boston, Philadelphia, and Charles Town to hear cases of trade violations.

Resistance to the Townshend Duties arose quickly in the colonies. Captains and merchant ship owners became enraged for two reasons. For many of them, smuggling had become a regular part of their trade with the West Indies. Customs officials played directly into their illicit activities by holding out their palms for bribes. Now, the Board of Commissioners would enforce their authority to take one-third the value of every captured smuggling ship and its cargo, and the new vice-admiralty court justices would prosecute captures, earning them little more than colonial wrath. Sailors on board oceangoing ships also harbored deep anger when the new laws went into effect. For generations, crews on merchant ships had been permitted to buy and sell goods "on their own accounts" at ports of call. Merchants and captains accepted this activity as a harmless means of adding to sailors' meager wages. But imperial law now prohibited the sale of any goods that were not written on the official ship's manifest. Although the violence that erupted between sailors and port officials at many colonial ports during 1768 and 1769 may not have been directly related to the Townshend Duties, the new parliamentary laws probably cemented many resentments along the waterfronts.

When port officials entrapped Henry Laurens, a prominent South Carolina exporter, on a minor technicality regarding a ship's entry and recording of cargo, colonists buzzed with indignation. When officials boarded John Hancock's sloop *Liberty* in Boston in June 1768, and subsequently seized it on the grounds that he held undeclared (and thus untaxed) imports in the hold of the vessel, townspeople reacted openly. An angry crowd gathered on the docks, threw the offending agents into the water, and marched to the customhouse to recover stores of goods held there. Hancock, one of North America's wealthiest merchants and a popular wine, paper, tea, and silk smuggler, eventually went to a vice-admiralty court for trial. The conditions under which he was tried outraged Bostonians. No jury heard his case, surly justices employed "judge-made law," prosecution witnesses gave perjured statements, and defense lawyers were denied certain rights in the "crown's court." As word about these conditions spread, the court was forced to drop the case. If such an exalted citizen's property and civil rights could be invaded so easily, asked many Bostonians, how secure could the rights of other "true born Englishmen" be?

The Townshend Duties also prompted colonists to consider whether they should allow any distinction between internal and external taxes. Perhaps, argued some, Parliament's authority over them did not extend to taxation at all. John Dickinson lashed out at the Townshend Act's external duties in his 1768 *Letters from a*

Farmer in Pennsylvania, twelve spicy pieces intended to arouse colonists to resistance once again. Dickinson believed that Parliament was almost always justified in regulating what colonists could trade, and where. On the other hand, it was *never* justified in legislating taxes to raise revenue on their trade without obtaining colonists' consent. Such laws, Dickinson argued, violated colonists' constitutional authority over taxation. Although he used strong words, Dickinson favored petitions and legislative responses to the Townshend Duties rather than violence.

While Dickinson argued about constitutionality, the Sons of Liberty led a new round of street actions in northern cities during 1768, and radical leaders appealed for a more far-reaching reaction to Parliament's new laws. Samuel Adams sent a "circular letter" to all the colonial assemblies in North America, proposing a united plea for repeal of the Townshend Duties and another pan-colonial congress. The Massachusetts assembly approved Adams's document, and the Virginia assembly replied enthusiastically. However, a copy reached the king's close advisers on the Privy Council, which ordered colonial governors to suspend the assemblies in the event of any organized challenge to the Townshend Duties. Meanwhile, Lord Hillsborough, the British secretary of state for the colonies, demanded that Massachusetts governor Francis Bernard force the assembly to rescind its approval of the circular letter. But Hillsborough timed his order poorly: ninety-two Massachusetts representatives affirmed the demand for repeal (only seventeen remained loyal to the crown) in June 1768, just as Hancock's trial proceeded. In both assembly and courts, said colonists, Parliament was assaulting "the cause of liberty," and "92" became a symbol throughout the colonies of resistance to arbitrary rule.

Colonists also organized another nonimportation movement in response to the Townshend Duties. In fall 1768, boycotters from Charles Town and Williamsburg in the South, to Philadelphia, New York, and Boston in the North, coordinated pledges to halt importation. Once again, merchants hoped to reduce the glut of goods in their warehouses. In addition, hundreds of shopkeepers, artisans, and housewives pledged to abstain from buying British goods for one year beginning January 1, 1769. Local newspapers printed the names of merchants who continued to import goods, and men and women vandalized stores in which retailers sold recently arrived British wares. Broadsides posted around Boston praised small producers and women for rejecting the corrupting influence of British "luxury and dissipation" and the goods "dumped on them, draining their very Livlihoods." During 1769, colonial imports fell by about 40 percent.

Unlike the first nonimportation movement, the second one brought together colonists of every social layer, in all regions, and in very large numbers. The boycott drew in consumers and small producers who never paid port duties or wrote orders to London merchants, but who dreaded the rising prices for items covered under the new acts. Daughters of Liberty, women of elite and middling means, denounced tea consumption in 1769. By early 1770, numerous rural women joined them and pledged to drink only "rye coffee" sweetened with maple syrup from their own woodlots. In Boston in early 1770, over three hundred "ladies of patriotic leanings" vowed to forgo imported sugar, tea, coffee, molasses, and "other superfluities." Women in New York City issued statements of solidarity to merchants, noting that their boycott of British imports was crucial to the movement's victory. In Providence, Rhode Island, women met regularly in public places to spin, while rural women in other northern locales announced their intentions to learn "the arts of weaving," a trade traditionally associated with men. Indeed, cloth making became more than a household task: when whole townships encouraged production of "homespun" and kept track of their collective progress, spinning and weaving became political activities. By denying their households the use of certain imports and supporting community textile production, hundreds of women were brought into public political participation. In all, thousands of colonists took another step toward translating their economic potential into a confident political community. Moreover, they began to associate the different roles of various colonists with a unified movement. For the first time, a number of colonists also identified people who joined nonimportation as "patriots," or defenders of longstanding political liberties against tyrannical encroachments from Parliament.

Toward Independence, 1770–1773

While the responses to the Townshend Duties gained momentum, merchants and policymakers in England grew ever more concerned about how to restore imperial political authority. Together, colonial protest movements and the crisis of imperial rule created mounting fears on both sides of the Atlantic. Added to the organized protests and official policies, however, was the increasing level of tension leading to persistent scuffles in the streets, bitter dialogues in the newspapers, and unforeseen bloodshed years before colonists declared political independence.

The Boston Massacre

Lord North became prime minister in 1769. Although he was a firm believer in Parliament's absolute sovereignty over the colonies, North was also aware that nonimportation was creating serious commercial and political difficulties throughout the empire. On March 5, 1770, North stood before Parliament to seek partial repeal of the Townshend Duties. An ocean away on the same day, British troops killed five civilians in Boston.

Circumstances had been building toward the Boston Massacre for some time. Since October 1768, Bostonians had tolerated some 1,700 British troops living and mustering within their town of about 18,000 people. Citizens walking to and from jobs, markets, and taverns constantly encountered armed sentries and off-duty redcoats. Townspeople resented that rank-and-file soldiers were permitted to compete for scarce jobs and accepted wages lower than desperate local laborers needed for survival. Children, many of them war orphans, wiled away hours taunting redcoats; tippling soldiers picked fights at night in alleys. It did not help that Samuel Adams fueled bad tempers by circulating his own inflammatory printed versions of incidents, or that crown officials deliberately strolled on the commons with off-duty soldiers in their scarlet uniforms.

Word reached Bostonians in January 1770 that violence had erupted in New York City. Laborers, artisans, and young orphans had turned to violence against redcoats garrisoned there. British troops answered by tearing down the city's Liberty Pole, the rallying point in many colonial towns for planning protest activities, sharing information, and posting notices of general political importance. A week of clashes between citizens and soldiers ensued in what historians call the Golden Hill riots.

On February 22, 1770, Boston events heated up, too. Several children pelted the home of a townsman known to have informed against smugglers. The informer leaned out of a second story window and fired his gun into the crowd, killing a young boy. A mammoth funeral procession, organized by the tireless Sam Adams, channeled the public outrage temporarily. But on March 2, local rope makers and carpenters harassed, then beat, three soldiers seeking work at John Hancock's wharf. The number of mobbing laborers and soldiers grew quickly until a commanding officer intervened and took his men back to their barracks.

Then after a weekend of relative calm, citizens and soldiers collided violently. The evening of March 5 was moonless and especially frigid. Despite the cold, a large crowd began to congregate near the customhouse—long a symbol of hated taxes and crown authority—where a lone sentry stood at his post. Children threw snowballs and shouted insults at him, as they had on previous occasions. But this night, the crowd grew to alarming proportions, and the sentry called for help from a barracks nearby. Captain Preston and seven soldiers arrived shortly, positioned themselves in front of the sentry, and held their firearms in a half-cocked position. Although Preston appealed to a number of Boston gentlemen to help disperse the crowd, his men grew restless as heckling youngsters dared them to shoot. At a certain point, someone shouted "Fire!" and as one soldier tripped over a chunk of ice, his gun went off. The other soldiers also fired, though without any order to do so. When the smoke cleared, eleven citizens had been hit. Five of them died, including a sailor of mixed Indian and African-American descent named Crispus Attucks.

No British soldier could fire on civilians without an order from a civil magistrate, even in self-defense, under penalty of hanging. As a military commander, Preston lacked the authority to give such a command. So who could have shouted "Fire!" on that bloody night? Perhaps one of the boys unintentionally pushed an overwrought soldier over the edge. Perhaps Sam Adams used the opportunity to escalate city tensions to a breaking point. In any event, the soldiers retreated to Castle William in the city's harbor. In the months to come, colonial lawyers John Adams and Josiah Quincy, Jr., defended Captain Preston and six of his men against murder charges. The court acquitted all but two of the soldiers; these two received "benefit of clergy," or a branding on their thumbs, and were released.

The Boston Massacre shook colonists everywhere. Where, asked inhabitants as far away as Georgia, would the standing army's potential for tyranny over innocent civilians lead next? Were these murders, asked frontier people at Fort Pitt, the inevitable outcome of Parliament's ill-conceived designs and laws against colonists? James Bowdoin, a future Massachusetts governor, penned *A Short Narrative of the Horrid Massacre in Boston* to circulate the view that British soldiers had planned the assault for some time. Engraver Paul Revere did his part, too, to produce an exaggerated version of the massacre. He illustrated a popular broadside showing the soldiers firing point-blank, together, into a defenseless crowd. Sam Adams organized yet another funeral attended by thousands of Bostonians.

The Boston Massacre As this reproduction of Paul Revere's engraving of the event shows, the soldiers and citizens were crowded into a small commons as tempers flared the night of March 5. The accuracy of this depiction of the massacre is questionable, however, since written depositions at the trial indicate the soldiers did not fire in unison and no command to fire was issued formally by an officer such as the one in this image. *(Library of Congress.)*

The Problem with Tea

At Lord North's urging, Parliament repealed all the Townshend Duties except the one on tea in April 1770. The tea tax would remind colonists of Parliament's sovereignty. Most colonial merchants sighed with relief, since repeal meant they could claim nonimportation a victory and place orders for goods from English firms to restore their depleted inventories. The Sons of Liberty, supported by many artisans, requested that nonimportation continue until Parliament repealed all legislation passed after 1763, but consumers wished to purchase imports again, and the movement declined by late summer 1770. When the Quartering Act expired and Parliament repealed portions of the Currency Act during late 1770, colonists took little notice and instead returned to business as usual.

Then, in 1772, tensions between spheres of the empire arose again. Early in the year, the British schooner *Gaspée* ran aground near Providence, Rhode Island.

Already the vessel's crew had earned notoriety in New England because they had arrested colonists who violated the Sugar Act, plundered unwary colonial vessels at sea, demanded bribes at port entrances, and preyed on coastal villages for supplies and shelter. Exasperated local populations could not resist going out, under cover of night, to burn the *Gaspée* to the waterline. British authorities dispatched a commission to round up suspects and take them to England for an admiralty trial—a blatant violation of colonists' right to a trial by civil jury.

While the residents of Providence made sure that the commissioners found no suspects, the local "Committee of Correspondence" warned neighboring colonies about the incidents. The Providence committee was one of many being formed by 1772 in New England towns, and eventually in all of the colonies, to spread information and tie colonists of the interior to leaders in coastal towns. Resistance leaders sitting in colonial assemblies used the committees as conduits of propaganda to tens of thousands of widely scattered farmers and craftsmen. Once people were linked in this way, they also began to take sides on important issues and commit themselves to a broadening resistance movement. In March 1773, Thomas Jefferson, Richard Henry Lee, and Patrick Henry urged Committees of Correspondence to report regularly "to all parts of the mainland."

Then, in May 1773, Parliament's Tea Act shattered colonists' hope for repeal of the odious duty and restoration of constitutional equilibrium in the empire. The British East India Company, one of the two largest corporations in the world at that time and holding a monopoly on English tea importation from the East Indies, hovered on the brink of bankruptcy due to financial mismanagement at home and misguided military engagements in India. Since some Parliamentary representatives held many shares in the company, they were keen to save it from ruin. As a result, company directors and key spokesmen in Parliament together agreed that colonists must cease their extensive smuggling and buy more company tea. Lord North, convinced that the East India Company was a pillar of England's international commerce and defender of the nation's interests in India, accepted this reasoning. Americans, North insisted, must buy tea only from the company, and port officials must suppress all smuggling into the colonies from the Dutch and French. To these ends, Parliament passed the Tea Act, which waived the company's obligation to pay import duties at English ports and permitted the company to sell tea directly to colonists without colonial middlemen interfering. How, asked American merchants, could they possibly compete against such blatant favoritism and the Company's resulting low tea prices?

North and his supporters in Parliament expected colonists eagerly to choose the cheaper East India Company tea. But in the heightened ideological climate of 1773, a far different dynamic resulted. The committees of correspondence quickly spread news of the Tea Act. Parliament's new offense, said committee literature and newspapers, was no less than a conspiracy to abolish the economic and political rights of colonists. The Tea Act, argued writers from Boston to Charles Town, took away colonists' right to consent to all legislative acts. Their response should be a complete boycott of East India Company tea and intercolonial agreement to turn around all East India Company ships headed to their shores. In New York City and Philadelphia, merchants gained promises from harbor pilots not to admit tea ships. In Philadelphia and Newport, broadsides posted on trees and taverns warned of "warm pots of tarr and feathers" for selling tea. Uneasy company agents wisely resigned their commissions.

In late November 1773, an East India Company ship named the *Dartmouth* entered Boston harbor with 114 chests of tea. Customs officers inspected the vessel and announced that the owners and captain had twenty days to pay the required Townshend Duty taxes on their tea, just as all legal colonial importers did. If they failed to pay, the cargo would be seized and sold at auction. Two more ships with another 128 chests of East India Company tea entered the port. A New England Quaker merchant owned one of them. Rather than violate the patriots' agreement to resist the Tea Act, he announced his intention to return his ship, and the offending goods, to England. Boston leaders John Hancock and Sam Adams, who feared that disgruntled citizens would take matters into their own hands, pleaded with Lieutenant Governor Hutchinson to release the Quaker merchant's ship.

Hutchinson, however, was determined to enforce the Tea Act. Already, Stamp Act rioters had destroyed his house; the Sons of Liberty had stolen his private correspondence in 1768 and smeared his reputation; and the legislature regularly threatened to withhold his salary. So he was not surprised when, on December 16, just hours before the twenty-day deadline, thousands of Bostonians gathered at a public meeting to denounce him. About fifty men from the crowd dressed as Mohawk Indians and headed for the wharf, followed by huge numbers of others. In the next few minutes, a few of the disguised colonists boarded the *Dartmouth* and hacked forty-five tons of tea out of their wooden crates. Authorities later estimated the value of the tea dumped into the harbor at a staggering £10,000. When the Boston Tea Party ended, people simply returned to their homes.

"The Bostonians Paying the Excise-Man" This London cartoonist's view of disorderly conduct was intended to arouse British opposition to colonial demands. Here, under the symbolic Liberty Tree, on which the Stamp Act is nailed upside-down, colonists of various classes tar and feather a tax collector and force tea down his throat. In the background, a tea party is under way. *(Library of Congress.)*

Tea parties took place in Annapolis, Maryland; Perth Amboy, New Jersey; New York City; and other coastal ports. Shocked when he heard the news, George III warned Lord North that the issue was whether "we have, or have not, any authority in that country." "Concessions," stormed the king, "have made matters worse." In the spring of 1774, Parliament responded with four Coercive Acts—colonists called them the Intolerable Acts. On April 1 the Port Bill closed Boston's harbor until colonists paid for the ruined tea, a measure Parliament knew would throw the city into economic distress. The Government Act annulled the colonial charter, made upper house delegates subject to the governor's appointment rather than election, and restricted town meetings to one a year under the governor's supervision. A new Quartering Act ordered the colony to garrison soldiers in barracks or private homes. The Administration of Justice Act (colonists called it the Murder Act) permitted crown officials who had been accused of serious crimes to be tried in courts outside the mainland colonies.

The crown hoped to make Massachusetts an example to the other colonies with this combination of acts, which attacked almost every cherished political and legal ideal in North America. But the plan backfired. A new round of violence ensued in northern cities. In Boston, John Malcolm, a port collector notorious for extorting money from importers, experienced "how well he appeared in black tarr and coop feathers" in fall 1774. George Washington, in Virginia, responded to news of the Coercive Acts much as many others did: "The cause of Boston . . . is . . . the cause of America." The New York assembly declared the acts a "hostile invasion" and agreed to send food to besieged Boston. From many regions, Massachusetts citizens received words of support and wagonloads of supplies.

Quickly on the heels of these acts, Parliament passed the Quebec Act of 1774. Although the Proclamation of 1763 stipulated that French people in Quebec would have a governor and elected assembly similar to most British colonies, the Quebec Act granted Canadians freedom of religion, restored old French civil law, allowed Canadians to hold crown appointed offices, and extended the jurisdiction of Quebec's governor into the Ohio Valley. American colonists' anger flared not only because the act encouraged the spread of "papacy" close to their own borders, but also because it permitted Canadian expansion into the area closed to Americans by the Proclamation of 1763. Virginia and Pennsylvania land speculators who had long coveted the rich Ohio lands for colonists worried that they would not be able to renegotiate the terms of the Proclamation Line. In addition, land covered by the Quebec Act fell within Virginia's charter privileges to expand "from sea to sea." Virginians immediately declared the Quebec Act "utter despotism," clear proof of Parliament's plot to deprive Americans of their "true English liberties."

Forging a Political Community, 1774–1775

By 1774, many colonists had joined repeatedly in protests against the actions of Parliament or local royal officials. Many regularly participated in committees that gave increasingly coherent expression to colonists' grievances. A significant minority of colonists moved steadily closer to understanding that their time in the

British Empire was probably limited. But in 1774 political relations in the empire reached a qualitatively new stage when Parliament passed a comprehensive set of laws to assert its sovereignty. A congress of colonial delegates met and replied to this new level of parliamentary "tyranny" with joint statements and pan-colonial organizations. When dozens of soldiers and citizens shed blood at Lexington and Concord in 1775, colonists were already much closer to forging a political community separate from their imperial inheritance.

The First Continental Congress

In September 1774, the First Continental Congress convened in Philadelphia. In the first intercolonial meeting since the Stamp Act Congress of 1765, fifty-five elected delegates from twelve colonies (excepting Georgia, Florida, Quebec, and Nova Scotia) met to discuss the Coercive Acts. The delegates agreed on their solemn purpose: suffering alike from Parliament's "tyranny laid against our liberties," they needed to formulate a common response. They readily acknowledged their differences of religious persuasion, territorial claims, professional training, sectional economic interests, and political beliefs. These differences had produced petty jealousies and conflicting perspectives in the past and could render the Congress totally ineffective. While each delegate risked losing the confidence of people who had sent him to these 1774 deliberations if he did not satisfy their local interests, each of them also understood the need to identify a unifying cause.

Delegates first established that each colony would have one vote, ensuring a basic equality among all the provinces. They then discussed a bold document brought by the Massachusetts delegates. These "Suffolk Resolves" declared colonial resistance to the Coercive Acts and announced preparations for a military defense against British tyranny. Delegates from New York, Pennsylvania, and Delaware did not yet wish for such far-reaching rejecting of Parliament's authority over them. Pennsylvania's moderate Joseph Galloway proposed instead a "Grand Council" that combined colonial and imperial authority for governing and taxing throughout the empire. John Adams spoke for a more radical point of view: the time for shared rule had passed, he asserted, and the Galloway plan was a vain hope for reconciliation. In October, Virginia delegate Patrick Henry voiced an emerging belief in a new identity that opposed British rule when he declared, "I am not a Virginian, but an American."

Delegates compromised these points of view in preparing a Declaration of Rights that condemned the actions of Parliament while still recognizing the king's sovereignty over them. In the declaration, the Continental Congress underscored that all colonists enjoyed certain rights, which were secured by "the immutable laws of nature, the principles of the English constitution, and the several charters" originally granted to the colonies. While Parliament had the right to regulate imperial commerce, efforts to destroy colonial systems of justice with new admiralty courts, to decree internal taxes, to close their assemblies, or to revoke crown charters were unmistakable signs of Parliament's utter corruption. Colonists had rehearsed these ideas many times in the preceding years, but in 1774 their unified voice in a delegated Congress added significant weight to the charges.

Without waiting for the king's reply, Congress initiated a third economic boycott in early 1774. A broad intercolonial Association Agreement urged colonists to halt importation of British goods after December 1, cease exportation of colonial commodities to England after September 1, 1775, and pledge themselves to nonconsumption of English goods. The association urged colonists to "encourage frugality, economy, and industry, and promote agriculture, arts and the manufactures of this country." Further, delegates "discountenance[d] and discourage[d] every species of extravagance and dissipation," including many of the gentry's public entertainments, and they called on all "virtuous countrymen" to "break off all dealings" with violators.

Congress's declaration and association were important new steps beyond local and colonial Committees of Correspondence and toward shaping a national political community. The delegates' endlessly busy committees laid the basis for much wider public deliberation that spilled over into pamphlets and newspapers that circulated across colonial boundaries. Hundreds of Daughters of Liberty made homespun wool and produced substitutes for imported goods. Women in areas committed to the association eagerly enforced its provisions. For example, in October 1774, fifty-one North Carolina women declared their "sincere adherence" to the association by abstaining from drinking tea and affirming their "duty" to do "everything as far as lies in our power" to uphold the "publick good." Even after official nonimportation ended, women from dozens of small towns urged their neighbors to continue with modest forms of dress, scaled-down funerals, and less ornate holiday celebrations as signs of patriotic support.

When the crown dismantled provincial governments beginning in 1775, thereby severing relations between governors and the people, the habit of working through independent committees became stronger than ever. Thousands of colonists helped forge a new intercolonial identity by joining these committees, declaring beliefs openly, and punishing those who wavered or disagreed. In order to enforce the association and convene special courts to hear cases of infractions, Congress authorized Committees of Observation and Safety. These same organizations called out local and colonial militia companies from time to time, and they became important testing grounds for the new language of *nation, America,* and *states.* Large numbers of colonists still had not chosen between remaining in the empire or declaring political independence. Nevertheless, they took a significant step toward independence in early 1775 when various colonies formed "provincial congresses," or new legislatures, which established a dual authority alongside the governments still run by royal governors.

Lexington and Concord

Although many colonists concluded during 1774 that they could no longer live happily in the British Empire, when did large numbers of them relinquish their identity as British subjects and call themselves Americans? The answer varies, depending on the colonists' region, political and religious persuasion, and social and economic condition. Many continued to hope that the Association Agreement and Declaration of Rights would restore harmony in the empire, and long after 1775, indecision and shifting commitments marked colonial politics. But certainly in the early months of 1775, the patriotic cause gained large numbers of firm supporters.

"A Society of Patriotic Ladies at Edenton in North Carolina" The British scorned women's involvement in public patriotic activities, as this London caricature makes clear. Here women are portrayed in many unflattering or scandalous poses, neglecting their children, mixing with slaves, and drinking heavily while they put their signatures to the Continental Congress's Association Agreement. *(Library of Congress.)*

Parliament once again discussed whether to punish the colonies or to seek a compromise. Hard-liners favored sending more troops to rein in the "unruliness of our children in America," and in early 1775 they pushed through legislation to restrict commerce to and from the colonies. William Pitt tried to soften these measures, but Parliament voted him down. In March, Edmund Burke, a parliamentary representative from Bristol and long a friend of merchants and great landed families in the colonies, eloquently appealed for conciliation. Further coercion, he insisted, would only alienate colonists from imperial authority. When authorities replace dialogue with military force, Burke reminded Parliament, "the cement is gone, the cohesion is loosened, and everything hastens to decay and dissolution." Far away in Virginia, assemblyman Patrick Henry made another impassioned speech at almost the same moment. "Is life so dear or peace so sweet as to be purchased at the price of chains and slavery? Forbid it, Almighty God! I know not what course others may take, but as for me, give me liberty or give me death!"

In Massachusetts, local militia members drilled frequently and towns stockpiled arms. The Committee of Safety, organized by the rebel provincial government, ordered the militia to be prepared to "rise up in a minute's alarm," hence the name minutemen. From Boston, Governor Thomas Gage responded to a rumor that activities had centered a few miles to the west in Concord. On April 18, 1775, he ordered about seven hundred British troops to seize supplies there. Riding quickly "to sound the alarm," Paul Revere and William Dawes warned colonists in towns along the road out of Boston that the British were approaching. At Lexington, about seventy minutemen met the redcoats, and after an inconclusive few rounds, eight colonists lay dead and one redcoat wounded. The British soldiers marched on to Concord, where they torched supplies and leveled a Liberty Pole. The smoke alarmed neighboring farmsteads, and soon great numbers of people flocked toward Concord. Over the next few hours, hundreds of minutemen and other citizens fired their muskets on the British redcoats. Refusing to fight in European-style formation, the minutemen used the camouflage of trees and stone walls, hid in barns, and popped out of farm buildings to fire repeatedly at the retreating regulars. By the end of the day, 73 redcoats lay dead along the sixteen miles of road back to Boston, and over 200 were wounded or missing; of the nearly 4,000 militiamen, 95 died. On the following day, thousands of Bostonians and country inhabitants came together to seize the British garrison. British troops and officials began evacuating the city by sea. Clearly, colonists had entered a new phase of resistance. But would it become a movement for independence?

CONCLUSION

In the wake of the French and Indian War, a series of events unfolded in mainland North America that at first seemed unrelated. Frontier violence erupted into the Cherokee War, the Paxton Boys' march on Philadelphia, the Regulator movements, and tenants' riots in many colonies. Urban tensions rose, too, some of them due to the usual postwar difficulties of reconstructing the economy, and others to the particularly heavy strains of this last imperial war in North America. Seen individually, or from a significant distance, any particular event could be viewed as one of the growing pains of an expanding and prospering people. Besides, asked many colonists, what did the affairs of a shoemaker have to do with those of an indigo planter? What did the troubles of Rhode Island have to do with those of South Carolina? At the end of the French and Indian War, colonists shared new lessons about paying for expensive imperial wars and the differences between their colonial militia and the British standing army. But within North America, their political and cultural identities remained separate.

Slowly, however, colonists began to perceive patterns in Parliament's thinking and actions toward them, and to experience patterns in their own responses to the tightening reins of political control over them. During the Imperial Crisis, Parliament moved beyond former disconnected policies to create a more deliberate plan for ruling the colonies. Its postwar legislation came in quicker succession than previous ones; its policies invaded colonial property and rights more thoroughly than previous laws. From the mid-1760s to the mid-1770s, colonists detected an intentional effort to suppress their liberties, and as their fears of tyranny grew, their protests intensified.

During the Imperial Crisis, transatlantic legislation and debate fueled profound political and cultural changes in colonial identity. At first, colonists relied on traditional forms of resistance: petitions, verbal appeals, pressure on neighbors and shopkeepers. As the frustrations of the Imperial Crisis continued, however, colonists added new forms of resistance, or intensified familiar ones: the Sons of Liberty, nonimportation boycotts, networks of committees, mob intimidation, personal violence. Public political activities also incorporated greater numbers of women of all classes, artisans, and servants. These would provide the seeds of a new, American, identity. Yet even in 1775, colonists remained fragmented in important ways. It was not yet clear that enough citizens wanted independence to declare a separation from the empire, nor did colonists envision what kind of society and governing structure might replace the British system. And most colonists did not yet think of themselves as "Americans."

SUGGESTED READINGS

Fred Anderson, *The Crucible of War: The Seven Years' War and the Fate of Empire in British North America, 1754–1766* (1999), is the most recent reappraisal of the immensely important events of those years. Another social look at the ranks is in Sylvia R. Frey, *The British Soldier in America: A Social History of Military Life in the Colonial Period* (1981). For political and social aspects of the French and Indian War, compare the important contributions of Naomi Griffiths, *The Contexts of Acadian History, 1686–1784* (1992); Francis Jennings, *Empire of Fortune: Crowns, Colonies, and Tribes in the Seven Years' War in America* (1988); and Howard Peckham, *Pontiac and the Indian Uprising* (1947).

For colonial discord on the frontier in the 1760s, see Richard M. Brown, *The South Carolina Regulators* (1963); Richard Beeman, *The Evolution of the Southern Backcountry* (1984); David Corkran, *The Cherokee Frontier: Conflict and Survival, 1740–1762* (1966); Bernard Bailyn, *Voyagers to the West: A Passage in the Peopling of America on the Eve of the Revolution* (1986); and Michael McConnell, *A Country Between: The Upper Ohio Valley and its People, 1724–1774* (1992).

Parliament's reassessment of the role of colonies is covered admirably in Thomas C. Barrow, *Trade and Empire: The British Customs Service in Colonial America* (1967); John Brewer, *Party Ideology and Popular Politics at the Accession of George III* (1976); W. A. Speck, *Stability and Strife: England, 1714–1760* (1977); and Robert Calhoon, *Dominion and Liberty: Ideology in the Anglo-American World* (1994).

For a readable account of the first legislation of the Imperial Crisis, and colonial responses, see Edmund Morgan and Helen Morgan, *The Stamp Act Crisis* (1965), and Ian Christie, *Crisis of Empire* (1966). For the Sons of Liberty, see especially Peter Shaw, *American Patriots and the Rituals of Revolution* (1981). For the deepening crisis in the late 1760s, see especially Michael Kammen, *Empire and Interest: The American Colonies and the Politics of Mercantilism* (1970), and for the increasingly violent 1770s see Hiller B. Zobel, *The Boston Massacre* (1970); Benjamin W. Labaree, *The Boston Tea Party* (1974); and Stephen E. Lucas, *Portents of Rebellion: Rhetoric and Revolution in Philadelphia, 1765–1776* (1976).

The process of coalescing colonial patriots and weeding out loyalists is covered in Ian Christie and Benjamin Labaree, *Empire or Independence, 1760–1776* (1976); David Ammerman, *In the Common Cause: American Response to the Coercive Acts of 1774* (1974); Richard D. Brown, *Revolutionary Politics in Massachusetts: The Boston Committees of Correspondence and the Towns, 1772–1774* (1970); David Conroy, *In Public Houses: Drink and the Revolution of Authority in Colonial Massachusetts* (1995); and Janice Potter, *The Liberty We Seek: Loyalist Ideology in Colonial New York and Massachusetts* (1983).

For the last phases of radicalization, see John Shy, *Toward Lexington: The Role of the British Army in the Coming of the American Revolution* (1965); Robert Gross, *The Minutemen and their World* (1976); and T. H. Breen, *Tobacco Culture: The Mentality of the Great Tidewater Planters on the Eve of the American Revolution* (1985). On the limits of radicalization, see Jay Fliegelman, *Prodigals and Pilgrims: The American Revolution Against Patriarchal Authority, 1750–1800* (1982), and A. Roger Ekirch, *"Poor Carolina": Politics and Society in North Carolina, 1729–1776* (1981).

Competing Voices

The Southern Frontier Erupts

Regulators Explain Their Grievances, 1769

Repeated clashes with Native Americans west of the colonial lines of settlement became an integral part of the Imperial Crisis. On the southern frontier, Regulator movements of discontented frontier settlers grew strong in South Carolina and North Carolina by the late 1760s. Regulators demanded representation in the colonial government, regular legislative and legal government, and recognition of their expansionist land claims against Native Americans. In North Carolina, these grievances combined with hatred of coastal planters. Finally, in January 1771, rural rioters were declared guilty of treason by the colonial assembly, and in May at the Battle of Alamance, vigilante violence escalated into war. North Carolina Regulators from the town of Salisbury justified their protests in an open letter to the colony.

To the Inhabitants of the Province of North-Carolina
Dear Brethren,

Nothing is more common than for Persons who look upon themselves to be injured than to resent and complain.... Excess in any Matter breeds Contempt; whereas strict Propriety obtains the Suffrage of every Class. The Oppression of inferior Individuals must only demand Tutelage of superiors; and in civil Matters our Cries should reach the authoritative Ear....

The late Commotions and crying Dissatisfactions among the common People of this Province, is not unknown nor unfelt by any thinking Person. No Person among you could be at a Loss to find out the true Cause. I dare venture to assert you [are] all advised to the Application of the Public Money; these you saw misapplied to the enriching of Individuals, or at least embezzled in some way without defraying the publick Expenses. Have not your Purses been pillaged by the exorbitant and unlawful Fees taken by Officers, Clerks, etc.... Have you not been grieved to find the Power of our County Courts so curtailed, that scarce the Shadow of Power is left[?] ... In Consequence ... very small Sums drags us to Superior Courts ... many at the Distance of 150 Miles. Add to this a double Fee to all Officers....

For what End was the Jurisdiction of the Courts reduced to such narrow Limits? Is it not to fill the Superior Houses with Business?... Is it not evident, that this was calculated for the Emolument of Lawyers, Clerks, &ct. What other Reason can be assigned for this amazing Scheme? none Brethren, none! ...

Exorbitant, not to say unlawful fees, required and assumed by Officers, the unnecessary, not to say destructive Abridgement of a Court's Jurisdiction, the enormous Encrease of the provincial tax unnecessary; these are Evils of which no Person can be insensible....

But whence received they this Power? Is not their Power delegated from the Populace? ... we have chosen Persons to represent us to make Laws, etc. whose former Conduct and Circumstance might have given us the highest Reason to expect they would sacrifice the true Interest of their Country to Avarice, or Ambition, or both.... [But] is it not evident their own private Interest is, designed in the whole train of our Laws? ... What can be expected from those whose ... highest Study is the Promotion of their Wealth? ...

... [As] you have now a fit Opportunity, choose for your Representatives or Burgesses such Men as have given you the strongest Reason to believe they are truly honest: Such as are disinterested, publick spirited, who will not allow their private Advantage once to stand in Competition with the publick Good ... let them be such as enjoy no Places of Benefit under the Government; such as do not depend upon Favour for their Living, nor do derive Profit or Advantage from the intricate Perplexity of the Law.

Are you not sensible, Brethren, that we have too long groaned in Secret under the Weight of these crushing Mischiefs? How long will ye in this servile Manner subject yourselves to Slavery? Now shew yourselves to be Freemen, and for once assert your Liberty and maintain your Rights....

Have they not monopolized your Properties; and what is wanting but Time to draw from you the last Farthing? Who that has the Spirit of a Man could endure this? Who that has the least Spark of Love to his Country or to himself would bear the Delusion?

In a special Manner then, let us, at this Election, rose all our Powers to act like free publick spirited Men....

Address of the Inhabitants of Anson County to Governor Martin. 1776

Just six years after Regulators of western North Carolina deluged the colonial assembly with such petitions, hundreds of the same colonists signed petitions expressing their "loyal support of his Majesty in America." Following the Battle of Alamance, many backcountry residents continued to seethe with discontent because coastal leaders still ignored their demands. Their western discontent against eastern leaders easily turned into their loyalist opposition to the patriot planters in 1776, as the following outline of Regulator grievances explains.

Most Excellent Governor:

Permit us, in behalf of ourselves, and many others of His Majesty's most dutiful and loyal subjects within the County of Anson, to take the earliest opportunity of addressing your Excellency, and expressing our abomination of the many outrageous attempts now forming on this side of the Atlantick, against the peace and tranquility His Majesty's Dominions in North America, and to witness to your Excellency, by this our Protest, a disapprobation and abhorence of the many lawless combinations and unwarrantable practices actually carrying on by a gross tribe of infatuated anti-Monarchists in the several Colonies in these Dominions; the baneful consequence of whose audacious contrivance can, in fine, only tend to extirpate the fundamental principles of all Government, and illegally to shake off their obedience to, and dependence upon, the imperial Crown and Parliament of Great Britain; the infection of whose pernicious example being already extended to this particular County....

> We see in all public places and papers disagreeable votes, speeches and resolutions, said to be entered into by our sister Colonies, in the highest contempt and derogation of the superintending power of the legislative authority of Great Britain. . . .
>
> We are truly sensible that those invaluable blessings which we have hitherto enjoyed under His Majesty's auspicious Government, can only be secured to us by the stability of his Throne, supported and defended by the British Parliament. . . .
>
> Duty and affection oblige us further to express our grateful acknowledgements for the inestimate blessings flowing from such a Constitution. And we do assure your excellency that we are determined, by the assistance of Almighty God, . . . to contribute all in our power for the preservation of the publick peace . . . and to see a misled people turn again from their atrocious offences to a proper exercise of their obedience and duty. . . .

The North Carolina Regulators represented many, though not all, of the settlers and migrants into the backcountry in the last colonial years. The content of their grievances may have sounded strange to foreign visitors, and certainly East Coast leaders believed that the elite had a clear right to determine the rights and privileges of everyone in their jurisdiction regardless of changing circumstances or unique conditions. But from the Regulators' point of view, westerners were asking only for the rights and privileges to which all members of the empire were entitled. Regulator petitions used familiar language to ask for the extension of familiar institutions into their settlements. Still, neither side resolved these tensions before the Imperial Crisis ended.

Questions for Analysis

1. What specific grievances do the Regulators express in the first document? Are these likely to arise elsewhere in North America? Why or why not?
2. What kind of people do the Regulators project themselves to be? Do you believe the image is accurate? What would you add about their social status, lifestyles, and ambitions?
3. Explain why violent regulators in 1769 "abhorred" violence in 1776? Are there different kinds of violence? different purposes that activate violence?
4. Why do the Anson County petitioners pledge support to the crown in 1776?
5. What impact would Regulator beliefs have on forging a unified American identity during the period to come?

6

Winning Independence, 1775–1783

Eighteen miles north of Philadelphia in late December 1777, Albigense Waldo, a surgeon in the Continental Army's Connecticut Line, watched exhausted patriot soldiers dine on "loathsome firecake," a pasty mash of flour and water. Of the dwindling army provisions, wrote Waldo, no more than twenty-five barrels of flour remained, and no meat, no fish, no salt at all. General George Washington's "ragamuffins" had just straggled into their winter quarters at Valley Forge, exhausted from fighting at Germantown, Pennsylvania, when they heard about the food shortages. To the cries of "No meat! No meat!" the troops added desperate pleas for something better to eat than the firecake that "turned their gutts to pasteboard."

Washington was ill prepared for the dilemmas that faced him that winter, and Waldo's reports offered the commander little solace. Officers had chosen to camp the roughly twelve-thousand-man army at Valley Forge because it lay on rolling high ground that could be defended from British attack and yet afforded a view of the British occupying Philadelphia. Washington also reckoned that Valley Forge was remote enough from the refugees fleeing Philadelphia to avoid depleting resources—food, fuel, and fodder—that would never be sufficient for both the army and the civilian population. Washington thought his troops could probably survive on the goodwill of local farmers and the abundance of nearby forests.

Instead, Washington recorded that his soldiers at Valley Forge endured "unmentionable distress" that winter. Even flour ran out by January, and foraging parties scoured the woodlands for small game. Soldiers lacked the most basic necessities of army life, including shoes and socks, jackets and shirts, soap, and utensils. They had lived for weeks virtually in the open and, now that the weather had turned cold, could not find craftsmen to build barracks. Washington ordered the men still fit for duty—about 8,200—to put up wooden huts fourteen feet square and sealed with clay from the rain-soaked ground. Each hut became home for at least twelve men; most had no straw for mattresses and slept on the frozen ground. Soldiers and camp followers crawled into the huts for days on end, emerging only to ransack nearby fields for corn stalks to boil. Over three thousand people died in camp that horrible winter, and hundreds of horses perished.

In their misery, the soldiers began to refocus their attention from fighting the British to finding scapegoats for their anguish. Many of them at first blamed the local farmers for withholding food and fuel. It quickly became obvious that troops, refugees, and civilians had "utterly scoured and laid waste" the region around Valley Forge. But supplies were not coming in from the outside, either. Licensed civilian storekeepers and merchant suppliers charged exorbitant prices to the troops for necessities. Wagoners embezzled supplies and sold them elsewhere or hired their vehicles to anyone who could pay cash. Rumors that farmers and millers were sending flour to New England almost provoked a general mutiny among Washington's men.

Then, too, some blamed the military suppliers, who offered "an endless stream of excuses" for failing to deliver essential goods. The army's Commissary of Purchases and Quartermaster General's department were devilishly unreliable. They had turned up precious little food, fuel, and fodder to send to Valley Forge, and yet they had "laid upon Congress very great charges for flour and pork never tasted" in the camp. Government contractors cut up blankets into four pieces and sold each one as a whole blanket; they adulterated flour with pebbles and weeds; and they transported wet gunpowder to the wrong places.

Despite the many examples of such "peculation" among both citizens and suppliers, few Americans knew that the primary sources of the widespread shortages were the transformation of an agricultural society into a war machine and the British blockades of their vital international commerce. By February 6, 1778, Washington wrote that his troops were starving and that "a general famine ravages the countryside" with "sickness threatening to carry us all away." The seven hundred women camp followers at Valley Forge busied themselves caring for the wounded, scavenging for scraps of fuel, and burying the dead. Still, even when soldiers began to desert the army altogether and to die in frightening numbers at Valley Forge, Washington forbid his troops from seizing civilian goods. Taking what was not given or sold to them, insisted Washington, would "corrode the moral fiber" of the Revolution. When American soldiers acted out of "selfish private interests" and "beyond the force of laws," their behavior was "unrepublican" and suited only the British regulars.

Chronology

1775	Second Continental Congress
	Washington appointed commander of Continental Army
	Battle of Bunker Hill
1776	Paine's *Common Sense* published
	Declaration of Independence adopted
	Cherokee attack North Carolina frontier
1777	Battle of Saratoga
	Howe captures Philadelphia
	Soldiers encamp at Valley Forge
1778	France enters the war
	Brant leads Iroquois in western Pennsylvania and New York
1779	Spain enters the war
	Philadelphia food riots
1780	Cornwallis invades North Carolina
	Dutch loans help the war
1781	Robert Morris becomes superintendent of finance
	Articles of Confederation ratified
	Cornwallis surrenders at Yorktown

Although the Continental Army at Valley Forge marched into battle six months later "in fraternity and brotherhood," their horrible winter highlighted important issues that Americans would confront as they sustained their war for independence and built a new system of government. Some of these issues concerned the character of a republican citizenry, especially when it tried to sustain a long revolution that did not succumb to the arbitrary authority of the English army and government. Others issues concerned the balance between political authority and individual rights. Even in the midst of their Revolution, Americans entered a discussion about what kind of government they wished to create and the character of the people who would live under that government's laws. They learned much in that discussion about their own frailties and contradictions—in particular, that no shared cultural, political, or racial identity yet made them one nation. Moreover, their discussion would continue for years after the Revolution.

- What ideas and experiences account for a large part of the diverse colonial population making the decision for independence, and these colonists' ability to stay committed at each turn of the war?
- Who joined the American patriots in the Revolution, who actively opposed independence, and who remained neutral?
- As the war progressed, what kinds of social divisions, shortages, and sacrifices did revolutionaries endure? How did revolutionaries win the war?
- To what extent were patriots motivated by republican values about individual character and the proper role of governments? by the desire for economic success and political self-government?

This chapter will address these questions.

The Decision for Independence, 1775–1776

It was one thing to petition for repeal of revolting legislation and burn stamp masters in effigy. These activities were typical methods of popular dissent in western Europe. It was quite another to set up a new government and raise an army against the imperial might of England. Yet that is what people in thirteen North American colonies did starting in 1775, even though few of them understood where such unprecedented opposition would lead them.

The Second Continental Congress

Colonial minutemen and citizens marched back from Concord to Boston in April 1775 and put the city under siege for the next two months. Governor Thomas Gage declared their activity treasonous but offered pardons to all colonists who turned in their arms and took an oath of allegiance to the crown. Very few did. Instead, thousands of patriots fortified Breed's Hill on the north side of Boston near Charles Town on June 16. The next day, General William Howe ordered his redcoats to assault the colonists hunkered down on the hill (and next to it, on Bunker Hill) in three reckless charges up the slope. The battle left more than 1,000 redcoats killed and wounded, including 92 officers, and nearly 450 colonists killed and wounded, most of them during their scattered withdrawal once they ran out of ammunition. The battle, known ever since as the Battle of Bunker Hill, was thus a British victory—although an extremely costly one—and enabled the British to hold Boston nine more months. At the same time, the battle convinced many northern farmers that—though untrained and poorly supplied—they could nevertheless effectively fortify a hill from which to combat the formal lines of the British standing army.

Elsewhere in 1775, royal governments collapsed as crown officials fled to safe havens or left the colonies altogether. Patriot leaders in the deteriorating provincial governments retreated into the countryside, where they created new sources of rep-

"Don't Tread on Me" A significant change from Franklin's segmented snake, which symbolized the divided colonies at the time of the Albany Congress (see pages 164–165), this image of the coiled rattlesnake on the flag of the Continental Navy became common after 1775. Army, militia, and naval flags abounded during the Revolution. *(National Archives.)*

resentative political authority. The first acts of these new governments including activating the Committees of Correspondence and arousing their militia to begin taking over "loyalist nests." In May 1775, Vermont's Green Mountain Boys under Ethan Allan, Connecticut's militia led by Captain Benedict Arnold, and the now-famous Massachusetts militia surprised and captured the British garrison at Fort Ticonderoga on Lake Champlain, New York. Other patriot militia occupied the fort at Crown Point eight miles farther north.

As this undeclared war dragged on, delegates convened a Second Continental Congress of "Confederated Colonies" in Philadelphia in May 1775. Like the first Congress, the second one was a voluntary meeting of representatives chosen by colonial assemblies to deliberate about matters of mutual concern to all Americans. At first, Georgia did not send delegates, stating that the colony was preoccupied with Creek attacks and slave resistance. But by September, backcountry settlers and Savannah merchants agreed to join other southern colonies that had entrusted Congress with their protection. The arrival of the Georgia delegation brought the number of colonies represented to thirteen.

Knowing that British officials would try to use Quebec as a staging area to strike at northern American provinces, the Continental Congress made appeals to Canadians in late 1774 and early 1775 to join its cause. Some colonists were certain that Nova Scotia would take up arms with them because of the large influx of New England migrants there. But Halifax became a tightly controlled British outpost during 1775, and one of the main cities to attract "loyalists"—colonists whose support for the crown endangered their lives. Similarly, the British military kept tight control of the multiethnic, multiracial population in East and West Florida. Assemblies of the British Caribbean possessions of Grenada, Jamaica, and Barbados opted to join the American independence movement, but the crown's military forces on the islands overwhelmed the rebels before they could arm themselves. In the future, these islands would also attract many fleeing loyalists.

So the thirteen colonies deliberated on their own. As a first step, the delegates resolved that "we must put ourselves in an armed condition" against the war in progress. Thomas Jefferson, a Virginia planter and lawyer who had steeped himself in Enlightenment ideas, noted the "frenzy of revenge" coursing through delegates' discussions. Colonists, wrote Jefferson, had a desire to raise "resistance in every corner of the continent."

But what kind of military force should Congress create? Most delegates reflected the general public's distrust of standing armies, especially since the French and Indian War, and asserted that they had no authority to create a centralized national institution. Perhaps the colonial militias would be adequate. Other delegates pointed out that the resistance movement "engaged a continent," which required a trained and centrally commanded force. Militiamen served short terms of enlistment; their loyalty often stemmed from serving under officers of their choosing and from their locales; and they balked at training or military discipline. A revolutionary war required very different terms of service. Furthermore, although militiamen proved time and again to be intrepid fighters, few went into battle with knowledge of sustained bloodshed and few understood that returning home between battles could be interpreted as desertion.

In June 1775, George Washington and John Adams presented a plan that addressed the objections to a standing army. Congress should raise a Continental Army of ten companies of riflemen from "among the best frontier marksmen" (rifled muskets had a much longer range of fire than conventional muskets) to supplement the Massachusetts militia now on the outskirts of British-held Boston. The next day, delegates voted unanimously to place the forty-three-year-old Virginian, Brigadier George Washington, at the head of the new Continental forces and dispatched them to the Boston area. A few days later, Congress gave Washington a staff of major generals and voted to issue $2 million in paper currency to fund the troops.

Congress had been able to create an army, a commander, a military staff, and an intercolonial currency without great public resistance because the crisis in Massachusetts demanded such measures in 1775. But the delegates did not constitute a central government. The Second Continental Congress had no authority to coerce colonies or citizens to support independence, nor had it defined the longer-range political goals of all "confederated colonies in congress." Some delegates favored an immediate call for political independence from the British Empire. Others openly denounced the gathering momentum toward such a split. Still others proposed a compromise. On July 5, 1775, John Dickinson of Pennsylvania presented the Olive Branch Petition to Congress, a document delegates voted to send to George III affirming colonial loyalty to the monarch, asking that British army hostilities cease, and proposing a sincere discussion of differences.

Although some leading colonists argued for compromise with the British government, many others sponsored stronger statements of colonial liberties. Dickinson himself helped Thomas Jefferson draft a Declaration of the Causes and Necessities of Taking Up Arms the day after Congress sent the Olive Branch Petition to the king. The Declaration of Causes denounced the actions of Parliament since 1763 and declared Congress's intention to defend the colonists' traditional English liberties with arms. In early August, a few congressional delegates began negotiations with Indians in the mid-Atlantic region, especially the Iroquois, to win their support, or at least their promise of neutrality. Congress appointed Benjamin Franklin as postmaster general in charge of coordinating intercolonial communication.

George III was still raging about British losses at Bunker Hill when he received the Olive Branch Petition in August. Lambasting the colonists as "traitors," "enemies of the Britons," he refused to read it. Congress now had little choice but to entrench itself deeper in war. In fall 1775, two regiments of the green Continental Army marched into Canada to secure support from citizens for the American cause before the British did so. General Richard Montgomery seized Montreal in November; Colonel Benedict Arnold trudged through Maine and reached Quebec in December. Montgomery joined Arnold beneath the walls of Quebec. Acting on rumors that their troops would leave when enlistment terms expired that month, the commanders attacked the city desperately on December 31. But redcoats killed, wounded, and captured hundreds of Americans. Montgomery died in battle and Arnold was wounded. Americans failed to take the city, and after holding their position outside the citadel for a few desperate months, the American forces retreated out of Canada.

As the Continentals marched north in late 1775, southern patriot militia forces engaged with loyalists, who took up arms in the countryside and in cities where redcoats had been stationed. In Virginia, the former Governor Dunmore organized slave regiments (see page 221) that defended crown interests bravely, but the colonial militia defeated loyalists, redcoats, and armed slaves by fall 1775. In retaliation, Dunmore's troops bombarded and scorched Norfolk, Virginia, on the last days of 1775, further alienating planters and small farmers from the crown's cause. Southern patriot merchants began honoring the conditions of Congress's Association Agreement, which stipulated a halt to all trade with Britain (see page 192). In retaliation, Parliament passed the Prohibitory Act outlawing all English trade with the colonies after December 1775. The stage was thus set for a long war in the South.

Common Sense

Although fighting had erupted during 1775, colonists did not rush to declare their independence from England. It was not until early 1776 that Thomas Paine, a recent English immigrant to Philadelphia, helped put into words the meaning of colonists' grievances and spurred deeper commitment to independence. While still

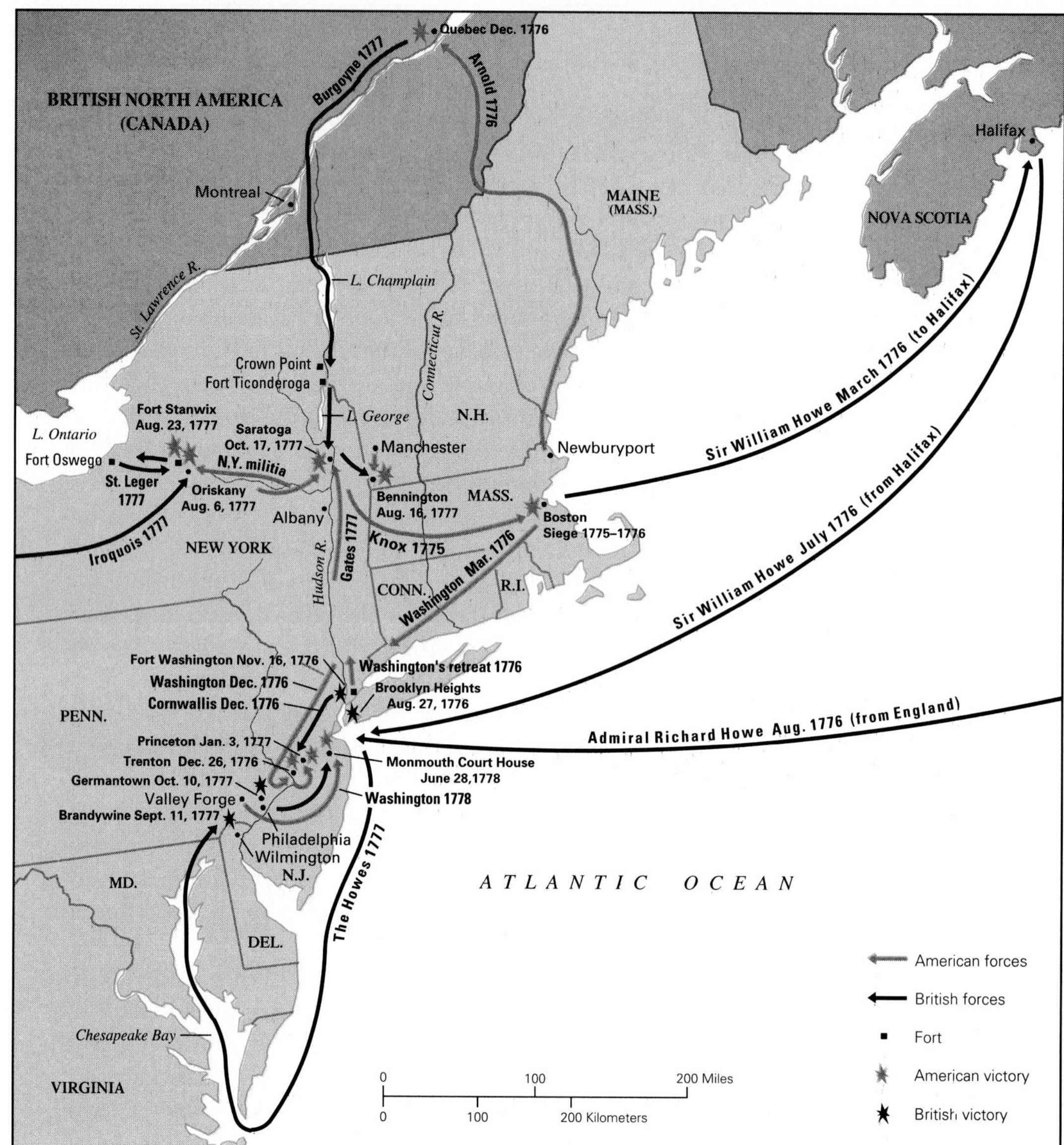

War in the North During the first months of the Revolution, the British made important advances against Boston and Philadelphia. By early 1776, British troops began invading New York and New Jersey.

in England working as a corset maker and then a petty tax collector, Paine wrote occasionally against crown policies. But he did not express any special interest in American affairs until he befriended Benjamin Franklin in London, and only when he reached Philadelphia in 1774 did his popular literary talents emerge. Paine took a job with the *Pennsylvania Magazine* in 1775 and became friendly with congressional delegates who frequented the public houses. Soon Paine agreed to take up his pen for the patriots' cause (see Competing Voices, page 239).

Common Sense, Paine's masterpiece, appeared in January 1776. In it, Paine used language of "common sense" to wipe away "ancient prejudices"; his metaphors came from familiar evangelical and republican traditions. He restated long-held beliefs about natural law and justice in colorful imagery that colonists could, and did, quote widely. And he put ambivalent and tentative thoughts into bold formulations about right and wrong. Most consequential in 1776, Paine shattered patriots' last vestiges of loyalty to the monarchy. "There is something exceedingly ridiculous in the composition of monarchy," wrote Paine, especially government under the "crowned ruffian," the "hard hearted sullen Pharaoh of England" who "hath little more to do than to make war and give away [political] places."

Colonists devoured *Common Sense.* They purchased over a hundred thousand copies before midyear. More colonists heard portions of the pamphlet, or read reprinted excerpts in newspapers, than any other statement of political and cultural beliefs during the era. They read it aloud in public coffee houses, passed it around in neighborhoods and ladies' teas, and posted selections on church doors. Shunning the details of this or that objection to public resistance, Paine's argument became a ringing call to arms.

Declaring Independence

The reconstituted colonial governments in New England, Virginia, and the Carolinas created committees and built popular support for independence through 1775. Colonists in the mid-Atlantic region, however, hesitated to go this far. Instead, they looked for ways to compromise with their traditional assemblies and governors. But these assemblies had increasingly become the last official bastions of loyalist control. When patriots finally drove them from the continent during mid-1776, some rebel governments "declare[d] the United Colonies free and independent states."

In Congress, Virginia delegates put forward a resolution on June 7, 1776, "That these United Colonies are, and of right ought to be, free and independent States . . . and that all political connection between them and the State of Great Britain is, and ought to be, totally dissolved." Moderates from New York, Delaware, and New Jersey stalled significant discussion of the proposal until July. A committee that included Franklin, Jefferson, John Adams, and two others began preparing a longer document elaborating on the Virginia resolution.

On July 1, Congress took a first vote on the redrafted resolution. Four colonies cast negative or inconclusive votes: Pennsylvania, South Carolina, Delaware, and New York. July 2 brought better results. After an entire night of deliberations, Pennsylvania and South Carolina switched their votes, and Caesar Rodney of Delaware raced on horseback through drenching rain to weigh in for independence. For the next two days, delegates combed through Jefferson's draft, and finally on July 4 twelve colonies approved the revised draft of the Declaration of Independence. Dickinson did not sign the final version, and delegates from New York held out.

What Paine had implored the general population to do, Congress now made official: a final break with the crown. The preamble of the document, one of the most stirring passages in American letters, established the fundamental republican principles on which patriots rested their actions. There were, wrote Jefferson, "self-evident truths" embodying the "inalienable rights" of citizens, rights each citizen enjoyed from birth that could not be taken away by any ruling authority. Governments obtained their "just powers from the consent of the governed" and, as John Locke had taught during the Glorious Revolution of 1688 (see page 98), could be overthrown if they violated the trust and consent of the people.

But congressional delegates did not spend much time discussing the preamble—after all, some said, matters that are "self-evident" and apply to "all men" do not require debate—and moved on to the body of the Declaration. There, the document listed numerous ways that the crown had violated the public trust and foisted unjust and unconstitutional acts on colonists; in sum, the king was "unfit to be the ruler of a free people." After this "long train of abuses," Congress had little choice but to dissolve the bonds of empire and vest political authority in the people as a whole. For years to come, Americans struggled to shape this new collective authority, "the people," into workable governments.

Delegates signed one official copy of the Declaration and hid it. Copies that did not include the signers' names—after all, they had committed treason and feared reprisals from loyalists—rolled off the press immediately, and an eager public finally knew what Congress had accomplished. The American experiment had been launched.

The Revolution in Earnest, 1776–1778

While Paine's pamphlet was galvanizing public sentiment and Congress was inching toward the Declaration, the North Carolina militia had defeated a loyalist Highland Scots force at Moore's Creek Bridge on February 27, 1776. Washington's new army fortified Dorchester Heights near Boston and pummeled the British until they evacuated the city on March 17. Colonists successfully defended Charles Town from British attacks in June. Many Americans believed they had virtually expelled the British from the rebellious thirteen colonies by then. But had they? Hopes for a short war were dashed as delegates put their names to the Declaration of Independence: a massive British flotilla of men and materials approached Staten Island, New York. As the war ground on and on, the level of sacrifice demanded from citizens and soldiers grew to unimagined proportions, almost impossible to sustain. By the third year of the war, political doubts, vulnerable governments, persistent scarcities, and mounting deaths threw the War for Independence into the balance.

A Year of Exuberance

Britain's professional standing army ranked among the best in the world, and the royal navy was indisputably the best. But by 1776, half its naval ships needed repairs, desertion and mutiny had drastically reduced the number of sailors, and mostly very young and very old men remained enlisted in the British fighting force for the duration of the war. Over thirty thousand German Hessian mercenaries joined English, Scottish, and Irish rank and filers, and over fifty thousand Americans became active supporters of the crown during the Revolution. Supplying such forces would be a constant difficulty. American privateers mobilized every available craft to prey on British supply ships. In fact, so many British vessels carried basic supplies that not many remained available for blockading American ports. To pay for these shipments, British citizens bore the steepest taxes in memory.

Americans enjoyed the benefits of fighting on home soil, where the civilian population provisioned them more easily and the "rage for libertye" in 1776 buoyed men marching off to war. About 220,000 men from sixteen to forty-five—a very high proportion of patriot adult males—served for some length of time as citizen-soldiers in the militia or enlistees in the Continental Army. During the opening months of fighting, the militia used effective guerrilla-like tactics, familiarity with the terrain, and ability to identify and intimidate loyalist neighbors to build support. Militiamen, many Americans noticed, did not give up on the patriotic cause in appreciable numbers because they made frequent trips home and had contact with kin and neighbors during battles.

In contrast, the Continental Army marched far from home, and men served fixed terms of longer duration than the militia. In 1776 Washington projected that he needed twenty thousand men to create an effective striking force; during the following months, about thirteen thousand men enlisted. To fill the gap, Congress assigned troop quotas to each provincial assembly, which in turn ordered local communities to supply specified numbers of soldiers. Committees of Public Safety helped enlist servants, the unemployed, and unmarried farm laborers, along with male heads of households.

Although freedmen served in northern militia units from the beginning of the war, Congress initially barred slaves and free African-Americans from serving in the Continental Army. As the war dragged on, the New England governments permitted free black enlistments in the hundreds and allowed slaves to enroll if their masters approved. Southern patriot governments avoided enlisting free African-Americans, but masters permitted hundreds of slaves in the Chesapeake region to serve as their own replacements. In all, probably five thousand black men served under patriot command, often in separate units.

Despite such enthusiasm, Washington often noted the failings of his men. Troops had little conception of sanitation, cleanliness, or sobriety, he lamented, and when soldiers' leaves came up, they departed from camps and battlefields regardless of the military circumstances. Lack of deference to commanding officers and fraternization among the ranks of soldiers plagued efforts to conduct campaigns. Overall, the army was relatively untrained and poorly armed. These problems loomed larger when the British focused on taking coastal American cities beginning in July 1776.

That month, General William Howe landed 10,000 troops in New York, intending to take the city, move up the Hudson Valley, and cut off New England from the rest of the rebellion. In the next weeks, over 8,000 Hessians and thousands more British troops arrived, along with a steady stream of supplies and large forces under the command of Admiral Richard Howe. The British won a stinging victory over the Continentals in the Battle of Long Island on August 27, 1776. Over 1,500 Americans lay dead or wounded, a huge loss given the army's small ranks. Washington had little choice but to pull his remaining troops, a ragged lot of what he called "scum," first out of Brooklyn Heights, and then back to Harlem Heights.

As huge numbers of well-armed British soldiers poured onto Manhattan Island, a poor woman taking shelter in a cellar full of gunpowder torched the city. Fires raged for days, gutting a quarter of New York. Another woman, the wealthy Quaker wife of merchant Robert Murray, detained General Howe long enough to help Washington evacuate his troops to White Plains, up the Hudson. But Howe had just taken Fort Lee, New Jersey, in November, and moved against Washington's troops at Fort Washington, New York, as patriot troops settled in. Howe took nearly three thousand patriot prisoners. Washington fled with his weary men and camp followers into Pennsylvania, anticipating relocation far to the interior. Fearful as the British front line crept closer, Congress abandoned Philadelphia and fled to Baltimore.

But before reaching a suitable location for encampment, Washington received reports about British positions that altered his plans. On Christmas night 1776, Washington crossed the Delaware River with about 2,500 men to surprise and rout celebrating Hessians stationed at Trenton, New Jersey. A second victory at Princeton on January 3 forced the British evacuation of New Jersey. Washington set up camp at Morristown, and Congress returned to Philadelphia. But political leaders began to worry out loud that British commanders planned to keep New York City, take Philadelphia for good, and, with the middle ground secured, turn north and

New York City Ablaze, 1776 Although the accuracy of this image has been challenged because it shows fires starting in multiple locations and suggests that the British were the instigators, the New York fire did level a large portion of the city. Wooden structures near the waterfront were ravaged within hours, and in another portion of the city, destroyed structures became home for hundreds of runaway slaves who took refuge in the city. *(Museum of the City of New York.)*

south toward the more difficult areas of New England and Virginia. Congress's assessment of this divide-and-conquer strategy proved to be correct.

War in the North could have ended very badly for the Americans in this first year if both sides had accepted all-out warfare. But British and American armies both avoided frontal assaults; each hoped to press the opponent into surrender and to avoid decimating whole regiments. British troops normally did not fight during the winter. Moreover, commanders had been indoctrinated to put down rebel governments, not to destroy whole peoples and their ways of life. Besides, taking Washington's army would require compliance with the rules of treason and war: trials of officers, hangings of resisters, whippings, maybe deportations of thousands of citizens, with the inevitable alienation of whole regions from the crown's authority. Of course, the British troops committed arson, confiscated property, and looted storehouses, but they hardly ravaged populations and towns. Howe's men ranged through New Jersey, extracting oaths of allegiance to the crown, living off the land, and imprisoning a few selected officers.

Indeed, both sides remained relatively cautious during the first year of war. Washington tried to draw the British into the countryside, away from supply lines and civilian populations, and permitted his troops to make a few stabs against the enemy to bolster their morale. British troops along the coastline and in cities made little effort to take over the hinterlands. But it turned out that such caution on both sides probably prolonged the war. The retreat into the countryside certainly aggravated the difficulties of supply movement and troop recruitment.

Philadelphia, Saratoga, and Valley Forge

General Howe believed that once he had New York City, the next step, and perhaps the winning maneuver, would be to capture Philadelphia. England's minister of war ordered a three-pronged attack. General "Johnnie" Burgoyne would march south from Canada; Sir Henry Clinton would hold New York City; and Colonel Barry St. Leger would advance east from Oswego in upstate New York. Together they would reinforce Howe's Philadelphia campaign. But Howe rejected the plan as too dispersed and undermanned; he decided to attack Philadelphia by sea. In June 1777, Howe sailed with thirteen thousand men from New Jersey to the Delaware Bay, where Americans fired fiercely on redcoats and prevented river pilots from guiding Howe's forces into Philadelphia. So the British fleet proceeded to Head of Elk, Maryland, landing on August 24. Hessian and British troops marched toward Philadelphia across the upper Chesapeake and southeastern Pennsylvania, scorching the countryside as they proceeded. In the Brandywine Valley of northern Delaware, Howe's troops inflicted heavy losses on Washington's forces on September 11. Two weeks later, Howe occupied Philadelphia. Congress fled once again, this time to Lancaster. Washington attempted to quash the redcoats at Germantown, but failed and retreated to Valley Forge.

Earlier that month, Burgoyne had taken Fort Ticonderoga. St. Leger's nearly 1,800 soldiers and Iroquois besieged Fort Schuyler in August but retreated when Benedict Arnold marched 1,000 American militiamen and Continentals against the fort. Burgoyne's nearly 7,800 troops began a march from Fort Ticonderoga toward Albany. However, American general Horatio Gates ordered his men to impede Burgoyne's advance by laying hundreds of trees across the trails, thereby starving the British troops now stymied in the backcountry near Saratoga, New York. When Burgoyne tried to resupply his forces by sending about 700 men into the nearby forests, John Stark's New Hampshire militia, about 2,600 strong, routed the British completely. Although Burgoyne's 650 Hessians made a final attempt to take Albany, militiamen from Massachusetts, New Hampshire, and New York poured in to support Gates and decimate the British. On October 17 the patriot militias and army surrounded and overwhelmed the weary British troops, capturing about 5,000 of them and securing their munitions. Burgoyne surrendered at nearby Saratoga.

Victory at Saratoga proved to be a turning point in the war because it demonstrated that colonial militia and the Continental Army could rout the British forces. Securing such huge portions of the interior boosted public patriot morale immeasurably at the end of 1777, just as soldiers withdrew to winter camps. Yet events at Saratoga contrasted sharply with what the military and civilian populations experienced in the next phase of the war. After the first year of fighting, army recruits tended to come from the most desperate ranks of society, many of whom enlisted for three years in order to collect a small cash enlistment bounty and a signed promise of 100 acres at the end of the war. Henry and John Laurens, South Carolina planter-merchants and ardent patriots, promoted a plan to enlist about 3,000 slaves in the army with the offer of freedom at war's end, but they failed to garner enough support. Morale sagged seriously in the North and South when the currencies issued by individual governments declined rapidly in value. By early 1778, the value of enlistment bounties shrank to almost nothing. Also, many recruits wearied of life in the field, most of them never having been far from home before, let alone gone off to prolonged war. Some panicked in the face of heavy fighting, and thousands walked away from battle.

The wretched winter of 1777–1778 at Valley Forge strained all of the problems related to recruiting and sustaining the army to the breaking point. Indeed, the troops' winter at Valley Forge has become notorious as a severe test of military endurance and civilian support, as well as a defining moment of the American commitment to political independence and their republican character. Alexander Hamilton, a young recent immigrant from the West Indies who served during the Revolution as Washington's aide-de-camp, thought that all republican virtue had vanished and, with it, the foundation for a new nation.

Helpless to enlarge his army and secure its necessary supplies, Washington appealed to Congress for measures to stem its total demise from desertion and demoralization. However, Congress at first replied that a number of stiff regulations already existed for treating drunkenness, insubordination, taking multiple bounty payments, desertion, and other infractions of military laws. Eventually, Congress enacted stiffer penalties—usually physical punishments—but Washington and his officers could not uniformly and consistently whip or imprison every delinquent soldier—there were simply too many. Repeated attempts by a soldier to desert were supposed to result in the death penalty, but Washington rarely ordered it because an execution produced even greater demoralization among the troops. He preferred to offer soldiers incentives to return to camp. Congress also devised incentives, including bonuses to soldiers who enlisted for three years and larger land bounties for those who stayed for the duration of the war.

Training in field tactics and the use of arms probably improved conditions in the army after the winter of 1778-1779 more than stiffer rules of conduct. Help came from the timely intervention of a few experienced foreigners. Baron von Steuben, a Prussian officer committed to the American cause, trained Continental troops in field duty and distributed a drill manual to intermediate officers that helped prepare the rank and file for more efficient fighting. Two others, the French Marquis de Lafayette and the German Johann Baron de Kalb, joined Washington at Valley Forge during that terrible winter. The Poles Thaddeus Kosciuszko and Casimir Count Pulaski also helped create an increasingly professional Continental Army.

The French Alliance

The victory at Saratoga not only boosted American morale but also convinced the French government to ally with the independence movement. Eighteen months earlier, before the Declaration of Independence had been drafted, the French firm of Roderique Hortalez et Compagnie had begun to receive large sums from the French government to smuggle gunpowder, clothing, and military supplies to Americans through the pitifully weak British blockade. In December 1776, Benjamin Franklin arrived in Paris as an unofficial liaison for Congress, winning the hearts and minds of the French people and working secretly with the courtier, Pierre Augustin Caron de Beaumarchais, to secure French supplies and privateering vessels. Then, once Philadelphia fell to Howe, King Louis XVI (reigned 1774–1792) agreed that Americans desperately needed French aid; Saratoga convinced him that Americans deserved it. The French foreign minister, the Comte de Vergennes, and Franklin worked out two agreements in February 1778. One granted Americans open trade with all French possessions. The other recognized American independence, committed French forces to fight in North America, and relinquished all French territorial claims on the continent (though American diplomats recognized France's claims on any West Indies conquests it might make).

British leaders grew desperate to prevent France's entry into the war. William Pitt stormed in Parliament that an American victory would crush the British Empire, and then collapsed into an illness that killed him a month later. George III fumed that if the Americans won their war, the West Indies and Ireland would be next to rebel. Lord North, the hard-liner who had so enraged Americans during the Imperial Crisis, wrote a plan for conciliation that he attempted to deliver to Congress in June 1778. But Congress, hoping for a quick end to the war now, rejected North's overtures. On May 4, 1778, Congress voted unanimously to ratify both treaties with France, thereby creating America's first alliance with a foreign nation.

North's ministry in turn declared war on France and ordered General Henry Clinton to pull out of Philadelphia in order to concentrate his forces in New York City. Washington's more highly trained forces met Clinton's retreating redcoats at the Battle of Monmouth Court House in New Jersey. There, a number of women joined the Continentals in battle, including the renowned Mary Ludwig Hays, "Molly Pitcher," who took her husband's place behind a cannon when he fell. The British won the battle but retreated to New York City knowing they would encounter formidable Continental forces from that time onward. Attempting to consolidate their strength, the British evacuated Newport during 1778, used New York City as a supply depot and prisoner camp, and ordered supporters of the crown to abandon the countryside for the greater safety of the city. Indeed, except for a few minor skirmishes, the war had ended in the North.

The Character of War

The Revolutionary War was much more than formal battles. In thousands of parlors and kitchens, women, servants, and children made persistent sacrifices. In local committees, experienced politicians and inexperienced new officeholders grappled with the tasks of raising troops and mediating disagreements among civilians about a range of issues, including taxation. And in the halls of Congress, American leaders argued over policies for arming, feeding, relocating, and punishing patriots. These arenas of discourse and decision making profoundly affected the future character of American life.

Armies and Taxes

As good republicans, patriots saw the British standing army as a threat to peace and a drain on public resources. As a consequence, Congress's creation of a Continental Army evoked ambivalent, sometimes hostile reactions. Citizens who had sacrificed year after year for the public good grew disgusted when Continentals ravaged the "neutral ground" between army fronts for forage, wood fuel, and food from their gardens. In May 1779, a Connecticut man wrote that "this whole part of the Country are Starving for want of bread, they have been drove to the necessity of Grinding Flaxseed & oats together for bread." Yet the "armed soldiery somehow believe we hide our bread, and tear down our barns to find it." Washington's troops at Valley Forge tore up fence posts to burn; Hessians on Long Island did likewise, so that "the cattle stray[ed] away."

Many citizens struggled mightily to be "true republicans." Stretching meager supplies and turning used goods into valuable army wares became synonymous with patriotism. Women organized war aid societies that mobilized scattered resources into substantial contributions. In 1776 almost four thousand Philadelphia women pledged to produce "soldier cloth" in their homes. Volunteer organizations such as the Ladies Association of Philadelphia, founded by Esther DeBerdt Reed and continued after her death by Sarah Franklin Bache (Ben Franklin's daughter), solicited door to door for money to purchase linen to make over 2,200 soldiers' shirts. Townswomen in Northboro, Massachusetts, spun 2,600 miles of woolen yarn, which they subsequently used to make uniforms. Baltimore women outfitted Lafayette's soldiers in new uniforms before their march into Virginia in 1781.

Women everywhere turned metal plates and pots into bullets and hemp into rope; households gave every firkin, wheel, sheet, and dried onion they could spare. Women managed farms and stores while men fought far away. Young people delayed marriages and schooling in order to contribute their energies to the war effort in whatever way they could.

Nearly twenty thousand women became "camp followers" who marched along with troops as cooks, washerwomen, and nurses. Generals' wives, including Martha Washington, Catherine Greene, Lucy Knox, Deborah Putnam, Molly Stark, and Kitty Stirling, traveled with the moving troops from time to time, too. Women became indispensable workers, spending hours every day toting heavy pots, small children, and baggage through rough terrain. At times, women and children traveled with troops—British and American—because they would have endured worse conditions at home. Hannah Winthrop identified with the plight of the British prisoners captured at Saratoga who were marched through Cambridge, Massachusetts, in November 1777. Along with the soldiers, there marched "a sordid set of creatures in human Figure . . . great numbers of women, who seemed to be the beasts of burthen, having a bushel basket on their back, by which they were bent double—the contents seemed to be Pots and Kettles, various sorts of Furniture—children peeping thro' gridirons

Nancy Hart A legendary frontierswoman from Georgia, Hart wielded a rifled musket against six Tories who invaded her homestead when her husband was gone to a neighbor's farm. When the Tories ordered her to cook a family turkey, she killed not the turkey but one of them and wounded at least one other soldier. The remaining soldiers were hanged by Hart's husband on his return. Hundreds of patriot women remained alone on remote farms for months at a time during the war. *(Library of Congress.)*

and other utensils, some very young Infants who were born on the road; the women bare feet, cloathd in dirty raggs, such effluvia filld the air while they were passing . . . ." Prostitutes followed both armies as well, and although officials frowned on "consorting," they could not eradicate it. A military court, for example, charged officer Adam Stephen with "taking snuff out of the Boxes of strumpets" in 1777, but the court returned him to his command without further ado.

Although most American patriots agreed to sacrifice comforts, or even necessities, for the revolutionary cause, few of them expected the deprivations to last long. Most people comforted themselves with the prospect that "our sacrifices at this moment will set the terms for our great plenty" once independence had been secured. For some time before the war, New England and mid-Atlantic farmers and craftsmen had developed a thickening web of market exchanges that stretched far beyond their immediate neighborhoods. During the nonimportation movements of the 1760s and 1770s, colonists argued that their exports were vitally important to the growing populations of England, the West Indies, and Europe, and that by halting importation from England, they could bring its merchants to their knees. The success of nonimportation had been predicated on colonists' frugality, albeit only temporary. But colonists also professed that nonimportation would spur their own manufacturing and lay the foundation for greater self-sufficiency as a people. In the face of constant difficulties plaguing all layers of society, this hope in America's future prosperity made the rigors of the war bearable.

Despite this underlying current of confidence, the war sometimes seemed to utterly sap the energy and will of citizens. No matter how many sacrifices they made, Americans heard constant pleas from every political and military corner for still more. Above all, Congress needed huge sums of money to keep troops in the field. But it faced formidable obstacles to raising funds because provincial governments had their own wartime burdens and their citizens abhorred taxation from any quarter. Furthermore, Congress had no accepted authority to lay taxes on Americans, and it quickly depleted the funds that wealthy patriots loaned to the revolutionary cause.

In order to create the circulating funds necessary to fight the war, Congress resorted in 1775 to the familiar strategy of printing paper money—$6 million at first, but quickly growing to $200 million by the time it stopped the presses in 1780. And to surmount its lack of power to force the circulation of this money, Congress distributed it to the individual provincial governments and required them to pass the laws that would permit Americans to pay their taxes with this "continental currency." Congress hoped that each of the thirteen governments would withdraw its quota of paper money through these taxes, thereby keeping the amount of circulating currency low and public trust high.

But the continental currency system instead created a crisis of public trust. By 1779, so little of the money had been withdrawn that depreciation became serious. At the end of that year, it took forty-two "continentals" to buy one specie dollar worth of goods. In March 1780, Congress tried to withdraw continentals from circulation and issue new ones, but with little success. By December, one hundred continentals had the value of one specie dollar. Making matters worse, reports of widespread counterfeiting of paper currency reached Congress.

Even with the printing presses running night and day, Congress required ever more currency. One important addition to the circulating money was Congress's certificates to wealthy individual Americans, which held their value because Congress secured them with part of a $6 million loan from France. Other French loans, and then Dutch ones, increased the acceptability of these certificates, as well as the paper money still in circulation. However, foreign loans, though they represented important diplomatic alliances, amounted to only a drop in Congress's leaky financial bucket.

Congress's circulating currency was also supplemented by its Loan Offices, whose appointed officers issued interest-bearing bonds in large denominations to wealthy Americans and made them redeemable by the states. The certificates carried first 4 percent interest, and then 6 percent interest after February 1777—neither rate as attractive as the 10 to 18 percent private loans made during the war. And, like paper money, the Loan Office certificates depreciated quickly until Congress closed Loan Office operations in 1781.

Each state also issued its own paper money, a total of over $209 million during the war. But only Delaware and Georgia required a "fund"—collateral—of real estate to back the currency with something of widely accepted value. Elsewhere, the states tried to redeem the currency in future taxes (hence their name "tax anticipation notes"), but the need for funds rose much faster than legislative tax laws could meet. Various taxes on goods, land, houses, licenses to operate businesses, and even crops were not unusual. But their burden became unbearable to many citizens, and by early 1779, petitions flooded state legislatures for relief from both the tax laws and the jail sentences imposed on those who could not, or would not, abide by them.

Prices and Wages

When farmers marched off to war and abandoned their fields, and when British blockades began to cut off necessary imports, prices skyrocketed. During 1778, some coastal towns reported over 1,000 percent price increases in daily necessities. Salt in Maryland and Virginia that sold for $1 a bag in 1776 went for over $3,500 by 1779—when it could be found. In April 1779, George Washington wrote that "a wagon load of money will scarcely purchase a wagon load of provisions."

Congress and the states responded by trying to regulate the flow of goods and their prices. Early in the war, Congress implored citizens to sell goods "at reasonable prices," and repeated this call over and over. Some farmers and small producers discovered they could hoard goods and take them to market when prices rose steeply. Others, when approached by military suppliers with government certificates to pay for goods, supported "open prices" that they could negotiate to their own advantage. In the cities, merchants complained that price controls thwarted "the nature of commerce," which they believed should "be as free as air."

Artisans, shopkeepers, and "citizen consumers" agitated for price regulations on food and fuel brought from the countryside. Popular committees tried to fix prices among townspeople by general agreement—and sometimes by force—but they met with only partial success. Congressional calls for delegated conventions to determine fixed prices also faltered or failed. A convention of New England delegates met in 1776 in Providence to establish a list of wages and prices for every conceivable job and commodity, but its measures "fell into dissipation" before the end of 1777. Elsewhere, regional coalitions of new states made similar unsuccessful efforts to regulate prices and wages.

Instead, governments representing new states tried to address alarming inflation and scarcities by imposing embargoes that would keep necessities at home. New England states also passed "land embargo" laws that prohibited sales across state lines of necessary goods such as cider, wood, linen, and fodder. Most of the new states also tried to douse farmers' temptations to hold back goods in order to force prices up by decreeing that dairy, meat, grain, and vegetable products must be given up for immediate sale to needy populations. Massachusetts wrote a model law in 1779 to prevent "monopoly and forestalling" in the countryside that permitted only bakers to keep on hand more staples than one family needed to get through a season. The law also created county committees to search for hoarded goods and arrest violators.

But regulations did not prevent frequent outbursts of violence over scarcities or price hikes, often under female leadership. Shopkeepers and housewives from two western Virginia counties stormed Richmond warehouses to "set free" supplies of salt in 1776. Women of Beverly, Massachusetts, and a few dozen citizens of East Hartford, Connecticut, seized hogsheads of sugar from merchants in 1777 and forced the offenders to agree to sell at a fair price in the future. Boston women descended on Thomas Boylston's store in 1777 demanding that he sell coffee at a fair price. As Abigail Adams later recounted, "a number of females, some say a hundred or more, . . . marched down to the warehouse and demanded the keys, which [Boylston] refused to deliver. Upon which, one of them seized him by the neck and tossed him into a cart," while other women "opened the warehouse, hoisted out the coffee themselves, put it in to the truck and drove off."

In many instances, "republican townspeople" who insisted that governments set prices with "more justice in them" resorted to prolonged violence. In Philadelphia, mobs demanding lower food prices were joined by sailors and artisans demanding higher wages; together, they stormed the streets for days in January 1779. When daily necessities became so costly that the poor faced starvation, broadsides wailed that "in the midst of money we are in poverty, . . . You that have money, and you that have none, down with your prices, or down with your selves. . . . We have turned out against the enemy and we will not be eaten up by monopolizers and forestallers."

For a while, Philadelphia authorities regulated the public markets and tried to impose fair prices. But new rioting broke out during April and May. Housewives and youth gangs taunted flour merchants whom they perceived to have caused artificial shortages so they could raise prices. "Men with clubbs etc. have been to several Stores, obliging the people to lower their prises," wrote the elite lady Elizabeth Drinker in her diary. But such "popular regulation" seldom lasted long before merchants returned to "open markets" of unregulated sales.

On October 4, some two hundred Philadelphia militiamen rose up against price increases and marched on the house of James Wilson, a lawyer who publicly supported the offending merchants. Lawyers, merchants, and army friends joined

Wilson at his house, and Captain Campbell of the Continental Army opened fire on the protesters. In the melée known as the Fort Wilson riot that followed, militiamen killed Campbell and five other men. After hours of conflict, public authorities arrested and fined fifteen of the militiamen, and in the next days they distributed food to the poor.

Protests about wages and prices occurred because many Americans perceived that the Revolutionary War challenged two cherished ideals. One was the belief that republican citizens should always put the "common good" before individual gain. Farmers who withheld food in the countryside and merchants who sent it to distant markets violated the common good, and the people had a right to protest the breach in customs. Second, many patriots believed that governments should be responsive to public need, especially regarding food, fuel, and clothing. But regardless of principle, Congress had no spare funds to relieve the poor, and Washington refused to share his meager army budget with the general citizenry. Some county governments in Virginia and Connecticut dispensed small amounts of relief to needy families, usually in the form of bushels of grain or sides of pork. But elsewhere, provincial and local governments, unable to solve the dire problem of poverty, encouraged the families of wounded and dead soldiers to seek private handouts. Indeed, patriots learned over and over that the "common good" and government accountability were very difficult to attain.

Loyalists

A great number of colonists made no enduring commitment to support or oppose the Revolution, but instead changed sides as circumstances suited them. But a significant portion of the population declared their allegiance to the crown. In 1775 and early 1776, thousands of loyalists rushed out of North America with a few of their household goods and financial assets. Most believed they would return after a short absence. Probably one-fifth of the white population in the thirteen colonies actively fought for the crown after 1775, and probably another fifth did not take up arms for the crown but continued to believe in its authority over the colonies. This was the core of the loyalist population. As many as fifty thousand of them joined makeshift militias, informal vigilante groups, and the British Army. More than eighty thousand left their homes to resettle in Canada, the West Indies, or England.

Loyalists shared a belief in the legitimacy of British rule in North America. This legitimacy derived not only from England's time-honored right to rule over the parts of its empire, but also from the benefits conferred by England's protection of colonial frontiers and commerce. But beyond this common ground, loyalists comprised a varied cross-section of colonial society.

Governors and their close supporters stood at the top of the list of loyalists, especially Lord Dunmore in Virginia, Benning Wentworth in New Hampshire, and Thomas Hutchinson in Massachusetts. Clergy of the Church of England and lawyers of established reputations joined loyalists ranks by 1774 and 1775, too, denouncing separation from the empire as illegal and unconstitutional. Even after the Continental Congress declared in June 1775 that support for recent parliamentary laws constituted treason, loyalists used the pulpit, tavern, and courthouse steps to win wider support for the crown. Some leading loyalists funded the publication of inspired broadsides that combined impassioned political rhetoric and shocking stories of their mistreatment by patriots.

Many wealthy merchants, great landlords, and substantial slave owners joined the patriots, but far more of them could not imagine breaking from the empire. For them, aristocracy, monarchy, and social stability itself hung in the balance. Deference, the fragile cultural foundation of political power over local populations in many areas, could dissolve without the bonds of empire to support it. Property, institutional stability, and cultural traditions depended on the imperial trading system, they argued. As the Sons of Liberty and hundreds of local committees gained their own voices, which challenged the status quo to its roots, families "of reputation and property" grew anxious about the "democratic mob" they saw rising throughout North America.

Large numbers of loyalists came from the middling and lower strata of colonists. They also came from all occupations, as well as all age and ethnic groups. Sometimes a colonist's loyalism stemmed not from support for the crown, but from opposition to patriots who owned the estates on which they lived. This was certainly the case for hundreds of tenants along the Hudson River. Throughout New Jersey, hundreds of small farmers, the majority of Dutch descent, joined the pro-British New Jersey Volunteers. On the eastern shore of Maryland, many struggling farmers became loyalists when the landed and slave-owning gentry became patriots. The Regulators of North Carolina tended to join loyalist regiments because of their deep-seated distrust of the patriot coastal gentry.

Religion and ethnicity motivated some colonists to become loyalists. French Canadians, almost always Catholic, affirmed their loyalty to the crown by the hundreds and called for protection from frontier patriots under the terms of the 1774 Quebec Act. German groups, especially recent immigrants who had moved quickly onto the far frontiers, believed their religious freedom depended on British rule. Highland Scots in the Carolinas organized fierce resistance to the patriot militia, largely because they still identified with their British heritage and worried that future waves of newcomers to the frontier would take their land and challenge their religious freedom. And the thousands of British soldiers stationed in hostile cities or the lonely backcountry often welcomed the chance to prove their loyalty to the mother country.

At least fifty thousand slaves ran away to British lines or British territories, most of them from regions south of Richmond. Thousands of slaves "took their freedom" and escaped to Canada or northern colonial cities, especially New York City. Hoping to find a refuge in Indian villages, many Virginia and South Carolina slaves fled into the wilderness. Large numbers also tried to pass as freed persons in Florida or northern cities. In 1775 hundreds of runaway slaves made it to Sullivan's Island, South Carolina, but patriot forces overran this refuge in December and returned most of the escapees to their masters. Over the ensuing years, however, hundreds of slaves drifted back to the island for shorter or longer periods of time. In New York City, runaway slaves from patriot-held areas took shelter in the homes of resident slaves and their masters to form a "slave city."

Hundreds of slaves accepted the offer to enlist in loyalist regiments in exchange for their freedom. In Virginia, as news of Lexington and Concord spread, Governor Dunmore announced he would arm all slaves who defended the crown and free them at the end of hostilities. In November 1775, he made this promise an official decree, under which some eight hundred slaves applied to fill British army ranks within a couple of months. Most of them were relegated to noncombat roles such as keeping camp, constructing bridges, foraging, and repairing wagons. In addition, smallpox and cholera ravaged the "tent cities" where slaves encamped separately. Still, as many as twenty thousand slaves enlisted in the private brigades of British commanders or in the ranks of the British army, and thousands more aided the loyalists indirectly as the fighting shifted into the South. Once the Revolutionary War erupted, these practical rehearsals for freedom turned into a surge of African-Americans joining the military fray—on both sides.

Aside from the Catawba in South Carolina and Oneida of New York, most Native Americans became loyalists, if they chose a side at all. The Iroquois, long torn between opposing imperial forces on the frontier, had grown fearful about westward migration. As the Revolution neared, the Mohawk leader Joseph Brant sought reassurances from the British that settlers' land grabbing would cease. In return, Brant guaranteed that most Iroquois villages would support the British.

Loyalists who remained in civilian areas during the war became vulnerable to patriot humiliations, seizures of goods, confiscation of estates, house arrests, and

Joseph Brant, Chief of the Mohawks (1742–1807)
Also called Thayendanegea, Brant became a commissioned officer of the British Army and fought against patriots near Canada for much of the Revolution. Before 1776, Brant had been befriended by Sir William Johnson, Indian superintendent in New York, and served against the French at the Battle of Crown Point in the Seven Years' War. Brant's accomplishments were not confined to warring: he learned numerous European languages in Connecticut schools, traveled to London in 1775, and translated the New Testament and Anglican prayer book into Mohawk. *(National Gallery of Canada.)*

suspension of their civil rights. Patriots hurled the epithet "Tory"—a term that once identified die-hard defenders of absolute monarchy, but came to designate all supporters of British rule in North America—at loyalists in all ranks of society. Tories in New York City and Philadelphia were forced to "ride the rails," a painful trip through the streets astride a fence rail, and in many places tarring and feathering continued for the duration of the war. Patriots hung a few particularly recalcitrant loyalists by their wrists. New treason laws made it a crime to speak or write against the patriot cause. Patriots also used existing British laws, especially bills of attainder, to seize loyalist presses and lands. And they tended to regard women according to English common law, as "under the care and authority" of their fathers and husbands, enabling them to disregard even sincere declarations of neutrality and confiscate family businesses and farms from the women left to tend them.

Spies, Prisoners, and Evaders

Secretive communications and interpersonal betrayals marked revolutionary activity from the beginning. As early as 1776, Washington issued orders to patriot agents to establish a spy base and "secret correspondence for the purpose of conveying intelligence of the Enemy's movements and designs." Washington also regularly received information from refugee loyalists and British army deserters. Both sides used fraudulent reports and disguised infiltrators. Farmers and businessmen who crossed combat lines to make deliveries made excellent spies. Washington, for example, relied on the resourceful John Honeyman, a New Jersey butcher and weaver who plied his trades within British lines. Honeyman persuaded Hessian commanders that Washington did not intend to recross the Delaware River and collected essential information for the patriot attack on Trenton, December 26, 1776.

On the other side, the Boston physician Benjamin Church became a member of the Massachusetts Provincial Congress, but he also supplied General Thomas Gage with information on Lexington and Concord before the British raid and alerted the British about fortifications at Bunker Hill. Patriots discovered Church's treachery in 1777, but not before he had become Director General of American army hospitals and chief military physician. Church spent the rest of the war years confined in a Connecticut jail.

One of the most notorious loyalist spies was Benedict Arnold, a hero of the Continental campaigns in Canada and Saratoga. But in 1779 he turned against the patriots' cause and became a paid informer for General Henry Clinton, the head of British forces in occupied New York City. In 1780 Arnold used his post at West Point to betray patriot movements, and then fled behind British lines when patriots uncovered the plot to deliver the stronghold to the enemy. Major John André, a promising young officer in the British army, had worked closely with Arnold at West Point until patriots captured him in the "neutral ground" of northern New York and sent him to the gallows on October 2, 1780. In subsequent months, Arnold led raids against his home state of Connecticut, and then Virginia. He retired with a handsome pension in England, where he heard a running stream of news about the deep hatred that Americans bore against him.

Each side held thousands of prisoners of war. Generally, the British soldiers fared better than Americans did, largely because patriots took captives to the countryside and gave them food and outdoor work. Lancaster, Pennsylvania, became a major place of confinement, though the neighboring towns of York, Carlisle, Reading, Lebanon, and Hebron hired out thousands of captives as farm servants and iron foundry workers. British officers, on the other hand, often moved about freely, buying extra food and clothing when it was available. Although the southern gentry and northern urban elite enjoyed the intellectual and social company of cultivated European officers and their families, local people often greeted the enemy with hostility. For example, when Baroness Riedesel, wife of the Hessian commanding general, arrived in Virginia with her two children, one householder refused the baroness extra food: "The corn we need for our slaves because they work for us, but you come here to kill us."

Many American prisoners endured horrid conditions in New York City prisons and British hospital ships anchored offshore, and great numbers of them did not survive the ordeal. The British deprived patriots of rations, fuel, and sanitation. Fewer than 800 of the 4,500 prisoners taken in the siege of New York and the flight to White Plains survived to be exchanged later in the war. Typhus, called "jail fever," claimed hundreds of lives, and starvation carried off hundreds more. The British also executed nearly 300 of the men taken in these early campaigns. Living conditions in the floating jails moored in New York and Charles Town harbors were abominable. Prisoners spent days below deck retching, ate meat and biscuits full of worms, and slept standing up. Guards treated complaints with beatings and shackles. In the New York jails alone, between 8,000 and 11,500 rebels died, more than all the men killed in military action during the Revolution. And neither side offered an effective form of prisoner exchange until very late in the war.

Patriots raised evasion of service to a high art by 1777. Congress and the states had two ways to recruit soldiers, both of them fraught with difficulties. One was to promise or directly pay cash bounties for enlistment. But congressional and state recruiters both tried to fill assigned quotas, and their competition for men bid up the bounties to such tempting amounts that unscrupulous citizens enlisted several times. By 1779, multiple enlistments were common in every state. In the second method of recruitment, state governments ordered local conscription officers to draft quotas of men. Officials accepted substitutes for drafted men—as European armies had for generations—and soon the practice of hiring substitutes to fight was a regular practice. In the South, masters tried to pass off their slaves into service, and in many cities, artisans hired handicapped or mentally unfit persons to report to camp, knowing that "the ringers" would be sent home and everyone would escape conscription. Dissenters such as the Quakers, Mennonites, and Amish made legitimate claims to be exempted on the basis of religious beliefs or pacifism, although some were fined heavily as a consequence. Moravians of North Carolina stated that "we Brethren do not bear arms," but they willingly gave financial and

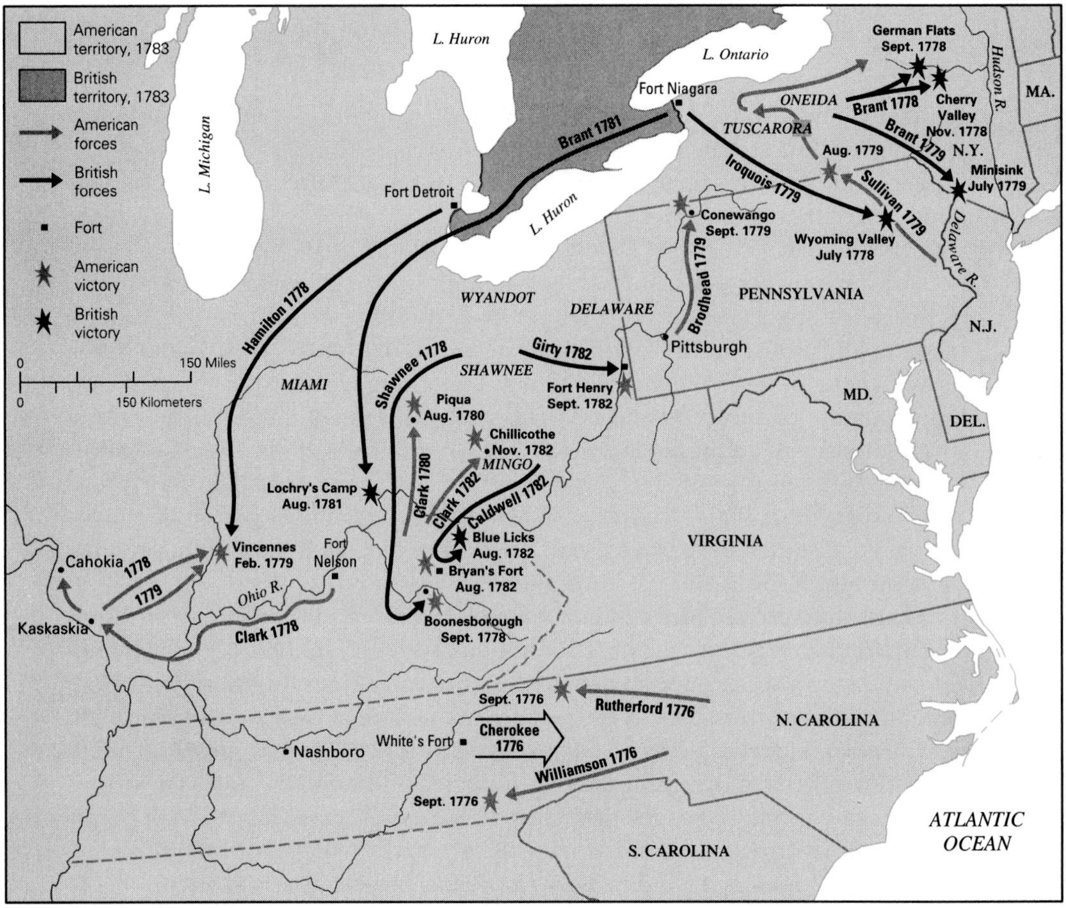

War in the West Although patriots won important victories in the Hudson and Mohawk river valleys during 1777, the Ohio and Pennsylvania frontiers remained vulnerable to British attacks.

material aid to patriots and worked in military hospitals. The result of all these factors was a fighting force of increasingly poor, propertyless men of doubtful commitment to the cause.

The New Republican Order

As the war dragged on, with its dire need for manpower, indecisive battles, low morale, and a crumbling economy, revolutionaries discussed what kind of political structures were suited to their republican character. When delegates approved the Declaration of Independence, they stepped out of the empire, but they did not replace their former colonial governments with new ones right away. Shunning aristocracy and monarchy, in their place the patriots created a weak central government during the Revolution. They also agreed to distribute most political authority separately to the thirteen former colonies. And it was in these jurisdictions that revolutionaries groped toward redefining what their particular republican rights and privileges would be. Although most patriots still believed that pure democracies were an unreliable form of authority, they readily dropped their identity as "subjects" of the empire and began to call one another "citizen."

From Colonies to States

Patriot leaders knew they were embarking on a great experiment. Their experiences expanding the power of the colonial assemblies, creating committees and congresses during the imperial crisis, and sustaining a war for independence focused many discussions on a single critical issue: how to refine the rights and obligations of citizens and their rulers. Often, they turned to classical and republican writers to express their ideas about good government. As Tom Paine had reminded Americans, "The word *republic,* means the *public good,* or the good of the whole." Benjamin Rush's words to Americans intoned that virtue, the opposite of corruption, came from deep within individuals: "Every man in a republic is public property. His time and talents—his youth—his manhood—his old age—nay more, life, all belong to his country." Rush, and thousands of Americans who put pen to paper in these years, believed that every patriot should exhibit republican virtue. But the day-to-day circumstances of the war revealed that virtue was fragile, and the wisdom of the ages taught that any government constituted on a republican basis could not endure. Moreover, opponents reminded revolutionary leaders that the English monarchy had already lasted for about a thousand years, whereas every republic had become corrupted and declined in a short time.

In order to make the ideal of republicanism a more practical reality, revolutionary leaders insisted on certain innovations. First of all, a virtuous citizenry required written constitutions comprised of explicit principles. The unwritten British constitution, made up of many centuries' worth of customs and precedents, could not be studied, known, and altered by a great number of citizens participating in politics. Further, written documents would be based on popular sovereignty—the principle that governments derive "their just powers from the consent of the governed," or "the people," as the Declaration of Independence set forth. Still, the Declaration did not prescribe what form of government should follow from this axiom. Nevertheless, during the Revolution, each former colony created distinct but compatible written republican constitutions that embodied popular sovereignty.

Second, Americans writing new constitutions believed that the most durable and just republics were small ones. The Baron de Montesquieu's *Spirit of the Laws,* a widely read treatise on different forms of government, cautioned that rulers should regularly consult the interests of the ruled. To do this, rulers should be physically near the people. Governments deliberating too far from the people could not enact wise policies. Distant governments out of touch with "the circumstances of their domain" eventually became sources of tyranny.

Numerous writers grappled with how to create new governments along these lines. In New Hampshire in 1776, an anonymous pamphleteer proposed in *The People the Best Governors* that all power should reside in one elected body, without property qualifications for any official position, and with universal adult male suffrage. Furthermore, the judicial branch also should be elected; most legislation should emanate from town meetings at the local level; and taxes should be raised and used in the towns or counties. Paine's *Common Sense* proposed a similarly democratic form of government, with no property qualifications for voting or holding office, and no upper council of wealthy lawmakers. Paine substituted a unicameral, or one-house, legislature instead, and he proposed to eliminate imprisonment for debt, protect small producers and commercial farmers, and educate all citizens. Pennsylvania's 1776 constitution incorporated many of these radical measures; Georgia's and Vermont's constitutions provided for unicameral legislatures.

John Adams proposed a different form of state government, one adopted by Virginia and then other states. Adams thought Paine's plan was far too democratic and too simplistic. He set out his own ideas in *Thoughts on Government* (1777), as a direct reply to Paine. Americans should abandon the "mixed government" of the unwritten British constitution, Adams wrote, under which three different social orders—king, lords, and commons—acted together. Instead, the powers of government should be divided among three separate branches—executive, judicial, and legislative. The legislature should have two houses, neither of which would base officeholding on social rank. Adams agreed with many radical patriots that governments should rest on republican virtue, the sacrifice of self-interest for the common good. Republics could not rule by force, but rather by talent, wisdom, and the consent of the governed. Government, he wrote in a famous metaphor, should mirror the diversity of society. But, Adams continued, the popular multitudes ought not to have whimsical authority over all officials. Justices should be appointed, not elected, and governors should have the power to veto legislation.

State delegations tended to write more democratic constitutions early in the war than they did later on. Some, as in Virginia and Georgia, started by defining individual, or civil, rights before proceeding to form their representative governments. They assumed that "the people" had to carve out the boundaries of their rights before they surrendered some of them to governing bodies. Among these rights were protection of property and life, abolition of hereditary privileges, frequent elections and short terms of office, trial by jury, religious toleration, and an extended franchise. Most of the early state governments also gave state legislatures sovereignty over all other parts of government. In 1776 Virginia created a legislature elected by qualified voters annually; the legislature was to appoint the governor, his council, and most state justices. Virginians denied their governor a veto power and strictly limited his powers to the area of appointing officials.

The differences between upper and lower houses of the early and more democratic state governments were minor. Candidates for the upper house did not need great property holdings to be elected, and three states permitted the lower house to elect the upper, which further restricted the rise of political privilege. In addition, these states created larger lower houses and began to create counties in their western regions that gained representation in government. As a result, men of modest means often held legislative seats. The early, more democratic states also created executive branches made up of committees, implemented voting by secret ballot, opened their legislative sessions to the public, and published proposed bills prior to voting on laws.

Some of the first new states not only unseated the wealthy, but turned out entire ruling factions. In Pennsylvania, for example, middling artisans, retailers, and professionals, many of them recent German and Scottish immigrants, asked why "men of great property" always led citizens when "men of modest means" were equally qualified? These groups formed an alliance that swept away the dominating Quaker elite and proprietary party. The new Constitutionalist party formulated many elements in the radical state constitution of 1776. Then, under the pressures of mobilizing the militia, taxing and regulating the economy of starving citizens, and quelling disorders on the frontier, the Constitutionalists found themselves in the unexpected position of resorting to force against their opponents, including many pacifist Quakers whom they disfranchised. Although many Scots-Irish and Germans played an important role in the Constitutionalist party after 1777, more experienced leaders could easily brush them aside during wartime.

Indeed, from 1777 on, new state constitutions began to reflect the more conservative reasoning of Adams's *Thoughts on Government.* New York established a bicameral legislature with the lower house determined by population, a governor with a strong veto power, an appointed judiciary, and property qualifications that restricted voting to only 40 percent of adult white men. South Carolina's constitution of 1778 required governors to have a debt-free estate of at least £10, 000, and other officials to own property as well. About 10 percent of the white male population were qualified to hold office, and only a small minority of men even qualified for voting. Maryland's 1777 constitution, the most conservative of all, adopted voting and electing requirements similar to those in South Carolina, but added that judges and high executive officers should sit for life.

Serious internal divisions in some states prevented easy resolution of their differences from the onset of constitutional discussions. In Massachusetts the divisions between east and west, older towns and newer settlements, established political privileges and rising ambitions, persisted for over four years. In the fall of 1776, the provincial government asked the towns for authorization to draft a constitution. In the past this request would have been granted without question. But by now, some of the towns had grown distrustful of central authority and wished to have newly created powers emanate directly from them. The government got just enough support to proceed, but when the delegates sent the constitution to the towns for ratification two years later, it was overwhelmingly rejected.

Massachusetts citizens had various opinions about the particular rights and obligations outlined in the proposed state constitution. But they generally agreed that a special convention should be assembled to discuss matters and draft a satisfactory document. Following John Locke's reasoning, some town leaders argued that the Declaration of Independence had torn down former governments, leaving citizens in a "state of nature," and that they now needed collectively to create a government from scratch.

In December 1779, state leaders did, indeed, organize a special convention in Boston, at which delegates wrote a draft constitution to be submitted to all free adult males for ratification. The resulting document stipulated annual elections for both houses of the legislature, the lower one chosen by the free adult voters of the towns and the upper one by counties according to property holdings rather than population. The constitution permitted the governor a veto, albeit a limited one. It narrowed the franchise to citizens worth £50 in real estate or £100 in personal property; officeholders had to meet higher property qualifications. Voters approved the Massachusetts constitution in spring 1780, and it became the most popular model for states formed in the next years. Despite its apparent bias toward elite officeholding, the Massachusetts constitution had been drafted in a special convention at which political discussion was open to middling citizens. The wider public discussions and deliberations in turn spurred leaders at the national level to consider the importance of this popular sovereignty for their political reforms.

Despite the differences in the various state constitutions, and despite the elitist qualities of some, American political culture became more democratic during the Revolution. Most new states reduced the authority of their executive branches. Most lower houses apportioned seats according to population, which gave all regions of the states an opportunity to send representatives to legislatures. Eight of the state constitutions incorporated statements of individual rights that followed from the premise that "all men are created equal." Furthermore, there was widespread discussion in every state about important issues such as the frequency of elections, the extent of suffrage, and the duties of officeholders. This open forum emboldened "men not quite so well dressed, nor so politely educated, nor so highly born" to become active in the affairs of their new states, and at times even to hold office. In their thinking, revolutionary Americans rejected "democracy" because they believed it inclined too easily toward mob rule and licentiousness. Instead, they chose the identity of "republicans" who entrusted government to men of superior genius and talent. But in practice, many more artisans and commercial farmers were serving in the lower houses by 1785. In a short time, large numbers of Americans who had never played a direct role in determining legislation or returning their "betters" to office would begin to identify their political interests with like-minded people and move onto the public stage of electioneering and party life.

The Articles of Confederation

As the Revolutionary War proceeded, the Continental Congress initiated a discussion about what powers a national government should have. Given that colonists had declared their independence from the coercive authority of one great empire, they wished above all to avoid another highly centralized government. As a consequence, the proposed Articles of Confederation set strict limits on the powers of Congress. Strong traditions of local governance within all the colonies reinforced this commitment to weak central power. The Articles stipulated that each province would have one vote in a national assembly, which would be one body without separate "chambers," and that the Articles be approved unanimously by all thirteen provinces in order to have effect. Once the Articles were approved, each province could send two to seven delegates to the new Confederation Congress, each delegate serving no more than three out of six years. Congress would determine most matters by a simple majority; important issues would require the approval of at least nine provinces. Congress could declare war and make peace, coin or print money, raise loans for public uses, regulate Indian trade, decide disputes between states and territories, run the postal system, and establish a system of weights and measures. But it could not tax citizens directly; rather, it had to request money or supplies from the thirteen provinces.

In November 1777, Congress submitted its draft of the Articles of Confederation to the thirteen rebelling former colonies for their collective ratification. By mid-1778, eight of the newly created states had ratified the Articles, but to take effect, all thirteen had to approve the document. Four more new states ratified in the next year, but Maryland held out. During deliberations in Congress about what rights a national government should have, one important privilege stayed in the hands of states and individuals: control over western lands. Now during the ratification process, Maryland's leaders demanded that Congress have more control over these lands. Otherwise, the eight large states with extensive land claims in the West would use occupation and sale of land to expand their political power to an inordinate degree. Marylanders did not wish to strengthen Congress, but rather to weaken the large states. Maryland's legislators demanded that large states "cede" portions of their western territories to Congress, creating a "national domain" outside of individual states' control. Speculators who held shares in western land companies went along, hoping to make special deals with Congress. Eventually, New York and Virginia ceded portions of their western claims to Congress "for the good of the public." Mollified, in March 1781, Maryland signed the Articles of Confederation.

By the time the Articles became law, most of the war had been fought. Indeed, certain members of Congress, known as the "nationalists," attributed the sorry state of the army and civilian living conditions during the war to the absence of an effective central governing power. Once the individual provinces approved the Articles, nationalists quickly proposed remedies for pressing problems. Most important, Robert Morris, possibly the wealthiest merchant in America, became the superintendent of finance in May 1781. By that time, Congress's currency was "not worth a continental" and ceased to circulate. Morris stepped in with a masterful plan to turn around Congress's dire financial condition. First he persuaded Congress to charter the first private commercial bank in America, the Bank of North America (BNA). In it Morris deposited the silver, gold, and bills of exchange loaned to America by Holland and France, as well as large sums of his own money. Morris then asked Congress to authorize a printing of new certificates, to circulate freely with the backing of BNA funds and to earn interest. In mid-1781 Morris initiated a new means to supply the army, a bidding system for supply contracts. Both the bank-backed certificates and the army contracts operated with "the full credit and name of Congress."

Morris wanted to do still more. With the support of his fellow nationalists in and out of Congress, he proposed amending the Articles of Confederation to allow him to create a national revenue based on taxes. Although citizens expressed widespread opposition to granting Congress authority to tax, twelve states approved the proposed duty on commercial imports, or "impost," by fall 1782. Only Rhode Island, or "Rogue's Island" to impatient nationalists, refused, but without this tiny state's vote, the duty—America's first proposed tariff—failed. Later that year, New York rescinded its support for the impost as well. Over 1782–1784, some provinces also began paying the interest on war debts and certificates directly to their citizens, bypassing Congress. In this way, Pennsylvania, New York, New Jersey, and Maryland took over, or "assumed," about one-third of their national debt by 1786, thereby undermining the authority Morris had so carefully crafted.

Given the significance of debt and taxes to the creation of central governing authority, nationalists grew fearful about state assumption. They began to perceive a profound division of interests between Congress and the thirteen provinces. Even as the war wound down and negotiators went to the peace talks in Paris, nationalists began to discuss ways to bolster the central taxing authority of Congress. They also knew they would have to revisit another issue: the disposition of western lands.

Winning the War, 1778–1783

Congress rejoiced over the French alliance of 1778, which secured money, soldiers, and guns for the patriot cause. But military victory was far from assured. Tensions in the West heated up until they erupted into unconventional forms of fighting involving Indians, Spanish, and frontier settlers of different political persuasions. In addition, Lord North commenced a brutal southern campaign that left Americans wondering, again, whether their virtue and sacrifice would lead to independence after all. In the end, while the British army floundered in an alien military environment, it was Americans' ability to withstand the bitter final struggles in the southern states that pulled them through.

The War in the West

In 1778, a year after France forged its alliance with Americans, Spain also declared war on Britain. Although Spain had not committed itself directly to the American cause, its armed strikes against Britain in various parts of the world indirectly aided the patriots. Spain tried to retake Gibraltar, but failed. Next, it tried to overrun British West Florida, and succeeded. Then, setting its sites farther west, Spain aimed to protect the Louisiana territory, which it had received as a gift from France by the Treaty of Paris in 1763. Spain had slowly built up trade and Indian diplomacy to prosperous levels around San Diego and San Francisco, California, and immigrants from the Canary Islands, Acadia, and French trading posts created viable towns with strong Spanish identities along the Mississippi River.

Elsewhere in the West, most Indians remained neutral unless their own immediate interests favored an expedient alliance with the British to defend their homelands. Only the Catawba, deep in the South, favored the American rebels during the Revolution. The Choctaw, Creek, Cherokee, and Chickasaw waged fierce war against the patriot backcountry in the South. The Cherokee, in particular, suffered from warfare on their lands, first in 1760 (see page 167) and again in 1776. By the end of the Revolution, Cherokee and Shawnee villages had been rebuilt far into the West.

Out in Ohio country, beyond the Appalachian ridge, the Revolution assumed characteristics that few Britons anticipated in 1776. Already the Iroquois and Cherokee had sold their claims to this vast area, and the Shawnee continued to regard Virginians with hostility even after surrendering their claims in the valley. Continued American expansion into the Ohio country revitalized Indian hatreds and enhanced tribal support for an alliance with the British. Indian allies of the British torched the American settlements at Boonesborough in 1778 and terrorized Americans by taking scalps in return for British bounties. From 1778 to 1781, Iroquois rampaged across the Wyoming Valley of east central Pennsylvania, joined by the Great Lakes Indians to fend off hostile settlers in the Ohio Valley.

George Rogers Clark, an inveterate Indian fighter still just twenty-six years old, led a combined force of American and French frontiersmen from Kaskaskia, Illinois, and militiamen from Virginia against an alliance of Creek and Ohio Indians during the winter of 1779. Clark's "Long Knives" held Vincennes, deep in the American interior, for some months before the Native Americans drove them out in 1781. But by then, Clark had taken the last of the British forts and established firm American claims over the entire region north of the Ohio River. Other battles, far from the diplomatic centers of the Revolution, engaged hundreds of Americans who died defending the wilderness from Indian, British, and French belligerents. For generations to come, these hostilities seethed. Frontier "buckskins" and American troops continued to shield the advancing line of European settlement, even when doing so required atrocities.

In the North, the Iroquois divided. Mohawk chief Joseph Brant, in alliance with the Seneca, helped loyalists and British troops raid patriot villages on the Pennsylvania and New York frontier. But in retaliation, patriots combined with friendly Oneida and Tuscarora to attack villages allied with Brant. The mighty confederacy of Iroquois nations almost disintegrated during 1779.

The War in the South

In late 1778, the British navy took Savannah, Georgia. From there, royal commander General Henry Clinton planned to launch an assault on Charles Town, South Carolina, and wage a pacification campaign in the southern countryside. Clinton would leave Lord Cornwallis in charge of southern forces while he returned to the north to attack Washington's army in New Jersey. This effort, Clinton knew, required full mobilization of redcoats and the aid of thousands of loyalists.

The first part of Clinton's plan worked with unprecedented success. Cornwallis took Charles Town from Benjamin Lincoln and his five thousand Continentals in May 1780, making it the single greatest surrender of the war. By July, Cornwallis had evicted patriots from the city, established military control of the state, and purged rebels from government. His forces organized rice production and export, and forced loyalty oaths (including promises to take up arms for the crown) on all able-bodied Carolinians. Cornwallis enjoyed the support of marauder loyalists under Banastre Tarleton, who chased about 350 patriots toward the North Carolina border during June, slaughtering all who stood in his way and then murdering those who surrendered. British officer Patrick Ferguson led another group of armed vigilantes against patriot settlements along the Santee River.

South Carolina patriots also mobilized vigilante raiders, whose unconventional methods of fighting became normal in the final Revolutionary campaigns. Under Thomas Sumter, a planter-merchant, eight hundred mounted raiders stormed Hanging Rock on August 6. Their target was not British soldiers but nearly five hundred loyalist settlers scattered in dozens of new homesteads. Sumter's riders overran the largely defenseless loyalists and then succumbed to looting and drinking. Meanwhile, commander Horatio Gates moved his wing of Continentals from

War in the South After the British invaded Georgia in 1778, their strategy was to move deep into the Carolina interior, where numerous battles tested the morale and endurance of both sides until the decisive patriot victory at Yorktown in October 1781.

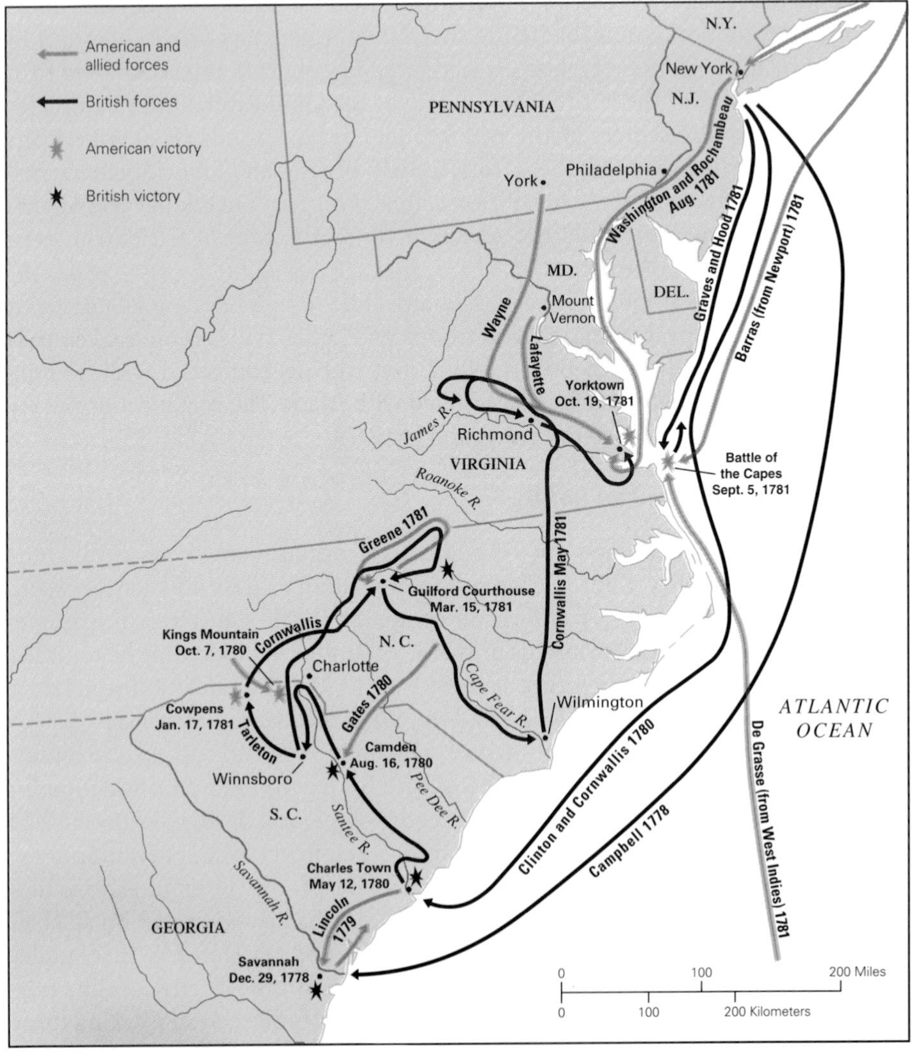

Maryland and Delaware into the South, where two thousand Virginia and North Carolina militia joined them. But at Camden, South Carolina, on August 16, Cornwallis leveled the combined patriot force. Two days later, Tarleton's bandits raided Sumter's camp at Fishing Creek, where they killed over two hundred and wounded up to three hundred patriots. Violence was common in colonial life, especially on the frontiers, but the massacres at Hanging Rock and Fishing Creek escalated partisan animosities to unheard-of levels. From then on, both sides threw themselves into a backcountry civil war that bore little resemblance to what regular armies or militiamen had been trained to do. Patriot leader Gates remained dumbfounded at the "murders and devastations" all around him.

With British now in control of South Carolina, many patriots feared reprisals from the thousands of slaves who had flocked to the British side. Unlike their counterparts anywhere in the North, southern loyalists not only professed their allegiance to the crown boldly, but also organized large fighting units that turned viciously against the rebels.

But the tide began to turn against Cornwallis in 1780. France dispatched five thousand troops under General Comte de Rochambeau. They arrived in Newport, Rhode Island, in July and August, and awaited orders to march against either Clinton's troops in New York City or Cornwallis's in South Carolina. In addition, patriots redoubled their efforts to defend the southern backcountry. Cornwallis had embarked on a plan to plunder any portions of the North Carolina frontier that did not join the British. In response, patriot riflemen from across the Blue Ridge descended on Patrick Ferguson's loyalists in early fall 1780. The bloody encounters that ensued involved mostly civilians on both sides. Finally, in a battle at King's Mountain, patriot woodsmen prevailed and captured about six hundred of Ferguson's men; in October they hanged a few loyalists and shot many prisoners. Local communities were quick to point out that patriot tactics were no less brutish than Tarleton's. Meanwhile, Cornwallis's advance into North Carolina ended.

Washington also replaced Gates with General Nathanael Greene, who entered South Carolina by land with a small number of Continentals in October 1780. At about that time, "the Swamp Fox," Francis Marion, recruited hundreds of patriot backcountry settlers from remote origins. Heeding Marion's advice that he divide his troops into small spearheads, Greene sent 300 men with Marion and another 300 riflemen with Daniel Morgan to encircle Cornwallis's troops. Morgan picked up about 700 militia as he crossed the countryside and set up camp with his back to the river at Cowpens, South Carolina. When Tarleton attacked on January 17, 1781, Morgan deployed first his militia sharpshooters, then the Continentals, and finally an armed cavalry, in a bewildering array of choreographed moves that decimated Tarleton's army.

Although Cornwallis held his ground at the Guilford Court House on March 15, 1781, it was a shallow victory because he had exhausted his troops by chasing Greene deeper and deeper into terrain that British cannon and wagons could not manage. Cornwallis confessed that he did not know where to go next. The British had almost no connection to coastal supply lines, while bases of support "plentifully fed" patriot troops in Virginia.

The Battle of King's Mountain This painting by Robert Windsor Wilson of the 1780 struggle between the "over mountain men" and redcoats depicts the close contact of soldiers. Toward the end of the Revolution, when most battles had shifted into the South, more frontier patriots banded together, often foraging in the backcountry woods and sleeping in the open for weeks. Many patriots from western counties of South Carolina hoped they would get more responsive government and internal development from the Revolution, as had the Regulators before them. *(Collection of the State of South Carolina.)*

Cornwallis decided to keep marching north, into Virginia. He set up camp at Yorktown in late August 1781. And there he and his 8,000 men waited while American and French forces regrouped and converged on them. Rochambeau and his 5,000 French troops were still fresh and ready in Newport, Rhode Island. When Washington found out that French commanders had steered their Caribbean fleet toward the Chesapeake, he asked Rochambeau to provide reinforcement in the bay outside Yorktown. Lafayette moved down the interior of Virginia's eastern shore to join them and French Admiral Count de Barras approached from the north by sea. From the water, American and French forces bombarded the British for nearly a month until mid-October, when Cornwallis realized he would not be reinforced by Clinton and his own supplies gave out. After two days of negotiations, he sent out from the trenches his second-in-command, General Charles O'Hara, to surrender. On October 19, 1781, the British admitted defeat to the "bloody colonials," whom they had regarded with contempt as inferiors for generations.

Victory at Last

The reasons for the American victory are not straightforward, but certain factors were critical. For one thing, the Continental Army matured over time and learned discipline and formal battle routines they needed when facing the redcoats in open battle. For another, American civilians, for all of their failings of virtue, sacrificed enormously over seven long years of warfare, from Lexington to Yorktown. Once they dismantled British government in most areas, Americans worked together to create new government structures and sustain the war. In addition, French troops, arms, and silver aided patriots considerably, and the Spanish navy provided well-timed modest support as well.

For their part, the British faced formidable difficulties supplying their forces in the interior of North America, especially when a recession developed in England and its subjects grew openly war weary. Britain also fought this costly and long war without European allies. Commanders Howe and Clinton usually chose cautious maneuvers and clung to the official rules of eighteenth-century warfare when Americans readily and regularly adapted to terrain and local circumstances. Nor did the British use their loyalist strength effectively: in the north, loyalists operated relatively autonomously from the redcoats at crucial moments, and in the south, loyalists formed vicious vigilante groups that drove large numbers of backcountry people into the arms of patriots. Finally, the Continental Congress, Continental Army, state governments, and civilian committees all provided vehicles for patriots to affirm and extend republican political authority throughout the countryside that was fundamentally at odds with monarchy. The British reason for continuing to fight in North America—restoring Americans to royal rule—became unrealistic.

The war need not have ended with the fall of Yorktown. After all, Clinton still held New York City. But when Lord North sensed that his own career had been dashed, he resigned in November 1781. In March 1782, King George accepted the new Rockingham administration's proposal to recognize American independence. The Continental Congress's representatives, Benjamin Franklin, John Adams, and John Jay, discussed the terms of peace with British and French officials for months. Eventually it became clear to the Americans that their French allies did not have the same objectives. The French wanted to divide up the colonies and give England rule over New York, Georgia, and the Carolinas. The American negotiators could not accept this; they claimed not only all thirteen independent provinces but Canada as well.

In November 1782, all the parties set their names to the Treaty of Paris, which recognized the United States to be "free Sovereign and independent States." Canada remained British, but the United States would extend to the Mississippi. In a separate treaty between Britain and Spain, Florida became Spanish once again. The Treaty of Paris permitted creditors to collect pre-war and wartime debts, in sterling, which in time created hardship for southerners. And Congress agreed to ask the states to consider returning all confiscated property to loyalists—which the states eventually declined to do. Finally, Britain agreed to withdraw its troops on the frontier—a provision that also went unfulfilled for many years. The Treaty of Paris was signed on September 2, 1783. It was followed by the exodus of thousands of British troops and loyalists, who left New York, Charles Town, and Savannah to begin again in St. Augustine, Nova Scotia, West Indies islands, and London.

CONCLUSION

The Revolution was the longest war in American history until Vietnam. Perhaps as many as one in ten of the available population served under arms. During its eight years, communities divided deeply and endured dire economic and social duress. And going into the war, few patriots expressed an identity as "Americans." For the majority of rebels, local attachments were the strongest ones. The war itself offered further challenges to soldiers and citizens concerning taxes, army recruitment and supply, and civilian survival.

But the struggle for independence did, indeed, prevail. Patriots committed to the movement for political independence believed that the existing imperial political and social system had become unbearable. As they advanced from declaring independence toward forming a new republican order, they began to formulate their alternative to life in the empire. A significant number of patriots must have been convinced—though to different degrees—that their victory would make their lives better in political, cultural, and economic terms. Although, for the most part, their plans did not include women or people of color, the ideal of republican citizenship for male heads of households underlay patriots' efforts to define the powers granted to Congress and new state governments. The need for alliances and material support from foreign nations also forced leading patriots to begin formulating the rebellious North Americans' relationship to existing nations.

Beyond this, the expanse over which patriots fought the war, and their many internal divisions, did not permit a singular vision of the future or a unified identity as Americans. The war taught as much about the limits of individual sacrifice as it did about the virtues of the revolutionary cause. The creation of new governments did little to settle questions about who should run them and who should benefit from their actions. At war's end, citizens of the new states were more divided than ever.

After 1781, people throughout the separate states faced the awesome tasks of demobilizing an army and reconstructing society. Many Indians and slaves felt entitled to land and freedom in return for their sacrifices during the Revolution. Thousands of relocated loyalists left homes and estates that needed to be disposed of; thousands more wished to stay in the new republic, but it was not clear how to reintegrate them. The Continental Congress had been too busy raising an army and financing a war to clarify much about its relationship to citizens or state governments. Republican rhetoric asked revolutionaries to sacrifice their private interests for the public good, but continual internal discord was the norm. Now that they had won the war, survivors would have to secure the peace among themselves.

SUGGESTED READINGS

There are some valuable general works on the American Revolution, each with a different perspective. For social portraits, see Edward Countryman, *The American Revolution* (1985); Steven Rosswurm, *Arms, Country, and Class: The Philadelphia Militia and the "Lower Sort" During the American Revolution* (1987); Alfred Young, ed., *The American Revolution: Explorations in the History of American Radicalism* (1976), and the older but invaluable Merrill Jensen, *The Founding of a Nation: A History of the American Revolution, 1763–1776* (1968).

For the political culture of the era, Jack P. Greene, ed., *The American Revolution: Its Character and Limits* (1987) is the best starting point. The most recent effort to synthesize historical scholarship is Gordon Wood, *The Radicalism of the American Revolution* (1992). For a series of detailed vignettes about ideas, political processes, and military events, see Jack P. Greene and J. R. Pole, eds., *The Blackwell Encyclopedia of the American Revolution* (1998).

For contrasting perspectives about the last efforts at compromise and the forging of oppositional currents, see John Brooke, *King George III* (1972). The biography by Philip Lawson, *George Grenville: A Political Life* (1984), represents an effort to show scholarly balance and fractured communication during the era.

For the Continental Congress's work and the Declaration of Independence, see Jack Rakove, *The Beginnings of National Politics: An Interpretive History of the Continental Congress* (1979); Pauline Maier, *American Scripture: Making the Declaration of Independence* (1997); Richard Ryerson, *The Revolution Is Now Begun* (1978); and Peter Shaw, *The Character of John Adams* (1976). The best single study of Paine and the urban scenario of Philadelphia is Eric Foner, *Tom Paine and Revolutionary America* (1976).

The exuberance of the first year is captured in Charles Royster, *A Revolutionary People at War: The Continental Army and American Character* (1980).

The social aspects of the war, on the field and off, provide some of the most fascinating reading about the Revolution. The best places to start are Robert Gross, *The Minutemen and Their World* (1976); Dirk Hoerder, *Crowd Action in Revolutionary Massachusetts, 1765–1780* (1977); Ronald Hoffman, *A Spirit of Dissension: Economics, Politics, and the Revolution in Maryland* (1973); and Michael Belleisles, *Revolutionary Outlaw: Ethan Allen and the Struggle for Independence on the Early American Frontier* (1993).

For frontier warfare, see Colin G. Calloway, *The American Revolution in Indian Country: Crisis and Diversity in Native American Communities* (1995); Barbara Graymont, *The Iroquois in the American Revolution* (1972); James H. O'Donnel III, *Southern Indians in the American Revolution* (1973); Alan Taylor, *Liberty Men and Great Proprietors: The Revolutionary Settlement on the Maine Frontier, 1760–1820* (1990); and Richard White, *The Middle Ground: Indians, Empires, and Republics in the Great Lakes Region, 1650–1815* (1991).

The best study about the corruption, doubts, and deceits of the Revolutionary War, especially related to the army supplying, is E. Wayne Carp, *To Starve the Army at Pleasure: Continental Army Administration and American Political Culture, 1775–1783* (1984). On the loyalists: Wallace Brown, *The Good Americans: The Loyalists in the American Revolution* (1969), and Robert Calhoon, Timothy Barnes, and George Rawlyk, eds., *Loyalists and Community in North America* (1994).

On army and militia life in the field, see the very engaging work of James Kirby Martin and Edward Mark Lender, *A Respectable Army: The Military Origins of the Republic, 1763–1789* (1982), and Holly Mayer, *Belonging to the Army: Camp Followers and Community During the American Revolution* (1966). For a more ideological study, which also explains many political twists and turns during the war, see Don Higginbotham, *The War of American Independence: Military Attitudes, Policies, and Practice, 1763–1789* (1983).

For the struggles over public commitment to the patriotic effort, many insights about daily local life are offered in Richard Buel and Joy Day Buel, *The Way of Duty: A Woman and Her Family in Revolutionary America* (1984).

The best book about forging new state governments is Gordon Wood, *The Creation of the American Republic* (1969). But Jack Rakove adds important dimensions to the state-level discussion about rights, property, and sovereignty in his new work, *Original Meanings: Politics and Ideas in the Making of the Constitution* (1996); and the older volume by Jackson T. Main, *The Sovereign States, 1775–1783* (1973), is still a valuable source on this subject.

Work on the southern campaigns often overlaps with portrayals of the frontier and Native Americans. See the indispensable studies, Jeffrey Crow and Larry Tise, eds., *The Southern*

Experience in the American Revolution (1978), and Ronald Hoffman and Thad W. Tate, eds., *An Uncivil War: The Southern Backcountry During the American Revolution* (1985). In addition, the final months of struggle are covered well in James O'Donnell, *Southern Indians in the American Revolution* (1973); John Pancake, *The Destructive War: The British Campaign in the Carolinas, 1780–1782* (1985); and Russell Weigley, *The Partisan War: The South Carolina Campaign of 1780–1782* (1970).

Important work assessing what patriots gained during the Revolution are Ira Berlin and Ronald Hoffman, *Slavery and Freedom in the Age of the American Revolution* (1983); John Ferling, ed., *The World Turned Upside Down: The American Victory in the War of Independence* (1988); and John C. Dann, ed., *The Revolution Remembered: Eyewitness Accounts of the War for Independence* (1980). All of these works illuminate, through local studies and personal portraits, the role of different social constituencies. The matter of new rights and obligations for women is treated admirably in Linda Kerber, *Women of the Republic: Intellect and Ideology in Revolutionary America* (1980), and Mary Beth Norton, *Liberty's Daughters: The Revolutionary Experience of American Women, 1750–1800* (1980); but also see the social framework of women's rural life in Joan Jensen, *Loosening the Bonds: Mid-Atlantic Farm Women, 1750–1850* (1986).

Slavery is treated in many of the studies listed above. For separate treatments that focus on slaves and free African-Americans, see Jeffrey Crow, *The Black Experience in Revolutionary North Carolina* (1977); Sylvia Frey, *Water from the Rock: Black Resistance in a Revolutionary Age* (1991); Gary Nash, *Forging Freedom: The Formation of Philadelphia's Black Community, 1720–1840* (1988); and Gary A Puckrein, *The Black Regiment in the American Revolution* (1978).

Two Views of the Imperial Crisis

Competing Voices

Daniel Leonard Condemns Rebellion, 1775

When events heated up in 1775, Daniel Leonard, a lawyer from an elite Massachusetts family, was forced to flee from his country home and take shelter in British-occupied Boston until he could escape, first to Halifax and then to Bermuda. Leonard wrote seventeen eloquent appeals to fellow colonists to remain loyal to the British crown. The selection that follows appeared in the *Boston Gazette* two weeks before Lexington and Concord.

> We have been so long advancing to our present state, and by such gradations, that perhaps many of us are insensible of our true state and real danger. Should you be told that acts of high treason are flagrant through the country, that a great part of the province is in actual rebellion, would you believe it true? Should you not deem the person asserting it an enemy to the province? Nay, should you not spurn him from you with indignation? Be calm, my friends, it is necessary to know the worst of a disease, to enable us to provide an effectual remedy. Are not the bands of society cut asunder, and the sanctions that hold man to man trampled upon? Can any of us recover a debt, or obtain compensation for an injury, by law? Are not many persons, whom once we respected and revered, driven from their homes and families, and forced to fly to the army for protection, for no other reason but their having accepted commissions under our King? Is not civil government dissolved? . . . [Is it not wrong and treasonous] for a body of men to assemble without being called by authority, and to pass governmental acts, or for a number of people to take the militia out of the hands of the King's representative, or to form a new militia, or to raise men and appoint offices for a public purpose, without the order or permission of the King or his representative; or for a number of men to take to their arms, and march with a professed design of opposing the King's troops . . . ?
>
> . . . We already feel the effects of anarchy; mutual confidence, affection and tranquility, those sweeteners of human life, are succeeded by distrust, hatred and wild uproars; the useful arts of agriculture and commerce are neglected for caballing, mobbing this or the other man, because he acts, speaks or is suspected of thinking different from the prevailing sentiments of the times, in purchasing arms and forming a militia; O height of madness! . . . Let us consider this matter: However closely we may hug ourselves in the opinion that the Parliament has no right to tax or legislate for us, the people of England hold the contrary opinion as firmly; they tell us we are a part of the British empire; that every state from the nature of government must have a supreme uncontrollable power coextensive with the empire itself; and that, that power is vested in Parliament. It is as unpopular to deny this doctrine in Great-Britain as it is to assert it in the colonies. . . .

Thomas Paine Urges Independence, 1776

Tom Paine had only recently come to Philadelphia in 1774, penniless and unemployed. But he quickly entered the circles of political discussion and became fast friends with the city's most important intellectual and political leaders. At their behest, Paine wrote a pamphlet that was intended to portray the Imperial Crisis in the sharpest relief and raise the level of commitment in America to the patriot cause. *Common Sense* did exactly that.

Some writers have so confounded society with government, as to leave little or no distinction between them; whereas they are not only different, but have different origins. Society is produced by our wants, and government by our wickedness; the former promotes our happiness *positively* by united our affections, the latter *negatively* by restraining our vices.... Society in every state is a blessing, but government even in its best state is but a necessary evil; in its worst state an intolerable one.... Government, like dress, is the badge of lost innocence; the palaces of kings are built on the ruins of the bowers of paradise. For were the impulses of conscience clear, uniform, and irresistibly obeyed, man would need no other lawgiver; but that not being the case, he finds it necessary to surrender up a part of his property to furnish means for the protection of the rest; and this he is induced to do by the same prudence which in every other case advises him out of two evils to choose the least.

...But there is another and greater distinction for which no truly natural or religious reason can be assigned, and that is, the distinction of men into Kings and Subjects. Male and female are the distinctions of nature, good and bad the distinctions of heaven; but how a race of men came into the world so exalted above the rest, and distinguished like some new species, is worth enquiring into, and whether they are the means of happiness or of misery to mankind....

In England a k— hath little more to do than to make war and give away places; which in plain terms, is to impoverish the nation and set it together by the ears. A pretty business indeed for a man to be allowed eight hundred thousand sterling a year for, and worshipped into the bargain! Of more worth is one honest man to society, and in the sight of God, than all the crowned ruffians that ever lived....

...America would have flourished as much, and probably much more, had no European power had any thing to do with her. The commerce by which she hath enriched herself are the necessaries of life, and will always have a market while eating is the custom of Europe.... Besides, what have we to do with setting the world at defiance? Our plan is commerce, and that, well attended to, will secure us the peace and friendship of all Europe....

It is repugnant to reason, to the universal order of things, to all examples from the former ages, to suppose, that this continent can longer remain subject to any external power.... Small islands not capable of protecting themselves, are the proper objects for kingdoms to take under their care; but there is something very absurd, in supposing a continent to be perpetually governed by an island. In no instance hath nature made the satellite larger than its primary planet, and as England and America, with respect to each other, reverses the common order of nature, it is evident they belong to different systems: England to Europe, America to itself....

> O ye that love mankind! Ye that dare oppose, not only the tyranny, but the tyrant, stand forth! Every spot of the old world is over-run with oppression. Freedom hath been hunted round the globe. Asia, and Africa, have long expelled her. —Europe regards her like a stranger, and England hath given her warning to depart. O! receive the fugitive, and prepare in time an asylum for mankind.

Generations after the Revolution, it became possible to explain the sequence of events leading up to colonists' declaration of political independence. But during the Imperial Crisis, the colonists were not necessarily clear about what was happening in the empire. Even in 1775, most colonists who protested parliamentary laws or chafed under the monarchy did not consider leaving the empire. A large number of people who would eventually become loyalists agreed with protesters that Parliament acted at least hastily against the colonists, and perhaps unjustly. The lines of distinction between patriot and loyalist were drawn slowly, haltingly.

Leonard, a member of the colonial elite, believed that the colonial majority should defer to the wisdom and experience of their rulers. He feared that colonists would destroy the best features of the traditional social and political order, and insisted that all rebellion was "the most atrocious offense" against civility and good government. The colonial independence movement had developed so gradually, Leonard observed, that few colonists realized how the "demagogues of a minority" had led many to "ill-founded views" and, by 1775, were prepared to take over governance of America from the traditional elite.

Paine had no fear of changing the old order. Indeed, he pleaded with colonists to realize that their critique of Parliament and colonial governors was just the first—not the last—step toward realizing their own tremendous potential as a separate people. More than any other writer in the last months before the rebellion, Paine measured the gap between the hesitating and loyal part of the population and the energized and organized revolutionary part—and declared it unbridgable. Committees of Correspondence, regular public acts of violence, the Sons of Liberty, nonimportation movements, and constant public discussion of differences—all of these, Paine knew, were the prelude to taking a final step toward declaring independence. It was that final step that he now implored colonists to take.

Questions for Analysis

1. What does Daniel Leonard believe are the boundaries of legitimate protest, and in what ways have colonists crossed those boundaries?
2. Compare each writer's view of what is troubling the empire. Who is to blame for the troubles, and what is the implied or stated remedy?
3. What does Paine believe is happening to America? What does he believe *should* happen?
4. Each writer has a view of "the people" and their rights. Find passages in each selection that capture those views.
5. How do Leonard and Paine define legitimate political authority? Identify passages that demonstrate their contrasting views.

7

The Federal Experiment, 1783–1800

In the first years of peace after the Revolution, Mercy Otis Warren confided fearful thoughts in her diary and in letters to friends. The Revolution's accomplishments seemed to be buckling under too many pressures—might it be in danger of ruin? As one of the most educated women of her generation, Mercy had put herself at the head of patriot women during the Revolution. Indeed, her famous family of lawyers and politicians had nurtured Mercy to be an enlightened public citizen. As a young adult, Mercy married Charles Warren, a prominent Boston patriot who encouraged her to develop her talents and revolutionary commitment to their fullest extent. "Having accepted my personal and political liberty," Mercy wrote, "I strained every nerve of my female constitution" to participate in the vibrant, sometimes stormy, public debates about the republican experiment that the patriots had undertaken.

But during the first years of peace, Mercy expressed worry in her diary and in letters to close friends that "all soon shall be lost." After all their sacrifices during the Revolutionary War, Americans were suddenly turning to self-indulgence, luxury, and greed. "A most remarkable depravity of manners pervade[s] the cities of the United States," she moaned. It was bad enough that wealthy people wished to restore "their dissipated habits" of dress and public entertainments so that "every principle of that republican spirit which requires patience, probity, industry, and self-denial" might vanish. But even worse, "multitudes of people" were buying more foreign goods than they could afford. Republican governments could never recover social order and reconstruct war-torn areas in the face of such pervasive, and perverse, popular indulgence. Moreover, observed Warren, even political leaders had become demagogues. But they could no longer point to British politicians as the source of moral and political corruption, for these qualities now characterized American political life.

How, she wondered, had such a remarkable reversal occurred? Mercy Otis Warren wrestled mightily in her writings to understand why Americans, in the postwar years, seemed to have lost their republican virtue. Her answers, some of them published, gave solace to other anxious observers of American political and cultural life. Warren insisted that the growing incidence of rowdy public behavior, disrespectful political discussions, and wanton purchasing and indebtedness were not inherent characteristics of Americans. No, Warren reassured her readers. At fault was the war. The Revolution had brought out citizens' best patriotic efforts, but it had also tempted them into dangerous behavior. Warren blamed the persistent "state of war; a relaxation of government; the sudden acquisition of fortune; a depreciating currency; and a new intercourse with foreign nations" for the chaos of the 1780s. The true identity of independent American citizens would emerge when they recognized their depravity and restored social order. Until then, Warren was not at all certain that Americans' republican experiment would turn out well.

But the problem did not stop there. Warren also feared that the remedies proposed in the federal Constitution of 1787 "overly corrected the dangers of licentious" political and cultural life by threatening to undermine "the people's liberties" that revolutionaries fought so hard to win. The new federal experiment could "unhinge" the so-called Spirit of '76. In the years to come, Warren felt compelled to part ways with the revolutionary leaders, many of whom she had admired, and to join opponents of the Constitution.

Ambivalence about the future of the republic transcended class and gender. Thousands of men and women shared Warren's anxieties about the uncertain, shifting conditions of the 1780s. The Revolution had introduced many changes—desired by some, dreaded by others—and more would follow that no one could have anticipated. While many people welcomed opportunities to alter social relations and develop a national identity according to a new vision of themselves, many others longed to restore public order and slow the pace of cultural and economic change during the 1780s and 1790s. The intense public debate that developed in these years divided Americans in many ways, and yet also inched them closer to a new national identity.

- Who participated in the widespread postwar discussion about American political and cultural identity?
- How would the new republic recover from the Revolution and extend the liberties that had been promised to Americans?
- What powers should the new states enjoy after the Revolution, and would they be adequate to protect Americans from both external threats and internal discord?
- Given the spectrum of social conditions in so large a nation, how would the great natural abundance of America be divided among citizens?

This chapter will address these questions.

The New Nation's Culture

The Revolution initiated a number of important transformations in American life. Despite their scorn for the British standing army, Americans created the Continental Army and sustained it through many years of warfare. Americans had also eagerly begun to discuss what forms of political organization might be appropriate for them and had created new republican states. Even so, in the years after Yorktown, issues of personal and institutional freedom remained largely unsettled and continued to concern Americans. But the independent republic was still, as one war veteran put it, "unsecured from the clutches of our own internal skemes [schemes] . . . and the claws of foreign powers." How, asked many Americans during the 1780s, would their new governments protect their liberties and extend their opportunities? For some time to come, they found no clear answers.

Religion

The Declaration of Independence made it impossible for King George III to reign over religious matters in his former colonies. Indeed, the Revolution initiated a widespread reorganization of North American religious denominations and numerous efforts to give churches a distinctive American identity. During the Revolution, many Anglican clergy retained their right to collect taxes for the established church and to sanction members' marriages. But slowly, new denominations such as the Methodists and Baptists, especially in the southern states, began to gain members. Religious dissenters rejoiced that political independence paved the way for official recognition of new denominations. In 1786 Thomas Jefferson submitted Virginia's Statute of Religious Freedom, which swept away many Anglican privileges and decreed that church attendance and financial support of clerical leaders would henceforth be voluntary. In 1789 a convention of bishops and clergy in Philadelphia recreated the Anglican Church's identity by establishing the Protestant Episcopal Church of the United States.

Religious freedom emerged by degrees in other areas of the new republic. In northern states, where the Congregational Church was strong and in some cases the established religion, legislatures continued to raise taxes for that denomination's support but permitted new ones—especially the Baptists—to earmark taxes paid by their members for their own clergy. Officially, most American states still stipulated that offices be held by Christians, or even Protestants, but many people agreed that they must not otherwise curtail freedom of conscience. For example, new Catholic and Jewish places of worship gained tolerance during the 1780s, and in predominantly Anglican strongholds, Presbyterians and Quakers began to spread. In 1774 colonists had registered loud protests against the crown's "papist" Quebec Act; less than a quarter-century later, in 1790, John Carroll of Maryland became the first Roman Catholic bishop in America.

While established denominations changed, new ones grew by leaps and bounds after the Revolution. On the frontiers, settlers without churches welcomed itinerant Baptist and Methodist ministers. Circuit riders reached out to new converts, invit-

Chronology

1783	Treaty of Paris
	British evacuate New York
1784	Treaty of Fort Stanwix
	Economic depression begins
	Spain closes New Orleans to American trade
1785	Shays's Rebellion
1786	Annapolis Convention
1787	Constitutional Convention
	Northwest Ordinance
	Publication of *The Federalist*
1789	French Revolution begins
1790	Judiciary Act
	Indian Intercourse Act
	Hamilton's funding and assumption plan
1791	Bank of the United States chartered by Congress
	Bill of Rights ratified
	Whiskey Tax passed in Congress
	Hamilton's Report on Manufactures
1791–1796	Slave revolts in Saint Dominique
1793	Congress passes Neutrality Proclamation regarding England and France
1794	Battle of Fallen Timbers
	Whiskey Rebellion
1795	Treaty of Greenville
	Jay's Treaty
1796	Adams elected president
1797	XYZ Affair
1798	Alien and Sedition Acts
	Virginia and Kentucky Resolutions
1799	Fries's Rebellion in Pennsylvania
1800	Jefferson elected president

ing the "awakened" to rousing camp meetings. At Cain Ridge, Kentucky, for example, thousands gathered for five days of gospel preaching under tents and in the open air, reveling in their distance from genteel religious traditions and their newfound emotional spirituality. No more learned clergy and rigid church hierarchies, they agreed. Revivalists urged their audiences to find personal religious self-reliance and independence from established institutions. In a few short years, these postrevolutionary changes would swell into what historians call the Second Great Awakening (discussed further in Chapter 9).

Servitude and Slavery

The Revolution's language of freedom and equality challenged many of the social dependencies and distinctions that existed in colonial society. New laws and social norms in the 1780s began to reform the degrees of legal nonfreedom that defined indentured servants, apprenticed youth, and certain religious and ethnic groups. White men, in particular, found it increasingly odious to bear any dependent status, including temporary servitude, because it was "contrary to . . . the idea of liberty" that all citizens now embraced. In a very short time, indentured servitude shrank to negligible proportions of the laborers in Philadelphia and New York. The term "servant" dropped from use in many areas. Instead, many immigrants who worked in urban households referred to themselves simply as "the help" and negotiated a range of privileges, including "freedoms to come and go as we please" once they completed their chores.

The condition of slaves and free African-Americans was dramatically different in the new republic. True, the calls for patriotic "liberty" raised hundreds of individual claims for manumission and spurred thousands of slaves to "take their freedom" by running away during the Revolution. In addition, tens of thousands of slaves, mostly in the Chesapeake and southern states, gained freedom during the fighting. The British army freed a majority of Georgia's slaves by sweeping them into its regiments during the second half of the war; the northern patriotic governments accepted hundreds of African-American volunteers, too. As many as one-fourth of South Carolina's black majority obtained their freedom from the advancing British troops. As the British fled Charleston and Savannah at the end, fleeing masters took thousands of slaves to the West Indies, Canada, and West Africa.

Some of the northern states abolished slavery during the war, though unevenly and for varied reasons. When Vermont became a state in 1777, its constitution abolished slavery. The 1781 state Bill of Rights in Massachusetts allowed some slaves to sue for their freedom in state courts on the grounds that they had been "born free and equal." Thousands of northern slaves in Massachusetts and New Hampshire simply walked away from the shops, forges, stables, and farms of their masters over the next years.

To ease the transition for white masters, Pennsylvania, Connecticut, and Rhode Island legislators provided for gradual emancipation. In 1780 Pennsylvania declared that all offspring born to slaves from that time forward could claim their freedom at age twenty-eight. In New York and New Jersey, where slaves accounted

Elizabeth Mumbet Freeman
This painting, done in 1811 by Susan A. Livingston Ridley Sedgwick, is of a Massachusetts former slave who sued her master for her freedom in 1781. In her court hearing, Freeman told the justices that she believed the "rights of man" should be accorded to all women as well, slave and free. She won, and became a domestic servant earning wages. *(Massachusetts Historical Society. Gift of Maria Banyer Sedwick, 1884.)*

for more than 10 percent of the population, gradual emancipation came even later. Only in 1799 did the New York legislature yield partially to demands from white abolitionists and black leaders by granting freedom to slave children when they reached age twenty-five. In 1804 New Jersey became the last northern state to grant gradual emancipation. Still, a decade into the new century, in 1810, more than 25,000 African-Americans remained enslaved in the North. In addition to those slaves who had not yet come of age for emancipation, hundreds were sold by their northern masters into the southern states before the deadline for emancipation. Masters also lied about the ages of their slaves in order to retain their labor.

Even when free, African-Americans voted only occasionally and almost never attempted to hold local or state office. In Delaware free blacks outnumbered slaves three to one by 1800, but new laws excluded them from full civil and political rights. By 1810, many northern free African-Americans believed "life is no whit better" day to day in northern cities, and "maybe just one whit better" without "master's heel on our backs."

Some free blacks prevailed against social prejudice and adverse laws to develop their talents, build community institutions, or become outstanding leaders. White and black philanthropists formed the Abolition Society of Pennsylvania during the 1790s to protect former slaves and ease the transition to freedom. The Quaker Anthony Benezet funded a school for free African-Americans, and the black Reverend

Absalom Jones established a huge congregation in Philadelphia known as St. Thomas's African Episcopal Church. Although freeholding, political rights, and property ownership remained the preserve of white society, free black churches, clubs, and schools sprang up in every northern city. By the 1790s, thousands of free African-Americans in the North and in the Upper South created the Baptist Association, Williamsburg African Church, African Marine Fund in New York, and numerous African Free Schools. A distinctive African-American voice appeared in Jupiter Hammon's writings about the failed promises of the Revolution and in Phillis Wheatley's poems describing her own mixed African and American heritages. "Every human breast," wrote Wheatley, "is impatient of oppression, and pants for deliverance."

In the southern states from Virginia to Georgia, social and economic advancement for free African-Americans was far more difficult than in northern states. Although many new congregations of Methodists and Baptists supported abolition during the early 1780s, the next decades witnessed their retreat from such positions. Methodist leadership carefully laid out new rules for church organization and membership prohibiting both freed and slave African-Americans from acquiring equal stature in congregations with white members. Virginia and Maryland permitted individual masters to manumit slaves beginning in 1782, and by 1810 they had freed about one-fifth of Maryland's slaves. Masters in Virginia freed a smaller proportion of their slave population, probably about 10,000 of the state's 300,000 slaves by 1790. Then, a 1792 law made manumission harder to achieve, sparking more instances of resistance and open revolt against masters' authority. In 1800 the freeman Gabriel Prosser attempted to lead a slave uprising in Virginia, but authorities quickly suppressed the revolt and hanged nearly forty slaves with Prosser (discussed further in Chapter 12).

Below the Chesapeake, slavery laws and daily treatment of bound labor tightened even more. In North Carolina the state government negated individual Quaker manumissions as early as 1776 and confirmed the right of masters to re-enslave African-Americans who had been set free during the Revolution in 1788. New North Carolina laws also stiffened penalties for runaway slaves headed toward the North. After 1800, expanding cotton cultivation created a huge demand for slave labor in South Carolina and Georgia, where planters dug new furrows to raise "white gold" and dug in their heels against efforts to free valuable slave labor. Because most slaveholders were also state and national political leaders, they were in a position to preserve the institution. For over twenty years after the end of the Revolution, these states imported slaves by the thousands. The number of southern slaves grew roughly from 400,000 in 1770, to 700,000 in 1790, and to 1.2 million in 1810.

Republican Womanhood

Many women accepted new roles during the Revolutionary War as heads of households, active business partners, spies, or producers for the army. As the war progressed, some women demanded more permanent authority over household decisions, while others decided to stay in retail businesses that male kin had established before the war. When women throughout the northern countryside sporadically pooled resources of textiles or food for needy soldiers, they learned important public economic and political roles. For example, women of the Philadelphia Ladies Association made shirts and coats for Continental soldiers and nursed the wounded taking refuge in the city. Many women also readily crossed military lines to supply troops, risks that sometimes brought valuable news, goods, and cash into their communities and families.

After the war, many circumstances thwarted these experiences of economic and political empowerment. For instance, farms did not recover uniformly once the troops were gone, which kept household purchasing power low and prolonged dire necessity for imported goods. The postwar recession also challenged the wits of women in cities and country villages faced with running a household. Women and children worked hard just to produce enough to survive. Continuing high prices provoked many community outbursts of rage. Women who had participated in riots to "liberate" goods from rapacious storekeepers' shops during the 1770s once again entered public arenas: driven by necessity, they forced millers to free up supplies of flour, fishermen to distribute their catches at discount prices, and urban retailers to unlock hoarded goods.

Despite reverses, many women persevered in their efforts to extend their new economic and political roles. Some demanded more equality within marriage and greater respect from the men in their lives. One target was the common law tradition of coverture, which denied wives legal personalities. Some women pleaded successfully with state legislatures to be allowed to keep the property of departed loyalist husbands, since it was their sole source of income. Others demanded to be treated equally in marriage, as when Lucy Knox wrote during the war that "there is such a thing as equal command" at home even if it did not obtain on the battlefield. Parents of middling and elite families began to shed traditions of arranging marriages and careers for their children, and to recognize the right of their children to choose their own spouses. Revised property and inheritance laws in some states gave women more authority over their own and their children's futures. Most states wrote new laws that broke the tradition of recognizing inheritance through the male line of kinship, and moved toward favoring the descent of property within married couples. Pre-Revolution laws allowing widows only the "use" of one-third of their deceased husbands' estates gave way to new laws favoring their outright ownership of that portion. Moreover, the northern states began to recognize not just the eldest son's privilege, but all sons' and daughters' roughly equal status in inheritance disputes. Every state except South Carolina liberalized its divorce laws soon after the Revolution.

The same Enlightenment and republican ideals that shaped the independence movement in general also inspired new thinking about women's education and family roles. By the 1780s, a few writers were suggesting that women were morally superior to men and enjoyed a greater facility with reading and writing. These idealized qualities equipped women to be "republican wives" and "republican mothers" who not only gained higher stature within middle-class and elite families, but who also bore most of the moral responsibility to nurture husbands and sons in these qualities. Republican wives would soften the aggressive entrepreneurial pursuits of men with profound patriotism toward civic affairs. Republican mothers would shelter their children from the temptations of immoral behavior and selfish materialism by providing a proper moral education at home.

While writers, artists, and politicians began to shape these ideal family and nurturing roles, some outspoken individual women began to demand more personal independence. The most outspoken advocate of women's education, Judith Sargent Murray, insisted that women "should be taught to depend on their own efforts, for the procurement of an establishment in life." Although many clergymen and politicians ridiculed such views as coming from "women of masculine minds" and "masculine manners," Murray stated confidently that she stood on the brink of "a new era in female history." Many male educators agreed with Murray, but they usually coupled the benefits of female education with women's inherent duties to nurture republican husbands and children. Benjamin Rush, for example, believed women "ought to have suitable education, to concur in instructing their sons in the principles of liberty and government." That is, women should not seek education for their own enrichment, but to produce a better citizenry of publicly minded men.

Liberty Displaying the Arts and Sciences America's republican virtue is portrayed as a refined woman who shares music, literature, and worldly wisdom with free African-Americans, whom she invites to become full members of the nation. She holds a pole with the cap of liberty perched on top, and a bountiful countryside fills the background. *(Courtesy, Winterthur Museum.)*

In fact, even though many women enjoyed a privileged moral role in their homes and widening opportunities in education, many legal and political rights remained closed to them. Legislators who relied on common law traditions to shape legal rights in the new states withheld certain fundamental privileges from women, or granted them partially. The New Jersey constitution of 1777 conceded to propertied widows the right to vote, but then revoked the privilege in 1807. Elsewhere, republican traditions and the common law together limited women's civic participation. For example, the requirement of property ownership for the franchise, long a treasured precept of the common law and republicanism, linked property to political commitment and independent political judgment and prevented women from voting altogether.

The Precarious Peace, 1783–1786

At first, congressmen and negotiators thought the Treaty of Paris (see page 235) was the best agreement Americans could have hoped to sign. In territorial terms, the new nation's frontiers provided tremendous potential for expansion. In commercial terms, Americans looked forward to rapid recovery and expansion into new, distant markets. But soon after diplomats John Jay, Benjamin Franklin, and John Adams returned from Paris, they realized this "parchment agreement" provided very little guarantee of peace or grounds for development. For years, pressing issues demanded congressional and state attention. Soldiers and loyalists, widows and rural debtors, merchants and army suppliers, among others, emerged from the war's stresses and strains with high expectations and many disappointments. These years, known later as the "Critical Period," tested the revolutionary experiment on numerous fronts.

Soldiers and Loyalists

As Americans waited from 1781 to 1783 for the war to end officially, Continental soldiers and officers grew restless in their camp at Newburgh, New York, just north of West Point. Over ten thousand men and about a thousand women demanded back pay and the bounties of land Congress owed them. Congress had promised to give life pensions at half-pay to officers who enlisted for the duration of the war; but Congress had made no payments. If the army disbanded once negotiators signed a peace treaty, officers believed they might never see that pay. So, in January 1783, a group of prominent officers petitioned Congress to commute their pensions into a single payment of five years' full pay.

Congressional delegates divided deeply over the officers' demand. While some delegates favored appeasing the Newburgh petition, a majority rejected it. Officers at Newburgh also disagreed among themselves. General Horatio Gates led a faction calling for a meeting to force Congress's hand; General George Washington countered with a meeting of his own on March 15, 1783. He appeared before his men knowing full well that if he could not calm the officers quickly, a military coup might shatter the tenuous Revolutionary victory before the peace treaty was even signed. In an emotionally charged speech, Washington acknowledged the officers' years of selfless sacrifices and then pleaded with them to retract their thoughts of coercing Congress and the American people to satisfy their demands. It worked. Within a week, the officers informed Congress they would not take action, and a relieved Congress granted the five-year bonus.

Washington needed more than personal charisma to calm the troops in those early months of 1783. Fortunately, he had firmly established military subordination to congressional authority. When he resigned in December, he was both a military and a civilian hero. Meanwhile, in late 1783, Congress permitted soldiers to begin returning home, some of them still short of pay and some with the assurance of getting cash or land bonuses soon. By early 1784, the Continental Army had become a shell of its former self.

While the army disbanded, large numbers of former loyalists sought the right to return home or to recover their abandoned belongings. Alexander Hamilton was one leading patriot who believed that these exiled "valuable citizens" should be welcomed back and restored to their property. He cited the Treaty of Paris provision that loyalists had twelve months to return and settle their personal or business affairs. Gradually, former loyalists resurfaced in colleges, churches, and even local political offices in major northern cities. Some states, including radical Pennsylvania, repealed anti-Tory legislation such as the test oaths administered during the Revolution. Connecticut legislators explicitly invited loyalists to share their commercial, inventive, and political genius in reconstructing the new state. Hamilton himself defended legal claims of loyalists who sued New Yorkers for restoration of their prewar property. Although many Americans feared that the "stain of loyalism" would mar the new republic's fragile identity, thousands of former loyalists quietly reintegrated themselves into a rapidly changing American society.

Commercial Decline and Recovery

Despite high hopes for recovery after 1783, Americans entered a prolonged commercial depression. For a few years the reduction in urban population and scarcities of building materials caused by the war hampered the ability of urban centers to recover. Even when the population of the original thirteen states began to grow again from natural increase and immigration, per capita exports did not keep up over the 1780s, for overall American households did not yet produce as much as they had before the war. Lowered levels of production meant fewer purchases of consumer goods—especially imports. In the South, tobacco exports recovered slowly because of ravaged fields and low European demand, which meant that southerners did not earn credits for necessary imports of manufactured goods. Virginia and Maryland farmers already had begun a significant shift from producing tobacco for export toward growing grain for export and local consumption. Overall, imports from England fell nearly 70 percent below pre-Revolution levels in southern states by 1787.

Although Americans had less money to spend during the depression, British firms continued to flood city stores with goods priced lower than American-made ones. In response to demands from artisans to protect their trades, some state governments placed high import taxes on imported manufactures. But merchants still needed to repay debts to English and other foreign creditors, and so gold and silver "flew like lightning bolts" from the country. To make matters worse, in 1784 Parliament passed a series of written decrees that closed off the West Indies ports to American ships, thereby stifling the long-standing trade between northern cities and Caribbean ports and upsetting the entire balance of commerce for the new states.

During the 1780s, American merchants began to cultivate new trading partners to substitute for their reliance on England. Trade with southern France and the French Caribbean provided some relief but not nearly enough long-term credit and, according to some Americans, far too many "luxuries" such as French brandy and silk. In 1784 a consortium of merchants sailed the *Empress of China* to new markets in the East, but it would take years to find the right products in sufficient quantities, and to build enough seaworthy vessels, to make many voyages to East Asia.

Debtor Relief and Shays's Rebellion

Most states owed large sums to private citizens for their loans of money or sales of goods and services during the war. Some legislatures raised average citizens' taxes steeply in order to acquire the revenue to extinguish these debts, mostly held by merchants and landowners. In an attempt to relieve their citizens of the burden imposed by higher taxes, many states tried two remedies: One, familiar to former colonists, was to print huge quantities of paper money in order to facilitate business and tax payments. The other was to pass "stay laws" that postponed repayment of debts that citizens owed to one another. However, so much paper currency entered circulation that its value declined rapidly, and stay laws increased the anxieties of merchants whose foreign creditors were kept waiting "because we have so little payment coming in from the countryside."

In Maryland, landowners in the legislature proposed staving off debtor discontent by replacing the poll tax, which had been a hardship for the poor for generations, with a property tax on lands. However, more conservative state leaders rejected the measure in 1785. In South Carolina, farmers gained a little relief when a new law permitted them to repay creditors in installments, thereby avoiding seizure of their land and goods. In Rhode Island, a large coalition of rural candidates won control of the state government in 1786 and proceeded to issue huge amounts of paper money. New laws declared the currency legal tender for all personal and public debts, which meant that creditors would have to accept the money regardless of its market value. Additional laws decreed that debtors could deposit partial payments of their debts with county judges if creditors refused to accept the legal tender. Merchant creditors expressed alarm that debts, which had always been defined as sacred personal contracts, could be wiped out by such "licentious and unchristian injustice" of "farmer laws." But so long as debtors controlled the state government, creditors had no recourse.

In Massachusetts, farmers did not gain a majority in the legislature and failed to get debtor relief legislation. Moreover, eastern merchant and creditor groups consistently rebuffed petitions from the countryside for paper money and approved of laws that kept raising taxes. By 1785, when many farmers and small producers in the western counties defaulted on their taxes or their mortgages, merchants, landlords, and sheriffs dragged them into court and repossessed their farms. As tensions grew during 1786, farmers in Springfield and Worcester began to hold meetings, what James Madison called "conventions of their own making," to protest high taxes and mistreatment by sheriffs and lawyers. In some areas, angry farmers closed the courts by force or set free their jailed neighbors.

By early fall, hundreds of western and central Massachusetts citizens had organized an extralegal army of "regulators" under Captain Daniel Shays, a local hero and Continental Army veteran. The "Shaysites" demanded lower taxes, restoration of homes to their former owners, and more political representation of western areas in the state government.

On January 25, 1787, Shays marched 1,500 men toward the Springfield arsenal to capture its 450 tons of military stores. The state militia, defending the arsenal, opened heavy artillery fire on the Shaysites, killing four and wounding twenty. At about the same time, the state legislature passed a Riot Act outlawing all unauthorized assemblies and inviting eastern merchants and lawyers to finance a special army to restore order in the western counties. With Governor James Bowdoin's help, a private army of 4,400 men marched west, caught up with the retreating cold and hungry Shaysites, and captured 150 of the rebels. The legislature subsequently voted acquittals for all but Shays and his coleader Luke Day. However, they did not vote tax reductions, and skirmishes between local authorities and tax resisters continued in western counties. In the next election, disgruntled farmers and artisans turned Bowdoin out of office.

In New York, Pennsylvania, Connecticut, and New Hampshire—and in the independent republic of Vermont—other debtors' rebellions arose. In South Carolina,

Country Politics in the 1780s During the uncertain decade after the Revolution, western counties of many states were filled with indebted small producers and farmers who began to play a more vocal role in local affairs and to hold local offices. However, taxes remained high, and wealthy men in state legislatures resisted the demands of overburdened debtors for relief. Here, an angry artisan throws a wealthy officeholder into the mill creek as sympathetic townspeople look on. *(Library of Congress.)*

North Carolina, Georgia, and western portions of Virginia, debtors sent petitions demanding changes in taxation policies, meanwhile resisting the collection efforts of their local sheriffs. From Canada and London, as well as their military posts in the West, British officials gloated that the "disunited States" verged on collapse, while in America urban elites and former revolutionary leaders lamented the "Anarchy and public Convulsion" in the states. Rural regulators, cried one Massachusetts gentleman in February 1787, seemed to be making "a declaration of war against the United States!" The stability and future of the Confederation, warned some, was in doubt.

Shaping the West

The Articles of Confederation of 1781 and the Treaty of Paris of 1783 (see page 235) established Congress's control over extensive new land beyond the former colonies. However, as Congress began efforts to settle, develop, and sell portions of this "national domain," some western claimants challenged Congress's jurisdiction, including new states, Native Americans, and independent settlers, known as squatters, who would occupy thousands of land parcels without legitimate titles. One early step toward resolving these overlapping claims came when New York, Virginia, and Massachusetts ceded land north of the Ohio River to Congress between 1781 and 1786. In future years, Connecticut ceded land in the Western Reserve south of Lake Erie, and New Hampshire and New York gave up claims to Vermont in 1791. These lands became known as the Northwest Territory. South of the Ohio River, Virginia, North Carolina, South Carolina, and Georgia ceded additional lands to the nation between 1792 and 1802 (see map).

Congress outlined tentative efforts to assert its authority over the West. In 1784 Thomas Jefferson drafted a land ordinance designed to divide the area into ten territories and to guarantee settlers self-rule—a constitution and government of their own choosing. Once a territory achieved population equal to the smallest of the revolutionary states, it could petition to become a state in the Confederation. Congress defeated Jefferson's plan because too many delegates feared it would shift political power to newly populated areas and create a frontier in which settlers would live "willy nilly" without orderly settlement and "fall to the level of the savages." Partly to satisfy these objections, Jefferson submitted an additional Land Ordinance in 1785 that provided for land surveys. Based on the old New England system of settlement, the revised ordinance divided land into townships of thirty-six sections, one square mile (or 640 acres) each (see map). The ordinance reserved one section for a local school, and four sections for future public use. Sections were to sell for $1 per acre, giving Congress sorely needed revenues and attracting thousands of small farm families to orderly communities.

However, most small farmers could not afford the $640 needed to buy a section, so sales under the congressional act were largely to wealthy investors. In 1785 Congress allowed the Ohio Company, a group of aggressive speculators, to purchase 1.5 million acres for $1 million dollars. Military veterans under the leadership of Manassah Cutler from Massachusetts, and ambitious investors such as William Duer from New York City, combined forces to underwrite this tremendous land grab.

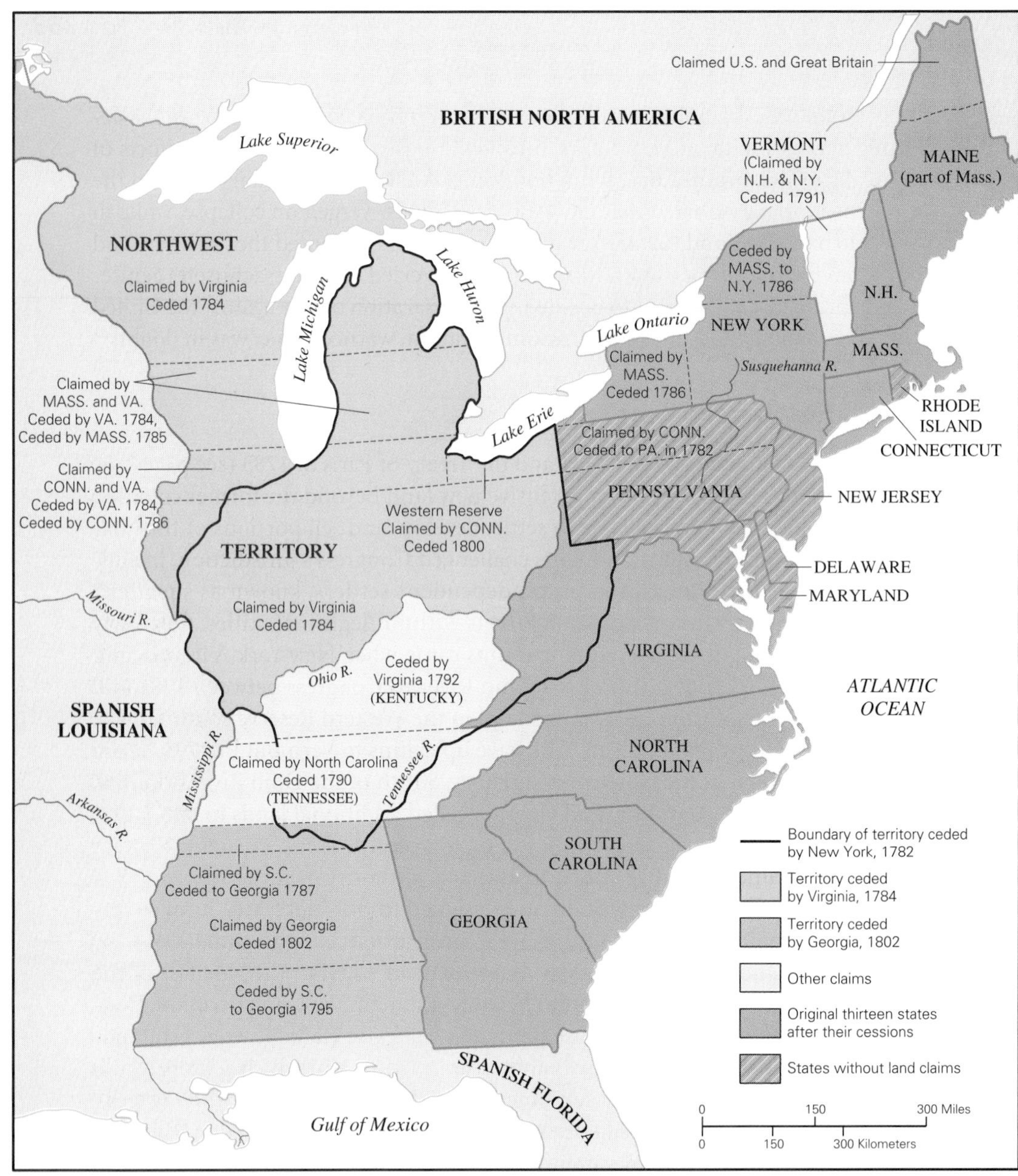

Cession of Western Land, 1782–1802 By the end of the Revolution, most of the new thirteen states claimed large areas of the western territory. Overlapping claims, based on the original colonial charters, as well as new waves of settlers fighting over titles to tracts of land, led to violence on the frontier and political confusion in Congress. A series of compromises among the states and federal government eventually resolved most disputes.

These "mushroom companies" paid for territorial land in revolutionary paper money and securities that its investors had purchased at drastically depreciated prices from thousands of farmers and small-time army suppliers.

Another threat to the Jeffersonian vision for orderly western settlement was the continuing presence of British troops on the frontier. In 1784 Congress appointed John Jay to negotiate with the British for the removal of these troops, but Jay failed.

Settlers attributed the diplomatic setback to Congress's indecision. Some Ohio settlements even threatened to leave the Confederation and seek protection from the British, while others decided to live without any government's authority. Acting on rumors of western discontent, Spanish officials hired Americans George Rogers Clark and General James Wilkinson to gather information from the "Kentucky wilderness" to see whether those Americans could be persuaded to live under Spanish rule. Wilkinson briefly tried to organize western Pennsylvanians into an independent state under the protection of the Spanish government. In another example of this "separation tendency," when Congress refused to let Vermont gain independence from New York during the early 1780s, the Green Mountain Boys negotiated temporarily with London for readmission to the empire as a colonial province.

Related difficulties unfolded in the South. Spain still claimed rights to the Mississippi River, but Americans in the Northwest Territory needed the river passage for exporting goods to southern and eastern markets quickly and cheaply. Hauling goods overland was a far more costly and dangerous undertaking for small producers in the Ohio Valley and Indiana country. When Spain disallowed American river transport from New Orleans southward after 1784, settlers in the Northwest and southern politicians promoting expansion fumed. John Jay stepped in again, attempting to persuade the Spanish minister, Don Diego de Gardoqui, to accept American sovereignty over the river, promising that Spain would enjoy equally "free transit" as Americans. When that proposal was rejected, he offered to recognize Spanish sovereignty over the waterway if Americans could trade freely at all Spanish ports on the river. Although the northern states would have been happy with this compromise, congressmen from the southern states blocked passage of Jay's plan.

Trouble with Native Americans also plagued efforts to settle the Northwest Territory. Many Americans assumed that, since European powers had recognized American dominion as far as the Mississippi River when they signed the Treaty of Paris, that dominion included a right of conquest over all peoples within those lands. But many Ohio Valley Indian tribes and New York Iroquois villages thought differently. With encouragement from British troops stationed just north of the Ohio River, Native Americans throughout the valley defended their homelands against advancing American settlement. Although Congress did not recognize any need to forge treaties with Indians in the territory, it nevertheless saw the diplomatic wisdom of trying to secure the frontier from continuous multisided warfare among Americans, British, and various Indian peoples.

But negotiation of treaties often dissolved into land grabs or the use of force against Indians. In the Treaty of Fort Stanwix in 1784, Congress's first agreement with an Indian tribe, the Iroquois ceded great areas of land to the United States, literally at gunpoint, and agreed to relocate to Canada or live on small reservations. In the Treaty of Fort McIntosh in 1785, Congress further secured national interests over the Ohio Valley, and the Wyandot, Delaware, Ottawa, and Chippewa villages succumbed to the rush of white settlers. Nevertheless, government surveyors worked quickly to measure and sell lands taken by treaty. By 1786, congressional efforts to "clear the savage forces" from the Great Lakes down to the Gulf of Mexico encompassed many Native American peoples, including the Creek, Shawnee, and

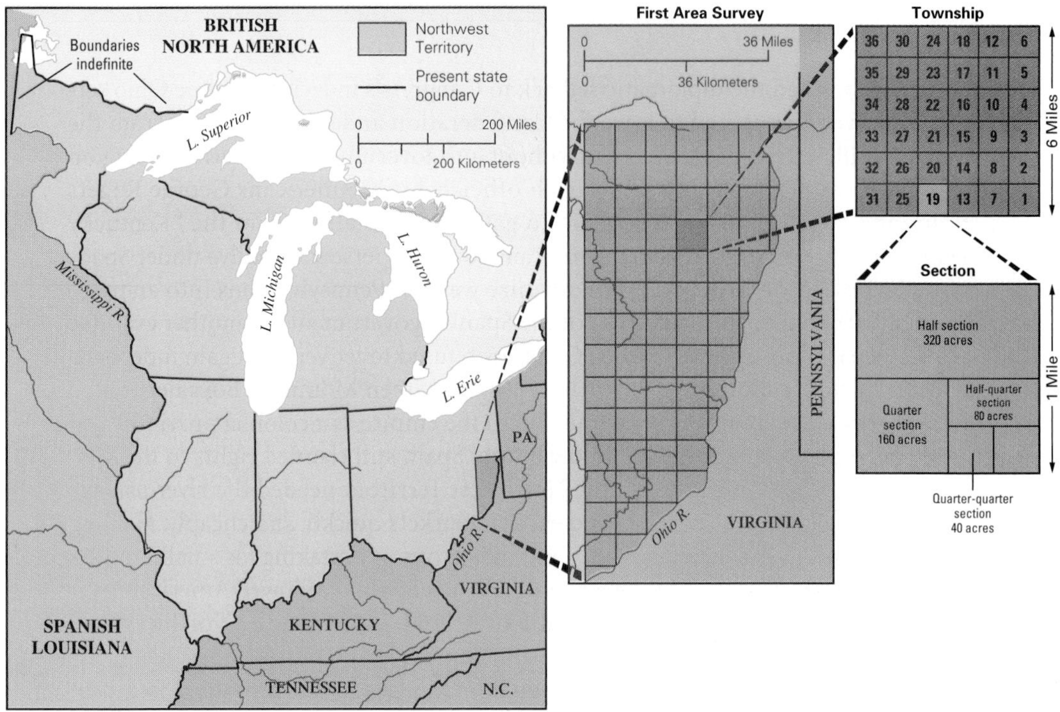

The Northwest Ordinance, 1785 This act provided for the orderly surveying of the extensive lands now under American jurisdiction following the Revolution. The Ordinance divided the land into townships of thirty-six sections of one square mile each. Although many Americans could not afford to purchase such large tracts of land, settlers continued to migrate westward in great numbers. The Northwest Ordinance of 1785 was later modified in 1787 to divide the area into three to five territories, give a structured government, and prohibit slavery in these new lands.

Miami nations. Because Americans had extracted these agreements by force, however, some Indians repudiated the measures and attempted to reclaim their sovereignty over their lands. For example, Mohawk chief Joseph Brant declared that the Iroquois were "equally free" as any Americans to claim rights over land.

Land companies, Indians, and government surveyors all complained about yet another "evil force at work against peace and order" in the West: the thousands of squatters who moved into areas ahead of surveys and heedless of Native American treaties. During the Revolution, hundreds of settlers had crossed the Appalachian Mountains into the fertile Ohio Valley. By 1785, over 30,000 farmers and traders occupied Kentucky territory (admitted as a state in 1792), and by the end of the decade, its population stood at over 74,000. The Tennessee territory (admitted as a state in 1794) held 36,000 people by 1790. From 1784 to 1788, settlers streamed from North Carolina into what is now eastern Tennessee, where they set up a quasi-government and called themselves the State of Franklin. Though they petitioned Congress repeatedly for statehood, national leaders feared the Franklin settlers would choose not to join the union and so refused the petitions.

Congressmen admitted that they needed a "strong toned government" to bring order out of the chaos of territorial settlement. So their last important act was to pass a modified Northwest Ordinance in 1787. It provided for the creation of three to five states in the huge Northwest Territory (future Ohio, Indiana, Michigan, Wisconsin, and Illinois), to be "admitted on an equal footing with the original states." In place of self-government, Congress decided that appointed judges and governors would provide greater stability in the West. Once a territory's population reached five thousand citizens, inhabitants would choose an assembly modeled on those of existing states. The governor would have an absolute veto over all legislation until the territory achieved statehood. Of great future significance, slavery was prohibited in the territories.

The Northwest Ordinance established principles for orderly occupation of the land, as well as the peaceful transfer of citizenship and government to new areas. It helped Americans view the different parts of the new nation as a coherent whole and deterred secessionist movements by giving settlers a means to become states and identify with national development. At the same time, the Ordinance established national claims against the Indians, Spanish, and French peoples in the West, claims that would be applied to the trans-Mississippi frontier in the future, and would in turn provoke fierce reactions from the Indians who occupied that land.

The Constitutional Convention, 1787

By 1786, Congress's credibility was fading fast. Its instability and lack of authority, insisted some critics, had become symbolically clear in its repeated relocations: from Philadelphia, to Princeton, New York City, Trenton, and Annapolis. Critics overlooked the substantial gains made by individual states in recovering from the Revolution. They also dismissed the very great contributions of the Land Ordinances, noting—correctly or not—that settlers would amass in the new region regardless of political provisions for survey, protection, and government. Instead, nay-sayers focused on the numerous difficulties facing the new nation and hinted that Americans were in danger of losing the entire republican experiment. What voices would rise above this din of fears and criticism—some of it founded, some of it fabricated—to organize effective political responses? What new social alignments did Americans need, and what new institutional forms?

Thinking Continentally

Advocates of a stronger central government had been prominent in American politics for some time. Earlier identified as "nationalists," or "men who think continentally," they began to call themselves "Federalists" in 1786. This cadre of national leaders included men whose views had been nurtured in long years of revolutionary struggle: Washington, Hamilton, Madison, Jay, Adams, Knox. To most Federalists, republicanism implied preservation of elite rule, an aristocracy of talent, the security of private property, and a hierarchical social order—conditions that many new state constitutions had begun to eliminate. Federalists believed that state governments had reached too far beyond the Revolution's goals, that they invited "democratic disruptions" by elevating "base layers of unpropertied citizens" above their rightful political and social stations. Just as colonists had successfully defended their liberty from British tyranny, now Americans had to guard against creating too much liberty.

Federalists were appalled by the violence of agrarian Shaysites in the backcountries of many states. But they knew that such violent challenges to the social order would end only when Congress found long-term remedies for the problems of the Critical Period. Since the Confederation's creation in 1781, argued Federalists, the states had focused on paying their own private and public debts, while neglecting to provide for the national debt. Moreover, the states were unable to reopen West Indies and Mississippi River trade that had been closed to American merchants by foreigners. Instead, they passed discriminatory legislation against one another, thereby fragmenting their potential for a great national commerce. Further, the states individually could not secure peace and orderly settlement in the national domain. It would take a strong national government to correct these, and other, ills.

The first step came in 1785, when George Washington invited representatives of Maryland and Virginia to a small conference at his Virginia home, Mount Vernon, to settle a dispute over use of the Potomac River. James Madison, perceiving that this agreement made a good beginning toward interstate cooperation, persuaded the Virginia legislature to call on all the states to meet at Annapolis, Maryland, to discuss additional commercial improvements. On September 5, 1786, delegates arrived at Annapolis from four mid-Atlantic states and Virginia, and New Yorker Alexander Hamilton immediately presented a report on international trade.

Hamilton, born in the Leeward Islands, where his mother taught him bookkeeping skills and introduced him to powerful merchant firms, rose to prominence quickly in New York's post-Revolution commercial and political life. His service in Washington's army, his defense of returning loyalists, and his efforts to raise national revenues during the 1780s exposed him to both the grandeur and the petty jealousies and corruption of public life. When the Annapolis Convention failed to correct the "anarchy of these disunited states," Hamilton urged fellow nationalists to call on Congress to hold a convention that might "render the constitution of the Federal Government adequate to the exigencies of the Union." The following February, Congress agreed to organize a convention, to be held in Philadelphia. Twelve states—all but Rhode Island—said they would participate.

At Philadelphia

In all, 55 delegates attended the Philadelphia convention at one time or another from mid-May to mid-September 1787. The average daily attendance, however, was about 35 men. Twenty-nine delegates had college degrees; 34 had practiced law; 24 had served in the Confederation Congress; and 21 had been officers during the Revolution. Many called themselves merchants and slave owners, but no artisans, small farmers, or free African-Americans came to Philadelphia to deliberate. Washington, Franklin, Hamilton, Robert Morris, and numerous other men identified with political, military, and legal leadership of the Revolution participated in the important convention deliberations. Because of his position at the head of the Continental Army, Washington was the obvious choice to preside over the convention. Madison rose hundreds of times to speak on the convention floor and tirelessly recorded summaries of delegates' speeches. His notes are the only relatively continuous record of those proceedings, which broke from previous practices and took place behind closed doors. Some leading patriots did not appear at the convention: Thomas Jefferson still served as minister to France, John Adams represented America in England, and Patrick Henry refused to participate in any design to reduce the powers of the states.

Most delegates came to the convention to revise the Articles. But an outspoken core of leaders was determined to achieve more far-reaching changes in the structure and functioning of the American republic. Accordingly, they asked the convention delegates to consider a plan that would replace, not revise, the Articles of Confederation.

Madison for the most part had drafted this initial plan, which Edmund Randolph of Virginia presented to delegates on May 29. It proposed a strong national government with one central "consolidated authority" over "the aggregate interests of the community" of all citizens. This "Virginia Plan" proposed a bicameral legislature with representation in both houses apportioned according to population. The legislature would choose the national executive and national judiciary, and it would have all the powers currently held by Congress plus the power to settle disputes between state governments. Congress would have the authority to veto state laws that contradicted the laws of Congress but it would not be able to tax citizens or regulate interstate and international trade.

After only two weeks of debate, the delegates agreed to some of the provisions of the Virginia Plan, including that representatives of a lower house would serve for three years and those of an upper house for seven years, and that a single elected person would hold executive power for seven years.

But the key issue of representation was a sticking point. Delegates from the smaller states argued that basing representation on population would naturally shift power to the most populous states. In June they countered this so-called large-state plan with their own small-state plan. Introduced by William Paterson of New Jersey, the small-state, or "New Jersey Plan," proposed to preserve as much of the existing Confederation structures as possible. It would have granted Congress new powers to tax domestic trade and goods, tax imports, regulate commerce, and demand state requisitions of money and goods. Most important, each state would have one vote in a unicameral Congress, which would guard against excessive influence of very populous states, in particular Virginia, Pennsylvania, and Massachusetts.

In addition to these two plans now on the floor for discussion and refinement, some delegates proposed extravagantly impractical measures. Hamilton, for example, put forward the idea that members of the executive and upper house of government hold offices for life—a proposal inspired by Britain's model of the monarch and peerage. When Hamilton's proposal met vigorous opposition in late June, he went home to New York for a month. Luther Martin of Maryland presented a plan almost the mirror opposite of Hamilton's: Martin insisted that the convention rigorously respect the integrity of the states and eradicate "all smell of aristocracy." When delegates soundly rebuffed him, Martin retreated to his home state to prepare for the long battle to defeat whatever plan emerged from Philadelphia. However, because the delegates knew what the voters would accept and what would best unite their range of views, most of these extreme ideas faded quickly from the convention floor.

In the oppressive heat of June and July, debate was often acrimonious. Gunning Bedford of Delaware threatened that if the large states insisted on proportional representation, "the small ones will find some foreign ally" to turn to. The large-state delegates were equally frightened that their entire republican experiment would fail if Shaysites, or dissenters anywhere, overran the fragile new state governments. As the convention deliberated during July, Secretary of War Henry Knox warned delegates that "a general confederacy has been formed of nearly all the Indians to the Northward of the Ohio" and was "preparing an insurgency against the republic." A compromise of their various interests was now of the utmost urgency.

The deadlock was broken starting on July 12 when Roger Sherman of Connecticut proposed what became known as the Connecticut Compromise, or the Great Compromise. Sherman's plan accepted proportional representation for the lower house of Congress, but gave each state one vote—or equal state representation—in the upper house. Terms of office were shortened to two years for the lower house (House of Representatives), six years for the upper house (Senate), and four years for the executive. An electoral college comprised of all representatives and senators would choose the executive.

The Great Compromise also established the principle of *federalism,* or the sharing of power between the states and central government. Delegates agreed that the central government should have certain powers to create particular supreme laws, enforceable on all individuals of the republic. Further, they gave Congress the authority to levy and collect taxes, settle disputes among the states, negotiate with foreign nations, and set the standards for citizenship. Congress would have veto power over state laws only in cases involving "the supreme law of the land," but it would set the terms of interstate commerce and frontier diplomacy, including enforcement of existing treaties with Indians and protection of citizens by the federal government, not the states. Finally, in addition to the specific powers reserved to central government, Article 1, Sections 8 and 10, of the final draft included a "necessary and proper clause" available for Congress's use in cases delegates could not foresee or immediately decide on. This so-called elastic clause provoked many disputes in years to come: some praised it as a green light for expansive government action, whereas others condemned it as a gift of excessive authority to national rulers.

The Great Compromise also addressed sectional interests between North and South. Southern delegates argued that although slaves were not citizens, they should be counted toward political representation. Northern delegates retorted that slaves should be counted for representation only if they were also counted for purposes of direct taxation. Few delegates wished to argue for the abolition of slavery although Gouverneur Morris stormed that slavery was "a nefarious institution." Most northern delegates believed that the provision in Article 4, Section 2, for the capture and return of runaway slaves was only a small concession to southern interests, especially because delegates at the Confederation Congress had recently agreed to prohibit slavery in the Northwest Territory. The dispute was resolved by what became known as the "three-fifths compromise": representation in the lower house of Congress would be determined by each state's free population plus three-fifths of "all other persons," namely slaves. In addition, southerners won a guarantee that the slave trade would continue—"the migration or importation of such persons as any of the states now existing shall think proper to admit," as it was termed in the final document—for the next twenty years.

Before delegates finished their business, they agreed to present the document to special ratifying conventions in each state for consideration. In this way, delegates hoped there would be a wider public discussion of the tremendous changes being proposed, while at the same time less opportunity for special interests to oppose the constitution from within the existing state governments. To avoid long delays and ensure passage of their controversial document, the delegates also stipulated that the Constitution would become law as soon as nine states had approved it.

On the last day of the convention, September 17, forty-two men remained in session. Three refused to sign the Constitution, and some indicated their reluctance to promote it publicly. Thirty-nine signers, however, put aside whatever misgivings they had and formally added their names to the document, knowing that they would have to argue strenuously for its acceptance. Their deliberations had been utterly secret, and their new document brushed aside the existing Confederation's written basis for a central government. But they believed they had devised the best alternative to the crises of the 1780s. Although delegates conferred popular sovereignty only on propertied white males in America, they hoped that widespread public discussion and special conventions would win over a more expansive "will of the people." Failing that, the republican experiment itself could fail.

The Public Debate

Once the states received copies of the Constitution, Americans began an intense discussion about whether to ratify the radical changes it proposed. They expressed a great spectrum of opinions about different provisions within the document, and they used the press, pulpit, and public podiums to spread their views into every social layer of society. Sometimes differences hinged on great political principles, and sometimes they derived from petty personal quarrels. Before long, however, the many issues at stake in this discussion polarized into two constituencies: Federalist supporters of the Constitution and Antifederalist opponents.

Both Federalists and Antifederalists appealed to the republican ideals of the Revolution to determine what kind of government and society was best suited to Americans' identity. But there were also significant differences between Federalists and Antifederalists. Federalists argued that government should have "majesty" and a significant degree of power over the lives of Americans. Too often, state and local governments succumbed to the "mischief of petty interests" that refused to compromise for the greater good. Citizens needed an "energetic" government to coordinate and develop the nation's great potential. Federalists also believed that both branches of the legislature should be filled with men of property, education, wealth, and "reputation."

Federalists published scores of newspaper essays and separate pamphlets, but their most influential writing appeared in *The Federalist,* a series of pathbreaking essays by the eminently influential trio of Madison, Hamilton, and Jay. *The Federalist* systematically defended central measures in the Constitution and depicted for its readers a bold new vision of federal power and government structure. During the months before the Constitutional Convention, Madison had studied the histories and constitutions of Western governments from ancient Greek to recent European times. Now, in *The Federalist,* he marshaled the wisdom of those classical works, and the practical experience of the convention itself, to argue for building the "energy" of government and expanding the territory of the country.

Madison's famous *Federalist* No. 10 took as its starting point a widely shared idea that political factions or parties were wrong because they represented only "partial interests" and were likely to arouse violent differences rather than protect the general welfare of a people. However, argued Madison, factions would arise inevitably in any republic, especially in one as large and dynamic as America. Furthermore, most people would not put public virtue first, but would serve their self-interests, which grew out of their individual liberty, above all else. Therefore, a strong republic would seek not to destroy but to regulate the natural interests that gave rise to factions. Such reasoning was a bold departure from traditional belief that governments and economies should seek to preserve themselves rather than to expand. Madison also reasoned that conflicts and negotiations in a dynamically expanding republic were natural and could be channeled creatively. Federalists generally argued that expansive commerce and westward settlement were important guarantees of a secure "republican empire." Madison, among others, thus turned America's great size, and its diverse, self-interested population, into virtues. And the federal government proposed by the Constitution would give institutional structure to the new nation.

Antifederalists arose in every locale and social strata of America. Some long-time state leaders, including George Clinton of New York and Patrick Henry of Virginia, provided their strongest voices. Clinton and Henry argued that the Constitution would create an overly centralized federal authority that would strip state governments of many legitimate powers. During the Imperial Crisis, republican rhetoric taught Americans that selfish interests of men in political power easily corrupted governments. Now, during the ratification controversy, Antifederalists reminded citizens that Federalists were proposing to create an equally dangerous, overly "energetic" national government, and to overturn the revolutionary goal of building effective states. Indeed, many states were recovering admirably from post-war crises under effective state leaders.

Other Antifederalists expressed more truly democratic sentiments. They warned against the "monied interests" and distant authority that would be created by the Constitution. Local governments, they contended, would be much more responsive to people's immediate needs. A few, such as New Yorker Melancthon Smith, believed that by concentrating political power in the hands of a wealthy minority, the Constitution would introduce dangerous class divisions. Many Antifederalists agreed with Mercy Otis Warren, who admitted that government needed more "dignity" and strength, but insisted that Americans had "struggled for liberty" and "the rights of man" too hard simply to hand them over to a few politicians deliberating in isolation from the "true interests of the people." Other Antifederalists cited the French Enlightenment political philosopher Montesquieu, who taught that republics should be small and roughly homogeneous in their "manners" or social composition. In such circumstances, contentious political factions and special interests would not corrupt public virtue. Governments should reflect their citizenry, and rulers should be responsive to public needs.

In the fall of 1787, elections were held for the state ratifying conventions. Only about 20 percent of Americans voted for delegates to these conventions, and some conventions—Delaware, New Jersey, New York, and Georgia—saw meager attendance. Predictably, public support for the Federalists came from coastal and urban areas; merchants, artisans, rising entrepreneurs, and shopkeepers all favored the Constitution in great numbers. But large numbers of laborers also supported the Federalist promise of commercial recovery and manufacturing protection. In the mid-Atlantic region, commercial farmers and southern planters enjoyed the benefits of an economic revival. Frontier Georgians found the Federalist promises of Indian defense and central political power appealing, given their weak position. And even though people in the unorganized territories did not vote on the Constitution, support tipped toward the Federalists in many frontier settlements.

Still, judging from the records of town meetings, petitions reprinted in the newspapers, state legislative discussions, and many personal memories, most Americans probably opposed the Constitution or were indifferent. Antifederalists dominated large portions of rural New England, western New York, central Pennsylvania, piedmont and southern Virginia, and large portions of the Carolinas. Average or poor farmers who were not well connected to the export economies of the coastal areas tended to agree with Antifederalist messages about the need for local control over politics. Few of these people expressed concern about shaping a great American nation, except to protest that such a goal would consume the resources of the states and raise taxes again.

Delaware, Pennsylvania, and New Jersey ratified in December 1787. Georgia and Connecticut followed suit in January 1788. Massachusetts weighed in sixth, but only after deep controversy. The state's Federalists slowly won over the strong Antifederalist majority by promising to include a list of amendments to the Constitution—something the drafters had rejected in Philadelphia—as a condition of ratifying. Then, once Maryland and South Carolina approved the Constitution with strong majorities, the approval of only one more state would secure ratification of the document.

On June 21 the New Hampshire convention squeaked out a slim majority and became the ninth state to ratify. But New York and Virginia, two of the most populous states and home to many leading Federalists, still had not acted. In the next days, brilliant and sustained Federalist oratory, as well as massive propaganda campaigns, secured ratification in both states—with winning margins of just ten votes in each convention. Then, once the matter was settled, a tremendous outpouring of public support followed. Thousands of New Yorkers marched in the streets in the summer of 1788 to celebrate ratification—lawyers and merchants headed the processions; craftsmen were arrayed next, according to the unspoken hierarchy of their various trades; and last came laborers. In contrast, North Carolina did not ratify until November 1789, and always-contentious Rhode Island bowed to the inevitable in May 1790—months after the first federal government was in operation.

How did Federalists win, given such great and protracted opposition? Certainly, the special ratifying conventions aided in their victory because they bypassed the likely political explosions in the state legislatures. Also, Federalists controlled much of the public press and marshaled much of the collective wisdom and experience gained from the revolutionary years. Many Federalist leaders had hammered away for years at the need to recast the Articles of Confederation. By 1787, many Americans believed that the multiplying problems of the new nation could not be solved by the states alone, which were the centerpiece of all Antifederalist alternatives. Although many Americans protested that the Constitution prolonged the existence of slavery, they agreed with Madison that "great as the evil is, a dismemberment of the union would be worse." Other Federalists asked, "If not this, then what?" Antifederalists, though eloquent defenders of revolutionary republicanism, had no coherent answer for the crises at hand.

"The Good Ship *Hamilton*" Ratification of the Constitution was celebrated with elaborate parades in major cities. Here, in New York, a float of the "ship of state" rolls past George Washington and members of Congress and fires a thirteen-gun salute. Despite the great opposition to changes proposed by Congress in the 1780s, and fears of federal government still lingering in 1788, the public expressed relief and joy that the "Critical Period" was over. *(Miriam and Ira D. Wallach Division of Art, Prints and Photographs, The New York Public Library. Astor, Lenox and Tilden Foundations.)*

 A New Political Nation, 1789–1791

Citizens throughout the nation had many reasons to be jubilant about the ratification of the Constitution. At last, sighed Federalists, there was a governmental structure suited to both the responsibilities of a rising nation and what some founders called "the genius of a people." But the controversy over ratification of the Constitution did not end when the document was narrowly approved. In the very first federal Congress, Federalists themselves began to quarrel over the appropriate taxation, commercial, defense, and other policies. Soon differences among Federalists became irreconcilable, and permanent political factions emerged. Outside Congress, too, the identity of the new nation was far from clear. Indeed, many Americans wondered whether they could become one nation.

The First Congress

Americans voted in the first federal election in November 1788, and the men they elected took their seats in the first federal Congress in late spring 1789. Of the ninety-one Congressmen, forty-four had either attended the Constitutional Convention or strongly favored ratification; only eight Antifederalists served in the first House session. Electors agreed quickly on Washington as president and John Adams as vice president, both of them strong Federalists.

Federalists knew that Americans followed every action of the new government with anticipation. The first federal administration not only would make laws but also would define the culture of national leadership. Some Federalists believed that the people wished to look with awe on the majesty of their rulers, as when John Adams proposed the title, "His Highness the President." Others, thinking that citizens should be reminded regularly of the government's great power, proposed to stamp coins with a "regal view of the president" and to adorn public buildings with busts and paintings of leaders "in majestic garb." Most Congressmen, however, rejected such "artificial chimera." Virtuous republican leaders, they insisted, should look and act like their constituents—the American people—not like the corrupt officials of the British Empire.

As president, Washington was aloof from the general population. He rode a carriage pulled by six horses and attended by liverymen, and he entertained members of the urban elite "in the grand style." Washington also conducted foreign affairs face to face and addressed Congress personally, according to the customs of royalty in Europe. But he also stemmed his use of the executive veto power and created a cabinet of department heads reflecting various points of view. He included Thomas Jefferson as secretary of state, Alexander Hamilton as treasurer, Henry Knox as secretary of war, and Edmund Randolph as the head of the justice department, or attorney general.

Congress's first major step was passage of the Judiciary Act in 1789, which established a six-justice Supreme Court, thirteen district courts, and three circuit courts that would hear cases appealed from the states. However, the apparent power given to these courts was actually quite limited because federal judges did not preside over a uniform national code of civil and criminal justice, but rather over the many bodies of state law. Differences between federal and state judicial interpretations thus began with the creation of the federal government.

Another of Congress's early actions was to pass the constitutional amendments known as the Bill of Rights. The Philadelphia convention delegates had determined that special provisions to protect individual rights and popular sovereignty were unnecessary elaborations of the federal government's powers. But Antifederalists revived pressure to amend the Constitution with guarantees of "essential rights." Madison reluctantly accepted the chore of collating over two hundred specific demands from state ratifying conventions and shaping them into a workable set of amendments. In June 1789, Congress considered Madison's list of twelve amendments and submitted them to the states; the ten provisions approved by the states became the Bill of Rights in 1791. Many of the amendments further restricted Congress's authority over citizens: they prohibited established (government-supported) religion; guaranteed freedom of speech, press, assembly, and petition; limited the quartering of troops in private homes, unreasonable searches of citizens and their property, and breaches of the common law; and secured many individual legal rights, including due process of law and the right of citizens to refuse to testify against themselves.

Hamilton's Plans

The first important signs of division in Congress came with efforts to repay Revolutionary War debts still outstanding. Most legislators agreed that the best source of government income was not direct taxes on property or private incomes, but import duties on commerce. Hence, the Tariff Act of 1789, which taxed tonnage of foreign ships coming to American ports and all imported goods, but at low enough levels to encourage merchants to expand business. Over the next thirty years, revenue from commerce provided 90 percent of the national government's income.

With a stable source of income guaranteed, it was finally possible to tackle the problem of federal debts. Hamilton submitted a "Report on the Public Credit" to Congress in January 1790. The report outlined three kinds of debts Hamilton believed Congress should repay: approximately $12 million owed to foreign countries, over $30 million owed to private American citizens, and another $25 million that the states had not repaid to private citizens. By consolidating all state and national debts into one fund, and repaying them from the national treasury, at an annual interest rate of 4 percent, the federal government would assure the world at large, as well as America's creditors, that the new nation could honor its obligations.

Congress readily agreed that foreign debts should be paid quickly and fully, since the political reputation of the country rested on its good credit abroad. But a prolonged discussion ensued about how, and how much, to pay private American creditors of the states and Congress. During the Revolution, congressional notes had depreciated from their face value to near worthlessness. Out of necessity, many soldiers and farmers sold off "continentals" at low market value in order to get cash.

But debate surrounding Hamilton's report—and possibly information he floated to insiders—fueled speculators' hopes that Congress would repay its debts at face values much higher than the market values, which in turn spurred a frenzy among speculators to acquire as much of the depreciated currency as possible. Hamilton's assistant secretary of the treasury, William Duer, formed a syndicate of speculators in the North; by the time Hamilton's report reached Congress, a few northern businessmen, merchants, and brokers controlled most of the national paper debt.

Hamilton's proposal also included provisions for "assuming" outstanding state debts and repaying them at face value. Since all of the southern states except South Carolina had already paid off most of their debts during the 1780s, neither those state governments nor their speculators stood to gain much by federal assumption. In the North, however, state debts were largely unpaid and became the objects of energetic speculation when Hamilton unveiled his plan. The sectional benefit to the North was not lost on southern congressmen.

Hamilton urged Congress to look beyond the private benefits for a few speculators and to contemplate the greater public welfare that his report set forth. Assumption and funding of the debts would enlarge America's reputation in a "world of watching nations" and secure the support of the country's wealthiest citizens to the goals of the federal government. The national debt, Hamilton argued, would become a "national blessing."

In his next report to Congress, in December 1790, Hamilton underscored this reasoning even more. Using the Bank of England as his model, his "Report on the Bank of the United States" proposed that Congress charter a central bank, which would then sell stock in the amount of $10 million to both private investors and the government. From these funds, the Bank would make loans to merchants, warehouse government revenues, and issue notes to investors. Did Congress have the constitutional authority to create such an institution? Hamilton thought so, pointing to the "necessary and proper clause" of the Constitution, an interpretation that became known as "loose construction."

Although acrimonious discussion challenged Hamilton's reasoning, President Washington approved the Bank's opening in Philadelphia in 1791 under a twenty-year charter. The Bank of the United States provided merchants with an international circulating credit, and many Americans benefited from Bank notes in ordinary business transactions for many years to come. Revenues from commercial tariffs poured into the government coffers, some of which was channeled into the Bank's backing fund. In April 1791, Hamilton convinced Congress to approve additional excise taxes on the consumption of wine, tea, coffee, and distilled spirits, the last of which also included a tax on whiskey produced in the frontier. The Bank quickly established eight branches around the country, and state governments had begun to specially charter their own banks.

With his plans for public credit and banking in place, Hamilton submitted his last proposal in December 1791, the "Report on Manufactures." It was an ambitious plan for using government resources to promote development. Certain that the British mercantile model was the best in modern Western times, Hamilton pored over the reports about American manufacturing conditions that Assistant Secretary

Alexander Hamilton, 1792
By modern standards, Hamilton was still a young man of thirty-seven when John Trumbull painted this portrait. By then, the great statesman and economic visionary had seen many of his plans to alter the American political economy come to fruition. *(Yale University Art Gallery, Trumbull Collection.)*

of the Treasury Tench Coxe laid before him. Hamilton also undertook an extensive refutation of the views popularized by Adam Smith. Smith, a Scottish Enlightenment figure whose 1776 tome, *The Wealth of Nations,* had captured widespread attention, urged policymakers and philosophers to abandon their faith in government regulation of trade and domestic production. Smith repudiated the subsidies, discriminatory tariffs, prohibitions, and embargoes that mercantilists often supported. Let demand for goods and services determine the level of production and prices, wrote Smith, and trust that the negotiations of buyers and sellers would create the best environment for market exchanges.

On the contrary, Hamilton believed government should protect "infant industries." His report was clear that inventions of new machinery, more skilled labor, and new technologies still lay in the future, and that investment capital was in short supply throughout America. But he believed that federal bounties for experiments in production, as well as higher import duties on foreign goods, would stimulate growth.

However, Congress consigned Hamilton's Report on Manufactures to rapid defeat. Entrepreneurs and artisans in the cities sputtered that Hamilton did not want to give them protective tariffs to keep out foreign competition. Farmers and southern planters slammed the Report as biased in favor of cities and the "money interest" in them. Merchants—otherwise important allies of Hamilton—were more concerned about shipbuilding and commerce than manufacturing. When word spread in late 1791 that Hamilton had encouraged a handful of prominent speculators to invest their "flimsy paper credit" in the transformation of Paterson, New Jersey, into a manufacturing entrepôt, the congressional report collapsed. Only in the next American generation would manufacturing gain effective government support.

Nevertheless, when judged by the enduring impact of the principles and institutions he promoted, Hamilton possibly influenced the framing of early national government and economy more than any other individual. The financial health of the country improved dramatically within a short time; foreign confidence in America revived, and foreign investment in government securities increased; commerce recovered and grew.

From Factions to Parties

The constitutional founders believed that Americans would live in a one-party nation whose federal structure of government would prevent factions from disrupting peace and derailing development. But even in the first Congress, debates about the national debt, banks, and manufactures revealed important differences emerging in that one party. Madison and Jefferson soon began to voice serious objections to Hamilton's plans, and their opposition became the basis for congressional divisions on important policies during 1791 and 1792. Hamilton's opponents believed that nothing less than the future of the revolutionary experiment was at stake. Their arguments generated a renewed public discussion about Americans' national identity. Soon, factional divisions in Congress spread throughout the republic. During the 1790s, these divisions coalesced into the first political parties in the nation.

Hamiltonians Versus Republicans

Madison readily admitted the wisdom of a national tariff in 1789, and he took the lead in shaping the Bill of Rights. But as soon as Hamilton presented his assumption and funding plans, Madison loudly voiced his fears that fellow Federalists in Congress were falling behind a scheme to favor a northern "monied interest" that presented grave danger to republican citizens. He recoiled from the "immorality" of speculators who bought depreciated wartime currencies from soldiers, widows, and descendants of wartime farmers and artisans with the calculated intention of redeeming them at face value if Congress passed Hamilton's plans. As an alternative to assumption of creditors' debts at face value, Madison proposed that Congress give the current holders only a prevailing market value for their securities—which would be far below their face value—and to return remaining amounts up to face value to the original holders of the money. This was high moral ground, but the House of Representatives rejected Madison's plan as utterly impractical, for it would be nearly impossible to find the original holders of revolutionary debts. Besides, many congressmen held securities and thus stood to profit from government's funding of private debts.

Madison rose again to protest another aspect of Hamilton's report on public credit, the federal assumption and funding of the state debts. Since southern states had repaid most or all of their revolutionary obligations, they stood to benefit very little by Hamilton's plan. Madison objected to the "injustice" of discriminating against an entire section of the country. So, in order to gain southern support, Hamiltonians agreed to place the federal capital on the Potomac River, a location that Madison believed reflected the "majesty" of an agrarian republican countryside that had not fallen under the "baneful influences" of urban corruption. As in 1787, political compromise temporarily calmed sectional animosities.

Four months later, Hamilton's plan for the Bank of the United States passed in Congress, but before President Washington signed the Bank bill into law, opponents exploded with objections. Jefferson raged against the creation of a national bank that would "enrich a monied power." The Bank, he charged, would benefit wealthy merchants and investors by granting them loans and paying them interest on their deposits, but would enable only a few to prosper from a fund created by huge numbers of average citizens. Such an institution was blatantly unfair. Moreover, there was a "decidedly unrepublican" blending of political and economic interests, according to Jefferson: thirty Congressmen owned stock in the national Bank, and "great numbers" of them owned some part of the government debt. But most important, Jefferson and Madison insisted that the Constitution did not give Congress the power to charter a bank as part of its "necessary and proper" functions, and to do so would exercise unwarranted central authority against the rights of the American people. Jefferson pleaded for a more narrow interpretation, or "strict construction," of constitutional powers. However, Washington was persuaded that the Bank would be a beneficial institution, and the act became law.

Rifts Widen

Madison and Jefferson did not have to marshal strenuous arguments against Hamilton's 1791 Report on Manufactures to sink it because both Congress and the American public rejected it outright. But by mid-1792, both opponents had concluded that Hamiltonians had set out to overturn the republic and establish a monarchy in America. Reaching out to state legislatures, public organizations, the press, and popular opinion in general, opponents of Federalist "designs and corruptions" began to organize outside Congress. Modeling themselves on the Sons of Liberty (see page 180), citizens formed "constitutional societies" and "rights watches" to "fully inform our neighbors far and wide of [Federalist] governmental encroachments." By the end of the year, dozens of "Democratic-Republican," or "Republican," societies simmered with dissent.

These clubs and public meetings often started with discussions of the Hamiltonian programs, but quickly included other issues. Thousands of miles away in 1789, the French people had initiated their own revolution that assaulted all remnants of feudalism, instituted a constitutional monarchy, and promised to build a republican society in time. Many Americans applauded the French Revolution's egalitarianism as a new stage in the development of republicanism and adopted the French term "citizen" as a democratic form of address. Many also associated the French Revolution with greater possibilities for open commerce among many nations and world peace—an attractive antidote to the stifling restrictions imposed in the British trade.

Federalists scoffed at this Jeffersonian optimism. By late 1792, France was at war with the monarchies of Prussia and Austria; internally, revolutionaries began to execute thousands of leaders in the church, aristocracy, and monarchical resistance in the Reign of Terror. Wealthy, deeply religious, and Hamiltonian Americans were repulsed when French revolutionaries beheaded Louis XVI in 1793, and even more when the French republic declared war against England. Federalist merchants in the northern states feared losing their British trading partners. Even if they appreciated the French experiment in republicanism, they needed English imports.

Washington tried to avoid American involvement in the wars that grew out of the French Revolution. In early 1793, he urged Congress to declare American neutrality. In response, Congress passed the Neutrality Act, which barred the ships of fighting nations from American ports and suspended America's obligations under the treaty of 1778 to defend France in any war with Britain.

The American public responded enthusiastically to the declaration of neutrality. Merchants interpreted the move as an invitation to trade openly with both French and British West Indies colonies. Commercial farmers in the Chesapeake and mid-Atlantic regions stepped up grain production because it seemed as though warring European countries would now become eager buyers. And port cities generally welcomed the prospects of high employment in trades related to shipping. Property values skyrocketed and urban people watched in awe as the nation's first building boom transformed coastal cities.

However, neutrality on the high seas did not tame political factionalism at home. Tensions rose again in April 1793 when Jeffersonians enthusiastically linked the activities of their Democratic-Republican clubs to the visit of French diplomat Edmond Genêt. "Citizen" Genêt spoke to huge crowds of pro-French Americans, who generously donated funds to support their fellow revolutionaries abroad. Young men signed up by the thousands to privateer against British and Spanish ships in the Caribbean. In mid-1793, Genêt challenged Washington's Congress to a debate about the neutrality policy, hoping to persuade it to declare war on Britain. Federalists assailed Genêt as an agent provocateur, and many Jeffersonians, or Republicans, despised his ill-disguised attempts to lure America into war. There was a collective sigh of relief when Washington demanded his recall in August 1793.

Although many Democratic-Republicans distanced themselves from the Genêt affair, their local and state opposition to the Federalists grew stronger than ever. More Democratic-Republican societies formed from Georgia to Maine, claiming the heritage of republicanism, decrying the presence of British troops on the frontier, and demanding removal of the Spanish from the Mississippi River. Federalists, they charged by 1794, ignored the urgent problems of the frontier as they defended monarchy, special privilege, and measures that sucked the life out of local government. For their part, Federalists replied that Democratic-Republican opposition was "self-created," or outside the authority of official institutions or constitutions. "Without the force of law," complained Federalists, "the lowest orders of mechanics, laborers and draymen" had nullified "the respectability we seek in statesmen."

By fall 1793, international neutrality on the high seas began to crumble. Britain declared a blockade against France, and the British began to seize American ships trading with the French West Indies and southern France. Within six months, British naval commanders had taken over 250 American vessels, forced thousands of American men to serve under them, and stolen sugar and indigo of incalculable value. American merchants failed to win compensation for lost property from British admiralty courts. In an effort to end this "piracy" against American shippers, Washington sent Chief Justice John Jay to London in spring 1794 with orders to negotiate a resolution.

Jay returned to America that fall with a more comprehensive document than Americans anticipated, but no direct resolution of their problems. In the first place, Jay's Treaty proposed that Americans make "full and complete compensation" to British firms for all debts outstanding at the onset of the American Revolution twenty years before. The treaty also permitted Britain to take French property from neutral—that is, American—ships for the duration of the European war, thereby erasing the tradition that "free ships make free goods." British arbitration panels would hear American claims for commercial compensation, but most West Indies ports remained closed to American shipping. The British agreed to withdraw their troops from six forts on the American frontier.

Democratic-Republicans proclaimed Jay's Treaty a fiasco. Jay had returned without provisions to compensate masters for slaves who fled to the British side during the Revolution; nor had he secured terms for peaceful trade between France and America; nor were there guarantees that British troops would leave the frontier. With some exaggeration, Jay said he could travel across the American continent at night by the light of fires burning him in effigy. Congress deadlocked in a debate about the treaty for months.

Then in 1795 Congress learned that Spain wished to negotiate an end to hostilities on the Mississippi. Envoy Thomas Pinckney, a southerner who supported open trade and American expansion into the Southeast, worked out an agreement with Spain to set its claims at the thirty-first parallel and open the Mississippi (plus New Orleans) to American shipping. Congressmen compromised factional and sectional interests by tying the Pinckney and Jay treaties together. The Senate then ratified Jay's Treaty in June 1795 with the required two-thirds majority.

The Frontier Besieged

In 1787 the Northwest Ordinance had recognized the independence of Native Americans from national government, and in 1790 the first federal administration reinforced this view with the Indian Intercourse Act. The act stipulated that only the federal government could negotiate the terms of travel and trade on Indian lands; created a federal licensing system and regulated prices of frontier trade; asserted that only the federal government, not individuals could acquire Indian lands; and instituted a treaty-making process.

Frontier people regularly abused the act, however. Traders cheated and cajoled Native Americans into unfavorable relationships; government agents used force to obtain Indian land by sham treaties; and American citizens carried on "private expeditions against the Indians" to obtain fertile land along the Ohio River. In 1790 chief Little Turtle led the Shawnee, Delaware, and Miami in a bloody victory against the American army forces. A year later the same confederacy of Native Americans attacked settlers in the Northwest Territory under Governor-General Arthur St. Clair. Over nine hundred Americans died in the days-long siege. Fighting continued for three years until Americans under the command of General Anthony Wayne defeated Little Turtle and his pan-Indian army in the Battle of Fallen Timbers on August 20, 1794. The following year, in the Treaty of Greenville, twelve Indian nations ceded the land that would become Ohio and Indiana.

At the same time, Spain was consolidating its territorial claims around the Gulf Coast from the Floridas to New Orleans, in California, and in the Caribbean. Most frightening for Americans, the Spanish tried to block American expansion through the Southeast by courting close friendships with populations of runaway slaves, Acadian refugees, and Native American peoples, as well as by closing off the lower Mississippi to American ships. Farmers from the Ohio country and planters in South Carolina and Georgia grew increasingly anxious about their ability to export goods and expand territorially.

In the 1790s, the Spanish Floridas flourished as a multiethnic, multiracial crossroads, laced with waterways that no authorities could effectively develop or police. Italians, Greeks, and Minorcans came by the hundreds, most of them Roman Catholic, and lived alongside the Seminole and black settlements created during the revolutionary era. In contrast to the southern American plantations to the north, a large free Creole population born in Spanish and French colonies of the Caribbean and South America thrived in Florida, as did hundreds of African and country-born runaways after the British evacuation in 1783. Remnants of Lord Dunmore's "Ethiopians" had formed maroon communities along the Savannah River, where they fought against a joint force of Catawba Indians and South Carolina and Georgia militias. Spain did not always encourage these maroon societies to settle in its empire, but runaway communities on the mainland were magnets for rebellious slaves fleeing Saint Dominique in 1796. St. Augustine's population reached nearly 50 percent free and slave black people by about 1800.

Washington confided to close advisers in 1794 his belief that persistent violence on the frontier put the entire republic in peril. At about that time, westerners began to inundate the administration with petitions decrying "the burden of great taxes for the support of government." They singled out Hamilton's excise tax as the most "unreasonable and unjust of all" because it fell hardest on "industrious citizens" farming in western Pennsylvania, North Carolina, and Kentucky. Because they risked the loss or spoilage of corn crops during transport on open flatboats down river—turbulent waters could capsize crops, and rains could wipe out a season's labor in a few hours—farmers converted corn into whiskey. For farmers still living in mud shacks, deeply in debt for their tools and land, producing spirits promised sure profits.

Western farmers had rallied in 1792 against sheriffs who attempted to collect the whiskey tax, and court officials who tried to fine and arrest violators. The Whiskey Rebellion broke out in 1794 when the local militia marched against tax collectors in

Mingo Creek, Pennsylvania (near Pittsburgh). Their cries were the familiar ones of the Stamp Act riots, Shays's Rebellion, and the French Revolution: "Liberty, Fraternity, and Equality, and no Excise." Farmers and distillers burned local sheriffs in effigy and broke open the courts here and there on the frontier. Angry protesters cried that the government had taxed westerners without their consent and imposed unjustified force against "a free people." Washington responded decisively to this threat against the new republic. He reasoned that if Americans successfully thwarted their government, Spanish, British, and Indians would follow. The president ordered an army of thirteen thousand federal troops, commanded by Hamilton and led by the commander-in-chief himself for part of the march, to suppress the rebels at once (see Competing Voices, page 283).

Parties and Interests

As he prepared to leave office in 1796, an exhausted sixty-four-year-old President Washington pleaded with Americans to avoid the "baneful effects of the spirit of party." Most of his listeners would have agreed; all healthy republics avoided party politics. Americans, Washington stated, should be actively "extending our commercial relations" around the world, seeking "peace and prosperity" in the exchange of goods and peoples. But they should have "as little political connection as possible" with foreign nations—otherwise, they would inevitably be drawn into costly and debilitating wars. Federalists and Democratic-Republicans shared this political philosophy. But in the world of practical affairs and fallible human beings, could they achieve peace and prosperity without political conflict?

The Idea of Political Parties

For generations, colonial and revolutionary Americans had believed in deference, social hierarchies, and rule by one's "natural betters." Of course, colonial assembly representatives had often divided into factions; but they usually based alliances on kinship, marriage, crown patronage, or rifts within the elite over land, commerce, or religion. During the revolutionary years, factions remained shifting and temporary alliances, and no state constitutions provided for permanent political divisions. Most Americans still expected that the "better sort" should naturally assume rule over all others and that only the crassly self-interested actively campaigned for offices. During the 1790s, Washington and Jefferson grew apart politically but shared scorn for parties. Even Madison's frank vision in *Federalist* No. 10 of factions arising in the republic did not portray such coalitions as permanent.

But these views slowly changed. The Revolution had nurtured belief in "the people," and new state legislatures had experimented with more democratic forms of rule. Although the Federalists had begun to create strong institutions and central political authority, they also stimulated opponents to speak out for more personal liberty and limited government. As a result, during the 1780s and 1790s, a great public debate considered the role of citizens in a republic, the nature of a standing army marching against the likes of the Whiskey Rebels, and America's status among nations. These political issues became more and more poignant in the cultural atmosphere of changing family and gender roles, shifting religion and educational life, new consumer goods and western lands.

In the fall elections of 1794, Democratic-Republicans showed rising strength in national congressional debates, local political societies, and state contests for offices. By 1796, conflicts over Hamiltonian programs, taxes, foreign affairs, and America's frontiers propelled citizens another step away from their colonial past and toward an uncharted political culture. By then, grass-roots contests between Federalists and Democratic-Republicans encompassed national issues. The presidential election thus became the occasion for a full-blown national contest, with candidates vying for citizens' votes at all levels of society and identifying with party-based policies. For the first time, parties held caucus meetings to choose candidates for office and determine how to reach voters with their messages. Newspapers spread the idea that two political "parties" were emerging: Federalists who supported "order," elite rule, and the Washington administration; and Democratic-Republicans (or just Republicans) who stood for the revolutionary heritage, democratic tendencies, a Bill of Rights, and "free government."

Toward a Party System

Thomas Jefferson resigned as secretary of state at the end of 1793 and joined Madison's opposition to the Federalists during Washington's second administration. Their efforts at first targeted Hamilton's programs, but they soon developed a separate view of the proper role of government that reached deeply into every aspect of American society. As a man of the Enlightenment, Jefferson was widely educated in science, agriculture, diplomacy, natural history, architecture, and political theory. He worked steadfastly toward religious toleration, broader educational opportunities, social refinement, and westward expansion. As a southern gentleman planter and slaveholder in the eighteenth century, Jefferson did not profess equality of the races. He believed in "moral improvement" for whites through the vehicle of agricultural, not urban, life, and he defined *personal independence* as the ownership of a parcel of land and *social independence* as continual westward expansion. On the other hand, a dependent people, such as England's city dwellers, could be known by their wage labor, factories, and luxury consumption. Jefferson had set out these ideas in the Land Ordinances of the 1780s, and they shaped his vision of America for years to come.

The nationwide appeal of Jefferson's vision became clear in the national election of 1796. The Federalists still had enough prestige, wealth, and experience in public life to win a majority in Congress and the electoral college. The latter chose Washington's vice president John Adams to succeed him as president. After rejecting the avid southern expansionist Thomas Pinckney for vice president, the electors turned to Thomas Jefferson to fill that office.

John Adams, a New Englander, had sparred with Jefferson on almost every important issue of the 1790s. As president, Adams upheld a pro-British foreign policy and grew increasingly irritated with continuing French seizures of American sailors, ships, and goods on the high seas. Following moderate Federalist policy, Adams attempted to negotiate compensation for losses and a more lasting peace with the French. But an American delegation sent to Paris discovered that three of the French prince Talleyrand's agents assigned to "treat with" them demanded a bribe before they would begin talks.

Although Adams fumed at the insult to American honor, he shrewdly turned the affair to his advantage. When Democratic-Republicans in Congress demanded proof of the French insults, Adams divulged secret correspondence, with the French agents' names changed to *X, Y,* and *Z.* As planned, the XYZ Affair aroused anti-French sentiment throughout America. The slogan "Millions for defense, but not one cent for tribute!" rang through the country. Congress passed an embargo act that stopped trade against France and authorized privateering against French ships. In May 1798, Congress allocated funds for a large naval buildup to defend the American coast against French attack. In July Congress repealed the entire treaty of 1778 and approved the recruitment of ten thousand army troops. From 1798 to 1800, the Adams administration in effect fought an "undeclared war" against the French republic.

As it became clear that the XYZ Affair would not cow Democratic-Republicans, Adams determined to repress political dissent in the country. Fearing that foreign subversives would flock to American shores, the Federalist Congress passed an Alien Act during the summer of 1798. The act permitted the president to order the imprisonment or deportation of noncitizens. Strictly speaking, Congress had been granted such a power to regulate immigration and naturalization of citizens under Article 1, Section 8, of the Constitution. The Alien Act's special targets included the Irish and Scottish dissenters with pro-French sympathies who publicly denounced the government's pro-British policies. To allay growing public fears of "foreign meddling" in policymaking, Congress also passed the Naturalization Act, which raised the residency requirement for citizenship from five to fourteen years. And as a capstone to Federalists' fears, Congress passed the Sedition Act, which prohibited exaggerated, ill-intentioned, or untruthful written attacks on Congress or the president. But the main Federalist mouthpiece, the *Gazette of the United States,* bordered on excessive silencing of the party's opponents when it raged that no opposition to the Federalists would be tolerated. "All who are against us are at war," stormed the *Gazette.*

In the next months, government officials arrested almost two dozen Republican editors and legislators for sedition. Matthew Lyon, who had come to America in 1764 as an Irish indentured servant, was one of them. Lyon had risen quickly in revolutionary years by profiting as a supplier to the patriot militia, acquiring confiscated loyalist estates, and ambitiously seeking political office in the new state of Vermont. In February 1798, the "scrapper Lyon," a Democratic-Republican from Vermont, spit at Connecticut House Federalist Roger Griswold. Griswold struck Lyon with his cane, and Lyon returned the blows with a pair of fire tongs. Because few Americans accepted the legitimacy of political parties and loyal opposition in those years, it seemed to many Federalists that Lyon had attacked the majesty of the republic itself. Under the terms of the Sedition Act, Lyon's subsequent accusations of Adams as full of "ridiculous pomp, foolish adulation, and selfish avarice," caused Lyon to serve four months in a Vermont prison. Independent-minded Vermonters, however, voted him into Congress that same year.

Today, silenced writers and politicians could turn to the courts for a ruling on provisions in the Bills of Rights, including freedoms of speech, press, and assembly. But in 1798, most Republicans viewed courts as bastions of Federalism. Few people knew what powers the courts had over citizens and legislation. Instead, Americans looked to their state governments as counterweights to the authority of the national government, and that is exactly how Madison and Jefferson mobilized sentiment against the Alien and Sedition acts. Prodded by Jefferson, the Kentucky legislature passed a resolution making the offensive congressional laws "void and of no force" and asserting the absolute authority of each state to "judge by itself" which federal laws to follow. A similar resolution in Virginia went even further, asserting that states had the right to nullify any powers exercised by the federal government that were not explicitly granted in the Constitution. The Virginia and Kentucky Resolutions of 1798 thus argued for a strict construction of the Constitution. In 1787 Madison had pressed for extensive national powers; now he was insisting that the states should use their powers to guard public virtue.

By 1798, Democratic-Republicans and Federalists were regularly airing their political differences in public, and both parties used fiery rhetoric to denounce opponents. Federalists portrayed Democratic-Republicans as "handmaids of the irreligious French devil" and "without scruple for our foreign reputation." Though they were somewhat fearful of the social consequences of tensions building between European nations, they continued to favor England's war against France. Federalists hoped to calm internal discord, too. But they formulated policies that added to citizens' burdens and led to new eruptions of violence, as when the Direct Tax of 1798 led to Jacob Fries's Rebellion in eastern Pennsylvania in 1799.

For their part, Democratic-Republicans took advantage of Americans' war weariness and called for an end to the shrill newspaper feuds, less government intrusion in citizens' lives, westward expansion, and commercial revival "on terms of equal freedom among all nations." Voters fed up with belligerence on the oceans and high taxes turned away from the Federalists. In the 1799 state elections, Pennsylvania and New York went over to the Democratic-Republicans, joining the Jeffersonians in southern and new western states.

Then, in 1800, electors handed Jefferson and Aaron Burr, both Democratic-Republicans, a majority of seventy-three votes each for executive office. It fell to the House of Representatives to decide who would become president. In a desperate attempt to prevent Jefferson's ascendancy, the Federalist-controlled House blocked ballot after ballot. Then, after thirty-five ballots, Hamilton begged his fellow Federalists to turn away from Burr—the "embryo Caesar" who, Hamilton argued, would stop at nothing to destroy federal authority and raise up contentious local interests—and accept Jefferson. At least Jefferson would preserve the federal union and the Constitution, even if on Democratic-Republican terms. And so the House ratified the "bloodless Revolution" that transferred power peacefully, but definitively, to a new party. It seemed to many observers that the American experiment might be preserved after all.

Mad Tom in a Rage, 1790 For years, Tom Paine was identified as a spokesman for the American revolutionary cause and a supporter of the new federal government. But when the French Revolution began, his support for the extension of American ideals of liberty to that foreign country drew scorn from Federalists, who thought Paine wanted to destroy America's strong central government. In this Federalist cartoon, Paine tries to dismantle the national government with the help of a familiar symbol of disloyal political opposition. Only after 1800, with Jefferson firmly in power, did many Americans accept the legitimacy of political factions or parties. *(Library of Congress.)*

CONCLUSION

Mercy Otis Warren agreed with a majority of Americans during the 1780s that the new states were handling the post-revolutionary recovery well, and that the Federalists exaggerated the problems of the Critical Period. She also agreed with many Americans that the Constitution of 1787 introduced dangerous tendencies to centralize political authority and stifle the creative energies of people in their locales. Like other Antifederalists, Warren was somewhat reconciled to the new national government by passage of the Bill of Rights, but she refused, ever, to accept Hamilton's plans. In her declining years, Warren hailed Jefferson's 1800 victory as a second chance for the republican experiment of the Revolution to succeed.

Jefferson himself called his triumphant election the "Revolution of 1800," but many other Americans understood that the Democratic-Republican ascendancy had come from below. Bitter partisan battles, originating in the differences between Federalists and Antifederalists, had shaped their political identity and their place among other nations. In the years between independence and the election of 1800,

Americans decisively shifted from support for a republic of stable and like-minded citizens to support for boisterous and factional politics that invited widespread public participation.

But if a new political era dawned, few Americans at the time understood its profound social, economic, and cultural significance. New England still harbored large numbers of Federalists, while the South nurtured leading Democratic-Republicans and the mid-Atlantic region defied clear political tendencies. Federalists drew much of their support from merchants, manufacturers, and commercial farmers, whereas Democratic-Republicans boasted the solid backing of wage earners, artisans, shopkeepers, new immigrants, religious minorities, southern exporting planters, and small farmers throughout the interior. While Federalists imagined the benefits of a "natural aristocracy," Democratic-Republicans dreamed of making a "decent living within the reach of the better part of mankind." Yet women, Indians, and African-Americans continued to be excluded from the franchise—and from the vision of both parties.

SUGGESTED READINGS

Religious issues during the revolutionary generation are presented best in Ruth H. Bloch, *Visionary Republic: Millennial Themes in American Thought, 1756–1800* (1985), and Nathan Hatch, *The Democratization of American Christianity* (1989). An assessment of slavery is made by the contributors in Ira Berlin and Ronald Hoffman, eds., *Slavery and Freedom in the Age of the American Revolution* (1983). The most compelling case study of emancipation in the North is Gary Nash and Jean Soderlund, *Freedom by Degrees: Emancipation in Pennsylvania and Its Aftermath* (1991).

Most studies about women's gains during the revolutionary generation draw guarded conclusions. See especially Jay Fliegelman, *Prodigals and Pilgrims: The American Revolution Against Patriarchal Authority, 1750–1800* (1982); Linda Kerber, *Women of the Republic: Intellect and Ideology in Revolutionary America* (1980); and Jan Lewis, *The Pursuit of Happiness: Family and Values in Jeffersonian Virginia* (1983).

An excellent recent study of the problems faced in commercial relations after the Revolution is John E. Crowley, *The Privileges of Independence: Neomercantilism and the American Revolution* (1993). The tremendous problems related to repaying the war debts owed by Congress and the states are clarified in E. James Ferguson, *The Power of the Purse: A History of American Public Finance: 1776–1790* (1967).

For Shays's Rebellion, start with the stimulating collection of essays in Robert A. Gross, ed., *In Debt to Shays: The Bicentennial of an Agrarian Rebellion* (1993), and the major work of David P. Szatmary, *Shays's Rebellion: The Making of an Agrarian Insurrection* (1980).

For the relationship of difficulties during the 1780s and the promise of prosperity and opportunity, see Merrill Jensen, *The New Nation: A History of the United States During the Confederation* (1950); Ronald Hoffman et al., eds., *The Economy of Early America: The Revolutionary Period, 1763–1790* (1988); and Cathy Matson and Peter Onuf, *A Union of Interests: Political and Economic Thought in Revolutionary America* (1990).

For the background to the Constitutional Convention, important starting points are Lance Banning, *The Sacred Fire of Liberty: James Madison and the Founding of the Federal Republic* (1995); Gordon S. Wood, *The Creation of the American Republic, 1776–1787* (1969); and Richard Beeman et al., eds., *Beyond Confederation: Origins of the Constitution and American National Identity* (1987). For the intellectual discussions embedded in the political struggles at Philadelphia, see Richard Bernstein and Kym Rice, *Are We to Be a Nation? The Making of the Constitution* (1987). For the ideas that shaped public discussions, see Donald

Lutz, *Popular Consent and Popular Control: Whig Political Theory in the Early State Constitutions* (1980); Staughton Lynd, *Class Conflict, Slavery, and the United States Constitution* (1967); and the Pulitzer Prize–winning contribution by Jack Rakove, *Original Meanings: Politics and Ideas in the Making of the Constitution* (1996). Richard B. Morris has composed short biographical sketches of the leading constitutional framers in *Witnesses at the Creation: Hamilton, Madison, Jay, and the Constitution* (1985).

Aspects of ratification of the Constitution are covered best in Steven Boyd, *The Politics of Opposition: Antifederalists and the Acceptance of the Constitution* (1979), a detailed account of the range of Antifederalist opposition to the Constitution during the late 1780s. See also the fine articles in Michael Gillespie and Michael Leinesch, eds., *Ratifying the Constitution* (1989), and the intellectual history by Michael Kammen, *A Machine That Would Go of Itself: The Constitution in American Culture* (1986). Two outstanding earlier studies that remain required reading on this topic are Jackson T. Main, *The Antifederalists: Critics of the Constitution, 1781–1788* (1961), and Robert Rutland, *The Ordeal of the Constitution: The Antifederalists and the Ratification Struggle of 1787–1788* (1966).

The first federal government is treated in Kenneth Bowling, *Politics in the First Congress, 1789–1791* (1990), and Stanley Elkins and Eric McKitrick, *The Federalist Era* (1993). Hamilton's plans are judiciously presented in the biography by Jacob E. Cooke, *Alexander Hamilton* (1982), and in John R. Nelson's excellent *Liberty and Property: Political Economy and Policymaking in the New Nation, 1789–1812* (1987).

The entangling web of foreign diplomacy, commerce, internal development, and political factionalism are presented in Ralph Ketcham, *Presidents Above Party: The First American Presidency, 1789–1829* (1984); Richard Buel, *Securing the Revolution: Ideology in American Politics, 1789–1815* (1972); and Daniel Lang, *Foreign Policy in the Early Republic* (1985). An older study that encompasses the Federalists' rise and fall at the national level is John C. Miller, *The Federalist Era, 1789–1800* (1960). For Federalist repression at the end of the century, see James Morton Smith, *Freedom's Fetters: The Alien and Sedition Laws and American Civil Liberties* (rev. ed., 1966).

Recently, historians have returned their attention to Federalists' opponents to understand the roots of Jefferson's appeal. See, for example, Joyce Appleby, *Capitalism and a New Social Order* (1984); Michael Durey, *Transatlantic Radicals and the Early American Republic* (1997); Alfred Young, *The Democratic Republicans of New York* (1967); and Richard Twomey, *Jacobins and Jeffersonians: Anglo-American Radicalism in the United States, 1790–1820* (1989).

For contentions on the frontier, see Stephen Aron, *How the West Was Lost: Kentucky from Daniel Boone to Henry Clay* (1966); Andrew Cayton and Frederika Teute, eds., *Contact Points: American Frontiers from the Mohawk Valley to the Mississippi, 1750–1830* (1998); Gregory Dowd, *A Spirited Resistance: The North American Indian Struggle for Unity, 1745–1815* (1992); Reginald Horsman, *The Frontier in the Formative Years, 1783–1815* (1970); and J. Leitch Wright, *Britain and the American Frontier, 1783–1815* (1975). On the Whiskey Rebellion, see Thomas P. Slaughter, *The Whiskey Rebellion: Frontier Epilogue to the American Revolution* (1986).

The rift that grew between Federalists and Antifederalists, then Democratic-Republicans, and finally the party of Jefferson, is analyzed in Joseph J. Ellis, *American Sphinx: The Character of Thomas Jefferson* (1996); Noble Cunningham, *The Jeffersonian Republicans: The Formation of Party Organization, 1789–1801* (1957); and Lance Banning, *The Jeffersonian Persuasion: Evolution of a Party Ideology* (1978). The ideas that supported political choices and policies are thoroughly covered in Buel, *Securing the Revolution*, cited above. For explanations of the ideology and structures of political parties as they first emerged, see both John F. Hoadley, *Origins of American Political Parties, 1789–1803* (1986), and the classic study by Richard Hofstadter, *The Idea of a Party System: The Rise of Legitimate Opposition in the United States, 1780–1840* (1969).

Subduing the Old Northwest

Competing Voices

Hamilton Denounces Frontier Scofflaws

Alexander Hamilton was furious with the open defiance of the 1791 Whiskey Tax on the frontier—so furious that he urged Washington to raise troops to crush the so-called Whiskey Boys. As the troops gathered for their march westward, Hamilton defended their mission with an article in a Federalist newspaper.

Shall the majority govern or be governed? Shall the nation rule or be ruled? Shall the general will prevail, or the will of a faction? Shall there be government or no government? It is impossible to deny that this is the true and the whole question. No art, no sophistry can involve it in the least obscurity.

The Constitution *you* have ordained for yourselves and your posterity contains this express clause: "The Congress shall have power to lay and collect taxes, duties, imposts, and excises, to pay the debts, and provide for the common defense and general welfare of the United States." You have, then, by a solemn and deliberate act, the most important and sacred that a nation can perform, pronounced and decreed that your representatives in Congress shall have power to lay excises. You have done nothing since to reverse or impair that decree.

Your representatives in Congress, pursuant to the commission derived from you, and with a full knowledge of the public exigencies, have laid an excise. . . . But the four western counties of Pennsylvania undertake to rejudge and reverse your decrees. You have said, . . . "An excise on distilled spirits shall be collected." They say, "It shall not be collected. We will punish, expel, and banish the officers who shall attempt the collection. We will do the same by every other person who shall dare to comply with your decree expressed in the constitutional charter, and with that of your representatives expressed in the laws. The sovereignty shall not reside with you, but with us. If you presume to dispute the point by force, we are ready to measure swords with you, and if unequal ourselves to the contest we will call in the aid of a foreign nation [British or Spanish frontier troops]. We will league ourselves with a foreign power."

Jefferson Condemns Excessive Force

Jefferson was astounded that thirteen thousand troops were sent against the distillers and farmers of western Pennsylvania. He saw the suppression of the rebels as an excessive use of force deployed to increase the prestige and power of the national government. In the following account, Jefferson writes to his friend James Madison (both living in Virginia at the time) lamenting the raid's potential to damage, rather than bolster, the public's image of its new national government.

The excise law is an infernal one. The first error was to admit it by the Constitution; the second, to act on that admission; the third and last will be to make it the instrument of dismembering the Union, and setting us all afloat to choose which part of it we will adhere to.

The information of our militia, returned from the westward, is uniform, that though the people there let them pass quietly, they were objects of their laughter, not of their fear; that a thousand men could have cut off their whole force in a thousand places of the Allegheny; that their detestation of the excise law is universal, and has now associated to it a detestation of the government; and that separation, which perhaps was a very distant and problematical event, is now near, and certain, and determined in the mind of every man.

I expected to have seen justification of arming one part of the society against another; of declaring a civil war the moment before the meeting of that body [Congress] which has the sole right of declaring war; of being so patient of the kicks and scoffs of our [British and Spanish] enemies, and rising at a feather against our friends; of adding a million to the public debts and deriding us with recommendations to pay it if we can, etc. etc.

The Whiskey Tax that Secretary of the Treasury Alexander Hamilton proposed, and Congress passed, in 1791 was especially damaging for the livelihoods of frontier farmers. With poor and costly transportation, they paid dearly to cart their surplus rye and corn to markets. Most of them chose to convert grain into the distilled beverages that a large consuming public on the East Coast readily purchased. Under the provisions of the bill, farmers who operated stills and refused to pay taxes on the transport of whiskey would be sued by the government. Trials would be held far from their frontier homes, under the jurisdiction of unfamiliar judges, and before juries certain to be prejudiced against the "ruffians of the west." Like western Regulators before the Revolution, the whiskey producers of Kentucky and western Pennsylvania were keenly aware that they lacked good government in their settlements. When the Whiskey Boys encountered sheriffs and government tax collectors, they were likely to tar and feather them, beat them, or burn their homes—in self-defense, they would say, and to protect their frontier enterprises from heavy taxation and unjustified assaults.

Questions for Analysis

1. How does Hamilton use the Constitution to support his argument?
2. On what grounds does Jefferson oppose the excise tax?
3. How do Hamilton's and Jefferson's views of the proper role of governments differ? How does each explain the limits of federal authority and the rights of citizens?
4. How does each author describe the activities of the army? of the western settlers? What do their characterizations reveal about their opinions of these people?

8

Striving for Nationhood, 1800–1824

Shortly before noon on March 4, 1801, Thomas Jefferson, the Democratic-Republican president-elect, walked from his lodgings at a Washington, D.C., boarding house through the muddy streets to the half-finished Capitol building. The city contained fewer than four hundred dwellings, most of them "small miserable huts" surrounding the seat of national government. The capital's first inaugural was likewise humble, a far cry from the grand procession of "carriages and lace cuffs" that heralded Washington's administration. Jefferson dressed as "a plain citizen, without any distinctive badge of office." His Federalist predecessor, John Adams, was not present when Jefferson stood quietly before Chief Justice John Marshall to take the oath of office. In his inaugural address, Jefferson announced his intentions to create a government more suitable for a republican people, to purge the government of lingering Federalist influences, and to respect the individual states.

Jefferson called his electoral victory the "Revolution of 1800," indicating that profound political and cultural change in the republic could occur without bloodshed. The electoral revolution, said Jeffersonians, represented a peaceful transition from the nation's founding political party, the Federalists, to a new party organization, the Democratic-Republicans. It also seemed to signal the decline of political processes based on deference and privilege, and the rise of new social interests, more economic opportunity, and greater democracy in government. As Jefferson said in his inaugural address, "We are all republicans, we are all federalists."

Bitterness among political opponents still lingered after the contentious election in 1800, but Jefferson's speech to Congress voiced hope that Americans could move forward peacefully. In contrast to the bellowing speeches of congressmen in years to come, Jefferson spoke barely above a whisper, insisting that his powers as president were strictly limited and that the great tasks of shaping the nation's growth and expansion required citizens to "unite in common efforts for the common good." He reminded listeners that the revolutionary experiment, the accomplishment of his own generation, was a work in progress. In addition to the victory of a war for independence, the American people now had to complete the "revolution in the principles of our government."

Hogs ran through Washington's streets, and Jefferson never expressed urgency about "citifying" the rural crossroads of Washington, D.C., or finishing the construction of government buildings. But to many Democratic-Republicans, the unrefined and unfinished nature of Washington suited the proper roles of national government: to be small in size and modest in its guardianship over the people. Over the next three decades, wide constituencies of Americans continued to believe that they could escape the dangerous tendencies of growth and rapid pace of development that could lead them to the brink of wars and breed internal cultural corruption. Public discussion and local political policymaking reflected Americans' yearnings for a republican citizenry. But expansion into new frontiers, the growing use of national government to create opportunities and divide resources, and continuing international controversies all threatened to annihilate the republican ideals that framed American political culture.

- How did the Jeffersonian Democratic-Republicans attempt to calm the bitterness of political factionalism, keep government small, and promote substantial development?
- What contributions did Hamiltonians make to shaping American institutions, internal development, and international commerce?
- How did America's expansion into new frontiers—in North America and abroad—affect other nations' interests?
- In what ways were Jeffersonians forced to alter their vision for America as the great public effort to define, secure, and develop the new American republic unfolded?

This chapter will address these questions.

Democratic-Republicans in Power

Democratic-Republicans founded their party on the ideals of republican citizenship and a responsive, local, and lean government. Their ideals emerged when America was still small in territory and population, and close to agricultural and craft pro-

Chronology

1801	Jefferson inaugurated as president
1803	Louisiana Purchase
	Marbury v. *Madison*
1804–1806	Lewis and Clark expedition
1807	Embargo Act
1808	James Madison elected president
1809	Tecumseh forms Indian alliance in territories
1811	Battle of Tippecanoe
1812	War of 1812 begins
1814	Hartford Convention
	Treaty of Ghent
1815	Battle of New Orleans
1816	Congress charters Second Bank of the United States
1818	Jackson invades Florida
1819–1820	Panic of 1819
	Missouri Crisis and Compromise
1819	Adams-Onís Treaty
1823	Monroe Doctrine pronounced in Congress

duction. For many Democratic-Republicans, Federalist policies seemed to be harmful, especially Hamilton's financial plans. But as the years went by, Democratic-Republicans—in office and in the public at large—witnessed the republic expanding and developing in unforeseen ways. Their notions about the ideal republican citizen and a virtuous republic required regular adjustments as the years passed. Changing Democratic-Republican policies reflected this adjusted thinking.

Simplifying Government

Jeffersonians had pledged themselves to creating a new political era of "simplicity and frugality." In practical terms, this meant bolstering the integrity of the states, "the surest bulwarks against anti-republican tendencies"; reducing government spending and repaying the public debt; restraining military buildup; and guarding the freedoms enumerated in the Bills of Rights. As the government paid off its debts, Democratic-Republicans would struggle mightily not to incur new ones and, in doing so, would wipe out the need for Hamilton's fiscal state. A small government, argued Jeffersonians, ruling over an expanding agricultural and commercial people, suited republican Americans the most.

In some respects, Jefferson's plan did suit the early republic, for the national government did not play a significant role in the daily lives of citizens at that time. The states still fulfilled many important functions related to education, law enforcement, promotion of the economy, and building roads. The national government had a small budget and very few employees. Washington, D.C., itself had the appearance of a country town during Jefferson's administration, and it did not grow nearly as rapidly as Cincinnati, Baltimore, New Orleans, and Wilmington.

Government expenditures, though never high in Washington's years, diminished even more in Jefferson's first administration. The fledgling navy almost disappeared; Jefferson cut military spending dramatically and kept only a few troops on the western frontier after 1803. Jefferson did not fire all Federalists from their positions, although he did reduce the number of clerks, post office employees, military officials, and diplomats, especially those whom corruption, incompetence, and reported scandal had touched. Nor did Jefferson hand-pick replacements with wild revolutionary ideas, as Federalists feared he would. Rather, he drew to Washington Democratic-Republican gentlemen of the highest social standing. He also used patronage, as Federalists before him had, to appoint loyal Democratic-Republicans to offices in New England, where Federalists had held majorities in many local and state offices for many years. However, Jefferson also reserved three key cabinet positions for Federalists.

Congress, acting on Jefferson's plea, abolished the Federalist excise taxes and Direct Tax of 1798, and allowed the Alien and Sedition Acts to expire. The national debt, which stood at about $80 million when Jefferson took office, declined to a little more than half that amount when happy voters went to the polls in 1804, and stood at about $43 million when he left office. Although major Hamiltonian institutions, including the Bank of the United States, continued to exist, Jeffersonians did not expand their operations or rely on them for the success of their goals.

The Judiciary and the Common Law

Jefferson promised "equal and exact justice to all" in his inaugural address, but many of his supporters in Congress believed that two obstacles stood in the way of achieving this promise. One was the Federalist Judiciary Act of 1801, which created many new circuit courts and added additional federal marshals and regional judges. The other was President Adams's numerous "midnight appointments" of loyal Federalists to these new posts just before he left office. Many Democratic-Republicans believed that Federalists would not apply their common law traditions properly. Although the common law blended precedents—decisions made in previous cases—with an intellectual tradition that embodied natural law and reason, in practice it had emerged during the regimes of monarchs, aristocrats, and great landlords whose interests often were upheld by Federalists and were opposed by Jeffersonians. Federalist court officials had supported wealthy landowners against settlers in the West who needed protection of their claims. Federalists also had upheld the monopoly privileges of old families against the energy and capital of new developers across the nation.

Throughout the 1790s, Federalists had insisted that Americans needed an independent judiciary, secure against attacks from political enemies or "mob democracy." They continued to support old, or prior, economic privileges against the encroachments of new wealth and enterprise. For example, Federalist courts often ordered new mills to cease operations when they diverted water for their use from the farms that lay nearby. These new enterprises, the judges repeatedly ruled, interfered with prior owners and "the established will of the community."

Many Jeffersonians challenged this long-standing legal wisdom. As products of radical intellectual changes during the revolutionary generation, they believed the law should change as American circumstances and people changed. Laws emerged, they held, from contentious interests and political negotiation, as a "positive law . . . which is the will of THE PEOPLE." Popular sovereignty, they insisted, should permeate the judicial process just as it should the legislative and executive. Jeffersonians also feared the "excessive interference" of Federalist courts in matters they felt should be left to Congress or state legislatures.

Now, in the early 1800s, Jeffersonians countered that the courts ought not to nullify legislation initiated by the people's representatives, nor should it hold back new development. In February 1802, Congress—overwhelmingly comprised of Democratic-Republicans—repealed the Judiciary Act, eliminating all the new courts and offices it had created. The following year, it began impeachment proceedings against select Federalist judges for their "dangerous opinions" that could "work the destruction of the Union." Congress then brought impeachment charges against Samuel Chase, a justice of the Supreme Court, for "intemperate and inflammatory political harangues" that threatened "to excite the fears and resentment of the . . . people . . . against the Government." This time, Jeffersonians had overstepped themselves, and the Senate acquitted Chase.

By the early 1800s, Jeffersonian thinking about the law began to reorient many court decisions and to have a profound effect on economic development. New interests demanded, and won, the right to take private property from prior users when their improvements brought "progress for great numbers" of citizens. The owners of new mills and small factories were permitted to flood farmlands, and ruined farmers had to accept reasonable compensation. By 1815, legislatures were granting private turnpike and canal companies the authority to cut through rural land holdings, and the courts upheld the "creative privilege" of these ambitious new interests.

But tensions between elected government representatives and justices remained strained during the Jefferson presidency. John Marshall, chief justice of the United States Supreme Court in 1801, was a strong Federalist. Appointed by John Adams, Marshall dominated the Court until his death in 1835. One of his major goals was to establish the principle that came to be known as judicial review, by which the Supreme Court had the power to strike down acts of Congress, a power granted to it by the Judiciary Act. In *Marbury* v. *Madison* (1803), Marshall established this principle of judicial review. William Marbury, who had been nominated a justice of the peace by Adams but then did not receive his commission when Jefferson took office, sued the government. Under the terms of the Judiciary Act, the court had the power to demand that James Madison, the secretary of state, hand over Marbury's commission. Marshall agreed that "it is emphatically the province and duty of the judicial department to say what the law is." However, he also declared that it was impolitic and illogical for the Court to force the executive branch to put Marbury in a position that was almost over by the time the case reached the court. Although at first this second part of his decision seemed to ally Marshall with the Jeffersonians, it was his firm stance on judicial review that became a hallmark of Marshall's entire tenure in office. In addition, Marshall's decisions invariably favored strong federal government over state government.

In *McCulloch* v. *Maryland* (1819), Marshall asserted Federalist principles and the implied nationalist powers of the Constitution even more clearly. When Congress chartered the Second Bank of the United States in 1816 (see below), it assumed the authority to deal not only with national funds but also with deposits to its branch banks made by the states as well. In turn, the branches of the Bank issued notes that circulated widely in the business community. Leading Maryland politicians grew unhappy with this arrangement, charging the Bank with excessive powers, and imposed a tax on the Bank's operations. Other states, disturbed over the national Bank's assumption of superiority over state banks, leaned toward following Maryland's example. A large group of Maryland depositors and lawyers insisted that the Second Bank of the United States was as unconstitutional as the first one

"John Marshall (1755–1835)," by Charles-Balthazar Julien Févret de Saint-Mémin, 1801 Marshall, who served as chief justice of the United States from 1801 to 1835, sat for this portrait his first year on the Court. A strong Federalist, he rendered many decisions favoring both the political and economic the power of the national government and gave the Court a major role to play in shaping the destiny of the early federal republic. *(Duke University Archives.)*

had been, and that any state had the right to tax institutions within its own boundaries. Marshall's Court took the Federalist approach to interpreting the Constitution, ruling that the Bank was "necessary and proper" for the functioning of national government. In addition, the court disallowed the Maryland tax, arguing that "the power to tax involves the power to destroy"—in this case, to destroy the national Bank (see Competing Voices, page 319).

In order to establish judicial review, Marshall sometimes took decisions out of state control and made them federal cases. In *Fletcher* v. *Peck* (1810), Marshall upheld that matters of constitutional interpretation should be heard in the highest courts in the land and, in this case, the principle that states could not impair "the obligation of contracts" between governments and individuals. *Fletcher* involved the Georgia legislature's grants of land to the Yazoo Land Company. When a newly elected state government tried to nullify the company's claims on the grounds of speculation and corruption in acquiring them, Marshall insisted that, regardless of company wrongdoing, the contract between Yazoo claimants and the state of Georgia must be honored.

In *Dartmouth College* v. *Woodward* (1819), Marshall interfered with the intentions of a state government in order to uphold older corporate claims of individuals. The trustees of Dartmouth had been fighting off efforts by the New Hampshire legislature to convert the college into a public institution, which, in true republican terms, would "serve the greater number" of citizens. They hired Daniel Webster, a formidable Federalist Massachusetts lawyer, to argue their case, which hinged on the original "corporate rights and privileges" inherent in the college's charter before the Revolution. Webster insisted that such institutional charters were contracts, and according to the Constitution such contracts must be held sacred. Despite strong opposition from some colleagues on the bench, Marshall's majority opinion supported Webster. In years to come, the nation's entrepreneurs benefited immeasurably from the reasoning about contracts articulated in the Dartmouth case, and creditors would find it easier to pursue their debtors in countless cases brought before courts. Even today, many courts respect the fundamentally Federalist principles of constitutional law established in the *Fletcher* and *Dartmouth* cases.

Defining Politics and American Identity

For generations, colonial Americans accepted a political process premised on deference toward elites, which required that most citizens remained aloof from the affairs of political decision making. In the postrevolutionary years, many new families moved into positions of political power, but they tended to perpetuate elite control of offices, and to exclude Indians, women, and (in most new states) unpropertied white men such as shopkeepers, carpenters, teamsters, seamen, and commercial farmers from governing the new nation.

During the 1790s, political discussion had become a noisy, participatory activity. Vote getting and office holding required close attention to an increasingly demanding citizenry. Using the language of republicanism, many Americans challenged hierarchical authority and called for more legal (though not social and economic) equality for free white men. John Adams had said Americans created a "government of laws, not of men," in which there would be no aristocracies of birth. Thousands of voters took his reasoning a step further and declared that in practice office seekers who wore powdered wigs and silver buckles would now have to share public offices with the middling, unadorned, citizens of the country.

As the public sphere of politics grew, many state governments expanded the franchise. After 1789, the very small percentage of adult white males who could vote slowly, but surely, grew. Four states created universal manhood suffrage in 1800; other states gradually reduced property requirements and restrictions on religious affiliation for voting or holding office. Connecticut and New York abolished property qualifications in the early 1800s. The new states of Indiana (1816), Illinois (1818), and Alabama (1819) permitted universal suffrage to free white men. These measures set the stage for more and more Americans to enter public political participation during the coming three generations. In the original New England states, 70 to 90 percent of eligible voters went to the polls during local and state elections by 1820. But over the years, as middling white men gained more political rights, the diminished place of women and African-Americans also became clearer—and eventually less tolerable.

The vibrant public political discussion of the early national years stimulated new forms of communication. On the eve of the Revolution, 37 journals, most of them weeklies, nourished the colonists' need for news. By 1789, printers put out 92, including 8 daily publications, and by 1810, Americans read 376 different papers, some weeklies and some biweeklies, with combined circulations of over 22 million. This was an amazing publishing effort, given that the population had reached only 8 million people by 1810, half of them under age sixteen and one-fifth of them slaves whom the law forbade to read. Post offices, libraries, taverns and public houses, and even street corners provided public venues for the constant buzz of exchanging news.

During the rising political factionalism of the 1790s, newspapers were not only the eyes, ears, and mouths of Federalists and Democratic-Republicans, they were also the focus of discussions about rights guaranteed by the Bill of Rights, especially freedom of expression. With the demise of the Sedition Act, Jefferson was able to assure Americans in 1801 that "error of opinion [would] be tolerated, where reason is left free to combat it."

In the next decades, the proliferating number of bookstores and book peddlers in the countryside attested to Americans' hunger for the printed word. Literacy rates in the coastal states rose rapidly, and literary societies sprang up in many locales. In New England the Connecticut Wits charmed readers with their biting commentary; in Philadelphia erudite circles of intellectuals and entrepreneurs joined the American Philosophical Society; and New York City's Tontine Society attracted the native and immigrant intellectuals of property. Combining the activities of newspaper printing, public speaking, book collecting and library subscription clubs, and organized distribution of printed tracts, some intellectual circles also drew urban artisans into their membership.

In their articles and novels, American writers reflected on the rapid changes of American life and sought to define a distinctive identity for the country. Frontiersmen in Kentucky, "unmannered and uncivilized" hunters in Georgia, the so-called new man rising from poverty to comfort, or the self-made servant who roamed from place to place working for entrepreneurs and tinkers—these kinds of characters fired the imaginations of early national readers. Simultaneously, some writers began to write histories of the colonies and the American Revolution, including Mercy Otis Warren's erudite 1805 account of the Revolution from a republican point of view. Michel-Guillaume Jean de Crèvecoeur's reflections on the postrevolutionary American character in *Letters from an American Farmer* (1782) and Parson Weems's laudatory and sometimes fabricated *Life of Washington* (1800) are examples of a new genre of moral and introspective writings that appealed to Americans widely. Crèvecoeur proposed that the "new man" of America was a blending of many cultures and represented the strongest characteristics of each one. Romantic fiction, initiated by William Hill Brown in the first American novel, *The*

Noah Webster's *American Spelling Book* This text created a sensation when it first appeared in 1789, and its popularity prompted many reprintings in the next years. Webster's efforts to create distinctive spellings of many commonly used words and expressions, and to teach basic literacy to the first generation of children after the Revolution, were significant contributions to an American national identity. *(Courtesy, American Antiquarian Society.)*

Thomas and *Andrews's FIRST* EDITION.

THE

AMERICAN

Spelling Book:

CONTAINING AN EASY

STANDARD of PRONUNCIATION,

BEING THE

FIRST PART

OF A

GRAMMATICAL INSTITUTE

OF THE

ENGLISH LANGUAGE.

BY NOAH WEBSTER, JUN. ESQUIRE.

AUTHOR of "DISSERTATIONS on the ENGLISH LANGUAGE."

Thomas and *Andrews's* FIRST EDITION.

With additional LESSONS, corrected by the AUTHOR.

PRINTED AT *BOSTON*,

BY ISAIAH THOMAS AND EBENEZER T. ANDREWS.

Sold, Wholesale and Retail, at their Bookstore, No. 45, NEWBURY STREET, and by said THOMAS at his Bookstore in *Worcester*.

MDCCLXXXIX.

Power of Sympathy (1789), also sold well, especially to the widening reading audience of women. Susanna Haswell Rowson's *Charlotte Temple,* published in 1791, provided a racy tale of seduction and abandonment, levened with moral cautions about the dangers of emotional entanglements.

Americans also purchased or borrowed copies of Noah Webster's *American Spelling Book.* First published in 1783, Webster's compilation of words and examples of their usage became the number one best-seller of secular texts by 1810. In 1828 Webster astonished Americans again by publishing the *American Dictionary of the English Language,* which attempted to replace "the King's English" with "more common sensical" spellings, such as *odor* instead of *odour,* and added many new technical terms.

As Americans strove to define their popular political life with the expanded suffrage and greater discussion of political issues in a growing press, they also developed a distinctive American cultural identity. Indeed, print culture and popular public involvement with the political process became intertwined. As America grew by leaps and bounds, Jeffersonian political culture enveloped settlers of the new states and waves of people in older regions who acquired new political rights. At the same time, Federalists became more and more associated with a worn-out, even irrelevant, approach to governing at both the national and local levels.

Expansion and the Agrarian Republic

While Jeffersonians limited the role of government in the civil and legal affairs of American citizens, and reduced the size and expense of government, they promoted energetic use of state and federal governments for internal improvements (discussed in Chapter 9) and westward expansion. This improvement and expansion, argued Jeffersonians, corresponded with republican ideals about what constituted a good citizenry and would cement people's political liberty under conditions of relative social equality and broad popular use of the land. Without relatively widespread ownership of modest parcels of land, argued Jeffersonians, Americans risked developing the crime-infested, immoral urban centers such as in Europe, falling into habits of luxury, and thereby creating the conditions for political despotism or monarchy. Horrifying European examples of great cities, overgrown central governments, excessive commercial wealth, and degrading manufactures had "destroyed the manners and morals" of whole nations. For Jefferson, the pinnacle of republicanism was the yeoman farmer becoming an independent landowner earning a comfortable living from the soil. It followed that the government ought to acquire "an empire of the west" and organize its settlement and use by a "virtuous, expansive people." Beside, argued many Jeffersonians, settlement of new western lands would establish America's claim over a great expanse of territory that might otherwise be "overrun by foreign foe" such as the Spanish, French, and British. And although Jefferson promised that western lands would remain cheap enough for yeomen farmers to afford, their sale would nevertheless provide government with additional revenue. However, as Americans expanded across abundant lands and integrated new settlements into the Democratic-Republican political culture of the nation, they also encountered numerous tests of their republicanism.

Lands of Promise

In 1800 the population of the United States stood at only 5.3 million, but already it was growing at the astounding rate of 3 percent per year. Greater numbers of people moved from place to place, occupying new lands or migrating from town to town, than ever before or since in American history. Much of this migration flowed in a westerly direction. In one stream, New England "Yankees" moved into Vermont and Maine, western New York, or even all the way to Pittsburgh, and then down the Ohio River. Since the late colonial period, dozens of small towns had become overcrowded. Younger sons and daughters, having run out of eligible spouses and employment opportunities, gambled on their future prosperity by packing up a few belongings and heading for the uncultivated fertile river valleys in unfamiliar terrain.

From 1790 to 1820, New York's population more than quadrupled; the newly settled western counties alone boasted over 800,000 inhabitants. About 400,000 more Americans splayed out into the Ohio Valley beyond. Some of these people bought their land from established land companies, including the Genesee investment group of British investors and the Holland Land Company of mainly Dutch speculators. The members of entire Congregational churches sometimes resolved to move together into New Hampshire or western New York. Other times, extended kin networks pooled resources for the long journey and difficult first years on new soil. Alongside these communities, a handful of American investors grabbed huge tracts of land at cheap prices and offered tenants attractive rental conditions. Most New England farmers preferred rent-to-buy conditions, by which they could be assured that their payments to landlords would eventually win them a freehold; few, however, realized this dream. Those who could not afford the rising cost of real estate out west simply squatted on available tracts of land.

Farmers left behind in New England adjusted to the loss of laborers and consumers by developing strategies to get higher yields of crops and better marketing of surpluses. Potatoes, turnips, and other vegetables "trucked," or taken by wagon to towns, became valuable additions to New England diets by the 1820s, while almost every farmer from Massachusetts to Virginia planted at least a little grain. New Jersey and Pennsylvania farmers practiced more crop rotation, fertilization, and deeper plowing, all of which increased farm yields and permitted more diverse cultivation. Better tools compensated somewhat for the sons who left their fathers' farms.

From the Chesapeake region, white tenant farmers and impoverished freeholders headed by the thousands into Kentucky and Tennessee (see map page 297). Meanwhile, planters in Virginia and Maryland lamented the loss of population in the older settlements. Whole counties that had once been full of valuable taxpayers and free laborers seemed now to be deserted. By 1800, a steady stream of families were moving through the Cumberland Gap (see map), lugging their belongings into the forbidding mountains and cutting trails with the crude agricultural implements they would need to clear land in years to come. Few Kentuckians held prior claims to lots; virtually all of them simply squatted on the land. They counted on "ancient traditions" to confirm their rights to the soil: settlers earned title to their lands by occupying them and building "improvements" of fences and homes in what was otherwise the "savage wilderness."

Squatters' rights remained a compelling reason why many farm families and small entrepreneurs risked much to move into the Northwest Territory or across the Southeast during the early 1800s. But squatters encountered solid opposition from speculators and land companies that held deeds to vast tracts of this land, courtesy of state legislatures that bowed to the demands of powerful investment collectives. In addition, many politicians in state legislatures agreed with land company agents that a more orderly occupation of the West was desirable, and only land companies could produce revenues from land sales that could be shared between investors and governments. In the scramble for occupation, title, and development of the Northwest Territory, squatters often lost their struggles for homesteads, or fought violently to defend their claims against encroaching land companies. Many of them became poor tenants scratching out a living, no better off on the cotton and hemp farms west of the Appalachian Mountains than they were before migration.

Not all migrants came from the Northeast and mid-Atlantic regions. Beginning in the 1790s, southerners pressed toward the Mississippi River, through Alabama and Mississippi, and then into territory west of the river. Some of the new settlements filled with small farmers and former Chesapeake tenants who were able to get a freehold. More migrants, however, were planters who reproduced the slave and export agriculture system of the older South. When Chesapeake area planters converted from tobacco cultivation to wheat, they sold off many of their slaves to migrating planters in the new southern territories (see Chapter 9), where the harshening realities of cotton and sugar cultivation required large amounts of labor. In addition, down to 1808, when the Constitution's ban on the transatlantic slave trade became effective, Georgia and South Carolina planters imported nearly 250,000 new slaves, about as many as they had brought in during the entire colonial period, to help make their expansive agriculture a success. Tidewater region planters who migrated into Kentucky and Tennessee also took large numbers of slaves with them. In all, by 1820, nearly 250,000 slaves were sold from the older plantation regions into the new cotton and sugar South, and almost 50,000 were relocated into the trans-Appalachian region. Indeed, the hope of the Constitution's framers that slavery would "fade from our national life" now seemed naïve.

These strands of migration, in which eastern and southern peoples carried their distinctive identities into the new western territories, slowed the rise of national identity. German-speaking communities could be found in 1820 in Lancaster, Pennsylvania, near Savannah, Georgia, and in Ohio country. People of Scots-Irish heritage rarely mingled and intermarried with those of New England Congregational backgrounds. Although newspapers enlarged the political participation of urban Americans and began to bring rural people closer to coastal events, only members of professions and economic elites participated in a national culture regularly. Even as the franchise widened, most people expressed political demands and obligations of citizenship in local and regional terms.

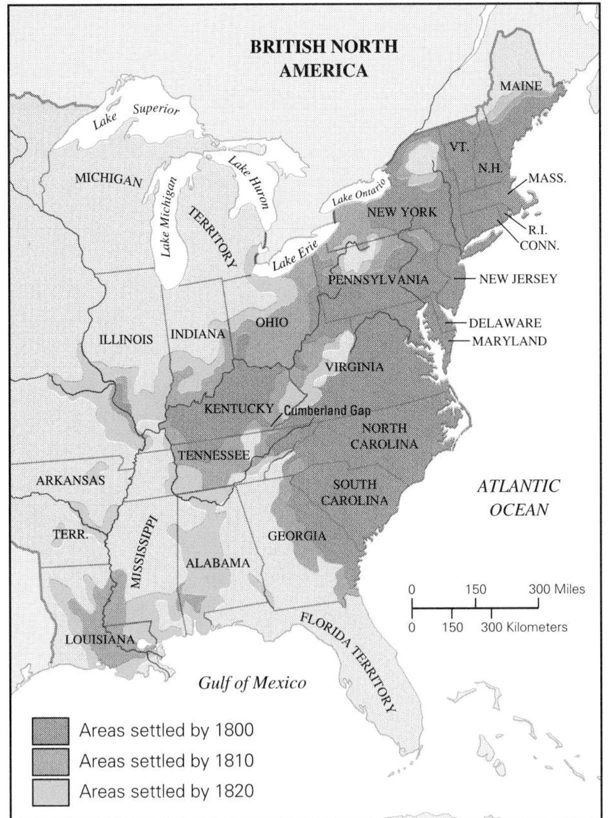

Early National Expansion
In the decades after the Revolution, waves of immigrants and migrating Americans spilled over the Appalachian Mountains. By 1820 a quarter of the nation's people lived in this trans-Applachian frontier. (Source: Adapted from *Out of Many: A History of the American People,* Combined Edition, Third Edition, by Faragher/Buhle/Czitrom/Armitage, 1997, Prentice-Hall, Inc., Upper Saddle River, N.J.)

The Louisiana Purchase

In 1893 historian Frederick Jackson Turner wrote a highly influential essay, "The Significance of the Frontier in American History." Turner believed that Americans had developed a unique national identity as a result of their experience of the West. The West of the early 1800s differed from the frontiers that colonial settlers had experienced. This new West had been defined as a national domain, much of it acquired through international treaties. Sectional contests, the presence of Indians, the "rudeness of nature," and other characteristics of the West imparted to American settlers a particular character: democratic, pragmatic, forward-looking, and individualistic. Of course, Americans adapted a great deal to frontier conditions in the early 1800s. New kinds of soil, distance from markets, and the difficulties of starting farms and stores required skills that settlers had not used in their former locales.

But Turner grossly underestimated the power of regional heritage, kinship, and cultural traditions that people brought with them into the frontier. And he virtually overlooked evidence that frontier settlers aimed to reproduce the institutions, relationships, and culture of their coastal homes. Moreover, success came slowly to most migrants. Democracy and capitalism did not naturally, or always, travel with migrants out onto the frontier. On the contrary, years of struggle and poverty marked the lives of most westward settlers.

Jefferson shared the deep convictions of most Americans about the significance of new land for settlement, as the land ordinances of 1785 and 1787 (see Chapter 6) demonstrated. In the Land Act of 1796, Federalists enunciated different goals—of raising great sums from sales of the national domain—when they raised the price of land to a minimum of $2 per acre in lots of 640 acres. Such terms of sale put ownership outside the typical family's reach, however. A new Land Act of 1801 reduced the minimum lot to 320 acres and permitted incremental payments, with discounts for paying in cash. Within the next eighteen months, families, land companies, and speculators purchased nearly 500,000 acres—more than the government had sold during all of the 1790s. The government sold over 500,000 acres each year for the rest of that decade.

Despite these efforts to provide yeomen farming families with cheap and plentiful tracts of land, security often eluded settlers. Speculators and greedy land companies continued to create a jurisdictional nightmare for many settlers, while Indian resistance continued to plague the Ohio Valley. The presence of foreign trappers and troops along important rivers added to migrants' anxieties about settling the West.

In 1800 Spain signed a secret treaty that returned the vast lands of Louisiana to France, though its local government and population remained Spanish. Two years later, Spanish officials in Louisiana began barring Americans from the vital port of New Orleans, a serious blow to farmers who needed that outlet for goods from the trans-Appalachian territories and to merchants trading with the frontier settlements. Meanwhile, word reached America that Napoleon intended to send forces to crush the slave rebellion of Toussaint L'Ouverture in Haiti. Secretary of State James Madison raised the possibility of American merchants trading beneficially with Toussaint's new government.

Wishing to avoid open conflict with France, Jefferson instructed the American minister in Paris, Robert R. Livingston, to buy New Orleans. To Livingston's surprise, in April 1803 Napoleon agreed to sell not only the port, but also the entire territory of Louisiana. By then, Napoleon's plan to retake Haiti had failed because rampant yellow fever and persistent slave resistance made landing impossible. And without Caribbean stations, Napoleon was also unable to launch efforts to subdue the vast Louisiana. Once the hope of securing Haiti faded, it made less sense to hold on to Louisiana, whose main purpose would have been to grow food for the slave islands. Napoleon also feared that if Britain followed through on its threat to invade French-dominated Europe, Americans would seize the opportunity to invade Louisiana.

Napoleon offered some 830,000 square miles to America for a mere $15 million. Jefferson quickly set aside arguments, many of them from his Democratic-Republican party allies, that making such a purchase violated the letter of the Constitution and was not "necessary and proper" for the running of the government. However, faced with the possibility of expanding the "empire for liberty," Jefferson waived these objections and used the treaty-making power of the executive branch to seal the deal with France.

More serious opposition came from Federalists, especially in New England, who feared that this new western land would "drain" people from the East and dilute the "civilized character" of the American people. Worse, westward migration would tip the balance in Congress toward an alliance of the West and South as new territories became states. Some Federalists in New York and New England circulated rumors of secession. As a first step toward forming a northern confederacy separate from the United States, they supported the candidacy of Aaron Burr, a disgruntled Democratic-Republican leader, for governor of New York in 1804.

Hearing of these threats to divide the country, Hamilton bristled with indignation, and Burr challenged him to a duel—formerly a means for aristocrats to settle disputes, but now illegal in most northern states. In July 1804 the two men drew arms in New Jersey, and Burr's gunshot wounded Hamilton fatally. Burr was promptly indicted for murder, but he fled west once his term of office was completed. There he plotted with the Louisiana military governor, General James Wilkinson, to seize the territory and perhaps portions of northern Mexico. The plan failed, and John Marshall, in his capacity as circuit court judge, tried Burr for treason. Marshall refused to interpret Burr's duel and western escapades as treason, and the court acquitted Burr. Further talk of a separate northern confederacy ceased, but the entire ordeal illustrated deep sectional divisions in the American political culture.

Lewis and Clark

Despite party factionalism and regional sectionalism, the public cheered news of the Louisiana Purchase, and land offices reported soaring sales of tracts on either side of the Mississippi River. Jefferson wanted detailed information about this "great unknown wilderness." Even in the 1790s, he had believed a convenient waterway might be found traversing North America to the Pacific Ocean. Earlier than that, fur traders had reckoned that the Columbia and Missouri Rivers might provide the best way through Indian territories and around Spanish settlements in California, Nevada, and Utah. In 1783 William Clark—a Virginian who had fought in the Revolutionary War in Ohio—declined Jefferson's offer to head an expedition into the trans-Mississippi West. Twenty years later, with the Louisiana Purchase completed, Jefferson had a more convincing argument. America, he pleaded with Congress, had a duty to displace all foreign nations remaining in the West and to make the Purchase secure for westward migration. By that time, Jefferson's view was supported widely by Americans, who viewed Louisiana as an expanse of land so large that it could provide hundreds of thousands of yeomen settlers with sizeable estates, and perhaps room to resettle Indians from east of the Mississippi River without disturbing white migration.

Jefferson asked Congress for money to send out an expedition and appointed Meriwether Lewis, his private secretary, to head the team. Lewis began in Pittsburgh in August 1803 with a keelboat and a Corps of Discovery crew that included seven soldiers, three young men eager to travel, and a pilot. Clark, now enthusiastic, joined the party two months later, at Clarksville, Indiana, with a handful of Kentucky woodsmen and hunters. Together they went down the Ohio River, to St. Louis; wintered over at Camp Dubois; and headed up the Missouri River from May 1804 through the summer and early fall (see map).

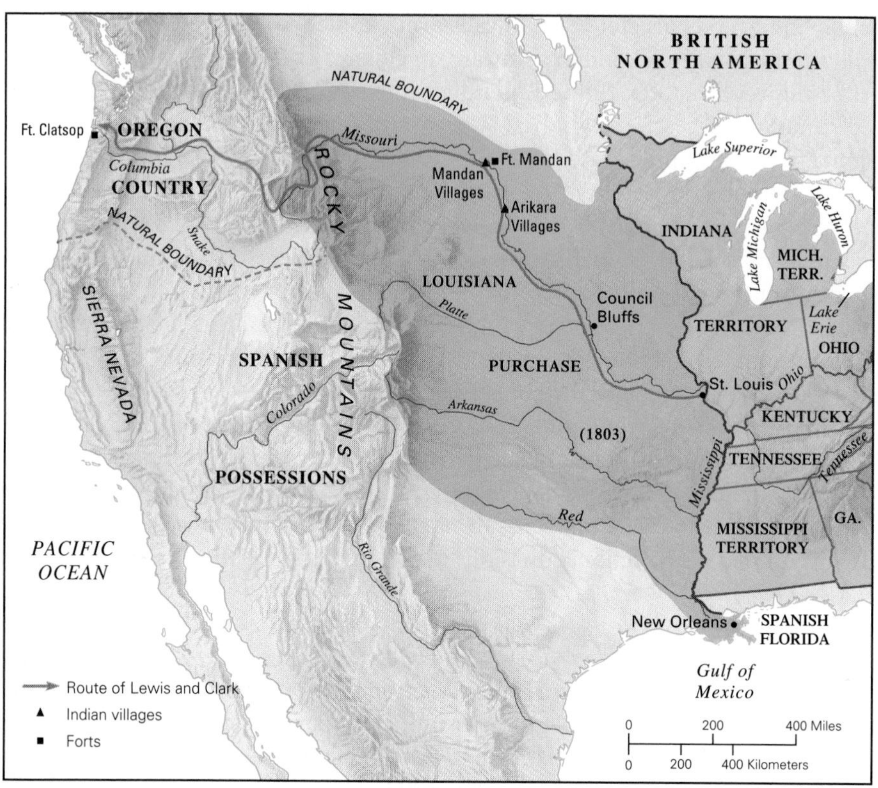

The Lewis and Clark Expedition and the Louisiana Purchase Acquisition of the vast Louisiana territory in 1803 made American dreams of westward expansion and Jefferson's "Empire for Liberty" seem possible to fulfill. Within a year, Lewis and Clark led an expedition into the farthest section of the territory and beyond. The explorers brought back from the Pacific coast news and artifacts that ignited widespread popular excitement about the West.

Word of the expedition spread through Indian villages ahead of the eastern strangers' arrival. By October 1804 the Mandan villages of the upper Missouri River teemed with excitement at the prospects of new trade and military support against their enemy, the Sioux. Chief Black Cat welcomed the Americans and informed them of their dire need for assistance. In previous years, "the smallpox destroyed the greater part of the nation," the chief told Clark. At one time, the Mandan had been numerous and "all the nations before this malady [were] afraid of them." But weakened by disease and hunger, the Mandan were frequent victims of the warring Sioux.

Lewis and Clark arrived at Fort Mandan with a full complement of twenty-nine men. They informed the Mandan leadership that President Jefferson expected them to forge bonds of friendship and trade, and that the Indians would in return pledge their loyalty to the American government of the East. Over the next months, Lewis and Clark's party gathered great amounts of valuable information about the culture of the Mandan and the environment of the region. In early spring 1805, the Americans hired several French-Canadian fur trappers and traders who lived in the Mandan villages part of the year to translate for them and accompany them on the remaining westward journey. In addition, they added the young Shoshone pathfinder, Sacagawea, to their expedition. Sacagawea, the wife of a French trapper, carried her baby through the rest of the trek, providing the Corps of Discovery with a signal to other Native American villages that they came in peace. In April they left with canoes and dugouts to navigate the Lemhi River, Salmon River, and the Lolo Trail to the Bitterroot Mountains. The Nez Percé helped guide the weary explorers through rough terrain, until they could descend to the Snake and Columbia Rivers. They reached the Pacific coast in November 1805 and wintered over near the mouth of the Columbia.

Lewis and Clark not only saw dramatically different terrain from their eastern homelands, they also encountered remarkable new cultures. Americans had only a vague knowledge of the Plains Indians, who lived on grasslands and hunted the great herds of buffalo. The explorers observed with amazement how the Indians shared the environment with the buffalo, their main source of food, shelter, and spiritual life. The buffalo's pathways determined Indian patterns of migration, the nature of their hunting, and the relationships with other Indian nations. North of the Plains, exploring parties met the Mandan and Minitari, who lived in numerous small groups in colder climates and river valleys in sedentary villages. Leading Mandan already served as middlemen for French and British fur traders when Lewis and Clark met them.

The expedition returned rapidly, by September 1806, because Lewis and Clark were eager to report their findings of friendly Indians, rich and varied landscapes, and the success of European traders and settlers in the far Northwest. Their reports, which were published soon after their return and distributed widely to an eager public, spurred settlement in the northern part of the Purchase. Americans took possession of the trans-Mississippi West for the first time, naming it, settling it, and transforming its landscape with great enthusiasm.

While Lewis and Clark were on their way back to Washington, D. C., Lieutenant Zebulon Pike set out in other directions. First he explored the Mississippi River from St. Louis to its source in northern Minnesota. Then he trekked across the southern half of the Purchase to Colorado, where he named one of the Rocky Mountain summits Pike's Peak. Continuing deep into territory held by the Spanish, Pike's party crossed the Rio Grande, passed into the Mexican desert, turned north and moved through San Antonio. Like Lewis and Clark's account, Pike's reports about the expedition prompted numerous plans for American settlement in those directions as well.

Indian Relations

Most people who settled west of the Mississippi River in the early 1800s did not plan to farm. Instead, this new area of American migration attracted speculators, fur traders, French and Spanish wanderers and bandits, confidence men waiting to lure travelers into uncharted areas, and a few adventurers from Kentucky and Ohio country picking their way west. These sparsely dispersed Americans encountered great numbers of Indians of varied cultures. In the Ohio Valley, north of the famed river, a loose confederation of Delaware, Miami, Shawnee, Potawatomi, and numerous villages of mixed populations fended off early American expansion. South of the river, the so-called Five Civilized Tribes of Cherokee, Choctaw, Creek, Chickasaw, and Seminole grew familiar with the imperial policies of both Spanish and Americans. Long before 1800, the tools and guns of Europeans had reached the Mandan, Hidatsa, Cheyenne, Arapaho, and others far to the West. After 1800, the relentless westward expansion of American people changed the Indian frontier decisively and devastatingly.

Most Americans generalized that all Indians were "savages" of inferior character, unsuited for republican citizenship. A few shrill voices demanded that Native Americans simply be pushed west, ahead of the tide and out of settlers' way. Many Americans, however, believed that large numbers of Indians could eventually be assimilated into white culture. Baptist, Moravian, and Quaker missionaries launched efforts to convert "the heathen" of western New York and Pennsylvania. The Society for the Propagation of the Gospel (1787) undertook to christianize and educate Native Americans in the Northwest Territory, though with only modest success.

The Indian Intercourse Act of 1790 stipulated that the government had to secure Indian lands by treaty, not by conquest or seizure. But this policy quickly became interpreted as the federal government's right to aggressively take Indian land, and the law did little to prevent the surge of westward white migration in advance of official surveys and treaty negotiations. Time and again, land-hungry Americans combined with state militias or the national army to crush Indian resistance to white territorial advances. Jefferson deplored the violence on the western and southeastern frontiers. His solution, hardly an adequate one, was to ask Indians to cede their lands peacefully in return for instruction in the agricultural ways of yeomen and "the culture of a more civilized nation."

Already in disarray because of internal wars, many tribes west of the Appalachians had become defenseless against white migration by 1810. Some served as interpreters and middlemen in the fur trade that extended around the Great Lakes and, in the case of John Jacob Astor's American Fur Company, to the far Northwest. This trade brought Native Americans useful goods such as blankets, iron pots, and hoes. It also brought harmful patterns of economic dependence, smallpox, and depletion of game on their hunting grounds. Other Indians fled west, and then fled again as wagons and sod houses spread out over the prairies.

Ultimately, Native Americans who assimilated into "civilized" American ways only accelerated their disorientation and fragmentation. But when villages chose to migrate farther west, they often met equally difficult conditions trying to share the same environments with Native Americans already present in an area. In either case, few villages survived the waves of American migration intact. Between 1790 and 1820, most Indians between the Appalachian ridge and the Plains beyond the Mississippi experienced some degree of disease, economic dependence on the East, cultural transformation, bitter political splits, or demoralizing accommodation—any or all of which accelerated changes in tribal life and introduced unforeseen trauma.

Of the Indians who chose extensive adaptation to white culture, the most successful were the Cherokee. In 1800 they still controlled vast acreage in western North Carolina, eastern Tennessee, and backcountry Georgia. But villages quickly succumbed to disease and warfare, and fleeing remnants of clans consolidated with villages far from ancestral soil. Meanwhile, settlers created new counties that encompassed Cherokee lands and imposed American law and economic institutions on reluctant individuals. Within the Cherokee nation, a bitter feud developed between families who wished to fight back against the southern state governments versus the accommodationist families who feared a destructive war with white armies if they resisted. John Ross, a leader of the "peace" group, helped accommodationists win internally and then create their own Cherokee National Council in 1808. The council organized dispersed villages under one governing body, wrote a code of law, and encouraged their people to become literate. One of their greatest scholars, Sequoyah, devised a Cherokee alphabet, and a few enterprising individuals printed a Cherokee newspaper. Most villages accepted a system of boarding schools run by missionaries, and many Cherokee set up their own stores, gristmills, and blacksmith shops.

Accommodation produced mixed results. Most Cherokee no longer lived as hunters but rather as sedentary farmers, seldom rising above poverty. A few prospered and acquired African-American slaves to work large tracts modeled on white cotton plantations. By 1827, the council oversaw distribution of a constitution, modeled on those of the southern states, which declared Cherokee status as an independent nation with sovereignty over tribal lands in Georgia, Alabama, North Carolina, and Tennessee. In 1829 the council made it an offense against the entire Cherokee people for any individual to sell land to a white settler. But accommodation eroded quickly when relentless white expansion raised the prospect of Cherokee removal far to the West (see Chapter 10).

The Shawnee of the Ohio Valley resisted the advancing line of white settlers until their decisive defeat at Fallen Timbers in 1794. Of the remaining population, many accepted the efforts of Quaker and Moravian missionaries to convert them and settle them on farms. Others chose to move west but found that a life of constant removal and hunting further weakened their diminishing numbers. Tecumseh, a young Shawnee warrior, led some of his people into the Indiana Territory around 1805, where the governor, William Henry Harrison, had been pressuring Delaware, Miami, and other tribes to sign treaties that carved out a series of reservations. That same year, Tecumseh's brother, Tenskwatawa, began sharing his spiritual visions with other Shawnee, visions in which the revitalization of Indians would occur once they rejected American culture, goods, and settlers. Tenskwatawa, also known as The Prophet, preached that turning away from American influences would restore the health, peace, and prosperity of the Shawnee.

Tecumseh drew on Tenskwatawa's powerful spiritual message to create a military confederation of many different tribes in the Michigan, Illinois, and Indiana region. After 1807, the British realized it suited their interest to send arms and food to this pan-Indian movement. By 1809, Tecumseh aroused the movement to active resistance against further white migration into their hunting lands: "the mere presence of the white men," he insisted, "is a source of evil." That year, Harrison presided over the signing of the Treaty of Fort Wayne, by which the Delaware and Potawatomi ceded nearly 3 million acres of land in Indiana. Tecumseh vowed defiance. He insisted that all Indians held this land in common, that no single Indian tribe could cede it forever, and that his alliance would defend such collectively used Indian lands "in a war of extermination against the paleface."

On November 7, 1811, Harrison advanced about 1,000 troops to the village of Tippecanoe, where in a pitched battle about 150 from each side died. Harrison claimed a victory, but in truth, the hundreds of Indians expelled from the area made war against vulnerable settlers throughout the interior of Michigan and Indiana territories. Tecumseh forged an official alliance with the British, while the word spread eastward that the frontier harbored more dangers than ever.

To the south, a young militia commander named Andrew Jackson urged President Jefferson to authorize a campaign against the Creek "Red Sticks" who refused to be removed from northern Georgia and Alabama. A planter from Tennessee who supported slavery, Jackson declared himself an ardent Indian fighter. But from 1808 to 1813, Washington politicians ignored his petition to exterminate the Creek. Finally, however, Creek atrocities against settlers became unbearable, and Jackson began a march with thousands of Kentucky and Tennessee militia into the heart of Creek lands. David Crockett accompanied him to the battle at Horseshoe Bend in early 1814, where over eight hundred Indians died—the heaviest losses in one battle in the entire history of U.S.–Indian warfare. Jackson, however, determined to subdue the Creek "completely." In the next months, he scorched the surrounding

Tecumseh (1768–1813) This Shawnee military leader had led Indian resistance to expansion into the northwest area of the trans-Appalachian region for many years by the 1780s. In that decade, as American settlement progressed rapidly into Kentucky, Tecumseh formed an alliance of midwestern tribes that engaged in numerous rebellions. Hoping to blend the support of the British and the fierce resistance of Indian peoples on the far side of the Appalachians, Tecumseh ultimately failed when an overwhelming American military force ended the uprisings. Tecumseh died at the Battle of the Thames in 1813. *(Field Museum of Natural History FMNH Neg #A993851.)*

region, constructed Fort Jackson at the center of the Creek nation, and declared American sovereignty over 22 million acres of traditional Creek soil.

International Relations, 1800–1815

George Washington had left office with the plea for "no entangling alliances," and into the early 1800s, many Democratic-Republicans accepted this wisdom. For many years they had recoiled from making English connections, but increasingly the French had also become suspect. Americans, insisted Jeffersonians, needed to blend their bounteous agriculture with overseas commerce to prosper: farmers could produce the foods that Europeans needed, and merchants could bring home the finished manufactures of more advanced nations. For Jeffersonians, these mutual relations shielded Americans from the dangerous concentration of wealth, corrupt cities, and degraded lives of wage workers that marked Europe. But Napoleonic designs on the Western Hemisphere endangered this view of trade and peace.

Spain in North America

After a long era of relative indifference, Spain began to grow uneasy about its dominion in North America. From the 1760s to 1783, Spain's King Carlos III maintained a keen interest in securing the vast lands north of New Spain that lay loosely within his empire: the Floridas, Louisiana, much of present-day Texas, and portions of present-day Arizona and California. Following the French example, Spanish viceroys throughout these borderlands pursued a policy of divide and conquer. Spanish officials forced Native American peoples who refused to sign treaties of submission into dependent trade relations or extermination. The Apache and Comanche of Texas entered years of fierce warfare, while the Pima, Pueblo, Navajo, and other peoples in Arizona and California succumbed to forced labor, liquor, and disease.

Spain's power in North America reached its highest point in the 1790s. Its hegemony stretched from East Florida across the Gulf Coast and beyond, through Texas and New Mexico. In California, Spanish landed estate holders and merchants ruled over numbers of Native American peoples and a rich environment. For several decades, the government sent missionaries and soldiers north from Mexico to set up missions and *presidios* from San Diego to San Francisco. Father Junipero Serra, a leading Franciscan priest, set up a series of missions that soon dominated California's lush valleys. Serra and his mission staff put thousands of Indians to work on the missions, sometimes by conversion, sometimes by force. Just before the American Revolution, a number of southern California mission Indians rose up against their Spanish rulers, the deplorable conditions of work, and rampant disease and death. They burned the mission at San Diego and organized rebellions throughout the countryside during the 1770s. But with their numbers reduced significantly by then, the southern California Indians were unable to reestablish their former village lifestyles.

Even as Spain subdued these outlying areas of its New World empire, its rule was being threatened in its eastern holdings. Pinckney's Treaty of 1795 had given Americans access to the Mississippi River and voided Spanish claims in the Ohio Valley. Then Spain tried to forge a strong alliance with France by giving up Louisiana in 1800, only to see France sell the region to America in 1803.

In 1808 Napoleon installed his younger brother Joseph on the Spanish throne. In Mexico *mestizos* (people of mixed Spanish and Indian heritage) and Indians rose up against royalist rule and declared their social and economic rights. In 1810 and 1812, revolts led by Father Miguel Hidalgo and Father Jose Maria Morelos demanded Mexican independence but were easily crushed by the Spanish authorities. In Texas, a few American settler-invaders, supported by the Mexican republican leader Bernardo Gutierrez, declared the province a republic in 1812, but they, too, fell into the hands of royalists who warred against American rebels, Mexican republicans, and homesteaders.

In 1810 American adventurers also occupied Spanish West Florida, claiming territorial rights that included several important rivers that drained to the Gulf of Mexico. Americans demanded annexation to the United States, which Congress granted in May 1812. During the War of 1812 (see below), American troops occupied Spanish West Florida and incited citizens to overthrow the Spanish governor. In 1817 Andrew Jackson marched into East Florida, where he seized Spanish citizens and forts under the pretense that Seminole Indians and Spanish troops had raided American settlements nearby. John Quincy Adams, the secretary of state under President James Monroe, took advantage of these open conflicts—though he disagreed with Jackson's methods—to force Spain into signing the Adams-Onís Treaty in 1819. Spain, facing rebellions in Mexico and throughout its South American colonies, was in no position to bargain.

Under the treaty, the United States annexed East Florida, took responsibility for paying the claims of its citizens against Spanish who had destroyed their property in the borderlands, and set a boundary between Louisiana and New Spain. In 1818 Adams had signed a separate treaty with England that secured the boundary between Louisiana and British Canada. Once British troops cleared out of the Ohio Valley, as they did in the years following the Rush-Bagot Treaty of 1817, Americans could rejoice in their undisputed possession of all territory west of the Appalachian ridge and south of the forty-ninth parallel as far as the Rocky Mountains.

The Atlantic Community

Jeffersonian leaders dreamed of building a lasting international peace, but they experienced a different reality when Americans encountered trouble abroad or when foreigners threatened American interests in North America. For example, between 1801 and 1806, naval vessels brought numerous reports that the Barbary states of Algiers, Morocco, Tripoli, and Tunis had launched raids against American trade vessels in the Mediterranean Sea. On many occasions, Jefferson and naval officials ordered armed ships into hostile waters to escort merchant ships, and they continued to express diplomatic concerns about the attacks against Americans in that part of the world.

The hope that the tensions of the undeclared war with France in 1798–1799 would not grow into open war also became strained once Napoleon came to power.

As Napoleon sent his armies across Europe from 1803 to 1814, Jeffersonian outpouring of support for the French Revolution diminished noticeably. Federalists and Democratic-Republicans agreed that Americans needed trade with both England and France. American ships carried food, cotton, and semiprocessed goods to both England and France, and foreign West Indies islands provided vital markets for American agricultural exports and goods for reexport to Europe. Yet after 1792, these ships became targets for French and British frigates, and by the end of the decade, the policy of neutrality was difficult for either political party to support.

By 1805, Napoleon's armies had overrun most of continental Europe, while Britain retained mastery of the high seas and had effectively blockaded France's international commerce. Democratic-Republicans and Federalists alike wished for neutrality in this new round of foreign belligerence, especially because nonalignment would keep trade with both France and England open. The government's official declaration of neutrality at first brought great profits for American grain and staples exporters; from 1803 to 1807, exports rose over 40 percent. And merchants who imported foreign goods from the Caribbean, transferred them to American ships at U.S. ports, and shipped them to Europe saw their trade rise over 400 percent.

Neutrality lost its luster after early 1805. Although Napoleon continued to rule on the continent, England's Royal Navy, under Lord Nelson, destroyed French and Spanish fleets at the Battle of Trafalgar (near the Straits of Gibraltar), and the English government passed the Essex decision, which stipulated that European countries could not open up their national and colonial trade to neutral nations during war if they normally prohibited that trade during peace. In effect, the decree attacked the most important sector of American trade, its reexport of French and Spanish West Indies goods through American ports to European buyers across the Atlantic. At the same time, Britain stepped up seizures of American vessels in the Caribbean and attempted to recapture thousands of British sailors who had deserted to American ships for higher wages and kinder commanders.

These incidents infuriated American merchants, especially in the New England states, which relied on the reexport trade as the "sinews of the republic." Jefferson agreed, and added that the British had delivered a serious blow to international protocols respecting neutrality. But he knew that Congress and the nation would not willingly enter another war, especially because Jeffersonians had reduced the navy to an insignificant force against the British fleet, the world's strongest. Hoping to secure a more enduring peace, Jefferson and his close supporters convinced Congress to pass a Non-Importation Act in 1806, modeled on the boycotts of the revolutionary crisis. But this time, the boycott of British imports failed to bring manufacturers and merchants in England to their knees because it was neither thorough enough to shut down trade nor fully supported by northern American merchants.

Meanwhile, British naval officials tried to recover their losses of sailors by capturing Americans. From 1803 to 1811, the British navy illegally impressed, or forced into service, some six thousand American sailors. In 1807 tensions erupted into open confrontation when the *Leopard*, a British ship, stopped the American

Chesapeake in American waters in order to apprehend deserters from the Royal Navy. When the *Chesapeake*'s captain refused to hand over any seamen, the *Leopard* fired its cannon, killing three men and wounding eighteen others; the British then took four men who may have been Americans.

As it became clear that nonimportation was a failure, Jefferson tried a different policy. He asked Congress for an Embargo Act in December 1807. Unlike the embargoes of the colonial years, which had halted either imports to, or exports from, certain ports, Jefferson's proposal barred American ships from sailing to *any* foreign port. He intended not only to cut off American markets for British finished goods but also to deprive British manufacturers of raw materials. This last-ditch effort to "peaceably coerce" the British resulted in disaster. As exports dropped during 1807–1808 to one-fifth their pre-embargo levels, the nation fell into a deep depression. Cities in the Northeast entered a phase of scarcities and gloom. Smuggling compensated for some loss of commerce and satisfied some consumer demand in northern cities. Coastal traders falsified documents or simply showed up at foreign ports not specified on their bills of lading. But these illicit tactics did not revive commerce. In the meantime, British shippers rejoiced in the lack of American competition and cultivated new markets in South America and the Far East.

Federalists could not bear to watch commerce languish, "for our trade is our civilizing influence." Hundreds of leading New England Federalists simply defied Jefferson's embargo. Their anger reached a fever pitch when the Democratic-Republican Congress passed a Force Act in 1808 to curtail American smuggling into Canada and the West Indies. The act, argued New Englanders, was another instance of Jeffersonians using excessive federal power, and this time it harmed American trade more than European. At one point, Jefferson ordered federal troops to Lake Champlain, New York, to arrest smugglers, but the local population defied national authority by burning goods on federal revenue vessels and retaking seized cargoes. Ironically, a few loud voices proclaimed that "rights belonging to the states" had been violated by federal officials who proclaimed to be Jeffersonians and yet "wear the mantle of our former foe," the Federalists.

Jefferson left office despondent about America's future. James Madison, also of Virginia and a good friend of Jefferson, assumed the executive office in March 1809 at a difficult moment. Almost immediately, Congress repealed the embargo, replacing it with the Non-Intercourse Act, which reopened America's trade with all nations except France and England. But Americans desperately needed these two highly important trading partners. So, in 1810 Congress added Macon's Bill No. 2, which tentatively opened trade with France and England but at the same time stipulated that the president might reimpose the Non-Intercourse Act on one nation if the other lifted its restrictions against American commerce. In September Napoleon's foreign minister in America announced that France would rescind the Berlin and Milan decrees and reopen trade with America, thereby putting Madison in the position of declaring hostility toward England. Madison gave England three months to follow France's lead, after which time he promised to reimpose the Non-Intercourse Act. England called his bluff: British officials refused to

"Ograbme, or, The American Snapping-Turtle," by Alexander Anderson, 1807 Congress passed the Embargo Act in 1807 in an effort to stop both English and French warring navies from harassing American shippers and sailors on the high seas. But the halt of exportation had disastrous effects on American commerce and did little to change foreign nations' policies. Few foreign merchants wanted to send goods to American ports if they could not secure exports for their return voyages. In addition, numerous mid-Atlantic American merchants smuggled flour and other goods out of their ports in violation of the embargo, as indicated by the "superfine" stamped on the bottom of the barrel. Jefferson has unleashed his snapping turtle, the Force Act of 1808, to catch smugglers and bring them to justice ("Ograbme" is "embargo" spelled backward). *(© Collection of The New-York Historical Society.)*

revoke their commercial restrictions and told Madison to withdraw the Non-Intercourse Act until France repealed every last measure against British trade. Madison faced a dilemma: either submit to the imperial authority of the former mother country or go to war.

The War of 1812

In November 1811, Congress voted to begin a military buildup in preparation for war with Britain, and in the following year the country entered what some scholars call the "second war for independence." War Hawks in Congress—a loose coalition of some Democratic-Republicans—believed the war was necessary to defend American citizens at sea and recover shipping and sailors from belligerent foreigners. War, declared the faction's congressional leaders Henry Clay and John C. Calhoun, would also defend western and southern land claims against Indians and

Spanish Florida. While most Federalists, now concentrated in New England and the northern mid-Atlantic region, feared the loss of commerce, War Hawks who stood behind Madison declared a war to defend America's maritime and territorial rights. The war vote in June 1812 clearly reflected this partisan and sectional alignment: all thirty Federalists and most northeastern Democratic-Republicans in Congress opposed a declaration of war against Britain, whereas the southern and western Democratic-Republican majority supported war.

Despite predictions that the war would end quickly, initial campaigns in Canada proved inconclusive and costly. At first, General William Hull's midwestern troops fell under fierce attack by Tecumseh during early 1812. But Commodore Oliver Hazard Perry's naval forces kept the region south of Lake Erie from falling into British hands, while General William Henry Harrison redoubled attacks against Tecumseh's forces and the British regiments that fell back from Detroit. Tecumseh died at the Battle of the Thames in October 1813, just as an American naval squadron burned and looted Toronto (then York).

Before Americans could claim victory over much of Canada, New England states withdrew both troops and financial support from any further invasions of "foreign British soil" at the end of 1813. Federalists in Congress tried to block national appropriations of funds and to roll back tariffs. Northerner Daniel Webster led their efforts to discourage enlistment in the American army and to prohibit recruitment of local militiamen into national forces. Democratic-Republicans appeared to many sectors of the country to have become the War Hawks, while Federalists shrank the military budget and sought renewed peaceful commerce.

But British warships stymied commerce along the American coastline, blocking trade and menacing civilian fishermen. In 1814, the Royal Navy rushed the shoreline of the Chesapeake Bay, overran coastal towns, and sacked the area around the capitol in Washington. The presidential house, still unfinished and cluttered with materials, was burned along with government buildings; Madison's household fled. Then, as the British troops headed toward Baltimore, Americans were able to turn them back at Fort McHenry, but fears of weak defenses gripped the South. In another couple of months, the British nearly took New York at the Battle of Lake Champlain, and by December 1814, it looked as if the British might cut off access to the sea through New Orleans.

Word arrived late in 1814 that Britain and its allies had defeated Napoleon. English negotiators now anxiously sought peace in order to lower taxes in England and reopen trade lines with America. But American enthusiasm was not universal. New England Federalists, whose loyalty had been lukewarm throughout the war, met in Hartford, Connecticut, to discuss reform of the Constitution or even secession from the union. Federalists, especially those in New England, wished to end the Democratic-Republican policies that had strangled their trade. The Hartford Convention called for a one-term limit on the presidency, restrictions on the length of national embargoes, and diminished presidential powers over foreign policymaking, the creation of new states, and trade restrictions. Although Federalist authority had declined too much to win these changes, their convention heightened anxieties brewing during "Madison's Little War."

The commissioners negotiating an end to the conflict finally recognized that they had deadlocked. Britain would not give up large portions of Canada and Florida, and America refused to set aside a large land reserve for the Native American allies of the British. On December 24, 1814, the Treaty of Ghent fixed the prewar boundaries as the grounds for peace. But how could the Democratic-Republicans sell the lack of territorial gains to the American public after three long years of war? Spirits sagged everywhere during late 1814, until word reached eastern newspaper offices and pulpits—before word of the treaty did—that General Andrew Jackson and his ragtag army of multiethnic, multiracial troops had decimated the British forces at the Battle of New Orleans on January 8, 1815.

Jackson's victory boosted morale immeasurably throughout the nation and elevated his own stature as a symbol of rugged individualism and frontier determination. The immense loss of life on the British side—some 700 dead and 10,000 wounded or imprisoned—contrasted sharply with America's mere 13 dead and 58 wounded. This lopsided victory, said some, proved the "RISING GLORY OF THE AMERICAN REPUBLIC." It also helped preserve Democratic-Republican political authority and consigned the Federalists to further obscurity. However, Monroe's subsequent two terms as president also proved to be years of deepening tensions and a fragmenting Democratic-Republican party system, which laid the groundwork for a new political party that war hero Jackson eventually led.

Postwar Political Culture, 1815–1824

Following the War of 1812, Americans welcomed a period of relative quiet in national political life and international relations. The Democratic-Republicans—now called simply Republicans or sometimes National Republicans—continued to dominate national policymaking, despite the crises of the two previous decades. In the postwar years, politicians of James Madison's and James Monroe's presidencies formulated bold new definitions of America's place in the world. Some would call the years from 1815 to 1824 an Era of Good Feelings. But was it? Seething crises in western development, Indian wars, and a shattering economic panic in 1819 reminded Americans everywhere that they still lived in a fragile republic.

New Frontiers

In 1790 only 5 percent of the American population lived west of the Appalachian ridge; by 1820, 25 percent did. The trickle of prerevolutionary migration into frontier lands beyond coastal settlement had become a river of people, wagons, and goods flowing into the Old Northwest territories and the southwestern area covering western Georgia, Alabama, Mississippi, and Louisiana. Who were these people? Almost 2.5 million native-born Americans, most of them in farm families, chose to leave the increasingly crowded towns and worn-out lands of the northeastern coast or Chesapeake regions. The end of the War of 1812 brought news that Indians had been defeated or removed and that British troops finally had cleared out. Then, too, Congress had slowly reduced the price of western land from its high of $2 an acre under revenue-hungry Federalists. The Land Act of 1820 reduced the price of land to $1.25 an acre, the minimum lot size to eighty acres, and down payments to only $100 cash. In addition, the act gave squatters the right to "preempt" Congress's terms and buy land even more cheaply when they made "improvements"—homes, fences, mills, and stores—to their plot. Of course, speculators continued to plague the "sturdy yeomen's" efforts to settle fertile expanses in the West. Overlapping claims and open violence among squatters, speculators, and trappers on the frontier made something of a mess out of Jefferson's landed ideal for the continent. But liberal land policies made the prospect of westward movement more attractive to hundreds of thousands of average Americans.

Migrants poured across western New York, through Utica and Syracuse, toward the new settlement on Lake Erie called Buffalo; across the turnpike connecting Philadelphia to Pittsburgh; out of Baltimore, itself a fresh new port city, toward new trading towns in the Ohio Valley; and down the Wilderness Road along the Appalachian ridge, through the Cumberland Gap, and into Kentucky. They clustered in settlements widely spread out on the frontier, along the fall line and rivers that provided milling power and transportation.

Each new frontier region reproduced parts of its migrants' former culture, while adapting to new frontier conditions as well. From New England came emigrants who were young, for the most part, and anxious to be released from the crowded towns and depleted soil of their home counties. They came, too, as families, often with foreknowledge about a particular spot where kin or neighbors had begun a settlement. But once they arrived at these promising locations, over half of the East's migrants moved on again within a few years. Rumors and newspaper accounts of even richer land still farther west kept pulling them into areas "just beyond the next rise or even to the horizon." People who stayed behind in the new territorial towns more often than not rose to political and economic prominence as boosters, developers, bankers, real estate agents, and merchants amid the constantly fluctuating population of newcomers. Southern planters favored the rich soil around Natchez, Mississippi, and brought large numbers of slaves to labor for them. They soon understood the rapidly rising value of cotton—"white gold"—and turned toward New Orleans for exporting it to Britain. A well-developed system of labor and agriculture was thus transplanted into unknown lands. Through market calculation and adaptation to new conditions, a few planters grew immensely rich in this delta region and drew planters from Virginia, the Carolinas, and Georgia to the new cotton belt after 1815. Still, some migrants from the South and East moved into the Northwest Territory and looked to a life on free soil without slavery.

Government and Development

By 1815, Republicans were often promoting policies that at one time only hard-line Federalists had advocated. By then, the early Jeffersonian vision of self-reliance had receded far from view. President James Monroe continued the "Virginia Dynasty" of Republican presidents, but he filled his cabinet with men from all regions and both parties. John Quincy Adams, with his New England Federalist pedigree, became secretary of state; John C. Calhoun, a southern War Hawk and emerging states' rights champion, became secretary of war. From the start, Monroe also identified closely with westerners such as Henry Clay, who advocated a stepped-up program of internal improvements.

Already in 1815, Madison had enunciated support for what contemporaries then, and historians since, call the American System. It included the promotion and funding by government of a Second Bank of the United States, protective tariffs, and a network of roads and canals. In the past, Jefferson and his close supporters had denounced such improvements as a plan to usurp power from local and state control. By Madison and Monroe's administrations, however, proponents of government-sponsored development had become more vocal in the press, and in Congress. Early advocates of the American System premised its benefits on a vision of America's mixed commercial and agricultural economy. More and more Republicans hoped for additional government aid to transportation and financial institutions that helped developers, but they hardly foresaw the elaborate networks of capital flows, factory systems, and wage labor that lay ahead.

In 1816 Monroe kicked off the American System with two important federal measures. Congress chartered the Second Bank of the United States for another twenty years, thereby explicitly promoting a strong national currency and large funds of capital for the rapidly growing economy. Despite continuing protests from agrarian-minded Americans, some "nationally-minded Republicans" joined Federalists in support of the Bank. Monroe's 1816 message to Congress also implemented the first truly protective tariff in American history, largely in response to the flood of manufactured goods that the British dumped at American ports once the eight long years of boycotts and battles came to an end. American craftsmen and small entrepreneurs grew outraged with the competition from England's cheaper goods. The tariff imposed higher duties on woolens, cottons, leather, fur hats, paper, sugar and candy, and iron products. For the time being, the Bank and higher tariffs answered the immediate needs of America's commercial and "infant" manufacturing interests. Later, however, they would be the subjects of profound disagreement among Americans of various economic and political persuasions.

The American System also encompassed energetic promotion of roads and canals under Madison and Monroe. However, as Republicans, both presidents believed the Constitution prohibited the use of federal funds for such projects because, they reasoned, most roads and canals would cut through portions of states, or benefit only two or three states. For the time being, development originated primarily in the minds and pocketbooks of state governments and private citizens (discussed further in Chapter 9).

The Panic of 1819

In the early 1800s, most Americans worked directly on the land or in small shops at crafts and retailing. Here and there entrepreneurs started small businesses, mechanized their mills, or hired wage labor, but few investors yet envisioned a true factory system. Indeed, the economy had many familiar characteristics until long after the

War of 1812. Merchants renewed their commerce with England and Europe after the war, importing finished goods and sending southern agricultural goods to foreign ports. English ships were beginning to sail east for cotton, but southern planters still did not grow much of that commodity. In addition, the English Corn Laws after the War of 1812 prohibited imports of American grain and flour, which diminished American sales abroad and forced shippers to begin looking for new markets.

At first, it seemed to many Americans that although the export economy did not recover and grow according to their postwar expectations, they could turn west for prosperity. Land offices opened up in the new states formed out of the Northwest Territory, and planters snatched up cotton-growing land in the Southeast all the way to the Mississippi River. Proliferating local banks offered easy credit to eager settlers who wished to purchase land, and eastern speculators teamed up, not for the first time, with directors in the Second Bank of the United States to promote the land-grabbing frenzy. Prices for agricultural goods rose rapidly, which fueled even more land hunger.

However, when the national Bank needed funds to make a last foreign payment for the Louisiana Purchase, it turned to local banks for a supply of specie. These local banks had been built on overextended credit to eager farmers and entrepreneurs, and although required to cover their loans with a specie fund, few of them provided that safeguard. In 1819 the national Bank's unmet needs drew attention to the inflated credit of the local banks, with the result of demolishing public confidence, then private credit. The subsequent failure of numerous banks meant that thousands of farmhouses and herds of livestock went up for auction, while recently purchased slaves went up for sale.

Once panic set in, a stream of bankruptcies followed and unemployment rose to alarming heights. Laborers by the thousands lost jobs, employers sliced wages to a small fraction of wartime levels, and farmers experienced foreclosures. In southern states, rapidly falling cotton and tobacco prices forced many planters to switch to grain production before they lost all hope of economic survival. The courts were jammed with lawsuits, families lost houses and farms, and young people despaired of setting up businesses of their own.

A wave of dislocation washed over every class, region, and occupation in America. Nearly half a million workers lost their jobs when city businesses failed. Homeless families roamed the streets of northern cities, and soup kitchens could not meet the growing demand for food. Moreover, the Panic of 1819 revitalized images of the famous credit and banking "bubbles" that had burst in previous centuries, including the specter of financial and institutional ruin brought on by unscrupulous individuals. Many supporters of Maryland's case against the Second Bank of the United States (see *McCulloch* v. *Maryland*, page 290) were motivated by such traditional considerations. But as the panic wore on, some Americans began to interpret economic trauma in different terms. Perhaps it was not deceitful individuals or poor judgment of risk, some observers mused, but structural problems with state and federal institutions, or political policies, that lay at the root of so much human misery. When the next panic occurred in 1837, Americans still had not abandoned their traditional view of banks and business failure, but they were increasingly prone to blame government officials—especially at the national level—for their hardships.

The Missouri Crisis

As economic panic gripped the country, the issue of slavery in the western states and territories riveted congressional attention. Since the Constitutional Convention and the Northwest Ordinance, political leaders had negotiated the expansion of slavery with great caution. With each new acquisition of land, with each surge of population into the West, the specter of slavery threatened to break the fragile terms of agreement among political and regional interests. With each territory's application for statehood, politicians cobbled together a fragile new consensus on the boundaries of slavery.

When Missouri applied for admission to the United States in 1819, Congress had not yet made provisions to allow or disallow slavery in the region west of the Mississippi River. Immediately, Missouri became the subject of sectional divisions between different parts of the country. Senator Rufus King of New York proposed that Missourians prohibit slavery while still a territory and enter the nation as a free state. Predictably, southerners wanted to transport their way of life and their system of labor into the new western lands. People in each section feared that a victory for

The Missouri Compromise After years of bitter Congressional debate, Maine was admitted as a free state, while Missouri became a slave state, in 1820. Although north of 36°30′ would remain free territory, a number of policymakers anticipated opportunities to create slave territories as the nation expanded.

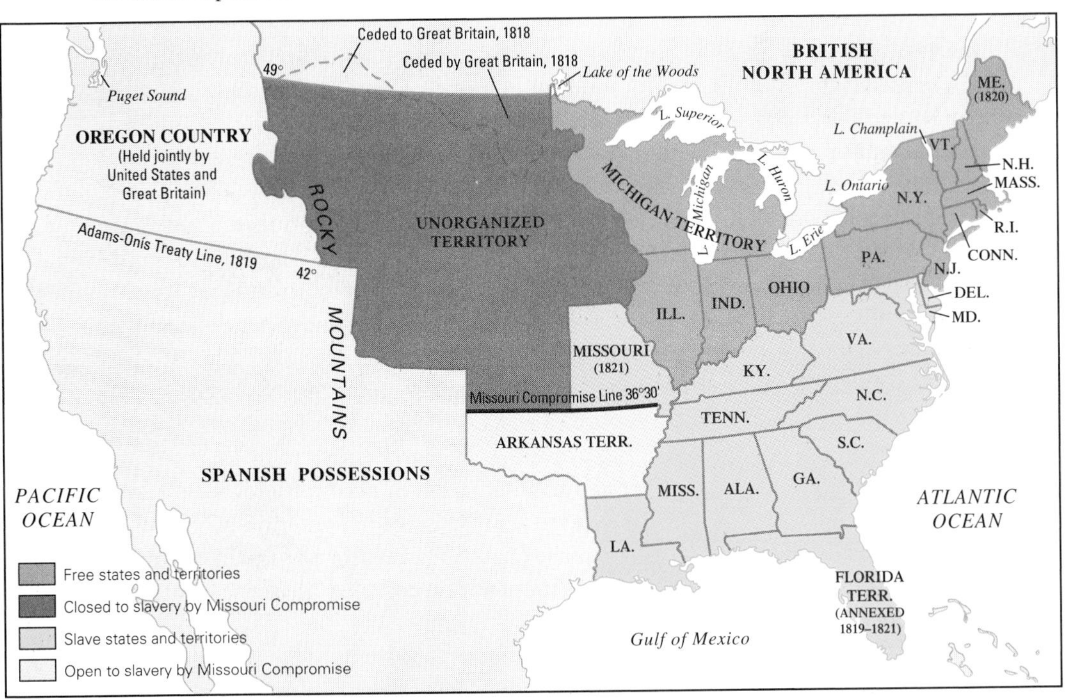

the other would shatter a delicate political and economic balance in the nation. If Missouri became a free state, argued southerners, the North would control Congress and its opposition to slavery would be imposed—by law and by force—on the southern way of life. Over recent years, insisted southern Old Republicans, an amalgamation of western and northeastern citizens had formed under the umbrella of "new-style" Republicans who wanted to channel resources for development and settlement to northern citizens. King's proposal intensified these fears, especially because northern public opinion favored it strongly.

During the months-long congressional debate about Missouri statehood, latent sectional arguments were laid bare. Many northern social reformers worried that unless the entire West was made free territory, "the future character of our nation" would deteriorate. Jefferson, from the more contemplative vantage of his home at Monticello, believed that the sectional divisions over slave and free territory were "like a fire-bell in the night, [that] awakened and filled me with terror." Fortunately for the southern slave owners' viewpoint, Maine had applied for statehood as this debate unfolded, which allowed Congress to work out what became known as the Missouri Compromise. Missouri would come into the nation as a slave state, Maine as a free state. Congress also extended Missouri's southern border of 36°30′ latitude to the Rocky Mountains (see map). For years to come, planters understood that they could spread slavery onto land south of the line, while they also negotiated strenuously to redraw that line farther to the north.

The Monroe Doctrine

America's sprawling empire provided a gigantic open space for settlement that was diplomatically and militarily—though not culturally—free of the influence of the Spanish and British empires. Optimism about westward migration increased every year. But adjacent to this frontier, in Latin America, the early 1800s were filled with instability. Liberation movements grew strong enough first to challenge Spain's and Portugal's rule over their colonies and then, by 1822, bring about independence from Old World hegemony in four important nations: Chile, Venezuela, Mexico, and Brazil. American newspapers responded in anxious watchfulness, expressing serious concern that France or Russia—far stronger nations than Spain—might attempt to undermine the new republics.

In March 1822, President Monroe urged Congress to recognize the legitimacy of the fledgling Latin American republics and thus implicitly disapprove of European aggression there. Over the next months, foreign ministers to England and America discussed the feasibility of a joint declaration of neutrality regarding Latin America and in defense of the struggling new nations against potentially belligerent foreign powers. Fears that France, because of its 1822 invasion of Spain, would be the first nation to attack the new Latin American states fueled the sense of urgency among American policymakers.

At first Monroe believed that the joint declaration would be America's best course of action; Madison and Jefferson agreed. But a bolder John Quincy Adams, who was less interested in protecting young republics in Latin American than in holding back the power of European nations in the Western Hemisphere, convinced the president not to ally with Britain on this issue. Instead, Monroe agreed to use his annual message to Congress in December 1823 to warn Spain and all other European powers to abandon all designs on the Western Hemisphere, especially the regions in Mexico and Latin America declaring themselves independent republics. In his speech, written by Adams, Monroe declared that "the American continents, by the free and independent conditions that they have assumed and maintained, are henceforth not to be considered as subjects for future colonization by any European power." This Monroe Doctrine, as it came to be known, pledged the American government to keeping unwanted European presence out of the Western Hemisphere. But it did not commit the United States to noninterference in Latin American affairs. For the time being, America's expansionist concerns turned westward, across the North American continent, but Latin American leaders remained wary about the United States' ultimate intentions.

CONCLUSION

The Revolution of 1800 that brought Jefferson into the presidency proved to Americans that their nation could withstand bitter political factionalism and witness a peaceful transfer of federal power. It also ushered in the long rule of the Republicans. The Louisiana Purchase added so much new territory that the republican ideal of an expanding agricultural yeomanry seemed to be secure for generations to come. The "second war for independence," from 1812 to 1815, demonstrated decisively that the new republic was strong enough to resist Britain's attempt to turn them into colonists again.

Jeffersonian political policies often reinforced the emerging national identity. They significantly reduced the presence of government, while also invoking federal powers to expand the "empire of liberty" and safeguard the country from foreign and Indian nations. Jefferson could rejoice during his retirement at Monticello that he had helped to restore toleration for different opinions in political life; that direct taxes on American property had been repealed; that the national debt had been reduced and would no longer be used to create stronger national power; and that the franchise had become more inclusive.

But the party that rose to national office on a platform of local control and international peace in fact tolerated Hamiltonian institutions to a significant degree and occasionally wielded federal power over citizens in Hamiltonian fashion. Moreover, sectionalism and regional contentions grew, rather than shrank, during the so-called Era of Good Feelings that followed the War of 1812. The Panic of 1819 shattered two decades of commercial growth, the Missouri Compromise brought to the forefront political disagreements rooted in deep moral differences among citizens, and the frontier continued to be a dangerous place filled with hostile Europeans, runaway slaves, and recalcitrant Indians. By 1824, Americans were poised to undertake a new experiment in rapid and transformative growth, while at the same time entering a new era of political strife.

SUGGESTED READINGS

The best studies of Jefferson's first years in the presidency include Lance Banning, *The Jeffersonian Persuasion: Evolution of a Party Ideology* (1978); Noble E. Cunningham, *The Jeffersonian Republicans and Power: Party Operations, 1801–1809* (1963); and Drew McCoy, *The Elusive Republic* (1980) and *The Last of the Fathers: James Madison and the Republican Legacy* (1989). A recent collection, Peter Onuf, ed., *Jeffersonian Legacies* (1993), offers fresh interpretations of the political and cultural Jefferson. For Jefferson's relationship to popular politics see Merrill Peterson, *Thomas Jefferson and the New Nation: A Biography* (1970); and for his relationship to Federalists, see Stanley Elkins and Eric McKitrick, *The Age of Federalism: The Early American Republic, 1788–1800* (1993). The political life in the national capital is effectively captured in James S. Young, *The Washington Community: 1800–1828* (1966). For the role of the courts in this era, especially the Supreme Court, see G. Edward White, *The Marshall Court and Cultural Change, 1815–1835* (1991).

Westward expansion in the early 1800s is best covered in Stephen Aron, *How the West Was Lost: Kentucky from Daniel Boone to Henry Clay* (1966). For aspects of settlement and conflict on the Old Northwest frontier, see Andrew Cayton, *The Frontier Republic: Ideology and Politics in the Ohio Country, 1780–1825* (1986); Robert Mitchell, ed., *Appalachian Frontier: Settlement, Society, and Development in the Preindustrial Era* (1991); and Thomas Slaughter, *The Whiskey Rebellion: Frontier Epilogue to the American Revolution* (1986).

Stephen Ambrose's *Undaunted Courage, Meriwether Lewis, Thomas Jefferson, and the Opening of the American West* (1996) is a spellbinding account of the Lewis and Clark expedition. For Native American relations with settlers going west, the best accounts are in Richard White, *The Middle Ground: Indians, Empires, and Republics in the Great Lakes Region, 1650–1815* (1991); Colin G. Calloway, *Crown and Calumet: British-Indian Relations, 1783–1815* (1987); and R. David Edmunds, *Tecumseh and the Quest for Indian Leadership* (1984), and *The Shawnee Prophet* (1983).

The best studies of the diplomacy and political policies related to commerce are Doron Ben-Atar, *The Origins of Jeffersonian Commercial Policy and Diplomacy* (1993); Roger H. Brown, *The Republic in Peril* (1964); Lawrence Kaplan, *"Entangling Alliances with None": American Foreign Policy in the Age of Jefferson* (1987); Bradford Perkins, *Prologue to War: England and the United States, 1805–1812* (1961); and Peter Onuf and Nicholas Onuf, *Federal Union, Modern World: The Law of Nations in an Age of Revolution, 1776–1814* (1993).

Two of the most informative studies of the War of 1812 remain Harry L. Coles, *The War of 1812* (1965), and Reginald Horsman, *The Causes of the War of 1812* (1962). A more recent work explains the political culture of public opinion and internal regional developments related to the war: Steven Watts, *The Republic Reborn: War and the Making of Liberal America, 1790–1820* (1987). The best biographies of Madison during these testy years are by Robert Rutland: *James Madison, The Founding Father* (1987) and *The Presidency of James Madison* (1990). For the Canadian perspective, see Pierre Berton, *The Invasion of Canada* (1980).

The political crisis of postwar America is treated admirably in Harry Ammon, Jr., *James Monroe: The Quest for National Identity* (1971), and James Banner, *To the Hartford Convention: The Federalists and the Origins of Party Politics in the Early Republic, 1789–1815* (1967). Recently, historians have returned to the topic of emerging American national identity. See first the older work by George Dangerfield, *The Awakening of American Nationalism, 1815–1828* (1965). Then look at the more cultural approach of David Waldstreicher, *In the Midst of Perpetual Fetes: The Making of American Nationalism* (1997).

The Missouri Crisis is explained in rich detail in Glover Moore, *The Missouri Compromise, 1819–1821* (1953). And for the Monroe Doctrine, the best treatments are Ernest R. May, *The Making of the Monroe Doctrine* (1975), and Dexter Perkins, *The Monroe Doctrine, 1823–1826* (1927).

The Government's Role in Building Institutions

Competing Voices

McCulloch v. *Maryland* (1819) and the National Bank

The Second Bank of the United States, chartered by Congress in 1816, evoked both intense public criticism and hearty applause. Among the Bank's supporters was Chief Justice John Marshall, whose Supreme Court heard a momentous case in 1819 that challenged its constitutionality. The Court unanimously rejected the challenge, and Marshall's opinion would stand as a landmark statement affirming the authority of the government to create powerful national institutions.

> We [justices of the Supreme Court] admit, as all must admit, that the powers of the government are limited, and that its limits are not to be transcended. But we think the sound construction of the constitution must allow to the national legislature that discretion, with respect to the means by which the powers it confers are to be carried into execution, which will enable that body to perform the high duties assigned to it, in the manner most beneficial to the people. Let the end be legitimate, let it be within the scope of the constitution, and all means which are appropriate, . . . are constitutional.
>
> That the power of taxation is one of vital importance; that it is retained by the states; that it is not abridged by the grant of a similar power to the government of the Union; that it is to be concurrently exercised by the two governments—are truths which have never been denied. . . . The states are expressly forbidden to lay any duties on imports or exports, except what may be absolutely necessary for executing their inspection laws. . . . The same paramount character would seem to restrain . . . a state from such other exercise of this power as is in its nature incompatible with, and repugnant to, the constitutional laws of the Union. A law absolutely repugnant to another, as entirely repeals that other as if express terms of repeal were used.
>
> On this ground the counsel for the Bank place its claim to be exempted from the peer of a state to tax its operations. There is no express provision for the case, but the claim has been sustained on a principle which so entirely pervades the Constitution, is so intermixed with the materials which compose it, so interwoven with its web, so blended with its texture, as to be incapable of being separated from it without rending it into shreds.
>
> This great principle is that the Constitution, and laws made in pursuance thereof, are supreme; that they control the constitutions and laws of the respective states, and cannot be controlled by them. From this, . . . other propositions are deduced as corollaries. . . . These are: 1. That a power to create implies a power to preserve. 2. That a power to destroy, if wielded by a different hand, is hostile to, and incompatible with, these powers to create and preserve. 3. That where this repugnancy exists, that authority which is supreme must control, not yield to that over which it is supreme. . . .

That the power to tax involves the power to destroy; that the power to destroy may defeat and render useless the power to create; that there is a plain repugnance in conferring on one government a power to control the constitutional measures of another . . . are propositions not to be denied.

If we apply the principle for which the state of Maryland contends, to the Constitution generally, we shall find it capable of changing totally the character of that instrument. We shall find it capable of arresting all the measures of the government, and of prostrating it at the foot of the states. The American people have declared their Constitution, and the laws made in pursuance thereof, to be supreme; and this principle would transfer the supremacy, in fact, to the states.

If the states may tax one instrument employed by the government in the execution of its powers, they may tax any and every other instrument . . . the mail . . . the mint . . . patent rights . . . papers of the custom-house . . . judicial process . . . to an excess which would defeat all the ends of government. This was not intended by the American people. They did not design to make their government dependent on the states. . . .

The question is, in truth, a question of supremacy. And if the right of the states to tax the means employed by the general government be conceded, the declaration that the Constitution, and the laws made in pursuance thereof, shall be the supreme law of the land, is empty and unmeaning declamation.

Niles's Weekly Register Denounces the Decision

The Court may have been unanimous in its judgment, but the people were not. Hezekiah Niles, the Baltimore editor of America's most influential weekly newspaper, wrote a scathing refutation of the Supreme Court decision. Not only had Congress exceeded its authority in 1791 when it established a federal bank, but it now tampered with the powers inherent in each state government. Following is an excerpt from *Niles's Weekly Register* in 1819.

. . . A deadly blow has been struck at the sovereignty of the states, and from a quarter so far removed from the people as to be hardly accessible to public opinion. . . . We are yet unacquainted with the grounds of this alarming decision, but of this are resolved—that nothing but the tongue of an angel can convince us of its compatibility with the Constitution of the United States, in which a power to grant acts of incorporation is not delegated [to the federal government], and all powers not delegated are retained.

Far be it from us to be thought as speaking disrespectfully of the Supreme Court, or to subject ourselves to the suspicion of a "contempt" of it. We do not impute corruption to the judges, or intimate that they have been influenced by improper feelings. They are great and learned men; but still, only men. And, feeling as we do—as if the very stones would cry out if we did not speak on this subject—we will exercise our right to do it, and declare that, if the Supreme Court is not mistaken in its construction of the Constitution . . . their sovereignty is at the mercy of their creature—Congress. It is not on account of the Bank of the United States that we speak thus . . . it is but a drop in the bucket compared with the principles established by the decision, which appear to us to be these:

1. That Congress has an unlimited right to grant acts of incorporation!

2. That a company incorporated by Congress is exempted from the common operation of the laws of the state in which it may be located!

. . . Our sentiments are on record that we did not wish the destruction of that institution but, fearing the enormous power of the corporation, we were zealous that an authority to arrest its deleterious influence might be vested in responsible hands, for it has not got any soul. Yet this solitary institution may *not* subvert the liberties of our country, and command every one to bow down to it as Baal. It is the principle of it that alarms us, as operating against the unresigned rights of the states. ▮

In 1791 Jefferson and Hamilton sharply disagreed about the constitutionality of the First Bank of the United States. Three decades later, Democratic-Republicans and Federalists were still debating whether the federal government had the power to establish such a strong central institution. Jeffersonians had struggled to diminish federal powers, especially in cases in which Bank directors had used the institution's funds to speculate in real estate and public improvements projects. Thus, the views expressed by opponents such as Niles remained strong and would challenge the Bank—as well as other institutions and developments associated with Federalists—repeatedly during the coming years. In Maryland, state legislators responded to the public outcry against such abuse of public banking powers by putting a high tax on that state's branch of the Bank and causing it to fold operations.

Federalists argued that the Bank, and many other institutions and improvements supported by the national government, were responsible for securing the republic's very existence. Chief Justice John Marshall, who steadfastly maintained his Federalist posture even when the party faded from prominence, also declared in *McCulloch v. Maryland* that the Second Bank of the United States was perfectly constitutional and stood above the Maryland tax law. He was therefore protecting the interests that favored a strong national bank and its functions in helping to promote the national economy. Further, Marshall's decisions in a series of cases challenging federal powers firmly held that the government had a constitutional right to establish national institutions "necessary and proper" for the running of the country and that no state had the authority to destroy them by taxation.

Questions for Analysis

1. What are the central points of Marshall's argument? What does the chief justice mean when he writes that "the power to tax is the power to destroy"?
2. Is Niles more concerned about the power of the Bank of the United States over Maryland citizens or about federal encroachments on the rights of the states?
3. What language in Niles's article would appeal to Jeffersonians in any section of the country?
4. Which parts of each argument speak to the particular issues raised by this case in 1819, and which speak to much larger issues concerning federal and state powers that arose frequently in early American history?
5. What would you say are some of the benefits of banks—whether state or national institutions—during this period of time, and what are some of their drawbacks?

9

An Emerging Capitalist Nation, 1790–1820

In September 1811, Nicholas Roosevelt boarded his steamboat *New Orleans* at the Pittsburgh docks and waived enthusiastically to friends and family who stood gawking on shore. Months before this, they had "united in endeavoring to dissuade" Roosevelt "from what they regarded as utter folly, if not absolute madness." It seemed to them that Roosevelt had joined the endless parade of visionaries, tinkerers, and deluded developers who kept trying to "tame" nature and "civilize" newly settled regions. In these early years of the new republic, many of these efforts failed. But a few of them succeeded spectacularly, and these in turn spurred new efforts to transform the landscape with human entrepreneurship.

Despite the misgivings of skeptics, Nicholas Roosevelt stuck by his plan to navigate the Ohio River by steamboat, thereby joining the many other Americans making internal improvements that reshaped the early republic. His hired craftsmen labored diligently under Roosevelt's watchful eye at the shipyard, until the morning when he turned to the crowds, shrugged off public doubts and private fears, climbed onto the *New Orleans,* and began a daring voyage past many budding Ohio River towns. Two days later, as the "grand lady" chugged downriver at eight miles per hour, curious onlookers flocked to Cincinnati's docks to deliver their own advice. One local merchant shouted, "Your boat may go *down* the river; but, as to coming *up* it, the very idea is an absurd one." Crowds at Louisville repeated the refrain of doubt, but the determined Roosevelt ordered his crew to take the *New Orleans* upstream a bit, which he hoped would convince townspeople how his investment could "make good headway *up* the river."

But having begun to replace scorn and cynicism with "universal incredulity" about the magnificent steamboat, Roosevelt then encountered "days of horror." Four days into the trip, the vessel met low water at the falls of the Ohio River. Once the water rose sufficiently, Roosevelt ordered full speed to descend through the falls. "The safety valve shrieked; the wheels revolved faster than they had ever done before, and the vessel . . . fairly flew away from the crowds on shore." Shortly thereafter, the captain recorded fire on board, then an earthquake that shook "the length of the Mississippi," and then numerous uncharted patches of sandbars that confounded the steamboat's pilot. Sparks from the steam engine's chimney lit clothes on fire, and smoke backed up into sleeping chambers more than once on the fourteen-day trip. No wonder the Chickasaw Indians who followed briefly in their small craft called the *New Orleans* a "fire canoe." But the steamboat survived the mishaps and finally reached New Orleans, achieving acclaim for a "voyage which changed the relations of the West—which may almost be said to have changed its destiny."

After the War of 1812, steamboats did not immediately replace the familiar keelboats and flatboats coursing down major rivers, but their powerful engines and greater carrying capacity became more and more familiar on the country's inland waterways. By 1820, at least a dozen steamboats made daily trips between New York City and Albany. Other "transportation wonders"—graded roads, canals, and eventually railroads—were also part of an incredibly rapid transformation of the American landscape.

New experiments shaped not only the landscape during the early 1800s, but urban and frontier life also underwent far-reaching change, and the cultural arenas of work, religion, and family were likewise deeply altered. Some observers marveled that Americans had become "a breathless people." But few Americans understood the consequences of the sweeping changes they experienced. Historians today still debate the nature and meanings of change in the early republic.

- How did new machines and technologies change commerce in the early republic? Who sought change, and who benefited from it?
- How did the far-reaching material innovations knit frontiers and settled areas together into one nation? How did they enhance differences from region to region?
- How did Americans react to economic and social change in the early republic? How did their reactions affect the cultural institutions of family and religion?

This chapter will address these questions.

Improvement and Invention

In some important respects, American life in 1790 continued much as it had in prerevolutionary years. Local attachments to family and neighbors, nearby markets, poor transportation and communication, hand tools and customary methods of

Chronology

1790	Slater opens first mill
	Federal patent law validates Evans's milling equipment
1793	Whitney invents cotton gin
1801	Cane Ridge, Kentucky, revival
1807	Livingston and Fulton send *Clermont* up the Hudson River
1807–1808	Jeffersonian embargo of American commerce
1810	First steamboats ply the Ohio River
1816	First protective tariff
1817	Erie Canal begun
1818	National Road finished to Wheeling, Ohio
1824	*Gibbons* v. *Ogden* puts interstate travel under federal authority
	Hall introduces the American System of Manufactures

farming, small farms with depleted soil in older regions and uncleared fields on the frontier, all were familiar to Americans. In the next thirty years, however, the pace of economic and cultural change accelerated. Farmers, entrepreneurs, and shippers swamped their state legislatures with requests for special laws to promote particular projects. New terms such as *development, expansion, improvement, refinement,* and *invention* began to be heard, and older concerns about protection, persistence, deference, and neighborliness faded. Many Americans tried actively to harness nature, inventing the belching, lurching contraptions that increasingly occupied the landscape after 1800. Edward Everett, a leading political orator, distinguished editor, and Harvard graduate, exulted that Americans had "the means of private comfort by the inventions, discoveries, and improvements" they made. They stood poised to transform their culture and take "first place in the world." Aided by "wise laws" and political security, experiments in internal improvement of the countryside and in manufacturing would flourish.

It followed that federal and state governments had a duty to grant funds and special privileges to build the infrastructure that connected peoples across great distances. That duty, wrote many Americans, rose to special importance in the early republic because people's demands for new roads, canals, and time-saving machines outstripped their ability to pay for them privately. The need for governments to fund improvements generously also derived from what many people believed to be the American experiment's mission to expand across the continent.

Roads and Turnpikes

In the 1790s, people who lived along the major eastern rivers benefited from their natural accessibility, easily exchanging imported goods or coastal manufactures for frontier timber and furs. But migrants into the Genesee and Mohawk frontiers of western New York, or into certain mountainous areas of Pennsylvania, lacked access to continuous riverways that led to the east, and their overland travel remained arduous. Even along the coastline, a coach ride from New York City to Philadelphia in 1800 took two days, and a journey to Boston four days. When George Washington died in Virginia in 1799, Kentucky inhabitants first heard the news nearly a month later. By 1820, travel by land was faster, but it still took a week to get from New York to Pittsburgh.

Frontier settlers found that the hardships of clearing land and starting farms in their new environment became even more difficult because of their isolation from goods, news, and kin. But if local barter and neighborhood self-sufficiency marked settlers' meager existence at first, they gradually overcame these conditions by looking to government. Their demands for the national government to provide roads, canals, military protection, and political representation equivalent to what easterners enjoyed were loud and long.

State and national political leaders were not deaf to these demands. While Jefferson attended to his controversial embargoes in 1807 (see page 308), his secretary of the treasury, Albert Gallatin, implored Congress to extend earlier efforts at "opening roads and making canals" throughout America. Since the 1780s local and state governments had occasionally poured resources into roads and canals they believed would make the citizenry "one and indivisible." But pressing political reasons persuaded Congress to fund even more of these projects, over longer distances. For one thing, the new states of Kentucky, Ohio, and Tennessee had enlarged the republic to daunting proportions, but they were still not a connected and secure part of the nation. Spanish, French, and British traders and wilderness settlers spread word to their governments that Americans in these new landlocked states might be willing to form new national allegiances with foreign powers. Frontier settlers often complained of their distance from the advantages of coastal cities and international commerce. When groups of them started speaking about forming republics under a British or Spanish flag, the American Congress and public opinion readily agreed about the urgency of Gallatin's message.

But unifying the country's parts was a formidable task. Traveling more than a hundred miles was likely to involve a combination of horses, wagons, flatboats, small sailing vessels, barges, or canoes. In 1800 most American roads were suitable for little more than foot traffic, and those that were designed for wagons easily turned to muddy swamps or became overgrown with brush. Even on the country's best roads, a traveler needed ten 16-hour days to get from Boston to Washington, much of it by walking.

Roads to the west of the Appalachian Mountains were so treacherous that in the autumn, after crops had been harvested, communities banded together to organize trains of pack animals to carry produce to Baltimore or Pittsburgh or Cincinnati. These trains afforded westerners a small amount of mutual protection and support

Rivers, Canals, and Roads to 1820 Migrants, developers, and policymakers joined together to create a dense transportation network in the early republic. These links were both the result of, and further spur to the rapid development of the nation's interior.

on a journey that was dangerous and lonely. Paths leading through valleys, over precipices, and into thick underbrush carried goods slowly, each animal carrying maybe two hundred pounds of goods. Needless to say, this method of transport made sense for farmers only if their crops brought prices high enough to cover the cost of transportation and provide a small profit. Although men and boys could drive hogs from Kentucky to Baltimore "on the hoof" and thus avoid most transportation costs, wheat was too heavy and too perishable to be shipped east profitably during the early 1800s, so many farmers converted it into distilled spirits (see the Whiskey Rebellion, Chapter 7). Farmers in Lancaster, Pennsylvania, were outraged that it cost as much to cart goods overland to Philadelphia as it did to ship them from Philadelphia to London.

Transporting goods by river and stream tended to lower costs and reduce time getting to markets, but water travel had perils of its own. Beavers clogged small waterways with their dams, flooding or freezing hindered traffic at certain times of the year, and mills often diverted the flow of water on once-navigable rivers. If a farmer got his wheat, ginseng, and maple syrup overland from, for example, western New York to Albany, he might have to wait months for the Hudson River to thaw and float his goods to New York City—if they did not rot or spoil in the meantime. Meanwhile, he paid fees for storage.

At the center of Gallatin's proposed system of internal transportation was a "great turnpike road, from Maine to Georgia, along the whole extent of the Atlantic sea coast," and "four first rate turnpike roads" to join the four main rivers flowing from the Appalachians into the Atlantic Ocean (see map at left). Already by 1807, some of the northern states had actively promoted new turnpikes by granting to private companies liberal charters that stipulated extensive land grants, rights to sell stock to the public, and provisions for taking tolls. One successful chartered company project, the Lancaster Turnpike, was "a masterpiece of its kind . . . paved with stone the whole way, and overlaid with gravel."

The War of 1812 prompted even more heightened interest in road construction when British blockades cut off most coastal shipping and forced coastal populations to rely more on inland producers for necessary goods. After the war, the momentum of public interest rose as more and more interests pressed for construction of roads to link east and west in "a system of internal improvements." Legislators in Pennsylvania and Massachusetts granted scores of special charters to private turnpike companies, while private investors sponsored numerous roads connecting settlers of the Ohio Valley to Detroit, St. Louis, and New Orleans.

The height of these efforts came when the federal government committed funds to build the National Road. In 1815 construction of a turnpike that was intended to lead from Cumberland in western Maryland, through southwestern Pennsylvania, to Wheeling, on the Ohio, was initiated. By 1818, this leg of the National Road was completed; by 1833, additional government allocations extended the road to Columbus, Ohio; and by 1850, the turnpike reached nearly to the Mississippi River at Vandalia, Illinois. Gradually, roads linked America's borderlands to the heartlands of the Northwest Territory and from there, to the oldest parts of the country. One New Yorker saw the trend as more than lines on a map: "The roads that connect trading interests and laws across the great spaces between us, have a tendency to mingle various manners, dress, and habits of people otherwise separated."

Steamboats and Canals

Comparing his early life before the American Revolution to his old age in the early 1800s, one New Jerseyan reflected that goods and people "flowed through our riverways as blood flows through arteries, the same in my declining years as in my youth." Americans had added the Ohio and Mississippi Rivers to their important "arteries," but they transported goods much the same way. Once inland transports reached points such as Pittsburgh or Wheeling, arduous overland trails gave way to relatively faster river travel by flatboats that could carry tons of bagged grain or a few head of livestock, downstream to Cincinnati, the mouth of the Wabash River, or even far down the Mississippi. Long into the 1800s, flatboats moved bulky goods more cheaply, more quickly—and often more safely—than Conestoga wagons could on the National Road.

But ambitious commercial farmers teamed up with entrepreneur-inventors to create even faster ways to get crops and people from one place to another, and to break down the distinctions that marked the different regions. "We wish," wrote a retailer in eastern Tennessee, "not to continue in the present rude condition in which you see us but to advance in our trades, and hence in our civilizing tendencies." The major problem they identified was getting their flatboats and canoes to go as easily upstream, against the current, as they could go down.

The answer was the steamboat. Harnessing steam power to drive watercraft was one of the early republic's great achievements, and the initiative to do so came from the same pragmatic considerations as the road and canal boom of the era. The first efforts to launch steam-powered boats came in the 1780s on the Delaware River between Trenton and Philadelphia, but technical difficulties led to failure. Then Robert Fulton, a long-time advocate of "energetically fund[ing] the unifying ties of internal commerce," teamed up with New Yorker Robert R. Livingston, who had acquired a twenty-year monopoly on all steam transportation along the Hudson River. In 1807 they sent the *Clermont* up the Hudson River to Albany. By then, Fulton and Nicholas Roosevelt had introduced innovations to improve steam adaptation to the centuries-old method of harnessing water power with wooden paddlewheels. Though builders continued to use white pine for the bodies of steamboats, as they had for almost two hundred years of shipbuilding, a sheet of metal covering the hull helped protect the "belching whales" from being torn apart from below or catching fire from stray sparks. Although many steamboats did catch fire, snag on tree trunks and sink, or explode, the benefits of faster travel soon outweighed initial fears of Fulton's "sea monster." It was the team of Fulton, Livingston, and Roosevelt that made the risky 1811 *New Orleans* project possible. By the end of the War of 1812, steamboats began making the unprecedented journey from New Orleans to the Ohio River and its tributaries. Soon after, steamboats regularly puffed up the Missouri River.

Enthusiastic witnesses felt certain that steamboats were an essential ingredient in realizing Jefferson's western "empire for liberty." "Our new steamboats," remarked an eastern traveler to Cincinnati, "take with all due speed the spirits [whiskey], candles, [corn]meal, barreled meats, and sundry barrels of country production, to the remotest points which few fellows can imagine in their life times; and they return with the refinements of a life their fathers left behind [in the east] long ago."

Steamboats introduced their share of trauma, including long mechanical delays at unfriendly trading posts, fires, choking engines, and bursting boilers in the "smoke-belching machines." Then, too, when steamboat enterprises proliferated, private in-

Fulton's Sketch of His Steamboat, 1809 Harnessing steam engines to furnace-heated boilers, and attaching both to wooden boats, transformed river travel and laid the basis for steam technology on the railroads decades later. Transport became faster and cheaper when steamboats could go against river currents and link people and markets more directly than in the past. Robert Fulton sent his first steamboat up the Hudson in 1807 and made this sketch to accompany his 1809 patent application. The idyllic setting he created fails to represent the horrifying fires and boiler explosions that occurred on a regular basis throughout the steamboat era. *(American Society of Mechanical Engineers.)*

vestors competed for rights to waterways and customers. In the absence of state and federal government regulations, it was only a matter of time before competitors wound up in court. In 1824 the Supreme Court, still under John Marshall's leadership, ruled in *Gibbons* v. *Ogden* that travel on the Hudson River passed through two or more states and was thus a form of interstate traffic under federal control. Any state monopoly issued in New York, the Court decided, unfairly hindered development and competition of new enterprises in other states. The ruling cleared the way for new enterprises to create even better transport of goods and passengers in years to come.

During these same years private interests and local governments initiated efforts to cut short watercourses through land to join busy river systems. Modest projects were begun in the 1780s and 1790s in eastern portions of Virginia, Massachusetts, and South Carolina. Soon these efforts developed into a canal-building craze. By the 1790s, every major coastal city had plans to cut canals into the interior. Some established lotteries to fund the projects with public money, while others allocated municipal and state funds to underwrite construction. Philadelphia immigrants and urban semiskilled laborers signed up by the thousands to dig the ditches connecting area waterways.

Then, in the early 1800s, wealthy investors teamed up with a few skilled mechanics to initiate greater engineering projects. Canals, they agreed, could follow natural highways of water that required only a little alteration to float heavier traffic. Barges could pass easily into the interior with only four feet of water, and mules trudging along towpaths could pull great loads. Sleighs, reasoned many early writers, could glide along the same waterways when canals froze over. At that time, engineers knew little of how to dig and line deep trenches, or how to make dam locks that would not burst under the force of sudden rushes of water. But they learned important skills from millwrights, surveyors, and shipbuilders.

Although engineering troubles or insufficient funds doomed many state canal projects to failure, Pennsylvania, Maryland, and New Jersey promoted some very successful systems that linked their agricultural hinterlands with coastal cities. One of these was the Schuylkill Canal, which linked Pennsylvanians for 108 miles when it was completed in 1826. By then, however, another state canal attracted far more attention because, upon completion, it profoundly transformed the lives of thousands of farmers and eastern peoples throughout the mid-Atlantic and New England regions.

This was the Erie Canal, an "artificial river" that was cut through portions of New York's Mohawk Valley wilderness, where no single river linked west to east, and where trappers and traders trekked by canoe and foot. Since the revolutionary era, public promoters felt certain that the region could become an abundant breadbasket if only transportation were improved. Hence the plan for the Erie Canal to slice across the region for 363 miles from the Hudson River to Lake Erie, thereby opening a continuous water route from New York City to Chicago.

In early 1817, Governor De Witt Clinton urged the state legislature to issue bonds to the public—in effect, to get loans from New Yorkers which the state would repay—to construct the canal. Over the coming years a work force of nearly four thousand unskilled laborers, many of them recent Irish immigrants, pulled stumps, cut stone, blasted cliffs, hauled rubble, mixed cement, tended the dozens of horses used to supplement human muscle power, and built over 300 bridges and 83 locks. Lack of prior experience in such work made the project a major outdoor school of engineering.

Early on, skeptics insisted on calling the project "Clinton's Folly" because of its unheard-of scale and exorbitant costs. But by the time it was completed in late 1825, the Erie Canal was a colossal success. Toll money poured in as the locks and towpaths teemed with drivers shouting at mules and oxen pulling freight-laden barges at about four miles per hour. Within five years, Erie Canal barges hauled over fifty thousand people a year to western territories. Syracuse, Rochester, Buffalo, and Erie became boomtowns that attracted migrants from cities and abroad to western lands and transported imported textiles, New England shoes, eastern cabinets and chairs, and numerous other items from seaboard cities into the frontiers. Foodstuffs, hogs, whiskey, hemp, and other farm goods meanwhile made their way east to eager urban consumers. Many New York City merchants pivoted their attention from financial markets in Amsterdam and dry goods purchases from London to the exploding demand from Buffalo and points west.

Between 1816 and 1840, other states cut nearly 3,400 miles of "ditches" linking towns of the interior to one another, and to vital people and supplies of the coastal cities. Canals extended like deep veins from Toledo to Cincinnati, Richmond to Lynchburg, or Philadelphia to Pittsburgh. They brought daily necessities to migrating people, took rich lodes of coal out of the Allegheny Mountains, and delivered farm products from the interior of the Old Northwest to river towns along the Ohio and Mississippi Rivers. Small trading posts such as Cleveland and Dayton in Ohio and Harrisburg in Pennsylvania became significant manufacturing and residential cities. By 1828, Cincinnati boomed with commerce that flowed from eastern cities along the Erie Canal, through the Great Lakes, down from Toledo, and out of Cincinnati along the Ohio to the Mississippi River and points south. Cincinnati had become not only a significant trading center, but also the Old Northwest's largest producer of steamboats.

Canals had a profound effect on the livelihoods and households of untold thousands of Americans by the 1820s. For one thing, the cost and time of transporting goods fell dramatically. Freight handlers and wholesale agents reported that a ton of grain could be shipped and hauled from Buffalo to New York City for about $100 in 1820; just five years later, this transaction cost only $9. By 1830, it cost fifty to seventy

Construction of the Erie Canal Thousands of workers and engineers, and hundreds of horse-powered cranes, labored to haul away rock and dirt, build stone locks, and reinforce the banks of the Erie Canal. Many of the workers were recent Irish immigrants who spent weeks at this hazardous work digging "Clinton's Ditch" and then stayed as farmers and townspeople on the frontiers transformed by the canal. *(Miriam and Ira D. Wallach Division of Art, Prints and Photographs, The New York Public Library. Astor, Lenox and Tilden Foundations.)*

times more to haul by wagon than it did to pay canal rates. When the costs of transport fell, so did prices that consumers paid for wheat and bread, salt and coal.

Canal towns continued to draw young men from sleepy eastern mill towns and rural villages, as well as from immigrant ships, into the countryside. Most hoped to find jobs and eventually set up farms near the conveniences and culture of growing river towns. By the 1820s, it had become clear that this migration would not merely transport the traditional ways of eastern families into the wilderness. New social and work relations developed as distances between producers and consumers grew. For example, international commerce had already spurred many mid-Atlantic and eastern rural families to give up local exchange of household products such as textiles, flour, barrels, or candles. Instead, they made clothing and bedding from "store-bought" fabric and bought more of their tools, while certain family members worked for cash incomes. One hundred miles and more into the interior, wives and daughters also made less of the cloth for family linens and clothing, and purchased more textiles from a local retailer. At the same time, many young women on the frontier continued to spin yarn at home on an "outwork" basis, which they sold for a little cash to agents of eastern manufacturers and merchants.

Mills and Manufactures

In 1791, when Hamilton proposed his Report on Manufactures (see page 269), Americans did not yet work in factories where many workers congregated under one roof, reported to work by shrill whistles, and stood before clanging machines all day. Fewer than one in ten adult white men "manufactured" items, and traditional hand tools were the norm. The workplace was often a home or a small shop, where diverse activities were performed by two or three craftsmen. At the same time, farmers did carpentry on the side, barrel makers shaved shingles when work was slow, millers ran small retail shops on the side, and most adults exchanged labor time with neighbors. Women from farms near major towns produced and sold large quantities of butter and cheese to eager consumers. Peddlers who rode about the countryside hawked the handcrafted goods of farmers, blacksmiths, and artisans. Bustling production often took place not in major cities, but in rural saw and gristmills, cider works, village smith shops, glassworks, and paper mills dotting the countryside.

The pace of handicraft work in the early republic had not changed noticeably since prerevolutionary decades. It was slow and irregular when demand was off, slow and regular when neighbors needed items. Artisans and skilled farmboys made yokes, shoes, baskets, and all manner of agricultural implements by hand. The rhythms of work fluctuated according to supplies of raw materials, as well as family and community demands on time.

But despite the defeat of Hamilton's bold plan for manufacturing and the persistence of traditional production, change was in the air by the end of the 1790s. Would-be manufacturers applauded the scurry of people to new western lands and the unprecedented energy people unleashed everywhere to "improve" their household income and comfort. They did not immediately introduce huge machines or build large factories, but instead entrepreneurs adapted new kinds of ownership and work to the existing forms of shop and home manufacturing. Some rising cabinetmakers, barrel makers, sail makers, silversmiths, and other skilled craftsmen who weathered the crises of the 1780s and 1790s (see Chapter 7) opened up their own shops, hired apprentices or wage laborers, and joined the civic enthusiasm to invest some of their profits in canals, real estate, or shipping services.

As western land prices and transportation costs fell, and as foreign demand for eastern ships and western agricultural goods rose in the early 1800s, many Americans experimented with more efficient ways of performing work and with perfecting or inventing labor-saving tools. For example, during the 1790s, a few tinkerers, working independently, began to improve the woodsman's axe, the farmer's iron plow, and the homemaker's kettle. Despite the federal Patent Law of 1790, few inventions brought profits or exclusive recognition to their developers, for local blacksmiths and clever farmers ignored the law and adapted innovations to their personal needs. Such was the "inventive spirit" that gripped Americans.

While some new products—cast-iron plows, for example—were too expensive for many individual farm families to purchase, other innovations were adopted by just a few individuals and had far-reaching consequences. Those of Oliver Evans must be included in the latter category. Between the fall of Yorktown in 1781 and the Constitution, Evans had progressed from an "improving farmer" and storekeeper in northern Delaware to the architect of a great flour mill that incorporated new mechanical devices to move, grind, cool, sort, and bag flour with top-notch efficiency. Ships pulled up next to Evans's redesigned mill without unloading, hauling overland, and then lifting grain to the grinding stones. A few workers unloaded grain directly onto conveyor belts, and Evans's mechanization made it possible to operate mills almost entirely "without the aid of manual labor," which in turn cut millers' costs tremendously. Evans substituted leather buckets and pulleys, conveyor belts, and revolving rakes for the men and boys whom millers normally hired.

Despite receiving only the third registered patent under the 1790 law, which gave him the sole right to make and market his milling inventions, Evans faced skeptical millers and contended with blacksmiths and wheelwrights who copied his inventions and undermined his potential profits. Nevertheless, Evans's buckets and pulleys transformed milling, one of the key industries in the early republic. Old mills in the mid-Atlantic region were converted and enlarged to accommodate Evans's machinery, and new mills were almost always built according to his plans. Between 1800 and his death in 1819, Evans also put steam engines into his mills, introduced steam-powered shovels for dredging canals near Philadelphia, and introduced large steam flour mills to far western towns such as Lexington and Pittsburgh. By 1840, nearly twenty thousand new mills incorporated some or all of Evans's ingenious ideas; between 1810 and 1860, the value of flour produced in such mills rose nearly 200 percent. And just as Evans had wished, flour became America's number one industry, while the number of artisans and laborers employed in milling declined dramatically.

A second innovation preceded, and paved the way for, America's factories: precision-made interchangeable parts. For centuries, craftsmen made their parts and assembled and repaired items in a single shop, creating each commodity from start to

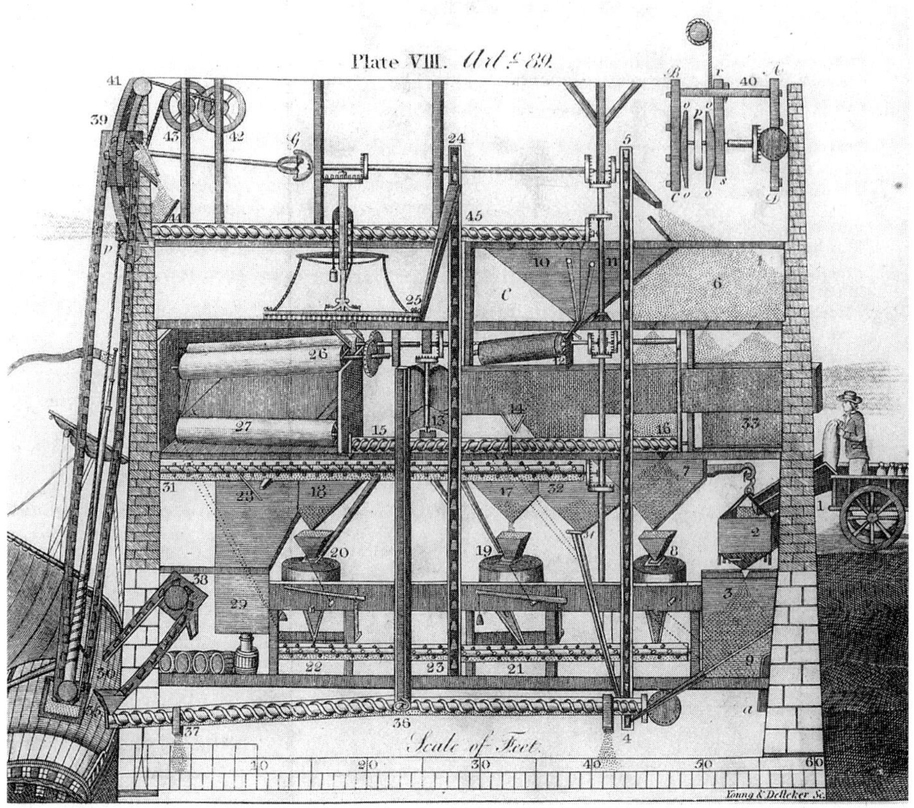

Oliver Evans's Mill Until Oliver Evans introduced a series of innovations in flour milling during the 1780s, the typical mill was far smaller than the one shown here and employed a number of local artisans. This etching from "The Young Mill-wright and Miller's Guide" (1795) emphasizes the greater scale of production and the absence of all but one worker at the more technologically efficient mills adopting Evans's equipment in the mid-Atlantic region. *(The Young Mill-wright and Miller's Guide, 1795.)*

finish. In the case of complicated machinery—such as guns and clocks—worn-out or malfunctioning parts had to be made by hand to fit the particular item. But in a couple of workshops, tinkerers strove to make milling machines that could grind each part to exact and uniform measurements. Then Simeon North, John Hall, and Eli Whitney each independently proposed that the separate parts of any product might be made from molds of standard sizes and assembled by semiskilled mechanics or, when one part broke or malfunctioned, purchased and repaired by the consumer.

In 1798 Whitney responded to the federal government's call for a steady supply of firearms "produced with . . . expedition, uniformity, and exactness" in America. Until then, both the government and consumers purchased expensive handcrafted firearms from artisans or imported French muskets that were available in large numbers, but were unreliable and costly. Whitney won a contract to supply ten thousand American-made rifles within a matter of months by implementing the principle of interchangeable parts. Whitney pretty much failed in his endeavor, however, and it was left to Simeon North, a Connecticut gunsmith, to fill the demand for weapons. By 1816, North had created milling machines to make many copies of each gun part. Within a short time John Hall was also using interchangeable parts to make rifles at the national armory at Harpers Ferry, Virginia. A Springfield, Massachusetts, armory was soon using the process as well.

These men participated in what is called the American System of Manufactures (not to be confused with the political program called the American System, discussed in Chapter 8). Their inventions did not transform manufacturing overnight, for many artisans continued to craft goods in their small shops. But larger machine shops appeared in coastal cities soon after the War of 1812, some of them owned by artisan-entrepreneurs who hired wage workers to produce the parts or build the engines used in more mechanized enterprises. Workers were taught specialized skills representing just one part of manufacturing pumps, power looms, grindstones, ornately lathed furniture wood, or smooth-bore gun barrels, and then reproduced the standardized parts over and over. By the 1820s, Eli Terry, Seth Thomas, and Chauncey Jerome mass-produced clocks for the homes of many middling families. In time, too, the American System of Manufactures encouraged farmers, lumberjacks, and miners to provide more raw materials to productive shops, while more consumers enjoyed these manufactured products because their prices fell.

A third innovation that preceded full-scale manufacturing involved the application of merchants' capital and credit to the traditional "putting out" system (see Chapter 7). Given the growing number of unattached and underemployed semirural people in New England and the mid-Atlantic, merchants had little difficulty encouraging some of them to transport raw materials such as cotton, leather, timber, or flax to central locations. Merchants then distributed these supplies to homes and small shops to be processed into the next stages of manufactured goods. Women and children welcomed the chance to earn a little extra cash by spinning yarn for merchants. Men and women who had looms could earn even more by weaving the yarn into cloth. The rough cloth was taken to mill sites owned by merchants and middlemen to be "fulled" by wetting, pounding, and smoothing it.

Putting out transformed work around Lynn, Massachusetts, where thousands of women and children earned low "piecework" wages by sewing together the sections of shoe leather that had been cut to patterns in central shops. After gathering the upper portions, merchants sent them out again to other workshops employing men who attached the soles. Farm families welcomed the piecework because it could be done between regular chores without responsibility for investing in materials or marketing finished goods. Some skilled artisans were able to endure the transition from traditional craft production to wage work by becoming manufacturers. However, most skilled artisans in Lynn who used to make whole shoes lost control over the process of shoemaking and the direct relationship with their customers. Some became shop foremen, but gradually most of them became workers who earned wages in large shops run by "bosses."

The cultural consequences of these gradual changes in Lynn were profound. As farm families did more tasks away from their land, they hired more occasional or contract laborers to work fields while they produced items for sale. Since Lynn artisans needed leather for shoemaking, some farmers in the region enthusiastically gave up plowing grain fields and turned to grazing cattle. As elsewhere, people in the coastal mid-Atlantic and northeast regions used more cash than ever before, which in turn stimulated purchases of food and textiles from storekeepers. Young girls who pricked their fingers with needles as they sewed leather uppers were glad to have "a modest contribution toward a new petticoat." Only later, when factories took young people further away from household chores, did they lament the impersonal drudgery that these changes introduced.

Samuel Slater and Family Mills

Inventions, interchangeable parts, available investment capital, and greater division of labor in the work force, all set the stage for industrialization in America. A further step toward industrialization was the appearance of so-called manufactories employing a dozen or more people. Although a few colonial and revolutionary Americans proposed factories for more efficient production or employment of the poor, none succeeded until the 1790s. Samuel Slater introduced one of the first.

In 1789 Slater defied English prohibitions on skilled mechanics leaving that country. Trained as a technician and manager of textile factories, Slater came to New York with the design in his head for Richard Arkwright's advanced cotton spinning machinery and water-powered loom. Beginning in 1790, Slater teamed up with Rhode Island merchant investors Moses Brown and Richard Almay to put together a highly efficient—for the time—factory system on the Blackstone River. Slater built and maintained the equipment of the factory and supervised the daily production of cotton cloth. Merchants Almay and Brown supplied the raw cotton. Women and young children spun yarn in the main mill, while handloom weavers—men and women—turned the yarn into cloth in nearby homes. Merchants took up the finished product to sell. In this first American textile factory, the skills of a mechanic and manager merged with the capital and commercial connections of merchants. The conditions of factory production mixed well with remnants of the putting out system.

Slater's factory had its problems, of course. Merchants from whom he bought imported equipment and southern cotton wished to be paid more promptly than traditional arrangements had taught him, leaving Slater often scrambling for cash to satisfy merchant creditors. Workers required their wages regularly, even when depleted supplies of cotton, lubricating oils, and timber for repairs caused work stoppages. Like most mills of its day, Slater's operations were set on a river because of the water wheel, but far from skilled repairmen and commercial linkages. In time, Slater grew exasperated with doubts and demands. He left this first business arrangement and went on to build about fifteen of his own textile mills during the early 1800s.

These mills generally employed thirty to eighty people, most of them children from seven to twelve years old who could be assigned tasks that required climbing onto equipment or crawling around amid moving parts. Slater started out employing the children of struggling local farmers, but after a few years he hired children from orphanages and the workhouses built to employ destitute families. Slater was not alone in hiring youths. By 1820, nearly half of Connecticut's wage labor force, and over half of Rhode Island's, were children. Up and down the East Coast, children worked in these earliest dismal, chilly factories for seventy-two to eighty-four hours a week.

During the 1820s, Slater looked for alternatives to child labor because state law required him to pay the children's parents an apprenticeship fee and to provide his young workers with a rudimentary education, which he deemed too costly. So he began to bring entire families to his mills, built houses for workers to rent, supplied looms for skilled weavers, and stocked local stores with daily household necessities. These arrangements seemed to be an efficient solution to the difficulties of getting and paying for labor. However, the families working for Slater were not always happy attending the church of his choice and shopping at stores he built and provisioned.

By the 1820s, many other rural mills dotted the countryside along with Slater's experiments. Most of them produced flour or textiles, spurred by the demand in cities during the embargoes of 1807–1808, the subsequent blockades, and the War of 1812. After the war, state and federal governments entered a long period of imposing tariffs on cotton cloth imports. By the 1820s, tariffs were high enough to protect America's "infant manufactures" of textiles using southern cotton and northern factories. That same decade, manufacturers began to cut their costs by hiring immigrant workers at wages lower than what Slater's rural American residents demanded. By his death in 1835, dozens of other cotton mills and nearly one hundred woolen mills had improved on Slater's plans.

Distinctive Lives and Lifestyles

The inventions and improvements of the 1790s to 1820s accelerated the transition from a life that had much in common with colonial times to one that resembled the industrial era to come. Most white Americans never traveled far from home, and most still relied primarily on face-to-face communication with one another. They worked and worshiped in very small communities, with neighbors ironing out their mutual concerns by personal negotiations. One traveler through the mid-Atlantic put it well: when a farmer or small businessman assessed whether his condition had improved over time, "he took his measure from the status of his neighbors—or at most, his travels to market."

Other observers remarked that commerce, transportation networks, maturing credit and banking institutions, and a flourishing inventive genius prepared citizens for unparalleled material prosperity and expansion westward in Jefferson's "empire for liberty." A postal service, newspapers, and celebrations of national holidays helped give restless Americans unifying experiences. Families who moved far from familiar surroundings enthusiastically melded their traditional ethnic and regional customs with those of their new neighbors.

Americans did not agree about the consequences of this experiment in growth. Did it unify them as a nation? Or did it underscore their ethnic, regional, and cultural differences? To many, it seemed that Americans were *both* more integrated and more separated. For all the changes wrought by the proliferation of new machines and the closing of great distances, there were still "Yorkers" in New York, "Yankees" making the most of rugged New England, "buckskins" in the western counties of southern states, and "cavaliers" on the large coastal plantations.

The Binding Ties of Commerce

Although commercial recovery from the Revolutionary War years was well under way by the 1790s, Americans still looked forward to breaking the ties of foreign dependence and discovering new markets of their own. Merchants did not anticipate that they could reach these goals by changing the way they conducted commerce. Relations, in fact, remained much the same in the early 1800s as they had been in the early 1700s. Merchants still tended to form limited, temporary partnerships and hired perhaps two or three clerks. Their transatlantic ships entered and cleared ports two or three times a year (though West Indies traders darted in and out of ports more frequently). And they relied on their personal reputations to find buyers and sellers in distant markets.

But two other important conditions gave northern merchants confidence after 1791 that America might become an important commercial nation. One of these

"Tontine Coffee House," by Francis Guy By 1792, daytime street life in New York City's commercial district had become a bustling mixture of merchants conducting business, artisans making containers and hardware related to shipping, and cartmen transporting goods. A wall of ship masts provides the backdrop to the shops and warehouses shown here, conveying the commercial optimism of the decade. *(© Collection of the New-York Historical Society.)*

was the creation of concrete government institutions that extended businessmen's capacity for commerce. Alexander Hamilton's plans to fund the national debt, assume the state debts, initiate the Bank of the United States, and develop a national taxing system (Chapter 7) allied important merchants and foreign investors with the Federalist government. The credit of the nation was, according to many commentators, tied intimately to the collective credit of its merchants. When state legislatures realized that banks provided the valuable services of making loans and warehousing capital for merchants, they chartered more and more of them. Soon farmers, artisans, and small entrepreneurs joined merchants in clamoring for more ready credit. By the War of 1812, nearly 200 state-chartered banks were dispensing loans and enjoying rising public support; by 1830, the number had grown to 330.

In addition to chartering banks, states granted many other kinds of corporate charters that protected would-be investors in risky ventures by stipulating their privileges—usually, the exclusive rights enjoyed by the corporation, its years of operation, and its exemptions from certain taxes or public claims. Corporations could also sell stock to their supporters and thus raise capital for projects such as roads, canals, and small manufactories. Once merchants began to prosper by the turn of the century, chartered corporations became an alluring form of investment for merchants' commercial earnings. State laws aided merchant investments by creating "limited liability"—or liability only up to the amount of an individual's original investment—when corporations failed and creditors came forward with unpaid claims. Before 1820, the states chartered over eighteen hundred corporations with limited liability.

The other important ingredient of America's commercial prosperity was the prolonged period of war (from 1792 to 1815) between England and France. War in Europe, though it confronted American merchants with dangers on the high seas, also offered them the chance for windfall profits. Both England and France desperately needed American grain, flour, timber products, and whatever foodstuffs were available. As demand rose, so did the prices foreigners were willing to pay American merchants, who in turn clamored for farmers and artisans to send goods from the countryside to their wharves for export. The structure of commercial relations did not, in itself, change during these years, but the sheer quantities of goods moving through American cities to foreign destinations was unprecedented.

Robert Oliver, probably America's first millionaire, began as a young agent for Irish merchants in the small town of Baltimore in 1783. For years, he studied America's trade with the Caribbean and South America as he performed his duties for the men who paid his commissions from Ireland, and as he formed safe partnerships with American merchants. By the 1790s, Oliver was ready to trade "on his own account," not only to West Indies markets for coffee and sugar, but to British and Spanish possessions in many parts of the world for exotic spices and silver. Oliver wrote that his success came from "calculated boldness," a combination of careful prediction, ambitious investments, and, he confessed, "good luck."

Stephen Girard shared many of Oliver's qualities. Girard migrated from France to Philadelphia in 1776, a man in debt to creditors in Bordeaux and without capital or connections to acquire a position in commerce. The Revolution pointed Girard toward many opportunities, but they failed one after another when the British seized his ships, debtors refused to pay up, and privateers preyed on his goods. After the Revolution, Girard expanded his links to the Caribbean, including a smuggling business with Haiti and Saint Dominique merchants that flourished. Over the 1780s, Girard fed starving Frenchmen with American flour, surviving the postwar depression and finally boasting about his great fortune by 1790. Admirers and critics alike called Girard "a walking tyrant" who "chewed up" ship captains and tenants, and who rejected the comforts of a grand lifestyle and the pleasures of close friendships. Yet Girard also improved his reputation by giving generously of his time and money to set up a hospital for yellow fever victims during the horrible August of 1793. "A rich man, such as I wish to be and shall be," he wrote, "must yet assure the public that he will not only take great risks to get his ships back and forth with goods in demand, but that he will be useful to citizens in general in times of crisis." Over the next years, Girard invested heavily in local enterprises such as coal mines, canals, and early railroads around Philadelphia.

War in Europe also provoked American merchants to experiment with new markets. A spectacularly bold venture by wealthy investors in Philadelphia and New York sent the *Empress of China* to Canton, China, with a cargo of ginseng in 1784. Upon its return the next year with silks, porcelain wares, and eastern teas, the sponsors pulled in an incredible profit of 30 percent. During the next few years, other combinations of merchants sent their ships to other uncharted Pacific destinations. Bostonian Robert Gray sailed around Cape Horn at the southern tip of Argentina, and up to the frigid waters of Nootka Sound west of Vancouver Island, where the Chinook Indians sold his dealers thousands of sea otter skins. Gray ventured across the ocean to China, sold the furs at unbelievably steep prices, and returned to Boston with eastern teas. In a few short years, fur traders would be sending shiploads of pelts back to the eastern states.

Financial institutions, European wars, and successful ventures on new shores revived coastal cities from roughly 1791 through 1807. Shipbuilding employed every available hand, ports buzzed with people moving goods in and out, and consumers welcomed cargoes from distant lands. Thousands of Americans invested small sums in the insurance companies, brokerage and real estate firms, and lending agencies connected to international trade. Ropewalks produced the cordage all commercial enterprise needed; coopers made endless wooden containers for shipping goods; carpenters built and repaired ships; sail makers kept busy; and metal tradesmen provided the small parts, hoops, chains, and bolts that held the wood and cloth together. Although many new firms did not survive the risks of business life in these years, many others prospered beyond their dreams.

The commercial revival of the early republic, and the resulting urban boom, spurred farmers to bring more wagonloads of goods to coastal markets. Burgeoning population growth in Europe created demand for foods such as flour, wheat, and rice, as well as woodcrafts such as chairs, barrels, and shingles. New towns and growing cities of the East Coast created additional demand for food and fuel from western counties.

Jefferson's Embargo of 1807 (see page 308) abruptly ended this commercial heyday. With prohibitions on exporting, most merchants would not take the risk of being caught on the high seas with illicit cargoes. A hardy core of traders kept smuggling during the embargo, but the majority of port merchants looked for ways to make a living within America. Moses Brown and his son-in-law William Almay of Providence, for example, had traded for years to far-flung international markets, but at the onset of the embargo, they linked up with ambitious small-scale entrepreneurs to start a textile manufacturing business. Dozens of merchants in New York City invested commercial capital in city real estate or western land companies during the embargo. Some commercial leaders in other port cities bought out craft shops or took control of supplying raw materials to them. In time, these merchant-manufacturers were able to monopolize production and markets for, say, iron kettles, birch brooms, or maple candy.

After a brief commercial revival when the embargoes ended, the War of 1812 put another damper on commerce. Foreign blockades and renewed (although more limited) American embargoes curtailed trade for four more years. After the war, Parliament passed so-called Corn Laws to keep shipments of grain and flour from America's mid-Atlantic region out of England. To make matters worse, England's cheap manufactured goods flooded American stores after 1815, undercutting new manufacturers. Then the Panic of 1819 put a halt to business everywhere (see Chapter 8). Merchants struggled to put their idle ships out to sea and groaned over bloated inventories of unsold goods, defaulting debtors, and a collapse of the real estate markets. Only a few would withstand the shocks of this period and return to commerce; instead, many turned their ambition to manufacturing. When commerce revived in the mid-1820s, new faces crowded the docks and coffeehouses where merchants organized their commerce.

Northern Agriculture

In 1790 nearly 90 percent of Americans worked primarily at cultivating the soil or raising livestock. Even in 1820, nearly 80 percent of America's labor force worked on farms. Indeed, land remained America's most valuable resource. In the Northeast and mid-Atlantic states, rural families still relied on neighbors and kin to help put up barns, thresh grain crops, lend tools, and share the endless tasks of maintaining and expanding farm production. No family could be entirely self-sufficient, and many signs pointed toward generalized interdependence throughout the settled parts of northern states, which extended inland roughly fifty to seventy miles from the coastline. Governed by the changes of weather, the soil, the tools to be had, available family and neighborhood labor, and good personal judgment, a rural head of household faced built-in limitations on his ambitions for prosperity.

Fathers passed on knowledge about farming to their sons by an informal apprenticeship, working side by side for years. The range of knowledge was very broad, for most families in the North still made and repaired their essential tools and household items. Because members of farm families made particular commodities that neighbors regularly needed, informal barter, borrowing, and sharing could somewhat compensate for—and stretch the benefits of—the intense personal labor each farm family applied to clearing land, planting crops, making basic clothing, and living day to day. In this sense, northern farms intertwined family life and work, the shared tasks of men and women, and household chores and public marketing.

In farm households in the 1790s, many young women performed the same tasks their mothers had, and their grandmothers as well. From December through May, girls and unmarried older sisters spent much of their time spinning and weaving. Elizabeth Fuller, a teenager in the 1790s, spent January and February spinning, and March through May weaving. On June 1 she pronounced, "Welcome sweet Liberty," and put down her tools to take up other household and garden duties. In one season she had produced 176 yards of cloth, enough for a year's worth of sheeting, underclothes, and children's outfits for a small family. Somehow, she would have to find time to cut and sew the cloth into usable items.

A few women confronted this seasonal and annual sameness, the lack of noticeable gain from revolutionary years, directly. Ruth Belknap, for example, knew very well that her condition in Dover, New Hampshire, was somewhere between the poverty she had seen in the cities and the rising prosperity of her genteel sisters. In a poem written in 1782, "The Pleasures of Country Life," Belknap poked fun at women who did not have to "toil and sweat," the "starch'd up folks that live in town, / That lounge upon your beds till noon, / That never tire yourselves with work, / Unless with handling knife & fork."

But the dream of sustaining a large family farm was becoming elusive for large numbers of northerners. Partible inheritance (see page 136) shrank farms to averages of 100–200 acres through many old areas of the Northeast. A few large holdings dotted prosperous counties in any state, but many families barely made it from year to year on small surpluses. Southeastern Pennsylvania, long held to be a prosperous "best poor man's country" was, by the early 1800s, stretched to the limit of its resources.

Under these conditions, many young men chose to migrate to western New York, Ohio, or Kentucky (see pages 295–297). People who stayed behind in New England often entered their adult years as tenants or struggling farm hands. Even freeholders with farms of their own had to adjust to the loss of so many young people to the western frontiers. One adjustment involved new agricultural techniques. To make up for natural disadvantages of the soil and loss of human labor power, farmers began to adopt "scientific" farming methods and to diversify crops. Potatoes caught on in New England, and orchards flourished in the mid-Atlantic states. Experimental crops such as oats and rye, when alternated with wheat, increased the fertility of the soil, while hay and Indian corn provided food for livestock. More and more farm families produced a variety of vegetables, fruits, and animal by-products for their own use. Retailers began to carry cast-iron plows, which dug deeper furrows with less effort than the brittle wooden or metal-tipped plows colonists had used. Agricultural improvement societies and newspaper articles informed the "scientific farmer" how to fertilize with manure and occasional crops of clover or rye and how to rotate crops, try new strains, hybridize plants, breed sheep, and graft seedlings. In some areas of Pennsylvania, Delaware, and Maryland, average yields of wheat rose from fifteen to twenty-five bushels per acre, which in turn provided millers with greater surpluses to grind for export. Many rural people in New England, New Jersey, Pennsylvania, and Maryland began to raise sheep for wool and cattle for meat, tallow, and hides for local markets. Industrious women and children made woolens and dairy products for neighbors and townsfolk.

In time, these experiments and adaptations by New England farm families also gave rise to new social relations in the countryside. More country storekeepers and increasingly familiar itinerant peddlers collected country surpluses for transport to markets far away, and also met rural demand for new American or imported goods. Along the riverways of Massachusetts, Connecticut, New York, New Jersey, and Pennsylvania, towns attracted enterprising capitalists who agreed to receive farm goods, arrange for their transport to major cities, advance credit and goods to rural families, and order new store goods from urban merchants. In addition, by the early 1800s, a number of the many landless young men in northern communities were willing to work for wages on other men's farms. To the extent that prosperous commercial farmers could afford their labor, some of these willing hands worked on a day-to-day or week-to-week basis during plantings or harvests.

By several measures, northern freeholders were modestly successful in the early republic. But they gauged their success according to conditions of their own times. Privacy was rare in most homes, given the size of families and the few small rooms they occupied (see Competing Images, page 360). Even when there was tea and a china service, families might lack fuel to boil the water; homemakers might revel that their house had window holes, even if it lacked windowpanes. But newspapers were replete with reports of land purchases, high yields of grain, investments in new farm buildings, and successful markets abroad. Visitors to the Brandywine River in northern Delaware remarked that its huge three-story mills "afford perhaps the best flour in the world." Estate inventories taken on the death of a household head show increasing quantities of store-bought clothes and furniture, mirrors, chinaware, playing cards, and other amenities. From Lancaster County, Pennsylvania, to Albany, New York, bustling communities boasted a considerable "refinement of manners."

The Old Northwest

The Jeffersonian vision taught that, in contrast to England and Europe, America had endless stretches of available land, offering equally endless opportunity for self-improvement. In the early republic, government policies made it cheaper and easier for New England farm families to acquire frontier land. Thousands marched westward out of New England, into New Hampshire and Vermont, then western New York, and into the Ohio valley. Other families moved out of Pennsylvania into Kentucky, joining the steady wave of migrants who clamored for private investors and federal government to provide "the amenities of bridges, roads, postal stops" to existing settlers and "incentives for a well-put sort of people" to move west. Above the Ohio River, agriculture developed mostly as an extension of New England and Pennsylvania ways of farming; south of the river, cotton and slavery took hold in Kentucky and Tennessee.

By the early 1800s, new western settlements produced enough not only for local exchange, but also for very distant markets that set the terms of sale and prices for their farm goods. Cheaper land, taken in huge amounts from Native Americans, lured struggling easterners far away from families of birth, while rising southern planters continued their restless search for rich soil. Thousands began to cross the Alleghenies, and by the 1820s, the West had its own communities of bankers, land speculators, developers, and "infant manufacturing" nestled along riverways.

Much of the Kentucky and Tennessee frontier during the 1780s to 1810s was first acquired by speculators with connections to state and federal legislatures, and with commercial or banking capital to invest. Robert Morris, the financier of the Revolution, snagged about 1.3 million acres in central New York for about 6 cents an acre at a time when the going federal rate for the small freeholder was $2 an acre. Morris sold much of his holding to British investors, who set up land offices in New York City and sold small parcels—often overlapping with other speculators' claims—to thousands of farm families moving west. Dutch investors in the Holland Land Company did likewise and added an important incentive for would-be migrant yeomen: in exchange for improving the land, the company offered short-term leases with the option to buy tracts, thereby attracting settlers who could not afford full payment up front. But the high interest rates on start-up loans, and the steep transportation fees farmers paid to get surplus crops to market, created frontiers of debt rather than new waves of independent yeomen. Within a few years, many migrants turned into long-term tenants paying rents to eastern landlords.

Frontier land clearing was backbreaking work, often lasting from sunup to sundown in the first seasons of setting up a farm. Poor populations occupied the fringes of existing Maine, Tennessee, and Louisiana towns, and gradually dotted the deeper interior. But frontier poverty was different from its urban counterpart: people on the frontiers tended to accept their poverty as a temporary condition of new settlements. As the first trickles of eastern and immigrant families risked hostile Indian encounters and greedy itinerant traders, they turned hardships into myths of heroic "injun fightin'" and spread stories about the bigger-than-life characters who were reputed to eat alligators raw or fist-fight their way through Indiana trading posts.

The Shenandoah, Mohawk, and Ohio Valleys changed markedly before the 1820s. The rough life of early settlers rapidly transformed into complicated networks of exchange. People of the growing river towns advanced from subsistence to modest comfort and, for some, to a fashionable life on the frontier. Farmers traded their log cabins for sided houses or even two-story frame structures. "We have within ourselves," remarked one 1819 newspaper editorial in Kentucky, "every improvement that will give us the appearance of Boston."

King Cotton Emerges

Since the early 1700s many observers believed that sectional differences between the North and the South surpassed all other regional distinctions. Northern free labor and wide ownership of property contrasted sharply with southern slavery, plantations, struggling poor farms, and enduring paternalism. Even the casual observer would readily identify the different uses of the land and kinds of labor systems. Diversified agriculture marked the northern countryside, whereas staple crop production dominated southern life. Free labor and slave labor contrasted sharply as work regimens, systems of discipline and reward, and ways of thinking. The North was full of talk about advancement, ambition, attainment. In the South, those who did not own slaves regarded prosperity and social status as out of reach, often permanently. Foreign travelers noted how the "great middle" of "generally educated and hard working" people in New England contrasted to both the "rude manners and easy solace in whiskey" of poor southerners and "passion for games of chance and courting rituals" among the planter elite.

The South was undergoing an important transition by 1800. Tobacco had always been a risky crop for Chesapeake planters. Prices depended on fluctuating international markets, and then the Revolution disrupted planting and shattered many planters' commercial connections in tobacco. Even before the Revolution, many Chesapeake growers had turned away from tobacco and toward grain crops, especially wheat. Afterward, agriculture in the region continued to diversify, as did the artisan crafts, milling, and transport services related to grain-based economies. Overseers taught slaves many new skills as barrel makers, smiths, and boatmen. But because grain required fewer intensive days of labor in a season than tobacco did, planters did not need as many slaves.

The result was a "surplus" of slaves in the Chesapeake during the early 1800s. Chesapeake slave families and communities grew rapidly during the first decades of the early republic. The slave population increased from about half a million in 1776 to nearly 2 million by the early 1820s. Compounding the surplus, the Constitution guaranteed the slave trade's existence until 1808, so planters continued importing—over 250,000 new slaves came into the country before the deadline. Fears rose among planters that their slave property would decline in value and idle slaves would become a burden to care for.

Planters responded to their dilemma in different ways. Some sent slaves to cities such as Baltimore or Wilmington to become "servants" to employers who paid the owner, not the worker. Under those conditions, slaves experienced life in the two worlds of plantation and city. Some of them never returned to the plantation, a small number eventually bought their freedom, and many tried to "take their freedom" by running away to Philadelphia or New York City for asylum in the growing African-American neighborhoods there. Emancipation, however, was not an option.

Increasingly, planters also responded to the "surplus" of slaves by separating large numbers of slaves from their families and selling them out of the Chesapeake into newly settled frontiers beyond South Carolina and Georgia. There, the lure of great profits from a new commodity—cotton—was building the demand for slave labor. In the area that would become known as the Black Belt, breaking new soil, establishing plantations, and bringing in harvests of "white gold" required a large labor force.

Cotton, known for centuries on other continents, was not a crop of choice in the American South until after the Revolution. Sea Island, or long staple, cotton grew well in the warm, moist tidewater area, but it did not thrive in the upcountry areas of new expansion. Short staple cotton was a hardier variety that gave large yields to upcountry planters, but it required long hours of labor to pick the seeds from the cotton fiber. Some planters reported that it took a slave all day to pluck seeds from a mere pound of cotton.

It did not take long for planters to begin calling for a solution to this dilemma—some kind of tool or mechanical device that would speed cotton production. In 1792 Eli Whitney became the first to create such a device. During his childhood on a Massachusetts farm, Whitney had repeatedly shown an aptitude for making labor-saving gadgets. At age sixteen, he turned away from farming to supply the Continental Army with nails made at his own forge. After the Revolution, Whitney paid his own way through Yale, but upon graduating, instead of becoming a lawyer, he resolved to pay off his heavy tuition debts by teaching plantation children in the South. On the way to South Carolina, Whitney stopped to visit his friend Phineas Miller, an overseer at the Mulberry Hill, Georgia, plantation of a Revolutionary War widow. There, Catherine Greene challenged Whitney to invent a machine that could separate the seed from the fibers of the recently introduced short staple cotton. Within ten days, Whitney came up with a small contraption he called a "cotton gin" (*gin* was short for *engine*). His small, hand-cranked box, in which a rotating cylinder fixed with teeth combed the seeds from the cotton, "made the labor fifty times less" for southern farmers readying cotton for market.

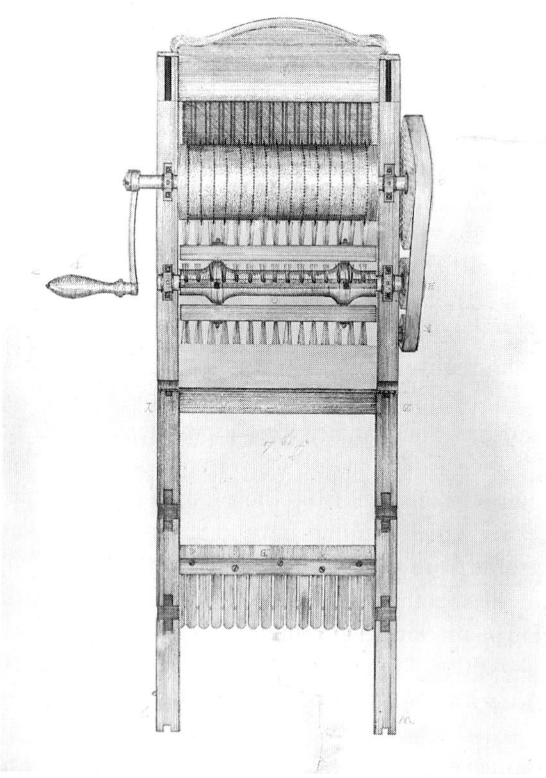

Eli Whitney's "Cotton Engine" The cotton gin, a simple mechanical innovation that planters adopted widely during the 1790s, made it possible to process cotton for English—then American—textile manufacturing at incredibly faster rates than the former method of picking seeds from the raw cotton by hand. The gin spurred agricultural expansion, international trade in cotton, textile production, and the demand for both slave field hands and free factory workers. *(Eli Whitney Papers, Manuscript and Archives, Yale University Library.)*

As the War of 1812 came to a close, England's accelerating industrial revolution stepped up mechanized spinning and weaving, and consequently consumed endless supplies of raw cotton. New England merchants eagerly sought southern staples to transport, as well as markets for finished goods coming out of northern states. New southern settlements—stretching from the fringe of South Carolina and Georgia into recently taken Cherokee and Creek lands, and farther westward into the territories of Alabama, Mississippi, eastern Tennessee, Louisiana, and Arkansas—drew planters from more crowded areas of the Chesapeake tidewater and Carolina low country. On these new lands, slaves who were experts in agriculture and planters who were well-connected to eager markets labored to produce short staple cotton.

The simplicity of Whitney's gin made it easy to copy, and thus cost him his opportunity to profit handsomely. The device was adopted rapidly and changed southern life almost overnight. A relatively insignificant experimental crop in the 1780s, cotton provided nearly 40 percent of American exports by 1810. By the 1820s, cotton represented over half the total value of exports. Only a comparatively few southern planters grew rich, but many thousands of small farmers and storekeepers benefited from rising production by providing cotton plantations with foodstuffs, leather goods, wooden tools and containers, and—paradoxically—textiles. Many northern merchants prospered from opportunities to ship cotton to England's and, eventually, New England's mills, and in turn to ship manufactures to southern states. Many of them invested the capital earned in southern commerce into New England's first manufacturing enterprises. In this way, the rise of the "Cotton Kingdom" boosted northern shipbuilding and commerce as well.

Republican Cultural Patterns

For Americans who lived through both the pre- and postrevolutionary period, the country seemed to be undergoing alarming change. The largest coastal cities were still commercial and administrative centers, but they were also becoming the entry point for numerous immigrating foreign peoples and rising numbers of poor and unskilled people, whose lives were strained to the edge of endurance. An emerging middle class also became visible in cities and towns during these years. These middling families with established reputations, often headed by entrepreneurs rising in fortune, had only just begun to define their place in American culture. This new middle class would begin to define its character and roles through the changing American family, and also in the wave of religious fervor initiated by the Second Great Awakening. Soon, cultural and religious change would sweep through middle-class households and congregations, into the remotest corners of western frontiers, and into the homes and hearts of the poorest Americans.

Immigration and Cities

Before the Revolution, North America's few thriving cities were intimate places in which rich and poor lived almost side by side. Merchants lived above or next door to their warehouses or stores; artisans worked in shops that fronted their family homes. The "lower orders" of poor, unemployed, and recent immigrants did not yet live in separate neighborhoods, but rather lived alongside the craftsmen and laborers of Philadelphia, New York, and Boston. Only the very wealthiest men of northern port cities shared political offices, which dispensed broad privileges to citizens or restricted their activities. Small clusters of wealthy families set prices for important commodities, regulated markets, licensed taverns and cultural events, and organized relief for the poor.

After the Revolution, the social intimacy of the cities changed dramatically. For one thing, cities grew rapidly and became far more crowded, receiving immigrants from abroad and migrants from the countryside in numbers that put a strain on urban housing and services. During the revolutionary generation, immigration had almost ceased, but then the devastating Napoleonic Wars displaced millions of Europeans from their homes, and some of them made it all the way to America. In the early 1790s, upheaval in the major Caribbean islands triggered a major exodus to safer conditions, including American cities. Overall, from 1783 to 1820, about seven thousand people arrived per year, most of them free Scots and Germans.

Free African-Americans, too, added to the ranks of city dwellers. Although freeing slaves in northern cities was a gradual, not a sudden and complete, process, communities of free African-Americans flourished in every major northern coastal city by the 1790s. Philadelphia's free African-American population swelled into the thousands as refugees of both the American and Haitian Revolutions flocked to the city, and as merchants and Quakers manumitted their slaves. More than half of New York City's 6,300 African-Americans were free.

In 1820 only five cities in the United States had populations over 25,000; New York City was growing the fastest, topping 150,000 by the 1820s. By then, over a third of Britain's people lived in large cities, but only about 7 percent of America's did. Nevertheless, the quality of America's urban life was changing quickly. For one thing, cities were becoming seats of manufacturing as well as commerce. Workshops and open-air work sites were being consolidated into "industries" under one roof. Milling and processing, often of the goods being imported to nearby docks, flourished. Increased production of shoes, textiles, hats, chocolate, flour, and many other items strengthened early manufacturing enterprises, too. By the 1820s, the country's largest coastal cities were poised to look both out over Atlantic ocean commerce and inward to their own productive energies.

Gaps between the rich and the poor had always been more pronounced in North American cities than in rural towns and villages. But the gap between these groups grew noticeably during the early 1800s. Most shocking to many observers was the glaring discrepancy between an upper-level citizenry that accumulated unprecedented amounts of household goods, real estate, and paper investments, and a down-and-out citizenry that multiplied in numbers but gained very little. A few merchant families at the pinnacle of society after 1800 controlled more real estate, dock space, and stores than the wealthiest prerevolutionary families and lived in far greater luxury. Although these families were few, their prosperity was conspicuous, especially compared with the economic hardships, epidemics, and twists and turns of wars that affected the lives of other city inhabitants.

During these early years of the century, the "middling sort" grew in numbers and social importance, especially in cities. Many lawyers, ministers, doctors, shopkeepers, tavern keepers, and ambitious entrepreneurs never attained great stature and wealth, but they shared a degree of comfort and occupational success, and they made an important mark on growing cities. Sometimes artisans advanced to become independent manufacturers, as was the case with Duncan Phyfe, a New York cabinetmaker "of exquisite taste and unparalleled skill," according to a prominent merchant. Then, too, there were expanding professions such as managers, stock agents, insurance brokers, and printers whose services rarely led to fortunes but did link these middling city residents to urban elites and distant places. But these links were at first tenuous, and the people entering the middling sort had much to prove. By the 1820s, the middling sort was striving to uphold cultural standards that would set it apart from the lower orders and emulate characteristics of the elite. Close observers insisted that the middling should be known by their habits of sobriety, hard work, family order and modest comfort, lack of indebtedness, obedient children, and civic involvement.

At the same time, more and more wage workers and unskilled laborers were pushed to deplorably low levels of subsistence. Eighty percent of an unskilled

"Family Group in a New York Interior," by Francois Joseph This painting from 1807 shows an ideal middle-class family at home in the North. The fine clothing, printed rug, mirror, silver tea set, writing desk, and other household items convey a level of comfort to which many Americans aspired. The division of men's and women's activities is also underscored here, especially men's literacy and women's nurturing role. *(Warner Collection of Gulf States Paper Corporation.)*

worker's wages was spent on clothing, shelter, and food for a family of four or more. City dwellers depended on farmers to come to them with most of their meats and vegetables. Prices could be high, and country producers did not always have sufficient surpluses to satisfy urban demand. Fuel, so plentiful in country woods, was expensive and scarce in cities during the early republic.

The poor made up 60 to 70 percent of urban populations by the 1820s. Their hardscrabble lives showed the strains of surviving in a very young economy that offered only unskilled work and few urban amenities. Those who lived to the age of twenty might expect to live on to the age of forty-five, but not much longer—a pattern that persisted for the next hundred years in America's crowded cities. Difficult hours and conditions of work, undernourishment, and misguided medical practices, all combined to shorten the lives of many poor people. Infant mortality was high and the rigors of childbirth often fatal to mother, child, or both. Families sometimes sent out their children to scavenge for bare necessities for hours each day.

Cities periodically became death traps: one-third of all city children died from cholera, yellow fever, measles, smallpox, and diphtheria during the early 1800s. Few people could afford the care of a physician, resorting instead to dangerous home remedies and self-diagnoses. Those who did turn to professional care might be treated to extensive bleeding, blistering, or purging. Even worse, cities could not yet provide clean water to neighborhoods. Philadelphia's water system required fee payments that the poor could not afford, and other large cities did not initiate running water systems until the 1840s. No wonder, then, that Philadelphians suffered regular epidemics in the 1790s. In early 1793, an outbreak of cholera created panic in the "better sections" of the city, from which the wealthy fled, while the poor died in terrifying numbers. Within months, 10 percent of the city's population had been buried, mainly by the free African-Americans who offered to stay behind and care for the ill. Little was known about disease prevention, and there was no cure for cholera. Efforts to quarantine people in their homes, to dispose of dead bodies quickly, and to clean up the filthy streets all gave minimal relief. Epidemics returned with a vengeance again in 1796 and 1797.

Republican Women and Families

While some northern states abolished slavery after the Revolution, few legislatures in the nation restructured women's rights or opportunities in the republic. Nevertheless, gender roles and family life changed markedly in the two generations following the Revolution. The country's astounding population growth was a major factor. Both high birthrates and stepped-up immigration during the early 1800s added to the boom. By 1820, America was a far more youthful place than in prerevolutionary years. Over half of the population was under twenty years old, and during that decade the country was the youngest it has ever been. And according to some contemporary writers, the rapidly rising number of young Americans fueled other centrifugal forces gripping the country. As one commentator put it, when "a nation becomes crowded," for so it felt in certain New England and mid-Atlantic communities, "its people move more frequently, its families depart from the warmth of kith and kin" to spread out across new frontiers. Sons and daughters, the pundit continued, reject the care and discipline of parents "at a tender age." Meanwhile, shrinking farms in New England and the mid-Atlantic continued to push sons westward where land was relatively cheap. Or, complained fathers, maturing sons left farming altogether for careers as craftsmen or seafarers.

In response to the sudden youthfulness of the country, many writers began to offer advice on child rearing and mothering. Some writers called on politicians to create unique ordinances addressing children's circumstances. Guidebooks implored parents to honor the individual personalities of their offspring and to avoid excessive punishment for small infractions of family rules. Orphans became the special objects of public attention, and during the 1820s, concerted efforts began to build workhouses and private orphan homes.

Another cause behind changes in gender roles and family life was the turmoil of the revolutionary years. Political independence heightened many women's expectations for personal economic independence and social justice, and during the next generation, those expectations challenged a lot of thinking about family roles. Some writers questioned whether husbands had the right to demand unquestioned obedience from wives; others spoke out stridently for women's legal control over their dowries and inheritances. After all, hadn't many women run households, acted on behalf of their husbands at stores and public markets, and protected family properties in the absence of husbands during the war? Hadn't many women sacrificed on battlefields for the patriot effort? Deborah Sampson Gannett, who had dressed as a man and served for seventeen months in the Continental Army, was proud that she had "burst the tyrant bands, which held my sex in awe."

In the early republic many widows continued a husband's business when he died; worked as servants, laundresses, or nannies; ran shops; or even migrated to frontiers to set up trading posts. Even when they traveled to find a spouse or to remarry quickly after the death of one, many postrevolutionary women lived on their own for certain periods of their lives. In marriage, awareness about spousal abuse grew, as did sensitivity about the vital tasks women performed within households. Young women increasingly shirked the fixed hierarchical roles of an earlier era, including their parents' choices of potential husbands. As they rejected arrangements of economic convenience, which might have brought them increased wealth or land holdings, they demanded marriages based on love and physical attraction. Together, middle-class men and women also began explaining that their marriages should be based on companionship.

Still, law and custom limited these changes. First of all, most of women's gains after the Revolution could be measured in emotional and domestic terms. When it came to property or public life, women still did not have equality within the marriage relationship. Husbands of the early republic retained legal, economic, and ideological authority over their wives. For example, few states granted women equal title to family estates during the marriage, and no state granted women clear and uncontested title to estates upon the death of a spouse. In the republican political culture, only propertied white men had legitimate authority.

Evangelical leaders also supported the divisions between men's and women's roles. They urged men to step into political controversies where they might exercise their civic rights, and at the same time recommended that women provide a stronger nurturing and spiritual role at home. In their "domestic sphere," women had unique abilities to sustain the moral life of the republic, including the rearing of children into valuable citizens. The older view that women were by nature intellectually inferior and sexually loose began to fade. A newer view proposed that, in their virtuous republican capacities, women were models of modesty, piety, and nurturing motherhood.

This new view of women applied largely to the elite and middle classes. Elite women became the arbiters of taste in manners and customs, while middling women accepted the weighty task of educating sons about "the principles of liberty and government" that they would take into public life. In rearing their children, republican mothers were required not only to teach the "practical arts" of housekeeping to their daughters, but also to instruct girls and boys in moral beliefs, personal habits, and social manners desirable in "children of means." Increasing divisions between public and private life, between work and home, also defined the role of middle-class women. As their fathers and husbands focused more attention on their public political and occupational roles, middle-class women took on more responsibility for managing households that were both a refuge from fast-paced public life and models of virtuous child rearing. Their homes would be "an elysium to which [a husband] can flee and find rest from the stormy strife of a selfish world."

Many poor Americans would have found it difficult to follow republican prescriptions for gender roles and family life. Often, they rented living space, indentured or contracted out their children, took in hours of outwork a day, or toiled at jobs away from home for barely living wages. Little time was left over for attending public lectures about child rearing, and little spare family income to buy copies of popular ladies' magazines such as *Mother's Monthly Journal.* For families who needed every hand gainfully employed, enrolling a child in school was unthinkable.

As widespread public discussions more firmly defined the roles of virtuous married mothers and wives—at least in the elite and middle layers—they also began to address America's unprecedented population growth. Back in the 1750s, New England women commonly bore eight to ten children; by 1800, more infants survived the first months of life, but the number of births was declining toward six to seven per woman. Over the next five decades that number fell to five. Thus, the population growth in that region, although still rapid, began to slow.

A number of factors account for reduced family size in the Northeast. As farm sizes shrank in older areas and young men migrated westward, the women remaining in older areas did not find spouses easily. As a result, they tended to marry later, which reduced a woman's fertile years during a marriage. In addition, scholars find much evidence showing that urban middle-class couples sometimes deliberately limited the size of their households—usually by abstaining from sexual intercourse—in order to provide a full education and an inheritance for each of their "tender republican citizens." The poor in cities did not necessarily limit family size deliberately, especially because a larger family of workers could produce a greater income. But when the rundown neighborhoods of the poor were struck by ravaging diseases, the young and the very old died in huge numbers. Parents in such vulnerable urban households could be left with only one or two children as women neared the end of their childbearing years.

Emotional and Rational Awakenings

The First Great Awakening of the 1740s arose out of quarrels in local communities and within existing congregations (see pages 149–152). In its wake, new evangelical denominations arose over the next three decades, including the Baptists and Methodists, and congregations of older denominations split in the tense conflicts. A second wave of revivalism from the 1790s to the 1820s had more diverse roots and spread into the newly settled western frontiers very rapidly. Moreover, it transcended regional differences and eventually doubled church membership in the nation. This Second Great Awakening fed on the discussions about equality of opportunity that permeated the new republic, and it unleashed a deluge of religious fervor based on widespread belief in the potential for universal salvation.

Early leaders of the Second Great Awakening believed the Catholic and Episcopal Churches were enclaves of privilege, wealth, and ritual control. Newer denominations of Protestants created alternatives that became magnets for people who were discontented with the older churches or who were drawn to the excitement of newly created Protestant churches. Presbyterians, in particular, attacked the top-down hierarchy of power in many Congregational and Anglican Churches and replaced it with a bottom-up election of laymen to church offices. Beginning as early as 1797, revivals spread from the Congregational churches of New England far into the countryside. Women left behind when marriageable men migrated westward, and facing the prospects of a bleak life of late marriage or no marriage at all, turned desperately to the awakening's preachers for consolation and hope. Some young women joined church missionary societies or charities that organized the urban poor and educated children on very distant frontiers. Indeed, in New England, women composed 70 to 80 percent of new members in Presbyterian and Baptist churches.

In the mid-Atlantic, Methodists began to decrease emphasis on the church's internal hierarchy and discipline, and to encourage widespread emotional participation of lay members, along with music, outdoor gatherings, and active recruitment from the lower ranks of cities and towns. By 1800, Quakers and Baptists, too, caught the fire of the Second Great Awakening, attracting thousands of converts to a more democratized religion in a republic devoted to promoting economic and political opportunity. Not until the 1820s, when more politicized and secular reform movements attracted the energies of anxious Americans, did evangelical fervor subside.

Around 1800, the tone and theology of revivalism also spawned a few religious sects that remained smaller in numbers than the great revival denominations, but that had an influence on religious and cultural life in America far beyond their numbers. In northern New England, for example, Universalists rejected the strict Calvinism of older days that still lingered in the Baptist and Shaker traditions. Instead, they preached that predestination was far too selective, that salvation could be universal among all declared believers.

The southern and western frontiers gave rise to even more inclusive and noisy proclamations of universal salvation for all believers. Spurred by eastern clergy who worried about "sin, vile sin, and lack of preparation for the coming of Christ," western missionary movements grew after 1800. Itinerant preachers "rode circuit" through newly settled areas or counties full of Germans or Scots-Irish immigrants. Presbyterian missionaries organized camp revival meetings throughout western South Carolina and portions of Ohio, Kentucky, and Tennessee. Earnestness, exhortation, and a hearty dose of exaggeration in the sermons of revival preachers could transport listeners for hours. Physical displays of religious conversion—trembling and quaking, calling out, "rattling" with uncontrollable "transportation to some other place beyond the ground we stood on"—infected masses of frontier people at a time. The burgeoning Methodist and Baptist churches appealed to deep emotional aspects of conversion. At Cane Ridge, Kentucky, Presbyterians, Baptists, and Methodists came together in 1801 for a days-long open-air revival that attracted some twenty thousand settlers. Throughout the new cotton belt in the Southwest, Baptist and Methodist preachers also drew African-American slaves into their churches, while in northern cities free African-Americans built independent churches of their own.

Other groups of Americans in the early 1800s also rejected the strict teachings of Calvinists, especially the insistence on declaring one's depravity before being saved. In place of Reformation-based sources for their religious convictions, certain ministers adopted the Enlightenment's message of reason, understanding, and individual free will. In New England, highly educated commercial and professional families drifted toward Unitarianism—the rejection of the Holy Trinity and its replacement with a single, indivisible God. Recoiling from the overly emotional aspects of camp revivals, Unitarians insisted that not the heart, but the head could comprehend "the idea of God." William Ellery Channing's Unitarian sermons drew directly from Enlightenment texts.

Moderate forms of rational religion also arose. Many Congregationalists resisted the intense fire of evangelicalism in favor of important reforms proposed by Methodists and Baptists. The prominent Congregationalist minister Lyman Beecher, for example, preached against predestination to his New England churchgoers. He accepted that although all humans had a natural tendency toward sinful ways, they could also choose righteousness through individual will. Samuel Hopkins, who as a young man had been inspired by the First Great Awakening's Jonathan Edwards, enjoined his congregants to find personal salvation first, and then reach out to the poor and unemployed with "disinterested virtue and generous pockets." Hopkins—and other dissenting pastors—connected public charity and work relief for the indigent to the inner joys of spiritual redemption.

Rational religion spread beyond the older regions into new settlements, too. Lane Theological Seminary in Ohio and the Andover Theological Seminary in

"A Camp Meeting at Eastham, Massachusetts, 1851" Religious revivals, often away from major population centers, immersed large numbers of people in prolonged searches for grace and redemption. At this New England camp meeting, typical of the Second Great Awakening, a number of repentant converts renewed church ties with enthusiasm and probably also became involved in social reforms such as temperance, asylums, education, and the abolitionist crusade. *(Gleason's Pictorial Magazine, 1851, Boston Athenaeum.)*

Massachusetts drew together the ministers, educators, and lay church leaders of Protestant denominations throughout eastern and western areas. Such gatherings provided a forum for discussing issues that touched many churches at once and became the basis for homogenizing matters of liturgy, recruitment policies, and missionary efforts. The American Sunday School Union (begun in 1824) was just one of the interdenominational societies formed as a result of these coordinating efforts. It served as a network for the transmission of cultural and political values, as well as a forum for extending the influence of Protestantism.

Whether in new churches or old, evangelical or rationalist, the new religious climate gave women unprecedented opportunities to take their rising moral stature as "republican mothers" out of the parlor and into the church, where they could join charitable agencies, mission societies, and moral educational experiments. In both old and new Christian denominations, religious leaders adapted republican thinking about the special virtues of women to church goals. Quaker women in Philadelphia and evangelicals in New York City set up relief agencies for the poor. Methodist and Baptist women in New England states organized special prayer meetings, some of which became vehicles for mass "conversion of souls." Magazines and broadsides advised young couples throughout the nation about Christian courting and "Christian child rearing." Seminaries and academies that combined classical and moral training opened their doors to young, middle-class women starting in the early 1800s. By the early 1820s, female missionary schoolteachers entered frontier towns as far away as Maine, Ohio, and Louisiana to extend the messages of the Second Great Awakening, as well as their own job opportunities.

One of the "leading lights of the awakened" was Charles Grandison Finney, an inspired young preacher who brought religious revival messages to the waves of new immigrants flowing into New York's frontier along the path of the Erie Canal. Life in western New York, where the canal transformed frontier life in a twinkling, exposed Finney to both the material prosperity introduced by canal commerce and the unsavory culture of drinking, gambling, prostitution, and "bald usury" that colored the boomtowns. In 1821 Finney was struck with "a wave of electricity going through and through me," which he "knew could be no other than God's pure love." Finney turned his own sudden personal awakening on the teeming populations of Rochester, Rome, and Utica, where he insisted that prosperous business families were obliged to reach out to immigrants and poor laborers with benevolence. During 1824–1826, middle-class women urged their families to attend Finney's meetings, and then reached out with evangelical zeal to help perfect the blacksmiths, millers, tanners, and other "lost" workers in western New York's canal towns. In 1832 Finney moved to New York City and carefully applied the drama and rhetorical flourishes that were used by politicians to his massive First Presbyterian congregation. "Vote for Lord Jesus!" cried Finney. Thousands did, and in 1836 Finney's "electorate" of church members funded the Broadway Tabernacle, a huge arena modeled on the theaters just down the street that had begun to draw hundreds of citizens to "godless" plays.

CONCLUSION

By 1800, commercial separation from England and increasing migration into the West carried the promise of change. Canals, mills, inventive technology, and new ways of doing work deeply affected lives everywhere. In this setting, citizens strove for the revolutionary ideal of the equal worth of all citizens in a republic, regardless of wealth and family name. Promoting vast economic experimentation, more Americans wrote about, and agitated legislatures for, the realization of economic opportunity. *Development, expansion, refinement, improvement, invention*—these terms filled the vocabulary of ambitious people in every nook and cranny. By 1800, profits in foreign trade and cotton sales not only recovered, but endowed thousands of people with new money to finance their dreams: to start up a store or blacksmith shop, invest in a new gadget, buy supplies for a frontier settlement, send a cargo to the West Indies, buy a slave, or launch a son in business. Large numbers of Americans plunged into enterprises, some recklessly and some with careful calculation.

Commerce and agriculture had only started to show more modern characteristics in the early 1800s, and so most social relations remained familiar. International commerce still lay at the vortex of economic recovery and progress, and important cultural differences persisted from area to area. Often a rural frontier community had more in common with another rural frontier community hundreds of miles away than it had with a nearby coastal city. Travelers remarked about the separate regional patterns of speech, dress, manners, ethnic concentrations, and even business practices.

Northern and midwestern agriculture was only slowly and sporadically becoming more diverse and productive, and the most crowded or land-hungry communities continued to witness a drain of young men toward western soil. Most of the North's farmers did their chores as generations before them had. In the South during this era, staple agriculture and slavery continued to dominate social relations and the nature of economic development. The spread of cotton cultivation became a harbinger of increasing differences between the South and America's other populous regions, the Old Northwest, the mid-Atlantic, and the Northeast.

But in many respects Americans still shared traditional lives, regarding the pace and character of change with ambivalence and anxiety. People in all regions still relied on the ties of neighbors and family to satisfy wants and needs. "Manufactures" were still performed more at home than in workshops and factories. Only a minority of Americans worked regularly for wages. Urban populations also coped with a bewildering array of class, ethnic, and cultural differences, aided by only a few of the institutions and services that rapidly growing cities required.

But the early 1800s saw the dawning of a great discussion that preoccupied Americans for generations to come: did they belong to a nation as Americans, or did they retain membership in a local community, an immigrant group, a church, an occupational skill, or a class? Migrating peoples of many kinds strove to "civilize" landscapes to their west, but it was not clear if they were making those lands suitable for many different peoples coming from settled coastal areas, or for one homogenized populace. Easterners celebrated their efforts to become a prosperous people, but they had not yet examined the political and cultural consequences of rapid change and competition. By the 1820s, it was becoming clear that attending to the community's welfare and the neighbors' needs were rapidly fading traditions. "Everyone knows," said a farmer near Norfolk, Virginia, "that the only job worth doing is one that brings rewards." During the next decades, open ambition, self-interest, and individualism grew. Soon it would infuse partisan political discussions as well. Americans would ask themselves more and more frequently whether their political and cultural experiment could simultaneously unfetter the individual liberties of Americans and build a republican nation.

SUGGESTED READINGS

A number of studies about early national development admirably weave together social policy and technology. See the path-breaking work, George R. Taylor, *The Transportation Revolution, 1815–1860* (1951), and the still valuable study by Carter Goodrich, *Government Promotion of American Canals and Railroads* (1960). The importance of water transport is treated in Erik F. Haites, James Mak, and Gary M. Walton, *Western River Transportation: The Era of Early Internal Development, 1800–1860* (1975). The best works on canal development are Nathan Miller, *Enterprise of a Free People: Aspects of Economic Development in New York State During the Canal Period, 1792–1838* (1962); Harry N. Scheiber, *The Ohio Canal Era: A Case Study of Government and the Economy, 1820–1861* (1969); Ronald E. Shaw, *Canals for a Nation: Canal Era in the United States, 1790–1860* (1990); and Carol Sheriff, *The Artificial River* (1996). For a more general study about changing technology in agriculture and manufactures, try Brooke Hindle, *Emulation and Invention* (1981).

The best overview of the era's manufacturing is Stuart Bruchey, *The Roots of American Economic Growth* (1965). Robert Dalzell, Jr.'s, *Enterprising Elite: The Boston Associates and the World They Made* (1987) looks at manufacturing from the vantage of the capitalists who initiated factories. Alan Dawley, *Class and Community: The Industrial Revolution in Lynn* (1976), examines the changing social relations of craftsmen and townspeople in one New England town. Thomas Dublin, *Women at Work: The Transformation of Work and Community in Lowell, Massachusetts* (1979), studies the effects of factory production on women. For the emergence of new awareness about work outside the home, see Bruce Laurie, *Working People of Philadelphia, 1800–1850* (1980).

During recent years, exciting work has been done on the relationship of society to new machines and industrial processes, including Brooke Hindle and Steven Lubar, *Engines of Change: The American Industrial Revolution, 1790–1860* (1986); David Jeremy, *Transatlantic Industrial Revolution: The Diffusion of Textile Technologies Between Britain and America, 1790–1830* (1981); and Judith McGaw, *Most Wonderful Machine: Mechanization and Social Change in Berkshire Paper Making, 1815–1885* (1987).

For the American System and family modes of early manufacturing, see Otto Mayr and Robert Post, eds., *Yankee Enterprise: The Rise of the American System of Manufactures* (1981); Merrit Roe Smith, *Harpers Ferry Armory and the New Technology* (1977); and Barbara Tucker, *Samuel Slater and the Origins of the American Textile Industry, 1790–1860* (1984). The organization of manufacturing and its effects on communities are thoroughly covered in Jonathan Prude, *The Coming of Industrial Order* (1983), and Philip Scranton, *Proprietary Capitalism* (1983).

Some of the best work on the nature of international commerce and the early republic includes somewhat older studies of particular port cities or merchant families. See, for example, Robert G. Albion, *Rise of New York Port, 1815–1860* (1939); Stuart Bruchey, *Robert Oliver: Merchant of Baltimore, 1783–1819* (1956); Edwin Dodd, *American Business Corporations Until 1860* (1954); David Gilchrist, ed., *The Growth of the Seaport Cities, 1790–1825* (1967); Freeman Hunt, *Lives of American Merchants* (5 vols., 1856–1858); and John B. McMaster, *The Life and Times of Stephen Girard, Mariner and Merchant* (2 vols., 1918). More recently, scholars have been examining the relationship of commerce to policymaking and shifting structures of the American market: among the most noteworthy contributions are Glen Porter and Harold C. Livesay, *Merchants and Manufacturers: Studies in the Changing Structure of Nineteenth-Century Marketing* (1971); Burton Spivak, *Jefferson's English Crisis: Commerce, Embargo, and the Republican Revolution* (1979); and Jeffrey S. Adler, *Yankee Merchants and the Making of the Urban West* (1991).

Manufactures, commerce, and agriculture took shape during the rise of many new institutions in the early republic, including courts and legal training. On the relationship of the law to development, Leonard Baker, *John Marshall: A Life in Law* (1974), Jonathan Glickstein, *Concepts of Free Labor in Antebellum America* (1991), and Morton J. Horowitz, *The Transformation of American Law, 1780–1860* (1977), are highly recommended.

The most important overviews of early expansion beyond the Ohio and Mississippi Rivers include Paul W. Gates, *The Farmer's Age: Agriculture, 1815–1860* (1960), and Malcolm Rohrbough, *The Land Office Business: The Settlement and Administration of American Public Lands, 1789–1837* (1968). Eugene Genovese's *The Political Economy of Slavery* (1965) offers an interpretation of distinctive southern development that departed from all previous interpretations and paved the way for intense scholarly debate. For additional views of southern agricultural society, see Stephanie McCurry, *Masters of Small Worlds* (1995), and John H. Moore, *The Emergence of the Cotton Kingdom in the Old Southwest* (1988).

The changing character of northern urban life, especially with respect to its immigrant and free African-American populations, is treated best in Leonard P. Curry, *The Free Black in Urban America, 1800–1850* (1981), and Christine Stansell, *City of Women: Sex and Class in New York, 1789–1860* (1986). For the development of neighborhoods and conditions of working people, see especially Elizabeth Blackmar, *Manhattan for Rent, 1785–1850* (1989); Paul Gilje, ed., *Wages of Independence: Capitalism in the Early American Republic* (1997); Howard B. Rock, *Artisans of the New Republic: The Tradesmen of New York City in the Age of Jefferson* (1979); Billy Smith, *The Lower Sort: Philadelphia's Laboring People, 1750–1800* (1990); and Ronald Schultz, *The Republic of Labor: Philadelphia Artisans and the Politics of Class, 1720–1830* (1993). Sean Wilentz, *Chants Democratic: New York City and the Rise of the American Working Class, 1788–1850* (1983), analyzes "artisan republicanism," and Edward Pessen, *Riches, Class and Power Before the Civil War* (1973), covers the gaps between rich and poor.

A unique study of one woman's domestic and community networks of meaning is offered by Laurel T. Ulrich in *A Midwife's Tale: The Life of Martha Ballard, Based on Her Diary, 1785–1812* (1990). For northern women's work in the early republic, see Jeanne Boydston, *Home and Work: Housework, Wages, and the Ideology of Labor in the Early Republic* (1990), and for exciting treatments of rural farm labor, Joan Jensen, *Loosening the Bonds: Mid-Atlantic Farm Women, 1750–1850* (1986), and Mary Ryan, *Cradle of the Middle Class: The Family in Oneida County, New York, 1790–1865* (1981). For southern women's lives, see Jan Lewis, *The Pursuit of Happiness: Family and Values in Jefferson's Virginia* (1983); Suzanne Lebsock, *Free Women of Petersburg: Status and Culture in a Southern Town, 1784–1860* (1984); and Kathryn K. Sklar, *Catharine Beecher: A Study in American Domesticity* (1973), which explores the extent and limits of women's southern lives.

Although dated, Whitney Cross's *The Burned Over District* (1950) is still a valuable study about the relationship of migration, expansion, and religion. Paul John, *A Shopkeeper's Millennium* (1979), is also helpful. For details about the revival movement of the early republic, see John Boles, *The Great Revival, 1787–1805* (1972), and Paul Conkin, *The Uneasy Center* (1995). An older but nevertheless useful cultural study of religion during the period is Timothy Smith, *Revivalism and Social Reform* (1957).

Competing Images

Houses in the Early Republic

Slave House *(© Collection of the New-York Historical Society.)*

One way to gain valuable insights into the variety of people living in America during the early republic, as well as their cultural views of themselves and one another, is to study their homes. Where people lived in relation to one another and the kinds of houses they built provide valuable clues about their identity, as these illustrations show.

Slaves' houses came in all varieties of styles, some African in origin and some adopted from European architectures. All known dwellings were one-story frame or thatch buildings with two rooms. Often the rooms were, in fact, closed off from each other, sharing a chimney between them and having two exterior doors. This suggests that two families, or two separate groups of slaves, lived in these dwellings. A single room could be shared by six to twenty-four slaves on Virginia plantations. However, some slaves lived as separate families with a two-room house of their own, usually about twelve by eight feet in size. On occasion, a skilled slave might have his own private dwelling. Most slave quarters had

Modest Farmhouse *(State Historical Society of North Dakota.)*

no windows or, at best, small holes cut by the slaves after construction. Slaves were often expected to add their own shelves and make benches for sitting and trunks for storage. Some dug root cellars in the interior floors or made smoke houses away from the dwellings. Masters might provide a blanket, cooking pot, and bed—or not.

Poor and middling white farm families tended to pass through stages of home ownership. Most started out with a bare-bones lean-to, often similar to slave houses, to get through the first seasons of planting or herding. Slowly, they accumulated the timber for a sturdier—though still impermanent—dwelling and a few household goods. Small clapboard dwellings in the countryside were often uncomfortable, especially as families grew. On the frontiers, the traditional log cabin or lean-to was usually a telltale sign that settlements were just beginning. Begun by the Swedes in Delaware, the log cabin was adopted by Pennsylvania settlers and spread into the West. One-room log cabins went up more quickly than frame houses did, and they did not require time-consuming planing, joining, sawing, nailing, and finishing, for which settlers often lacked the tools. In time, log cabins also became symbols of American myths of rugged individualism, frontier simplicity, and family self-sufficiency.

Working people of northern cities also lived in cramped quarters. The very high cost of shelter—rents rose over 200 percent in cities during the Revolution—prohibited most families from occupying much space. Single-story dwellings in Philadelphia measured eleven by fourteen feet, to perhaps twelve by eighteen feet. Many families took in boarders to help with living expenses and rents; few had separate kitchens and instead cooked

Frontier Cabin
(The Oakland Museum.)

Urban Working-Class Rental *(Philadelphia Historical Commission #40232.)*

Mount Vernon *(Mount Vernon Ladies' Association.)*

meals where they gathered to warm themselves, at the fireplace. On the outskirts of growing cities, immigrant and poor families flocked to tenement housing or makeshift lodgings. To create additional space for increasingly crowded neighborhoods, landlords rented out subdivided basements, cellars, attics, and even sheds behind dwellings.

By the early 1800s, successful master artisans were able to separate their living and working spaces. In many cases, their hired journeymen no longer lived with them but instead found their own poor lodgings in declining neighborhoods or emerging suburbs. Middle-class masters, in contrast, moved into single-family federal-style row housing that was both newer and more spacious. Grocers, printers, craftsmen in the luxury trades, and other high-end middle-class producers distanced themselves from the activities of markets and shops. Small manufacturers and professionals tried to live as close to the homes of wealthy merchants and rich retailers as they could afford.

Affluent urban families lived in two- or three-story homes, often made of brick. The houses tended to be narrow across their fronts, like working people's homes, but far deeper from front to back. Wealthy Americans usually had servants who performed their many tasks in outbuildings such as kitchens, stables, and wash-houses. Southern planters' lavish mansions stood in the landscape as stark contrasts to the housing of most white tenants and homeowners, and all slaves. Members of America's elite, whether great planters in Virginia or wealthy merchants in New York City, embellished their status by displaying their wealth in expensive architecture.

Questions for Analysis

1. As your eyes move from one picture to the next, how would you describe the differences in types of homes? Think not only about size, comfort, and protection, but also about family activities, privacy, and status.
2. Is the housing of poor white farmers and craftsmen, especially on the frontier, very different from slave quarters? In what ways would living conditions be different on the frontier, compared with slave quarters, even if the houses themselves are the same?
3. How should we compare the living spaces surrounding rural houses to their urban counterparts?
4. How might space have been organized in urban middle-class homes? Where were businesses located? servants' quarters? kitchens? entertainment areas?
5. Why do you think planters built such large mansions, especially compared with modest white farmers' households? What were the different purposes of spaces in planters' mansions?

10

Transforming the Political Culture, 1820–1840

Wagon wheels stuck in the muddy ruts of Washington, D.C., streets on March 4, 1829. Taverns and inns teemed with throngs of country people, many of whom had traveled hundreds of miles to attend the presidential inauguration of General Andrew Jackson. Jackson's own trip to Washington had seemed to ratify his commitment to "the common man" and the "civilizing" transformation of the West, for he had traveled down the Cumberland River and up the Ohio to Pittsburgh by steamboat, and finished his journey on a new turnpike. Jackson entered the nation's capital with great dignity, barely acknowledging the masses who wished to view him because, as he later divulged, he wished to impress on his constituents the gravity of the political transformation they were about to experience.

But Jackson was helpless to suppress the multitude's excitement over the Democratic Party victory in the 1828 national election. On inauguration day, thousands of people packed the street in front of the Capitol building and held their breath, rapt, as Jackson read a speech of no more than ten minutes. Most of the "monstrous crowd of people" could not have heard Jackson's exact words, but they did not need to. They were certain, wrote the doubtful Daniel Webster, "that the Country is rescued from some dreadful danger." Another observer wrote that this "free people, collected in their might," was "an imposing and majestic spectacle, . . . without distinction of rank, collected in an immense mass around the Capitol." Then, when Jackson completed the oath of office, they broke into roaring huzzah's and strode with Jackson to his new home in the White House.

But if this day demonstrated unprecedented popular support for a new president and the victory of a new "Democratic" Party, the scenes that followed also introduced Americans to "this new animal, this mob Democracy" that had been unleashed by fundamental changes in the country's political culture. The crowds followed Jackson right into the White House for the traditional reception, where they shed all gentility. "A rabble, a mob, scrambling, fighting, romping" pressed in through doors and windows. "Cut glass and bone china to the amount of several thousand dollars had been broken in the struggle to get refreshments," according to Mrs. Margaret Bayard Smith, whose husband was president of the Bank of the United States branch in the city. The "country farmers" shredded draperies and put their filthy boots up on stately furniture.

In the jostling that soon consumed Jackson's hard-drinking well-wishers, "ladies fainted, men were seen with bloody noses and such a scene of confusion took place as is impossible to describe." Supreme Court Justice Joseph Story decried "the reign of King 'Mob,'" the excesses that, unfortunately, had to be expected from a democracy of ordinary citizens. High society gentlemen in attendance at Jackson's reception demanded that "the hoards" be thrown out onto the White House lawn, "with the bowl of punch."

The disruptions at the White House were frightening to an older breed of politicians and social elite. They believed that order had given way to destruction of property, that respect for elite rule had yielded to a dangerous popular democracy. "Old Hickory," as campaign organizers called Jackson, had little in common with either the Virginia dynasty of previous presidents or the New England gentility of the Adams family. Instead, Jackson had steadily gained widespread popularity during the 1820s as a leading representative of "the common man" in American life, and he had pledged to launch a new political experiment grounded on the needs and interests of this kind of American.

- What conditions and values gave rise to the new political culture called "the era of the common man"?
- How did Jacksonian democracy depart from the traditional republican political culture of the postrevolutionary period?
- What did Jacksonians do in office, and how did their politics and policies represent the values and aspirations of most Americans?
- In what ways did Jacksonians reflect what it meant to be an "American" politically and culturally? How did other groups of people interact with Jacksonians to create important new meanings of "Americanness"?

This chapter will address these questions.

Chronology

1821	Van Buren's Bucktails win in New York, broaden franchise
1823	Monroe Doctrine pronounced
1824	J. Q. Adams elected president
1828	Tariff of Abominations passed
	Jackson elected president
1829	New York Working Men's Party formed
1830	Jackson vetoes Maysville Road Bill
	Indian Removal Act
1832	Nullification crisis begins
	Jackson vetoes Second Bank charter
1834	Whig Party organized
1836	Van Buren elected president
1837	Panic of 1837
	Charles River Bridge v. *Warren Bridge*
1838	Trail of Tears begins
1840	Harrison elected president
	Independent Treasury Act
1841	Harrison dies; Tyler becomes president

Popular Politics, 1820–1828

Following the War of 1812, local and state elections began to turn away some of the men whom John Jay, a Federalist and former Supreme Court justice, identified as "those who own the country." Politicians boasting great wealth, landholdings, and powerful family dynasties watched in amazement as the old deferential order gave way to men of modest means but powerful ambition and political aspirations. The criteria of personal disinterest and leisure time to rule eroded, and in their place Americans praised self-interested men on the make.

The word *democracy* appeared in the American vocabulary with greater frequency. Even before the war, preacher Elias Smith sang out praises of democracy: "The government adopted here is a DEMOCRACY. It is well for us to understand this word, so much ridiculed by the international enemies of our beloved country.

The word DEMOCRACY is formed of two Greek words, one signifies *the people,* and the other the *government* which is in the people. . . . Let us never be ashamed of DEMOCRACY!" This was in 1809; by the 1820s, others also praised "the common man" and declared that America had entered the "age of the self-made man." Privilege and elite rule were being replaced, rapidly, by middling white men who gained rights at the voting polls and in the public political life of the nation. But even as this boisterous new political culture took shape, few of its supporters or critics understood the profound changes it would bring in American life.

Extending the Right to Vote

Most of the state constitutions written during the revolutionary years restricted political rights because Americans believed that very few people had enough republican virtue to make public decisions wisely. Republicans of the revolutionary years believed that their liberty was safeguarded by a government run by "the better sort," or men who held the required amounts of property—often stipulated as land—to govern with personal disinterest and wisdom. Thus the first generation of political leaders were men who enjoyed the benefits of wealth and education.

For many years after the Revolution, most people thought that what was needed to govern a republic—the virtues of property, wealth, and education—rested in a few great men, but not in political parties. Parties, or factions, were self-interested and scheming by definition. And democracy, or the direct rule by the mass of people, would be as disastrous as tyranny; democracies in large geographical areas were inherently unstable, contentious, and changeable. Although historians give the name First Party System to the quarrels that took shape during the 1790s and the contested years of Alexander Hamilton and Thomas Jefferson, no true parties existed at that time. Politicians did not recognize the claims of factions or permanent interest groups, only of individuals. Hamiltonian Federalists and Jeffersonian Republicans locked horns in important factional conflicts over policies and principles after the Revolution, but most of them continued to believe that politics ought *not* to be based on contests for the right to rule.

Slowly, Americans began to recognize that factions were becoming a part of their political culture. Starting in the 1790s, discussions about equality, liberty, and virtue challenged the basis for the old republican view of elites ruling. Voices rose against property qualifications for holding office, the small number of men in government, and the restrictions on male citizens' right to vote. The throngs of Americans living in new states west of the Appalachian Mountains demanded political participation in the republic. One of their strongest demands involved expanding the suffrage, or the right to vote, to at least portions of this western population. In 1792 Kentucky entered the Union with provisions to let every adult male vote. In 1796 Tennessee became a state and required males over twenty-one to pay only very low taxes in order to vote. Ohio followed Tennessee's lead when it gained statehood in 1803. Constitutions written for the new states of Indiana (1816), Illinois (1818), and Alabama (1819) included provisions for a broad male franchise.

Older states in the East expanded the right to vote, too. Maryland and New Jersey eased property qualifications for voting early in the 1800s, in hopes of keeping farmers from moving West. Sometimes factional infighting among the elites of coastal states resulted in a wider franchise for middling citizens, granted in efforts to win popular votes for one faction or another. This was the case in Connecticut where, by 1817, all men who paid taxes or served in the state militia could vote. Many small farmers there turned their backs on Federalist rulers and voted for the Republican candidates who claimed to have won them the ballot. Western counties in South Carolina put up fierce fights to achieve the franchise and won it in 1810. In New York, Republicans promised to give most white men the right to vote, which in turn helped the party gain more state government seats in 1821; the state legislature made good on its promise that same year. In fact, most of the older states followed the precedents of the frontier by dropping qualifications for voting. By 1825, all white men could vote in every state except Rhode Island, Virginia, and Louisiana; by 1840, nearly 90 percent of adult white males in America could vote for their local, state, and national leaders (see map).

Universal White Male Suffrage As a comparison of these maps shows, most new states admitted to the Union during the early republic did not require voters to own property. In addition, many older eastern states liberalized voting requirements during these years. However, this increasing democratization of white men's voting rights did not extend to women and was increasingly taken away from free African-Americans in various states. (Source: Adapted from *Out of Many: A History of the American People,* Combined Edition, Third Edition, by Faragher/Buhle/Czitrom/Armitage, 1997, Prentice-Hall, Inc., Upper Saddle River, N.J.)

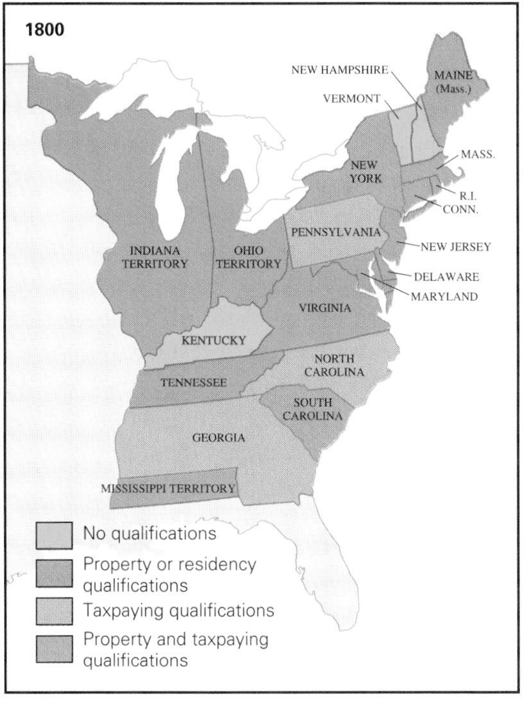

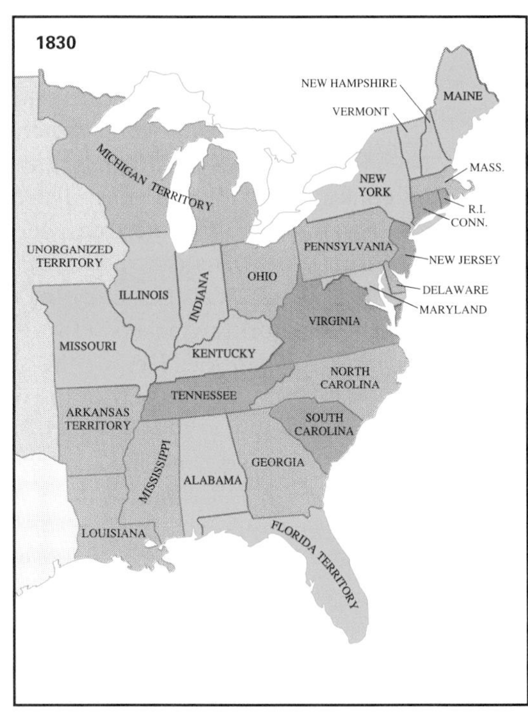

This process of expanding the franchise had a tremendous impact on political life in the nation. The visiting gentleman Benjamin Latrobe was astounded by the transformation in American political life. The extended suffrage, he declared, "planted a germ which has gradually evolved, and has spread actual and practical democracy and political equality over the whole union." When all can vote, he continued, distinctions of class and reputation begin to disappear. Men of modest means and moderate education are more trusted, said Latrobe, than men of great wealth and superior professional training. Americans had "what may be called an unlettered majority" governing at all levels. By the 1820s, others also called this phenomenon a "democracy," and extended its meaning beyond merely "majority rule" to encompass the political culture of ordinary white men deliberating together regardless of family name, occupation, or wealth.

As politics became more democratic, men who had never dreamed of attaining prestige and power stepped into important positions. But it was not always easy for farmers, migrants, and middling craftsmen to attain local and state offices. On the western frontier, for example, small farmers and town traders looked forward excitedly to electing men like themselves, or men who would be responsive to their demands for cheaper land, "squatters' rights," abolition of debtors' prisons, lower taxes, and protection from Native Americans. But more often than not, the new men who took office in state legislatures were businessmen and land speculators who helped steer funds for pet projects or important legal privileges to their supporters. Entrepreneurs poured money into buying legislative support and lobbying for roads, bridges, and right-of-way privileges that suited ambitious group interests. Bankers demanded more charters for local banks, and speculators demanded statutes to evict small landholders or squatters. In order to serve their interests, these men mobilized average voters into more or less coherent political groupings. "Factions" and "parties" had shed their stigma in the face of pragmatism, and membership in all kinds of political organizations soared by the 1820s.

Not all Americans gained these rights of political participation. In several mid-Atlantic states, legislators who formulated new voting laws neglected to discuss the half-million free African-Americans who resided there. Some states expressly denied African-Americans the vote, even as they democratized requirements for white citizens. In 1821, at the same time they were loosening the requirements for white men, New York lawmakers set very high property requirements for African-Americans wishing to vote. Despite the optimistic promise of the Northwest Ordinance, which prohibited slavery in the territories north of the Ohio River, some new states were among those that forbade African-Americans from voting. Only gradually did a few New England states grant free African-American men the franchise before the Civil War. And in the southern states, old and new, the harsh daily reality of slavery underscored the denial of the franchise to African-Americans, free and unfree.

Women were forming an unprecedented number of voluntary organizations in which they could express independent views and wield public influence. However, none of the first state constitutions of the revolutionary years granted women the right to vote (although New Jersey legislators made a temporary provision to grant white women this privilege, they revoked it in 1807). Moreover, across the nation, official policy and rhetoric increasingly defined participation at the polls as "manhood suffrage," which reinforced the exclusion of women from the polls and political party life. In addition, the formal disfranchisement of women echoed the trends that set women apart socially and culturally in a "separate sphere" (see Chapter 9).

Popular Participation

By the 1820s, American politics was not just a matter of voting in periodic elections, nor was it limited to forming constituencies to instruct candidates and watch their behavior in office. Politics had become an ongoing discussion of attitudes and expectations for the early republic's future. Through politics, Americans negotiated access to the nation's abundant natural benefits.

Huge numbers of Americans participated directly in this public political culture. One gauge of this was the great number of public meetings that involved expansive audiences. Sometimes artisans and small retailers feared that these huge public gatherings would become forums in which the outmoded elite could claim popular support for the right to rule. Sometimes members of the elite grew just as fearful that popular politics would get out of hand and "democracy will indeed take the form of mobocracy." "Do we see there the solid, substantial, moral and reflecting yeomanry of the country?" asked one critic of a large rally. "No. They comprise a large portion of the dissolute, the noisy, the discontented, and designing of society." Organizers of public gatherings, however, were overjoyed that they included not only a cross-section of the electorate but also many others who lent valuable collective support even when they could not vote in the 1820s.

Another measure of expanding public political participation was the rapidly growing demand for newspapers and other printed materials, a sign not only of expanding literacy but also of widespread desire to absorb news from many sources and to be connected more deeply to people and goods who were great distances away. By 1826, printers were adopting steam-powered presses and the public was clamoring for printed material. For example, the moral reformers of the American Tract Society invested in one of the new presses and churned out millions of religious pamphlets. At the same time, newspapers were undergoing dramatic change. Printers not only churned out thousands of copies of each issue before the news was old, they also reduced the price of newspapers so that dailies, covering regular news from a spectrum of political viewpoints, reached millions of Americans by the early 1830s. By 1835, publishers produced about nine hundred newspapers, sixty-five of them urban dailies.

In 1833 New York printed the first "penny press," which came out in a smaller format and contained a new kind of content. Instead of the commercial news that merchants sought, or the lists of retailers' goods and land auctions that traditionally filled many columns of colonial newspapers, the new press at first publicized workers' demands for a ten-hour day and better wages and connected artisan needs to the activities of the existing political parties. The penny press flourished, and soon included even more popular news about scandals and tragedies of the moment, as well as local social and political gossip, stories of murder, fallen morality, racial violence, and Indian frontier wars. By 1836, the penny press of Philadelphia, Boston, New York, and

"The County Election," by Caleb Bingham (1854) The political culture of the era involved white men of all social strata in the activities surrounding elections. Even on election day, as this image shows, gentlemen appealed to farmers and artisans for their votes, while neighbors gossiped, traded horses, or passed the time with heavy drinking. Near the humble men climbing the stairs to be sworn in for voting—symbolizing the "common man"—is a banner that proclaims "The Will of the People The Supreme Law." *(Private Collection.)*

Baltimore carried regular news about local and regional political affairs alongside the latest scandals.

Another vehicle of popular politics was the expanding public entertainments available to Americans of this bustling era. For a small admission fee, hundreds of townspeople could attend traveling stage productions and lectures, dramatic readings of plays and poetry, or demonstrations of medical breakthroughs. Unlike previous generations, who had shunned such spectacles, Americans of the 1830s and 1840s flocked to open-air shows and indoor auditoriums for performances. Actors continued to produce Shakespearean comedies and tragedies, mixing these performances with popular melodramas and blackface minstrel shows, in which white performers blackened their faces and parodied masterpieces of literature or music in racial stereotypes. It did not take long before local politicians—and soon, national candidates—realized that these shows provided important opportunities for promoting political issues and stumping for votes.

An Old Order Passes

In the early 1800s, leading Republicans had hoped to end the nation's political factionalism. They sought to achieve compromise among sectional interests and welcomed into their fold the remaining Federalists. They praised the one-party system. After the War of 1812, President Monroe strove for an "Era of Good Feelings" to wash away the contentious spirit of party politics. Factional wrangling did not disappear, and local interest groups continued to fight over access to precious resources, but Americans widely shared the desire to trade the strife of the constitutional era and the war for "the calm that ensues when all political interest dissolves." President Monroe was certain in 1816 that "the existence of parties is not necessary to free government."

But then the Panic of 1819 hit, and the Missouri Crisis reminded Americans that they did not agree about how to shape the West. By 1824, the good feelings had dissolved into renewed political disputes. The War of 1812 had convinced some Republicans that a strong government was necessary. Congressional Republicans began to discuss the merit of a national bank, higher tariffs, and federal support for development. Young Henry Clay from Kentucky and South Carolina's influential John C. Calhoun hailed from the Republicans but became advocates for important measures formerly associated with Federalists. Opposing them were representatives clustered around Republican Presidents Madison and Monroe who favored strict construction of the Constitution and modest use of national government for development.

The new style of popular politics was making the Republicans who held state and local offices appear old-fashioned. Traditionally, politics was conducted through personal and factional channels, and groupings of politicians were merely temporary expedients. But by the 1820s, thinking about parties was changing rapidly. A new breed of politicians and the rise of countless voluntary organizations that brought people together publicly gave credibility to the idea that political parties were good, not simply necessary evils. Parties, the new view held, provided an arena in which contentious interests could negotiate their differences, which in turn would produce harmony and stability in the republic. To perform such a valuable service not only to elites but to all American citizens, parties should become permanent and establish their own rules for party loyalty and electoral strategies for putting party candidates into offices.

These new views took root in state legislatures gradually. In South Carolina small planters and farmers catapulted John C. Calhoun into power after 1800. A Richmond Junto took control of Virginia's state politics after the War of 1812, and in Tennessee new men rose quickly to take over the state by 1822. In New York, voters were willing to overlook Governor De Witt Clinton's origins from "old money" and "aristocratic privilege" because he promoted aggressive state development, especially the Erie Canal. But they criticized his habit of giving out political favors to loyal family and friends. This was, the popular press insisted, too reminiscent of the political patronage used in colonial days.

A rising middling layer of political activists in New York and other states resented the persistent power of old families such as Clinton's in the Republican fold. Martin Van Buren represented this disgruntled group, a new breed of citizens active in politics. Thousands of other local political leaders were also ambitious in business, excited about the fast pace of American life, and fed up with the privilege that came from long family lineages and inherited wealth. Van Buren, whose political savvy earned him the nickname "Little Magician," took the lead in New York. He rose to prominence from within the party by denouncing lingering tendencies to rule by dispensing personal favors. Political leaders, Van Buren insisted, ought to be "guided by higher and steadier considerations" than their own individual power and influence.

While Clinton served as New York's governor and Irishmen dug the Erie Canal, Van Buren worked steadily after 1819 with other disaffected Republicans to form a faction known as the Bucktails (because of the deer tails they pinned to their hats). The upstart Bucktails won two-thirds of the seats to an 1821 convention for ratifying a new state constitution. At the gathering, Van Buren's supporters won provisions to limit the use of political patronage, streamline the structure of party politics, and redefine manhood suffrage to include thousands more voters. Henceforth, argued the Bucktails, their party should represent the collective will and interests of its members in the state and nation; its policies should reflect the constituencies that conferred authority on elected officials.

When the new constitution took effect—adding to the electorate men who paid taxes, served in the militia, or entered the employ of the state to work on its roads—more than four-fifths of New York's adult males enjoyed the right to vote. In the years to come, family dynasties built on the fortunes of commerce began to cede political authority to rising professionals, entrepreneurs, and manufacturers who expressed new political interests. Men who held offices pledged to heed the demands of constituents, to adhere to majority rule, and to give up seeking personal influence.

Van Buren's Bucktails also thought hard about how political parties could assess the popular will and how parties could create internal loyalty. In addition to setting up a party press to disseminate the party stance on current issues, Van Buren spearheaded the formation of a legislative caucus. The caucus would function as a subgroup that would meet to decide on party positions and to map out strategies for persuading members to support these positions. Van Buren and his swelling body of supporters insisted that masses of ordinary people were willing and able to form a political community that was not built on influence, fortune, or great reputation. In the new-style political party, declared Van Buren's supporters, "individual partialities and local attachments" had little place compared with the "INTERESTS AND PERMANENCY OF THE REPUBLICAN PARTY" itself. Loyalty to the party dissolved all other distinctions between individual citizens and became the sole criterion of a person's political identity. Officeholders would not be chosen by virtue of their family ties and name, their personal attachments to men of wealth and fame, or even their accomplishments in business and culture. Party membership could not be secured by gentlemanly letters of introduction or personal friendships. Only loyalty to the party machine and party rules merited consideration for membership. It followed, said many Van Buren Republicans, that patriotism would never bind citizens so completely to the republic as patronage could. Love of country and virtuous behavior "are not half so strong as personal interests and private influence." For the next twenty years, the transformed New York Republicans, called the Albany Regency, ran state politics and provided a model of the new politics for other states—and eventually for the national government.

The Jacksonian Persuasion

As state leaders were shaping new party politics, Van Buren joined a group of ambitious first-term senators packing off to serve in Washington. For years Van Buren worked hard to transform his vision for party loyalty and patronage into a national Democratic Party. It was fitting that a new kind of politician would advance his goals. Andrew Jackson, a military hero of the War of 1812 and a rising politician out of the West, stood ready to challenge the old Republicans. During the 1820s, the popular press called Jackson "Old Hickory" in honor of his humble backcountry origins. Under Jackson's leadership, however, the Democratic Party itself was never humble; rather, it helped shape the swelling political culture that professed the grand ideals of equality, democracy, and unfettered opportunity.

Gathering Momentum

In 1824 the long-dominant Republicans fractured irreparably into five factions, each presenting a candidate for president. John Quincy Adams of Massachusetts and Henry Clay of Kentucky distanced themselves from the party's Jeffersonian heritage and argued for strong nationalism and government intervention to promote economic development. John C. Calhoun began to speak loudly now for a states' rights position he would develop more in years to come (see pages 382–383), drawing his support almost entirely from the Lower South. Andrew Jackson stood for traditional Jeffersonian ideals in 1824, including limited government and an agricultural foundation. Finally, William Crawford, the most traditional Jeffersonian of all and drawing from a more southern constituency than Jackson, became too ill to pursue the campaign to its end. Overriding the issues, however, was the fact that electors who had the job of casting votes for presidential candidates tended to adhere to local and regional loyalties. This had the effect of splitting the electoral college votes so that no candidate received a majority; Calhoun dropped out of the race in order to accept the vice-presidential nomination, leaving Jackson to receive 99 electoral votes, Adams 84, Crawford 41, and Clay 37. So once again (as in 1800), the House of Representatives decided the presidency.

Congressman Clay, who believed Adams would promote his beloved American System (see Chapter 8) and make him secretary of state, mobilized New England and Ohio Valley representatives to throw their support to Adams, who won the office. But Jackson rightly fumed that he had the greatest number of electoral votes and charged the House with sealing a "corrupt bargain." The southern voice of John C. Calhoun chimed in that the Adams-Clay alliance was "the most dangerous stab, which the liberty of this country has yet received." Both Jackson and Calhoun felt personally slighted; but even more, they feared an alliance of northern and western states against southern interests.

These fears were partially justified. Once the portion of Clay's American System related to internal improvements came up for discussion in Congress, it became clear that Adams favored the entrepreneurs and developers of the Northeast, as well as the commercial farmers of new western states. Southerners knew they would fall behind developmentally if left to raise most of their capital for improvement from state revenues while other sections enjoyed federal favor. Politically, southern congressional power would weaken if other sections developed rapidly and grew in population. Joining these southern opponents were many small family farmers in recently settled areas who feared the vigorous national government that Adams and his coalition promoted with the American System. Everywhere in America, voices insisted that the state legislatures, not Washington, should continue to shape development.

Opposition proved stronger than support for the Adams-Clay proposals, which largely went down to defeat in Congress and ended up in the laps of state legislatures once again. There, the clamor for improvements created the grounds for more "mixed enterprise" funded by states, counties, and eager private interests. In addition, states became the main authority to grant special charters for the expanding banking system.

Sectionalism intensified surrounding the Adams administration's higher tariff policies, too. Southern leaders as different as Thomas Jefferson and John C. Calhoun denounced rising import duties that would fall heavily on their states. In 1824 Adams's administration imposed a 35 percent protective tax on imported manufactures, including the vital imports of woolen and cotton cloth and iron goods. Mid-Atlantic politicians and voters from rural areas expressed dismay over the duties, since they still imported large quantities of the covered goods. Rising manufacturers who understood the benefits of high protective duties were still a small group, but New Englanders in crafts and manufacturing, especially in coastal areas, approved of the Adams tariffs as well.

Van Buren and other opponents of Adams were eager to use sectional tensions over tariffs to build support for a new party. Disregarding the long-term benefits of higher tariffs, and the immediate benefits of protectionism for manufacturers and small producers in America, Van Burenites simply wished to meld together as much voter support as possible for the 1828 election. They struck a bargain between southern and mid-Atlantic voters that was probably as consequential as the Adams-Clay deal in 1824. In the first place, Van Buren's coalition proposed to help small producers of New York, Pennsylvania, Kentucky, Ohio, and Tennessee (and thereby win their votes) by imposing higher import duties on certain unfinished goods: flax, hemp, lead, molasses, iron, and raw wool. Secondly, the coalition agreed to support northeastern manufacturers' demands for an import duty of nearly 50 percent on all imported British cloth. This 1828 "Tariff of Abominations" enraged the South. Southerners complained that since they had to import so many manufactured goods that they, as a planting agricultural society, did not make, they would suffer disproportionately from both the high duties on foreign imports and the high prices of American alternatives.

Southerners also feared that the huge federal revenue collected from the rising import tariffs would be funneled primarily into the northern states. Blind to the benefits of protection and revenue for all areas of the nation, they blasted a haughty, paternalistic, and "north-loving" President Adams for sanctioning tariffs that undermined the southern way of life.

Southern Congressmen also blocked Adams's efforts to forge diplomatic agreements with South American leaders in these years. In the wake of successful liberation movements, which threw off powerful imperial authorities and moved slave populations closer to freedom, Adams wanted to establish mutually beneficial hemispheric ties. But many leading southern planters insisted that this would send the wrong signals to their slaves and backcountry yeomen, even to the point of risking "the contagion of revolt" among their own slaves.

In short, the hopes Adams entertained about healing sectional rifts within the nation proved to be a mirage. As the next presidential election drew near, sectional controversy about tariffs continued to seethe. When voters turned Adams out of office in 1828, a new political party and a new presidential agenda inherited these "lamentations on taxes." Van Buren's coalition now had to join this southern opposition to its constituents of other regions.

Storming Washington

By 1828, Senator Van Buren led an awesome political machine poised to sweep Andrew Jackson into the presidency. Jackson's would be the first modern campaign in which ambitious new office seekers would be encouraged to "run" for office instead of "stand" for election. It was the first national campaign that promised to reward prominent supporters with offices and that built political coalitions on the grounds of loyalty to party members and programs.

In the North, Van Burenites mobilized the press and appealed for support from prominent voluntary societies and artisan clubs. In the South, they claimed the memories of Jefferson, Madison, and Monroe. They also drew in the planter elite by tapping Calhoun to run for vice president with Jackson. From the Old Southwest, especially Tennessee, Jackson could count on many supporters because of his frontier roots and his long record of promoting federal and state aid to the region.

Jackson was born in 1767 to a poor Scots-Irish family in the Carolina backcountry, where he came of political age following the American Revolution. By the time he was a teenager, he had been a prisoner of the British during the Revolution and had lost parents and brothers to the era's epidemics of cholera and smallpox. But his fortunes improved when he settled down to study law in North Carolina. He moved to Nashville to acquire land and slaves as he earned his reputation at the bar and married into an elite local family. Jackson also earned a reputation for fighting and dueling, but despite his rough public persona, the new state of Tennessee sent him as a representative to Congress in 1796.

In a few years Jackson's ambitious, forceful frontier personality caught national attention when he led a bloody series of raids against the Creek Indians in the South in 1813–1814. His victory at the head of a multiracial band of troops at the Battle of New Orleans in 1815 catapulted Jackson to national heroism. His escapades against the Seminole Indians in Spanish Florida in 1817–1818 enhanced his fame among a public that overwhelmingly favored his strategy of "clearing the frontier for the advance of civilization."

Jackson's presidential campaign drew in not only every region, but also many types of Americans. "Equality among the people" was one of his most appealing

Andrew Jackson, by Ralph Earl (1833) Jackson rose to political prominence based on his bold command of troops at the Battle of New Orleans in 1815 and his readiness to use force against Indians on the southeastern frontier. *(Memphis Brooks Museum of Art.)*

phrases, one that encapsulated widespread hostility to privilege, great wealth, and special interests in law and business. Immigrants and traditional artisans who did not directly benefit from new manufacturing enterprise applauded Jackson's verbal attack against rising tariffs of the American System; to them, lower tariffs implied that merchants would have fewer costs to pass on to consumers for imported items. When Congress passed the Tariff of Abominations, Jackson won support from the South by distancing himself from what he called the tariff's "great excesses." Yet at the same time he took credit for helping mid-Atlantic farmers gain higher duties protecting goods they produced, thereby shielding farmers from foreign competition. Small producers and squatters of the Old Northwest shared Jackson's hostility to Native Americans. In general, Jackson suited the restlessness of the nation, the entrepreneurial spirit gripping every region, and the rapid pace of a market revolution that was sweeping away old social elites and making room for ambitious rising interests.

Jackson swept the electoral votes in 1828 and became Americans' first president from the West. That year more than a million voters came out to choose a presidential candidate, and the popular vote would continue to rise through the 1830s. The wider franchise, the expanding arenas of public political activity, the unabashed development of "interests" and "opinions" allied with political parties, and the consolidation of party loyalty—all of these propelled Americans toward the Jackson coalition. And although universal male suffrage was still a novelty, voters overwhelmingly chose "the Jackson party."

Patronage, Democracy, Equality

Eventually, voters adopted the name Democratic Party to identify the coalition of interests formed around Andrew Jackson. Scholars have never agreed about who rallied to the Democratic Party banner, or exactly why. However, certain Americans were more likely than others to support the Jacksonian persuasion. Men in cities whose wealth was new, men of small means and large dreams about internal development, and men whose entry into the professions came by way of apprenticeships rather than a college degree—these provided fuel for the Democratic Party revolution. So, too, did obscure men without social position or recognized family names; and the great numbers of foreign immigrants coming into the cities and frontiers flocked to Jacksonian meetings. Even without the right to vote, large numbers of working women, as well as midwestern and southern farm women, favored Jackson's promises to help their families get ahead.

Jacksonians in Washington gained the reputation of being loyal but "lacking in fame or distinction," and the president filled federal offices with them. As he put it, "In a country where offices are created solely for the benefit of the people, no one man has any more intrinsic right to official station than another." Traditional concern for honor, dignity, leisure, and expensive appearances faded quickly. In their place, voting Americans assumed officeholders should be very much like them, that they would come from the same constituencies, have the same party loyalty, and formulate policies that reflected the interests of Democratic Party members.

Out of an intensely loyal party leadership, Jackson chose an informal group of advisers, called his "kitchen cabinet," which included rising newspaper editor Francis Preston Blair, speechwriter Amos Kendall, attorney Roger B. Taney, and the president's ever-present campaign manager and political engineer, Secretary of State Van Buren. Beyond this, Jackson also expanded the long-standing system of patronage in government, whereby loyal supporters and trusted confidants were rewarded with government positions.

With the Democratic Party securely established, and Van Buren's brainchild of disciplined party loyalty becoming a reliable feature of the Democrats, it was a small step for Jackson to rotate officeholders into and out of positions, according to their devotion to building the party. Leading Democrats reasoned that frequent and regular rotation of officeholders had the advantage of extending access to political positions to greater numbers of average party members. Moreover, nobody would hold any one office long enough to create insidious factions built on personal interest.

But Jackson's methods were soon known as the "spoils system," for as one senator put it, the Democrats popularized the view that there was "nothing wrong in the rule that to the victor belong the spoils of the enemy." In the spoils system, Jacksonians did not flinch at ousting political opponents from post offices, surveying offices, military supply posts, and other positions of government appointment. What was at first an egalitarian appeal to rotating officials slowly became a system of selective rewards. Jackson and his party loyalists justified such measures as the legitimate creation of "influence" that cemented the country together against frightening fast-paced changes in the era.

Apart from political offices, Democrats also attached central importance to the rank-and-file membership of the party. The emerging Democratic Party took hold of the expanding male franchise and the rise of popular political activity and channeled those trends into the party's goals. The Democratic Party's leaders proclaimed it to be a party of mass participation that would unite Americans across geographic barriers into one grand organization. Democrats, insisted the party newspapers, would knock down the walls that divided southern gentry from white voting yeomen, northern merchant princes from artisans, educated professionals from commercial farmers. This would not be a party of particular private interests or rival elites, but rather inclusive and attentive to public opinion. This would be a party of "the common man."

At the same time, many Americans argued that the Democratic Party would provide an umbrella over the great variety of voluntary societies and contending voices rising from the unleashed energies of the early republic. The Democratic Party would give Americans a unifying voice, with a national structure. In place of the horrifying prospect that huge numbers of separate interest groups would clash, and eventually self-destruct, in their aggressive selfishness, the Democratic Party would coordinate equality of opportunity.

Slowly, deference toward a would-be American elite gave way to a boisterous political culture based on representative government by "the common people." Admitting that equal wealth and equal reputations among people were impossible in so diverse and vast a country, many writers nevertheless insisted that the legal and civil rights conferred by representative government should fall equally on all citizens. William Findley had heralded this attitude in the 1780s when he said "no man has a greater claim of special privilege for his £100,000 than I have for my £5." From Connecticut, Abraham Bishop wrote that ordinary people had too long felt the "humiliation" of "wealth and power . . . a leading cause of all the slavery on earth." Rule by the traditional gentry could not endure, he believed, for Americans were progressively shedding their "fear and awe" of the elite, the "delusions" of the past which made the majority into fawning sheep of the "well fed, well dressed, chariot rolling, caucus keeping" elite of his New England. Once upon a time, Americans had believed in rule by "the better sort of people." But now, this notion was "thoroughly contemptible and odious," for "the people rule themselves."

Bishop, like so many enthusiastic optimists of his era, exaggerated. To opponents, Jacksonian patronage was a form of political favoritism; the rhetoric of mass participation did not guarantee any particular mandate for policymaking; and talk of democracy and equality all too often turned out to be more like wishful thinking than social reality. Still, Jacksonian rhetoric and the Democratic Party gave meaning and hope to huge numbers of Americans who wanted to participate and prosper in the early republic.

The Experiment in Action, 1829–1836

The Democratic Party developed a mass organization that prided itself on supporting democratic ideals of widespread suffrage and political participation, as well as greater economic and social opportunity for new and ambitious interests. In addition, many Americans believed it was essential to expand the country's territorial influence and increase its economic development. But Americans had still not worked out how much power the government should have to fulfill those goals. Once in office, Jackson had few misgivings about exercising extensive executive power to achieve the conditions he believed appropriate to those ideals. Jackson boldly relocated whole peoples, destroyed central national institutions, and attacked major components of the American System.

Indian Removal

Removing Indians from their homelands to distant places was not new; it had been going on for generations of European settlement in North America. Following the American Revolution, land-hungry settlers applied intense pressure on Native Americans in the Ohio and Mohawk Valleys. Treaties repeatedly attempted to set boundaries between peoples and to establish political and territorial rights that distinguished between Americans and "foreign nations" of Indians. Giving up land for a limited degree of sovereignty suited many Native Americans because the exchange tended to avert further destructive wars. But they paid an extremely high price for accepting the lesser evil of treaties: relocation to reservations—land with fixed boundaries that was often distant from their original homelands—and the shrinking size of their "nations."

During the War of 1812, Andrew Jackson began a phase of systematic violation of the foreign nations theory. Instead of negotiating treaties, he insisted that Indians were the "subjects" of the United States and led expeditions against the Creek who lived in Tennessee, Georgia, and Alabama, taking millions of acres of new land. John Quincy Adams tried to support the rights of Native Americans in southern states during his presidency. But popular and planter pressure to take ever more land thwarted his efforts. So, too, did missionaries who believed that establishing separate reservations neglected the responsibility of Americans to assimilate and "civilize" Native Americans. With Congress's support, starting in 1819, missionaries gained huge public funds and the government's blessing to teach in Indian schools, convert villages, and train the native people west of the Ohio River in "settled agricultural ways."

By the 1820s, then, competing views vied for favor and put the future of Native Americans in jeopardy. Few experts could answer the recurring question: What kind of political, legal, and social relationship would American citizens have with the quarter-million Indians resident on land claimed by both peoples? The answer was easy for southern planters who wanted to expand cotton production onto Indian lands, and elsewhere a widespread commitment to racial inequality and popular demand for "opening the West" bolstered their view. Jackson readily accepted the intricate web of economic development, westward expansion, white male democracy, Indian dispossession, and slavery.

Policies and beliefs reached a new stage when, in 1825, national officials and a group of Creek Indians signed a treaty to cede extensive land to the state of Georgia. When the Creek National Council repudiated the deal made by only a small number of their members and vowed not to move from their lands, Georgia's Governor George M. Troup appealed to Congress to enforce the treaty. He blamed the Creek resistance on Adams's earlier desire to be an "unblushing ally of the savages." Soon Congress extinguished all Creek land claims, based on the 1825 treaty, and state troops removed reluctant Creek to new homes farther west.

This pattern of disputed claims and eventual forcible removal of Native Americans would be repeated over and over for years to come. By the late 1820s, white westerners clamored for extensive resettlement of Native Americans to lands far west of the Mississippi River. Some advocates of removal wished simply to clear the land of "heathens," often coupling their demands with racist intonations to white Americans' "civilizing" influences. Others, including President Jackson, believed that the only humanitarian response to the "inevitable march of American empire," which was the American republic's right and proper goal, was to help relocate Native Americans for their own protection.

In 1827 the Cherokee, whose land covered portions of Tennessee, Georgia, Mississippi, and Alabama, met in council and adopted a constitution inspired by American representative government. They then proceeded to declare themselves a separate nation within the boundaries of the United States. The Georgia legislature, already practiced in removing the Creek, would have none of this "independency" and retorted that the Cherokee lived as the guests of the state, protected by federal troops at Americans' expense. When Cherokee leaders appealed to Jackson for support, he stated flatly that any state of the American union was "sovereign over the people within its borders." To underscore the rights of individual states, he also recalled federal troops that had been protecting the Cherokee, and in 1830 he urged Congress to hurry passage of an Indian Removal Act, which offered Native Americans new lands west of the Mississippi River in return for abandoning their ancient claims in the southeastern states (see map).

A small group of Cherokee accepted the terms of this offer, exchanging about 100 million acres of eastern land for $68 million and about 32 million acres of land "with clear title forever" in the West. Other Cherokee, however, stood firm. The following year, leaders of many villages defended their claim to be recognized by the federal government as a separate nation according to provisions in the U.S. Constitution; their case, *Cherokee Nation* v. *Georgia,* reached the Supreme Court in 1831. There, Chief Justice John Marshall struck down the Cherokee definition of their status and declared all Indians within the United States to be "domestic dependent nations" that could not enjoy full recognition as separate foreign governments. So far, Jackson and northern Democrats were satisfied that the court denied Cherokee claims.

But in an appeal case, *Worcester* v. *Georgia* (1832), Marshall went on to rule with the majority of the Court that the state of Georgia could not exert its state law

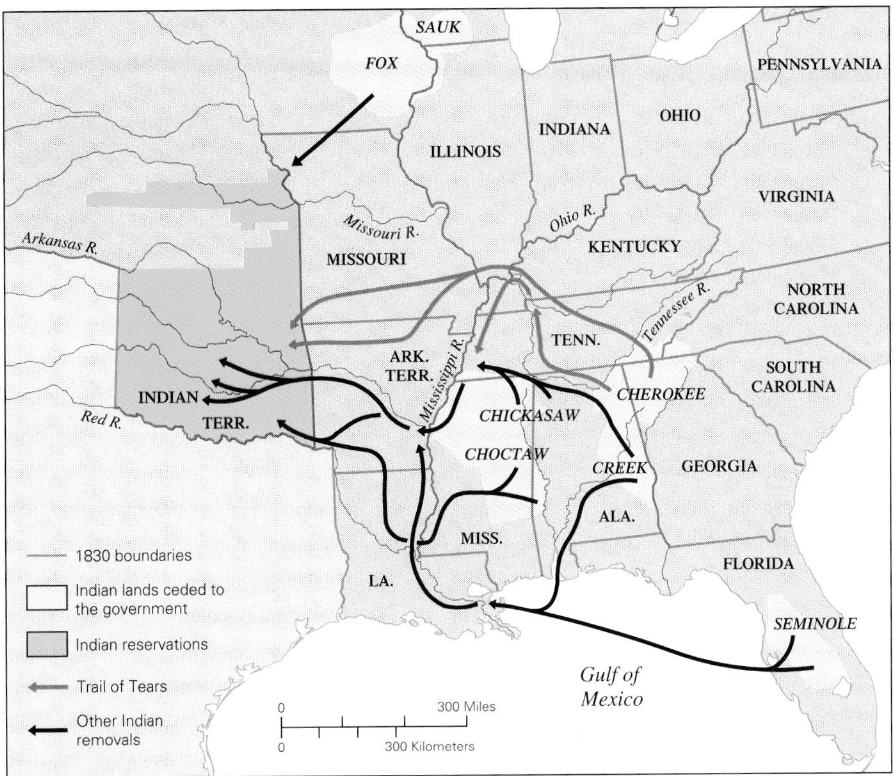

Indian Removal in the 1830s Jacksonian policies established a large Indian reserve west of the Mississippi River, which became the new residence of numerous eastern peoples. The Cherokee called their forced migration to this reservation the Trail of Tears.

against the Cherokee, for they had "territorial boundaries, within which their authority is exclusive" and protected by the laws of the federal government. This time, the decision to place the destiny of the Cherokee in federal hands quickly drew Jackson's wrath. "John Marshall has made his decision," Jackson supposedly fumed; "now let him enforce it."

Jackson tested the Indian Removal Act in 1832 when he ordered federal troops into western Illinois to forcibly remove Chief Black Hawk and the Sauk and Fox peoples following him. For years, tensions had been seething between these Native American people and the rising tide of new settlers. Now, when Jackson increased pressure on Native Americans by applying the federal law and sending troops onto that frontier, Black Hawk refused to be removed to lands across the Mississippi. He fled with whole villages, including about 1,000 warriors, into Wisconsin Territory, and on August 3 lost nearly 850 Indians in a brutal daylong massacre at Bad Axe.

Farther south, the Cherokee and Seminole peoples resisted the same strategy of forcible removal by federal troops. In Florida the Seminole recruited runaway slaves, fur trappers, and Spanish allies to fight federal troops and the state militia in a guerrilla war that lasted nearly a decade. Although about 2,000 Cherokee began to leave their ancestral lands under the terms of the earlier treaty signed by a minority of their people, over 17,000 Cherokee remained to resist General Winfield Scott's army beginning in early summer 1838. Scott's troops forced about 14,000 Cherokee to begin a brutal march that covered over 1,200 miles. Three thousand Indians, mostly the aging and very young, starved or died of exposure (see Competing Voices, page 401). The designated "Indian Territory," in today's Oklahoma, became home to a few thousand remaining demoralized Cherokee. Their miserable march is remembered as the "Trail of Tears."

Tariffs

Jacksonians often proclaimed that the national government should have diminished power over citizens. President Jackson understood this to be a mandate for cutting back, and maybe ending, federal support for internal improvements under the American System. His most direct means for doing this was to use the executive veto power to reject congressional proposals for aid. In fact, Jackson used his executive veto power more than all presidents before him combined.

In 1830, for example, he vetoed the Maysville Road bill, a favored project of Henry Clay's that would have used congressional money to expand the National Road through the Cumberland Gap. Advocates from the West proposed tapping federal funds to extend the road from Maysville, Ohio, to Lexington, Kentucky. But Jacksonian voices insisted such improvements should stay in the hands of states. Using federal funds for projects that Jackson believed would benefit particular state interests and were not a clear national interest not only drained the government of precious revenue, but also gave new meaning to the pre-Revolutionary Republican fears of corruption. Jacksonians further feared that to generate federal funds for projects associated with the American System, politicians clustered around Clay would seek higher and higher federal taxes on commerce. "Republican principles," declared Jackson, required a reduction of taxes and abolition of the national debt. Most important, states and their citizens, and not the national government, should decide how to invest their money.

Following the Maysville veto, Jacksonians set out to dismantle other parts of the American System, including protective tariffs and national banking. Jacksonians inherited Congress's 1828 Tariff of Abominations. During the campaign, Jackson had denounced aspects of the tariff (although he had supported some measures of the law), gaining many votes for the Democrats as a result. But once he was president, Jackson could not ignore the sectional tensions created by rising import duties. South Carolina was particularly anxious that northern and western interests had combined to harm southern interests. Living in perpetual fear of slave revolts and lurching international prices for their staples, southern planters nevertheless focused the blame for their precarious situation on the import duties that had been rising with each new national tariff law.

Calhoun returned to his state of South Carolina after the election to organize protest against the new Tariff of Abominations. He authored a pamphlet (anonymously, since he was then vice president), *The South Carolina Exposition and*

Protest, which condemned the tariff and pronounced the doctrine of nullification. The doctrine had a long theoretical pedigree, dating at least from Antifederalist opposition to the creation of a strong national government in the 1780s, and involving no lesser men than Jefferson and Madison when they had objected strongly to the use of national power in the Alien and Sedition Acts of 1798 (see page 288). For decades, in fact, dissenting interests had argued against the unjust and unconstitutional creation of national powers that annihilated states' rights. Now, in 1828, Calhoun declared that the national government rested its authority on the false claim that somehow it embodied "the will of the people," or the sovereignty of all Americans collectively. Such sovereignty could not exist, according to Calhoun, because the states were prior to, and continued to hold more authority than, the national government. As a consequence, true sovereignty could reside only in the people acting through their state governments. States were thus perfectly justified in forming special conventions to decide whether to support or nullify—to make void within that state—any national law. Even if the weight of most other states were brought to bear against a particular state's nullification, the latter's actions were, insisted Calhoun, perfectly constitutional. In addition, the dissenting state always held the right to secede from the republic.

Despite his resolve to decrease the authority of the national government and correct the upward rise of tariffs, Jackson opposed South Carolinian efforts to nullify an act of Congress in the name of states' rights. In early 1830, Jackson and Calhoun sat in on a congressional debate over the issue. Senator Robert Hayne of South Carolina rose to defend nullification, expressing fears that the North represented only one part of the nation's people and goods. Indeed, he continued, the North wished to crush other regions of the nation, especially the South, under the weight of oppressive tariffs. Senator Daniel Webster replied in a speech lasting nearly two days. The republic, he declared, was not a compact of states but of all citizens. Webster posed the horrible specter of Americans drenched in blood if states started to separate from the republic. Personal and collective liberty could not be secured with each state acting on its own, Webster insisted. In defense of a national perspective, and congressional policies, Webster demanded "liberty *and* Union, now and forever, one and inseparable."

Calhoun and Jackson listened intently to this Webster–Hayne debate, which had extended the issue of tariffs to the much weightier matter of states' rights, which in turn developed into a sectional argument about federal powers over western lands and slavery. Fearing that the web of interrelated issues could divide the Union, Jackson quickly announced his reply about the tariffs and the impending nullification crisis: "Our Union. It must be preserved!"

But in 1832, Congress exacerbated southern fears by passing yet another tariff that increased duties on imported cloth and iron goods, and although the new law removed some of the "abominations" of the 1828 tariff, it did not significantly lower rates. South Carolina's governor and legislature immediately contested the measure as an assault against the southern way of life. In November 1832, a convention of businessmen and planters in the state adopted an Ordinance of Nullification, which declared the tariffs of both 1828 and 1832 null and void. The ordinance further declared that port officials would not collect those duties in South Carolina after February 1, 1833.

Jackson's reply was swift and firm. South Carolina's ordinance, Jackson intoned, broke with the principles of the federal Constitution and was "unauthorized by its spirit, inconsistent with every principle on which it is founded, and destructive of the great object for which it was formed." In January 1833, he asked Congress for a Force Act to use the army and navy against southern violators and threatened to invade South Carolina to enforce national law, if necessary.

At the same time, Jackson agreed to help Congress move in the direction of reducing tariffs, thereby permitting South Carolina to save face, rescind its nullification ordinance, and keep peace in the union. Calhoun, disturbed by the turn of events toward physical confrontation, resigned as vice president, got himself elected to the U.S. Senate, and worked with Henry Clay to create a plan of reduced duties for the Tariff of 1833. When their compromise tariff passed in March in Congress, sectional interests quieted temporarily.

Banks

While disputes over tariffs built toward the nullification crisis, Jackson and his supporters became embroiled in equally divisive disputes over the national bank. Since 1816, the Second Bank of the United States had operated with a twenty-year charter from Congress; the government owned 20 percent of the stock. Many supporters of the national Bank agreed that it helped control the flow of money in the country and that it checked the tendency of state banks to issue too much paper money. The Bank did this by periodically calling in state loans and requiring the state banks to have a sufficient supply of specie, or gold and silver, on hand to cover their financial obligations to depositors and the national bank.

Through the 1820s, the Bank was successful in these functions. However, by the end of the decade the land- and credit-hungry settlers of the Midwest were demanding more credit from their infant local banks than the institutions could support. When the national Bank began to call in large amounts of the paper credit issued by these local midwestern banks, farmers and shopkeepers on the frontier suddenly felt pinched to repay loans for real estate and businesses. Longer-term development, and their immediate survival, they complained, was being stymied by "eastern monopolies" with control over their purse-strings.

Settlers' hostility to the Bank had deep roots in the past, even before the American Revolution, and had been nurtured through the subsequent decades of conflict between central and local institutions. By the late 1820s, western fears of being controlled by bankers and brokers hundreds of miles away grew volatile. Few Americans truly understood the regulatory functions of the Bank. They usually simply feared its authority to close the local institutions that gave them credit for purchases of land and farm supplies. Without that credit, another panic, like the one of 1819 and its ensuing depression, would be the inevitable result.

Another group of Bank opponents included wealthy easterners and leaders of chartered banks in the Midwest, who wished to create powerful competing state institutions over which they could wield control. It was not large banking per se, but the Bank of the United States and its president, Nicholas Biddle, in particular, that drew their angry protests. As friends of Jackson, they appealed to the national government to reallocate banking power to the states.

The charter of the Bank would expire in 1836, but in 1832 Biddle's supporters, including Henry Clay and Daniel Webster in Congress, sought an early recharter of the Bank of the United States. In moving early, they anticipated they represented a majority point of view. Banks were springing up everywhere that businesses operated and settlers arrived in America. They dispersed paper money, gave liberal credit, and expanded public confidence in bold development projects. Bank loans "knitted people together as tightly as roads and canals," observed one traveler to Ohio. They helped unleash more of the burgeoning energy of myriad Americans who had a lot of imagination but very little capital. And at the center of it all, the national Bank helped build confidence that central government existed in partnership with citizens.

However, when Congress framed a new charter for the Bank of the United States in July 1832, Jackson and his supporters rejected the bill with a thundering NO. Jackson vetoed the proposal for recharter, despite predictions that such an action could cost him the popular support he needed for the next presidential election. Further, he sealed his veto with a stinging public pronouncement of his views about the Bank. In a veto message that summarized the Jacksonian insistence on restricting the scope of federal institutions, Jackson invoked both constitutional principles and popular mythology about the Bank. Following Jefferson's strict construction of the Constitution, Jackson insisted that Congress lacked the authority to charter a national bank at all. Pointing to foreign investments in the Bank, Jackson evoked strong nationalist fervor favoring only "purely American" institutions. Borrowing from the anti-Bank rhetoric of previous generations, Jackson also convinced his audience that national banks were "subversive of the rights of the States" and "dangerous to the liberties of the people" because they embodied special privileges and shut out "the farmers, mechanics, and laborers" of the republic. When the Senate failed to override Jackson's veto, the proposal to recharter the Bank went down to defeat.

Jackson's veto message, as well as his firm stance against the unfolding crisis with South Carolina, electrified the political process during the presidential election of 1832. Jacksonians built an emotional appeal and carried it directly to voters. For the first time in American history, parties developed platforms and used party conventions to nominate candidates. Henry Clay's National Republican (forerunners of the Whig Party) ticket won only 49 electoral votes, while Jackson's Democratic slate tallied 219. It was clear to most observers that the Democrats swept up the support of northeastern working men, western farmers, rising entrepreneurs, shopkeepers, and ambitious professionals who favored Jacksonian attacks against privilege and Jacksonian promises of economic opportunity.

Riding on this crest of electoral support, Jackson moved boldly in 1833 to squelch the existing Bank before its charter expired. Declaring that his electoral victory was a mandate to "kill the Bank," and not waiting for congressional approval, Jackson appointed his friend and adviser, Roger B. Taney, as secretary of the treasury

"The Race Over Uncle Sam's Course," by David Claypool (1833) In this pro-Whig cartoon, Henry Clay and his American System are winning the race for national excellence and political control of the White House. Jackson stumbles over the ruins of the national Bank he has destroyed with the presidential veto, while Martin Van Buren, not a "Little Magician" but rather a monkey, faces toward the past and clings to the tail of the Democratic Party. Notice Jackson's Napoleonic cap and feather, representing his military dignity earned in the war of 1812, are flying off his head. *(Trustees of the Boston Public Library.)*

and instructed him to remove the government's gold and silver reserves from the Bank. This had the effect of removing the secure backing for printed money and threw banking into disarray. Taney ordered the specie to be deposited in selected state banks, soon known as Jackson's "pet banks."

Nicholas Biddle, director of the Bank, was outraged over these measures and set out to use the Bank to puncture Jackson's popularity. In very early 1834, Biddle called in bank loans to merchants and developers in the Northeast, hoping to tighten credit and make business leaders angry with Jackson. Biddle's maneuver succeeded in turning business leaders against Jackson, but it also threw the country into a sharp recession when credit networks collapsed near the end of the year.

While Biddle acted through the Bank, Jackson's congressional opponents introduced a resolution to censure the president. In March, Henry Clay, the resolution's author, sternly warned that the Bank crisis was "a war." "We are in the midst of a revolution, hitherto bloodless, but rapidly descending towards a total change of the pure republican character of the Government, and the concentration of all power in the hands of one man." Bank opponents, however, could not hold back Jackson's plan to destroy "the monster institution." By 1836, Jackson and his supporters had transformed the Bank's headquarters in Philadelphia into a state bank, thus symbolically affirming that Jacksonians had accomplished one of their major objectives.

Changing Legal Doctrines

Related to Jackson's goal of annihilating a "monster institution" such as the Bank was his intent to create power and privilege for new economic interests emerging throughout the nation by the 1820s, some of which were still fragile. The courts proved to be a useful vehicle for this "creative destruction" of "ancient rights," especially in one important Supreme Court case.

In 1785 the Massachusetts legislature had given to a corporation called the Proprietors of the Charles River Bridge the right to put up a bridge linking Charlestown to Boston. For years the proprietors enjoyed exclusive privileges to channel citizens across their bridge and to collect tolls for its maintenance. But then in 1828, the state government permitted a consortium of Boston merchants to build a rival Warren Bridge. The proprietors of the first bridge sued the new corporation, charging that their original contract gave them permanent exclusive privileges according to the U.S. Constitution's "necessary and proper" provisions in Article I, section 10 (see page 291).

Daniel Webster agreed that the Charles River Bridge Proprietors had an "original vested property right" in the bridge and argued their case. In 1837 the case made it all the way to the U.S. Supreme Court, where Justice Joseph Story wrote the minority opinion supporting Webster's reasoning about the Proprietors. As Story insisted, when the exclusive privileges granted by one legislature could be taken away by a subsequent one, there was "no surer plan to arrest all public improvements founded on private capital and enterprise." Projects that protected and furthered the public welfare, he went on, were far more important than the whims of changeable political bodies. Even when men made personal profits by investing their capital, they most likely promoted the public welfare and deserved the court's support. "There must be some pledge that the property will be safe," Story argued. These words seemed to echo what the Federalist and nationalist Chief Justice John Marshall might have argued had he not died in 1835.

However, in *Charles River Bridge* v. *Warren Bridge,* the majority of the Supreme Court did not share this older view of contracts and private property. Instead, the forceful reasoning of Roger B. Taney swayed a majority of the justices to knock down the old charter. Taney, hand-picked by his close friend Andrew Jackson to be the new chief justice, scoffed at the notion of protecting old property rights against the creative impact of new ones. It was the duty of courts to set aside outmoded contracts and thereby promote development. Unless the courts could use such a power, "we shall be thrown back to the improvements of the last century," Taney reasoned, "and obliged to stand still." New bridges, turnpikes, and canals "are now adding to the wealth and prosperity, and the convenience and comfort" precisely because new interest groups can hope to gain their own charters for development projects. This argument for dynamic growth, or "creative destruction" of exclusive property rights, would have far-reaching consequences for businesses, technologies, and railroads in the years to come.

The Taney Court championed other decisions that paved the way for the state governments to charter new privileges or waive legal obligations for fragile new enterprises. In *Briscoe* v. *Bank of Kentucky* (1837), for example, the Court ruled that despite constitutional prohibitions against the states issuing their own currencies, a state-chartered bank could issue notes and regulate their circulation. In addition, the Court supported movements in many of the states to chip away at chartered monopolies, contractual arrangements, and legislative statutes formulated for powerful groups of citizens. In so doing, the Court applauded efforts to allow more business risk and let individuals enjoy, and profit from, more "democracy of the market place."

Dissenting Strains, 1832–1840

Jacksonian democracy did not shape every aspect of the new American self and society. It faced competing ideals in the popular culture, in some religions, and among economic interests. In politics, dissent from Jacksonian policies did not at first take shape as a rival party, but by 1832, opponents of Jackson and the Democratic Party began to rally together in significant numbers. At first they clustered around aspects of the American System, affirming that the government should have a strong role in economic development. In Congress, some outspoken critics adopted the name Whigs to symbolize a return to the spirit of late-colonial opposition to the arbitrary power of Parliament and the crown. Eventually a widespread Whig persuasion focused political discourse on all aspects of political, economic, and cultural development. Outside the Whig fold, but also unhappy with the Democrats, labor radicals stepped forward with their own criticisms of the increasingly unequal social relations in the rapidly changing republic. And just as dissenting strains of thought and action began to coalesce around viable new political organizations, another financial panic spun Americans into renewed depression.

The Whig Persuasion

As a political party, the Whigs took shape gradually. Daniel Webster of Massachusetts, Henry Clay of Kentucky, and John C. Calhoun of South Carolina, senators whose sectional interests otherwise put them at odds with one another, shared an opposition to Jacksonian policies over the period 1828 to 1834. In the election of 1832, these congressional leaders were still identified with the fading National Republican Party and campaigned in the old-fashioned way: seeking support from influential people in high places while ignoring most of the electorate. But when Jackson's raucous parades, picnics, and rallies that year gave him a landslide victory, his opponents adopted the ways of the political party system set in place by Van Buren, with its mass appeals to public opinion. Starting in 1834, Jackson's opposition began calling themselves Whigs and soon formed coalitions that, by 1835, were taking shape as a new political party. Between 1834 and the national election of 1836, Whigs aimed to take control of national politics from the Democrats, holding regular party meetings, nominating candidates, and formulating a political platform just as Democrats did.

Clay was the most charismatic Whig leader, and the most ambitious. Five times Clay tried—and failed—to become president. At age twenty-nine he had become a U.S. senator, and at thirty-three he was Speaker of the House of Representatives. In the next years "Harry of the West" wielded immense power in Washington, eventually serving twenty years in the Senate. In some respects, Clay shared characteristics with Jackson. Both were slave owners; both came from a southern heritage and lived in the new West. Both believed deeply in the ideal of the self-made man and exhibited inexhaustible ambition. But as the foremost architect of the American System, Clay became identified with the national institutions and developmental plans that required strong government intervention in the economy, which Jacksonians had attacked for years.

Like Jacksonians, Whigs were a coalition of interests from all sections of the country. But important political, cultural, and economic issues set them apart from their opponents. Many Americans were drawn to the Whig Party because they believed that Jackson violated his own rhetoric and took too much power from local and state levels of government, using it to enhance his own strength as president. Like abusive monarchs of the past, "King Andrew" had not put the running of government into the hands of the American people. Instead, he had used strong presidential authority to dramatically alter the direction of the country on behalf of "the people." Many Whigs criticized the Democrats' blatant peddling of patronage and influence, which horrified significant numbers of Americans. When, as president, Jackson ousted officeholders and replaced them with Democratic loyalists, critics lambasted his rash of appointments as a "monarchical tendency."

Oddly enough, many Whigs who feared Jackson's strong use of personal executive power also feared the rise of "the common man" Jacksonians adored. Many Whigs charged Democrats with wooing immigrants and Catholics while ignoring the justified claims of rising middle-class, entrepreneurial, and Protestant interests. Numerous people in the 1820s and 1830s recoiled in alarm and anger at what America was becoming. Men on the make and eager land-grabbers were symptomatic of growing evils. It was also becoming impossible to ignore the harsh realities of poverty, unemployment, and shabby living conditions in the cities. Social critics of the 1820s and 1830s pointed to northern urban centers that seemed to be growing more and more like the dangerous, crime-ridden European cities that Jefferson warned them never to emulate.

The intellectual Whig leaders responded to these observations by reviving the argument that a natural hierarchy of ability existed in all developed societies, and that it would of course produce natural inequalities of wealth. But it was misguided to believe that although "the common element" grew in numbers, it should rightfully rule the country. Whig leaders in the states worried that inexperienced, ambitious, and "unrefined" men were governing as Democrats. Philip Hone, a gentleman-politician and conservative leader of the Whigs said in 1834 that Democrats intended to "bring down the property, the talents, the industry, the steady habits of that class which constituted the real strength of the Commonwealth, to the common level of the idle, the worthless, and the unenlightened" who flocked to the Democrats.

Throughout the northern and mid-Atlantic regions, the Whig Party attracted many business leaders in manufacturing and traditional commercial families. The party also appealed to small businessmen and professionals, who believed that Whigs would actively promote Clay's American System. They favored an active role for the federal government respecting internal improvements, protective tariffs, federal subsidies to help the states with regional projects, and banks at national and state levels. Although many Jacksonians and Whigs shared enthusiasm for successful enterprise and energetic mobilization of resources, Whigs expressed deep concern about Jacksonian efforts to dismantle government regulations and central institutions such as the Bank. In addition, rising businessmen, textile and iron manufacturers, and skilled workers in the North hoped for Whig protective tariffs.

In the western and mid-Atlantic states, people found the promise of federal aid for development very appealing. Commercial farmers, rising country merchants, skilled craftsmen of small towns, and the entrepreneurs of the fast-growing towns in the Ohio Valley and Great Lakes regions wanted active governments to invest in canals, bridges, and banks. Clay assured midwestern farmers that the Whig Party would support grants of funds and land subsidies for these internal improvements.

Whigs were a loose enough coalition to include certain important southern voices, too. Some southern Whigs were not keen about rising tariffs and internal improvements that seemed always to benefit northern interests. Planters defended

Henry Clay Even after defeat in the presidential election, Henry Clay continued to command tremendous respect from political leaders and citizens alike. He also continued to be a tireless advocate of internal improvements, American manufactures, and government sponsorship of growth in general. *(Metropolitan Museum of Art, Gift of I.N. Phelps Stokes, Edward S. Hawes, Alice Mary Hawes, Marion Augusta Hawes, 1937.)*

slavery as superior to a working class; they promoted large-scale paternal landholding as opposed to the rootlessness of urban and rural northerners who owned no property. Southern Democrats who controlled state offices often supported these same positions, but they also represented traditional planter authority. New southern Whigs made a bid to break with the patriarchy of the past and create a more energetic planter elite that was attached to commerce, banking, internal improvements and—by extension—interests in the northern states. These entrepreneurial planters, joined by coastal merchants and urban bankers, mobilized support from many nonslaveholding white farmers on the frontier who had chafed under elite state rule since the Regulator days of the 1760s (see page 152).

The Whig Party was able to attract such widespread support for its candidates in 1836 and 1840 because it combined both economic individualism and moral reform. The latter drew not only great numbers of voting men but also many nonvoting women to the Whig persuasion. Party leaders formulated high moral standards that became a model by which to conduct their own lives, as well as to judge the failings of certain other Americans. "Reform" and "improvement" would be available only to Americans of moral superiority which Whig middle-class reformers tended to link to their efforts at eradicating poverty, disease, excessive consumption of liquor, ignorance, and slavery during the 1820s–1840s. Sometimes, these Whig political reform efforts translated into an echo of traditional elite rule and suggested Whigs' suspicions of lower class whites. Many middle-class Whigs also linked their claim of moral superiority to the republican family ideal, which set "true Whigs" apart from large numbers of poor, working-class, and immigrant families.

By 1834, the Whigs had coalesced strength sufficiently in their individual states to win a majority of the seats in the House of Representatives. In the 1836 national election, the Whigs took 49 percent of the popular vote and seriously undermined the Democratic Party's strength in every geographical and social sector of the country. However, the Whigs lost the electoral vote by a landslide to Martin Van Buren, master builder of the Democratic Party and modern elections.

Workingmen's Parties

The rapidly changing political and cultural structure of America altered workingmen's lives dramatically during this era. Artisans in northern cities joined together more frequently during these years to protest that immigrants and migrating rural people degraded their skills and social stature. Ambitious entrepreneurs, they charged, were hiring low-paid semiskilled laborers to build toll bridges and canals. Some found the causes of their declining standard of living in the poor immigrants and female workers in outwork shops. In cities, prices for everyday necessities rose quickly after 1820, so that stagnating wages could not be stretched as far to pay a family's rent and fuel bills.

At first, workers formed mutual aid societies to provide benefits to families when a head of household became incapacitated or died. Although these organizations created important social and cultural links among working people, they were never adequate. And working people still lacked viable public institutions for relief and reform. Eventually, many urban workers would be attracted to the Democratic Party and would vote for its candidates. But during the 1820s, the issues of economic opportunity and political democracy were often discussed outside mainstream party developments, and sometimes in opposition to them.

Among the ardent critics of Democrats and emerging capitalism in the 1820s, Thomas Skidmore stands out. Like so many other young men of his generation, Skidmore began life in a poor New England family but as a teenager began to travel and work odd jobs. In his early twenties, Skidmore settled in Wilmington, Delaware, and conducted numerous experiments on machines and scientific instruments. Skidmore moved on to New York in 1819 as a machinist, just when the city entered a phase of tremendous commercial and manufacturing growth. During the next decade, countless artisans and wage workers were displaced from traditional skills and edged into low-paying putting-out systems or piecework arrangements. Skidmore was among them when they began to raise independent voices of protest.

For years, artisans and machinists in coastal cities had eagerly played roles in the literary, educational, and inventing movements of the early republic. Many of them just as eagerly read and wrote for the newspapers and broadsides that gave expression to workingmen's own popular culture. Public speeches, as well as evening meetings of educational academies and philosophical societies, brought together large congregations of workers regularly, while enthusiastic urban parades reinforced the spoken word.

Republican ideas helped workers understand and criticize this bewildering era. They taught that property conferred a "stake in society" and therefore white citizens should own it widely and in roughly similar amounts. Independent urban artisans believed this property was not just of the landed kind—as traditional republicans proposed—but also their hard won skills and their entitlement to enjoy the fruits of their labor as workers and citizens. These beliefs sharpened many artisans' understanding about how their work was changing during these years, and they offered elements of a critique against harsh aspects of capitalism. This "artisan republicanism" mixed the largely political character of Jacksonian democracy with an economic assessment of labor's conditions more generally.

Artisan republicanism's message about work quickly became the basis for organized political action. Between 1827 and 1837, Skidmore and others rose to become leaders among urban artisans, intellectuals, and immigrants who organized workingmen's parties in opposition to the Democratic and Whig Parties. In 1829 various strands of unrest came together in the New York Working Men's Party. Its first activity was to organize protests against bosses who tried to lengthen the working day from ten to eleven hours. In the coming years the "Workies" also demanded banking that was accessible to all laboring people, abolition of corporate monopolies, taxation based on wealth, and better education for their children. Starting in the fall of 1829, committees began to write a new political program and to select candidates for election to the state legislature.

Skidmore's formulations about the problems artisans and urban workers faced lay at the heart of the subsequent campaigns. The current social system, Skidmore argued, was more like slavery than freedom for most working people, for it took away most of their entitlements to hold land and enjoy their property, and put most people in a condition of want. Skidmore's solution involved abolishing the legal and property structure, as well as the political system, that characterized capitalism in early national America, and substituting for them a more equal ownership of land for everyone. A new political party of the poor and workers, he was sure, could achieve more equitable redistribution of property and citizens' rights.

A meeting of over five thousand people hailed Skidmore's plan in October 1829 and carried it as their standard into the political fray. Two weeks later, the Working Men won about one-third of the votes cast in New York City for candidates to the state legislature and put one of their members in office. But the elation over such a stunning success at the polls soon evaporated, for within a few short weeks, other political and social persuasions invaded the Working Men. Just then, Democrats were offering powerful new alternatives in northern local areas to old political elites. Urban social reformers siphoned off some working-class discontent into temperance and evangelical movements, where laboring people's voices were stifled by the stronger ones of middle-class leaders or manufacturers who had different economic interests. Calls for property redistribution were overwhelmed by the worthy, but less radical, demands for state-funded education and development projects.

Still, for decades to come, alternative working-class parties would arise out of the same rapidly altering master–artisan relations that characterized towns and cities throughout the North. Many of them shared the Working Men's point of view and drew strength from the ways that Skidmore and others had built a viable protest movement based on their republican heritage. Some new organizations grew out of economic grievances, while others stressed the need to extend political rights when exiting parties failed them. For example, in 1831 New York City's female seamstresses faced a cut in their already-low wages and piecework rates. In response to their grinding poverty, crowded tenement living, long hours of work, and little hope of change for their children, 1,600 women organized the United Tailoresses Society and demanded decent pay at mass strike meetings. But without help from organized and unorganized male journeyman, who generally scorned women laboring outside the home, the strikes were doomed to fail.

In the mid-1830s, newspaper editor William Leggett became a leader of New York's Equal Rights Party (called Locofocos by critics), which believed that Democrats should have extended their opposition to the national Bank to state bank charters as well. Only hard money and private transactions were legitimate. In addition, Locofocos attacked Democratic and Whig quarrels over special government legislation to regulate this or that aspect of the national economy. Only absolute freedom of individual opportunity in the market place could create economic justice. All people, Leggett wrote, should enjoy "the free exercise of their talents and industry." The Equal Rights Party was one of many crusades for entrepreneurial equal rights, a laissez-faire approach to development that arose against fears of "monopolistic privilege" that dissenters detected in both of the established parties.

By the 1830s, huge numbers of urban people were attracted to radical political alternatives, while these alternatives in turn drew opposition from the two major

Labor Organizes Politically

The symbol of the arm and hammer and its caption, "By Hammer and Hand All Arts Do Stand," appeared for the first time in 1836 in the newsletter of the General Trades' Union in New York City, which called for all working people in the city to support the tailors brought to trial on charges of "conspiring" against employers for higher wages and better conditions. The broadside, printed the following year, announced another general meeting of city workers. It was common to compare the struggles of unionists in the 1830s to the revolutionary struggle for liberty half a century earlier. *(Top: "The Union," July 14, 1836; New York Public Library, Rare Books; bottom: "New York City Labor Troubles, 1837," Library of Congress.)*

Working Men, Attention!!

It is your imperious duty to drop your *Hammers and Sledges*! one and all, to your post repair, *THIS AFTERNOON*, at *FIVE* o'clock P. M. and attend the

GREAT MEETING

called by the papers of this morning, to be held at the CITY HALL, then and there to co-operate with such as have the GREAT GOOD OF ALL THEIR *FELLOW CITIZENS at Heart.* Your liberty! yea, your *LABOUR!!* is the subject of the call: who that values the services of HEROES of the *Revolution* whose blood achieved our Independence as a Nation, will for a moment doubt he owes a few hours this afternoon to his wife and children?

HANCOCK.

parties, the courts, and powerful employers. But working people's organizations met their greatest obstacles with onset of the Panic of 1837 and the ensuing depression. Many labor radicals returned to the northern Democratic Party. Labor leaders gave up mass meetings to arouse support for social reform and concentrated their battles at the workplace. Efforts to organize unions, primarily of the unskilled, and to put decent wages into workers' pocketbooks became more prevalent than electoral struggles in the late 1830s.

The Panic of 1837

Although Jackson had tried to reduce the power of the national Bank and stem a rising tide of overextended credit by creating "pet banks" around the country, Americans continued to clamor for loans and credit to buy land and start businesses. The chartered state banks were able to respond to this public demand because large quantities of Mexican silver flowed into America from foreign trade and were dispersed into the state banks, thus creating new backup funds of "real and natural value." In the rush to get loans, citizens hardly noticed that their demand for ready cash outstripped the supply of silver, resulting in inflation. The newspapers noted only a few complaints when prices of real estate, food, and basic services rose rapidly by 1835. Southern planters paid little attention to the rising interest rates they paid on loans to purchase land and slaves. Speculators grabbed millions of acres of western land in 1835 and early 1836 with little more than flimsy pieces of bank paper.

Jackson did notice the inflation, however, and ordered legislation to restrict its feverish rise. In 1836 the Treasury Department issued a Specie Circular, which stipulated that land could be purchased only with gold or silver. Bankers in the Midwest and South curtailed loans in response to the order and called in outstanding debts. Struggling farmers and small planters began to feel pinched.

The impending disaster also had foreign causes. For years foreign—primarily British—investors had been pouring capital into northern transportation improvements and southern cotton expansion. But when the British economy fell on hard times by 1833, and its textile mills cut back on southern cotton imports, the international economy began to break down. Cotton prices fell and planters could not repay debts to state banks; the banks in turn faltered in their obligations to English creditors. Many southern banks closed their doors in early 1837.

In March, Van Buren took office. A month later, public fears about the country's financial stability spread to the northern states. Soon the panic set in. Merchants in New York and Philadelphia witnessed declining commerce; many declared bankruptcy. Average consumers and small investors flooded to the banks and demanded withdrawals of their savings in silver and gold, but the banks could not cover such demands and suspended specie payments. Eventually, the international and banking credit crisis reached small businesses, infant manufacturing, and farmers throughout the northern countryside. People could not pay their taxes, and cash was in such short supply that stores and toll ways closed. Public panic reached new heights when state governments announced that they could not finance bonds earmarked for canal building or their debts to private enterprises. British investors responded to the snowballing crisis by halting the flow of foreign credit into the American North.

The depression that overtook the country was worse than in any living American's memory. Prices rose steeply, store goods became scarce, unemployment skyrocketed in the cities, and farmers despaired of selling their surpluses to impoverished townspeople at any price. With little hope of recovery coming soon, the infant labor movement lost leverage with employers. Hysterical mobs of citizens banged on the closed doors of banks to recover their savings—to no avail. "The volcano has burst and overwhelmed New York," wrote Philip Hone, a wealthy Whig whose son lost a thriving business in 1837; then, there was a "dead calm . . . all is still as death. No business is transacted, no bargains made, no negotiations entered into . . . all is wrapped up in uncertainty."

These were bleak years for Americans everywhere. As businesses failed and eight hundred banks closed, thousands of city dwellers lived off their wits in the streets, and mobs broke open grocers' shops and flour mills to get food. Into the 1840s, Democrats charged Whigs with rushing into development and supporting dangerous speculation. Whigs charged Democrats with recklessly destroying the national Bank and the money system of the nation. The federal and state governments did little to help Americans, partly because government resources in those years were utterly inadequate to the great tasks of economic recovery, and partly because the nation lacked institutions to aid the bank directors, investors, and unemployed workers who had fallen into the doldrums.

The Election of 1840

The depression, which lasted until 1843, had a profound impact on politics. The Democratic Party won back the support of many workers, now unemployed, who left their fragile radical labor organizations and returned to the Jacksonians seeking protection of their declining living standards. At the same time, though, the party's "hard money" policies and attacks on national banking alienated other constituents during the deep crisis after 1837. Farmers in the Midwest and mid-Atlantic regions, and consumers everywhere, blamed "tight-fisted" Jacksonians for the foreclosures and shortages of goods. Others insisted that destroying the Second Bank of the United States had crushed important new internal improvements projects, and the Specie Circular's requirement of gold and silver to pay for land undermined the great republican promise to make western settlement possible for the average citizen. Whig politicians pointed out that Democrats had affirmed their commitment to less government involvement in people's lives just when it was most needed to lift them out of the depression.

Democratic president Martin Van Buren heightened public fears that shortages of money and goods might lead to a total collapse of the republic. In 1837, he proposed an Independent Treasury Act. As a long-time opponent of Jackson's "pet banks," which had held the redistributed government reserves of gold and silver in various states since 1833, Van Buren used his executive authority to call in all the federal government money in those banks. He then put it in a central treasury,

Election Scene in Cincinnati During the 1840 election campaign, mass public meetings occurred across the country in support of the Democratic, Whig, and Liberty Parties. In Cincinnati, shown here in a local etching, Whigs put up a "triumphal arch" emblazoned with a banner blending calls for universal white male suffrage and territorial expansion. Flags proclaimed "Protection to Industry, A Sound Currency, A Protective Tariff." *(Cincinnati Museum Center.)*

where it was to sit unused. The act, though delayed, was finally passed in 1840 at the end of Van Buren's presidency.

This was far from the kind of national banking that Whigs such as Clay and Webster favored, and it became fuel for the presidential campaign that year. Moreover, "Van Ruin," as the Whig press called him, did nothing to protect citizens, as the tariffs, improvements, and federal investments that Whigs promised with their American System would have done. In 1840 the Whigs passed over the ambitious Clay and nominated William Henry Harrison, a military hero of the Battle of Tippecanoe and the War of 1812, who hailed from the heartland of Ohio. Virginian John Tyler joined him on the ticket. With little substantial platform of his own, Harrison nevertheless eagerly accepted his party's leadership. He also adopted the Democratic style of appealing to popular culture to transmit political ideas. Using mass outdoor meetings and popularizing fictitious images of Harrison living in a simple log cabin, Whigs stumped enthusiastically across the nation. Thousands of women, though unable to vote, flocked to meetings to hear the moral intonations of Harrison's Whig supporters and organized political fundraising through their churches and benevolent societies. Whigs borrowed the language of the Democrats to reach "the common man" and concocted snappy slogans of their own, especially "Tippecanoe and Tyler Too."

The 1840 national election marked the first time in American history when two organized political parties appealed for the votes of a mass electorate. Although scholars have called the earlier rivalries between Federalists and Republicans the "First Party System," the leaders of those groupings neither recognized each other as permanent parties nor admitted to organizing campaigns to win over the electorate. By 1840, the electorate was far larger—a full 80.2 percent of adult white males voted that year—and the reading public far more eager to know what each party promised. Large crowds turned out to hear Whig and Democratic candidates, and a new conception of "constituencies" made the parties sensitive to demands of ordinary citizens. Through the years of controversy between Democrats and their opponents, eventually coalesced into the Whigs, a "Second Party System" had emerged.

Although the Whigs gained a majority in Congress as well as the White House, Harrison died of pneumonia within a month of his inauguration. His successor, John Tyler, was a former Democrat who supported states' rights and split from that party during the nullification crisis. As president, Tyler was only nominally a Whig, for he was critical of the American System's economic nationalism. He vetoed measures intended to create a Third Bank of the United States and raise tariffs, which prompted his own Whig Party to pass a congressional resolution that effectively expelled him from the party organization. Undaunted, Tyler went on to reject Whig proposals to raise the price of western land in order to generate national revenue. Instead, he supported Congress's Preemption Act of 1841, which permitted settlers to claim up to 160 acres freely and purchase it later at the low price of $1.25 an acre. Whig leaders in Congress and the northern states grew exasperated in the next couple of years when Tyler's western expansionist goals grew to include the annexation of Texas to the union. Few politicians disagreed with the assessment that Tyler acted more like a Democrat than a Whig.

CONCLUSION

The jostling crowds that cheered President Andrew Jackson's inauguration were rapidly leaving the world of Jefferson and Hamilton behind. Political parties had become acceptable vehicles for negotiating differences and policy reform. White men's right to vote, an inclusive political culture, and the nation's territory were all expanding. An emerging American identity celebrated ambitious, entrepreneurial, and individualistic activity. Jackson entered Washington with a solid popular mandate to democratize American political life, extend opportunities for development and prosperity, diminish the American System, and put more control of institutions in state and local hands. The Jacksonian experiment made important strides toward accomplishing these goals between 1829 and 1840. Even after 1840, Democrats continued to make room in their party for Irish and German immigrants in northern cities, poor farmers in the North and Midwest, small planters in the South, and skilled and unskilled workers in cities and towns everywhere. And Democrats continued making their claims to be the party of expansive opportunity for white males, of states' rights, and of an enlarged republic.

The social costs of these accomplishments were great, as the tensions over Indian removal, tariffs and nullification, and banks attest. Moreover, the ideal of releasing people from restraints and regulations had varied results. On one hand, it shrank the government's authority over Americans' lives and paved the way for tremendous entrepreneurial activity. But on the other hand, it increased the gap separating privileged Americans from the vulnerable "common man," and from Indians and slaves. Numerous dissenting working-class organizations and reform efforts arose to seek redress of these growing inequalities. But few of them could withstand the panic and depression that swept across the country for years starting in 1837.

For their part, the Whigs also contributed immensely to the American identity emerging during these decades. Whigs reminded Americans that their ambitions and fast-paced growth required checks; it needed control, order, regulation, and morality. For decades after the Whig Party faded out of sight, what it stood for—active federal support for internal development, protective tariffs, sales of national lands to create federal revenues, and moral and social control of the disadvantaged by the middle class—would be embodied in one or another major party. Clay's American System lived on in new guises, overlaid with Jackson's praise for democracy, white men's territorial expansion, and occupational mobility. Years after the Whigs' departure, Abraham Lincoln unabashedly identified with their political goals. "The legitimate object of government," wrote Lincoln, "is 'to do for the people what needs to be done, but which they can not, by individual effort, do at all, or do so well, for themselves.'"

SUGGESTED READINGS

Assessing the role of popular opinion and participation on the development of parties has enjoyed a revival of interest in recent years. See especially Jean Baker, *Affairs of Party: The Political Culture of Northern Democrats in the Mid-Nineteenth Century* (1983); Kenneth Cmiel, *Democratic Eloquence: The Fight over Popular Speech in Nineteenth-Century America* (1990); and Harry Watson, *Jacksonian Politics and Community Conflict* (1981). Two somewhat older works that tied the Second Party System closely to public sentiment and support are Ronald Formisano, *The Birth of Mass Political Parties, 1827–1861* (1971), and Marvin Meyers, *The Jacksonian Persuasion: Politics and Belief* (1957). A still older and, in its time path-breaking, view of Jacksonians as rising entrepreneurs and urban artisans is Arthur Schlesinger, Jr., *The Age of Jackson* (1945). Myers would later link Jacksonians to rural agrarian values.

For leadership and the party system, the best places to start are Merrill D. Peterson, *The Great Triumvirate: Webster, Clay and Calhoun* (1987); Donald Cole, *The Presidency of Andrew Jackson* (1993); Richard Latner, *The Presidency of Andrew Jackson: White House Politics, 1829–1837* (1979); and Richard P. McCormick, *The Second American Party System* (1966).

Scholarship about Indian removal and reservation policies during this era is voluminous. One of the older works that provides a useful overview is Grant Foreman, *Indian Removal: The Emigration of the Five Civilized Tribes of Indians* (1953). For work that is strongly critical of Jacksonian policies, see Robert Berkhofer, Jr., *The White Man's Indian: Images of the American Indian from Columbus to the Present* (1979); Angie Debo, *And Still the Waters Run: The*

Betrayal of the Five Civilized Tribes (1972); Michael Paul Rogin, *Fathers and Children: Andrew Jackson and the Subjugation of the American Indian* (1975); and Anthony F. C. Wallace, *The Long, Bitter Trail: Andrew Jackson and the Indians* (1993). Robert Remini's *Andrew Jackson and the Course of American Empire* (1977) is more sympathetic to the Democratic Party's western policies. J. Leitch Wright, Jr., in *Creeks and Seminoles* (1986), gives a wide-angled view of Indian life overall.

The best work on nullification is William Freehling, *Prelude to Civil War* (1966). For the bank wars of the Jacksonian years, see the following three works: John McFaul, *The Politics of Jacksonian Finance* (1972); James Roger Sharp, *The Jacksonians Versus the Banks: Politics in the United States After the Panic of 1837* (1970); and Peter Temin, *The Jacksonian Economy* (1965).

Rising alongside the Jacksonian persuasion was the Whig culture and party development, and this is treated most evenhandedly by both Maurice Baxter, *Henry Clay and the American System* (1995), and Daniel Walker Howe, *The Political Culture of the American Whigs* (1980). For cultural life during the Jacksonian years, start with the readable and engaging work by Paul Johnson, *A Shopkeeper's Millennium: Society and Revivals in Rochester, New York, 1815–1837* (1978); John F. Kasson, *Rudeness and Civility: Manners in Nineteenth-Century America* (1990); and Keith Melder, *Beginnings of Sisterhood: The American Women's Rights Movement, 1800–1850* (1977). On workingmen's parties and the urban economy, the best case study is Sean Wilentz, *Chants Democratic: New York City and the Rise of the American Working Class, 1788–1850* (1983). And the best one-volume sweeping synthesis of the era is Charles Sellers's *The Market Revolution: Jacksonian America, 1815–1846* (1991).

Cherokee Removal

Competing Voices

The Cherokee Nation Opposes Removal, 1830

Understandably, Native Americans often resisted removal from their homelands. In 1829, when the federal government approved policies to forcibly relocate the Cherokee from the Southeast to reservations west of the Mississippi River, tribal leaders delivered well-rehearsed speeches against such injustices. Following is one of their most forceful replies.

We are aware, that some persons suppose it will be for our advantage to remove beyond the Mississippi. We think otherwise.... Not an adult person can be found, who has not an opinion on the subject, and if the people were to understand distinctly, that they could be protected against the laws of the neighboring states, there is probably not an adult person in the nation, who would think it best to remove; though possibly a few might emigrate individually. There are doubtless many, who would flee to an unknown country, however beset with dangers, privation and sufferings, rather than be sentenced to spend six years in a Georgia prison for advising one of their neighbors not to betray his country. And there are others who could not think of living as outlaws in their native land, exposed to numberless vexations, and excluded from being parties or witnesses in a court of justice.... We are not willing to remove; and if we could be brought to this extremity, it would be not by argument, not because our judgment was satisfied, not because our condition will be improved; but only because we cannot endure to be deprived of our national and individual rights and subjected to a process of intolerable oppression.

We wish to remain on the land of our fathers. We have a perfect and original right to remain without interruption or molestation. The treaties with us, and laws of the United States made in pursuance of treaties, guaranty our residence and our privileges, and secure us against intruders. Our only request is, that these treaties may be fulfilled, and these laws executed.

But if we are compelled to leave our country, we see nothing but ruin before us. The country west of the Arkansas territory is unknown to us.... All the inviting parts of it, as we believe, are preoccupied by various Indian nations, to which it has been assigned. They would regard us as intruders, and look upon us with an evil eye. The far greater part of that region is, beyond all controversy, badly supplied with wood and water; and no Indian tribe can live as agriculturalists without these articles. All our neighbors, in case of our removal, though crowded into our near vicinity, would speak a language totally different from ours, and practice different customs. The original possessors of that region ... have always been at war, and would be easily tempted to turn their arms against peaceful emigrants. Were the country to which we are urged much better than it is represented to be, and were it free from the objections which we have made to it, still it is not the land of our birth, nor of our affections. It contains neither the scenes of our childhood, nor the graves of our fathers....

Andrew Jackson's Second Annual Message to Congress, 1830

Although in 1829 and 1830 many Americans raised strong voices against Jackson's calls for Indian removal, the president's annual address to Congress in December 1830 turned a deaf ear to such protests.

It gives me pleasure to announce to Congress that the benevolent policy of the Government, steadily pursued for nearly thirty years, in relation to the removal of the Indians beyond the white settlement is approaching to a happy consummation. Two important tribes [Choctaw and Chickasaw] have accepted the provision made for their removal at the last session of Congress, and it is believed that their example will induce the remaining tribes also to seek the same obvious advantages.

The consequences of a speedy removal will be important to the United States, to individual States, and to the Indians themselves. . . . It puts an end to all possible danger of collision between the authorities of the . . . governments on account of the Indians. It will place a dense and civilized population in large tracts of country now occupied by a few savage hunters. . . . [I]t will incalculably strengthen the southwestern frontier and render the adjacent States strong enough to repel future invasions without remote aid. . . . It will separate the Indians from immediate contact with settlements of whites; free them from the power of the States; enable them to pursue happiness in their own way and under their own rude institutions; will retard the progress of decay, which is lessening their numbers, and perhaps cause them gradually, under the protections of the Government and through the influence of good counsels, to cast off their savage habits and become an interesting, civilized, and Christian community. . . .

. . . I have endeavored to impress upon them my own solemn convictions of the duties and powers of the General Government in relation to the state authorities. For the justice of the laws passed by the states within the scope of their reserved powers they [the states] are not responsible to this government [the federal one]. As individuals we may entertain and express our opinions of their acts, but as a Government we have as little right to control them as we have to prescribe laws for other nations.

With a full understanding of the subject, the Choctaw and the Chickasaw tribes have with great unanimity determined to avail themselves of the liberal offers presented by the act of Congress, and have agreed to remove beyond the Mississippi River. Treaties have been made with them . . . and they have preferred maintaining their independence in the Western forests to submitting to the laws of the states in which they now reside. These treaties . . . give the Indians a liberal sum in consideration of their removal, and comfortable subsistence on their arrival at their new homes. . . .

Humanity has often wept over the fate of the aborigines of this country, and Philanthropy has been long busily employed in devising means to avert it, but . . . one by one have many powerful tribes disappeared from the earth. . . . [T]rue Philanthropy reconciles the mind to these vicissitudes as it does to the extinction of one generation to make room for another. . . . Philanthropy could not wish to see this continent restored to the condition in which it was found by our forefathers. What good man would prefer a country covered with forests and ranged by a few thousand savages to our extensive Republic, studded with cities, towns, and prosperous farms, embellished with all the improvements which art can devise or industry execute . . . ?

> . . . The waves of population and civilization are rolling to the westward, and we now propose to acquire the countries occupied by the red men of the south and west by a fair exchange, and, at the expense of the United States, to send them to a land where their existence may be prolonged and perhaps made perpetual. . . . To better their condition in an unknown land *our* forefathers left all that was dear in earthly objects. Our children by thousands yearly leave the land of their birth to seek new homes in distant regions. . . . These remove hundreds and almost thousands of miles at their own expense, purchase the lands they occupy, and support themselves at their new homes from the moment of their arrival. . . .
>
> And is it supposed that the wandering savage has a stronger attachment to his home than the settled, civilized Christian? Is it more afflicting to him to leave the graves of his fathers than it is to our brothers and children? Rightly considered, the policy of the General Government toward the red man is not only liberal, but generous. He is unwilling to submit to the laws of the States and mingle with their population. To save him from this alternative, or perhaps utter annihilation, the General Government kindly offers him a new home, and proposes to pay the whole expense of his removal and settlement. ▮

Wholesale removal of peoples was not new in the 1830s. The earliest settlers had "removed" Indians to "reservations," and the British "removed" Acadians from their homeland during the turmoil of the Seven Years' War in the 1750s, some as far away as Louisiana. Jefferson, along with many statesmen and policymakers in the early republic, advocated removal of Native Americans on the grounds that the savage, dangerous frontier needed to be made safe for westward movement.

A few bold voices kept up the opposition to removal, including Protestant missionaries on the frontiers and Ralph Waldo Emerson, the transcendentalist philosopher and essayist. Emerson's speeches would arouse thousands of New Englanders against slavery in years to come. In 1830 his published letters to President Martin Van Buren reminded readers of the moral and legal wrongs of removal.

At the same time, the Seminole resisted encroachments on their lands violently. The Cherokee chose to use American courts to challenge alien political policies and lost their court battles. Once the reservation lands called the Indian Territory had been set aside across the Mississippi River, voices of protest faded. More and more Indian peoples were placed within its boundaries during the 1830s and 1840s.

Questions for Analysis

1. What words and phrases do the Cherokee people use to express opposition to removal? Is the language reminiscent of other contexts?
2. Review in this textbook other examples of people who had been removed from their homelands and compare the Cherokee, and the condition of removal, with these other groups.
3. Describe the national context in which removal took place. Why did Indian removal become such a pressing issue during the 1820s and 1830s?
4. Trace the Trail of Tears on the map on page 381, and speculate as to what the great distance from home and different geography might have meant to the Cherokee.
5. According to Jackson, how will removal be good for Indians? for Americans?

11

Industry and Reform in the North, 1820–1850

In the spring of 1836, a "Horrid Murder" shook New York City. A twenty-three-year-old prostitute, Helen Jewett, was found axed to death in her bed; to hide the crime, her killer had set the room on fire. Educated, beautiful, and cultured, Jewett was well-known as a fun-loving "exceedingly fair and highly accomplished" courtesan who mingled with scores of the city's best-placed men of commerce and politics.

Richard Robinson, a young merchant's clerk who had come to New York from an upstanding Connecticut political family, had been seen frequently with Jewett at cultural events in the city. Because of his association with the prostitute, Robinson gained instant notoriety as the prime suspect in this "deed of darkness." Officers in the city's newly created police force arrested Robinson, questioned him, and escorted him to the dim and dank Bridewell prison. There were no other suspects.

Newspapers up and down the coastline, many only recently transformed from genteel weeklies into popular "penny press" dailies that battled for the attention of an eager public, carried the Jewett story for weeks into the summer of 1836. In fact, New York's *Sun, Transcript,* and *Herald* not only raced to typesetters day after day with each new breaking detail but became the arbiters of public opinion about this sensational crime.

At first New Yorkers were certain that Jewett had been brutally victimized. Friends told reporters that she mingled with respectable people, attended plays and public entertainments in the finest of imported clothing, and was "set apart" from the other women of waterfront brothels. But as the summer of 1836 wore on, reports in the popular press shifted from sympathy for Helen's plight to her supposed nature as a seductress. Some writers suggested that perhaps New York City was not a morally healthy place for so upstanding a citizen as Mr. Robinson. Perhaps, some reporters insisted, only "depraved minds" could revel in the details of so lurid a crime and conclude that a man of Robinson's stature was capable of an ax murder. Jewett, others began to write, was a "panderer of vice," a "dangerous" woman because of the very nature of her trade. Her character was suspect because of the public places she frequented. Hundreds of men each night were "beguiled" by the "winning smiles" of "ladies of the night," including Jewett.

Weeks of investigation revealed no new facts; no new public evidence pointed toward Robinson's actual innocence or guilt. But during 1836, the popular press mobilized a court of public opinion that subtly redirected guilt from Robinson to Jewett, and eventually a court acquitted Robinson. These were violent times, as the press kept reminding readers. Jewett's trade was one form of flagrant disregard for social propriety that major cities experienced regularly by the 1830s. In addition, gangs roamed freely in New York streets after dark; heavy drinking in public places led to frequent brawls; and the many laborers, sailors, and migrants passing through the city created an atmosphere of suspicion and tension.

Very uncommon things happened in this "Era of the Common Man" during which Helen Jewett met her fiery end. Both Jewett and Robinson reminded readers about the temptations and dangers of cities for the unfortunate poor and the unwary outsider. The pace of American life was not only quickening, it was also manifesting qualitative changes introduced by new technology, institutions, consumer goods, and relations in workplaces. As Americans crowded into coastal cities and spread into distant frontiers in unprecedented numbers, they were simultaneously exhilarated with feelings of opportunity and abundance, and disquieted with fears about deep and rapid change.

- How was northern life transformed during the 1820s to 1850s? Who welcomed new cultural and economic opportunities, and who resisted them?
- As industrialization unfolded in the North and upset social relations, how did the democratization of institutions and political culture continue to grow, and how did tensions among ethnic groups and social classes intensify?
- Who stepped forward to address the imperfections and unevenly distributed benefits of this developing northern society, and what kinds of reforms did they propose? What did these popular reform movements have in common with elite intellectual currents?
- In what ways was a distinctively American culture beginning to develop, despite regional, ethnic, class, and other differences?

This chapter will address these questions.

Immigration and Urbanization

Contests between Jacksonian and Whig persuasions grew out of fast-paced and deep-running changes in American life. From the 1820s to the 1840s, people in the North continued to experience those changes in sometimes unsettling ways. Politically and socially, they wrestled with how to address rapidly changing circumstances with institutional experiments. Immigration of new national groups introduced additional ethnic and religious distinctiveness throughout the older settled areas of the region, accompanied by tensions that both Jacksonians and Whigs needed to address. In addition, cities underwent an exciting—and sometimes frightening—degree of transformation in these same years. They not only made room for the cultures of new immigrants, but also became the centers of government and business institutions built by northern elites. At the same time, cities became laboratories of restructured working conditions in which the new material comforts of a rising middle-class arose beside unimagined crowding and poverty.

Old Cities and New

From the 1820s through the 1850s, New York City became America's largest metropolitan collection of people, and its most productive manufacturing city. At first glance, this claim seems far-fetched, for the city had few sources of fast-running water to power mills. Moreover, although the city had increasingly crowded living conditions, it did not have many large factories producing manufactured goods in massive quantities. New Yorkers had risen to prominence through commerce and for generations had imported cheap manufactures of daily goods from abroad.

Along with New York, Philadelphia, Boston, and Baltimore also grew by leaps and bounds during this era. More than a third of the people in the New England and mid-Atlantic regions lived in cities, the highest degree of urbanization in the country. Sustained by commerce and bolstered by milling and transportation services, these cities continued to expand. They became the nation's premier centers of credit and banking, importing and retailing, booming real estate development, and immigrant ghettoes. Although they were not yet centers of industrialization, these showcase cities nevertheless developed institutions and cultural life to complement their unprecedented economic vitality during these years.

One development that propelled coastal northern cities forward during these decades was the rapid rate of population growth in and around them. By the 1830s, huge influxes of immigrants arrived from England, Germany, and Ireland, along with a steady flow of rural people looking for a better chance after the disruptions of American and European revolutions and wars. Whereas fewer than 9,000 newcomers landed at American ports in 1820, about 23,000 came in 1830, and 84,000 in 1840. During the decade of the 1820s, about 129,000 people arrived from foreign countries; during the 1850s, the incoming tide rose to over 2.8 million newcomers (see graph page 408).

Chronology

1820s	Slater mill system spreads
1823	Boston Associates open Lowell mills
1826	American Society for the Promotion of Temperance founded
1827	Working Men's Party founded in Philadelphia
	Public schools movement emerges in Massachusetts
1830	Charles Grandison Finney preaches in Rochester
1833	The *New York Sun,* first penny paper, begins publication
1834	National Trades Union formed
	Female Moral Reform Society founded
1837	Panic begins
1841	Beecher publishes *Treatise on Domestic Economy*
1844	Mormon leader Joseph Smith killed
1847	New Hampshire passes first ten-hour-workday law
1848	Seneca Falls Convention for women's rights
	Oneida founded
1854	Thoreau publishes *Walden*

The influx of English continued throughout this era, especially during years of epidemic diseases and crippling crop failures. But by the 1830s, large numbers of Irish had also become conspicuous in northern American states as they fled unemployment and destitute poverty throughout their overpopulated country. In the next decade, this immigration into America swelled enormously when a blight struck three out of every four acres of Ireland's staple crops of potatoes, producing a famine that drove massive numbers of people out of the countryside. From 1847 to 1854, between 100,000 and 220,000 Irish entered America per year. Most came from tenant farming conditions, but few had the resources to buy even the cheapest land out West. As a result, the Irish crowded into tenement housing or, in the case of young men who migrated ahead of their families or came seeking their personal fortunes, followed the canal and railroad projects that cut into the countryside. Thousands of young Irish men stayed in eastern cities to work on the waterfronts or at unskilled labor, while young women sought work as domestic servants and seamstresses. Most were able to get only the worst-paying jobs, often unskilled and temporary. As Catholics and outsiders, the Irish overwhelmingly gravitated to the political umbrella of Jacksonian Democrats. In Boston, this political choice contrasted sharply with the Whig control of many city institutions and reinforced Irish

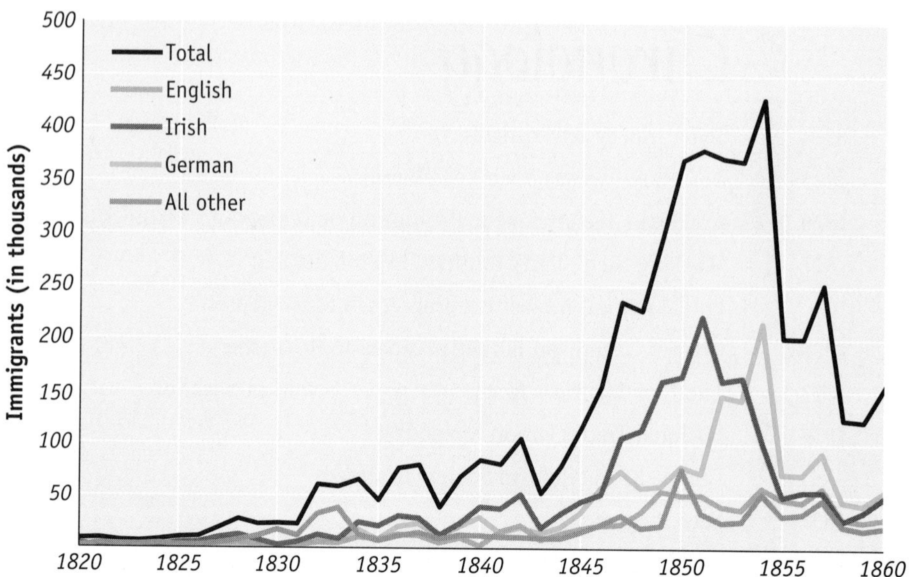

Immigration During the 1820s to 1850s Although large numbers of British and European peoples continued to come to America during the 1820s and 1830s, their numbers increased manifold by the mid-1840s due to political upheavals and economic hardships in many nations. Only with the return of relatively better times in the 1850s did immigration subside temporarily. (Source: *Historical Statistics of the United States,* 1975 edition)

distinctiveness. In Boston, the Irish "East Enders" created a lively community, sustaining their separate religion and distinctive cultural ways. Their neighborhood raised funds to marry and bury residents who were penniless; nuns and priests of the Catholic Church attended to the health and educational needs of Irish families.

German immigration into America differed markedly from the Irish experience. For generations there had been a sizeable German population in Pennsylvania. By the 1830s, when difficult European conditions promoted a new wave of German immigration to America, established German-speaking communities were already in place. But most Germans during the 1830s and 1840s came on the return voyages of southern cotton and tobacco ships, and were thus dropped at the ports of New Orleans and Baltimore. From those places, many Germans ventured up the Mississippi River to St. Louis and points east along the Ohio River. A large number of Germans crossed into Texas, where they obtained a land grant from Mexico. Unlike the Irish coming at the same time, Germans arrived with money or valuables needed to set up farms and shops. In addition, German families carried numerous skills into their new lives in the midwestern settlements. In and around St. Louis, Cincinnati, San Antonio, Chicago, and Milwaukee, Germans made a considerable mark on cuisine and culture. Thousands of German families took advantage of declining land prices to acquire prosperous farms.

Sustained heavy immigration contrasted starkly with the declining birthrate of older resident American families. By the 1820s, most American-born women bore fewer than the formerly typical eight children. By the 1850s, they bore on average only five, while at the same time over 300,000 people came to America per year until the Civil War impeded the flow temporarily during the 1860s. By then, Americans noticed two salient characteristics of these trends: a great proportion of the American population was foreign-born—nearly 20 percent—and the immigrant and native populations together were incredibly young. In the crowded urban centers of New York and Philadelphia, 50 percent of the population were under sixteen.

Some visitors to American coastal cities felt overwhelmed by the crowded confusion of burgeoning populations that clamored for goods and services. Others joined the more optimistic observers who sought ways to harness the energy of growing populations (see Competing Voices, page 442). Hard work, proliferating new businesses, and rising consumer demand for basic necessities would avert the entrenched poverty and periodic famines of Europe. Bakers, builders, tailors, leather workers, toolmakers, and many other trade groups both hired the new population and satisfied its demand for goods.

Frontier Cities

Beyond America's oldest settled areas, Great Lakes cities such as Rochester, Buffalo, and Chicago, and river cities such as Cincinnati, St. Louis, and Columbus, became the focal points of booming manufacturing and transportation services for America's vast rural population of grain and meat producers. Ambitious people in coastal areas took advantage of their prize locations near superb waterways and deep bays, as well as their connections to consumers and merchant exporters, to expand their ties to the interior. Although Illinois had been remote from Americans' imagination and development plans during the century's early decades, Chicago became the greatest midwestern city by the late 1850s. Not industrial development, but rather distribution and transportation services, turned that old Indian trading town into an overnight wonder. Farmers and ranchers came to Chicago's markets and stores from hundreds of miles away; railroad workers settled down near Chicago when they were laid off at this western terminus; insurance brokers and shopkeepers enjoyed steadily rising business in this booming region.

Out on the Ohio River, Cincinnati (see page 328) continued to bustle and boom, becoming the country's third-largest industrial center by 1840. Key to the city's rapid rise were its varieties of opportunity for manufacturing and the adaptability of its entrepreneurs to many kinds of work. Through midcentury, most young people in Cincinnati still labored in small shops using tools that would have been familiar to colonial artisans in metal trades and food processing. But blacksmiths, for example, while still providing horseshoes and chains, also added machine parts and huge carriage wheels to their regular product lines. And about one-fifth of Cincinnati's working population, which was increasingly German and Irish, made their primary living by work in factories. Skilled craftsmen in the furniture business, for example, still finished chairs and sofas, but machines increasingly helped them cut, bore, and plane the wood frames. Too, entrepreneurs began to reorganize factories so that skilled craftsmen no longer handled the entire production process, but instead specialized as upholsterers, carpenters, or finishers.

In both cases—adapting to machine technology or retooling as specialists—craftsmen earned decent pay. The same was not always true for Cincinnati's unskilled recent migrants, who were taken into the meatpacking and sewing industries for periods of time, given low wages, and turned out of employment when business slowed. In their households, wives and daughters supplemented family incomes by taking outwork making "men's rough clothes." They were paid by the piece, earning barely enough to put another meal on the table after hours bent over a needle.

Rich and Poor

Who enjoyed the new goods and services cities offered? This Era of the Common Man was, in fact, one of widening distinctions among Americans. Nowhere was this clearer than in northern cities, where in 1830 the top 1 percent of New Yorkers held 40 percent of the total wealth; the top 4 percent held 75 percent. Boston and Philadelphia approximated these figures, too. Each northern city had its few families who rose "from rags to riches," from modest means as wage earners or from distressed immigrant status to eminent stature in the elite. The complex of mill operations at Waltham, Massachusetts, depended on the investments of a few tightly knit families whose fortunes came from shipping services. Anson Phelps, whose ships carried cotton for southern exporters during the 1820s and 1830s, invested a commercial fortune in iron mines, forges, and rolling mills in Pennsylvania and Connecticut. John Jacob Astor arrived in New York from Germany in 1784 with little in his pockets; by exploiting the western fur trade and city real estate markets, he had become the wealthiest man in America by the time he died in 1848.

These fortunes, however, represented a tiny proportion of northern Americans. Far more numerous by the 1840s were the "middling sort" of somewhat less affluent businessmen, merchants, artisans, and successful immigrants who benefited from opportunities for advancement during the era. Most had adapted quickly to the depression conditions of the late 1830s, or had never invested wildly to begin with. This growing section of the population included new managers, tellers, brokers, insurance agents, and medical and legal "experts." Hundreds of former artisans in every northern city put on white collars to go to work each day by the 1840s, and their numbers grew steadily. Meanwhile, the elite of major cities remained committed to marrying and forming business alliances among themselves, in efforts to protect "dilution [of their class] by the rising shopkeepers."

The homes of wealthy and middle-class people in cities changed dramatically between the 1790s and 1840s. By the latter decade, families of modest incomes could enjoy iron cook stoves, rugs and window coverings that gave warmth and comfort, tubs in which to bathe with plenty of soap, and oil lamps and cheap candles for illumination. The increasing manufacture of textiles, soap, bread, and other necessities outside the home enhanced the household mistress's role as a consumer rather than a producer. By the 1820s to 1840s, middling housewives also aspired to hire domestic servants to take over the routine sweeping, scrubbing, polishing, sewing, cooking, and other chores of their households. According to popular advice manuals, the "perfect home" would be a bustling scene of servants working under the supervision of a "truly republican" middle-class household mistress.

By midcentury, the sewing machine was beginning to change one of women's ceaseless forms of toil: producing family clothing and linens. Sewing machines, invented by Elias Howe and Isaac Singer, not only reduced the amount of time it took to make necessary items, they also spread interest in fashion, which began to change more frequently. Although most homemakers did not themselves own sewing machines before the late 1800s, ready-made clothing fell in price as it came closer to being mass-produced. First imports, then American-manufactured outerwear, became cheap enough for most families to have a few outfits. Quilts became more decorative and elaborate in design, whether made at home or purchased. However, the sewing machine became a curse for many young women and spinsters who earned a living finishing textiles manufactures. Manufacturers preferred to set up the machines in shops, where work discipline replaced the sociability and convenience of outwork at home.

Most urban residents were poor. Despite the flow of people to the frontier and job opportunities provided by proliferating development projects, large numbers of people remained in cities who did not fare well. Travelers at the end of the colonial

Woman with Singer Sewing Machine The Singer sewing machine, patented in 1851, dramatically changed the way women produced clothing and fabric household items. The machine's continuous and rapid stitching was first adapted to factory production of ready-made clothing for men and women, but soon it became a highly desirable commodity in middle-class households. *(Private Collection.)*

era had marveled at the relative absence of persistent poverty and the apparently small gap in wealth between rich and poor. By the 1840s, however, visitors to northeastern cities gasped at the poverty of waterfront and tenement areas. Modern scholars estimate that by 1840, the top 5 percent of the population in large cities owned about two-thirds of all the wealth, with about 15 percent of artisans attaining somewhat prestigious positions as shop owners, small importers, or mill managers. But 50 to 70 percent of artisans and immigrants could barely make ends meet.

The urban poor usually lived in the rapidly rising new tenements of old urban neighborhoods. In contrast to the wealthy, who were relocating to the nation's first true suburbs, most city residents could not afford to pay to have water pumped from local rivers through the city's wooden pipe system. Water for drinking, cooking, bathing, and cleaning was only one essential item that proved difficult and costly to obtain. Most of the poor in the city also foraged outside their neighborhoods for fuel and daily food. Owning a home was beyond the means of most workingmen's families, and beyond the housing supply of most cities. About two-thirds of the average laborer's wages went to feed his family. If he was unfortunate enough to lose a job, or worked only occasionally, his wages would not even stretch far enough to provide food. In those cases, other family members took jobs carrying dirt and stones, hauling lumber, or mucking out horse stalls; some sold vegetables from small family gardens or scavenged through the alleys. Winters often forced families into charity shelters or workhouses.

While elite neighborhoods became elaborate arenas for carriage drives, flowering gardens, and grand parties, the tenement districts of northern cities decayed alarmingly. Many tenements, lacking running water and seldom heated, crammed ten or more people into each one-room apartment. Tiny shacks filled alleys behind shops, and large families squeezed into the basements or garrets of already-full tenements. Public officials hired to investigate the conditions of New York City's Corlaers Hook neighborhood found "hideous squalour and deadly effluvia, the dim, undrained courts oozing with pollution, the dark, narrow stairways, decayed with age, reeking with filth, overrun, with vermin; the rotted floors, ceilings begrimed and often too low to permit you to stand upright; the windows stuffed with rags . . . gaunt, shivering forms and wild ghastly faces, in these black and beetling abodes."

Large communities of free African-Americans rooted themselves in northern cities, but their living conditions often were difficult. Philadelphia had the largest free African-American community, about 22,000, by the 1820s, but all cities attracted families and individuals looking for education and job opportunities. Although in terms of wages and lifestyles, few free African-Americans ever attained the comforts of urban middle-class whites, notable achievements marked the 1820s to 1840s, including thriving networks of black newspapers and circular bulletins, lending libraries, and Baptist and African Methodist Episcopal (AME) churches. Black communities developed intricate social means of absorbing runaway slaves and recently manumitted freedmen into the strangeness of urban freedom.

But the law did not recognize equal rights and citizenship for freedmen. In addition to suffering disenfranchisement (see page 368), free African-Americans who excelled at an occupation often were victimized by resentful white workers. And the generalized view of African-American inferiority proved an insurmountable obstacle for many struggling families. Often denied access to jobs, white schools, and the protection of civil institutions, African-Americans reinforced neighborhood and kinship networks of self-help and protection. For blacks, segregated housing and exclusion from public buildings became the norm in northern cities.

Order and Disorder

The pace of change and the obvious inequalities in the North's urban environment erupted into violence of many kinds during the mid-1800s. Fathers, whether they suffered from job stress, status anxiety, or alcohol abuse, did not always live up to the era's expectations for an affectionate, well-ordered family. Mothers at home sometimes cracked under the pressure of both working for wages and managing all the household chores in cramped living quarters. Even women who enjoyed the labor of servants sometimes could not withstand the accompanying pressure to exhibit republican moral perfection.

Domestic violence and the chaos of crowded tenement life spilled out onto the streets with growing frequency, too. By the late 1820s, theatergoers noticed a marked increase in outbursts of violence during and after performances, and within a few years the "respectable crowds" of middle- and upper-class attendees established separate theaters from those of the rowdy lower class. Raucous amusements on the waterfronts or in lower class-neighborhoods—including circuses sporting exotic animals, feats performed on horseback, wrestling, and wild dancing—frequently became sites of crime. Taverns that served as places to congregate for gossip and sociability saw their share of commotion as the night wore on. Orphan gangs and young men's clubs in rough neighborhoods fought over space to play sports or simply linger. Groups of single males, and sometimes of females, banded together temporarily to lash out at targeted officials or institutions. The popular press fed a growing public hunger for lurid details about "horrid murders," labor strikes, sailors' brawls on the docks, and "shocking drunken rages." Only a few writers pointed out that elite members of society also resorted to violence at times, as when congressmen engaged in fistfights in the revered halls of government. More commonly, observers were preoccupied with the activities of the "dangerous classes" at the bottom of the social ladder.

Racial and ethnic differences fueled the tensions in northern cities. In the late 1820s, Boston erupted frequently in nightlong rioting between immigrant Irish and American-born populations, or between white working-class youths and African-Americans. In 1829 in Cincinnati, white rioters, in response to rumors of generalized southern emancipation, descended on free African-Americans who owned homes and shops and drove the majority of them out of town. The Cincinnati riots reflected the atmosphere in most new states west of the Alleghenies. White westerners, eager to overturn the prohibitions in the Northwest Ordinance against slavery (see pages 258–259), also talked about removing all African-American people from those states. Perhaps because of its large African-American community, Philadelphia became the worst center of race rioting. Almost yearly, mobs attacked some part of the black community, and repeated acts of personal violence marked city life from 1820 to 1850. A violent race riot involving hundreds of Philadelphians convulsed the city in "fiendish brutality" for nearly a week in 1834. The mounted state militia restored order only with difficulty. In the ensuing investigations, arrested rioters vented their resentment against African-Americans who competed for scarce jobs, a common grievance in northern ports. Remarkably, in 1835 white and African-American workers protested together for shorter working hours in Philadelphia and New York City.

Only in the 1830s did the middle class of northern cities begin to establish a few of the professional institutions associated with keeping public order. The colonial system of rotating responsibility for the night watch among citizens, or occasionally appointing constables, could not deal adequately with these explosions of violence. Without systems of law enforcement, cities of the early republic had little or no means to investigate crime. In New York City, citizens who volunteered to keep order chose only to aid the infirm and give street directions to strangers, fleeing at the hint of unruliness. In some quieter coastal towns, constables gradually took on the duty of inspecting suspicious situations and entering buildings to arrest criminals or deliver court orders. In 1833 the city of Philadelphia hired a few policemen to patrol the streets, but in the face of angry mobs, they were helpless.

When New York authorities called out armed militia to suppress disorder, mobs often broke down the authority of such a volunteer force by winning over militiamen who had neighbors or relatives in the crowd. The result, all too often, was chaos in the streets, escalated violence, and more deaths. Starting in 1845, New York's city government finally created a professional police force that held itself more aloof from the grievances of people in the street. A paid, trained, and uniformed presence reinforced the distance of policemen from ordinary people. By the 1850s, most city governments had created police forces of their own.

The Accelerating Industrial Experiment

At an 1833 "Exhibition of American Manufactures," rural storekeepers and laboring Philadelphians ogled at more than seven hundred articles of every conceivable kind, a cross-section of the manufacturing that was flourishing in the Northeast after 1820. Along with textiles in an array of textures and patterns, there were fine-fashioned tea sets, porcelains, cabinets and chairs, and clocks. New power machinery demonstrated how, in the corridor stretching from New England to Maryland, entrepreneurs processed wheat, timber, and leather into useful commodities. Exhibits showcased goods from paper mills that sprang up all around Philadelphia, and from the iron and metalware foundries that clustered around mining and transportation networks in New Jersey, Maryland, and Pennsylvania.

Northern Americans were poised to begin their industrial revolution during these decades. Industrial experiments would begin in both coastal cities and the agricultural hinterlands. Ambitious entrepreneurs everywhere used the familiar ingredients of water, wood, and human muscle to build and power new laborsaving machines, inventing contraptions that brought together new groups of laborers or created the need for new skills. Many observers marveled at the increasing pace of goods moving through the countryside, coaches roaring through city streets, and mail traveling to distant correspondents. Wonderful new goods lined storekeepers' shelves. Others, however, noticed that along with early industrialization came considerable upheaval in the ways Americans worked and lived together.

Coastal and Frontier Farming

From the 1820s to the 1850s, the majority of working men still labored hard on the soil as heads of rural households. But New England's poor soil and diminishing farm size continued to encourage migration westward. By the 1830s, more and more families journeyed farther and farther west to settle land that offered greater yields. "The grass out here [in Michigan]," wrote one young man to his mother back in Vermont, "is greener, higher, and makes the cattle all grow bigger."

Families who chose to stay in New England, New York, and Pennsylvania accelerated changes in farming technologies and cultivation strategies that began in a previous generation. By the 1840s, farm families fertilized and rotated crops more than ever. They plowed deeper in order to churn up rich new soil, and they gave up their traditional scythes for more efficient cradles to harvest grains. New journals taught them how to be "scientific farmers," while skilled woodworkers and blacksmiths sold their skills for wages at neighbors' farms, sometimes for a season and sometimes under contract for a year. These "by-employments" provided important supplemental cash income for struggling families.

Northern farm families also continued to produce more and more for growing local markets in nearby cities and towns. A shipment of milk, eggs, and fruits on the Erie Canal might prove stale when it reached city consumers, but deliveries from farms just five miles out of town provided variety and freshness. Consumers in Philadelphia counted on the produce of adjacent Lancaster and Chester Counties, as well as of New Castle County in Delaware; farmers' wagons crushed together on city streets during market mornings. Likewise, Long Island and Hudson River valley farmers delivered hundreds of loads of food to New York City weekly. Once railroads created fast transportation between East and West, distant farmers shipped durable fruits and vegetables to cities: peaches from Delaware, apples from western New York, onions and greens from the mid-Atlantic.

The lives of northern farm women did not change as quickly as the lives of urban and immigrant women who worked for wages in other people's homes and shops. Farm wives and daughters still spun wool, churned butter, prepared meals and preserved foods for the future, tended gardens and helped press cider, threshed wheat, and collected fuel wood. But in areas that lay near roads and canals, or within rapidly growing eastern counties, change became apparent. Once cheaper imports of cloth and household implements became available, women could devote more time to making marketable goods that brought in household cash, including butter and cheese for sale in town markets. Young women around Pittsburgh took homemade butter to storekeepers who stocked bolts of cloth, sugar, iron kettles, and other desirable goods. When the storekeeper's barrels filled with butter, he hauled them to Philadelphia markets, where an array of imported clocks and mirrors, as well as local craftsmen's cabinets and shoes, enticed "country buyers" thinking of their female customers back home. Indeed, these marketing trips drew women into active public exchanges on a scale that had been discouraged by supporters of women's "separate sphere."

Farming on the frontiers of the Old Northwest Territory, beyond the Appalachian ridge, took on its own distinctive characteristics as the area became heavily settled between the 1820s and 1850s. Families along the Ohio River specialized in corn and pork production by the 1820s and developed links to southern plantation buyers. In the next two decades, new waves of migrants flooded into Ohio, Indiana, and Illinois. They tended to follow the transportation improvements that tied them to more easterly markets, which demanded more wheat than corn and pork. On the heels of a third wave of migration during the 1840s, farmers on the frontier of southern Wisconsin, eastern Iowa, and southern Michigan provided huge quantities of wheat to hungry city dwellers.

An important attraction luring pioneers into these new frontiers was the availability of land and its declining price. In 1836 public land sales reached an all-time high of nearly 20 million acres, much of it acquired in the Old Northwest Territory. Settlers could purchase eighty acres of government land for about a hundred dollars. Thousands of young men borrowed from fathers, kinsmen, and banks to acquire their "stake." If they did not have cash left over for tools, household goods, seed, and animals, farmers could rent from well-endowed landowners. Tenancy, after all, had long been the best stepping-stone toward improvement and possibly even independent farm ownership. Hired itinerant laborers soon became another regular feature of western settlements. In fact, scholars estimate that tenants and itinerant laborers made up at least 25 percent of the western rural population. This proportion roughly equaled that in the Northeast. However, in the older states, landless men tended to experience downward mobility, whereas landless men on the new midwestern frontier could still hope to succeed.

Although such prosperity came to some frontier families, many trans-Appalachian migrants persevered through years of hardship. Crop failures and bankruptcies took their toll, as did lack of medicine in the unhealthy spring thaws or enough warm clothing in the brutal mid-Western winters. But slowly, second-generation frontier families improved their lots. Log cabins with a single room in which to eat, cook, sleep, and produce family necessities in time gave way to slightly larger and more comfortable clapboard dwellings. Gradually, with traditional hand tools and weary animals that were shared by whole neighborhoods, settlers cleared lots from the woods. Fences—building them and repairing them—occupied even more time than they had in colonial years, but eventually pioneers could hold the wolves at bay.

Transportation, Communication, Invention

America was still very much a commercial nation in the 1820s and 1830s. In addition to intricate coastal and Caribbean networks of importing and exporting, merchants plied the Atlantic highway with cargo ships, and numerous new packet lines carried passengers great distances. The Black Ball Line between New York City and Liverpool, for example, moved thousands of travelers and their belongings each year. By 1845, fifty-two trans-Atlantic packets offered similar services. "Square-riggers" ran on regular schedules from New York; others touched at Savannah, New Orleans, Charleston, and St. Augustine. That same year, the first clipper ship, *Rainbow,* took to the seas with its long, narrow hull and great spans of sail. For two decades, clippers moved people and goods faster than ever imagined, on both the Atlantic and the Pacific, and captured the imaginations of journalists and novelists worldwide. Only after the Civil War would Americans give up the glamour of the clipper ship for the greater cargo space and durability at sea of the steamship. A joint venture in 1838 of the British and American Steamship Navigation Company tried to traverse the Atlantic by steam navigation, but into the 1850s transatlantic steamships retained their sails as a backup.

In addition to international commerce, many Americans also attached the word *commerce* to the energetic transformation of the countryside. The transportation revolution (discussed in Chapter 9) was moving people and goods at unprecedented speeds, simultaneously linking and segmenting regions of the nation. By the 1820s, some writers even put internal commerce above foreign trade, as when a Pennsylvania governor insisted that "foreign commerce is a good" undertaking, "but of a secondary nature, [for] happiness and prosperity must be sought for within the limits of our own country." Americans shifted their focus not only from

Clipper Ship Card: *W. B. Dinsmore* With its sleek hull and legions of sails, the swift clipper ship commanded much of the passenger and cargo travel along the East Coast, into the West Indies, and as this advertisement boasts, to San Francisco during the 1840s. Faster and safer than most long-distance overland travel (the express package carriage in this view was also common in America during the era), clippers also "outran" steam vessels and became the fastest mode of transport to the West Coast during the Gold Rush. *(Museum of the City of New York.)*

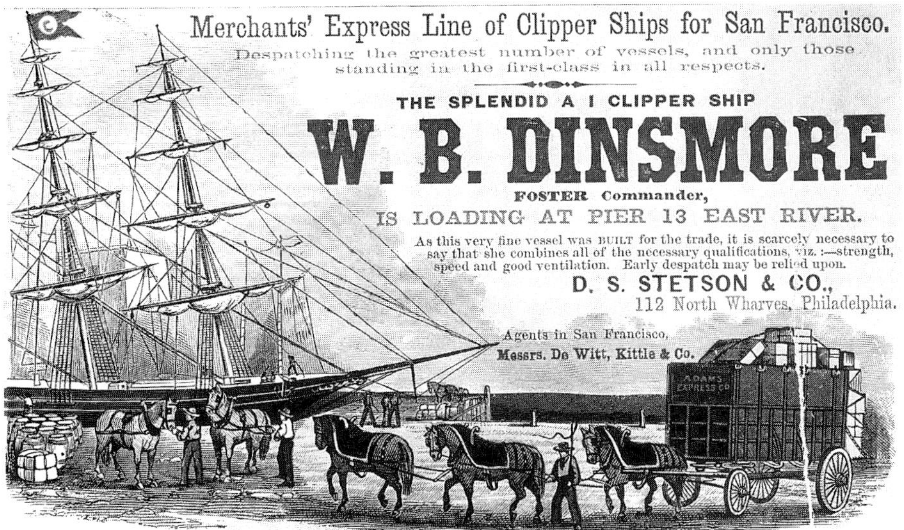

external to internal commerce, but also from skepticism about the effects of commerce to a celebration of its transformative powers. Even the ardent southerner John C. Calhoun had exulted in 1817 that commerce would "bind the republic together," and indeed by the 1820s, hundreds of canal ditches and turnpikes threaded through the American countryside. On rivers, goods and people could move against downstream currents at unimaginable speeds of 10 to 20 miles per hour.

In the momentum building toward industrialization, developers and inventors strengthened their partnership with local, state, and national governments to accomplish projects that had widespread consequences. For example, Samuel F. B. Morse spent years tinkering with devices to send coded messages over long distances. But until he received federal government funds as capital for equipment and workers' wages, Morse was unable to prove his vision. When, in 1844, Morse completed the first telegraph line and sent a message over wire from Washington to Baltimore, the public marveled at such "instantaneous communication." In the past, it had taken days to send commercial reports from New York merchants to Charleston shippers, or to let folks in Boston know the outcome of policy deliberations in Washington. The telegraph transmitted such news at once, allowing it to reach millions of Americans. Within a few months, plans unfolded for connecting the Northeast to other regions with Morse code.

Improvement and invention—supported by government funds, eager manufacturers, and ready consumers everywhere—often began in the North and spread quickly to other regions. Manufacturers in Boston and New York adapted French food preserving techniques to airtight "tin cans" that began to replace glass containers in the 1820s. Northern retailers carried Gail Borden's condensed milk in cans by the late 1830s. The John Deere steel plow, which made its appearance in 1837, speeded the cultivation of new land. Down in Virginia, Cyrus Hall McCormick perfected his "grain cutter," or reaper, a horse-drawn machine that enabled a farmer to harvest ten times more wheat per day. As soon as he patented the reaper in 1834, northern manufacturers began to market it. By the late 1840s, Midwestern wheat farmers were buying McCormick's reapers as quickly as they could be produced. The cast iron stove replaced fireplace cooking and changed northern middle-class women's daily routines forever.

"We live in a most extraordinary age," wrote Daniel Webster in 1825. "Events so various and so important that might crowd and distinguish centuries, are, in our times, compressed within the compass of a single life." As another observer put it, "Every man seems born with some steam engine within him, driving him into an incessant and restless activity of body and mind." Each person, he wrote, seems to be involved with "a thousand projects, and only one holiday—the 4th of July—working from morning till night with the most intense industry."

The railroad captured Americans' relentless pursuit of improvement more than any other innovation during this era. During the 1820s, engineers and politicians in the East set out to "tame and transform" the countryside and tie coastal cities to backcountry regions without reliable waterways. In 1828 the Baltimore and Ohio Railroad laid 13 miles of track; by the end of 1831, the entire country boasted just 73 miles. But in the early 1830s, Charleston merchants funded a plan to link their business to Hamburg, Georgia. Other lines were spreading out from Boston. By 1840, 3,000 miles of track stretched most of the length of the Northeast, and another 5,000 miles linked internal settlements to the coastline during the 1840s. By 1860, Americans traveled on 30,000 miles of railroad bed, much of it forming a spider web of connections linking New England and New York to the Old Northwest; rail lines linked Boston, Albany, Buffalo, Philadelphia, Wheeling, St. Louis, and Pittsburgh.

Until the late 1850s, canals continued to carry more goods—and more safely—through northern and midwestern regions than railroads did. Most rail lines serviced local areas for short distances and ran on their own gauges (the width between the rails). Varied gauges meant that goods and people had to be transferred from one train to another if the distance to be covered spanned more than one line, which proved expensive for shippers and consumers alike. In addition to this inconvenience, the iron straps holding down wooden rails often snapped loose and shot up through the thin floors of passenger cars. Fires that started in wood-burning engines or from stray hot coals caused much shrieking when clothing and luggage ignited.

Still, railroads stimulated iron companies to produce rails and employed craftsmen to provide skilled wood and metal work. Immigrants quarried the stone for rail beds and moved with construction crews to lay new rail or to transport supplies to frontier work sites. Indeed, by the 1850s, there was no mistaking the cultural and economic impact of the "iron horse." Not the Erie Canal, but the railroad boosted Chicago from a sleepy village to a boomtown during that decade. Many thriving river towns faded from prominence as flatboat transportation was replaced by the roar and smoke of trains that joined newer settlements elsewhere. Wealthy Americans who had made fortunes in commerce, lending, or real estate poured their capital into railroad development, and eager foreign investors purchased nearly 25 percent of the bonds that funded U.S. railroad construction.

Exciting Trial of Speed As this view of the locomotive "Tom Thumb" shows, one of the first steps toward developing railroads involved attaching a tiny soot-belching brass steam engine to a passenger carriage, which sped down the rails at a full eighteen miles per hour. Not everyone would hail the demise of horse-drawn transportation in 1830 when Tom Thumb appeared, but in the next three decades, governments and private entrepreneurs together funded construction of thousands of miles of railroad track. *(Museum of the City of New York.)*

Before the Civil War, local and state governments throughout the North and Old Northwest also provided a major stimulus for railroad construction. Politician-businessmen enthusiastically aided railroad development, just as they had promoted canals and turnpikes in the previous generation, by favoring special laws of incorporation, loopholes in tax legislation, and incentives to underwrite development bonds, or by giving direct loans to groups of developers. State and federal governments gave valuable land bounties that totaled nearly 20 million acres by the eve of the Civil War and many millions more in years thereafter.

Northern Labor

Until the early 1800s, most Americans believed that regular labor was reserved for society's middle class and "lower sort." Gentlemen aspired not to work. But the growing political culture and the rapidly changing social structure in America evoked new thinking: working at a useful occupation became a requirement for virtue and goodness in a person. Inventors and developers received public acclaim, and politicians seeking high offices in the North shed their associations with leisure and gentlemanly status, donning the mantle of "an honest working man." Happiness, argued clergymen and politicians, came from industriousness. Speeches and outpourings in newspaper articles insisted that the future belonged not to the "idle wealthy" but rather to the "industrious laboring people," which would include laborers, craftsmen, professionals, intellectuals, and often merchants.

No doubt, some independently wealthy gentlemen claimed to be hard-working only to gain the hearts and minds of voters. But the new attitude nevertheless supported dramatically changing structures of work in the North from the 1820s through the 1850s. At the beginning of this era, over two-thirds of the clothing and shoes, blankets and linens, and processed foods consumed in the North still came from households relatively nearby. In the next decades, however, new technologies, new forms of business organization, and new ways of doing work accelerated and expanded processes that had only begun in the early years of the century. Rising entrepreneurs and ambitious investors began to reorganize the traditional craft shops that dotted the rural landscape. A new breed of "mechanics," or semiskilled workers with extensive practical knowledge, entered every niche of bustling northern life. Tinkerers, improvers, and gentlemen changed this or that small part of a work process, slowly altering old ways of producing after many little experiments with primarily wooden materials.

Most Americans still believed that the ideal setting for these transformations was the countryside. As Jeffersonians had warned for years, cities brought crowding, poor health, and temptations to do evil; manufacturing in cities would only exacerbate these tendencies. Most commentators regarded factories with suspicion, not as places of exciting opportunity. Even workers in the early factories tended to think of themselves as temporary wage earners who would soon leave. In addition, entrepreneurs required moving water to power machinery and transport goods, as well as timber for fuel and construction, both of which were plentiful in myriad rural locations. And since these early "manufactories" remained small handicraft shops with five to ten workers, owners did not yet have to be concerned about recruiting great pools of labor from urban immigrant neighborhoods.

Even in the largest northern cities, factories were still rare before the 1840s. More often, the rapidly growing immigrant neighborhoods became the source of workers in the putting-out system (see page 335). Working for a pittance in garret shops, basements, unlit apartments, and even on rooftops, immigrants and poor native-born Americans accepted pieces of cut fabric from "bosses," who subdivided the work into "bits and parts" throughout the neighborhood. While they watched children, mothers sewed pieces of precut cotton fabric into shirts or petticoats. Girls and boys sat for hours stitching the leather uppers of shoes and then delivered them back to shops where men pieced the tops onto soles. In growing northern cities, this putting-out system eroded workers' ability to see unshaped materials slowly become a useful article.

Entrepreneurs in this system controlled the raw materials, made decisions about how to break down the work, and determined the piecework pay rates. Although bosses touted the convenience for women of working in their homes at traditional needle arts, piece-rates were always appallingly low, and bosses could withhold work when markets were slow or dump inhuman amounts of sewing on young people. In addition, putting out this piecework undermined artisan shops and hastened the demise of the apprenticeship system in northern cities, a trend foretold in Lynn, Massachusetts. Traditional skilled craftsmen who made an entire pair of shoes, a range of iron products for farming, or complete wooden tools and butter churns relinquished work to entrepreneurs who subdivided their trades among women and children in homes. Masters who once worked side by side with apprentices had to adapt or close shop. Between 1820 and 1850, weavers, silversmiths, cabinetmakers, shoemakers, tailors, shirt makers, and other craftsmen in northern cities watched helplessly as their old ways of life faded.

Disruption of the apprenticeship system contributed to the second very consequential development for workers in this era: the breakdown of paternalistic social relations in traditional crafts. In their place, the widespread introduction of wages marked a shift toward "free labor" social relations. Wage workers had the right to seek work wherever they could find it and to leave a job without breaking obligations to a master. Employers stipulated a wage at the time of hire, in addition to work rules and hours; in time, they took less responsibility for the living arrangements and moral conduct of workers. At first, these changes seemed to offer men, women, and even children a measure of the independence that all republican citizens deserved, and to clarify the value of a worker's time and skills applied to a job. Moreover, free labor implied the antithesis of the coercion inherent in slavery. Republican thought held that all white male citizens had a right to decent employment. Free labor was the mutual commitment by employers and workers, which, as one prominent labor leader explained, "decency required should be a living wage" from the employer in return for "faithful execution of the

Shoemakers, 1850s Daguerreotype Perhaps surmising that their small craftsman's shops would be eclipsed by factories and large businesses before long, these shoemakers proudly evoke the era rapidly fading from view. Their clothing—although probably cleaner and in better condition than during regular work—places them among humble working people, as do their tools and finished leather products. *(Library of Congress.)*

tasks" of a job by workers. Claims to freedom could have meaning only because they were morally binding.

It was a small step to extend the meaning of free labor from personal mobility and individual rights to include significant social values. Northerners who lionized the honest workingman celebrated the value of hard work, self-discipline, abstinence from drinking, and the absence of personal debt or obligations to others. Attaining these personal virtues, many argued, was the first step toward upward mobility and possibly the proprietorship of a business and a middle-class lifestyle. From that platform, in turn, the free citizen could begin to promote the upward mobility of still other virtuous workers.

However, this optimism about free labor was counterbalanced by important limitations in the new wage relations. Now, employers could fire workers at will, terminate a company without further obligation to workers, and eradicate the benefits and paternalistic protection that many artisans enjoyed in the past. And free labor ideas often obstructed workers' collective efforts to protect jobs or create community networks for their mutual protection and benefit. Occasionally, when wages were depressed during the 1830s, hungry workers tried petitions, slowdowns, and strikes to persuade employers to meet their perceived moral commitments.

Efforts to form trade unions revived after the worst of the Panic of 1837 had passed. But employers often blacklisted—or refused to hire—workers who became visible and vocal organizers. In New York, Connecticut, and Pennsylvania, employers in the clothing and shoe making trades went even further. They claimed sole power to hire and fire any worker, and fought vigorously against "closed shops," or businesses that required all workers to belong to a particular union. Carrying their argument to the state supreme courts, employers argued that they had a "sovereign right" to control their work forces, and that most union contracts represented "conspiracies" against the superior authority of employers to control the conditions of work. Time and again, in state after state, the courts agreed that each worker should bargain separately with the employer for the best hours and wages, and that employers must have control over working conditions and the fate of "the boss's goods." By and large, then, courts agreed with employers that free labor could not be construed as a collective ideal. Wage work was a matter of individual choice, individual competition for pay and advancement, individual attainment or failure.

The Lowell Experiment

America's first factories were small places. Usually, a few entrepreneurs pooled capital, introduced familiar technology or simple new machines, and hired wage labor from the neighboring countryside. Rapid population growth at home and rising demand abroad spurred early mechanization of milling and refining sites in the countryside. The mechanical improvements of Oliver Evans's mills and the simple cotton gin of Eli Whitney "answered our needs expertly," and Samuel Slater's first family mills suited an agricultural lifestyle (see Chapter 9). Boot and shoe manufacturing was more centralized in the countryside, too, as were papermaking and tanning, once small handicrafts associated with the forests and rural herds of livestock.

By the 1820s, entrepreneurs in New England and mid-Atlantic states began to bring together capital and labor along waterways to form larger factories that further consolidated and mechanized textile production. In Dudley and Oxford, Massachusetts, Slater added to his putting out enterprises with a series of complex mill sites that brought workers away from their homes. However, he had to contend with local farmers who feared that he would divert the flow of streams to run his mills and objected to transitory workers who would use roads and schools without paying taxes. Slater's workers, charged local journalists, were transient and antisocial, an "unsettled bunch" that contrasted with the "settled citizenry." By 1831, Slater petitioned the state government to form a separate mill town of Webster, which subsequently adopted independent ordinances about factory sites and mill workers' lives.

Factory conditions such as these did not arise overnight. The most famous complex of great red brick structures, built at Lowell, Massachusetts, arose out of decades of incremental change that set the stage for the town's system of manufacturing. Beginning in the 1780s, many farmers supplemented their work on poor New England soil with cattle herding, lumber milling, orchards, and woodworking. In time, some skilled craftsmen and jacks-of-all-trades prospered and invested in roads, canals, banking, and distilling.

In Waltham, Massachusetts, prosperity from this diversification laid the foundations for new elite families without connection to old colonial networks. The new local elite around Waltham were mostly merchant shippers who carried cotton, the "white gold" grown and picked by southern slave labor. Some prosperous merchants reinvested their profits in cotton shipping, while a few others bought up the water rights along Massachusetts rivers, where they set up foundries and mills that added to their fortunes. During the War of 1812, they began to put spinning machinery into shops and to hire young women to process raw cotton into thread. This was the "Waltham system."

In the 1820s a third group of investors, some of them new to the area, took control of textile production from Waltham's new elite and consolidated operations in small factories. By 1823, they had moved operations to the town named for the merchant and investor Francis Cabot Lowell, and from that location they sent agents out into the countryside to recruit women from struggling farm families. So successful was this complex of people and production that it attracted the attention of prominent merchant businessmen in Boston, who in 1830 took over a large portion of Lowell's operations. These Boston Associates, linked by birth and marriage, owned shares in numerous banking, insurance, and canal projects. Many of them had made fortunes in the China and India trades, and kept a close eye on possibilities for transporting southern cotton exports in their ships.

Soon the Associates introduced copies of the famous English power looms used for weaving thread into cloth. Unlike Slater's method of dispersing spinning and weaving tasks to different places, the Lowell system integrated all aspects of textile manufacturing in one place. Raw cotton entered one end of the mill complex of six buildings, and finished cloth emerged from the other. The Lowell mills were four stories high, with almost all the machinery hooked up to a huge central water wheel by shafts and belts.

Very early on, the Lowell factory was converted to a limited liability corporation, which allowed the owners to pool their individual resources but limit their individual risk: in the event of failure, only company assets could be used to pay outstanding debts. Backers thus gained confidence in the long-run possibilities of the Lowell system, which attracted more capital. Indeed, by 1835, Lowell was a complex of fifty-two mills employing more than twelve thousand people at the juncture of the Merrimack and Concord Rivers.

Unconventionally, Lowell's owners initially chose a work force of young women who did not bring mechanical skills from the countryside. Most of them had lived and worked on typical New England farms all their lives, but during the 1820s, they came by the dozens to sign contracts promising to stay in the mills at least a year and obey all mill rules. In the early Lowell years, the idea of single, unmarried ladies leaving home for months to work for strangers shocked observers. But the Lowell owners assured skeptics that their "operatives" would be well cared for under the work rules, religious training, and moral rectitude enforced on their premises. Pleasant dorm-like living quarters in wooden frame buildings, encircled with white picket fences, gave the visual impression that Lowell was a home away from home.

"Lowell girls" often reinforced arguments about the benefits of their new factory life in these first years. In letters to their families and friends, as well as in private diaries, they wrote about why they chose to enter the factory: it added cash to the family income; it gave them a chance to escape the drudgery of farm life; and it put them in touch with fashion, education, and the wider New England culture. The three dollars a week in wages was also a strong incentive. Mill work was a "freer life" for eleven-year-old Lucy Larcom, who wrote fondly about Lowell in her old age. Boardinghouse supervisors and factory overseers gave glowing reports about the productivity and happiness of the operatives.

But within a few years the operatives began to voice discontent. Air in the mills was hot and filled with cotton lint, and the machines were dreadfully noisy. The work—hour after hour, six days a week—was tedious. Far away from home, and from male company, gulping down monotonous meals, and subject to the whims of the company managers on the work floors, the young women argued for relief from the constraints imposed on them in their twelve-hour workday. But the company replied by tightening rules of behavior in the mills and imposing harsh penalties for infractions. Living by a regimented schedule marked by the peal of bells—awakening to bells, reporting to work by bells, going to lunch and returning again by the same bells—grated on workers' nerves. Within a few years, the work itself was degraded by giving each Lowell girl an unskilled or semiskilled task, for which she was paid a meager wage; the title of operative was reduced to "hands." Viewed by the mid-1830s as less than a whole person, as an extension of the machines, many a Lowell hand had little but her wages to look forward to.

Even leisure time was regimented at Lowell, including time spent in sleeping quarters and on Sundays. In defiance of rules for reporting to dorm rooms at night, one young female worker wrote, "I now make my own wage, and I shall make my own private time too." After regular working hours, the young women increasingly insisted, the Lowell Company had no right to control their living conditions and leisure pleasures. Operatives' complaints were seconded by a number of outside observers who drew bleak pictures of the young girls working away from home. Seth Luther, a carpenter who helped construct some of New England's early textile factories, wrote indignantly about the deplorable conditions of farm girls at Lowell and immigrant children hired at neighboring factories. Long hours, severe punishments in "whipping rooms," and the absence of fresh air and time to play, all contributed to the dour, short lives of factory hands. Women worked "like slaves for thirteen or fourteen hours every day" in the "prisons in New England called cotton mills." "Cotton mills where cruelties are practiced, excessive labor required, education neglected" had become "palaces of the poor."

In the 1830s, verbal discontent grew to open violations of mill rules and printed protests in the mill hands' paper, *The Lowell Offering*. Then in the years preceding the Panic of 1837 (see Chapter 10), falling credit and cotton markets compelled mill owners to squeeze more productivity from their workers or cut wages—or both. When the Lowell owners imposed wage cuts because of competition from textile producers elsewhere and deteriorating economic conditions, Lowell girls "turned out" in strikes. Starting in 1834, nearly eight hundred hands turned out when their wages were summarily cut about 25 percent. The cut pushed the value of their labor as "daughters of freemen" "below decency." But wages continued to fall. Again in 1836 owners reduced wages and the mill girls struck; when they failed for a

New England Spinning Mill Interior, c. 1850 Compared with the modern American factory, the relatively simple machinery, small shop floor, and exposed leather bands attached to power equipment shown here seem truly to be from an earlier era. Compared with the small craft shops still prevalent during the 1840s, however, this early New England textile mill would have been a startling environment in which to work. The women mill operatives probably came from the farms in the surrounding countryside. Their conditions of work would have been notably different from those of the shoemakers on page 422. *(George Eastman House.)*

second time, many young women lost hope that the mills could offer them decent opportunities, and they returned to the countryside.

For those who stayed in the mills, conditions worsened. In fact, female hands were gradually replaced by impoverished Irish male immigrants desperate for jobs. Nevertheless, spokesmen such as Luther, and their ardent pleas for regulation, led the state of Massachusetts to pass the country's first child labor law in 1842, one that prohibited children under twelve from working more than ten hours a day. Elsewhere in the country, male skilled workers were demanding a ten-hour workday, which inspired the New England Female Labor Reform Association of Lowell and its surrounding mills to petition the Massachusetts government for similar reform. The ten-hour proposal they sent in 1845 fell on deaf legislative ears, as did one in 1846 supported by ten thousand signatures. Only in 1847, when women workers in Nashua, New Hampshire, refused to stay on the job after sunset, did their state pass a ten-hour-day law; other states reluctantly followed with similar laws in the coming years.

Varieties of Social Reform

Immigration, urbanization, and industrialization called forth many critics and reformers from the 1820s to the 1850s. Some of them expressed their beliefs through literature and the fine arts. Others, fueled by the moral fervor of the Second Great Awakening and the perceived duty of emerging middle-class families to be models of virtue, set out to identify and uplift idle, sinful, criminal, intemperate, and impoverished citizens. They implored "unrefined and unmannered" American-born and immigrant people to follow their example of upstanding behavior. Some reformers started institutions to control or rehabilitate individuals deemed "deviant" from reformers' middle-class ideals. Others founded movements for profound moral and social reform across American society. By the 1840s, an array of organizations promoted individual self-improvement—especially the avoidance of drinking and gambling—and benevolent agencies strove to put the idle to work and to reform the criminal and insane. As the reform momentum built, organizations grew and their efforts took a qualitative leap into political struggles to secure rights for women and freedom for slaves.

Individualism and Improvement

Through the 1820s, important voices continued to associate America's territorial expansion and growing social complexity with political democracy and economic opportunity. The articulate French observer Alexis de Tocqueville traveled widely in old and new regions of the nation during the late 1820s. Tocqueville believed that restlessness with their current condition was the most salient characteristic of the nation's citizens. Its results were, in part, the widest spread of democracy anywhere in the world. Ceaseless climbing from one rung of the social ladder to another, an "innumerable crowd of those striving to escape from their original social condition," marked American life. Few adhered to traditions of accepting their "station"; few now wished to be ruled passively by their "betters."

But by 1820, it was clear to many others that northern prosperity was not universal. Since the early 1800s, boom alternated with bust; spells of bountiful harvests seesawed with stark years of scarcity; floods of imported "necessaries and superfluities" dried up during seasons in which few ships docked at urban ports. Jobs came and went, wages rose and fell, apparently in little correlation with skills or personal diligence. The Panic of 1837 blew like a frigid chill through the country, and the subsequent depression from 1837 to 1843 froze hundreds of thousands of Americans in icy unemployment and debt.

Journalists, intellectuals, businessmen, and farmers all tried to understand this fluctuation of good and bad times. Few of them identified structural or institutional causes for crises. But individualism, often promoted as the basis for collective prosperity in America, seemed to backfire all too often and without apparent cause. How could so many ambitious and virtuous individuals fail to achieve success?

By the time Tocqueville was writing, voices of optimism were being drowned out by misgivings about individualism and free market forces. For example, merchant

Samuel Mitchell in New York lamented that too many Americans wanted not only their independence from England, but "to be equally independent of each other." And when "every man is for himself alone and has no regard for any person farther than he can make him subservient to his own views," then lawlessness and "savagery" lay around the corner. Skeptics pointed toward the fearful rise in murder, suicide, theft, prostitution, and children's gangs. Under the guise of middle-class respectability, some entrepreneurs were enticing unwary consumers with underhanded deals and price gouging. At the same time, upstanding middle-class people recoiled from the dirty children and their haggard mothers living in urban hovels. Too many people, regardless of class or national origin, seemed to have lost their self-discipline and resorted to the liquor bottle when poverty or business failures overcame them. Too many people had lost all respect for civic responsibility, social manners, and public order. It seemed all too clear that some Americans could not handle their new republican liberties of political democracy and free labor.

What could be done? Some observers in the North proposed that the growing number of disadvantaged people required external help to attain "their true promise" as improved individuals. At first, a few intellectuals broke away from mainstream churches and literary circles and proposed that "perfection" would occur not within society, but within the individual. A few people dedicated to moral self-improvement and the regeneration of virtue in America, they proposed, would initiate small self-contained societies; in time, these societies would grow and prevail over the corrupted elements of American life. From the 1830s to 1850s, however, these separatist efforts were gradually eclipsed by larger movements that sought to reform American life with direct action. Women's rights activists, for example, protested the hypocrisy of advocating universal personal improvement, and then denying fully half of the population the opportunity for such fulfillment. Religious reformers such as Charles Grandison Finney confronted the powerful appeal of individualism with the equally powerful attraction of social harmony, what he boldly called "the complete reformation of the whole world." And, as detailed in Chapter 12, a growing number of abolitionists contended that individualism, political democracy, and free labor were thriving at great cost: the perpetual enslavement of an entire race.

Temperance

Temperance reformers had a big job on their hands. By 1830, Americans drank more than five gallons of distilled spirits per person each year, or more than any European nation admitted and over three times more than Americans consume today. Whiskey, rum, and hard cider were regular features of the working day, and of leisure time. A thousand distilleries operated in New York City during the 1820s, and the cost of distilled beverages sold by the glass in dram shops declined to easy affordability over the coming years.

However, concerns about public order and private health were also growing. Reformers linked excessive drinking to domestic violence, loss of valuable family income, loss of time on the job, and public rowdiness. But the root of the problem, most of them insisted, was the tradition of drinking throughout the day both on the job and after hours. The developing middle class deplored this habit. Businessmen began to forbid their work crews from drinking on the job; some urged workers to give up alcoholic beverages for good. Within a few years, a large movement to enact temperance legislation had formed, spearheaded by middle-class clergymen, entrepreneurs, and Whig politicians in the North.

In terms of the sheer number of members, the American Society for the Promotion of Temperance, founded in 1826 by evangelical reformers intent on leading drinkers toward prayer and personal conversion, was the largest reform organization of the era. Connecticut evangelical minister Lyman Beecher was the movement's early leader. Beecher, echoed by hundreds of local temperance chapters of the Society, warned that drinking inevitably led to poverty, adultery, social crime, and brutalities against family members. By 1834, millions of Americans had met in public gatherings, confessed their "fall into the sin of drink," and taken "the pledge" to stop drinking altogether. In 1836 the newly organized American Temperance Union moved beyond individual reform and brought its full weight to legislative halls, where it demanded laws to shut down dram shops and to license taverns more strictly. As that legislative crusade continued, the Panic of 1837 and its ensuing depression led skilled artisans and rising manufacturers to give up a drinking lifestyle they could no longer afford. People flocked to join temperance societies that required stern pledges of abstinence. Great numbers of women—the wives, mothers, and sweethearts of working, and drinking, men—found the combination of familiar republican language and stirring evangelical influences a powerful force against the "evils of drink." Women's groups, some called the Martha Washington Societies, worked for temperance legislation despite their inability to vote. Finally, the legislative crusade against liquor scored a success in 1851 when Maine became the first state to go dry by banning the sale or manufacture of any alcoholic beverages. Over the next years, other states would pass "Maine laws" as well.

Asylums and Prisons

Like the temperance movement, efforts to address so-called deviant behavior led individual reformers to propose government legislation. Those efforts also linked popular evangelicalism with middle-class presumptions about molding a moral society. Helen Jewett, for example, was a "fallen woman" in the eyes of this middle class; she had resisted the "cleansing power of prayer" and had spurned decent employment and marriage. The Female Moral Reform Society, founded in 1834 by middle-class women in the North's burgeoning evangelical movement, avoided ridiculing prostitutes and instead targeted the poverty that drove most women into prostitution. The society organized charity, work, and soup kitchens for them. At about the time of Jewett's murder, these reformers were also seeking legislation to enact penalties for clients as well as prostitutes brought to court. Although those efforts largely failed during the 1830s, the Moral Reform Society earned public acclaim for identifying the male clients of prostitutes in New York City and publishing their names. In this way, the burden of prostitution shifted somewhat away from individual women who seemed to have no other economic choice, and onto the shoulders of government and its institutions.

Reformers also stepped into the lives of people defined as criminal or insane. For generations, colonists and early national Americans did not distinguish clearly between these two kinds of people. Individuals who could not cope with the demands of social laws and moral standards—whether out of willful criminality or unwitting insanity—had been entrusted to their families or given temporary relief in tiny public institutions. But by the early 1830s, reformers in major cities protested that a maturing and crowded America required a more systematic approach. They demanded not only larger institutions, but also more enlightened responses to those who had been born into physically or mentally challenging situations or who had fallen on hard times. The criminal and insane, noted reformers with disgust, had been thrown together into dank and filthy rooms where they were neglected or subjected to unjustified cruelties. Every individual, they insisted,

The Stepping Mill, 1823 Reformers who grew concerned about the growing number of vagrants in already-crowded northern cities began to build establishments for putting the idle and poor to work in the 1820s and 1830s. Treated virtually as prisoners put to hard labor for six months at a time, vagrants made rope, paved city streets, or, as this illustration shows, worked the treadmill, or "stepping wheel." Bellevue (New York) Hospital's wheel was a twenty-foot-long cylinder attached to millstones; it was turned by sixteen "inmates" for eight minutes at a time. The city's mayor hoped the mill would induce forced workers to find meaningful employment. *(© Collection of the New-York Historical Society.)*

could be personally improved if given the proper environmental and educational conditions.

A leading proponent of this view was Dorothea Dix, who during the 1830s spent years investigating the treatment of insane women. In 1843 she reported to the Massachusetts legislature her horror at finding "the mixing of impoverished and ravaged" poor women with hardened criminals in the same cells. No efforts, she found, had been made to bring hundreds of women—"degraded, beaten, naked, and chained"—back into society; instead, they were locked up and "utterly ignored." Traveling thousands of miles for dozens of speaking engagements, Dix was able to awaken lawmakers to the need for more humane treatment for the insane. By the late 1850s, most states had created separate institutions for criminals and the insane. During the same decade, other reformers joined forces in northern states to move away from random private charity for orphans and the poor, toward the creation of public orphanages, hospitals, shelters, and immigrant aid societies.

Zealous reformers also hoped that by building "model prisons" in rural settings "away from the rigors of our cities," they could create conditions for teaching self-discipline and an orderly personal lifestyle—the first steps toward reintegrating criminals back into civil society. But these hopes failed. Even in new prisons, inmates' daily lives became regimented; guards watched, directed, and some said "herded" them. Absolute silence was imposed for long periods of time, prescribed Bible readings assigned. Separated from one another in individual cells, prisoners experienced isolation to the point of widespread depression and suicide in the early years of these experiments. The model prisons of Auburn and Ossining ("Sing Sing") in New York became focal points for journalists' outrage.

Family Roles and Education

During the early 1800s, wealthy and middle-class Americans idealized their families as moral institutions that nurtured republican virtue. Women in these families owed their first allegiance to their homes, where they raised and educated their children to become patriotic adults and comforted husbands who "retreated each day from the rigors of business and politics" to the haven of the family domicile. But by the 1820s, many middle-class women were taking their "female" responsibilities outside the home in very important ways. Urban voluntary associations distributed religious pamphlets, instructed children of orphanages in moral character, or taught in Sunday schools, which were activities suited to the presumed moral character of women. Women who attended evening lyceum lectures or enrolled in extensive instruction from clergymen sometimes stepped out of their prescribed female roles to join political activists in the abolitionist movement. Catharine Beecher, a writer and speaker as talented as her father Lyman, traveled widely to deliver public lectures on numerous subjects. Beecher, who authored a much-read *Treatise on Domestic Economy*, provided an inspirational model of a woman "building the moral government of God," promoting temperance, and tirelessly supporting educational and health institutions.

These activities also drew attention to the place of children in American families. Middle-class children enjoyed a diversity of entertainments and educational opportunities by the 1840s. They were schooled in academic subjects, dance and the arts, and etiquette. Novels and newspaper stories provided strong moral messages for children, instructed parents in childrearing, and became workbooks for household education of "young republicans." But children in working-class and immigrant families lived very differently. They often made vital contributions to household incomes by sewing for wages, earning pennies a week at shipyard jobs, or tending the small gardens alongside rundown homes. Poor children sometimes spent hours a day scavenging for food and fuel. Formal education was obviously out of the question.

Although few observers suggested that these growing social differences among children might be remedied by the wholesale reform of the American economy, many middle-class reformers fought for far-reaching educational reforms that would affect children of all social layers. Women active in their churches were among the first to stress childen's natural innocence and openness to moral instruction, rebutting colonial views of children as inherently sinful (see page 114). And for republican women who strove to nurture their children to be good republican citizens, it was a short step to believe that long-term, institutional education would benefit all children and strengthen the moral fabric of America. Before the Civil War, a variety of private and public schools appeared.

Northern states started public schools during the period from 1790 to 1820, most of them meeting in a room at the teacher's house or at church. By the 1820s, girls and boys attended in about equal numbers, and they came out of the schools with solid foundations in reading and accounting. Private academies also took root in the North and proved especially important for women who sought a frontier missionary career or the polish to rise in middle-class society.

In 1827 Massachusetts passed the first law to support public schools with taxes, thanks to the efforts of Horace Mann, the first secretary of the state Board of Education. Within a few years, white children from age five to nineteen could obtain a free education in numerous subjects. States throughout the North began to train female teachers in free "normal schools" and to monitor curriculum to include basic skills. By the late 1830s, school buildings were a regular feature of most northern and western towns (the South was slower to reform education). Oberlin College, founded in Ohio by leading religious and abolitionist activists from the East, was the first school of higher education to admit women, beginning in 1837. Oberlin also admitted African-Americans. Meanwhile, Mann crusaded during the 1840s to have all schools separate children by age, in order to encourage children with peer reinforcement, and then by ability within their age groups, in order to pace children's learning according to ability.

Teacher-training programs helped prepare some young women to take positions in the new schools, but most teachers relied on their background in religious and classical private education to give them a grounding as educators. By the mid-1820s, single young women left the security and comfort of eastern families by the dozens to take up positions in schoolhouses on the distant frontiers of Maine, Wisconsin, or

Indiana. Many young ladies were such welcome members of struggling frontier communities that they were asked to give advice on household accounting, land surveying, or the feasibility of building this or that manufactory. Families named their newborn children after the teachers who brought "so generous a portion of the mental life" to lonely settlers. But frontier teachers expressed their own lonely sentiments in letters to family members, lamenting the rapid onset of homesickness, depressingly low pay, and absence of eligible marriage partners. Teaching was still not a viable career for most young women.

Despite the increasing availability of public education, not all children went to school very long. Urban boys often attended sporadically and then left at age fourteen to begin a job as a retailer's clerk or a grocer's errand boy, thereby providing a necessary addition to their family's income. Rural children attended school for two or three months a year, depending on when their families could release them from work.

Women's Rights

Middle-class women who identified with republican ideals of home and motherhood entered every reform movement of the era, believing that women could make important contributions to changing the lives of wayward or unfortunate people around them. They also generally continued to accept the duties of their separate sphere. But a few outspoken and ambitious women sought more: to create conditions of legal, social, and emotional equality among men and women. In 1848 Elizabeth Cady Stanton and Lucretia Mott organized a convention in Seneca Falls, New York, to discuss these goals in an organized manner. Like many other women's rights advocates, Stanton and Mott had already been active in the growing movement to end slavery, and from that experience they appealed to the republican ideals of the Declaration of Independence for their women's rights platform. All men and women, their founding document proclaimed, "are endowed by the Creator with certain inalienable rights." To spark public awareness and action, delegates resolved to "employ agents, circulate tracts, petition the State and national legislatures, and endeavor to enlist the pulpit and the press on our behalf." Separate spheres of public and private activities for the genders, the convention concluded, perpetuated women's inequality.

Susan B. Anthony joined Stanton and Mott in 1851 and became one of the movement's powerful organizers. Hailing from a Quaker family in Massachusetts, Anthony had already begun her reform career in the temperance, moral reform, and antislavery movements in previous years. She left the teaching profession after experiencing repeated gender discrimination there, resolved that women had to organize and lead their own reform efforts. Anthony developed networks of female "captains" who could mobilize hundreds of women throughout New York to muster thousands of petition signatures on short notice. She trained women to speak before legislatures and to lobby energetically for the right to bring suit in courts, to retain all property they brought into marriage if the union dissolved, and to keep their own wages when they worked. Northern local groups expanded Anthony's teachings to include struggles for women's custody of children when they lost husbands, and guarantees of women's entry into places of higher education and seminaries. They made some modest legislative gains. For instance, between 1848 and 1858, women in some northern states were guaranteed protection of family property on the death of a husband, a measure that indirectly helped wealthy women because it ensured that their husband's property remained a family inheritance and did not pass into the clutches of creditors. A more radical demand was for the right to vote. Reformers declared "we do not seek to protect woman, but rather to place her in a position to protect herself," which the right to vote would aid. This more sweeping demand for female suffrage would, of course, remain unmet for decades to come. However, able leaders of the wider women's rights movement had laid a foundation of leadership and experience by the Civil War. This early women's rights movement set important precedents for women writing and speaking on behalf of their gender.

Intellectual Currents

The printed and spoken word traveled much faster after 1820, but its effects were varied and sometimes ambiguous. On the one hand, ideas and stories in newspapers, information about goods and their prices, and itinerant amusements brought people of many backgrounds closer together, especially in the political culture. On the other hand, popular culture and intellectual life in this era also illuminated differences, just as occupations, origins, and social status divided Americans into different groups.

Susan B. Anthony, 1852
Anthony was one of the most tireless female reformers of the era. Along with Elizabeth Cady Stanton, Anthony founded the Women's State Temperance Society in New York in 1852, and together they were active abolitionists and female labor reformers. Later, Anthony was an outspoken suffragist as well. *(Susan B. Anthony House.)*

Clergymen continued to be important intellectual leaders of communities. During the 1820s, for example, Lyman Beecher led efforts to prevent businesses from operating on Sundays. Throughout the North, church members galvanized behind political lobbying and neighborhood petitioning in support of the era's many moral reforms. Religious institutions drew in hundreds of thousands of members, provided instruction and inspiration to involve members in active reform, and then linked them back to public educational, temperance, and other reform movements.

Some religious groups gave up trying to reform society around them and opted instead for escape into isolated communities. Members left churches of both the older Protestant denominations and the newer evangelical churches to found "utterly purified" sects. In 1830 Joseph Smith came forward to announce that he had received the Book of Mormon teachings from an angel in a vision, leading him to found the Church of Jesus Christ of Latter-Day Saints. Members of the new religion, known as the Mormons, developed strong communal discipline and very quickly became economically successful wherever the church had members. But their success in living self-sufficiently and apart bred jealousy in non-Mormon neighboring communities, whose hostility drove Smith's followers from place to place. Harassed in New York, they moved on to the frontier of Ohio, then across Indiana and Illinois, into Missouri. From 1839 to 1844, Mormons thought they had found the perfect location for their growing number of believers in Nauvoo, Illinois. But once again, intolerant neighbors besieged them. This time, local authorities arrested Joseph Smith and his brother, claiming their crime was the Mormon practice of polygamy, or marriage between one man and many wives. Once in jail, a mob attacked and killed the two men. A new leader, Brigham Young, relocated the Mormons in 1846–1847 to Salt Lake City, far from the all-too-familiar persecution. There, in the unfamiliar challenging western environment, the struggling community eventually thrived.

Some eastern evangelicals developed exaggerated fears of imminent disaster, perhaps an apocalypse, and promoted extreme responses to the era's rapid change and economic turmoil. William Miller, a New England Baptist preacher prophesied that the Second Coming of Christ would happen on October 22, 1843. Until then, conditions would deteriorate throughout the nation. Rejecting the spirit of reform during the era, Millerites sold their worldly goods, bid farewell to family and neighbors, and prepared for their ascension to heaven on the Day of Judgment. When the anticipated Coming did not arrive, Millerites revised the date and continued to wait.

Other radical sects believed that their perfection did not require a Second Coming and entry into the next world; rather, they could achieve "heaven on earth" in their own ideal communities. Over a hundred of these communitarian—or utopian—societies were generated between the Revolution and the Civil War, although the greatest number of them existed during the 1840s. One influential group was the Shakers, founded in 1744 when Mother Ann Lee left the Quakers to establish a community of equal brothers and sisters that would replace the traditional family. The Shakers also practiced celibacy. During the 1830s they settled in communities established on the fringe of existing towns totaling about six thousand members in eight states.

Another kind of utopian society, radical free-love advocates, gathered at Oneida, New York. Founded by John Humphrey Noyes in 1848, Oneidans agreed to form one family in "complex marriage," in which any "saved" man or woman could have intercourse with any other, but in which only certain males were selected to father children, who were in turn raised communally. Shocked outsiders viewed Oneida as scandalous, but the community survived for many years as a successful economic enterprise, producing first animal traps and then flatware.

Socialist utopians formed New Harmony, Indiana, in 1825 under the leadership of the Scottish intellectual-industrialist Robert Owen. Owen believed that private property lay at the root of unemployment and poverty, so his community adopted carefully planned work regimens and an ethic of group sharing. But New Harmony's goals were too lofty, and the community folded within a few years. From the start, it was overcrowded, so inclusive as to invite constant infighting, and so bookish that residents neglected agricultural production.

Also scattered through the midwestern states were the "phalanxes," or huge social complexes designed by the French intellectual Charles Fourier. Fourierism purported to divide work tasks "rationally" according to suppositions about personality, age, gender, and physical stature. Fourierists rejected the creed of individualism and competition, substituting communal ownership.

Some utopian experiments functioned as retreats for reformers who sought intellectual and emotional closeness. In Massachusetts, Brook Farm in West Roxbury and Hopedale in Milford allowed temperance, women's rights, educational, and antislavery reformers to talk and write together, and to sustain themselves with farm labor. Fruitlands, a communitarian experiment near Concord, Massachusetts, that attracted radical intellectuals, set out to farm productively but foundered when members spent too much time studying and writing. All in all, cooperative and socialist communities sprang up in dozens of spots across the northern states. Although they proposed important intellectual and social alternatives to mainstream American life, their numbers always remained modest compared with the many thousands of members joining the middle-class voluntary associations during these years.

In another small but influential trend, elite institutions promoting intellectual pursuits flourished in the northern states by the 1820s. After its modest beginnings before 1800, modeled on the Royal Society of London, Philadelphia's American Philosophical Society (APS) gained a reputation for entertaining statesmen and scientists of note. APS members heard scientific papers presented by members and invited guests, and shared ideas about how to promote Philadelphia's growth. The Boston Athenaeum began lending books in 1807, and New Yorkers revived a subscription library that had begun in colonial years. Both brought together gentlemen and interested middle-class citizens to attend lectures or share reading material. Starting before the War of 1812, Boston's *North American Review* regularly published information about European intellectual trends, thereby bringing the professional, business, and political elite of New England more directly into world affairs.

Out beyond the major towns, however, intellectual life was a mixture of influences carried from the East and those arising from new conditions in the West. In large river towns such as Lexington and Cincinnati, settlers enjoyed regular traffic with eastern cities, which allowed both printed and word-of-mouth exchange of news. Their civic leaders and local merchants who wished to influence distant politicians or promote local improvements held meetings that sometimes became a form of public entertainment. But many settlers in Ohio country found little to read except the omnipresent religious tracts of the Society for the Propagation of the Gospel or the Methodists. Almanacs and collections of tall tales sold much better than literary magazines to new populations just settling in.

Even in the more cultured East, the gap widened between the fine arts embraced by the elite and the maturing popular culture of urban middle and working classes. Middle-class women began to crave the American-authored sentimental novels that became immensely popular starting in the 1820s. Recoiling from the rapid pace of change and the rank individualism rising all around them, sentimental authors appealed to inner feeling, family security, and social sincerity. Sentimentalists warned against dangerous eastern cities and Mississippi River boomtowns that were filled with untrustworthy predators. Prostitutes, confidence men, frauds, and cheats would subvert, without a shred of remorse, any virtuous young woman who failed to tread a moral path. Most of these stories adhered to a moral formula that idealized middle-class republican motherhood and the sheltering home. Heroic women cheerfully met the most trying of circumstances and prevailed against a cruel world to create lovingly nurtured families. Along the way, many of these "republican novels" reinforced the ideology of separate spheres and the rewards of nurturing virtuous republican citizens. Sentimental works also taught women how to behave in public, how to entertain at home "in the genteel manner,"" and even how to dress for various ritual occasions. Ironically, women wrote most of these novels and journalistic pieces, thereby breaking into public professional circles that were typically closed to them.

Eastern writers who appealed to a popular audience—though one still bound by literacy and the ability to buy printed volumes—often chose themes drawn from the frontier experience. Daniel Boone, the hearty individualist of mythical proportions, provided the model for Natty Bumppo in James Fenimore Cooper's *Leatherstocking Tales*. One of these epics, *The Last of the Mohicans* (1826), portrays the march of civilizing tendencies across the Old Northwest and the tragedies of wiping out Iroquois villages. A few years before that, Washington Irving mesmerized middle-class readers with his stories about Rip Van Winkle and the Headless Horseman, both of whom were characters set in rural simplicity. Other writers populated their work with realistic details drawn from everyday life and elevated them to romantic national icons. Authors praised the mundane chores of farmers, the Saturday night impromptu dances of Irish immigrants, the meticulous jottings in a retailer's account book, and the frontier "school marm."

Paralleling these new literary styles, many artists also tried to capture on canvas what it was to be an American. Thomas Cole founded the Hudson River school of painting that romanticized the landscapes of New York's Catskill and Adirondack Mountains in frankly nationalistic tones. Karl Bodmer and George Catlin captured the dramatic scenery of the West on canvas during the early 1830s and thus helped impart to eastern and southern viewers a sympathy for the vast expanses of land and the Indians being displaced from it. Naturalists also put into watercolors and oils the birds, mammals, and varied flora of places few Americans would ever visit. Yet great numbers of Americans embraced these printed and painted scenes of unknown frontiers as a part of their national identity.

A small but influential group of intellectuals known as transcendentalists arose during the 1830s. Professing that the material world was inferior to the spiritual and intellectual life of individuals, a core of New England radicals abandoned their urban and industrial communities and went to live at Brook Farm. Many of them were Unitarian ministers and scholars of German and English romanticism, a movement that stressed emotion, imagination, and freedom from social conventions. Foremost among the transcendentalists, Ralph Waldo Emerson articulated the philosophy that there existed an ideal reality, the Universal Being, which transcended ordinary life. Each person, insisted Emerson, could intuit this reality quite apart from government, churches, or social clubs. As he wrote in one famous essay, "Nature," in 1836, individual existence is best perfected directly in the natural world, where "standing on the bare ground—my head bathed by the blithe air, and uplifted into infinite space—all mean egotism vanishes . . . the currents of the Universal Being circulate through me." On the lecture circuit, Emerson spoke to packed rooms around the country about the virtues of America's cultural separation from Europe. Ironically, Emerson probably did not intend to inspire young people to achieve business and professional success, but his praise for individualism had that effect. Like Finney's mystically converted Christian and Cooper's self-reliant Natty Bumppo, Emerson's morally perfected individual was beyond the reach of corrupted civil society. As most transcendentalists did, Emerson vehemently opposed slavery and expressed horror to his huge audiences when, in 1850, Congress passed the Fugitive Slave Act, which guaranteed the return of runaway slaves to masters.

"Niagara Falls," by Frederic Edwin Church (1857) Church's painting of Niagara Falls captured the grand scale and magnificent beauty of nature that landscape artists of the Hudson River School were depicting during the era. In addition to being one of the highly idealized subjects of art, Niagara Falls was quickly becoming a popular resort area for visitors who took guided tours of this sublime attraction. *(The Corcoran Gallery of Art.)*

Henry David Thoreau, a friend of Emerson's, took the transcendentalist message about individualism further. Thoreau left the Massachusetts communities around him and, for a short time, opted for a hermit's life in the woods at Walden Pond (near Concord). *Walden, Or Life in the Woods* (1854), his most famous work, stingingly rebuked the "get-ahead generation" who sought lives of rank materialism and ended up leading "lives of quiet desperation." Another transcendentalist, Margaret Fuller, toured widely in the 1840s and wrote about the great social and intellectual potential of women, if only they could be released from the constraints of conventional norms. And Walt Whitman, whose *Leaves of Grass* (1855) exploded poetical traditions, tried to capture Emerson's call to have an "original relation" with nature. Each person, Whitman insisted, could reach a state of equality with "divine nature" and thereby reach equality with all "souls of our democracy."

Some contemporaries denounced the transcendentalists in New England as dangerous radicals. Thoreau and Fuller, feared clergymen and journalists, would bring down the exciting transformations and opportunities of life in the 1830s–1840s, and either return Americans to rustic simplicity or create the appalling spectre of women's equality. Traveling through the transcendentalist circle briefly, novelist Nathaniel Hawthorne has his adulterous couple in *The Scarlet Letter* (1850) rejected by their community for violating the norms established for orderly living. Their individual redemption can occur only outside the community, in the next world. In Herman Melville's *Moby Dick* (1851), the obsessively self-reliant Captain Ahab cannot hope to capture the great white whale that took off his leg unless he commands the cooperation of a large crew. In the end both individualism and cooperation fail against the forces of nature. Despite these and many other works critical of Emerson's celebrations of individualism, his message was more in keeping with emerging middle-class values and remained an important validation of the era's middle-class reforms.

CONCLUSION

From the 1820s to the 1850s, many Americans in northern society enjoyed unparalleled opportunities to acquire new land, become manufacturers or entrepreneurs, fill their homes with new goods, and offer their children education and cultural enrichment. But during this era, the republic also confronted waves of impoverished new immigrants who crowded into cities that rarely had adequate resources and jobs. The Panic of 1837 and its subsequent depression left huge numbers of people destitute, and changing patterns of work shook social relations between bosses and workers, and within families, to their very foundations.

Americans responded in varying ways to the rapid economic and social change of the era. Many celebrated the unleashed material prosperity that a rising urban middle class enjoyed. Others shuddered at the apparently hastening moral decline, increasing social and economic inequality, and entrenched indifference toward abolition of slavery and women's rights. As Americans framed it in those years, the greatest challenge was simultaneously to enjoy the marvelous changes around them, elevate individual opportunities for advancement, and yet also give the nation institutional and moral coherence. Reformers tried to meet that challenge. Their experiments brought mixed, sometimes modest, results. But the scope and zeal of reform movements, and the range of their efforts to reform Americans, was as unprecedented as the depth of the problems they addressed.

SUGGESTED READINGS

The immigrant group more studied than any other in this era is the Irish. Oscar Handlin's, *Boston's Immigrants* (rev. ed., 1959), was a path-breaking work that looked at especially the Irish adaptation to life in the American city. See also Hasia Diner, *Erin's Daughters in America* (1983). For studies that integrate immigrant groups into their views of urban growth, politics, culture, and services see Thomas Bender, *Toward an Urban Vision* (1975); Elizabeth Blackmar, *Manhattan for Rent, 1785–1850* (1989); and Stuart Blumin, *The Urban Threshold: Growth and Change in a Nineteenth-Century American Community* (1976). Sean Wilentz, *Chants Democratic* (1983), is a fascinating case study of the social history of artisan republicans in New York City before the Civil War.

The starting place for understanding the sweeping changes occurring throughout the North is Norman Ware, *The Industrial Worker, 1840–1860* (1964). The best recent studies of northern industrial change highlight social tensions of emerging classes, as well as the struggles of households to confront altering labor and cultural conditions. Among them are Mary Blewett, *Men, Women, and Work: Class, Gender, and Protest in the New England Shoe Industry, 1780–1910* (1988); Jeanne Boydston, *Home and Work: Housework, Wages, and the Ideology of Labor in the Early Republic* (1990); Alan Dawley, *Class and Community: The Industrial Revolution in Lynn* (1976); and Thomas Dublin, *Women at Work: The Transformation of Work and Community in Lowell, Massachusetts, 1826–1880* (1979). An especially enlightening look at gender during early industrialization is Sylvia Hoffert's *When Hens Crow: The Women's Rights Movement in Antebellum America* (1995).

For "rural industrialization," the best work to date is Anthony F. C. Wallace, *Rockdale: The Growth of an American Village* (1977). Steven J. Ross's study of a midwestern city in *Workers on the Edge: Work, Leisure, and Politics in Industrializing Cincinnati, 1788–1890* (1985) is highly recommended.

An important, though dated, overview of the reform movements of this era is Carol Bode's *The Anatomy of American Popular Culture, 1840–1861* (1959). Ronald Walters's *American Reformers, 1815–1860* (1978) offers one of the first comprehensive treatments of reform movements. Steven Mintz, *Moralists and Modernizers: America's Pre–Civil War Reformers* (1995), is a more recent survey of all major reform movements, with an emphasis on the ideas and beliefs that motivated reformers.

For arguments about the centrality of women in antebellum reform, start with Lois Banner, *Elizabeth Cady Stanton* (1980); Ann Douglas, *The Feminization of American Culture* (1977); and Lori Ginzberg, *Women and the Work of Benevolence* (1990). The overlapping, mutually influential roles of religion, gender, temperance, and medicine are sorted out in Barbara Epstein, *The Politics of Domesticity: Women, Evangelism, and Temperance in Nineteenth-Century America* (1981). Also see the enduring valuable work by Charles Rosenberg, *The Cholera Years: The United States in 1832, 1849, 1866* (1962). Contemporary medical theory and medical practice are best presented in David Rothman, *The Discovery of the Asylum* (1971); Paul Starr, *The Social Transformation of American Medicine* (1982); and Ian Tyrrel, *Sobering Up: From Temperance to Prohibition in Antebellum America* (1979).

Keith J. Hardman, *Charles Grandison Finney, 1792–1875* (1987), is a highly readable account of the reform revival movement in the North. For educational reforms, see Carl F. Kaestle, *Pillars of the Republic: Common Schools and American Society, 1780–1860* (1983);

and for intellectual currents, start with Cathy Davidson, *Revolution and the Word* (1986). New work emphasizes that what once passed as "highbrow" culture may have been more pervasive in American society; see especially Richard John, *Spreading the News: The American Postal System from Franklin to Morse* (1996); David Reynolds, *Walt Whitman's America* (1995); and Bryan J. Wolf, *Romantic Re-Vision: Culture and Consciousness in Nineteenth-Century American Painting and Literature* (1982).

For popular culture generally, the most representative studies include Ann Fabian, *Card Sharps, Dream Books, and Bucket Shops: Gambling in Nineteenth Century America* (1990); David Grimsted, *Melodrama Unveiled: American Theater and Culture, 1800–1850* (1968); Peter Dobkin Hall, *The Organization of American Culture, 1700–1900* (1982); and Karen Halttunen, *Confidence Men and Painted Women: A Study in Middle-Class Culture in America, 1830–1870* (1982), which surveys sentimentalism and the new middle class of the North. A useful survey is Jack Larkin's *Reshaping Everyday Life, 1790–1849* (1988).

The more far-reaching plans of utopian reformers are surveyed in Lawrence Foster, *Women, Family, and Utopia* (1991), and Carl Guarneri, *Utopian Alternative: Fourierism in Nineteenth-Century America* (1991).

Competing Voices

Equality and Opportunity in the Cities

From "The Sanitary Condition of the Laboring Population of New York"

John H. Griscom mercilessly criticized the daily life of certain New York City neighborhoods during the early 1840s. Few residents, he insisted, owned enough real or personal property to do more than scrape and survive, and Griscom's contemporaries and modern research have validated this claim. As a doctor and an active social reformer, Griscom appealed to middle-class residents' sensitivities—as well as their pocketbooks—to make changes on behalf of the poor. His graphic portrayals of urban poverty evoked widespread response from reformers.

It may well be questioned, whether improvement in the physical condition of the lower stratum of society, is not a necessary precedent, in order that education of the mind may exercise its full and proper influence over the general well-being. . . . But without sound bodies, when surrounded with dirt, foul air, and all manner of filthy associations, it is vain to expect even the child of education, to be better than his ignorant companions . . . .

The system of tenantage to which large numbers of the poor are subject, I think, must be regarded as one of the principal causes, of the helpless and noisome manner in which they live. . . . The tenements, in order to admit a greater number of families, are divided into small apartments, as numerous as decency will admit. Regard to comfort, convenience, and health, is the last motive. . . . These closets, for they deserve no other name, are then rented to the poor, from week to week, or month to month, the rent being almost invariably required in advance, at least for the first few terms. . . .

Very often, perhaps in a majority of the cases in the class of which I now speak, no cleaning other than washing the floor, is ever attempted, and that but seldom. Whitewashing, cleaning of furniture, of bedding, or persons, in many cases is *never* attempted. Some have old pieces of carpet, which are never shaken, (they would not bear it,) and are used to hide the filth on the floor. Every corner of the room, of the cupboards, of the entries and stairways, is piled up with dirt. The walls and ceilings, with the plaster broken off in many places, exposing the lath and beams, and leaving openings for the escape from within of the effluvia of vermin, dead and alive, are smeared with the blood of unmentionable insects, and dirt of all indescribably colours. The low rooms are diminished in their areas by the necessary encroachments of the roof, or the stairs leading to the rooms above; and behind and under them is a hole, into which the light of day never enters, and where a small bed is often pushed in, upon which the luckless and degraded tenants pass their nights, weary and comfortless. . . . The almost entire absence of household conveniences, contributes much to the prostration of comfort and self-respect of these wretched people. The deficiency of water, and the want of a convenient place for washing, with no other place for drying clothes than the common sitting and bed room, are very serious impediments in the way of their improvement. . . .

The subject of *sewerage* is destined to be one, which of necessity must ere long occupy the attention of the people and the government . . . the rain water cisterns [are] useless, the bottoms of them have in many instances been taken out, and they have been converted into cesspools, into which the refuse matter of the houses is thrown. . . . [A]n immense mass of offensive material, will thus be soon collected, its decomposition polluting the air, in the immediate precincts of our chambers and sitting rooms, and generating an amount of miasmatic effluvia, incalculably great and injurious. Discharge all the contents of our sinks and cesspools, through sewers into the rivers, and we will avoid two of the most powerful causes of sickness and early death. . . .

From "Society, Manners, and Politics in the United States"

Michael Chevalier, French ambassador to America during the early 1830s, took note that the franchise was very widespread in the North and most free urban male residents lived without fear of expressing their political and cultural beliefs. Indeed, Chevalier concluded that, in contrast to most of Europe, in America the "commoners" ruled. America, he wrote, was a dynamic and youthful country, and relatively middle class throughout, as the following passage shows.

There is one thing in the United States that strikes a stranger on stepping ashore . . . it is the appearance of general ease in the condition of the people of this country. While European communities are more or less cankered with the sore of pauperism, for which their ablest statesmen have as yet been able to find no healing balm, there are here no paupers, at least not in the Northern and Western States, which have protected themselves from the leprosy of slavery. If a few individuals are seen, they are only an imperceptible minority of dissolute or improvident persons, commonly people of colour, or some newly landed emigrants, who have not been able to adopt industrious habits. Nothing is more easy than to live and to live well by labour. Objects of the first necessity, bread, meat, sugar, tea, coffee, fuel, are in general cheaper here than in France, and wages are double or triple. . . . The term *democrat,* which elsewhere would fill even the republicans with terror, is here greeted with acclamations . . . .

The architectural appearance of Cincinnati is very nearly the same with that of the new quarters of the English towns. The houses are generally of brick, most commonly three stories high, with the windows shining with cleanliness, calculated each for a single family, and regularly placed along well paved and spacious streets, sixty feet in width. Here and there the prevailing uniformity is interrupted by some more imposing edifice, and there are some houses of hewn stone in very good taste, real palaces in miniature, with neat porticoes . . . and several very pretty mansions surrounded with gardens and terraces. . . .

The appearance of Cincinnati as it is approached from the water, is imposing, and it is still more so when it is viewed from one of the neighbouring hills. The eye takes in the windings of the Ohio and the course of the Licking [Rivers], which enters the former at right angles, the steamboats that fill the port, the basin of the Miami canal, with the warehouses that line it and the locks that connect it with the river, the white-washed spinning works of Newport and Covington with their tall chimneys, the Federal arsenal, above which floats the starry banner, and the numerous wooden spires that crown the churches. . . . The population . . . lives in the midst of plenty; it is industrious, sober, frugal, thirsting after knowledge, and if . . . it is entirely a stranger to the delicate pleasures and elegant manners of the refined society of our European capitals, it is equally ignorant of its vices, dissipation, and follies. ■

Bustling with enterprise, teeming with both newcomers and resident elites, and rapidly reproducing the institutions associated with modern urban life, northern cities drew the close attention of many writers. The pace of life, the variety of goods and entertainments, and the frightening crush of people in such relatively small spaces gave many cities the appearance of European cities, and separated them starkly from the majority of rural Americans.

But observers could not agree about the meaning of urbanization, or even its true characteristics. Critics were biased against many urban developments, usually because they were believed to harbor numerous threats to the virtue and stability of republican citizens. Admirers, however, thrilled at the pace of change and the excitement of cultural diversity and urban conveniences. Critics tended to record the dangers, filth, and immorality of city life. Supporters reveled in the ceaseless, restless ambition of citizens who took advantage of opportunities for real economic gains.

Arguably, both critics and supporters of the nation's urbanization drew attention to conditions that demanded many different kinds of responses. By the 1830s, a triumvirate of interests—courts, lawmakers, and investors—was beginning to initiate reforms to regulate, control, investigate, and simply understand this amazing social change. Often, they relied on the writings of astute observers such as Griscom or Chevalier to shape their proposals. Just as importantly, however, these writings became important printed vehicles for shaping public opinion about cities. In time, many observers would shift from recording primarily the material conditions of urban life to making more poignant judgments about the ethnic, religious, and class components of cities.

Questions for Analysis

1. Find details in each account of urban life that have drawn the attention of the writers. What sights, sounds, and smells do they record with displeasure or distaste? What pleases them?
2. What underlying judgments do you detect about city dwellers in each piece? Are their concerns about material conditions colored with any ethnic or class biases?
3. What, if anything, do older cities like New York have in common with newer cities like Cincinnati?
4. What cultural and economic differences arose between Americans who settled in the eastern seaboard cities and those who settled in America's interior?
5. Can we attribute some of these different characteristics to ethnic origins, others to social class, and still others to environment? Explain.

12

Slavery and Plantation Culture, 1820–1850

Thomas Garrett of Wilmington, Delaware, did not suspect how different the spring of 1845 would be from the ones that had preceded it. For twenty-five years, since 1820, this Quaker iron merchant had devoted his fortune and risked his physical safety to run a "station" of the Underground Railroad from his home. That spring he agreed to assist an African-American family of eight, along with four additional Maryland slaves, in their joint escape to freedom. Sam Hawkins was a freed man but his wife, six children, and traveling companions were slaves. Earlier in the year they had "gone missing" from their Maryland plantation, and their master had chased them right into Middletown, Delaware, where the slaves were captured and jailed. Garrett convinced the judge to release all of the slaves, based on a legal technicality. But when he then tried to take the group to Wilmington, the same court trumped up a new charge, this time also implicating Garrett: the court said he was now harboring fugitives. They fled, night and day, on foot and in hired wagons, until they reached deep into Pennsylvania. Still fuming, however, the slave owner sued Garrett and all who had assisted him for the value of his missing property.

By 1845, "Conductor" Garrett had provided over two thousand slaves with safe havens on their journeys from slavery to freedom. His "station stop" in Delaware, a border state, was strategically important for runaways. This made the suit against Garrett all the more significant to citizens of both Delaware and Maryland, and in 1848, when the case was tried at the New Castle

Courthouse, with U.S. Supreme Court Justice Roger Taney presiding, hundreds of people followed the proceedings closely. Taney read out a guilty verdict and ordered Garrett to pay a fine of $4,500, the sum total of his remaining fortune.

As Garrett left the courthouse, stamped by the press as a lawbreaker and now facing poverty, he paused on the steps to address Taney. "Thou hast left me without a dollar," Garrett reminded the harsh court. But he then assured Delawareans that he would continue in his moral choice to take slaves out of the southern states to freedom. "If anyone knows a fugitive who wants shelter," he challenged Taney and state authorities, "send him to Thomas Garrett and he will befriend him."

Thomas Garrett, born the year Delaware's delegates signed the Constitution, sacrificed his fortune and risked his personal safety time and again for slaves he did not know. When the Thirteenth Amendment to the Constitution guaranteed freedom to slaves, African-Americans praised Garrett as their Moses. He was one of hundreds of whites and free African-Americans who operated the Underground Railroad in every state, and who struggled mightily to end slavery in the South.

As this struggle unfolded, free African-Americans endured difficulties that often made the pursuit of freedom seem indistinguishable from the condition of slavery. Despite the formal rights of citizenship for all men, runaway slaves who blended into northern society and manumitted ex-slaves experienced constant discrimination on the job, in the streets, and in churches. Slaves in the South suffered even more direct legal, physical, and emotional affronts as the southern plantation system spread territorially and "King Cotton" ruled the southern economy. Still, as southern planters sharpened arguments justifying their way of life, two other developments qualified their domination in the South. One was the rapid growth of the small farming yeomanry, many of whom had little expectation of owning slaves or becoming prosperous, and great numbers of landless tenants who did not even own land. The other was the continuing efforts by slaves to preserve African ways and adapt African cultural inheritances to Euro-American culture. To varying degrees, slave communities throughout the South created distinctive identities within the dominant planter culture.

- What was the range of attitudes about slavery in the North? in the South?
- What made southern culture and economy distinctive from the cultures and economies of the North and West?
- How did slaves create separate cultural ways from their masters and other white people within the South?
- What tensions developed between planters and slaves? between small farmers and great planters?

This chapter will address these questions.

Abolition and Antislavery Movements

Runaway slaves, freedmen in northern states, and Underground Railroad activists appealed persistently for a more widespread assault on slavery. By 1820, Americans had nurtured their republican beliefs about personal independence for decades,

Chronology

1800	Gabriel's rebellion
1808	External slave trade legally ends
1816–1819	Boom in cotton prices
1817	American Colonization Society founded
1822	Vesey's rebellion
1827	First African-American newspaper, *Freedom's Journal*
1829	Dew's defense of slavery appears
1831	Garrison begins publishing *The Liberator*
	Nat Turner's rebellion
1833	American Anti-Slavery Society founded
1837	Lovejoy killed
1852	Stowe publishes *Uncle Tom's Cabin*
1854	Fitzhugh's *Sociology for the South* appears
1857	Helper releases *The Impending Crisis*

and the antislavery movements in England and the Caribbean inspired some Americans to think similarly. In 1808 Congress outlawed the importation of slaves into America, just as the Constitution had mandated; and in 1820 the Missouri Compromise prohibited slavery in much of the vast Louisiana Purchase. But for a growing number of white and black Americans, these were only first steps against the blot of slavery.

Gradual Emancipation and Colonization

The American Colonization Society, founded in 1817, urged masters to manumit, or set free, their slaves in return for compensation and worked to transplant freed slaves to Africa. The society established a West African colony called Liberia. Many colonization advocates, including Thomas Jefferson, believed that although slavery was a moral wrong, blacks themselves composed a "separate nation" that would never be able to mix in white American society. Members of the society in New England and New York agreed that even employed free blacks in their cities were failing to "civilize in both their mental and spiritual capacities." Several states denied or restricted African-American suffrage (see Chapter 10).

The colonization movement also attracted southern developers from Virginia, Maryland, and North Carolina who believed that abolishing slavery would be the South's first step toward the economic and social development that northerners enjoyed. Like Thomas Jefferson, many of them argued that emancipation without colonization could trigger a race war. As he promoted aspects of his American System, Henry Clay repeated this view. Other southerners opposed emancipation altogether but supported the Colonization Society because it could help remove free African-Americans from their region and thus make it safer for slavery.

One of the era's most radical utopians, Frances Wright, established a community based on the principles of gradual emancipation and colonization. Wright came from a wealthy Scottish commercial family, but at a very young age she dreamed of living in America and pursuing her ideal of becoming a social reformer. In 1824 she arrived with the celebrated French hero of the American Revolution, the Marquis de Lafayette, and stayed as a guest at Thomas Jefferson's Monticello. Jefferson encouraged Wright to found a utopian community of whites and freed blacks who would live together in full equality. In 1825 Wright gathered over thirty freed adult slaves in Nashoba, in western Tennessee, a settlement that eventually grew to over two thousand acres. Settlers were to earn their emancipation by clearing and planting the land, while their children were to receive an education suited to their eventual cultural and civic entry into American society. By 1828, however, Nashoba had failed to prosper agriculturally or to attract many additional recruits. Wright migrated to New York with Robert Dale Owen, the son of utopian Robert Owen (see page 436). There, she lectured widely to mixed audiences of men and women on the evils of capitalism and the benefits of universal compulsory education and women's rights. By the 1830s, Wright's early advocacy of gradual emancipation seemed very tame compared with her bold crusading for the northern working class.

Immediate Emancipation and Rebellion

Most free African-Americans rejected colonization because it denied them rights that, as Philadelphia's Bethel Church members said in 1817, "the Constitution and the laws allow to all." Thousands of African-Americans had already established themselves in the North after the Revolution. Independent churches, schools, and benevolent organizations were beginning to knit a community of African-Americans recently freed and born free, runaways, and urban African-American servants and slaves. Colonization directly jeopardized these efforts and denied these communities the opportunity to develop in confident freedom.

A growing number of free African-Americans believed that inadequate progress toward ending slavery justified open rebellion. David Walker, who had come from North Carolina to Boston in the 1820s, was familiar with slave conspiracies to take over southern plantations and cities. He sponsored the first African-American newspaper, *Freedom's Journal,* in 1827 to arouse northerners to help slave resisters. But two years later, fed up with the reluctance of white northern society to compel southern slave owners to free their slaves, Walker wrote *Appeal . . . to the Colored Citizens.* Walker's appeal warned that slaves would rise up in arms and take their freedom by force from masters in the South, with or without northern help.

Frederick Douglass, son of a white father and Maryland slave mother, escaped to the North as a young man. Douglass was a rare individual who had learned to read and write when he was a slave, and despite the physical and psychological brutalities of a harsh "slave breaker" to whom he had been sold, became a skilled ship caulker. By the mid-1830s, Douglass became the foremost African-American abolitionist in the North, although for years his white audiences bristled at his eloquent speeches on behalf of emancipation.

American Anti-Slavery Society

Frederick Douglass, Harriet Tubman, and Sojourner Truth were leaders in the black abolitionist movement that demanded an immediate end to slavery, but the thousands of free African-Americans who joined over fifty abolitionist societies fanned out far beyond the leaders. By the 1830s, a number of white opponents of slavery identified more closely with slaves who resisted and rebelled than with arguments for colonization. With moral urgency, evangelical ministers and women's rights organizations insisted on the sinfulness of slavery and masters' debilitation of slaves' inherent moral goodness. Theodore Dwight Weld, for example, was the son of a Congregationalist minister and had listened raptly to Charles Finney's sermons in New York State. Weld decided to take similar messages of moral reform on tour through New York and into Ohio, where he reached out to temperance and educational reform societies before he focused his greatest talents on abolition. In 1834 Weld convinced some of the students at Lane Theological Seminary in Cincinnati to form an antislavery society. When seminary president Lyman Beecher objected to this extension of the seminary's work beyond academic instruction, the antislavery

Frederick Douglass, 1848
Ten years after he escaped from slavery in Maryland, Douglass became a highly regarded orator for the abolitionist cause and equal rights for women. Although he lectured tirelessly to white, as well as mixed white and black, audiences during the 1840s, Douglass became weary of waiting for legislators to emancipate slaves and came to regard violence as necessary for abolition of the institution. *(Chester County Historical Society.)*

supporters moved to Oberlin College, where they were encouraged to study the relationship between religion and universal freedom.

Secular northern reformers joined religious leaders to rebuke merchants involved in the slave trade and organize lectures to raise public consciousness about the southern institution. William Lloyd Garrison was among the most tireless opponents of gradual and compensated emancipation. During the 1820s, he collaborated with Quakers in Baltimore to put out the *Genius of Universal Emancipation,* a serial that ardently promoted immediate emancipation. In 1830 Garrison spent a few weeks in jail for writing against a slave trader, his fine paid by Arthur Tappan, a prominent wealthy merchant from New York who was at the time affiliated with Oberlin College. Not to be silenced, Garrison in 1831 started *The Liberator,* a major voice for immediate emancipation that condemned the American Colonization Society. Even the Constitution, wrote Garrison, was "a covenant with death, an agreement with Hell" because it failed to abolish the institution of slavery.

Garrison and *The Liberator* became a magnet for radical abolitionists during the 1830s. In 1832 they joined to form the New England Anti-Slavery Society, which in 1833 was recast as the American Anti-Slavery Society. Weld, Garrison, Tappan and his brother Lewis, along with about sixty other white and free African-American abolitionists, developed a program that they hoped would attract massive numbers of middle-class Americans. Although some delegates to the society's first meetings called for "direct action" against slave owners in the South, the majority adopted the strategy of "moral suasion." This more moderate stance proved effective in attracting members: over the 1830s some 250,000 northerners joined the Anti-Slavery Society.

The society had two approaches. One was to reach out to great numbers of uncommitted Americans. Using the organizing method of evangelicals, abolitionists sponsored huge, hours-long public gatherings and arranged home visits in immigrant neighborhoods. And with financial donations from wealthy members, they kept antislavery printing presses churning day and night. In 1835 more than a million pieces of literature rolled off the presses and into the hands of northerners. That same year, the society flooded the fledgling post office with hundreds of thousands of antislavery pamphlets.

The second strategy of the American Anti-Slavery Society was to agitate for specific legislation from state and federal governments. Prominent merchants, transcendentalists such as Emerson and Thoreau, and some state-level Whig politicians pressed for congressional action. In the mid-1840s Thoreau would link together northern urban violence, a brewing war with Mexico, and southern slavery in stinging writings. In 1848 he published anonymously his famous essay, "Civil Disobedience," which advocated individual resistance to government wrongs and professed his belief in a moral law higher than man-made statutes.

As rank-and-file abolitionists stuffed envelopes for the post office to deliver in 1835, the movement mobilized supporters to circulate hundreds of petitions calling on Congress to stop admitting slave states into the Union, remove the "three-fifths compromise" from the Constitution (see page 263), abolish slavery in the nation's capital, and end the slave trade within America. Over the next three years, Congress received almost 500,000 petitions; more than half the signers were women.

Women and Emancipation

Few women stepped forward to speak against slavery in mixed male and female audiences in the early 1830s. But their numbers grew in the following years, especially as women's rights organizations took form and evangelicals coalesced moral outrage against slavery. The Philadelphia Female Anti-Slavery Society, founded by Lucretia Mott in 1833, and the Boston Female Anti-Slavery Society, founded by Maria W. Chapman in 1835, formed the core of growing female abolitionist networks that raised funds, operated printing presses, organized speaking engagements, taught free African-American children, and helped run the Underground Railroad.

Angelina and Sarah Grimké left their father's South Carolina plantation to join abolitionists in Philadelphia, where beginning in 1836 they lectured frequently to men and women. When challenged by clergymen and politicians for their bold entry, as women, into this highly charged reform movement, Angelina retorted, "It is a woman's right to have a voice in all the laws and regulations by which she is governed." In 1838 Angelina married Theodore Weld, and together with Sarah they compiled one of the era's best-selling books, *American Slavery as It Is: Testimony of a Thousand Witnesses* (1839). Culling excerpts from southern newspapers, the authors put together thousands of accounts of physical punishments, dehumanizing descriptions of runaways, and cold testimonials of masters.

For years, the Grimké sisters insisted that the treatment of women and slaves had many points in common, and by 1840, they associated women's traditional position in society with "domestic slavery." At the Anti-Slavery Society convention of 1840, Garrison agreed that women should have an equal right to participate in the abolitionist movement, a measure that prompted many middle-class northerners to leave the Society and found the all-male American and Foreign Anti-Slavery Society. Along with Garrison, Abby Kelley, Lucy Stone, Lucretia Mott, and Elizabeth Cady Stanton continued to combine abolitionist struggles with the reform of women's lives. Sojourner Truth, one of many African-American women to speak out during the 1830s and 1840s in public forums, linked women's rights in the North directly to women's rights under slavery. In her stinging rebuke of the treatment women received under slavery, Truth asked, "I have ploughed and planted and gathered into barns, and no man could head me—and ar'n't I a woman? I have borne thirteen children, and seen most of 'em sold into slavery, and when I cried out with my mother's grief, none but Jesus heard me—and ar'n't I a woman?"

Although Harriet Beecher Stowe never joined an antislavery organization, her famous 1852 novel, *Uncle Tom's Cabin,* found its way into more homes, and hearts, than any antislavery pamphlet did. Daughter of minister Lyman Beecher and sister of Catharine Beecher, Stowe advanced moral reform as a central message in her writing. The title character, Uncle Tom, endures abuses and agonies

Sojourner Truth She gained her freedom from slavery in 1827 and became one of the earliest participants in the women's rights and abolitionist movements. Excluded from a discussion of women's rights at an Akron, Ohio, convention in 1851, Truth rose to her full six feet height and demanded of the white women around her, "Ar'n't I a woman?" Already, she was widely known for her chilling lectures about the cruelties and indignities of slavery. In her lap, Truth has the daguerrotype of Frederick Douglass shown on page 449. *(Massachusetts Historical Society.)*

familiar to many slaves, including runaways who described their personal stories in detail to Stowe and then became incorporated into her book. Other characters also deeply touched northern Americans who read about Tom's sale and separation from his children: Eliza Harris, who risks running away and carries her son across the icy Ohio River to freedom, and little Eva, who dies in the midst of the system's cruelties.

Stowe believed that family life lay at the foundation of all moral authority, and that mothers in their spheres were indispensable for halting the political crises of the Union in the 1850s as sectionalism intensified. Joining a growing list of female reform authors, Stowe articulated slavery's degradation of families and women: slave women, unlike white women, had no separate sphere, and not many slaves were granted the basic right to nurture their own children in families. *Uncle Tom's Cabin* sold over 350,000 copies quickly after publication and continued to be America's most celebrated novel for years. It was tremendously popular abroad, too, and its wide acclaim would influence English attitudes toward the South for years to come.

Southern Society

It was obvious to Frenchman Alexis de Tocqueville, touring America in the late 1820s, that the nation was divided sectionally. The root cause was also obvious. "Almost all the differences which may be noticed between the character of the Americans in the Southern and Northern states," he wrote in 1831, "have originated in slavery." Slavery and the production of exportable agricultural crops had long dominated the southern way of life. Planters who turned to cotton in the early 1800s renewed their commitment to slavery and plantation agriculture, and to the acquisition of ever more land. The distinctive sectional characteristics that set the South apart from the North did not erode, as some Americans had predicted after the American Revolution, but instead deepened.

A Distinctive Economy

Production of the staple crops tobacco, sugar, hemp, rice, and cotton was based on certain conditions found exclusively in the South. For example, soil conditions and climate were better in the South than in the North for growing tobacco; cotton requires long warm seasons and abundant spring rains, conditions that characterized large areas of the coastal South from Virginia to Texas. In addition, English textile manufacturing created seemingly endless demand for all the cotton southerners could produce, and Whitney's cotton gin aided planters in meeting that demand. In addition, territorial expansion and declining government prices for western land beckoned southerners into unsettled areas that they believed were suited to cotton production.

As the older sections of the Chesapeake turned to cultivating more cereals, especially wheat, the production of tobacco moved west, mainly into Tennessee and Kentucky, during the 1820s to 1850s. In this same region, hundreds of farmers also began to plant hemp, a product used to make rope and coarse cloth. Although hemp was protected during the 1820s and 1830s by a steep tariff on foreign imports, the market was modest and fortunes were few.

On the other hand, along the ribbon of tidewater land through North and South Carolina and along the coastline of Georgia, rice planters prospered. To prepare rice marshes and maintain the canals and floodgates, great numbers of slaves populated the rice districts. For the planter who could invest heavily in slaves and land, rice often generated huge profits through these decades. So did sugar, a product that had made many Caribbean planters wealthy and drove hundreds of thousands of Caribbean slaves to early deaths. Although sugar grew well only in tropical climates, a few bold Louisiana planters won protective tariffs covering New Orleans and proceeded to grow rich on newly settled American soil by driving thousands of slaves mercilessly. Like rice, sugar required heavy capital investment, both in slaves and in machinery for grinding and boiling the cane. Sugar harvests were the most demanding of all slave work regimens: crews had to work fast and often through the night to cut the ripened cane, haul it to the sugar mills, tend the milling machines that ground the cane, and then boil cane in vats.

King Cotton, however, would surpass all other staple crops in the amount of land it covered and the number of slaves it consumed (see maps). In 1830 southern states produced about 720,000 bales of cotton; in 1850, nearly 3 million bales; and in 1860, almost 5 million—about 60 percent of the value of all American exports. Cotton exporting was thus unquestionably profitable for many planters—despite periodically rising prices paid for slaves and fluctuating prices received for crops—and it supported the livelihoods of numerous northern merchants who carried the raw cotton to industrial destinations in England, traded slaves to southerners, and returned from abroad with textiles for American buyers. Northern investors, such as the Boston Associates who financed the Lowell mills, planned for the day when they themselves would be able to process southern cotton into finished American textiles.

Southerners' emphasis on plantation agriculture tied them intimately to the credit, services, and goods provided by northerners, and precluded channeling many resources into other ways of developing their region. For one thing, a much smaller proportion of southerners lived in cities before the Civil War than northerners; nine-tenths of southerners lived in rural areas. Although New Orleans, Mobile, and Charleston attracted many immigrants, a large proportion of them continued migrating to northern cities. Charleston and Savannah grew far more slowly than New York City or Boston before 1860, and many southern states had no significant port city. The two exceptions were Baltimore and New Orleans. Baltimore grew to over two hundred thousand people by 1860, capitalizing on its position as a primary port for the Chesapeake region's agricultural exports of grain and flour, hides, and cotton. New Orleans, at the mouth of the Mississippi River, was a major crossroads between western settlements, the Ohio Valley, and southern plantations.

Travelers who headed inland from southern ports were immediately struck that the South had far fewer canals than the North. Antebellum (before the Civil War) newspaper editors often noted that the South had only about 30 percent of the country's railroads and no more than 15 percent of the country's factories. Some of these factories were impressive works, including the large iron foundries and rolling mills in Richmond, Virginia, and an armory at Harpers Ferry in northern Virginia. In addition, some of the largest gristing mills in America dotted the Maryland and Virginia countryside. William Gregg used his promotional skills and personal capital to construct the Graniteville, Georgia, cotton mill in 1846. He then put up a model village not unlike Lowell in design, including homes, a school and church, a library, a hospital, and a massive stone factory that became a marvel to Georgians and a workplace for many of them. The Tredegar Iron Works in Richmond hired skilled slaves from area planters to produce the military goods, boilers, steam engines, axes, saws, and other iron products shipped widely outside the South. In addition, southern state governments joined with private investors to create banks that gave generous credit for development projects and new railroad lines from 1830 to 1850, which in turn speeded up expansion of the plantation system into Louisiana, east Texas, and what would become Oklahoma.

Nevertheless, southerners invested far less of their collective capital in industry, education, and transportation before midcentury than northerners did. Planters created more wealth by investing in slaves and land than by building factories and schools. Consequently southern development lagged further and further behind

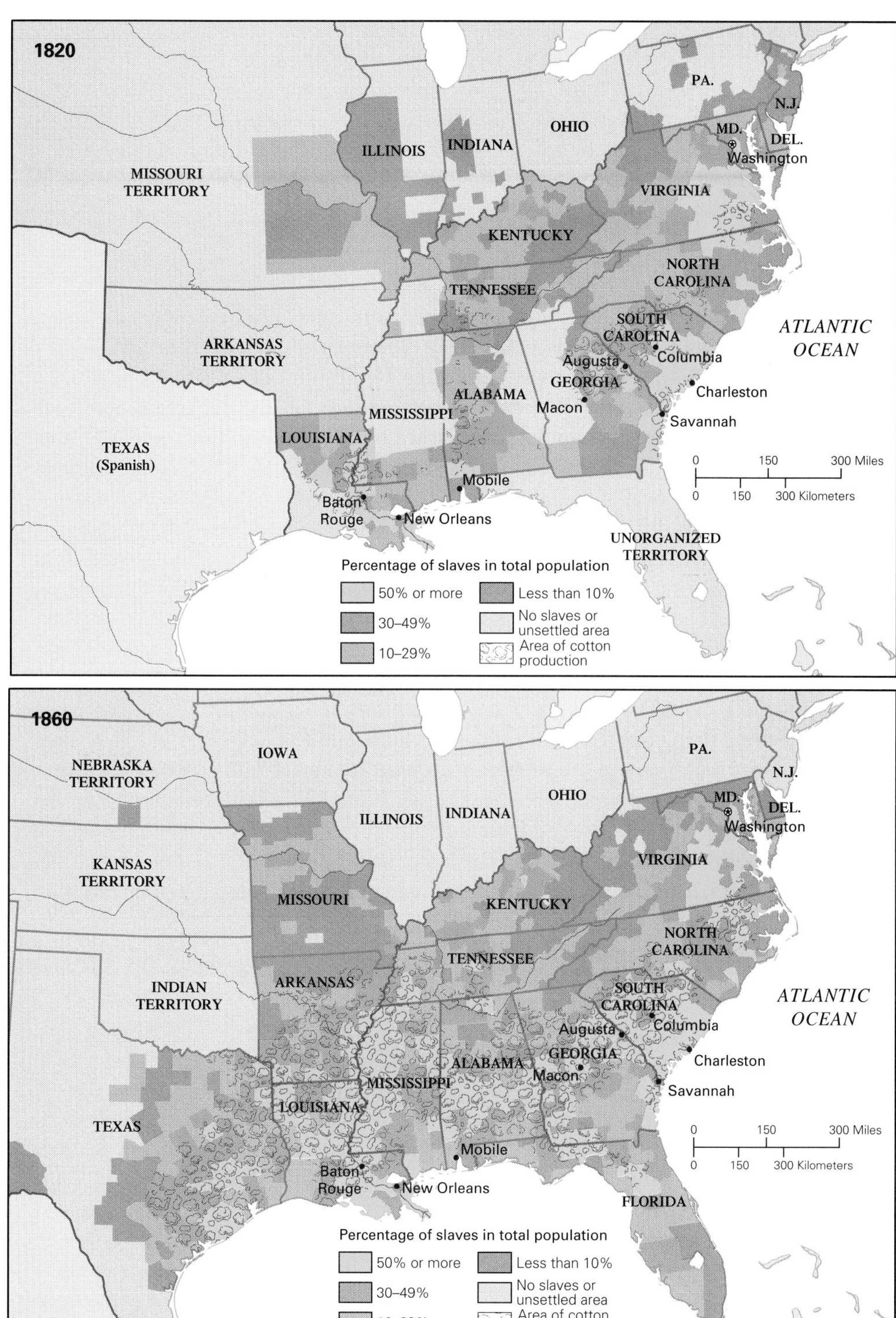

Slavery and Agricultural Expansion, 1820–1860 Although Americans were migrating westward in great numbers for many reasons by the 1820s, the expansion of plantation agriculture determined the spreading influence of slavery more than any other factor. By the 1850s, over 50 percent of all southern slaves worked in cotton fields, increasingly those of new western states. Rice, hemp, and sugar accounted for about 15 percent of slave work.

rapidly growing northern trade and industry. Moreover, no southern state instituted a public school system before midcentury. As long as cotton remained highly profitable, most planters concluded that internal improvements and factories were unwise and risky business ventures.

Expansion

Jefferson's vision of filling the West with hard-working white freeholders collapsed quickly south and west of the Ohio River, where cotton agriculture and slavery spread. Although the Panic of 1819 (see page 313) produced a dramatic decline in cotton and land prices, and thousands of new planters failed, even greater numbers of planters and slaves undertook the westward trek by the late 1820s. Already, hundreds of planters had settled in Kentucky, Tennessee, and Missouri. Georgia planters demanded the removal of Indians in order to expand cotton production. Unprecedented expansion during the 1820s and 1830s into new lands of Alabama, Mississippi, and Louisiana—what would become the southern "Black Belt"—and then during the 1840s into Texas set the framework for King Cotton's rise and the removal of entire Indian populations (discussed in Chapter 10).

Forced to move with their masters, or sold from older eastern plantations where they had become "surplus labor" as tobacco production declined, thousands of slaves were wrenched from family and community roots in the Chesapeake in the early 1800s. Setting out from Virginia, Maryland, and the Carolinas, slaves walked for days or weeks across rough terrain to east Tennessee and the new southern states. Having been separated from loved ones, from the pride and material benefits of working at diverse skills, and from customary negotiated arrangements with a master, relocated slaves then began the backbreaking work of starting new farms. Auctions and sales of slaves, and the forced marches to new plantations, spread slavery's influence remarkably quickly. By the 1830s, planters carried slaves and cotton production across the Mississippi River into Texas, as well as southward into the former Spanish territory of Florida.

The Slave Trade

The Constitution stipulated that American involvement in the international slave trade should cease in 1808, and during the twenty years after the American Revolution, the northern states had discussed and passed laws providing for gradual emancipation or manumissions. Successful revolts in Haiti during the early 1790s, and rumblings of additional independence movements in the Caribbean, produced enough fear in southern states that their legislators prohibited all importation of foreign slaves. England's Parliament abolished the international slave trade in 1807, and there was much talk of moving forward with general emancipation of slaves in the Caribbean during the next years.

But King Cotton was becoming so profitable that southern planters entered the smuggling business energetically during the 1790s and clamored for reopening the foreign slave trade, which South Carolina did in 1804. Slave auctions flourished: over forty thousand Africans were imported into Charleston alone before 1808 when the constitutional prohibition became national law. With King Cotton's even more rapid expansion following the War of 1812, middling and large planters saw slavery as their only way to remain prosperous. Because the Constitution prohibited future slave importation, their prosperity had to be based on the rising birthrate and internal buying and selling of slaves. Planters in Maryland, Delaware, Virginia, and Tennessee who had converted to grain production required fewer slaves for labor and offered hundreds of thousands of slaves for sale into the new southern states after 1820. Some scholars estimate that about half of the slaves in the Upper South were sold "down the [Mississippi] river" or to masters in the Black Belt states. The new states along the Gulf Coast accounted for one-third of the South's slaves by 1860.

The transplanting of slaves from one region to another was fraught with hardship and marred by violence. The breakup of families was common. Although relocating

Slave Trade, Watercolor by Lewis Miller The internal slave trade, primarily from the Chesapeake to the new areas of cotton expansion, broke up the families and settled lives of thousands of slaves. Sales of "surplus" slaves profited white planters in the older states, while also helping populate the new plantations beyond the Appalachian Mountains and in the emerging Black Belt. Usually, the slaves were "driven" by foot, chained together in coffles. *(Colonial Williamsburg Foundation.)*

planters sometimes took all of their slaves to new states, planters who stayed behind often sold individual slaves to middlemen who transported them to new masters far away. Many bankers and merchants—both northern and southern—served as brokers for the internal slave trade. With private capital, they bought slaves, hired white middlemen to escort them to their destinations, and received payments from auctioneers in Black Belt cities. Richmond and Charleston had "slave pens" for collecting groups of slaves before sending them by ship to booming auctions at cities such as Natchez, Mobile, or New Orleans. Slaves herded overland to internal plantations usually wore chains; drivers linked slaves together in "coffles."

African-American Culture

The widespread dislocation of slave communities and the demands of plantation labor introduced new challenges to slave culture, family life, and even survival. But during the decades before the Civil War, slaves continued to build communities within the plantation system, as they had throughout the eighteenth century. As they accommodated to plantation regimens of relentless work and masters' ultimate power over their lives, slaves combined their own African-American values and attitudes with selected European ones to form a distinctive slave culture within the dominant planter culture. This culture provided many slaves with the means to endure, and at times to resist, the inherent cruelties of the South's "peculiar institution."

Family and Community

Living conditions for slaves varied widely, depending on the size of the plantation, the "settledness" of the region, and the individual planter. Generally, small planters gave their slaves sleeping space in their houses or barns. Sometimes they shared the same food, though often they ate their meals separately. The great planters typically constructed separate slave quarters that consisted of cabins with dirt floors. The cabins might house ten to fifteen slaves, which could represent two or three families; thus they lacked privacy and sometimes even enough room for everyone to sleep indoors. As one observer noted, "More disease and loss of time [at work] on plantations was engendered from crowded negro cabins than from almost any other cause." Travelers to southern states noticed that American slaves lived more comfortably than European peasants; ornaments, brooms, cupboards, fences, hand-held mirrors, and other amenities captured outsiders' attention. Separate quarters also offered a place for rest and the evening meal apart from white people, a place to gather around a fire for stories, or a vegetable garden to supplement the typical diet of salted pork and corn. Masters supplied clothing, usually consisting of a homespun cloth shirt or two, two pairs of pants, and a pair of shoes for a man, and a few yards of homespun cloth for women to make their own and their children's smocks for a year. Some slaves were permitted blankets and coats, but many slaves complained that they were hardly adequate in the cold winter months.

Laws barred slaves from forming contracts, so whites did not legally recognize slave marriages. Indeed, the great planters in the Black Belt often forced unrelated mixed groups of slaves to live together under one roof, although slaves shunned unions with cousins and often identified strongly with families of birth and joined in what passed as marriage in the slave community. Farther to the north, in longer-settled regions of the Carolinas and tidewater Chesapeake, slaves more successfully established ties of romance, obligation, and kinship than in the new cotton region. The end of legal slave importation in 1808 slowed the introduction of new slaves from abroad and increased the proportion of African-Americans born and raised on Chesapeake or Carolina soil. Plantation agricultural work was arduous in these old regions, but it did not kill slaves at nearly the same rate as Louisiana and Caribbean sugar "factories" did. As a result, in the Chesapeake and North Carolina regions, slaves could develop the cultural habits and emotional links that grew out of familiar long-term relationships. By the early 1800s, families of three or more generations of slaves, with both parents playing a role in child rearing, became regular features on Virginia plantations.

Slave families and kin groups solidified their bonds with many cultural practices. One was to give newborns African names, a simple but meaningful way to cement lineages and reaffirm origins. In Virginia and Maryland, however, slaves often took names of English derivation and then passed on the names into the next generations, naming sons after fathers, uncles, or grandfathers, or daughters after grandmothers. Repeating names through the generations linked kin to kin and established patterns that evoked order in an otherwise cruel and arbitrary existence. In addition, slaves used kinship terms for nonrelatives, which helped knit together extended households and communities. Children, for example, often addressed all older women as Auntie or Granny.

Although state laws did not recognize slave marriage, some masters encouraged slave parents to wed and live together because they believed stable relationships led slave women to have more children, a future source of profit for planters. For their part, slaves sought marriage as a sanction of their intimacy and bonds of love or to avoid the shame their traditional cultures associated with unwed motherhood. But unlike male-dominated white marriages, which limited women to restricted public and private roles, slaves grounded marriage on greater equality. The fact that men and women often shared the same fieldwork and the same degraded powerlessness over their condition supported such an attitude. Married couples also helped sustain oral memories of kinship and could work together to teach survival skills and provide comfort and protection to young people. Yet masters who encouraged slave marriages also could separate slaves from each other, especially in the internal slave trade. Some 10 to 15 percent of slave marriages ended when one partner was sold away, and a similar proportion of children experienced the breakup of their families.

Fears and uncertainties created by these conditions made it important for slaves to forge bonds in the wider slave community. Mothering was shared throughout the slave quarters on large plantations, with most or all women cooperating to provide for children's daily needs. When slave women died in childbirth or were sold away, children could count on the maternal care of the wider community. Slave children who lost parents might be "adopted" by the family who shared the same cabin. On very large plantations a slave who worked in the master's house could assume the care of a few children if necessary. Over time, bonds strengthened between unrelated women and children, so that on some large plantations masters and overseers could not identify slaves by their families of birth.

Under slavery, African-Americans often retained traditional symbols, songs, art forms, and rituals from their countries of origin, although masters tried to prevent slaves from practicing their African traditions openly. Religion also offered many slaves opportunities for personal and internal solace in a harsh and potentially uprooted life, although planters interpreted many aspects of African religions as superstitions, pagan folk beliefs, or even witchcraft. Many masters tried to control whether and how slaves adopted Christianity. Fearing that slaves would take the biblical messages of equality and individual responsibility for spiritual regeneration too literally—and rebel against their condition as a result—masters hoped to transform slaves into docile, obedient workers by stipulating what elements of Christianity slaves might share with whites. Some of them forbade slaves to gather in African-American churches and insisted that they attend white church services where masters could control religious experiences. Pulpits became forums for preaching obedience and justifying the inequalities of slavery with Scripture.

Despite such interference, slaves adapted elements of Christianity to their daily needs and their traditional religions. As one ex-slave put it, "Dey law us out of Church, but dey couldn't law 'way Christ." Slaves attended frequent prayer meetings and impromptu religious gatherings. Many West African peoples traditionally believed in a Supreme God above all others in the pantheon of gods, which brought them closer to Protestant beliefs. Both West African religions and Protestant Christianity emphasized benevolence, forgiveness, and the promise of eternal life in some form. Additional beliefs in reincarnation and elements of ancestor worship divided some West Africans from European Christians, but in the tidewater, slaves often merged Anglican worship with African religious customs. Closer to the Mississippi River, many slaves brought Catholic influences into folk traditions after 1800. When the Second Great Awakening swept through the slave communities after 1790, Baptists and Methodists welcomed African-American preaching and separate slave churches.

Aside from attendance at white churches on Sundays, slaves in the Old Southeast observed many African religious traditions from day to day. They preferred to honor their own dead at night funerals and bury slaves at places of their own choosing. Native African languages, music, and dances persisted long into the 1800s throughout Louisiana and Mississippi. African "call and response," as well as group singing, endured in most areas of the slave South. Often, slaves adapted song lyrics to plantation work:

> We raise de wheat, Dey gib us de corn;
> We bake de bread, Dey gib us de crust;
> We sif' de meal, Dey gib us de huss;
> We peel de meat, Dey gib us de skin;
> And dat's de way, Dey take us in . . . .

Spirituals such as "Steal Away" and "Go Down, Moses" joined slaves emotionally and reminded them of the promise of deliverance in the afterlife and the hope of freedom in this life. Slaves often rejected teachings about original sin, and many who turned to Christianity openly shunned Calvinism's predestination. African-American preachers emphasized not internal conversion experiences but an externalized mission to mobilize the chosen people of God to liberate humanity. Nevertheless, slave religion did not lead toward mass rebellion because such a move would have been suicidal. Rather, slave Christianity imparted personal dignity and serenity, as well as group affirmation that slaves could transcend their shared hardships spiritually. Thus, whether African-Americans stressed their African heritage in their American environment or adapted English culture to their African legacy, distinctive communities emerged. These communities not only gave order and meaning to slave lives; they also helped slave men, women, and children create strategies for resisting the worst abuses of masters and southern laws.

Slave Men and Women at Work

The kind of work slaves did, and the treatment they endured, varied depending on the size of the plantation and its main activities. Over half of the South's slave owners had only one to five slaves and depended on the diverse skills of these individuals to accomplish many farm tasks. Moreover, regional differences between Delaware and east Tennessee, for example, and South Carolina or Georgia required drastically different work regimens. The cotton economy did not develop on Delaware soil in the same way, or to the same extent, as it did farther south. This, and strong antislavery sentiment (despite its officially remaining a slave state), accounts for the shrinking proportion of slaves and their special positions in Delaware. By 1860, when the number of slaves had shrunk to 2 percent of the state's population, many slaves had purchased their freedom and lived in daily contact with white commercial farmers and entrepreneurs.

In contrast, by the 1850s, 75 percent of slaves in the South lived on large plantations where freedom was a remote dream. Laboring from sunup to sundown, or longer at harvest times, distinguished field hand conditions on staples plantations from urban or small-farm lifestyles. Large planters were less likely to pay attention directly to the health of slaves than yeomen who lived in closer contact with the African-Americans they owned. In either case, however, few white planters understood much about basic nutrition, adequate housing, sanitation, and medical treatment. As a result, mortality rates for slave infants and children up to age five were double the rates for white children. Work regimens often denied pregnant slave women sufficient rest, which put their newborns immediately at risk. Malaria, yellow fever, and cholera claimed many babies and children, as well as undernourished adults. The harsh work on sugar plantations and in lumber camps along the Gulf of Mexico coastline of Mississippi and Louisiana created unusually high rates of chronic dysentery and cholera that killed many slaves within months of their arrival from the distant Chesapeake.

The "gang" and "task" systems of labor continued to divide slaves in different regions, depending on which staple crops they cultivated (see Chapter 4). In the rice and indigo fields of the Carolinas, tasking slaves were permitted a wide range of independent activities once they completed their stipulated tasks. Although slaves in rice fields stood knee-deep in water for hours, and their work regimens shortened life, they nevertheless had some means to negotiate with their masters certain modifications of rules about length of time at tasks and the quality of the finished jobs. This bargaining led to "the custom of the place," or the arrangements negotiated between slaves and masters. As a result, many slaves in the rice fields of South Carolina won periods of time to work in their own vegetable patches, trade with neighbors, find jobs off the plantation that earned food or household amenities, or simply rest.

Gang labor continued to apply in the Chesapeake, where tobacco plants had to be tended continually and slaves worked under the watchful eye of the master. As planters switched to wheat production, they easily modified gang labor to suit the intensive physical needs of planting and harvesting seasons. In tobacco and grain country, gang work lasted from sunup to sundown, often under the supervision of black drivers, or hired white overseers, and the system offered little incentive to work quickly. Chesapeake planters observed that "nothing can be conceived more inert than a slave . . . he moves not if he can avoid it; if the eyes of the overseer be off him, he sleeps." But gang labor was ideal for spreading King Cotton. Planters moving into the Georgia upcountry by the early 1800s brought the gang system to their new cotton plantations. Over time, they extended it to Alabama and Mississippi. Cotton growing required intensive plowing and planting, constant weeding with a heavy hoe, and painful separation of the ripe cotton from bolls that pricked slaves' stiff fingers. Each of these jobs was performed by large gangs that worked at the fastest pace a driver could squeeze from the slaves—the harshest might demand a grueling 150 pounds of cotton a day. Gangs in Chesapeake tobacco and wheat country were unable to negotiate working conditions as liberally as tasking slaves, although sometimes they effectively prevented the sales of particular members of their quarters or acquired additional clothing by agreeing to higher quotas or longer workdays.

It was not unusual for slave women to work in the fields with black men at tasks considered by white society to be too difficult for or unsuited to white females. While aging slave "grannies" cared for their children, many slave women worked with men to cut down trees, clear land for cultivation, and haul logs by leather straps attached around their chests. Slave women plowed cotton with mules and hoed fields to prepare them for planting; they helped build roads and repair wagons. A white observer at a Mississippi cotton plantation in 1852 remarked about slave women's stamina under extreme adversity: "Twenty of them were plowing together, with double teams and heavy plows. They were superintended by a male negro driver, who carried a whip, which he frequently cracked at them, permitting no dawdling or delay." On some plantations men did most of the heavy hauling and women sorted cotton lint and graded it, but this kind of separation was by no means universal, or even typical. As one fugitive slave insisted, "Women who do outdoor work are used as bad as men."

In addition to the unfailing duties of fieldwork, slave women worked at a variety of other tasks. They tended the slave and white children, who often mixed freely until age seven or eight, when slave children went to work. Other slave children began working at an early age doing light chores around the blacksmith shop, running errands to neighbors, or cleaning in the master's house. All were forbidden by law to learn reading and writing. Adult female slaves chosen to work in the "big house" cleaned, cooked, nursed, laundered, and sewed for the master's family. Some young women undertook weaving for masters and slaves on the plantation. Although this work was physically less demanding than the rigors of hoeing and picking cotton, it required long days (and sometimes nights) away from family members. It also involved the constant supervision of white people issuing orders and corrections. House slaves, unlike field hands, usually had to show subservience and respect or face severe punishments, especially when the "big house" filled with guests. When they returned to slave quarters, women often had to grind corn into meal or hominy, cook for their own families, and tend to the many chores of providing for others.

The rigors of field- and housework were sometimes broken up by opportunities for travel or group activities. Slave women with special skills, including seamstresses, cooks, and midwives, might travel to neighboring plantations and local towns as hired-out labor. Midwives were perhaps the most well-traveled of all slaves, since their services were needed in masters' families, neighboring slave quarters, and yeomen farmers' homes. Many masters relied on the medical knowledge of slave women to heal their slaves, which brought these specialists into contact with slaves and white people across a wide area. At the end of the week, Saturday afternoons might become occasions for group laundering or quilting. Sometimes slave women even slipped away to hold their own prayer meetings.

Skilled slave gardeners, blacksmiths, carpenters, tanners, and mechanics often worked in the master's house. Although such assignments brought slaves certain privileges, especially relief from fieldwork, being skilled could increase their chances of being sold away from their families or hired out to harsher masters. For example, on the docks of Natchez slaves worked as carpenters, chandlers, teamsters, sail makers, rope makers, and general deckhands alongside free African-Americans. Other slaves were hired out as miners, ship or dock hands, lumber camp workers, or forge men at iron mills. But for slaves hired out to the sugar mills of Louisiana planters, the backbreaking work of cutting and boiling cane was hardly a welcome relief from house labor.

Resistance and Rebellion

Slaves endured hard work, whippings, the sexual advances of masters, verbal abuse, and daily degradations of many forms. One ex-slave, recollecting her childhood spent with an unrelentingly cruel master on a small farm, said "that cowhide . . . would cut the blood out of you with every lick." Another, Harriet Jacobs, was rarely whipped or punished, and had more material comforts than "the torrent of Irish crowding our cities." But Jacobs was the victim of repeated sexual abuse by her "unprincipled master" and tormented verbally by her "jealous mistress," for whom "no terms were too vile for her to bestow upon me." Once pregnant, her master denied his role, and Jacobs's only close relative, her grandmother, turned her away for a few agonizing days. They reconciled, however, and in time Jacobs went into hiding in an attic for seven years until she could escape to New York City and Boston.

Slaves' resistance to abuses took many forms. Some tactics were subtle, as when slaves appeared to accommodate work orders but in reality set their own limitations to work or poked fun at drivers and masters. Other forms of resistance were riskier, such as pilfering supplies, slowing down completion of a task, sabotaging crop production, damaging tools, or using effusive apologies and praise of the master in order to avert suspicion and punishment for misdeeds. Frederick Douglass repeatedly told his white audiences about the use of deceit and guile among slaves: "As the master studies to keep the slave ignorant, the slave is cunning enough to make the master think he succeeds."

Leaving a plantation or factory without authorization was a more dangerous step for slaves to take. Some slaves who left work without permission simply intended to "go visitin'" family members or kinfolk on a nearby plantation, though the punishments for such travel and neglect of work duties could be serious indeed. Others wished to "disappear" temporarily just to show the master that escape was possible. Still others attempted to run away permanently and find their way to freedom. In Georgia and the new Black Belt states, running away was far more perilous than in the older states. To begin with, few slaves knew a safe haven to run to, especially once Spain ceded the Floridas to America in 1819. In addition, harsh work weakened slaves' ability to run far enough to attain freedom or thwarted their will to try. And rumors spread quickly that the forests and creeks of the Old Southwest were filled with hostile Native Americans and bounty hunters. Sometimes African traditional beliefs warned about vile creatures in swamps, forests, and mountains. By the 1840s, planters in Louisiana and Mississippi regularly hired slave catchers and their trained attack dogs to track fugitives.

Still, despite the odds, over a thousand slaves "took their freedom" by running away each year during the 1840s and 1850s. Most of the runaways were men between sixteen and thirty-five; many had work skills and could read and write. Women were much less likely to run away, perhaps because of their attachments to nurturing children. A network of white and black antislavery activists aided escapees with passage on the Underground Railroad. Both the law and slave catchers fought efforts to conduct slaves to freedom, posing a grave risk to everyone concerned in the enterprise. Many brave white abolitionists, including the Quaker merchant Thomas Garrett, sacrificed their time, money, and sometimes their reputations, to such efforts nevertheless. But the most valuable source of support came from free African-Americans in cities such as Richmond, Charleston, New Orleans, Baltimore, and Wilmington. In these communities, runaway slaves could find temporary refuge on their way north, secure food and new clothing, perhaps find a sponsor or escort to a safer region, or simply merge their identities with the free African-Americans around them. Some runaways, rather than moving on, devoted themselves to helping others escape. Harriet Tubman, an escaped slave and prominent abolitionist lecturer, worked tirelessly on the Underground Railroad. Tubman returned to the South nineteen times despite the danger of being re-enslaved or murdered each time she organized a trip to bring out slaves.

Open and organized group resistance to overseers and cruel masters was not frequent. It was most likely to occur where free African-Americans and slaves came in contact with one another or where runaways knew that a safe haven might harbor them. One intended revolt, in 1800, involved the plan of Gabriel Prosser, a liter-

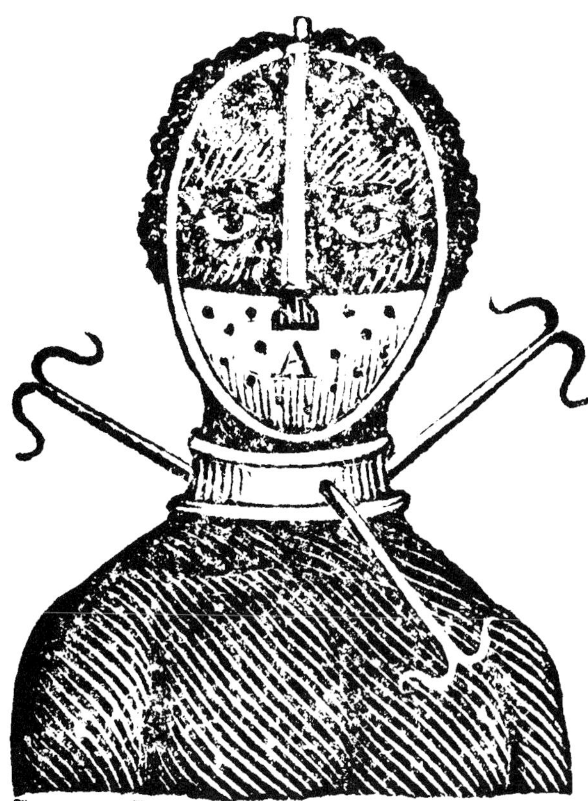

Torture Mask The laws of southern states had long stipulated that masters could use whatever means they deemed necessary to prevent slave runaways and insolence. In the early 1800s, some planters adopted this so-called restraining mask to punish slaves. *(Library of Congress.)*

ate blacksmith, to take over Richmond. With about a thousand slaves from the area, and the expectation that recently freed black people from Haiti would join them, Prosser declared "Death or Liberty." Although the rebellion was quashed at the last minute, and planters assented to the hanging of nearly forty slaves as examples to potential future resisters, Richmond residents had been seriously shaken.

Then, in 1822, Denmark Vesey's Charleston plot unfolded. Vesey, a free African-American, had the double distinction of owning his own carpentry shop and having an outstanding reputation in the city for eloquent speaking. Moreover, he had recently become a preacher. Many southern white leaders at the time were still proclaiming that the Missouri Compromise (see page 315) had given them the right to extend slavery into the trans-Mississippi West. Vesey shared his disgust over this interpretation of the compromise with his congregation. Gullah Jack, a folk medicine man from the South Carolina low country who spent time in Charleston, grew close to Vesey and together they connived to take the city. The conspirators planned to steal guns from the Charleston arsenal and horses from private stables, and then rally the support of widely dispersed house slaves to murder whites in their homes. Eventually the slaves would reach the docks and sail to freedom in Haiti.

Vesey and Gullah Jack convinced about eighty city and country slaves to join them, including the house slaves at the governor's mansion in Charleston. But two weeks before the appointed insurrection day, a reluctant recruit informed the authorities about the plot. When confronted, the leading insurgents denied the charges and deterred officials, but when the charge was raised once more by another house slave, Charleston authorities did not wait for proof. For days, slaves were grabbed up, thirty-four hanged alongside the swinging corpse of Vesey, and thirty-seven sold down the river to new masters. But not all the conspirators were caught, and the Charleston elite lived on for years in fear that a new revolt might be brewing. Leading citizens even appealed to the local government to close off the city to visitors. White citizens destroyed Vesey's church, and in late 1822, the South Carolina legislature enacted a law requiring that all black sailors be confined in local jails while their ships were in port, an attempt to limit contact between Charleston's slaves and free African-Americans who might have dangerous ideas.

In 1831 the violence that David Walker predicted shook the Chesapeake region. Nat Turner was a slave from Southampton County, Virginia, a self-taught, widely respected leader among the region's African-Americans, and something of a religious visionary. He had been promised his freedom, but a second master refused to grant it, while a third master separated Turner from his wife. Despite the kindly treatment of his current master, Joseph Travis, Turner became embittered. He professed to have experienced a religious vision of whites and blacks "engaged in battle," where "blood flowed in streams." Following a conversion experience, Turner believed he was destined to direct his inner rage at slave masters. Along with five others, Turner killed Travis on August 20, 1831, and then ran from plantation to plantation killing the white people they encountered and offering freedom to the slaves. Fifty-five whites died, but when a group of mounted and armed planters rounded up the nearly sixty runaway slaves, action came to a halt. Vengeful militiamen rampaged through the countryside and armed cavalry murdered dozens of slaves, hoisting fifteen of their heads on poles to send clear signals of their intentions. Trials of about fifty slaves resulted in twenty hangings. Eventually Turner himself was caught and met the same end. Although no other serious slave revolts broke out before emancipation, southern whites shuddered collectively for years as successful runaways provided constant reminders about discontents.

Free African-Americans

The American Revolution's language of political independence, and both patriot and British offers of freedom to slaves who aided their causes, inspired many slaves to break away from their bondage. After the Revolution, gradual emancipation provisions in northern states increased the numbers of free African-Americans, and private manumissions or self-purchases gained freedom for some former slaves. George Washington, for example, provided in his will for the manumission of his slaves. But increasingly, southern planters limited these opportunities for freedom, especially after Nat Turner's bloody revolt. Slaves turned to the more desperate measure of running away to cities where they could blend anonymously with free African-Americans.

Some slaves worked long years to buy freedom for themselves and their families. James L. Bradley "made collars for horses, out of plaited husks," according to his memoirs. With a little money from this work, Bradley bought a pig and tended a small plot of corn for feed; in time, he bred a large number of hogs, which he sold, along with small amounts of tobacco. After five years, Bradley bought time from his master to work odd jobs "morn and night," until he purchased himself for $700. In 1849 John H. Hammond told fellow South Carolinians that "whenever a slave is made a mechanic he is more than half freed." For many whites, including Hammond, this was reason enough to limit such opportunities for slaves. For other whites, slaves were a valuable addition to the labor force, as when railroad owners in Lynchburg, Virginia, or Nashville, Tennessee, hired slaves, or when the tobacco and hemp factory owners in Virginia and Kentucky did likewise. Scholars estimate that in the 1840s and 1850s between 5 and 10 percent of southern workers were hired slaves, some for a few days and some for a year at a time.

By the time of the Civil War, 500,000 African-Americans were free, about half of them living in southern states. Most free African-Americans, whether southern or northern, were landless rural laborers or tenants of white landowners. In North Carolina and Arkansas, the majority of the free black population continued to work for white planters or remained indebted to the white business class. But large numbers of free blacks migrated into southern cities such as Savannah, Charleston, Memphis, and Natchez, alarming white populations. In Washington, D.C., 30 percent of the population remained enslaved in the 1830s and 1840s, but fears among the white population grew as many slaves gained the right to live apart from masters in wooden shantytowns where they mingled with free slaves and all too often slipped from the grip of their masters.

In both the South and the North, African-Americans hardly enjoyed the unmitigated blessings of free society. Indeed, they usually lived somewhere between freedom and slavery. Courts, businesses, and schools frequently denied free African-Americans formal legal rights in practice. Immigrant Irish, German, and other peoples forced African-Americans out of jobs as horse tenders, domestic workers, barbers, and tailors in cities such as Richmond, Charleston, New Orleans, and Mobile. In St. Louis the black population became increasingly more rural, edged out of the city by immigrating unskilled workers from Europe. Most free African-Americans survived on meager wages at dreary jobs as carters, laundresses, horse handlers, barbers, carpenters, quarrymen, and road crewmen. A few former slave women in each city landed employment as nannies and housekeepers, their paltry wages sometimes the sole income for their families. Free black men hired themselves out in large numbers to sugar plantations in Louisiana by the 1850s, and to small shops as coopers, carters, and carpenters in Virginia and Maryland.

Nor was freedom for ex-slaves always secure. For example, slave traders such as James H. Birch of Washington, D.C., built a network of kidnappers and tricksters who abducted free African-Americans from northern homes and sold them into slavery in Louisiana, Mississippi, and Texas during the 1840s. In Washington, D.C., white citizens feared the rapid influx of free African-Americans, possibly because the city also had become an important location for large slave auctions and a crossroads for slaves being shipped from the Chesapeake to Georgia and South Carolina. The nation's capital enacted Black Codes in 1808 to control the liberties of freed slaves migrating into the city. These new laws imposed fines and whippings for public gatherings after 10 P.M., for "tippling" in local taverns, and for "nightly and disorderly meetings"—the latter measure outlawing virtually all social and religious gatherings of the city's African-Americans. In the wake of Nat Turner's rebellion in Virginia, Washington's Black Codes became even harsher; for example, a black person who struck a white person could have his ears cut off.

A few free African-Americans in Washington, D.C., reached middle-class status, owning property and serving in benevolent and religious organizations. George Fisher, for example, ran a blacksmith shop on East Capitol Street; Spencer Johnson made shoes to order at Pennsylvania Avenue and Twenty-first Street. The Reverend John Cook ran the Union Seminary, a private high school for free men of color, started in 1834, as well as the Young Men's Moral and Literary Society. By the 1850s, nearly 10 percent of blacks in Washington, D.C., owned property. Although the city boasted almost thirty schools for white girls, journalists widely noted that African-American girls got a far better education at their one female academy.

Washington, D.C., did not have the most stringent Black Codes. An 1806 Virginia law required newly manumitted ex-slaves to leave the state within a year or face re-enslavement; Maryland followed with a similar law of its own. Chesapeake laws also took away free African-Americans' rights to sue or serve in courts, and by 1830, it was nearly impossible to gain manumission. Throughout the South, free black people were forbidden to carry firearms or gather in meetings; were systematically denied the right to file lawsuits or to be tried by juries in criminal cases; and were required to carry "freedom papers" proving they were not slaves. Ex-slaves were not permitted to vote, hold office, or serve in the militia. In verdicts requiring punishments, laws stipulated that all black people—slave and free—would receive the penalties reserved for slaves.

Even the southern cities that had permitted all residents to own property and run businesses began to curtail the activities and opinions of free blacks in the 1840s and 1850s. Free black tradesmen in Charleston had to carry identification papers and wear badges attesting to their legitimate employment. The white community of Natchez deported numbers of poor free blacks during the 1840s under the pretense that they were "incendiaries" and "abolitionists."

Some free African-Americans overcame great adversity to achieve distinction. A few, often through self-education, attained public recognition and wealth, such as the surveyor and architect Benjamin Bannaker and the merchant Robert Sheridan. The nearly one thousand free African-Americans of Natchez who lived in abject poverty regarded with scorn the few ex-slaves who became prominent businessmen in the city, some of whom owned slaves and cultivated cultural relations with the white community. In Charleston, elite free black people offered goods and services to a white clientele who also permitted free blacks to educate their children in separate schools and to move about the city freely. Free African-Americans ran hotels, stables, and mills in and around Charleston. Urban ex-slaves who had advanced up the economic ladder considerably in the early 1800s often lived in white neighborhoods; some even acquired slaves to work in their shops.

Free African-Americans in Philadelphia at first joined the churches of white citizens (though they sat in separate sections), but in 1794 Reverend Absalom Jones

Free African-American Poet Frances Watkins Although freedom eluded all but a small proportion of slaves before the Civil War, those who gained freedom often prevailed against difficult conditions to become outstanding intellectuals. Frances Ellen Watkins Harper used her talents as a poet and lecturer to champion the antislavery cause. She became the first woman faculty member at Union Seminary in Ohio in 1850 and then moved to Pennsylvania in order to help with the Underground Railroad. *(Library Company of Philadelphia.)*

founded the first African-American Baptist church. Nearby in the same city, Reverend Richard Allen began the first Methodist congregation of African-Americans. Allen was born a slave in Philadelphia in 1760 but, as a teenager, had been sold with his family to a farmer in Delaware, where the fires of Methodism inspired Allen's master to let him buy his freedom. After the Revolution, Allen first became an itinerant Methodist speaker and then a minister who gained high esteem in Philadelphia's abolitionist and Methodist circles. But after witnessing years of discrimination, including separated pews for worship in churches and separate burial grounds, Allen decided to answer the burning desire of free African-Americans to control their worship. Allen was equally dissatisfied with proposals for gradual emancipation and colonization. In 1816 Allen brought together a number of breakaway African-American church members to found the African Methodist Episcopal (AME) Church, America's first independent black denomination.

Bringing talents together into new organizations often gave additional strength and autonomy to free African-Americans living in the North. Groups of freedmen founded societies for mutual aid, separate medical care, or dissenting religious worship. Numerous African-American women participated in efforts to found schools in northern communities. Freedmen's organizations also overlapped with the membership and activities of antislavery organizations. Sojourner Truth, David Walker, and Frederick Douglass helped build bridges that strengthened both African-American churches and abolitionist societies. In the South, AME churches gave slaves a degree of temporary autonomy from white religion and the slave institution. Denmark Vesey, the fiery speaker who inspired his congregation to the point of revolt, was an AME preacher.

Planters and Yeomen

Great plantation mansions rose out of the southern landscape here and there, as if to remind all viewers that the profits of slave labor would concentrate in the hands of a very few wealthy families. But very few southern landowners had twenty or more slaves on their plantations. The great majority of white planters occupied land between and around the great plantations stretching from Virginia and Tennessee to Louisiana and Texas. From poor tenants and itinerant white laborers, to middling white farmers—some of whom owned one to five slaves—this numerical majority enjoyed few of the cultural, economic, and political privileges that elite planters did. The planter's paternal identity vis-à-vis his slaves contrasted sharply with middling and poor white southerners' anxieties over slave competition for jobs and challenges to their belief in free white labor. Nevertheless, landowning yeomen and landless tenants constantly interacted with great planters and experienced the effects of the slave system daily.

Planters

In the 1850s only one-third of southern white people owned slaves—18 percent owned fewer than five, 16 percent owned five to twenty, and only about 2.5 percent owned more than twenty. As late as the eve of the Civil War, only about 46,000 planters in the South owned twenty or more slaves; fewer than three thousand white men owned over one hundred. But slave owners, especially the elite among them, shaped much of the culture, politics, and economy of the South, and they fiercely defended their interests against encroachments from small farmers in the region and against all critics outside the region. Some planters' mansions commanded awe and conferred authority by their opulence. The estate became a site for displays of elegance, grace, and constant expensive entertainment.

Tidewater and low country plantations that rose before the Revolution represented enduring property and power in the hands of a few men. After 1800, planter expansion into Kentucky, Louisiana, and Mississippi added a layer of new elite families. New Orleans and Natchez planters sometimes boasted hundreds of slaves and hundreds of thousands of acres producing cotton for ready shippers at the docks.

Some planters also enjoyed many hours a week of leisure reading, horseback riding, or "gaming" with neighbors. Most planters, though, were businessmen who attended carefully to surveying crops, reviewing slaves' work and planning work regimens, keeping account books and notations, and scouring the newspapers for pricing trends and commercial conditions. Many planters tried to furnish all of their own food and supplies and trained slaves to be carpenters, blacksmiths, weavers, and coopers. Even among planters who owned many slaves, mansions were rare until the 1850s. More typically a home of a few rooms stood amid outbuildings for cooking, tanning, dairying, and other chores related to provisioning a household.

Whether cultivating great wealth or sustaining a more modest productive enterprise, southern planters relied on the ideology of paternalism to maintain their supremacy over both slaves and wives. Paternalism taught that the complex social network of a plantation was a family, with the planter acting as the master and father of both his white household and his slaves. His wife and children, as well as his slaves, all fit along a continuum of roles. The master had to provide the basic needs of everyone in this "family" and was expected to treat both white and black members humanely. Wives, in return, would obey according to what their roles dictated, as would the master's children, as would slaves. Paternalism offered the ideal of constituting all plantation relations into "a harmonious whole." Masters had not only plentiful privileges and absolute control over the lives under their authority, but also the duty to provide necessities and protection for grateful family members and obedient slaves.

Masters in the Chesapeake region and parts of the new Black Belt supervised their plantations personally as businessmen. This put them in direct daily and personal contact with slaves, giving masters many opportunities to enforce their authority when necessary, but also requiring them to maintain a delicate balance of respect and solicitation of the welfare of slaves. Also, since the importation of slaves nearly ceased after 1808, any expansion of the master's slave labor force would have to come from domestic sales and natural increase. Thus, to encourage safe and regular childbearing, masters had to ensure at least a minimum of care for the physical and emotional well-being of slaves. Again, this afforded slaves at least some opportunity to negotiate conditions of work and leisure and to obtain small items of sustenance or comfort. Planters slowly gave up the most severe forms of punishment, including castration, branding, and physical mutilation. Still, these small measures did not indicate so much a master's moral or emotional conscience as his attention to profits. Supervisory methods constantly reaffirmed the status of slaves as inferior and "childlike," and the use of coercion—including whipping and withholding food, for example—was always a potential threat.

Paternalism gave the plantation mistress especially difficult burdens. In addition to cultivating all of the virtues that women everywhere were supposed to share—obedience, chastity, purity, and piety—the planter's wife and daughters managed the household slaves, spun and wove, cared for sick family members and slaves, arranged hospitality for visitors, and did the countless daily tasks that large households entailed. But overlaying this arduous routine, southern women bore the additional burdens of paternalistic ideology, which created an image of southern plantation mistresses at odds with their daily lives. Although plantation mistresses bustled ceaselessly about their homes, they were expected to refrain from "drudge work" and to delegate as many responsibilities as possible to master-husbands. Ideal southern mistresses were supposed to have very little real control over important domestic decisions, and thus to have far less authority in their "sphere" than northern women claimed. Ideal southern master-husbands, unlike northern men, were supposed to have extensive control over their households and to dominate all work and social affairs as they did in their plantation fields.

Plantation mistresses differed from northern female homemakers in another sense: southern ladies were strictly prohibited from entering public activities, and thus were shut off from important arenas of social reform. The isolation of rural plantations reinforced the social and emotional distance of white women from friends and kin, too. Although they often were surrounded by slave women of all ages, the chasm of differences between the races could not be easily bridged. The scholarly record shows some remarkable efforts by plantation mistresses to befriend or defend female slaves. Some softened the harshness of cruel masters by defending a slave's version of misdeeds, by handing out apples or molasses at slave quarters, and by helping at the birth of slave babies. Many pleaded on behalf of slaves who came to masters with minor requests for favors. And there are numerous stories of mistresses who entrusted slaves with arranging secret meetings with suitors or delivering love letters. Annie Broidrick, a white woman raised on a Mississippi plantation, recounted late in her life that "many a romantic tale was confided by mistress and maid to each other during the hours the hair was being brushed." But in the final analysis, as most of these recollections note, the more dominant note was one of great social and emotional distance between the races of women in plantation households.

Yeomen and Tenants

By the 1850s, when the slave population reached its zenith before emancipation, fully 65 percent of southern white heads of households did not own slaves. But few

Varieties of Racial Family Roles Although voluntary racial mixing had been scorned by much of American society for generations, white and black people actually lived in many different family and community arrangements. African-American women were nannies and nurses, field hands and washerwomen, mothers and lovers, indispensable to many planters' households as well as to their own in slave quarters. Although most African-American women remained the most subordinate members of southern society, this young lady enjoyed a special relationship to the white infant, who was probably in her care. *(J. Paul Getty Museum.)*

landowning yeomen or landless tenants challenged the appropriateness of elite planter domination and slavery in the South. After all, many of them admired wealthy planters and hoped to rise into a better condition themselves through the acquisition of slaves and cultivation of fertile soil. The republican ideal, so acclaimed by Thomas Jefferson, taught that a piece of independently held land was the starting point for true citizenship and a virtuous personal life.

Yeomen—independent landowning farmers—in the older tidewater areas produced food for their own families and sometimes for the plantations nearby. Upcountry Georgia farmers who lived on land once held by Cherokee Indians added livestock grazing to their agriculture and sometimes earned small amounts of cash from sales of a bale or two of cotton after each harvest. Occasionally, an upcountry yeoman fared better than his neighbors and was then able to buy more land, or even to become a slave owner. Those who moved farther into the interior found that the rich soil of the Shenandoah, Ohio, and other river systems yielded large crops of corn and wheat or provided extensive grazing for herds of cattle and sheep.

Southern yeomen clung to the Democratic Party's promise to expand America's western empire on behalf of the common man during the 1830s. For some this implied opportunities to rise into the ranks of the slave-owning political leadership, while for others the promise held out hope for the more modest acquisition of a small landholding and perhaps a couple of slaves—enough to secure "freedom" from domination by great planters or wealthy developers. In addition, landownership and its association with white male suffrage created a common bond of white racial superiority over blacks. And yeomen also cherished the ideal of self-sufficiency or modest comfort that could distance them from both the northern industrialization many southerners feared and the indebtedness of landless poor southern white families around them.

These beliefs tended to obscure the widening cultural and economic gap between yeomen and the great planters. Economically, most yeomen could not expect to grow wealthy, for their production of one to six 400-pound bales of cotton per year could not compare with the hundreds of bales that a great planter might produce. In addition, the small amounts of cotton sent to market put the farmer in touch with the distribution and pricing mechanisms that great planters controlled. Many yeomen needed the services of local millers and blacksmiths, who might be connected closely to the functions of the great plantations. In those cases, elaborate arrangements among many parties got the yeoman's grain gristed on the plantation mill in return for leather hides, barreled pork, or some other farm product. If he wished to get cotton to port cities, a yeoman needed help from well-connected planters. If he acquired slaves, a yeoman might hire them out to needy planters. If he needed workers, he might rent slaves from a planter. Sometimes the ledgers of farmers show detailed exchanges of labor time between farms and large plantations. But most yeomen, struggling just to squeeze a decent crop from their 150 to 200 acres, depended on regular cooperation among white neighbors to get in the harvests. Indeed, slaves themselves expressed a preference for being owned by a great planter rather than a yeoman, for the wealthy master tended to have greater economic security, which in turn offered the prospect of more enduring ties in slave quarters and perhaps family life. Although some yeomen prospered enough for modest comfort, many of them, as one ex-slave told it, "lived by scanty means, at the edge of their survival and mine."

Just as the spectrum of landowning yeomen included successful farm families that might have slaves and struggling farmers who barely survived from one year to the next, so there was a spectrum of landless southern whites throughout the South. Away from the tidewater and lowlands of plantation slavery, where hills and then mountains rose out of the countryside, the soil was less hospitable for growing cotton, and many would-be yeomen found it impossible to attain the ideal of owning a self-sufficient farm. Tilling the worst land, often far from waterways leading to markets, poor hill-country whites often fell outside the definition of republican yeomen citizens. Many of these poor whites focused on production for household consumption and local exchange, raising hogs, sheep, and cattle along with food crops. Neighbors borrowed tools, seed, and household goods from one another; they traded at small country stores for notions, salt, and yard goods; and they bartered with friends for food, tool repairs, midwifery services, and harvesting. Unlike plantation mistresses and rising yeomen, upcountry farmers' wives did household chores with their daughters and worked in the fields as well.

With little hope of acquiring land, many poor whites became the tenants of yeomen or planters, or moved from job to job in search of stability or survival. One-third of Georgia's upcountry farmers were tenants on other men's land. In the far western parts of North Carolina, South Carolina, and Virginia, from 40 to 50 percent of white people owned no land. The lowlands of Alabama and the pine barrens along the Atlantic coast were also home to large numbers of struggling poor whites. Throughout these areas by the 1830s, thousands of laborers, tenants, and occasional wage workers lived in utter poverty, surviving on minimal food of poor quality and enduring long bouts with debilitating diseases such as pellagra, hookworm, and anemia. And as King Cotton took over more and more of the best soil in new states, and the price of land skyrocketed, the yeoman ideal receded further and further beyond their reach. During agricultural harvests and in factories, poor whites and black slaves—both hired temporarily—might work side by side. Some landless poor whites rented land from planters hoping someday to repay their debts and save enough to buy a small tract.

The relationships between poor whites and slaves were filled with tension, for while most landless tenants and occasional laborers shared the yeoman's ideal of becoming independent landowners, in reality they had much in common with slaves and free African-Americans. Some sympathetic whites helped slaves escape and hide in obscure places. Some entered petty business deals to deliver liquor or extra food to slaves who were forbidden these items by planters. Planters often accommodated this trade by lowering the prices of flour, salt pork, or fabric that they sold to slaves in hopes of undermining trade outside their plantations. But, as one planter in Mississippi noted, there were "poor whites within a few miles who would always sell liquor to the negroes, and encourage them to steal, to obtain the means to buy it of them." In this way, the lines between free whites and slaves were often temporarily blurred.

Defending Slavery

For generations, presses, politicians, and pulpits had justified slavery to southerners. Historical examples of slavery in the Bible and in Classical Greece and Rome had bolstered arguments by colonists in the 1600s that for some people to be in permanent bondage to others was "the natural condition" (see Chapter 2). In the early 1800s, writers deemed slavery an evil developed by colonial ancestors and a burden borne by southern planters. Jeffersonians had dared to imagine the South without slaves, through discussion about "civilizing the dark races" and colonization of slaves in communities outside America.

Once the southern cotton boom was under way in the early 1800s, it became increasingly difficult for planters to contemplate emancipation of individual slaves. Some began to argue that the entire economic system of the South required slavery. Thomas Jefferson and a few others had proposed that slow individual manumission and colonization might be a viable response to slavery, but they also feared the mixing of the races and defended slavery as a "necessary evil" in national life. As Jefferson put it, "We have the wolf by the ears; and we can neither hold him nor safely let him go. Justice is in one scale, and self-preservation in the other."

Indeed, the nation did not move toward individual or general emancipation. Southern slave codes passed during the early national years ensured slavery's continuing existence. Northern and western states explicitly limited the rights of free African-Americans, some by imposing a property requirement for voting, some by prohibiting African-Americans from serving on juries or testifying against whites in courts, and some by closing public services, transport, land offices, and schools to African-Americans. The Constitution itself provided that seats in the House of Representatives would be determined by a count of the whole white population and three-fifths of the black population; runaway slaves would be returned to their masters; and the international slave trade could continue for twenty more years, until 1808. Moreover, a federal Fugitive Slave Act in 1793 encouraged kidnappers and bounty hunters to seize free African-Americans from northern neighborhoods and sell them into slavery.

But by the 1820s, disquieting ambiguities troubled southern planters. Although the Missouri Compromise of 1820 opened the door for expanding slavery west of the Mississippi River, the same act granted free African-Americans the right to vote in Maine, thereby heightening sectional fears between North and South. Some southerners believed that creating a free state, Maine, transcended a simple balance of political representation; it encouraged "convulsive and destructive" northern antislavery sentiment to grow.

And antislavery sentiment *did* grow. In one of their more spectacular efforts, abolitionists conducted a massive petition drive to flood Congress with requests to abolish slavery and the slave trade in Washington, D.C. But Congress was swayed by strong southern opposition to the petitions, and by prodding from President Andrew Jackson, to pass a gag rule in 1836 that prohibited discussion of the petitions in the House or Senate. Already, southerners had acted forcefully against the presence of petitions in their states, as well as use of the federal postal system to circulate them. In 1835 a proslavery mob broke into a Charleston post office and confiscated batches of antislavery petition forms and literature, which they proceeded to burn. Now, with support from Congress to stifle national discussion about slavery, planters became more arrogant in their defense of the institution.

By the early 1830s, Southern defensiveness about slavery was entering a new phase. As one far-seeing southerner put it in 1833, "So interwoven is it [slavery] with our interest, our manners, our climate and our very being, that no change can ever possibly be effected without a civil commotion." Although he added that "the heart of a patriot must turn with horror" from such national violence, the coercion inherent in slavery, the potential and real violence between the races, and the sheer numbers of black people in southern states had both entrenched the slave system and aroused opposition to it.

In their majority, southern legislators, printers, and clergymen defended their culture, including slavery, paternalism, and planter domination. In addition to passing laws that tightened their grip on slaves, southern leaders also articulated arguments in their press and pulpits that solidified their commitment to the so-called peculiar institution. For example, the constitutions of Louisiana, Alabama, and Mississippi included language permitting slavery. By 1835, every southern state passed additional laws to restrain the movement of slaves and to monitor or restrict public gatherings, dances, and African-American church services. With the exception of Kentucky, Tennessee, and Maryland, all southern states forbade slaves from learning how to read, and many outlawed manumissions. Slave patrols—vigilante groups of poor white men who whipped and tortured slaves caught without passes after curfew—became a regular feature of country roads and southern cities.

The violence based on racial attitudes associated with southern slavery spread through northern and midwestern communities in the 1830s to 1850s. For example, Irish immigrants mobbed antislavery activists in New York and Boston because the immigrants feared cutthroat competition for jobs should southern slaves be emancipated and move north. Free labor beliefs taught American-born and immigrant workers that slaves shared their aspirations for cheap land and decent wages.

Violence spilled out into the territories and new western states, too. In the Old Northwest, an area guaranteed by Jefferson's 1787 ordinance to remain free soil, "black laws" attempted to exclude or expel free African-Americans, and these were in turn enforced by self-appointed groups of white "slave police." In border states, white violence against blacks on plantations carried over into factories where slaves had been hired out by masters, and it threatened to break out whenever both races gathered together publicly, as at revival meetings or July 4 celebrations. In Alton, Illinois, the abolitionist editor Elijah P. Lovejoy endured the destruction of his printing press by angry mobs not once, but four times, before he was killed in 1837 by "border ruffians" who wished to spread slavery into Kansas.

In settled border states and Chesapeake-area cities, too, violence reached new levels by the 1830s. Northern abolitionists charged slave traders with "stealing" free African-Americans and selling them into slavery far from their homes. The New England Anti-Slavery Society called the traders "inland pirates" who had little concern for the true status of their "human cargo." In cities, racial tensions also grew between whites and blacks working in households and small shops, and occasionally individual confrontations took place. After Nat Turner's Rebellion in 1831, Chesapeake region planters advocated more stringent Black Codes. But codes did not satisfy everyone, and the animosity of white mobs toward free and slave African-Americans turned ugly. For example, in Washington, D.C., in 1835 a slave desperate for his freedom tried to murder the widow of the U.S. Capitol architect, Mrs. William Thornton, which provoked white retaliation. Angry young whites banded together for days in what was later called the "Snow Storm" and rampaged through the city's streets destroying black homes and businesses. For years, mob violence was periodically incited with the cry of "Avenge Mrs. Thornton!"

In addition to racial violence, legal restrictions, and increased abolitionist activities by the 1830s, some of slavery's southern supporters developed their justifications for the South's "peculiar institution" further. James Henry Hammond, a South Carolina planter who became a legislator in the 1830s, wrote that slavery was neither evil nor immoral because "civilized gentlemen" had organized the system rationally and efficiently. If slaves' privileges had been withdrawn and their punishments had grown harsh, it was the fault of abolitionist agitators who aroused slaves to disobedience. William Harper, a distinguished South Carolina jurist and advocate of nullification, insisted that evidence pointed to "some form of slavery in all ages and countries," and thus planters were unexceptional in that regard. Moreover, since slaves' "nature tended to the immoral," and prominent passages of both the Old and New Testaments of the Bible could be interpreted to dictate the permanent inequality of the races, masters simply followed the principles of benevolence when they subjected African-Americans to slavery.

Thomas R. Dew, a Virginia apologist for slavery, expanded the arguments of some southerners who found fault with John Locke's teachings about natural rights (see Competing Voices, page 482). All individuals, argued Dew, do not have inherent, God-given equality of rights within societies. Moreover, Locke was wrong in positing that at one time individuals came out of their "state of nature," or primitive competitive condition, to join in societies with rules and governments. Instead, Dew argued that the social order had evolved slowly over time, that it was suited for stability rather than legal changes or revolutions, and that it was an organic whole of mutually dependent people, not a set of "artificial" markets and institutions. Humans, insisted Dew, had strikingly different capacities from birth and could function only in pyramidal relationships of authority, especially across racial lines. People organize themselves, said Dew, more around their duties than around their rights. It was the duty of white masters to shelter, feed, protect, and permanently own black people.

During the 1850s, George Fitzhugh took the proslavery argument another step. In his influential books, *Sociology for the South; or, The Failure of a Free Society*

(1854), and *Cannibals All! Or, Slaves Without Masters* (1857), Fitzhugh argued that southern slaves actually lived in a condition of greater freedom than northern "wage slaves"; black slaves were tended by paternalistic masters in a "community of interests" from cradle to grave, whereas northern workers were hired, paid less than a decent wage, used up, and turned out into the world again if illness or old age made them useless to the employer. Fitzhugh was a respected Virginia lawyer and planter, and when he expressed the belief that northern industrial life had succumbed to impersonal market forces, in which profits were the sole aim of factory owners and wages the sole aim of workers, southerners nodded in agreement. Masters, wrote Fitzhugh, established cultural examples for poor whites and slaves to emulate. They lived a refined life that not only reflected their profits from the labor of slaves but also set a tone of civility and public virtue in the South that slaves grew to respect. Many years before this, John C. Calhoun had argued that slavery made it possible for the master race to perfect itself culturally and intellectually.

No matter how convoluted these intellectual arguments for slavery became, most of them rested on the assumption of African-Americans' racial inferiority. Those who accepted such a premise could then argue that force, restrictions, and of course slavery naturally followed. Slavery was not only a fitting condition for all people of African descent; it was the best framework for raising up, or "civilizing," African-Americans. Dew felt certain that "slaves of a good master are his warmest, most constant, and most devoted friends." Yet even the poorest whites did not need such paternalistic "friendship" because they supposedly were not racial underlings.

Not all southerners defended slavery, and a few of them turned against the institution. In the mid-1830s, the Grimké sisters left South Carolina and became outspoken abolitionists; the Kentucky antislavery spokesman James G. Birney became the abolitionist candidate for the Liberty Party in 1840. In 1832 Virginia's backcountry small farmers struck out against the great planters of the coastline when, fearing more rebellions like Nat Turner's, they forced the state government to discuss the feasibility of gradual manumission. By the 1840s, some yeomen complained about the difficulties of purchasing land and slaves, both of which were becoming more expensive, and their consequent inability to enter the ranks of slave owners.

Other small farmer whites fiercely resisted the encroachments of banks, railroads, and creditors reaching from coastal regions into the backcountry. These people did not aspire to become slave owners, but rather to sustain their republican independence against the southern system of slavery with its political and economic elite. They were no less racist than northern white people who feared the economic competition and cultural presence of African-Americans in their communities, nor than their southern counterparts who owned great landed estates. Hinton Helper, a North Carolinian who left the South to join northern abolitionists, wrote *The Impending Crisis of the South* (1857), in which he argued that unlike northern free labor's plentiful opportunities for economic advancement, southern slavery held non–slave owning whites in thrall to the dominant plantation and labor system. The true victims of the slave and plantation system were nonslaveholding whites. Although Helper intended to stimulate poor white sentiment in the South against both African-Americans and the institution of slavery, yeomen demands in southern politics continued to be subordinated to planters' elite power over all of southern political life.

CONCLUSION

Both northerners and southerners agreed that slavery was the basis for understanding the South. Slavery was the linchpin of southern rural and urban life, white and black culture, economy and politics. Despite the small number of large plantations compared with yeoman farmsteads and tenant tracts, it was staples agriculture and the slave labor system supporting it that set the South apart from the North most fundamentally.

Slavery unquestionably grew during this era, both numerically and territorially. Despite the official end to slave importation, the institution grew tremendously from the 1820s to 1850s. From fewer than 700,000 in 1790, the slave population in the South mushroomed to nearly 4 million by 1860. As slavery officially ended in the Caribbean, the numbers of "country-born" slaves in the American South rose dramatically. In 1860, 95 percent of America's blacks lived in southern states from Delaware to Texas, accounting for 25 percent of the southern population.

The "peculiar institution" spread to numerous new states in those years, too, and its defenders looked forward to its continuing expansion far beyond the Mississippi River. The Missouri Compromise gave southern expansionists hope that the southern way of life—its slavery, plantation agriculture, and planter paternalism—might defeat the ideals of free labor and independent family farming that northerners propounded. Despite the great disparity of social and economic conditions between rich planters and impoverished yeomen and tenants in the South, most white people agreed that slavery was necessary for their mutual survival.

But the southern way of life was fraught with inherent instabilities. Slaves built resilient communities within the great plantations and benefited from ongoing exchanges with yeomen for small household comforts. They mitigated the daily drudgery and brutality of work with song, sabotage, slowdowns, and other small acts of defiance that affirmed slaves' dignity to everyone who took notice. And they ran away in ever-increasing numbers during the 1830s and 1840s, to hiding places in the South and free cities of the North.

Faced with the volatile nature of master–slave relations, the growing movements of moral reformers and abolitionists, and the persistent political and cultural tensions of westward expansion, southern slave owners defended slavery more and more anxiously as the 1840s unfolded. By the 1850s, southern fears about the consequences of northerners transplanting their culture and economy into new territories became shrill. As slavery, King Cotton, and the southern way of life continued to expand over these years, so did the routes of the Underground Railroad and the number of eager northerners moving into the West. Indeed, Abraham Lincoln grew up in a heartland of racial tensions that stretched at first across the Allegheny Mountains, then to the Mississippi River, and then beyond.

SUGGESTED READINGS

David B. Davis, who wrote *The Problem of Slavery in the Age of Revolution, 1770–1823* (1975), was among the first scholars to place American antislavery activities into world perspective. Influential studies of the northern abolitionists include Lawrence Freidman, *Gregarious Saints* (1982); Gilbert Barnes, *The Anti-Slavery Impulse* (1933); and Ronald G. Walters, *The Antislavery Appeal: American Abolitionists After 1830* (1976). A fine biography of the movement's most important African-American leader is William McFeely, *Frederick Douglass* (1991). For the backlash against the abolitionist minority, see Leonard Richards, *"Gentlemen of Property and Standing": Anti-Abolition Mobs in Jacksonian America* (1970).

For an overview of southern social and economic life, see the highly informative work by David Roller and Robert Twyman, eds., *The Encyclopedia of Southern History* (1979). For views about the extent of southern economic and social development before the Civil War, see Fred Bateman and Thomas Weiss, *A Deplorable Society: The Failure of Industrialization in the Slave Economy* (1981); John Boles, *The South Through Time: A History of an American Region* (1995); and Ronald L. Lewis, *Coal, Iron, and Slaves: Industrial Slavery in Maryland and Virginia, 1715–1865* (1979). Kenneth M. Stampp's *The Peculiar Institution* (1956) turned the tide of most earlier scholarship by arguing that slavery was both immensely profitable and, from the slave's vantage point, socially horrible. In 1965 Eugene Genovese's work, *The Political Economy of Slavery,* proposed a dramatically new interpretation that questioned profitability arguments by introducing a distinctive southern mindset and regional departures from the rest of the nation. Since Genovese, many new lines of inquiry have developed. For example, Robert W. Fogel and Stanley L. Engerman, *Time on the Cross: The Economics of American Negro Slavery* (1974), argues for the profitability, though not the long-term viability, of slavery; Herbert G. Gutman, ed., *Slavery and the Numbers Game* (1973), challenges this view. James Oakes, in *The Ruling Race: A History of American Slaveholders* (1982), agrees slavery was profitable, but does so from the vantage of the small slave owners; Oakes argues that the South was capitalist. Fogel reexamines his own and others' work about slave productivity and well-being in *Without Consent or Contract* (1988). Michael Tadman, *Speculators and Slaves: Masters, Traders, and Slaves in the Old South* (1989), offers one of the finest studies of the internal slave trade of the South.

The most influential work on slave culture in the Old South is Eugene Genovese's *Roll, Jordan, Roll: The World the Slaves Made* (1974), which argues for great variety of slave experiences and paternalism of masters. Important objections are made to Genovese's contentions in Oakes, *The Ruling Race.* For rich details about slave culture also see George Rawick, *From Sundown to Sunup* (1972); Stampp, *The Peculiar Institution;* John Blassingame, *The Slave Community: Plantation Life in the Antebellum South* (1979); John Boles, *Black Southerners, 1619–1869* (1983); and Charles Joyner, *Down by the Riverside: A South Carolina Slave Community* (1984). To add details about the legal, demographic, and general social condition of slaves in every part of America, see the recent overview of scholarship by Peter Kolchin, in *American Slavery, 1619–1877* (1993). For an intellectual history of slave culture, the most important contribution is Lawrence Levine, *Black Culture and Black Consciousness* (1977).

Engaging portraits of free African-Americans abound in Ira Berlin's *Slaves Without Masters* (1974); urban and factory slavery are covered in the highly readable Robert Starobin, *Industrial Slavery in the Old South* (1970). For women's experiences as free African-Americans and slaves, start with the comprehensive overview by Jacqueline Jones, *Labor of Love, Labor of Sorrow* (1985); the biography by Melton McLaurin, *Celia, A Slave* (1991); and Deborah G. White, *Ar'n't I a Woman? Female Slaves in the Plantation South* (1985). Slave revolts have been reassessed recently in the work of Douglas Egerton, *Gabriel's Rebellion: The Virginia Slave Conspiracies of 1800 and 1802* (1993), and Stephen B. Oates, *The Fires of Jubilee: Nat Turner's Fierce Rebellion* (1975).

For the ideology of southern white planters, see standard overviews by Wilbur Cash, *The Mind of the South* (1941); Randolph Campbell and Richard Lowe, *Wealth and Power in Antebellum Texas* (1977); Bruce Collins, *White Society in the Antebellum South* (1985); and Clement Eaton, *The Growth of Southern Civilization, 1790–1860* (1961). A biography with deep insights into the southern mind is Drew G. Faust, *James Henry Hammond and the Old South* (1982). Still very important is George Fredrickson, *The Black Image in the White Mind: The Debate on Afro-American Character and Destiny, 1817–1914* (1971). For ways in which planter, small farmer, and slave experiences overlapped, see Donald G. Mathews's *Religion in the Old South* (1977).

The best works about plantation mistresses are Catherine Clinton, *The Plantation Mistress: Woman's World in the Old South* (1982), and the long but rewarding Elizabeth Fox-Genovese, *Within the Plantation Household* (1988). Recent scholarship on southern society often focuses on yeomen, tenants, and upcountry poor folks. See the very influential work by Lacy Ford, Jr., *Origins of Southern Radicalism: The South Carolina Upcountry, 1800–1860* (1988), and J. William Harris, *Plain Folk and Gentry in a Slave Society* (1985). To these, the interested reader should add Robert Kenser, *Kinship and Neighborhood in a Southern Community* (1987), and Stephanie McCurry, *Masters of Small Worlds* (1995).

The literature about southern planters' defense of slavery is prodigious and often includes valuable collections of documents to supplement scholarly opinion. Start with the comprehensive work of Larry Tise, *Proslavery: A History of the Defense of Slavery in America, 1701–1840* (1987), and the introduction and readings in Drew Gilpin Faust, ed., *The Ideology of Slavery: Proslavery Thought in the Antebellum South, 1830–1860* (1981). For a provocative and influential interpretation of the southern mentality, see Bertram Wyatt-Brown's *Southern Honor* (1982).

Competing Voices

Southern White Views of Slavery

Dew on the Virtues of Slavery, 1831

Thomas R. Dew, a wealthy planter and slave owner, was also president of the College of William and Mary when he wrote *The Virtues of Slavery, The Impossibility of Emancipation* in 1831. As a stalwart defender of slavery, Dew objected to a debate about the feasibility of slave emancipation that had taken place that year in the Virginia legislature. It was one of the last times southerners openly and genuinely debated emancipation, and Dew's point of view would become overwhelmingly prevalent in the coming years.

We have now, we think, proved our position, that slave labor, in an economical point of view, is far superior to free negro labor; and have no doubt that if an immediate emancipation of negroes were to take place, the whole southern country would be visited with an immediate general famine, from which the productive resources of all the other States of the Union could not deliver them.

It is now easy for us to demonstrate the second point in our argument—that the slave is not only *economically* but *morally* unfit for freedom. And first, idleness and consequent want are, of themselves, sufficient to generate a catalogue of vices of the most mischievous and destructive character. . . .

The great evil, however, of these schemes of emancipation, remains yet to be told. . . . Two totally different races, as we have before seen, cannot easily harmonize together, . . . and even when [the black person] is free, . . . idleness will produce want and worthlessness, and his very worthlessness and degradation will stimulate him to deeds of rapine and vengeance. . . . [L]iberate [our] slaves, and every year you would hear of insurrections and plots, and every day would perhaps record a murder. . . .

[Thomas Jefferson] has supposed the master in a continual passion—in the constant exercise of the most odious tyranny, and the child, a creature of imitation, looking on and learning. But is not this master sometimes kind and indulgent to his slaves? . . . We may rest assured, in this intercourse between a good master and his servant, more good than evil may be taught the child; the exalted principles of morality and religion may thereby be sometimes indelibly inculcated upon his mind. . . . Look to the slaveholding population of our country, and you every where find them characterized by noble and elevated sentiments, by humane and virtuous feelings. . . .

Let us now look a moment to the slave, and contemplate his position. Mr. Jefferson has described him as hating, rather than loving his master. . . . We assert again, that Mr. Jefferson is not borne out by the fact. . . . We have no hesitation in affirming, that throughout the whole slaveholding country, the slaves of a good master are his warmest, most constant, and most devoted friends; they have been accustomed to look up to him as their supporter, director and defender. Everyone acquainted with southern states, knows that the slave rejoices in the elevation and prosperity of his master; and the heart of no one is more gladdened at the successful debut of young master or miss on the great theatre of the world, than that of either the young slave who has grown up with them, and shared in all their sports, and even partaken of all their delicacies—or the aged one who has looked on and watched them from birth to manhood, with the kindest and most affectionate solicitude, and has ever met from them all the kind treatment and generous sympathies of feeling.

Helper on the Impending Crisis, 1857

Hinton Helper was a middle-class non–slave owner from North Carolina who moved north to gain advanced education and write professionally. During the 1840s and 1850s, he joined his voice to many others in advocating more southern manufacturing, transportation, and education to overcome decades of dependence on the outside world. Helper also concluded that slavery denied nonslaveholding white southerners the opportunities for advancement that free white northerners enjoyed. In 1857 he put these views together in *The Impending Crisis of the South: How to Meet It.*

Our theme is a city—a great Southern importing, exporting, and manufacturing city, to be located at some point or port on the coast of the Carolinas, Georgia or Virginia, where we can carry on active commerce, buy, sell, fabricate, receive the profits which accrue from the exchange of our own commodities, open facilities for direct communication with foreign countries, and establish all those collateral sources of wealth, utility, and adornment, which are the usual concomitants of a metropolis, and which add so very materially to the interest and importance of a nation. Without a city of this kind, the South can never develop her commercial resources nor attain to that eminent position to which those vast resources would otherwise exalt her. . . .

Whether Southern merchants ever think of the numerous ways in which they contribute to the aggrandizement of the North, while, at the same time, they enervate and dishonor the South, has, for many years, with us, been a matter of more than ordinary conjecture. . . . Let them scrutinize the workings of Southern money after it passes north of Mason and Dixon's line. Let them consider how much they pay to Northern railroads and hotels, how much to Northern merchants and shop-keepers, how much to Northern shippers and insurers, how much to Northern theatres, newspapers, and periodicals. Let them also consider what disposition is made of it after it is lodged in the hands of the North. Is not the greater part of it paid out to Northern manufacturers, mechanics, and laborers, for the very articles which are purchased at the North. . . . They have shown their wisdom in growing great at our expense, and we have shown our folly in allowing them to do so. Southern merchants, slaveholders, and slave-breeders, should be the objects of our censure; they have desolated and impoverished the South; they are now making merchandize of the vitals of their country. . . .

What about Southern Commerce? Is it not almost entirely tributary to the commerce of the North? Are we not dependent on New York, Philadelphia,

Boston, and Cincinnati, for nearly every article of merchandise, whether foreign or domestic? Where are our ships, our mariners, our naval architects? Alas! Echo answers, where? . . .

We are all spendthrifts; some of us should become financiers. We must learn to take care of our money; we should withhold it from the North, and open avenues for its circulation at home. We should not run to New York, to Philadelphia, to Boston, to Cincinnati, or to any other Northern city, every time we want a shoe-string or a bedstead, a fish-hood or a handsaw, a tooth-pick or a cotton-gin. In ease and luxury we have been lolling long enough; we should now bestir ourselves, and keep pace with the progress of the age. We must expand our energies, and acquire habits of enterprise and industry; we should arouse ourselves from the couch of lassitude, and inure our minds to thought and our bodies to action. ∎

For generations, Americans in every state and every walk of life debated whether slavery should exist. In the early 1800s, many outspoken southern planters and intellectuals argued that slaves should be emancipated. Their views usually held that slavery ran against the moral and economic interests of the region. But they wrestled with the question of where and how freed slaves should live, since even people who opposed slavery believed blacks inferior to whites. Gradually, even this qualified support for emancipation began to fade in the South. Political differences with the North became shriller, expansion into the West became a more aggressive enterprise that involved national and international negotiation, and southern poor whites and yeomen bolstered the need for a more rigid defense of slavery. Indeed, Dew joined many other voices in defense of slavery; he was impervious to compromise in national politics and closed to an alternative lifestyle and labor system.

As Helper learned from having lived in the North, active opposition to slavery grew slowly and advocates of complete, immediate emancipation were a minority of citizens in that section of the country. Nevertheless, their numbers and influence grew after 1830. Alongside abolitionist organizations, the budding Whig Party often attracted citizens of northern and western areas who believed that an end to slavery should somehow be sought. When Helper published his work in New York at an especially difficult moment in sectional tensions, his views about the growing gap between between slave owners and non–slave owners within southern white society helped galvanize northern views.

Questions for Analysis

1. What are the main differences between these two writers' views? Do they share any common ground? Explain.
2. According to Dew, why should slavery not only exist but expand?
3. How might opponents have responded to Dew's defense of slavery?
4. According to Helper, what are the causes of southern "backwardness"? Does he point mainly to personal characteristics of southern people, or to the entire social system and economy of the South? How legitimate do you find his arguments?
5. What kind of conversation might Helper have had with a northern abolitionist?

13

The Westward Experiment, 1820–1850

Some time during 1845, brothers Jacob and George Donner, prosperous farmers in Illinois, caught the "emigration fever" and decided to head west to California. They sold their land, houses, farm equipment, and most of their household belongings. They talked their friend James Reed into moving his family west with theirs, and together they bought oxen, cattle, bagged and barreled food, and heavy Murphy wagons. Advice books instructed them to hire teamsters who could guide them through rough terrain and across forbidding rivers that stretched out beyond Independence, Missouri, for two thousand miles.

The plan was daring but not unusual. Already thousands of Americans had left behind land, jobs, and culture to move west. But from the start, the Donners and Reeds met with more than their share of disappointments, failures, and setbacks. The Donner and Reed men were already in their sixties; each had remarried, and together they had sixteen children, some of them infants. On arriving at Independence in May 1846, they learned that most of the twelve hundred westbound wagons that spring had already left with their guides and would soon cut north for Oregon. In a week or so, they took heart when they caught up with a group of fifty California-bound wagons. But even being surrounded by other migrants provided little comfort during the days and weeks of trekking from the Missouri River to the Rocky Mountains, over land believed to be "almost wholly unfit for cultivation." Dust storms, thunderstorms, mud, stinging alkali dust, stubborn mules, and bad water strained their tempers. Anger rose easily among the women by the end of May, and George Donner flinched in disgust at the sight of some migrants beating their weary cattle and dogs to keep them stumbling forward. Word of conflict with Mexico raised the nagging possibility of a war in progress at their California destination.

During a welcome rest at Fort Laramie, the Donner and Reed men pored over a map showing what was called a "shortcut" around the southern edge of Salt Lake City that would take them into California more quickly. A couple of California trappers who overheard them warned about the dangers of taking a large number of wagons, animals, and people through the shortcut, adding that the route had never been attempted by wagon trains. The map, insisted the trappers, was little more than "the plan of that madman and speculator, Lansford Hastings," who hoped to lure settlers away from the well-trodden path into Oregon and set up his own independent republic in northern California. At that very moment, in fact, Hastings was rounding up a private army in California to replace the Mexican–Spanish settlements with the "Pacific Republic."

But knowing that they had to reach the far side of the mountains before snow began to fall, the Donners and Reeds decided to lead about twenty of their party's seventy wagons toward the Continental Divide and the shortcut that skirted around the southern edge of the Mormon settlement at Salt Lake City (see page 435). By July, the mountains loomed before them, higher than they had ever imagined. As they traveled through the Rockies—one or two exhausting, plodding miles a day—they glimpsed a searing desert that promised to test them severely during the days ahead. As oxen tired, families threw out precious household goods; some abandoned their wagons and carried what they could, while others quarreled bitterly over meager supplies of food. Hostile Paiute Indians killed cattle and dogs, and a few members of the party died from exhaustion. The Donner brothers realized when they reached the Humboldt River that the "shortcut" had saved no time at all.

On September 30 the Sierra Nevada faced them. A trapper along the way insisted that all the seasoned "mountain men" up ahead believed snow would be late that winter and thus would not block passage for the wagon train. But it did start to snow, and as the weary migrants trudged up the first rising eastern slopes, the weather worsened. Several of the worn-out travelers decided to wait out the storm at an abandoned cabin they spotted at the base of the foothills. Another group totaling about sixty men, women, and children continued through the foothills of the Sierra Nevada but then fell back to the cabin, where they put up four poor huts and crammed themselves in. A third party, including the Donners and some of the Reeds, pressed on. When they became trapped in the thickening drifts they huddled together under hides.

As hunger gnawed, the ill-fated Donner–Reed party of fifteen first caught a scrawny coyote and a single owl, then ate their dogs, oxen, and horses. Foraging parties failed to find anything more, except grass and moss. After nine days and nights out in the cold, they saw another blizzard darken the skies and two men, then two children, died. Their corpses became food for the starving survivors. Four more of the party died over the next twenty-three days out on the mountainside. Back at the

Chronology

1821	Mexico gains independence from Spain
	Santa Fe Trail opened to Americans
	Austin settles Texas
1830	Indian Removal Act
1834	Mission movement in Oregon Territory begins
1835	Texas revolts against Mexico
1836	Battles of the Alamo and San Jacinto
	Texas Republic founded
1841	Oregon Trail wagon trains begin
1843	Frémont initiates California migration
1844	Polk elected president
1845	Texas annexed as a slave state
	O'Sullivan popularizes "manifest destiny"
1846	War with Mexico begins
	Bear Flag Revolt in California begins
	Wilmot Proviso
1847	Notion of "popular sovereignty" announced
	Mormons begin migration to Salt Lake, Utah
1848	Treaty of Guadalupe Hidalgo
	Free-Soil electoral gains in the North
	Taylor elected president
1849	California gold rush begins
1851	Government reservations policy for far western tribes begins

encampment, thirty-seven of the sixty migrants perished in the grueling struggle for life. When the blizzard broke, seven of the Donner–Reed group made it out and reached the safety of Sutter's Fort, where they organized a rescue party to bring back a few more of the stranded survivors.

The Donner–Reed tribulations were remarkable only because so many people in that wagon train died, but many others perished as they moved west on the overland trails. The trek always brought difficulties, as young and old alike made their way through blistering deserts and across forbidding mountains, testing their endurance and will every mile. But the promise of land—plentiful and fertile—lured hundreds, then thousands, of Americans into the Far West from the 1820s to 1850s. Indeed, just a few months after the terrible Donner–Reed disaster, thousands more migrants set out in their footsteps on the strenuous trip to California and Oregon. Within a year, a handful of settlers near Sutter's Fort, California, would discover flakes of shiny yellow and initiate a massive rush for gold in the same deadly foothills.

Many easterners believed the "American imagination" had riveted completely toward Oregon, California, Texas, and other trans-Mississippi territories. They watched in amazement as extended families and whole towns uprooted themselves and carried their identities and culture into what was then an unknown wilderness. Others observed that, especially during the 1840s, the political agendas of existing state governments and federal officials were driven more by the West—how to acquire its lands, how to shape its future—than any other issue. What seemed equally remarkable to many Americans was how quickly far western frontier communities established familiar institutions and laws.

- What hardships did Americans face on their trek into the West? What experiences might have been exhilarating or inspiring? What kinds of communities did they build in the strange new lands beyond the Mississippi?
- What ideas did westward migrants share about their right to occupy the West, the kind of culture that should develop there, and the government's role in supporting the daunting tasks of transforming the western landscape and defining legal rights?
- What tensions arose between native inhabitants and western settlers, and between native inhabitants and new migrants from the North and South?
- What were the U.S. government's goals in the Mexican War, and why did so many Americans come to oppose the war?

This chapter will address these questions.

A Great Transfer of Peoples

By the 1820s, Americans had spilled over the Allegheny Mountains and into the farthest corners of the Northwest Territory. Settlements dotted the Midwest as far as the Mississippi River. Beyond the river, however, only the heartiest individuals explored, mapped, trapped furs, and undertook religious missions. But those conditions were about to change. In the next four decades, a swelling number of Americans turned their attention to the trans-Mississippi West, lured by the hope of attaining a large tract of productive soil or beginning over after the Panic of 1837 and its subsequent depression. Promoters and publishers told exciting stories about the lush environment out west. Guides offered advice about what goods to take and how to navigate the overland trails through varied landscapes. By the 1840s, the West was fixed firmly in Americans' national imagination; it had become their manifest destiny to "conquer space" beyond the Mississippi—whether by unflagging settlement or by irresistible force. Migrants streamed west by the thousands every spring, but few of them were sufficiently prepared for the dangers and hardships of the trail, and few succeeded quickly and to the degree they imagined possible at their far western destinations. Americans truly knew the promises and perils of moving west only after they arrived there.

Manifest Destiny

The trans-Mississippi West captured intense public interest by the 1820s. The budding popular print culture brought curious readers exotic details about scenery and peoples in that remote region, while landscape artists and naturalists added a visual dimension to people's knowledge. Grand depictions of the West in newspapers, novels, and painting suited the efforts of both southern planters and northern entrepreneurs who wished to expand into and develop the West. By the 1840s, these words and images—often exaggerated and romanticized—fueled a sense of urgency spreading through much of the population to join the swelling trans-Mississippi migration.

These optimistic perceptions of the West overlapped with darker, more aggressive notions stemming from widespread beliefs about race and political rights. In 1845 Democratic newspaper editor John O'Sullivan helped focus these other ideas about the West when he declared it an urgent necessity for Americans to carry their influences into the West, to "civilize" Indians and Mexicans with American culture and Christianity, and if necessary forcibly eject Spanish, French, and British people from the continent. In a December 1845 article, O'Sullivan gave these impulses a term that soon became popular: it was, he wrote, "our manifest destiny to overspread the continent and to possess the whole of the continent which Providence has given us for the development of the great experiment of liberty and federated self-government entrusted to us."

O'Sullivan's bold statement of manifest destiny came just as Americans recovered from the devastating depression that followed the Panic of 1837. Expansion seemed to offer new, perhaps unlimited, arenas for markets and resources. Senator Thomas Hart Benton of Missouri urged Congress to support taking control of the Pacific Coast's harbors from Mexico, which would provide launching points for transoceanic trade. The God-given right to expand also dovetailed with the great revivalist movements sweeping over the East, which in turn spawned numerous missionary efforts to transform the Indian peoples of the West. Moreover, by the 1840s, the West offered an escape from the fearful pace of industrialization and urbanization, a chance to return to the imagined Jeffersonian ideals of an agricultural people spreading out over space. Manifest destiny infused these ideals with justifications for preparing that space to receive migrating Americans—clearing it of other peoples, by force if necessary.

In reality, westward migration was not as full of opportunities as settlers believed it would be. Nor did the great spaces of the West ensure that social and political relations would be harmonious. Often, as settlers shaped new lands with old tools—customs and institutions long familiar in the East or South—they put equality and justice to severe tests. People from many different regions and backgrounds frequently clashed openly over what kind of life to build in the West. Many endured rude poverty for years; others succumbed to despair or returned home.

Sponsors and Entrepreneurs

Intrepid individual explorers, wilderness entrepreneurs, and active government intervention shaped many aspects of western development. For example, the fur trade represented both an economic incentive to explore the open wilderness everywhere in North America, and the energetic first forays into coveted lands for future settlers. John Jacob Astor began amassing the fortune that catapulted this poor immigrant to the topmost elite of New York City by diligently extracting furs from the far Northwest along the Pacific in the early 1800s. Simultaneously, the Hudson's Bay Company of fur traders and shippers accumulated great riches from the fur trade north of Astor's claims in Canada. By the 1820s, ambitious American newcomers competed with the Hudson's Bay Company and quickly upset its domination. They accomplished this by reorganizing the purchase and transport of furs into a highly efficient system. For generations, western trappers had pieced together a system of trapping, skinning, and transporting hides through informal trade and personal connections. Now easterners, led by the Rocky Mountain Fur Company of merchants and bankers, sent agents to certain central locations at designated times of the year to purchase hides. The trade fairs in this "rendezvous system" allowed trappers to bring their bundles of furs to closer points for trade, and to buy or trade for necessary supplies without traveling to St. Louis or other supply terminals hundreds of miles to the east.

Trade fairs were already a regular part of Indian life in the Far West. Mandan villagers, whom Lewis and Clark had met early in the century (see page 300), gathered once a year to trade, gossip, conduct business, and play games. Once Americans joined the trade fairs system, Indian culture changed rapidly. For one thing, the flow of manufactured goods from east to west grew steadily, and the fairs became crossroads of peoples and goods that blended elements of the western wilderness and eastern cities. For another thing, some easterners came to live permanently in the West. "Mountain men" who spent most of their mature lives trapping deep in the Rocky Mountains often married Indian women and learned many dialects of Indian languages. Sometimes the encounters between mountain men and long-time Indian residents of an area produced fear and conflict; but typically, Indians tolerated trappers or even cooperated in fishing and hunting efforts during nomadic winter seasons. One of these men, Jedediah Smith, made a career of fur trapping along the Platte River, across the Rockies, and throughout the northern parts of Mexico's western possessions. Smith's reputation for fair dealing in the beaver trade stretched from Independence, Missouri, to San Francisco, California.

By the 1840s, trappers had all but depleted the beaver supply of the far western frontier. Settlers, too, had begun to implement the familiar pattern of wearing down forests, interfering with Indian activities, and introducing their own diverse cultural ways into the West. Reflecting on environmental strains, one trapper lamented that "lizards grow poor, and wolves lean against the sand banks to howl." At the same time, the first wave of adventurers into the West bequeathed well-trodden trails for the permanent settlers who came in the next generations, as well as reports of people and sights, and maps of western geography that gave confidence to untold numbers of families. Many mountain men hired themselves out as guides for the first families coming to Oregon and California during the 1840s. Others related stories about their exploits to eastern journalists, who in turn embellished and romanticized the lives of mountain men and gave their excited readers somewhat false hopes about the tempting possibilities for personal success in the West.

Government help for western development came indirectly and directly. When Congress granted legal rights-of-way across federal land or timber rights along proposed routes, government indirectly helped private companies fund new railroads. Furthermore, railroad companies aided in the collection of knowledge about the Far West when they sponsored exploration and mapping for their own business purposes. Most ambitious of the railroad company efforts was the Northern Pacific Railroad's surveys during the 1850s for a potential transcontinental route. In this case, the government granted company investors unprecedented privileges to exploit land in the public domain.

Direct government support for westward migration had begun at the federal level when Jefferson boldly purchased the Louisiana Territory in 1803. Subsequent federal funds for scientific exploration that began with Lewis and Clark (discussed in Chapter 8) was extended to efforts at mapping, exploring, and then exploiting other parts of the trans-Mississippi West. Zebulon Pike led expeditions in 1806 and 1807, with government forces, to the Rocky Mountains in Colorado. Although the Spanish captured him in their territory and took him into Mexico, Pike took advantage of confrontation to record his observations about the region that one day would become Texas. After the War of 1812, the government became an active partner in transforming the West, providing land bounties to veterans of the war, funding troops to remove Indians year after year, and erecting forts to house soldiers whose job was to enforce treaties between America and Indian nations. In 1819–1820, the government dispatched Major Stephen Long to try to remove British fur trappers on the Great Plains. Long returned with maps and journals documenting aspects of "arid and forbidding" life there. During 1843–1844, John C. Frémont, who had much to do with the founding of California and the decline of Mexican power in the West, mapped the overland trails to Oregon and California.

The Westward Impulse

Development in the trans-Mississippi West was thus spearheaded by a combination of adventurous entrepreneurs, corporate enterprise, and government activity. But thousands upon thousands of families and small groups of settlers proved equally influential in transforming the western landscape in the years before the Civil War. The diaries and letters of people who went west after 1820 often expressed optimism about what lay ahead. "Each advanced step of the slow, plodding cattle," wrote one woman on her way to Oregon, "carried us farther and farther from civilization into a desolate, barbarous country. . . . But our new home lay beyond all this and was a shining beacon that beckoned us on, inspiring our hearts with hope and courage." By the 1840s and 1850s, the "shining beacon" sometimes represented the West's role as a new religious homeland. Just as often it heralded the republican promise of acquiring a family freehold or a planter's desire to relocate slaves and staple crop cultivation.

The rising tide of migrating families blended their belief in their "manifest destiny" to conquer the West with their belief in the need to build democratic institutions. The West, said many observers, had leveling tendencies. That is, migrants to new lands could abolish the irksome effects of rule by "ancient families" and rebuild institutions to suit their democratic aspirations. According to many optimists, so much mobility, so much mingling of people from various backgrounds, so much mutual reliance for life's necessities must surely impart a democratic spirit in frontier people. At a minimum, moving west promised a fresh start. Indeed, the popular belief in the power of the West to transform American sectional and national identity endured throughout the 1800s, until it was codified into Frederick Jackson Turner's powerful essay of 1893 (see page 297).

Numbers seemed to confirm these beliefs. By the 1820s, the Old Northwest Territory had been converted into states and was on its way to being integrated into the nation's development. Thousands of small farmers who had streamed out of Virginia and Maryland were sending large quantities of corn and pork products to hungry easterners. By 1820, nearly 25 percent of the American population lived west of the Appalachian Mountains. In the next decade, another large swath of settlers moved out of New England, through Vermont and New Hampshire, and then into Michigan, Iowa, and Wisconsin, where wheat farms and stock grazing dominated. Unlike in the crowded East, farms in the new midwestern states were large. The stubborn sod required that cast iron plows be traded in for more durable steel plows, and scythes for more efficient self-raking reapers that harvested much larger yields of cereal crops after the 1830s. A new tier of southern states—Alabama, Mississippi, and Louisiana—attracted thousands of planter families to field and forests that once were home to Creek Indians. Planters in North Carolina noted an "Alabama fever" which "has carried off vast numbers of our Citizens" and slaves to the far Southwest. By the late 1830s, more than a third of the American population lived west and south of the original thirteen states, spreading up to the Mississippi River. By 1860, over half of the nation's people lived west of the Appalachian Mountains.

Land out west also got easier to claim and cheaper to buy. The Land Act of 1820 had established a minimum price of $1.25 an acre, and a minimum purchase of eighty acres (compared with the 640-acre minimum set in the Northwest Ordinance of 1785), with a down payment of $100. Although thousands of families claimed farmsteads in western New York and Pennsylvania, and then in Ohio, the prevalent mode of land acquisition remained speculation in the 1820s. Congress's Preemption Acts of 1830 and 1841 allowed squatters—people living on land for which they had not paid and did not own a survey map and title—to stake out up to 160 acres and pay for it later at $1.25 an acre, provided that the claimants had built a house and "improved" the land. The purpose of preemption was to give small farmers a better chance to make a start in the trans-Mississippi West, and to undermine speculators' efforts to grab the most desirable lands. To some extent, the law worked. By the Graduation Act of 1854, the government stipulated that land not sold quickly would go down in price over time, the lowest price being 12½ cents an acre thirty years after the first offering.

Transportation improvements encouraged more rapid migration across natural barriers, and hastened the integration of different regions. Already the roads and canals of the American System linked the new states to coastal populations. By the 1850s, another mode of transportation—the railroads—made it possible to envision the movement of people and goods over even greater distances, at far more rapid speeds and much lower costs. As prices for transport of goods fell dramatically, western lifestyles were enriched by a variety of foods, clothing, tools, and household comforts. Rapidly growing cities such as Louisville, St. Louis, Detroit, and Milwaukee developed complicated social and cultural linkages between older eastern centers and trans-Mississippi settlements. Mills, packing plants, food

Cincinnati in 1843 One of America's fastest growing western cities by the 1820s, Cincinnati had a booming dockyard jammed with steamboats and flatboats, as well as expanding neighborhoods filled with a blend of eastern and southern settlers, slaves and free African-Americans, and foreign born immigrants who provided diverse labor skills and a cultural richness equal to that of coastal cities. *(Rare Books & Special Collections, Cincinnati Public Library.)*

processing industries, shipbuilding, tool making, and numerous other enterprises attracted thousands of immigrants and semiskilled eastern workers to the new urban centers of the West, which became the steppingstones for movement into the far western frontiers.

Making the Trip

Not all people who moved West remained optimistic about the opportunities and benefits of leaving home. Although many families relocated their homes and businesses more frequently in the 1800s than we do today, it may have been a more traumatic experience then than now. Migrants who entered the Susquehanna, Mohawk, and Ohio Valleys in the first part of the century severed their familiar roots and encountered strange, sometimes fearful, environments and peoples. Some left family and friends behind forever. Abraham Lincoln's family, for example, moved to five different locations, leapfrogging from Virginia, to Kentucky, to Indiana, to southern Illinois, and finally to Springfield, Illinois. Still, these early migrants traveled far shorter distances than the pioneers who ventured along the great trails leading westward from the Mississippi River toward the Rockies and the Pacific Ocean.

Westward-bound migrants usually launched their journey from Independence, Missouri, which was already far from their eastern and southeastern homes. From this point they pressed on for another grueling two thousand miles to Oregon or California (see map). Travel was slow and perilous. The walk was tedious and lonely for many people on the trails, and often utterly exhausting. The famous Murphy wagons, called the "clipper ships of the West," were three by sixteen feet in dimension, barely large enough to contain a family's worldly belongings and the necessary supplies for the trip, and rarely allowing room for sleeping or riding. A full Murphy wagon required ten or twelve mules to pull it, but even then, the five-foot-high iron-rimmed wheels creaked over dry Plains soil, stuck in muddy ruts, and broke from their axles on steep mountain climbs.

The trip to Oregon cost more than most families had on hand, so before starting out, a farm family usually sold most of their tools, land, household goods, and livestock. With the proceeds, they purchased oxen and wagons, extra clothing, seed to get themselves through the first phase of settlement, and a minimum of implements for housekeeping and land clearing. Families then banded together for mutual support in wagon trains. They came from all settled areas east of the Mississippi River—from midwestern farms, from the upcountry of the southern interior, from small towns and cities everywhere. Most migrants could not have been truly poor, given the high cost of outfitting a wagon, buying oxen and supplies, and paying a guide. The typical head of a wagon train family was a man who wanted a larger farm, a better-stocked and prosperous retail store, or a career as an independent provider of insurance, banking services, or some craft skill.

All but the most feeble walked alongside animals and wagons, and everyone helped guide precious livestock and goods through difficult terrain or across swift rivers, often on rafts. At Independence or some other embarkation point east of the

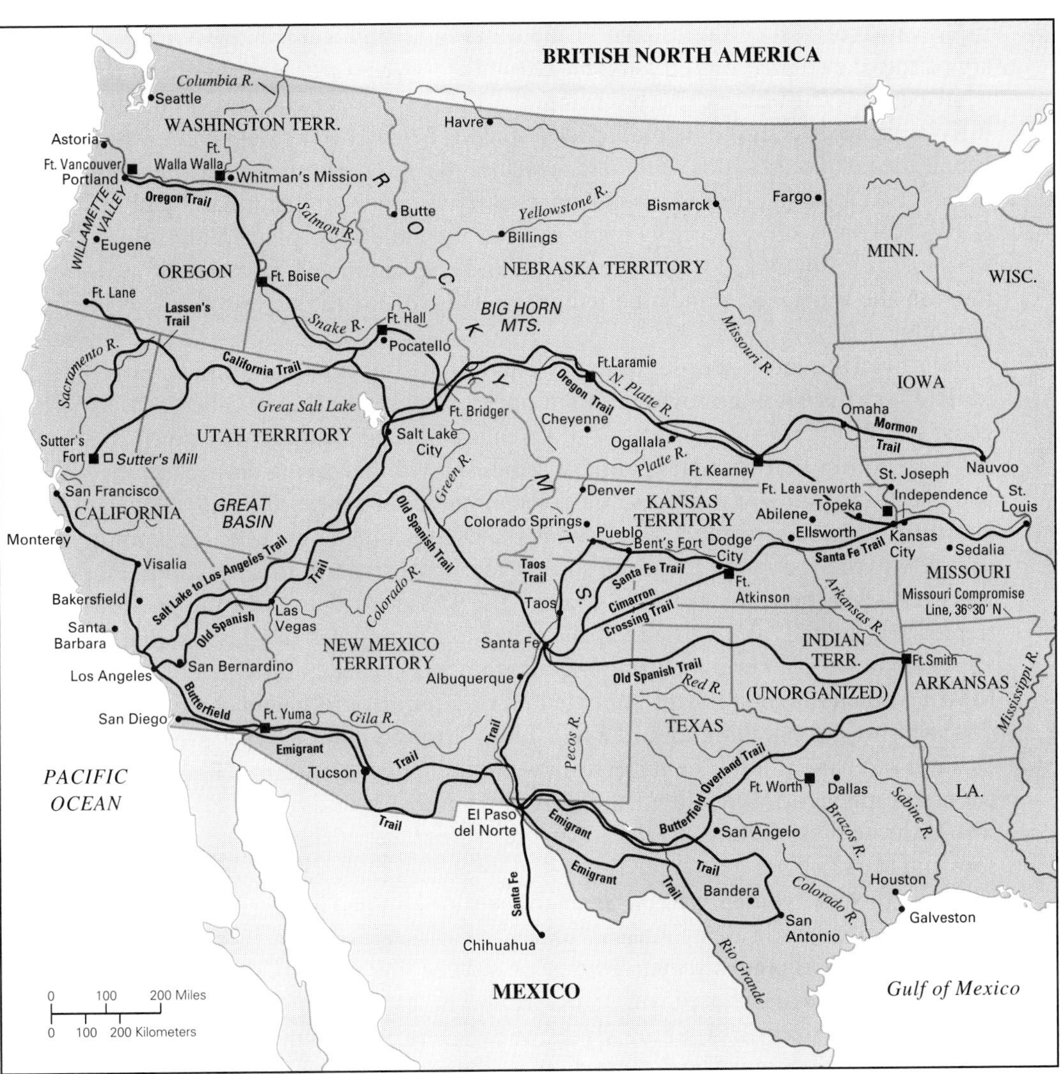

Western Trails, 1820 to 1850 As the United States acquired territories west of the Mississippi River and organized new western settlements and governments, citizens carved out trails through vast stretches of prairie, mountains, and lush forests. Oregon and California attracted huge numbers of migrants before Nebraska and Kansas territories did.

Mississippi, migrants often hired a guide to keep them on the unfamiliar trails west of that river. Trains started out in the spring once the grasses of the Plains began to turn green enough to feed the livestock, and they covered about twelve to fifteen miles a day through the rugged grasslands, dusty prairies, mountains, and mud pits. Long periods of travel without water alternated with broad rivers that drenched or even drowned the trekking parties. Then, once across the Columbia River leading to Oregon, or the Platte River on the way to California, formidable mountains loomed ahead. The typical trip took about six months.

Extremes of heat and cold, dryness and wetness, boredom and exhaustion regularly disheartened migrants crossing the Great Plains. Many more Indians died than white people in frontier skirmishes before the 1850s, but a popular perception that Indians regularly attacked helpless circled wagons heightened anxiety. More white people died of diseases such as cholera, which causes severe vomiting, diarrhea, and dehydration, than of arrow wounds. Almost every wagon train that made it past the Rockies carried women recently made widows and children orphaned on the way west. All in all, however, it was not the heroic and tragic moments that marked most time on the trails, but rather the tedium of fatigue and the pangs of low food rationing.

The overland journey upset women's lives deeply. To begin with, women rarely initiated the decision to move and often opposed what one diarist called a "wild goose chase" of "men with notions of splendor in their heads." Also, given the reigning notion that women's primary duties were child rearing, housekeeping, and "cultivating the social virtues," the constant physical labor of the trail, in open-air camps, required tremendous adjustments. Often women's experiences did not square with the vision of republican society advancing intact across the continent. Margaret Chambers, for example, crossed the Missouri River with the greatest trepidation and felt "as if we had left all civilization behind us." In addition, loneliness and the loss of familiar sustaining attachments caused endless grief for uprooted women. Lavinia Porter lamented leaving family and friends behind and doubted she was marching toward a new Zion: "I would make a brave effort to be cheerful and patient until the camp work was done. Then starting out ahead of the team and my men folks, when I thought I had gone beyond hearing distance, I would throw myself down on the unfriendly desert and give way like a child to sobs and tears."

Nevertheless, women were vital in the work of transplanting thousands of Americans to new soil. They washed clothes and dishes, boiled beans, picked and prepared fruit along the way, mended clothes and bedding, tended children, and did many other chores associated with "women's work." But women moving west also performed many of men's traditional jobs, and the line between men's and women's "spheres" of work blurred, and often disappeared, on the trail. They gathered buffalo chips for fuel, helped drive cattle and dogs through rough country, built rafts and repaired bridges, and took over leading the entire family through all kinds of terrain when their husbands fell ill with cholera or mountain fever. When Eliza Farnham's husband collapsed "under the tremendous sufferings of that terrible journey," she "yoked and unyoked the oxen, gathered fuel, cooked their food, drove the team, hunted wood and water . . . and for months performed all the coarser offices that properly belong to the other sex." Most women banished thoughts of socializing—at least regularly—with other women or sharing childcare responsibilities, since each family worked incessantly on the trail to sustain only itself. When trekkers had to discard belongings to lighten the wagons or consolidate loads if oxen died, they threw out mirrors, clocks, tea services, and other amenities of a "comfortable home," further demoralizing many women. Indeed, what woman of that era could identify the dilapidated, cramped Murphy wagon as a true home?

Life on the Trail Although the passage from east to west was fraught with muddy trails, steep ravines, ice-cold rivers, and in the case of these two migrants, no visible passage across seemingly endless prairie or meadow, it also offered the minor pleasures of a trailside meal and conversation. Although most westward migrants would not have had the tinned fruit and meats this later image shows, the landscape and the wagons did not change much over the years. *(Kansas State Historical Society.)*

Even if these conditions were temporary, some roles and beliefs about the proper social places of men and women were subtly, but permanently, changed on the overland trails.

The Indian Territory

Popular opinions about the Far West often distorted or ignored the reality of the Native American presence. The romantic view of Indian life captured in the art and literature of the 1820s–1850s usually excluded the reality of removal and warfare on the western frontier. By the 1830s, many Indian peoples had been removed from their homelands to a region across the Mississippi designated by Congress in 1830 as the Indian Territory. Covering today's Oklahoma, Kansas, and Nebraska, and bordering on the grasslands of the Great Plains, the Indian Territory became home to numerous peoples from east of the Mississippi. From the Old Southwest, Chickasaw, Choctaw, Creek, and Seminole joined the Cherokee in the southern portion of the territory. Together, these were known as the Five Civilized Tribes when the U.S. government planned for their removal to the Indian Territory. From the Old Northwest, Fox, Shawnee, Delaware, Wyandot, and numerous others were resettled in the northerly portion of the territory.

The purpose of establishing this reserve stemmed from the same reasoning that Thomas Jefferson enunciated years before: that until Indian peoples became "civilized," they would not be able to coexist with those of European origin. At first policymakers in eastern states and Congress believed that the Indian Territory lay far enough beyond the advancing white frontier to avoid racial mixing and conflict; the "civilizing process" could safely begin at arm's length But white people moved west much faster than predicted, and by the 1830s, they were following the Santa Fe trail into and through the Indian Territory. In the next years, the overland trails to Utah, Oregon, and California encroached even more on Native American lands. Many newly removed Indians had few means to resist dependency on unscrupulous migrants, peddlers, and speculators for goods and services because the land was unfamiliar and they had moved with few belongings. Others remained more aloof. In the area that is now Oklahoma, the Cherokee, Chickasaw, Creek, Seminole, and Choctaw established thriving new communities under very trying conditions. Despite efforts by overland trail traders and eastern merchants to make these tribes economically dependent, the Indians set up their own systems of law, education, and religious worship. Within the southern Indian Territory, an elite even arose that used slaves to cultivate cotton for shipment to New Orleans.

Removal policies and direct confrontations with federal troops did not weaken the resolve of many Native American peoples to resist the advancing line of land-hungry speculators and frontier families. In some places in the West, Indian resistance became more desperate as the flow of migrating settlers and the government forces sent to protect them became stronger. But Indian resistance had little impact on determined waves of migrants and major federal policies. For example, a number of recently settled Indian tribes in the northern part of the Indian Territory gained permanent reservation lands in 1851, only to lose them three years later when the federal government established the Kansas and Nebraska Territories and opened them up to white migration. Immediately, three overlapping tensions erupted into open conflict. In the first place, would-be white settlers, already steeped in sectional conflict over slavery's expansion, had little patience for the claims of Indian residents on the land. Second, Indians tried unsuccessfully to adjust old ways of agriculture and hunting to the requirements of farming on the arid land of the new territory. Third, in addition to migrating white people, the Sioux, Arapaho, Comanche, Cheyenne, and Kiowa from the Great Plains encroached, sometimes in huge numbers, on the eastern tribes who settled in the Indian Territory. As a result, the entire region remained inhospitable for years to come.

Destinations and Encounters

Americans' convictions about manifest destiny were a powerful influence not only on the northern and Great Plains migrations, but also on developments in the southwestern territories. While eastern and midwestern migrants set their sights on the Oregon territory during the 1830s, Texas was the logical place for southern planters to expand in that decade. But Mexico controlled Texas, as well as the great stretches of land west to California and east to Florida. As American migration and settlement grew in all of these areas during the 1840s, tensions with Native Americans and foreign nations also raised questions about what kind of people would live there and what kinds of political structures and cultures would develop.

Mexico and Its Territories

For three centuries, explorers and rulers attempted to extend Spain's jurisdiction throughout the North American borderlands. Through the 1700s, pockets of mission labor developed from San Francisco to San Diego, while internal trade was linked to coastal commerce at Santa Fe, New Orleans, along the Gulf Coast to the Floridas and St. Augustine. Multiracial crossroads dotted Spanish jurisdictions, which were otherwise thinly settled because of forbidding environments, few immigrants, and hostile and dense nations of Native Americans. *Presidios,* originally forts built to protect Spanish and Mexican interests in the new territories and to confer political authority over local populations, soon became the central sites for exacting tribute and forced labor from Indian populations. In California, thousands of Indians experienced the profound cultural, political, and religious shock of giving up semisedentary ways for the rigid work rules and settled cultivation introduced by Mexican and Spanish settlers.

Bit by bit, however, Spain relinquished its hold on the borderlands. In 1795 Pinckney's Treaty gave access to the lower Mississippi River and trade at New Orleans to Americans. In 1800 Napoleon forced Spain to return vast and ungovernable Louisiana to France. Then, in 1811 and 1813 Spain ceded portions of West Florida to the United States. By the terms of the Adams-Onís Treaty, written in 1819 and ratified by Congress in 1821, East Florida also became United States territory.

But Spanish and Mexican cultural influences remained strong across these lands. Many settlers of Spanish and Mexican descent inhabited the territory north of the Rio Grande River and the Southwest. During the early 1800s, Spanish traders maintained a strong presence in Santa Fe, preventing American merchants from dominating the southwestern trails and overland commerce. Spanish officials treated overland migrants and explorers harshly when they wandered into Mexico. Businessmen and merchants of Spanish descent continued to protect runaway slaves who made it to New Orleans and St. Augustine early in the 1800s, hiring skilled African-Americans and tolerating their distinct cultural and religious practices.

Conditions in the borderlands began to change significantly in 1810 when the Mexican Revolution erupted into war against Spanish royalists. While popular leaders led masses of people in an independence movement in Mexico, a combination of Mexican and American settlers declared the Republic of Texas in 1812. Although the Republic could not resist Spanish royalist troops' onslaughts, Mexico gained its independence from Spain in 1821. Immediately, the new rulers in Mexico invited American merchants to send agents through the forbidding deserts and Comanche lands to trade at the forts and trading posts hugging the Arkansas River's banks and the Santa Fe Trail winding through the Southwest. Around the city of Santa Fe, people of Indian, Hispanic, and European descent began agricultural settlements to supplement the commercial activities in town.

To the east of Santa Fe in Tejas, or Texas, another mixed population emerged. Over two thousand Spanish-speaking residents, or *tejanos,* clustered around missions and *presidios,* as Mexican-Spanish settlers had done in southern California, and also settled in the surrounding countryside on large ranches. There, legendary skilled *vaqueros,* or cowboys, herded cattle and poor laborers worked as agricultural tenants on the difficult Texas soil.

For generations, Spanish administrators regarded the *tejanos* as very distant from the center of imperial rule in the New World. Still, settlements at San Antonio, Nacogdoches, and Goliad provided outlying buffers against hostile Indians and French encroachments, much as settlements on the fringe of Spanish Florida had guarded against British expansion for generations. But the nomadic Comanche and Apache thundered through the outlying *tejano* settlements on regular raids. The Comanche consistently resisted efforts to incorporate their people into settled villages, choosing instead to follow the buffalo herds in their traditional way of life. Following independence, the new government attempted to reinforce the policy of building the outlying settlements of mixed Spanish and Mexican peoples. But the towns and ranches remained weak, and the Mexican government remained concerned about its ability to govern its extensive territories. Having correctly anticipated that American settlers would flow into Louisiana, and then into Texas, the Mexican government offered certain conditions to migrating Americans instead of trying to eject them. To the Germans who began entering the trans-Mississippi region in the early 1820s, and then the southern cotton planters who expanded across the river, Mexican officials offered protection against hostile Indians in exchange for their becoming Mexican citizens and Catholics. In return, Mexican officials looked forward to collecting much-needed tax revenue from Americans and transforming the area into prosperous ranches and agricultural settlements.

The first person to accept this offer was Moses Austin, who in 1821 received a grant of eighteen thousand square miles inside Texas, supposedly unencumbered by any Indian or foreign title. The possibility of acquiring free land in Texas without even a survey amazed Americans moving west. Moreover, Mexico permitted the American land agents for Texas to give out stupendous grants of 4,605 acres to each applying family, more than enough land to mitigate the requirement to relinquish American citizenship for Mexican and become nominally Roman Catholic.

Some two dozen additional settlements quickly began along the Sabine, Brazos, and Colorado Rivers. A few early parties of immigrants adopted the *tejano* ways of cattle herding. But since the Mexican government ignored the presence of slavery in Texas, even when Mexican law forbade it, most of the new settlers turned quickly to growing cotton for export through New Orleans. Indeed, Austin's son, Stephen, welcomed southern Americans who treated Texas as a convenient steppingstone in the spread of plantation life westward. Few planters actually became Mexican citizens, and most refused to adopt the Catholic religion once they lived in Texas. When Mexican officials denied Americans the right to establish local governments modeled on their experiences east of the Mississippi, Americans nominally pledged their support to Santa Anna, the head of the Mexican government, but in reality simply rejected Mexican government and laws and lived as they wished. By 1835,

27,000 white settlers and about 3,000 slaves had moved into Texas, greatly outnumbering the 3,500 *tejanos* in the region.

The Alamo and the Republic of Texas

From the Mexican authorities' point of view, their northern province of Texas had become unmanageable by 1830. The government announced its intention to bring Texans more closely in line with the laws and customs of Mexico. New legislation restricted the flow of Americans, outlawed slavery, regulated trade of Texans with foreign powers, and prohibited Texan taxes of many kinds. Americans in eastern Texas wrote to family and contacts across the Mississippi that they were being treated like the British had treated "the American colonists of old." Some believed the appropriate response was to "rebel against the injustice," just as American revolutionaries had. Adding to Americans' belligerence was their association of many Mexicans' swarthy complexions with the skin color of southern slaves. Given southern racism's close ties to skin color, its introduction into Texas helped sharpen white Americans' opposition to Mexican laws.

In 1833 Texans petitioned Mexico's president and commander of the army, Antonio Lopez de Santa Anna, for an independent state of Texas. Stephen Austin went to Mexico City that July. For months, the Mexican government ignored Austin, prompting him to write impatient letters to fellow Texans to the north. Finally Santa Anna granted not independent statehood, but full protection from Indian attacks and other rights afforded to Mexican citizens. However, as Austin started back to Texas with the heartening news, Mexican officials arrested and jailed him for his earlier letters against their government. Moreover, while Austin sat in jail for about eighteen months, Santa Anna transformed his power structure in Mexico virtually into a dictatorship. By mid-1835, when Austin finally rode home, the border between the two countries had become a staging ground for intermittent bloody skirmishes and widespread Texan fears of Santa Anna's unruly troops.

In the fall of 1835, revolutionary fervor spilled over into open warfare. Stephen Austin led a joint force of American Texans and *tejanos* in taking San Antonio and Goliad from the Mexicans. In November 1835, a small group of Texas town representatives met and organized a provisional government. On March 2, 1836, Americans meeting at a convention proclaimed Texas an independent republic and, under Austin's leadership, established a constitution that legalized slavery. Four days later, Santa Anna led a massive attack to retake San Antonio. A small garrison of Americans and *tejanos* made a stand behind the adobe walls of the Alamo, a former mission in the city. Their small numbers were no match for Santa Anna's four thousand troops. Davy Crockett, a frontiersman who joined Americans defending the fort, and Jim Bowie, known for the sturdy hunting knife he perfected, were among the 187 who died in the siege. Moving on to Goliad, Santa Anna rounded up and executed 371 American rebels and declared victory over two major Texan strongholds on March 27.

The American press began to spread news about the rebellion—and the massacres—within days, and an outpouring of nationalistic support for Texas

Siege of the Alamo This contemporary woodcut conveys well the direct assault made by Mexican and Spanish troops who scaled the walls of the mission. *(Texas State Library & Archives Commission.)*

mushroomed. Perhaps, argued many northern journalists and southern observers alike, a great influx of Americans into Texas would help resolve the conflict. After all, Monroe had enunciated stern warnings against Spain's imperial goals in the Western Hemisphere in his famous Monroe Doctrine speech to Congress in 1823 (see page 317). Many publicists now insisted in 1836 that the same warning should apply to Mexico's influence in North America. Almost overnight, packet boats from New York City set sail with thousands of young men, and sometimes whole families, who believed that in exchange for their help in a few brief skirmishes against the "papal scourge of Mexicans" they would be granted huge land bounties by the federal government.

Santa Anna thus pursued a growing force of combined American and *tejano* rebels, who were commanded by General Sam Houston. Houston was a seasoned military leader and former Tennessee governor who had served in battle under Andrew Jackson. On April 21, 1836, Houston's nearly 800 men voted to attack Santa Anna's resting troops at the San Jacinto River in east Texas. Raising the cry "Remember the Alamo!" they overwhelmed the greater number of nearly 1,300 Mexicans. Nine Texans died at the river, and 34 more were wounded; on the other side,

63 Mexicans fell, and 730 were taken prisoner. Among those captured was Santa Anna, who quickly agreed to grant independence to the new Republic of Texas north of the Rio Grande River. Citizens of the Republic granted Sam Houston its presidency.

However, when Santa Anna returned to Mexico City in 1836, his own congress refused to accept the terms of the peace treaty. In the coming months, the Mexican congress also rejected President Andrew Jackson's offer to buy the northern province, largely out of fear that Americans also coveted the New Mexico province adjacent to Texas. Meanwhile, Texans petitioned the American Congress in 1837 for annexation of their territory to the United States, which alarmed many Americans. Northern congressional representatives, led by the former president John Quincy Adams, joined Whig leaders throughout the North and Midwest to oppose admission of a fourteenth slave state when the application came before Congress. Southern Democrats, however, favored annexation and the prospects of extending slavery across the Mississippi into a new state. Jackson remained ambivalent about annexation, but in March 1837, he met Democrats halfway with a measure to grant diplomatic recognition to Texas, which implied that American military aid could be used against future Mexican belligerence. Many proslavery Texans—as well as many angry northern abolitionists—interpreted the measure as a first step toward annexation.

Meanwhile, American settlers in the Republic struggled mightily from 1836 to 1842 to impose more of their culture and political ways on the *tejanos*, first by depriving them of their property in outlying areas, and then by taking over their businesses in towns. Many *tejanos* fled to Mexico, leaving behind their land claims for Americans to seize. Although most towns in Texas remained more Mexican than American in cultural terms, they were becoming magnets attracting a growing immigrant population that had been living under the customs and laws of American society. In this environment, ethnocentrism flourished, as well as the conviction that "Mexico and the United States are peopled by two distinct and utterly unhomogeneous races." Texan Americans thus justified their continued appeals for annexation to the United States during the presidencies of Democrat Martin Van Buren and Whig John Tyler.

Oregon

Oregon, the destination of choice for most Americans who crossed the continent in the 1820s and 1830s, encompassed present-day Oregon, Washington, Idaho, small sections of Montana and Wyoming, and a portion of Canada. The United States and Britain held the territory according to a joint occupation treaty signed by the nations in 1818. At first, most of the early settlers who ventured so far were either mountain men who hunted beaver and other small game, or skippers who stopped along the coast for trade. Britain's Hudson's Bay Company kept a fort at Vancouver that attracted local Chinook Indians, French and American trappers, and traders from Hawaii. Races and nations mixed behind the walls of the British company's garrison in a multicultural environment on the far northwestern frontier.

By the 1830s, a few permanent American and French Canadian settlements took root in Oregon's Willamette Valley, also known as French Prairie. Eliza Farnham, just married in western New York, set out in February 1836 with a small party that made its way first by wagon to Pittsburgh, then by riverboat to Liberty, Missouri, and then by horseback to Fort Walla Walla on the Columbia River. On July 4, 1836, Eliza became the first white woman to cross the Continental Divide through the Rockies. A number of female missionaries from both Protestant and Catholic societies soon followed, many of them joining the migrations of family and village groups from the Midwest.

But it was not until 1842 that midwestern farmers began to arrive in Oregon. As the Panic of 1837 dragged on into a long depression that racked both urban and rural communities in the Midwest and East, hundreds of families made plans to leave after the spring rains and arrive on the far side of the Rockies before the winter snow. Few were concerned about arriving too late to clear land and plant their first crops, since news about the natural abundance and lush forests of Oregon's Willamette Valley seemed to promise plenty of alternatives to cultivation that first year in the new land. In addition, Hudson's Bay Company stores extended generous credit to newcomers. About five thousand settlers had followed the Snake and Columbia Rivers into Oregon by 1845. Among them were several Presbyterian and Methodist missionaries who made largely futile attempts to assimilate local populations of seminomadic Oregon Indians into American and Canadian religious and cultural ways.

Others soon followed in response to promoters' guarantees of autonomous local self-government and "free land," although the latter had been taken without treaties between the newcomers and local Indians, and without resolution of land rights between British and American claimants to the region. "Oregon Societies" and "Western Emigration Societies" published exaggerated reports of the riches beyond the Rockies. The Oregon fever began to take hold of midwesterners who had been hit hard by the depression following the Panic of 1837, and during 1843 and 1844, a rash of newspaper articles advised what to take and what routes to follow toward the Rockies. No need for heavy steel plows in Oregon, said journalists; leave them with the tough sod of the prairies, and bring only "your wooden plow, your scythe, and gentle oxen."

Some pessimistic voices continued to decry the dangers of the Great American Desert east of the Rockies and moan about the impossibility of getting wagons and livestock through the South Pass in what is now western Wyoming. Horace Greeley, the editor whose urgent appeals to "Go West! Young Men, Go West!" peppered his *New York Daily Tribune* before trans-Mississippi migration was truly underway, was by 1843 urging readers to "not . . . move one foot" beyond St. Louis. "It is," insisted Greeley, "palpable homicide to tempt or send women and children over this thousand miles of precipice and volcanic sterility to Oregon."

By 1846, Oregonians from many eastern areas wrote a constitution that legally prohibited slavery and defined liberal rules for voting and officeholding among the white population. "Oregon Conventions" convened in the new towns, pledging residents to shed "the lawlessness of the trail" and the "singleness of each family's survival." Instead, townspeople assembled under elected officials, adopted constitutions familiar in eastern counties and states, and instituted particular rules "for the purpose of keeping good order and promoting civil and military discipline" in their new homeland. The scattered farmsteaders of Oregon created networks of kinship and barter for goods and services until they could establish links to the East. Many homes regularly accepted boarders just arriving from the Midwest, exchanging shelter and food for the labor of newcomers during the fall harvests.

California

In 1821, when Mexico gained independence from Spain, the California territory was a crossroads of cultures. Nearly 200,000 Native Americans of many languages and cultures occupied the varied landscape. Over 22,000 labored under the control of Mexican and Spanish descendants in the *presidio* system that had been implemented generations previously. About 8,000 descendants of Mexican and Spanish settlers also lived at California's *presidios.* Some of them had intermarried with the local *mestizos* of Spanish-Indian heritage, while other Mexicans formed an elite of *californios* who remained separate from the "mixed bloods."

No more than a handful of Americans lived in California during the 1820s, most of them having entered Oregon first and then traveled into the Sacramento Valley searching for farmland or trapping furs. However, American and Russian ships cruised the coastline of California regularly. Their captains traded manufactured goods and provisions for sea otter and cattle hides, meat and tallow. *Californios* controlled most of this maritime commerce with the outside world, especially the very lucrative business with the Russian American Fur Company, headquartered in Alaska, which contracted for huge quantities of hides in exchange for textiles and iron tools. *Californios* also supplied Russian trappers and company employees with provisions when their ships lay over at coastal harbors.

The *presidio* and foreign trade systems changed dramatically after Mexican independence. Authorities opened California trade to ships of all nations, and in 1832 the Mexican government freed Indians from the *presidios.* Two consequences resulted. First, foreign merchants sent agents to live permanently in coastal California towns, where they competed for business with *Californios.* In time, many American settlers intermarried with this resident elite and became Mexican citizens, but they introduced many new cultural ways and often depended on America's eastern commercial establishment for credit and trade. The changing business climate was less accommodating to Russian fur traders, who all but abandoned trade with California by the 1840s.

Second, the Indians freed from life in the *presidios* left a vacuum of labor, which in turn contributed to the rapid breakdown of Indian agricultural production. In its place, Americans introduced new arrangements on the land. At first, because population was sparse, it seemed that new settlers might reinstate forced labor. When Johan Augustus Sutter came from Switzerland to California in 1839, he became a Mexican citizen and obtained a lush tract of land in the Sacramento Valley. To tend his vast cattle ranch and work his sawmills and mines, Sutter brought in forced Indian labor and built a walled compound to protect his supplies and provide living quarters for himself and his laborers. When a few Americans began to trickle into California by the early 1840s, Sutter's Fort provided valuable supplies to newcomers.

These venturesome Americans had a keen desire to establish independent farms in California valleys and be free of *californio,* Mexican, and Indian influences. Shortly, they would join the struggle to wrest California from Mexican control altogether.

Expansion and Sectionalism, 1840–1848

The widespread belief in America's manifest destiny and the growing tide of westward movement had momentous political consequences during the 1840s. Negotiations with the Indian tribes in the western areas and with the foreign nations vying to settle the West required skillful diplomacy. The American public had unquestionably riveted its attention beyond the Mississippi, but its attitudes alternated between optimism and belligerence, leaving politicians struggling over the appropriate policies to shape America's future in the West. One thing became certain to attentive Americans by the 1840s: their manifest destiny could not be secured peacefully. Events in Texas, Oregon, and California proved that. While settlement and diplomacy gave way to aggression and warfare, however, a strong opposition to both forceful acquisition of western land and the expansion of slavery also emerged in the 1840s.

Annexation and the Election of 1844

Americans in the Republic of Texas relentlessly pursued annexation to the United States after the battles at the Alamo, Goliad, and the San Jacinto River in 1836. Annexation became more and more appealing to southern Americans, especially as a means to prevent a rumored possible alliance between Texas and England, which would surely deprive the South of room to expand King Cotton. In political terms, the extension of slavery under the terms of the 1820 Missouri Compromise threatened to deepen sectional differences, but many southerners and midwesterners agreed that perhaps new states in the West might "add leavening" to politics and "balance the ship of state." Despite the spread of slavery, argued many close observers, most governments of the nine new western states between 1800 and 1840 also expanded white male suffrage.

In fact, optimism about balancing political and cultural interests in the West was miscalculated. Westerners, it turned out, raised many new demands for state and federal resources for defense, Indian treaties, viable government, and internal improvements. Each request for resources provoked an intense political battle among congressional factions. Throughout older portions of America, the press, pulpit, and American street corner persistently turned images of western opportunity and abundance into discussions about how to serve one or another sectional or partisan interest.

By 1844, Texans were again engaged in bloody skirmishes with neighboring American immigrants, Mexicans, and Native Americans. Some Texans fled the border area. Annexation had become a deeply divisive issue in American politics, especially because many Americans—whether for or against the annexation of Texas—believed that the very survival of the Republic was at stake. A huge shift in

American public opinion had been taking place in the early 1840s, from fear of another international war to support for annexation even if it required Americans going to war to win Texas. Many voices proposed that England's and America's joint occupation of Oregon equally stood in the way of resolving conflicts with western Indians and setting up orderly government for new settlers in the Oregon territory. Swept up in the public discussion about America's manifest destiny to expand against all opposing cultures and political systems, and riveting their attention on the westward migration to Texas and Oregon territories, great numbers of Americans accepted war as a viable means to secure the West.

The election of 1844 concentrated the political focus of the nation on these issues. President John Tyler hoped to gain popular support for his reelection by announcing his desire to annex the Republic, even though this position departed from a large portion of his Whig Party constituents in the North. But his political expectations were dashed when Secretary of State John C. Calhoun, a Democrat and a strong voice of the slave owners, introduced an annexation treaty to Congress in June 1843 before Tyler could announce his own intentions. Then Tyler's own Whig Party censured him and turned to the ever steady Henry Clay as its presidential nominee in 1844. As usual, Clay represented a compromise position: he was not opposed to Texas annexation, but he refused to promote it actively out of concern that he might alienate sectors of the Whig Party.

In contrast, the Democrats pulled out every stop for manifest destiny and annexation. Party leaders rejected the northern stalwart, Martin Van Buren, and chose an ardent expansionist from Tennessee, James K. Polk. During his campaign in 1844, Polk swept up the strength of southern and midwestern expansionists by making the annexation of Texas and the acquisition of other trans-Mississippi lands part of the United States. Although some Democrats were at first skeptical about supporting this "dark horse" candidate, Polk assured southerners that he would not only annex Texas but also support using federal funds for southern development. In addition, Polk earned midwestern support when he gave them hope that the federal government would subsidize removal, and possibly wars against, Native Americans.

Texas was not the only trans-Mississippi territory that preoccupied the American public and policymakers in 1844. Polk also pledged to bring the huge territories of Oregon, New Mexico, and California into the American republic if he should win the presidency. These promises appealed not only to the thousands of migrants by now setting out for the West each year, but also to the American people generally. Fear that Mexico would reincorporate Texas into its customs and laws, and fear that England and France had developed interests in coastal trade with Texas and California, churned up more ardent cries for manifest destiny at any cost. Although many fears were exaggerated, Polk believed he had a mandate to negotiate for, or go to war for, Texas, Oregon, and California territories. And although England probably had no intention of wresting California from American interests, many high-ranking officials imagined the worst. The American minister in Mexico said it "will be worth a war of twenty years" to keep England out of California.

Polk's slogan, "Fifty-Four Forty or Fight," reflected the growing commitment to defend manifest destiny. Instead of dividing the Oregon territory with England, the

Polk and Dallas This campaign flag clearly illustrates Polk's support for Texas annexation during the 1844 presidential race. While the existing twenty-six states are represented by stars ringing Polk's portrait, the "Lone Star" of Texas is still outside the Union. *(Collection of Janice L. and David J. Frent.)*

Democratic Party ran on a platform of keeping all of it for American expansion. Though the electoral college vote favored Polk widely over Clay in 1844, Polk's popular vote margin was narrow. Clay's middle-of-the-road stance on annexation and southern development was widely appealing to many sectors of the American people, but his ability to capture enough electoral votes to win in 1844 was hampered by a split in Clay's Whig Party. Antislavery Whigs deserted Clay and ran their own candidate, James G. Birney, under the Liberty Party banner. Formed in 1840 to oppose slavery, the Liberty Party ran the first antislavery campaign at the national level in 1844. Its 62,000 supporters at the polls could not unseat either major political party, but they made Clay's defeat more certain.

In any event, Polk and leaders from all major parties interpreted his victory as a mandate to annex Texas and acquire all of Oregon and California. But public opinion in the nation remained deeply divided in early 1845. What turned many northern congressmen toward support for Texas annexation was repeated news that England, France, and Mexico were negotiating how to serve their mutual international interests by keeping Texas independent and not annexed to the United States. Persistent fears of foreign dangers swayed enough northern votes to favor annexation, and in March 1845 the resolution passed in Congress. In December, Florida and Texas became the fourteenth and fifteenth slave states. By June, after months of holding firm on his commitment to end the joint occupation of Oregon, Polk signed an agreement with English officials to make the territory American soil from the forty-second to the forty-ninth parallel. That same month, John Frémont, an explorer who may have hoped to gain great power in California, joined his small force with a larger group of California rebels who wished to oust Mexicans. Together the Americans declared the Bear Flag Republic. But before the meaning of this declaration could be sorted out by Americans west and east of the Mississippi, the disputes in Texas, Oregon, and California had merged with a far wider war to win the entire Southwest.

The Mexican-American War

By early 1845, settlers between the Nueces and Rio Grande Rivers were involved in bloody border skirmishes once again. President Polk had sent General Zachary Taylor to the Nueces River with about 3,500 men and orders to defend Texas, which officially only lay north of the Rio Grande, if Mexico invaded. The area between the Nueces and Rio Grande continued to be disputed by Texans and Mexicans. At the same time, Polk ordered Pacific naval forces to seize California's ports if Mexico initiated a war, and he spread word to diplomats in the region that he would not suppress internal rebellions by Americans who attempted to take California. He singled out the Bear Flag Republic for special praise. In November 1845, Polk further pressed his goals by sending a secret envoy, John Slidell, to Mexico with orders to offer up to $40 million to Mexico's President Herrera to set the Rio Grande as the Texan border and to grant the United States the western Mexican provinces of New Mexico and California. The Mexican government could not give Slidell an audience without precipitating internal discord. Just as Congress was voting to make Texas a new state, without Mexican approval, Polk responded to the Mexican rebuff of Slidell with an order to General Taylor to advance his forces south to the Rio Grande. Americans everywhere knew that Mexico still claimed this soil.

Mexico ended diplomatic relations with America as soon as Texas gained statehood and then ordered all non-Mexican armed parties to leave California, including John C. Frémont and the men in his hire. Frémont went to Oregon temporarily, but returned when he learned that a small group of Americans in Sonoma were about to declare California free of Mexican rule. Lansford Hastings had been luring migrants off the overland trails that led to Oregon and onto "shortcuts" across dangerous terrain into California in order to build support for his own independent republic; it had been Hastings who influenced the Donner–Reed party's disastrous decision to alter its route in 1845. Now in early 1846, Frémont feared for the safety of the misguided settlers and the diplomatic reputation of the United States, not to mention his own future as a statesman in the West. In an effort to strengthen and guide the emerging revolt, Frémont returned to California and joined his forces with groups of rebels seeking to defend their land claims against Mexico, as well as to remove all Mexicans from the territory. In June 1846, California's new settlers followed the earlier Texas example and declared its separation from Mexico as the Bear Flag Republic. For the next two years, rebels fought to win California from the resident Mexicans and to secure statehood from the American federal government.

Meanwhile, American and Mexican troops collided briefly along the Rio Grande in April 1846—precisely what Polk needed to take a war message to Congress:

"Mexico has passed the boundary of the United States, has invaded our territory and shed American blood upon American soil." Despite strong hesitation in many American quarters, as well as Mexican authorities' desire to end hostilities if possible, Polk seized the moment to add, "War exists, and, notwithstanding all our efforts to avoid it, exists by the act of Mexico herself." Congress responded with a declaration of war on May 13, 1846 (see map).

Polk sent General Taylor into northeastern Mexico to capture the cities of Palo Alto in May and Monterrey in September 1846. At the same time, Colonel Stephen Kearny marched hundreds of midwestern volunteers across forbidding dry lands to Santa Fe, where they accepted the city's surrender. Kearny's force then proceeded to southern California, where he occupied the region with the help of American naval forces and Frémont's irregulars.

Although it appeared that American forces had secured a vast stretch of southwestern lands, Mexico refused to negotiate peace and instead chose to keep fighting. In February 1847, Santa Anna, who was once again at the head of Mexico's troops, attacked Taylor's forces at Buena Vista but was repulsed by the Americans. Within a month General Winfield Scott attacked the coastal city of Vera Cruz with an amphibious force and crushed its resistance. But it took until September for Scott to lead his forces to Mexico City and put an end to the country's resistance. Along the way, brutal battles took a heavy toll on Mexican and American troops, and both sides reacted to battle casualties by retaliating with rape, robbery, and banditry.

But once Mexico City fell to the American forces, the war was over. The chief clerk of the State Department, Nicholas P. Trist, carried papers into Mexico City that outlined Polk's terms for peace, and on February 2, 1848, both sides signed the Treaty of Guadalupe Hidalgo. Mexico ceded California and all land in Texas north of the Rio Grande River. In addition, Mexico ceded the vast territory of New Mexico (today's Nevada, Arizona, Utah, and part of Colorado). The United States agreed to pay Mexico $15 million in settlement and to assume about $2 million in claims by American citizens for war damages. In all, the United States was enlarged by about 1.2 million square miles and acquired jurisdiction over hundreds of rebel Americans in the territories and nearly eighty thousand Spanish-speaking people.

Internal Tensions

At first, the Mexican-American War was immensely popular in certain regions of the country. Expansionist leaders in Congress, including Stephen A. Douglas, a young Democratic senator from Illinois, championed the war. To many midwesterners, gaining the New Mexico and California territories seemed to be the logical next step in America's manifest destiny to expand to the Pacific Ocean. To many in the South, the press was correct to declare that "every dollar spent there, but insures the acquisition of territory which must widen the field of Southern enterprise and power in the future." The burgeoning penny press also whipped up public enthusiasm for the war, especially the newspapers closely allied with the Democratic Party. By the 1840s, reporters following the troops in Mexico could use the recently invented telegraph

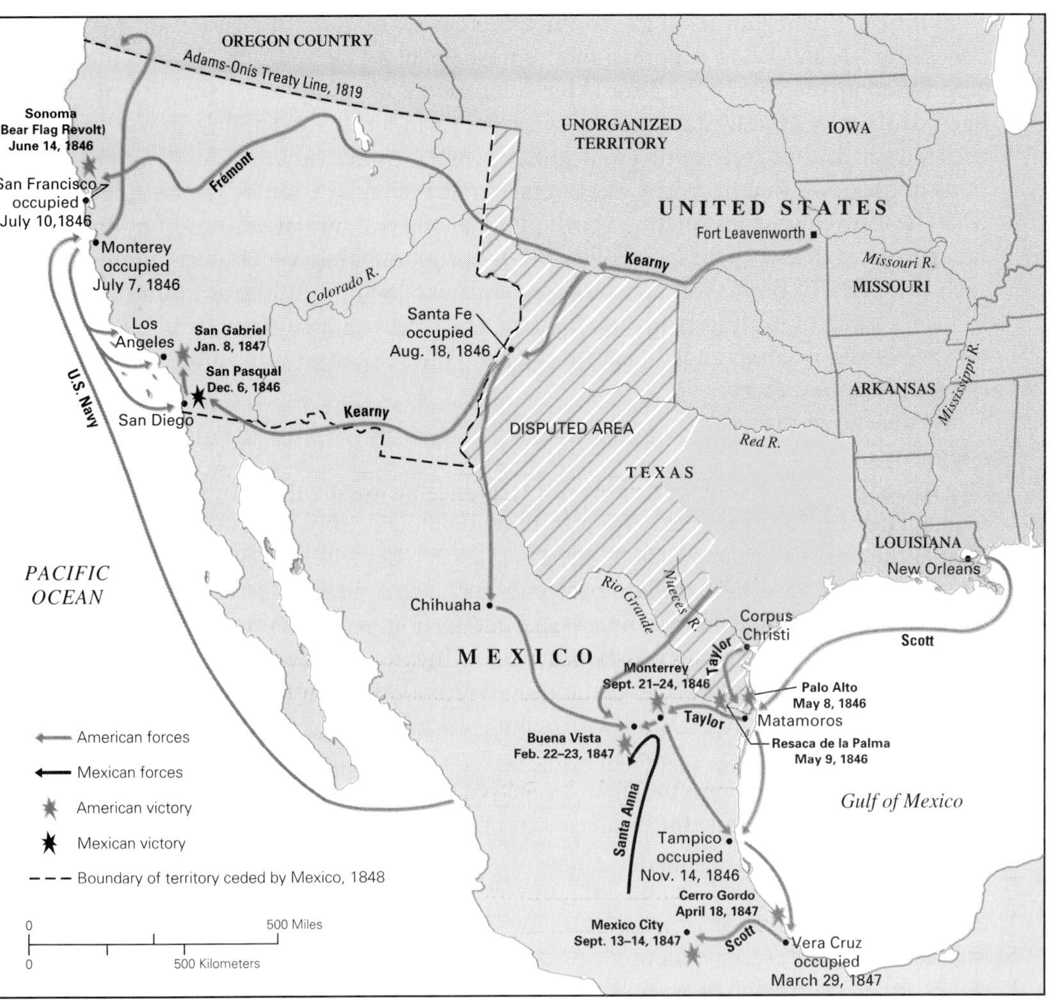

The Mexican-American War, 1846–1848 American troops fought in many regions of the Southwest and Mexico during this war. After claiming the disputed area shown here, the army took land to the Rio Grande, then New Mexico and Alta California. Later on, all of California fell to American naval control. General Winfield Scott finally invaded Mexico at Vera Cruz, and occupied Mexico City in the final major confrontation of the war.

to relay up-to-date information to their editors in eastern cities, who in turn printed stories for an eager public about "war atrocities" in Mexico. Reports straight from the battlefield were read out on street corners and in local gathering places, making it a more immediate, emotional experience than a war on foreign soil would otherwise have evoked. Taylor's and Scott's victories in early 1847 were cause for widespread celebration throughout the South and Midwest, largely because the news arrived quickly and directly from the scene. In May 1847, New York City organized perhaps its largest parade to that time; observers estimated that over 400,000 people took to the city's streets to glory in Scott's successful landing at Vera Cruz.

But from the beginning of the conflict, there was also loud opposition to "Mr. Polk's War." Many Whig congressional representatives believed that, despite the blood shed in 1845 along the Texas-Mexico border, Polk had provoked additional open conflict by sending Taylor deeper into Mexican lands and had precipitously declared war without attempting to negotiate peace. Suspicions about Polk's intentions in Mexico—that he might want to take over the entire country—intensified when he took charge personally of both political and military organization of the war instead of delegating responsibility to subordinates. Whig leaders charged that such co-opting of power was an excessive use of presidential authority, not unlike Jackson's forceful dealings with the Bank of the United States and Cherokee removal. Northern Whigs added that the goals of Polk's expansionism suited primarily southern slave owners.

By the end of the war's first year, opposition expanded to northeastern farmers and many northern small manufacturers and retailers who grumbled that the military struggle was draining federal resources away from essential internal improvements. The Mexican-American War proved costly indeed. About 13,000 Americans died in the war, and nearly 50,000 Mexicans. Taxes rose steeply in every state, and war expenses topped $100 million before its end. The Massachusetts state legislature passed a resolution condemning Polk's declaration of war as unconstitutional. In that state, essayist-philosopher Henry David Thoreau objected to rising taxes to pay for what he considered an unjust war. Rather than pay, Thoreau chose to go to jail (though only for a night) and returned to Walden Pond to pen the much-read essay, "Civil Disobedience." Thoreau gained a wide hearing for his view that when a government acted in an immoral manner, individuals had a right—in fact, a duty—to resist it. Since then, his model of civil disobedience has inspired many leaders, including Martin Luther King, Jr.

Political tensions were also building in Washington by war's end. When Trist returned to Washington with the signed treaty between America and Mexico, Polk was furious. Given Scott's tremendous victories, Polk believed by late 1847 that American forces should overrun all of Mexico and take much more territory than he had at first told Trist to negotiate for. To Polk, Trist had foolishly ignored the opportunity to win all of Mexico in the treaty's final terms. However, this hyperaggressive expansionism contrasted with widespread war-weariness by early 1848. Whig congressional and state leaders, as well as popular intellectual leaders such as Ralph Waldo Emerson, cried out that Americans had enough war and high taxes. Even some southern War Hawks believed that taking Mexico invited political disaster for Americans. Senator John C. Calhoun, for example, articulated a widespread racist argument that it was sufficient to take the "nearly vacant" lands of Mexico's former northern provinces, but that to take into America "the colored and mixed-breed" Mexicans who lived south of the Rio Grande would "taint" American politics and culture immeasurably.

Polk relented and accepted the treaty with Mexico. In fact, in the short span of three years, he had attained most of his political goals, including the acquisition of 1.2 million square miles of new territory—Texas, Oregon, California, and the huge New Mexico territory—increasing the size of the United States by some 70 percent. Still, many statesmen and citizens continued to question the means by which Polk and his circle took such vast lands, and to doubt the necessity of the Mexican-American War. Abraham Lincoln, for example, reflected many years later, "The act of sending an armed force among the Mexicans was unnecessary, inasmuch as Mexico was in no way molesting or menacing the United States or the people thereof; and . . . it was unconstitutional, because the power of levying war is vested in Congress, and not in the President."

The Wilmot Proviso

The war with Mexico drew Americans everywhere into a protracted political discussion, often very heated, about the meaning of the West and how it would be shaped by settlement and policies. Many important issues were subsumed in support for, or opposition to, manifest destiny in the West. Among them were concerns about pursuing diplomacy and relations with foreign nations, protecting settlers already in the western frontiers, heeding the demands for government and statehood that poured from the West regularly during the 1840s, and spreading the "civilizing tendencies" of American culture into the "untamed" West. But no issue was more divisive in American political and cultural discussions about the West than slavery.

When, for example, Daniel Webster intoned in 1846, "We want no extension of territory; we want no accession of new states. The country is already large enough," he went on to clarify that if America grew any larger, southern slave interests would rush into the new territories. Webster's view did not win many adherents during the war's early months of feverish patriotism, but slowly this view gained support in Congress. David Wilmot, a Democrat from Pennsylvania, rose during a congressional discussion about appropriations for the Mexican-American War to propose that slavery be banned in any territory acquired from Mexico. The South could keep slavery as it existed, he conceded, but under no circumstances should it be carried into the new territories.

Wilmot's Proviso of August 1846 provoked congressional representatives and state leaders to make an important decision about slavery in the territories. The result was jarring to every political interest in the nation: southern Whigs joined southern Democrats against the proviso, while northerners of both parties supported it. Party loyalty, which had been so strong since Jackson's early days in office, broke down over this all-important issue, and sectional loyalty replaced it. In the coming years, both parties would remain unable to pull their northern and southern wings together over matters related to slavery and the admission of new territories to statehood. Any decisive stance on these issues would only drive deeper wedges between members of either party, based on sectional interests. Once again, the American political culture was in crisis.

More lay behind Wilmot's proposal than strong feelings about slavery. Like many fellow Democrats, Wilmot feared the rising influence of abolitionists in the North and Midwest. The Liberty Party had been growing steadily since 1840, and its nearly 62,000 northern votes in the 1844 election had come from both Whigs and Democrats. The Liberty Party proposed to unseat all senators who held slaves, which would have decimated the southern states' power in that body. The party also proposed to keep out of the Union any territories that held slaves when they applied for statehood, to end slavery in the District of Columbia, and to crush the interstate slave trade.

The founders of the Liberty Party had first become politically active in the abolitionist movement during the 1830s. Voters who sided with the party in 1844 realized that its platform of strong antislavery positions could win only in the North, and that a Liberty Party victory would split the Union. Their votes nevertheless showed that thousands of Americans wished to express opposition to slavery in an official way. Outside the Liberty Party, the majority of northern citizens did not wish to abolish slavery in the South but hoped to secure expansion in the new states exclusively for white people. This majority coalesced into the free-soil movement after the 1844 election. To free-soilers, slavery was not necessarily immoral; it was an economic and political threat to the manifest destiny of white male expansion in free territories. Free-soilers supported a strong Union, even if that meant allowing slavery to continue to exist in the southern states. But the northern values of individualism, political liberty, and small free farms could be achieved in the unorganized territories and new western states only if slavery was prohibited there.

During the mid-1840s, free-soil support swelled among northerners and midwesterners who wished to halt the spread of slavery into the new territories. Reasoning in pragmatic terms, free-soilers argued that the southern plantation system would compete directly with white farm families moving into the Ohio Valley, and in all other regions across the Mississippi. Many free-soilers took cues from the labor movement of the 1830s and 1840s, which often promoted the values of free labor: hard work, personal independence, and the sanctity of individual property. Southern slavery was antithetical to these values, argued free-soilers. Some of them also believed that southern poor whites, by virtue of choosing to live in the South, did not hold the values of free labor either.

By 1848, these views coalesced into concrete political action. When Secretary of State James Buchanan proposed to extend the Missouri Compromise line to the Pacific Ocean—thereby admitting slavery into most of today's New Mexico, Arizona, and southern California—free-soilers attracted to their banner great numbers of Americans who wished to shape the West in the political and cultural image of the free labor North. The Free-Soil Party was born.

While many Free-Soilers came out of abolitionist backgrounds, and many party members believed free white and free African-American people could live well together in all of the free states, a constituency in the party adamantly opposed any mixing of races. As northern political radicals pointed out, only a few outspoken abolitionists sought true social and economic equality among the races of North America, and they tended to join radical abolitionist organizations. The majority of people in the North regarded African-Americans, whether slave or free, as inferior to whites. Moreover, African-Americans would compete for economic opportunity and employment in newly settled areas just as they did in the eastern states. Thus that a constituency of Free-Soilers reflected this majority and wished to cleanse the new territories of all African-American people came as no surprise to William

Lloyd Garrison, or to Sarah and Angelina Grimké. Already Indiana, Illinois, Iowa, and Oregon had enacted laws prohibiting African-Americans within their boundaries, though officials were unable to enforce the laws consistently.

The Election of 1848

By the time male citizens turned out to vote in 1848, the Treaty of Guadalupe Hidalgo had stretched America's boundaries around vast new lands. Streams of new settlers were beginning to determine the character of territorial life. But in 1848 American policymakers and citizens had still not resolved the central issue of the Wilmot Proviso: whether slavery would exist in the new territories.

Nor did the campaign for the presidency in 1848 give voters decisive choices. All three national party candidates declined to take a stand on the principled questions of freedom or slavery. Instead they developed their positions based on pragmatic political considerations. The Democratic Party candidate, Lewis Cass of Michigan, risked losing northern voters if he spoke out directly for slavery in the territories, and he risked losing southern voters if he said nothing at all about slavery. He chose the most ambiguous middle course available: the government should adopt a policy of popular sovereignty. This doctrine would leave the decision about slavery versus freedom to the citizens of each territory. It sounded very democratic since it would put decisions about the character of the territories in the hands of locally elected bodies of the Jeffersonian and Jacksonian "common man." In reality, Cass and other leading Democrats knew that popular sovereignty was no solution to sectional divisions at all. For one thing, every territorial and state government would be made up of the same political parties that argued about slavery at the national level. Divisions along party lines in the new territories would probably develop as mirror images of party disputes in older areas. For another, Cass's proposal for popular sovereignty also failed to say when and how a territory would choose its slave or free status, leaving it up to the various party factions and sectional interests of older regions to influence territorial outcomes.

The Whig Party also contributed its share of sectional and political confusion to the campaign of 1848. Instead of choosing the ever-willing Henry Clay to run, the party picked General Zachary Taylor, who was far from being a typical Whig. Taylor was, in the first place, not from a strong Whig center in the North or Chesapeake, but from Louisiana. Furthermore, as a slaveholder, he could not appeal to abolitionists, as so many leaders of his party could. In addition, where many of his party had opposed the Mexican-American War, Taylor had catapulted to heroic stature because of his military role in the war. Whigs hoped that Taylor would attract the votes of party members in every national region, including southern and midwestern Democrats who applauded Taylor's slaveholding and expansionist stance. To have such broad appeal, Taylor avoided taking a clear position on the issue of slavery in the territories.

The third national force in the election, the growing Free-Soil Party, scooped up the votes of northern Democrats who opposed the Mexican War's benefits for southerners, Whigs who did not thrill to Taylor's background and qualifications, and Whigs who had already associated themselves with the principled position of the Liberty Party and now wanted to vote their convictions in 1848. With the former Democrat Martin Van Buren as their presidential candidate, third-party supporters backed the slogan, "Free Soil, Free Labor, Free Men."

The Free-Soil Party gained 291,263 votes, or 10.1 percent of the popular vote. Almost all of the party's support was in the Northeast and Midwest, especially among small farmers and urban workers who wanted to improve working conditions and halt the extension of slavery. Although the Free-Soil Party did not officially endorse abolitionism, many free African-American leaders, including Frederick Douglass, welcomed the party's campaign as a good start in the much larger effort to end slavery everywhere. The Free-Soil turnout was enough to divide the Democrats (electoral votes of the powerful states of New York and Pennsylvania went to Van Buren) and to dampen the Whig victory. Taylor won the presidency with only 47.4 percent of the popular vote, as the candidate of a party he hardly seemed to fit, and without addressing the most serious issues dividing the country.

Gold!

One month before Mexico ceded California and New Mexico to the United States, James Marshall, an employee at one of Sutter's mills, found flakes of gold about as large as dimes in the millrace. Soon, all hands around the mills and mines on Sutter's land dropped their usual work to pan for gold. Within six weeks the news had spread, and men began to leave jobs from as far away as Monterey and San Francisco to join others who were reporting modest finds of gold from streams. By June 1848, "gold fever" was epidemic in California, and by September, ships returning to Boston and Philadelphia, as well as wagons returning to Independence, Missouri, reported that a few people had struck it rich.

When a couple of miners produced actual gold nuggets and little bags of gold dust, the news spread like wildfire and the initial California rush became a torrent of prospectors. Until 1849, only about fifteen thousand Americans had traveled overland to California; in 1849 alone, some eighty thousand men, women, and children left their farms and urban jobs in the East and Midwest to race to the western foothills of the Sierra Nevada Mountains. Later called the "forty-niners" because of the year most of them went west, gold seekers crossed the plains on the Overland Trail or took ships to San Francisco. Prospectors came from every walk of life, from every state and territory, from Mexico, Europe, and China, to stake claims in California. Within a year, they transformed California from a ranching and mining outback into a chaotic mixture of peoples from all around the world.

Chinese immigrants arrived by the hundreds during 1849 and 1850 to mine for gold, most with the expectation of returning home quickly. The first waves of Chinese were primarily men, and they often lived apart from American camps in their own "Chinatowns." Their success in extracting gold from the hillsides added to the intense economic competition of the gold rush, and resentment and racial stereotypes of Chinese appearances and customs developed quickly. When over twenty thousand more Chinese came to San Francisco in 1852, they seemed to whites to flood the port with a "foreign danger," and open racism became a regular feature of life in the city.

San Francisco had become a boomtown overnight, thanks to the discovery of gold. In little more than a year, it grew from 1,000 to 35,000 people, all of whom needed housing, food, mining supplies, and work animals. Tents rose out of the mud, as the swelling population burst the seams of makeshift city neighborhoods over and over. Saloons sprang up randomly. Fortunes, said many small entrepreneurs, were easier to make from needy prospectors and land agents than from hunting for gold. Agents of eastern merchants flocked to the city to sell shiploads of sugar, coffee, tea, rum, iron tools, pots and kettles, guns, and other necessities of frontier life. One ambitious entrepreneur was Levi-Strauss, a German Jew who brought his tough canvas material to San Francisco with the hope of manufacturing tents. But the sturdy cloth proved more useful in the form of men's pants. Miners soon learned from advice manuals that in addition to "your mule, your lamp and your pan," every miner would be grateful to carry along "a pair of well-sewn Levi pants."

Out in the mining camps and foothills where the prospectors worked, people survived with minimal comforts and many hardships. Amid the stench of people living together with little concern for public sanitation or personal hygiene, careless

The Bar of a Gambling Saloon By 1855, the California gold rush had attracted a variety of people, for a variety of purposes, to mining country and had converted small trading posts to thriving cities. Against the ornate background of this drinking establishment in San Francisco, men from many continents made business deals, discussed commercial and political news, and shared the same cultural space. *(© Collection of The New-York Historical Society.)*

campers often polluted water, and diseases took their toll as a consequence. Nor was the camp diet healthy; most miners lived on the boring fare of stale bread, beans, and salt pork. Few took the time to hunt or fish—which may have required going far from the camps overnight—and many neglected to build decent shelters for the rainy winter months.

Mining camps attracted people willing to provide services, usually at excessive cost. Because few miners were willing to take the time to do everyday chores, those who had money or small bits of gold would pay others to do the chores for them. Cooks, tailors, and laundresses made decent money in the camps, if they survived the ravages of disease, theft, and absconding employers. Saloonkeepers, prostitutes, and boarding house owners often met early deaths because of violence, venereal disease, or drug or alcohol abuse, although a few made fortunes and returned to the East.

Violence was a regular feature of this camp life. "Claim jumpers"—men who robbed successful miners of their gold or stole their claim papers—hung about in most mining camps, ready to engage in all manner of mayhem. Chinese, African-American, and Mexican miners endured especially harsh racist attacks; many minority miners were driven from their claims, taunted into leaving, or beaten brutally. Although Americans had entered California before 1848 as "foreigners," the wave of Americans entering the new republic assumed it was their right to dominate the territory and designated other groups of people as foreigners. Americans subjected the Chinese, in particular, to demeaning mining taxes.

Few of the forty-niners found any gold at all. And once the quest had depleted their savings and hopes, it was difficult to return to their former homes. Large numbers of them went to work for mining companies for wages. Where individual miners with their pans or picks could tap only the surface of potential deposits, organized mining companies pooled large amounts of capital to buy expensive machinery and probe deep for gold. In fact, after the first rush of independent prospectors into the foothills of the Sierra Nevada, it was wage workers who mined most of the California "Mother Lode" that stretched over one hundred miles southward from Sutter's Mill.

By the mid-1850s, individuals and companies had extracted more than $10 million in gold from California's mountainsides, and the gold rush was all but over. In its wake a multicultural population, some of it made affluent by the boom and some of it left desperately poor, made another transition to settled agricultural and commercial life in California. All of the undercurrents of tension among different races remained, especially in blatant forms of racism against the growing Chinese population. In addition, the California Indians who had lived in large numbers in the central valleys fled or died when waves of eastern migrants took over the environment. New settlers cultivated orchards and vineyards and vegetable fields that disrupted the ecological balance of Indian hunting grounds. To the south and west, along the coastline, Americans forced *californios* off their lands and legally annulled their former Mexican grants, compelling them to become another minority component of unstable communities in post–gold rush California. By 1860, the scramble for valuable mineral wealth had moved into Arizona and New Mexico. At first, copper mines yielded new fortunes; soon, silver was discovered at the Comstock Lode in Nevada. By the end of the Civil War, nearly $300 million in silver had been added to the world supply of precious metals.

CONCLUSION

By 1848, it seemed that Americans were fulfilling their "manifest destiny" to win and transform great stretches of land beyond the Mississippi River. The American government had secured over a million square miles in three years, by treaty and by war. The American people were moving onto that land with enthusiasm despite the tremendous hardships of life on the trails. Advancing over the Louisiana Purchase, Florida, Texas, the huge territories of New Mexico, California, and Oregon, Americans were occupying the landscape in successive frontier communities at an unprecedented pace. By 1860, nearly 350,000 people attempted the trek from Independence, Missouri, to Oregon and California.

Migrants carried many experiences from their former lives into the West. At the same time, many of them also tried to forge distinctive new communities in their adopted western homes. In either case, the processes for "civilizing space" in the West were not as easy and peaceful as promoters and publicists told Americans they would be. Almost 34,000 trans-Mississippi migrants before the Civil War died of exposure, disease, accidents, or hunger and fatigue before their wagons rolled across grasses and along the deep ruts that are visible even today. The majority of sojourners into the West also adjusted their expectations and endured hardships beyond the imagination of even the most accurate newspaper reporters of the era. Most settlers in the 1840s and 1850s did not replicate, or better, their farming efforts in the East. Most did not set up family farms as Jefferson and so many others envisioned for "the empire of the West," but instead trapped and hunted, mined, lumbered, constructed new towns and roads, provided services to newcomers, carried merchandize and the mail, fought Indians, and defended military claims. Their wives faced life-altering hardships on the overland trails, and then set up their new homes in communities fraught with scarcity, sometimes with violence, and almost always with lonely remoteness from the domestic culture they left back in the East.

Wars, especially the Mexican-American War, played an important role in gaining trans-Mississippi territory for Americans' goals. A powerful combination of ideas about their manifest destiny, their sectional quarrels over slavery and free soil, their anxieties about foreign alliances against America, and their restless migration into the West, all guided large numbers of Americans toward the conviction that a war with Mexico was necessary. As Americans in Texas continued to petition for annexation, as Americans in Oregon pleaded for orderly government and government aid, and as Americans in California declared their republic and sought annexation, a groundswell of sentiment rose favoring the tremendously costly war with Mexico. However, as the costs in lives and tax monies sapped the nation, public support for the war declined during its later months.

The West also focused Americans' deepening sectionalism and political divisions. The reformers and developers who shaped eastern and midwestern political culture from the 1820s to early 1840s turned their attention more and more to shaping the future of new territories. Discussion about the future of slavery could not be separated from territorial acquisition. Every political candidate for major office feared confronting the issue squarely, and yet all compromise positions failed to glue the rapidly shifting political forces into a viable national party. The election of 1848, one of America's most divisive, put a Whig in office who had southern identity and sentiments. It came at a time when territorial acquisitions made America a continental nation, but also when sectional tensions over the identity of the West and the existence of slavery rose to new heights.

SUGGESTED READINGS

Clyde Milner et al., eds., *The Oxford History of the American West* (1994), contains numerous essays that summarize old and new scholarship about many relevant topics. Patricia Limerick, Clyde Milner, and Charles Rankin, eds., *Trails: Toward a New Western History* (1991), brings together new work that stresses the role of the federal government in shaping the West and the multicultural character of frontier life.

Important starting places for understanding manifest destiny and expansionist ideology in nineteenth-century America include the standard work, Frederick Merk, *Manifest Destiny and Mission in American History: A Reinterpretation* (1963), which explains the sense of mission carried into frontier development; and Henry Nash Smith, *Virgin Land: The American West as Symbol and Myth* (1950), which analyzes the images of the West that inspired migration. See also Thomas Hietala, *Manifest Design: Anxious Aggrandizement in Late Jacksonian America* (1985), and Reginald Horsman, *Race and Manifest Destiny: The Origins of American Racial Anglo-Saxonism* (1981).

Early 1800s promotion of migration and exploration can be traced in Jennifer S. H. Brown, *Strangers in Blood: Fur Trade Company Families in Indian Country* (1980); James P. Ronda, *Astoria and Empire* (1990); Theodore J. Karaminski, *Fur Trade and Exploration: Opening of the Far Northwest, 1821–1852* (1983); and Dale Morgan, *Jedediah Smith and the Opening of the West* (1982). For the earliest experiences of migrants on the trails, see the engaging studies by Richard Bartlett, *The New Country: A Social History of the American Frontier, 1776–1890* (1974), and Sandra Myres, *Westering Women and the Frontier Experience, 1800–1915* (1982).

Indian experiences with Americans in the trans-Mississippi West before the Civil War are covered in the lively work of Robert Utley, *The Indian Frontier of the American West, 1846–1890* (1984), and Richard White, *"It's Your Misfortune and None of My Own": A New History of the American West* (1991), which is also a cultural and environmental study of the always-changing frontier and the many peoples who shaped it.

Ray Allen Billington's *The Far Western Frontier, 1830–1860* (1956) remains the best overview of the overlapping destinies of Texas, California, and Oregon in this era. For more detailed accounts of the Lone Star Republic and its struggle for annexation, see Gene Brack, *Mexico Views Manifest Destiny, 1821–1846* (1975), and Arnaldo DeLeon, *The Tejano Community, 1836–1900* (1982). David Weber, *The Mexican Frontier, 1821–1846* (1982), is one of the finest studies of the borderlands before American settlement transformed the region. The stories of Americans on the overland trails to Oregon and California are legion, but the best summaries include Leonard J. Arrington and Davis Bitton, *The Mormon Experience* (1979); William Bowen, *The Willamette Valley: Migration and Settlement on the Oregon Frontier* (1978); Malcolm Clark Jr., *Eden Seekers: The Settlement of Oregon* (1981); and John Mack Faragher, *Women and Men on the Overland Trail* (1979).

The best accounts of Texas and annexation, in addition to Billington's standard account, are Frederick Merk, *Slavery and the Annexation of Texas* (1972); David Montejano, *Anglos and Mexicans in the Making of Texas, 1836–1986* (1987); and David M. Pletcher, *The Diplomacy of Annexation: Texas, Oregon, and the Mexican War* (1973). For the progress of the war, Jack Bauer's *The Mexican War, 1846–1848* (1974) and Robert Johannsen's *To the Halls of the Montezumas: The Mexican War in the American Imagination* (1985) provide thorough coverage. The nature of Polk's actions regarding Texas and America's role in the war are treated with balance in Paul H. Bergeron, *The Presidency of James K. Polk* (1987), and portions of William Freehling, *The Road to Disunion* (1990), give valuable insights about tensions within the South regarding expansion, slavery, and the war.

Following the Mexican-American War, the years of political turmoil are engagingly related in Chaplain W. Morrison, *Democratic Politics and Sectionalism: The Wilmot Proviso Controvery* (1967), and Joseph Raybeck, *Free Soil: The Election of 1848* (1970). The best study of political party changes in the 1840s is Joel Silbey's *The Shrine of Party: Congressional Voting Behaviour, 1841–1852* (1967).

For the California gold rush and that territory's rapidly changing character, see John W. Caughey, *The California Gold Rush* (1975); William Greever, *Bonanza West: The Story of the Western Mining Rushes, 1848–1900* (1963); and Neal Harlow, *California Conquered: The Annexation of a Mexican Province, 1846–1850* (1982). For the consequences of multicultural contact in California, the most important studies include Robert H. Jackson and Edward Castillo, *Indians, Franciscans, and Spanish Colonization: The Impact of the Mission System on California Indians* (1995); Charles McClain, *In Search of Equality: The Chinese Struggle Against Discrimination in Nineteenth-Century America* (1994); and Leonard Pitt, *The Decline of the Californios: A Social History of the Spanish-Speaking Californians, 1846–1890* (1970).

Competing Voices

The Passage West

The Hope of a New Zion

Mrs. Priscilla Evans was a Mormon pioneer who walked the thousand miles from Iowa City to Salt Lake City in 1856. Not all westward trekkers were from eastern towns and midwestern farms: Priscilla was a recent immigrant from Wales, and among her fellow travelers were newcomers from Germany, Denmark, Sweden, and Holland. Together, they pulled handcarts filled with their belongings for five months of muddy spring rains and scorching summer heat. Unlike many less fortunate settlers who perished from exposure and hunger on the arduous journey, the pregnant Priscilla arrived at her destination, healthy and ready to create a new home with her husband.

> We took a tug from Penbroke [England] to Liverpool. . . . I was sick all the way. We landed in Boston . . . then travelled in cattle cars . . . to Iowa City . . . [where] my husband was offered ten dollars a day to work at his trade of Iron Roller, but money was no inducement to us, for we were anxious to get to Zion. We learned afterwards that many who stayed there apostatized [fell from religious grace] or died of cholera.
>
> When the carts were ready we started on a three-hundred-mile walk to Winter quarters on the Missouri River. There were a great many who made fun of us as we walked, pulling our carts, but the weather was fine and the roads were excellent. . . .
>
> We began our journey of one thousand miles [from the Missouri River] on foot with a handcart for each family. . . . There were five mule teams to haul the tents and surplus flour. Each handcart had one hundred pounds of flour, that was to be divided and [more got] from the wagons as required. At first we had a little coffee and bacon, but that was soon gone and we had no use for any cooking utensils but a frying pan. The flour was self-raising and we took water and baked a little cake; that was all we had to eat.
>
> After months of travelling we were put on half rations and at one time, before help came, we were out of flour for two days. We washed out the flour sacks to make a little gravy.
>
> There were in our tent my husband with one leg, two blind men . . . a man with one arm, and a widow with five children. . . . The tent was our covering, and the overcoat spread on the bare ground with the shawl over us was our bed. My feather bed, and the bedding, pillows, all our good clothing, my husband's church books, which he had collected through six years of missionary work, . . . all had to be left in a storehouse. We were promised that they would come to us with the next emigration in the spring, but we never did receive them. . . .
>
> No one rode in the wagons. Strong men would help the weaker ones, until they themselves were worn out, and some died from the struggle and want of food, and were buried along the wayside. It was heart rending for parents to move on

and leave their loved ones to such a fate, as they were so helpless, and had no material for coffins. Children and young folks, too, had to move on and leave father or mother or both.

Sometimes a bunch of buffaloes would come and the carts would stop until they passed. Had we been prepared with guns and ammunition, like people who came in wagons, we might have had meat, and would not have come to near starving. . . . We were much more fortunate than those who came later, as they had snow and freezing weather. Many lost limbs, and many froze to death . . . they got started too late. My husband, in walking from twenty to twenty-five miles per day [had pain] where the knee rested on the pad: the friction caused it to gather and break and was most painful. But he had to endure it, or remain behind, as he was never asked to ride in a wagon. . . .

The Lure of California Gold

In January 1848, when the first news leaked out that sawmill carpenters near Sacramento had found gold nuggets in the millrace, most people just laughed. But James H. Carson, a loner and adventurer, had few attachments to hold him in the East. "Just a little of the golden stuff would fix me fine," he wrote to relatives. Carson reached northern California where a few early prospectors were already panning the streams, hopeful of becoming rich if they survived camp conditions.

. . . I was knee deep in water, with my wash-basin full of dirt. . . After washing some fifty pans of dirt, I found I had realised about four bits' worth of gold. Reader, do you know how an *hombre* feels when the gold fever heat has suddenly fallen to about zero? I do. Kelsey's and the old dry diggings had just been opened, and to them I next set out. . . . I saw Indians giving handsful of gold for a cotton handkerchief or a shirt—and so great was the income of the Captain's trading houses that he was daily sending out mules packed with gold. . . . The population then there (exclusive of Indians) consisted of about three hundred—old pioneers, native Californians, deserters from the Army, Navy, and Colonel Stevenson's volunteers. . . . Every one had plenty of dust. From three ounces to five pounds was the income per day to those who would work. The gulches and ravines were opened about two feet wide and one foot in depth along their centres, and the gold picked out from amongst the dirt with a knife. . . .

Honesty (of which we now know so little) was the ruling passion amongst the miners of '48. Old debts were paid up; heavy bags of gold dust were carelessly left laying in their brush homes; mining tools, though scarce, were left in their places of work for days at a time, and not one theft or robbery was committed. . . .

We lived on beef and beans—beef dried, fried, roasted, boiled and broiled, morning, noon and night; as much as every man wanted, without money or price; and with a change, at times, to elk, venison and bear steak. . . . The discovery of gold raised the price of stock in proportion with everything else. Horses and mules in the mines were worth from two to four hundred dollars; cattle from one to two hundred dollars per head. I have seen men . . . ride them from one digging to another—take their saddles off, and set the animals loose (never looking for them again), remarking that "it was easier to dig out the price of another, than to hunt up the one astray."

> The morals of the miners of '48 should here be noticed. No person worked on Sunday . . . [they] spent it in playing at poker, with lumps of gold for checks; others, collected in groups, might be seen under the shades of neighboring trees, singing songs, playing at "old sledge" and drinking whisky. . . . We had ministers of the gospel amongst us, but they never preached. Religion had been forgotten, even by its ministers, and instead . . . they might have been seen with pick-axe and pan, travelling untrodden ways in search of "filthy lucre" & treasure that "fadeth away," or drinking good health and prosperity with friends.

Americans of the early republic only glimpsed the possibilities for westward movement into Jefferson's "empire for liberty," but by the 1840s, waves of settlers crossed the Great Plains into Oregon Territory. Some turned south into California, which became a state by 1850. This conquest of space did not happen overnight, and it did not happen easily. Many bloody battles with Indians and Mexican-Spanish residents, and disputes with people of European nations, took place as Americans followed their manifest destiny. At the same time, Americans debated whether they would extend free labor or slavery into the new lands they took over.

The result was a succession of frontiers filled not only with sturdy yeomen and successful entrepreneurs, but also with speculators, bankers, squatters, poor immigrants, failed gold-diggers, tenant farmers, and widows and orphans. A great number of migrants satisfied their deepest longings for modest success in a new life, and a few of them got rich. Priscilla Evans and her husband gradually prevailed against harsh Utah conditions. She bore twelve children and lived to know some of her grandchildren. James H. Carson led an altogether different life, but one equally representative of the thousands of single men and women who left trades or farms behind in order to begin a life anew on the far western frontiers.

Questions for Analysis

1. In what ways are these two accounts similar and in what ways different? Are these two individuals drawn to the West for the same reasons?
2. How do you think frontier life affected families, especially women and children? How was traveling west different for single men than for married men?
3. In what ways do each of these accounts emphasize the successes of frontier life? What are some of the difficulties migrants faced?
4. What do you think the journey and resettlement might have been like for less inspired farm families than the Evanses, or for less successful miners than Carson? Could you rewrite these accounts in other ways?
5. What do these accounts tell us about the variety of experiences and lifestyles on the far western frontier? What details strike you as uniquely far western, as opposed to southern or eastern?

14

The Sectional Challenge, 1848–1860

John Brown's leather tanning businesses in Ohio and northwestern Pennsylvania during the 1830s and 1840s had been sadly unsuccessful. His try at sheep ranching in Massachusetts flopped. Year after year, Brown endured not only business failures, but also the tragedies of his first wife's death, unrelenting hunger and disease among his children, the death of four beloved infants, the mental illness of more than one growing son, and the persistent poor health of his second wife. Unbowed, he tried to teach his sons to seek virtue in backbreaking farm labor and to take solace in family Bible readings. Somehow, his family grew and some of his children survived.

John Brown called all of his family's hardships and losses "small things" in comparison to the "one great thing" that sustained his passion and anger over the years: the existence of slavery. Although Brown failed in worldly occupations, he very successfully raised his children to be obedient, both to God's laws and to their father's will, and to struggle against slavery with every fiber of their beings. As a young man, Brown concealed many fugitive slaves who had crossed the Ohio River seeking freedom in the North. He befriended leading abolitionists in the Northeast and worked on a plan to raid the South, destroying planters' property and convincing slaves to run away. Deeper and deeper into the South, explained Brown, the "forces of Christian liberty" would march, until "floods of our bound brethren . . . flowed into northern freedom."

Brown moved his family to North Elba, New York, to farm an estate donated to him by the prominent abolitionist Gerritt Smith. There, Brown and his growing sons continued to ferry runaway slaves along the Underground Railroad to points farther north.

Once the government opened the Kansas Territory for settlement, Brown began to send his sons, one after another, into the West to farm. But soon they wrote home that "border ruffians" from Missouri and southern slave states were crossing into Kansas bent on establishing large slave plantations. John Brown the abolitionist could not sit idly by. He planned his own relocation to Kansas, leaving his wife and youngest children in New York, and raised funds for hundreds of Sharps rifles. By 1856, Brown was ready to do battle in "the inevitable war against that prime of all evils," slavery.

Naive? Visionary? Insane? Brown's plan was all of these. In May 1856, Brown gathered his living sons and sons-in-law in the Kansas Territory and led them in the massacre of five proslavery men and their sons on the Pottawatomie Creek. Even after his son Frederick was killed on a subsequent raid, Brown insisted that "the holy war" against slavery had to continue. Back east in October 1859, he decided the moment had arrived to enable southern slaves to "take their freedom" and force slave owners to die defending their odious system. With thousands of dollars from northern antislavery supporters, Brown purchased cases of weapons. He led eighteen heavily armed veterans of the battles in Kansas to the federal arsenal at Harpers Ferry, Virginia. There, "God's angry man" and his liberators seized the arsenal, killed a number of local citizens, and waited for a massive slave rebellion to catch fire.

But not many southern slaves even knew about Brown's plan, and no uprising occurred. The local militia, armed planters, and a detachment of U.S. Marines commanded by Colonel Robert E. Lee descended on the arsenal where Brown's men held out. A number of Brown's "antislavery warriors" died within hours, and the military took Brown prisoner. Virginia state authorities charged Brown with treason and ordered him to be executed on December 2, 1859. His hanging provoked some of the largest mourning parades the North had ever witnessed. The entire sequence of events sent shock waves through the South.

Public opinion about Brown's raid on Harpers Ferry was divided. A Richmond newspaper reflected that "the Harpers Ferry invasion has advanced the cause of disunion more than any other event that has happened since the formation of [the] government." In the North, members of the new Republican Party, which stood opposed to slavery in the territories, kept their distance from Brown's scheme. Republican Abraham Lincoln believed the martyr was little more than "an enthusiast" who "fancie[d] himself commissioned by Heaven to liberate" slaves. "He ventures the attempt, which ends in little else than his own execution." Stephen A. Douglas, the prominent Democratic senator who was in the forefront of discussions about the future of the western territories, used the Harpers Ferry episode to berate abolitionists and radical Republicans. Brown's raid, he charged, was "a natural, logical, inevitable result of the doctrines and teachings of the Republican party." Democrats elsewhere used correspondence between Brown and his northern abolitionist friends to fuel southern animosity.

Chronology

1848	Taylor elected president
1850	Compromise of 1850
	California admitted as a free state
	Know-Nothing Party formed
1851	Stowe publishes *Uncle Tom's Cabin*
1852	Pierce elected president
1853	Gadsden Purchase
1854	Kansas-Nebraska Act
	Indian Territory reorganized
	Republican Party formed and Whigs dissolve
1855	Bleeding Kansas
1856	Pottawatomie massacre
	Brooks assaults Sumner in the Senate
1857	*Dred Scott* decision
	Lecompton Constitution
	Lincoln-Douglas debates
1858	Brown's raid on Harpers Ferry
1859	Lincoln elected president
1860	South Carolina secedes

But numerous abolitionists and Unitarian ministers, including Thomas Wentworth Higginson and Theodore Parker, stepped forward to praise Brown as "the Christian martyr of a mighty cause." Henry David Thoreau called Brown "an angel of light" on a very dark issue, a principled individual in a "sea of murky indecision." Undoubtedly, many Americans interpreted Brown's violence as the logical consequence of the tensions that racked the territories and the sectional disputes that worsened with each passing month in 1859. But like his opponents, Brown's supporters were not raising controversial issues, or confronting violence over the matter of slavery, for the first time. Indeed, during the stormy decade of the 1850s, numerous Americans strove desperately to produce compromises that might repair or repress the deep divisions that split them. Their repeated failures raise significant questions about those last years before the Civil War:

- What was the role of western frontier development in the long-term sectional divisions between northern and southern Americans?
- What kinds of compromises did political and cultural leaders attempt to forge in these contentious years?
- Who spoke out for each section, each major interest, and what arguments did they give for their political proposals and personal beliefs? What was the role of new political party alignments?
- Why did compromise ultimately fail?

This chapter will address these questions.

Territory and Politics

If Alexis de Tocqueville had returned to America a generation after his first visit, he would have seen a dramatically altered nation. Over 2 million acres had been added to the geography, and the weight of America's population was shifting steadily westward. The Old Northwest and the Old Southwest had been organized into states. Each region had already passed through its rudimentary frontier stages and acquired many of the signs of maturity that marked the coastal states. But farther west, great new land acquisitions beckoned citizens to cross the Mississippi. Northerners and southerners divided over how to settle these new lands, with people in each section believing they were entitled to transplant their own, incompatible, social and cultural systems. How would the federal government resolve the sectional and territorial disputes that emerged as people began to settle in these new lands?

Political Ambiguities

When Whig Zachary Taylor won the presidency in 1848 with less than half the popular vote, the deep divisions in American political life became evident. Neither Democrats nor Whigs could sustain party unity across sectional lines. Issues and loyalties that had previously molded party identities across regional lines were rapidly dissolving into purely sectional alignments. Many northern Whigs who supported the Wilmot Proviso voted for Taylor, but a large number of northern and midwestern voters abandoned both parties to vote for the Free-Soil Party's candidate. Northern Democrats who were expansionists but did not want slavery in all of the new territories were helplessly divided from southern Democrats who demanded slavery's extension. With all eyes focused on the trans-Mississippi territories, each party seemed irreparably torn on the greatest question of all: freedom or slavery in the West?

From a southern point of view, Texas continued to be a logical place for planters' expansion, and the Wilmot Proviso's proposed denial of slavery in huge amounts of the West would unfairly limit southern expansion. John C. Calhoun reiterated his states' rights doctrine, insisting that the territories were jointly owned by the existing states and any citizen of any state had the right to carry his property (including slaves) into newly acquired lands. Congress, he argued, had no constitutional au-

Harpers Ferry Arsenal, 1859 John Brown and his band of supporters entered this national arsenal with the intention of laying hold of its munitions and using the site as a staging point for a general slave uprising out of the South. Although the buildings shown here were fortified, the arsenal site as a whole was easily surrounded and taken by federal and state troops. *(National Archives.)*

thority to regulate or exclude slavery in the territories. Other southern Democrats, more pragmatic than Calhoun, were willing to negotiate some extension of slavery into the territories without arguing for the principle of slavery on all new American soil. Still other Democrats, especially in the Midwest, adhered to popular sovereignty, which postponed national decisions about slavery in the territories and put all future decisions about statehood in the hands of "the people."

During the 1850s, support for popular sovereignty grew in states north of the Ohio River and in new territories west of the Mississippi River. But few Americans understood how and when such popular sovereignty should be exercised. Should it be determined at the time settlers organized the territory, or at the time they applied for statehood? And should it be granted by a constituted legislature, by delegated convention, or by a general vote of all white citizens? The question was put to the test soon enough. California continued to grow even after the gold rush frenzy subsided. Early settlers had sent back word to families in the East that the environment was lush and farms would "instantly prosper, should you only take the risk and come NOW." Miners and farmers alike wished to have California organized as a territory and to elect "a regular representative government."

Here was a chance to test popular sovereignty. Few planters had migrated into California to that time, so the convention that wrote a constitution and applied for statehood during 1849 heard few proslavery voices raised. In addition, Democrats in California tended to be Irish and poor southern migrants who were hostile toward African-Americans, slave or free, on racist grounds. The application sent to Congress expressed the California majority's desire to be admitted as a free state.

But President Taylor had his own political goals that did not accord with popular sovereignty or having California settlers vote independently on the issue. He responded to California settlers' demands for statehood as soon as he took office in March 1849, advising that they apply immediately, skipping the phase of territorial jurisdiction. Taylor's goals were threefold. In the first place, he hoped his call to bring California into the Union quickly would give members of the national Whig Party a unifying cause. Second, he hoped admitting California as a free state would attract Free-Soil Party members, as well as northern and midwestern Democrats, to the Whigs. Third, he wished to bring California into the Union as a free state without challenging the slave South directly, and without testing the political efficacy of popular sovereignty.

But southerners were stunned when, at the end of that year, Taylor simultaneously presented Californians' application for free statehood and recommended that New Mexico also be admitted as a free state. In addition to thwarting southern planters' expansionist aims, two more free states would upset the political balance in the Senate. In 1845 the admission of Texas and Florida as slave states had given the South a political edge of fifteen slave states, to thirteen free. The admission of Iowa (1846) and Wisconsin (1848) as free states restored parity to the Senate. Now the California–New Mexico proposal threatened southern interests again. Some southerners additionally feared that California's admission as a free state would encourage Free-Soilers and Whigs to unite forces long enough to carve up the remaining land between the Mississippi and California into many more free states. For the rest of 1849, Congress remained deadlocked.

The Compromise of 1850

Congressmen openly recognized that the future of slavery, and the rights of southerners to compete against northerners for each section's way of life in the territories, were on the line in early 1850. Voices for and against slavery were becoming shriller each year, and sectional interests seemed more divided with each occasion for making political harangues or casting controversial votes.

Neither northerners nor southerners would give up their territorial imperatives, their desire to expand. Each section believed in manifest destiny, though on different terms. Each argued for the correctness of its position based on "fundamental rights": many northerners appealed to the virtues of republican free labor and the rights of individual white male citizens, whereas many southerners defended states' rights and the sanctity of personal property, including slaves. Just as it was impossible to negotiate freedom or slavery, it was impossible to reconcile "rights" as sectional interests defined them.

By 1850, it also seemed clear to spokespeople from both North and South that two antithetical cultures and economies were facing off. Southern writers defended cotton and slavery as the "resources of great wealth" in their section, the basis for "cementing the most consequential of alliances with our brethren of other nations." Cotton, southerners pointed out, continued to be America's principal export and the source of a few tremendous fortunes, of southern planters' expansion across the Mississippi River, and of a population of about 4 million slaves by the 1850s. To this, some added the argument that slavery was a blessing for African-Americans who otherwise would not survive in a bitter, racially divided country (see Chapter 12). The North, in contrast, had established a form of "wage slavery" that hired and fired at will, refusing to care for workers in sickness and old age.

But northerners were correct to retort that although cotton production and slave labor had made a few southern planters fabulously wealthy, the southern way of life was not the source of America's economic vitality. The interdependent relations of manufacturing in the North and farming in the Midwest, linked by canals and railroads, created more dynamic development than occurred in the South. The North also had a far greater share of the country's cultural institutions, intellectual energy, and newspaper and communications systems. Northerners, in turn, accused planters of willfully declining to "improve" southern poor and middling white farmers, and of largely turning their backs on mining, manufacturing, and transportation development.

These arguments, delivered in the fog of political frustration and fractured party politics of the early 1850s, exaggerated the real differences between North and South. But they represented opposed values and moral systems that lay deeply embedded in the political reality of the decade.

With the California–New Mexico proposal before them, Congressmen confronted the difficulty of reconciling their varied goals. As they were discussing California, Utah applied for statehood as well, and the slave state of Texas was virtually at war with settlers in New Mexico who wished to form a free state. Antislavery forces from northern states were also loudly demanding that Congress abolish slavery in the District of Columbia, while southern planters bemoaned the rising number of slave runaways and clamored for their return. Accusations flung at northerners of harboring southerners' property raised the issue of their violating federal law.

In early 1850, Congress began an eight-month-long debate encompassing all of these touchy issues. Three veteran congressmen, representing the three major settled sections of the country, struggled mightily during those months to achieve a political compromise. It was the last time each would try to impose his imprint on policies that addressed the most pressing matters facing the nation.

Henry Clay, the Kentuckian present at the debates over the Missouri Compromise and a long-time advocate for development in the Old Northwest, gave a brilliant speech despite a "burning fever" that sent him from the Senate floor immediately afterward. The "Great Pacificator" urged that both North and South make some concessions for the sake of averting national political disaster and possibly the breakup of the Union. If necessary, he implored northern congressmen, they should agree to a fugitive slave law that would appease southern complaints.

Calhoun, at the brink of death from tuberculosis at the age of sixty-eight, sat and listened to a colleague read the speech he had prepared. Predictably, he repeated the southern states' rights position and now added that the North must leave slavery alone and keep the Senate balance of slave and free states. Calhoun asserted once again the South's right to secede from the Union to preserve its way of life.

Massachusetts senator Daniel Webster was also sixty-eight and ailing. Though a northerner, Webster did not support abolitionism during the debate. Indeed, he appealed to abolitionists to compromise to prevent the South's secession. "I speak today," he said, "for the preservation of the Union." Why, he reasoned to the overflowing chambers, should Congress legislate at all about slavery in the territories; the South would never extend slavery into the West because cotton would not grow there (a point about which Webster was quite wrong).

Antislavery congressmen, though a minority, were by 1850 skeptical that any compromise was possible. William Henry Seward, a New York Whig, wished to contain slavery within its existing boundaries and eventually exterminate it. In reply to Calhoun, Seward invoked "a higher law than the Constitution, which regulates our authority over the domain . . . the common heritage of mankind." Salmon P. Chase, an Ohio lawyer, then U.S. senator, and later governor of Ohio and chief justice of the U.S. Supreme Court, was well known for defending fugitive slaves. In response to southern frustrations over escapees, Chase argued for termination of all fugitive slave acts.

The president had intended to address the Senate himself and insist that southern representatives relinquish some of their demands. But he died suddenly on July 9, 1850, and Millard Fillmore assumed the task of moderating the Senate's deep divisions. Fillmore was not as keen as Taylor had been to force southerners to give ground. Already Clay had composed an elaborate plan for compromise, a puzzle with all the pieces of sectional interests laid out in neat order. Fillmore, however, passed on the job of presenting and motivating the compromise to rising, ambitious younger senators. Stephen A. Douglas of Illinois, just thirty-seven years old, was one of Fillmore's chosen spokesmen. Douglas won acclaim for ushering the Compromise of 1850 through Congress.

The Compromise of 1850 had four central tenets when it finally became a package plan in September. First, southerners won a new Fugitive Slave Law that replaced the 1793 law and now required federal officials to aid planters seeking runaway slaves in free states. The law denied slaves caught outside the slave states a right to testify on their own behalf or to have a jury trial over flight from their masters. Second, the compromise admitted California as a free state and created the territories of New Mexico and Utah, which were to be admitted on the basis of popular sovereignty. Third, it set the western boundary of Texas farther to the east than Texans wished, thus giving more land to New Mexico. In compensation to Texans, Congress assumed $10 million in debts still unpaid to citizens who suffered losses in the conflicts with Mexico before Texas statehood. Fourth, the act abolished the slave trade in the District of Columbia, although it permitted slavery's continued existence.

For now, most southerners pulled back from their threat of secession, and thousands of northerners demanded printed copies of Webster's moving appeal for compromise. Clay traveled through the country delivering over seventy speeches to

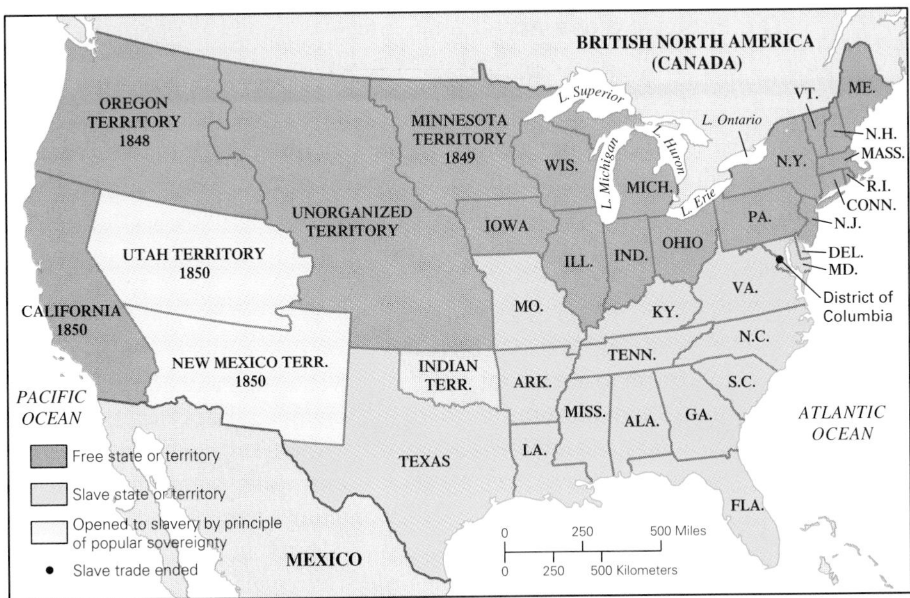

The Compromise of 1850 By the time Congress negotiated a new territorial arrangement for the trans-Mississippi West, America was a continental nation. By the terms of the compromise, California was admitted as a free state, the borders of Texas were fixed, and in the region covered by Utah and New Mexico territories, popular sovereignty would decide future status.

the public, pleading for conciliation. But hidden behind the votes that passed the Compromise of 1850 were ominous signs of continuing discord. Most important, in Congress it was moderate northern Democrats and moderate southern Whigs who favored compromise most. But some congressmen also expressed extreme views. Antislavery leaders such as Seward opposed the package, as did ardent proslavery leaders such as Jefferson Davis, both of whom argued fiercely in the Senate against the compromise.

In the southern states, proslavery Democrats lamented the loss of Calhoun, who died soon after his statement to the Senate, and regrouped around strong new leaders, making clear their intention to break with southern Whigs in order to defend slavery. These "fire-eaters" urged fellow southerners to boycott northern goods and shipping services, though the years of cotton and slavery prosperity made such appeals hopeless.

In the northern states after 1850, many Whigs who favored direct prohibition of slavery in the territories broke with their party leader and president, Fillmore, to denounce his advocacy of popular sovereignty. As Salmon Chase wrote from Ohio, "The question of slavery in the territories has been avoided. It has not been settled." Poet John Greenleaf Whittier and numerous outspoken clergymen gave harsher judgments. Ralph Waldo Emerson, the prominent philosopher, transcendentalist, and abolitionist, denounced Webster's call for compromise: "The word *liberty* in the mouth of Mr. Webster sounds like the word *love* in the mouth of a courtesan."

The Fugitive Slave Act

Scholars estimate that, by 1850, southern slave owners were losing about a thousand runaways a year. Some planters placed the estimate much higher, no doubt because of their fear that the Underground Railroad, "a freedom train to the cellars and closets of abolitionists," had become a widespread success. Now, with the Fugitive Slave Act, called the "Bloodhound Bill" by angry northerners, southern slave owners could demand the return of slave runaways and the punishment of those who harbored fugitives with heavy fines.

Many northerners saw the act as an affront to legislators, courts, and human dignity. Moderate Democrats and Whigs, who had been on the periphery of slavery discussions to this time, began to attend public antislavery meetings and donate funds to help the Underground Railroad. Some northern mobs jumped slave catchers who entered Boston and New York and attacked local officials who tried to enforce the act.

Slaves who were captured by mercenary slave catchers often were removed from the reach of legal support and court protection. Sometimes free African-Americans were abducted from their communities and sold into slavery. In *Twelve Years a Slave,* Solomon Northrup recounted his harrowing ordeal: a free black, he had been kidnapped in Washington, D.C., and served various masters for years before he could get word to friends to bring legal proof of his status. Stories such as Northrup's, published in 1853, spurred abolitionists to seek sterner measures to circumvent the Fugitive Slave Act. In response to previous fugitive slave laws, some states had passed "personal liberty laws" that made enforcement difficult by prohibiting the use of local jails for federal purposes.

Once the federal act went into effect in 1850, abolitionists added extralegal actions to their arsenal of resistance. More than once, angry mobs broke into courtrooms, seized runaways being tried for escape, and secreted them to upstate New York or Canada. In Syracuse, New York, one-third of the townspeople poured in through the doors and windows of the courthouse in 1851 to rescue a runaway slave and then helped him hide until state authorities stopped investigating. In the so-called Border States of Maryland and Delaware, Quakers who had long been active on the Underground Railroad helped large numbers of slaves evade the catchers from South Carolina and Georgia, risking steep fines and federal imprisonment for their efforts. While Daniel Webster lamented these actions, and President Fillmore declared them "mob rule," wider community sympathy with the abolitionists grew by the month. Antislavery societies organized mass meetings more regularly. Prominent abolitionist William Lloyd Garrison spoke to throngs of outraged city folk in 1851, declaring of the Fugitive Slave Act, "We execrate it, we spit upon it, we trample it under our feet."

Between 1851 and 1854, federal troops mobilized repeatedly to protect court proceedings against African-Americans and to give slave catchers safe passage back to the South. Armed abolitionists, led by the Unitarian minister Thomas Wentworth Higginson, stormed the Boston federal courthouse in 1854 to snatch back Anthony Burns, a runaway slave who was being sued by hired slave catchers. Although the mob failed to secure Burns's freedom, the president was fearful enough to send in artillery, marines, cavalry brigades, and a convoyed federal vessel to transport Burns back to the South. Even when members of the Boston abolitionist societies raised large sums to buy Burns's freedom, the president ordered the federal attorney on the case to deny the purchase. As Burns was walked in irons toward the dock, Bostonians lined the streets, standing in silence, dressed in black funeral garb, to show solidarity with the fugitive slave.

Although many attempts to free runaway slaves from the clutches of southern planters' paid hirelings failed, public sentiment grew stronger against slavery and against the government's Fugitive Slave Act. Abolitionists grew bolder, and some began to speak out in favor of violent resistance. Frederick Douglass, already a respected abolitionist leader in the North (see Chapter 12), called on citizens to resist "the bloodhound kidnappers" with the same force perpetrated against runaways. Increasing numbers of northerners believed that the new federal law had not helped compromise between the sections at all. Instead, it "brought the notion of slavery into our northern cities, it made all people of a particular color slaves, whether that be true or no." Not many northerners granted African-Americans true racial equality, but many now called the institution of slavery wrong. For Harriet Beecher Stowe (see page 451), the Fugitive Slave Act was an unforgivable assault on the dignity of both African-Americans and the moral integrity of families, white and black, everywhere.

"Practical Illustration of the Fugitive Slave Law" Many northerners, including some who opposed slave emancipation, found laws requiring the capture and return of runaways to be demeaning and impractical. In this cartoon the southern slave owner sits astride Daniel Webster, who voted for the act, while abolitionist William Lloyd Garrison takes aim in defense of runaways. *(Library of Congress.)*

The Election of 1852

Because President Fillmore supported popular sovereignty and had enforced the Fugitive Slave Act, Whigs rejected his candidacy in 1852. Clay and Webster had died. Seward, the New York antislavery spokesman, had become party head unofficially and put forward General Winfield Scott for nomination. Scott, another military hero candidate, was at first rejected by southern Whigs, but after many ballots, the northern wing of the party achieved his nomination. The 1852 convention, however, proved to most Whig leaders that their days as a national party were numbered. Southern Whigs had become increasingly disaffected, and many now left the party rather than support Scott. Northern abolitionist Whigs expressed disappointment that their party did not take a firmer official stand against slavery. Though individual Whigs continued to win national offices and maintained a strong presence in the government, the Whigs never ran a presidential candidate again.

Democrats did not have a clearer program or stronger unity than the Whigs in 1852, but they accommodated their sectional divisions enough to win the election. Large numbers of northern Democrats had made it clear they would support neither the extension of slavery nor popular sovereignty. So party leaders quickly rejected nominations for candidates who held southerner Calhoun's radical position that planters had a right to carry their property anywhere in the Union. After some debate, they also spurned potential nominees who supported popular sovereignty, even party stalwarts such as Lewis Cass, Stephen A. Douglas, and James Buchanan.

In Franklin Pierce, however, the Democrats found their man. Pierce had little name recognition—which in 1852 implied less chance of deepening party divisions—and he was a northerner who supposedly supported southerners' expansionist interests. Pierce pledged to enforce all parts of the Compromise of 1850, including the Fugitive Slave Act. At election time, it seemed that Pierce was a wise choice. The Democrats won a resounding popular majority, scooping up disaffected southern Whigs and sustaining a strong northern Democratic vote among workers and immigrants. Many Free-Soil voters left their party happy with Pierce's pledge to enforce the Fugitive Slave Act. Some of them hoped popular sovereignty in the West would lead to free states, as in California.

Scott won a significant popular vote in 1852, larger than Taylor's in 1848, but he carried only four of the thirty-one states. Even more, deep sectional differences would not go away. Popular sovereignty was widely appealing to Americans of many persuasions for it seemed to straddle sectional disputes with a viable democratic solution to territorial expansion. Californians' decision to enter the Union as a free state reassured northerners that popular sovereignty might be a panacea. But many leading southerners still favored the Calhoun position, and many leading northerners still touted an abolitionist stance. Pierce's response to these sectional extremes was not to seek compromise between the sides, but rather to ignore them. Like his predecessor Polk, Pierce diverted American attention to foreign expansion.

Renewed Foreign Expansionism

The 1848 revolutions in Europe seemed to bolster beliefs that manifest destiny made possible the spread of democracy and "civilizing tendencies" outside America. Ardent expansionists even suggested that their successes with manifest destiny had inspired the transformative liberal bourgeois revolutions in France, Germany, Italy, and Hungary. And they cheered again when President Franklin Pierce's envoy to Japan, Commodore Matthew C. Perry, returned with a path-breaking commercial treaty. Manifest destiny, according to some Democratic newspapers, would meld "the advanced peoples" of the world together "in peaceful markets" and among ever-expanding chosen peoples.

Over the 1840s, northern American merchants had actively pursued new markets in the Far East. Trade with China had declined markedly, but at first other trans-Pacific nations were reluctant to initiate commercial relations with America. Between 1846 and 1852, federal negotiations with Japan began to open doors for American merchants, and in 1854 Perry obtained a first treaty with Japan to begin modest mutual trading. President Pierce declined Perry's offer to use his squadron to take possessions in the area, primarily Formosa. But Pierce did extend Perry's commercial treaty and sought closer diplomatic relations with Japan. In 1854 he sent Townshend Harris to obtain these goals. It took numerous negotiating sessions with Japanese officials, at which Harris used his long experience trading in that part of the world to invoke traditional Japanese fears about the power of China, Russia, and Europe—fears Americans promised to help allay. Finally, in 1858 Japan signed a sweeping commercial treaty with American diplomats in Edo (later Tokyo) Bay. In the future, this treaty would bear important cultural and political fruits for both nations.

Pierce's support for expansionism extended within the Western Hemisphere as well, to Cuba, Mexico, and Nicaragua. Since the Mexican-American War a number of southern Democrats had pressed for an invasion of Mexico to secure additional territory. Polk had rebuffed this demand gently but remained interested in buying Cuba from Spain. A growing "Young America" movement within the Democratic Party coalesced around the ideas of a broader manifest destiny encompassing even more hemispheric territory, all earmarked for the southern plantation economy. Young Americans supported stirring up an anti-monarchy revolution in Cuba, which they hoped might lead to the island's becoming an American slave state. They secretly funded three expeditions to invade the island, called filibusters (from the Spanish word *filibustero,* or "piratical adventure"), led by the Cuban exile General Narciso Lopez.

On one of these filibusters in 1854, Spanish officials in Cuba confiscated an American ship in violation of international port regulations. Pierce demanded the release of the *Black Warrior* and its cargo, and turned to Congress for sanction to seek redress and apologies from Cubans and Spain. Secretary of State William L. Marcy threw his weight behind negotiations for indemnity and the return of the *Black Warrior*. But when northern Democrats balked at the possibility of going to war to establish a new slave state, Pierce had no choice but to accept lesser terms from Spain. Pierce also agreed to end the filibusters. He issued a proclamation that the federal government expected all private forces to cease their activities and abide by international neutrality laws.

But other interests still worked against Pierce. Once efforts to purchase Cuba from Spain for $130 million failed later in 1854, Marcy instructed Pierre Soule, the American minister in Spain, to meet with the British minister, James Buchanan, and the French minister, John Y. Mason, to set up an alternative plan to pressure Spain into giving up Cuba. In October they sent Pierce a message, now known as the Ostend Manifesto (the ministers met in Ostend, Belgium). "If we possess the power," it said, Americans were justified "by every law, human and Divine" in taking Cuba by force. When, two weeks later, administration insiders leaked the manifesto to the press, northerners raged against "the dirty plot" and forced Pierce to give up efforts to acquire Cuba.

But that was not the end of the filibusters. William Walker invaded Nicaragua four times, setting himself up as ruler of the country first in 1855 and inviting southerners to take up great landholdings from displaced local farmers. In 1856, after Walker declared the reintroduction of slavery in Nicaragua, he was happy to receive both Pierce's commendation for setting up an independent "republic" and the Democratic Party's endorsement of his rule. Neighboring Hondurans, however, drove Walker out of power in 1857, and he met his fate in front of a firing squad in Honduras in 1860.

A New Party System Emerges

Events in Cuba and Nicaragua showed Americans who did not already believe it that extending manifest destiny forcefully into other countries could fail. It showed Democrats that such efforts—especially when they ended in failure—could not build party unity. In 1854 Democrats, in an effort to survive as a national party, pinned their hopes once again on popular sovereignty and the expansion of slavery.

The Kansas-Nebraska Act

While the Young Americans pressed for imperialist expansion abroad, others revisited the matter of territorial expansion at home. Following the Mexican-American War, many Americans immediately turned their attention to settling California and Oregon. Politicians feared that the new western territories would break away from the Union if the existing states did not quickly integrate them into eastern life. Entrepreneurs saw the new lands as opportunities for development. But getting people and their trappings to the West presented challenges (see Chapter 13). Going by sea, across the isthmus of Panama or around South America, cost too much and took too long.

The only feasible way to link East and West was by railroad. Promoters hoping for government aid and huge fortunes put forward numerous plans for transcontinental lines, but it soon became clear that the government would subsidize only one line. Immediately, sectional interests came into the fray, since the favored proposal for a rail line would not only confer riches on the developers but also increase population and trade in the entire area that the line traversed.

Southerners proposed the Southern Pacific Railroad, which would run through Houston, Texas, all the way to Los Angeles, California. But the best route would have to cut through a portion of land in northern Mexico, where the mountains gave way to lower plains. A few leading southern expansionists, including Secretary of War Jefferson Davis, pushed for additional negotiations to acquire a swath of land for the railroad. Davis arranged for James Gadsden, a South Carolina railroad promoter, to be appointed minister to Mexico and commissioned to work with Santa Anna to acquire about thirty thousand square miles for $10 million.

Northerners protested this "wasteful use of public monies to buy a desert." But southerners retorted that the Gadsden Purchase would enable developers to cut a Southern Pacific route through completely American soil and, compared with other proposed lines, across fairly gentle terrain. The Senate approved the Gadsden Purchase in 1853.

Together, northern entrepreneurs and politicians realized that their success in getting a northern railroad line approved by Congress might depend on routing it through organized territory. Until 1854, however, a vast expanse separated the northern free states and the new possessions of California and Oregon. The Nebraska territory was still unorganized. However, overland trails had cut through the area for many years, and land-hungry migrants were pressing from the East.

In 1854 Stephen A. Douglas pounced on the opportunity to simultaneously organize this huge northern area for settlement and make a northern railroad possible, thereby counterbalancing southern goals. Douglas introduced the Kansas-Nebraska Act, which would open up the lands inside the northern part of the Indian Territory to migrating Americans, who would then set up a government and seek statehood for two territories—Kansas and Nebraska—according to popular sovereignty. Douglas's measure thus proposed to ignore treaties with Indians in Kansas and displace the many tribes living in that portion of the Indian Territory, there in the first place by the process of removal. The measure's popular sovereignty provisions also reopened the question of slavery in the territories.

Douglas had another goal, too. As a prominent railroad promoter, and a senator from Illinois, he wished to bring the much-discussed transcontinental railroad line through Chicago instead of the more southerly St. Louis, or the very distant New Orleans. In order to win congressional approval, not to mention funds and land grants to build such a line, land west of Iowa and the Minnesota Territory had to be organized into territories, and eventually new states. Southerners, quite predictably, resisted the formation of Kansas and Nebraska unless they were open to slavery. Northerners viewed the region as a contiguous part of free-soil states.

Douglas believed his solution to a potential congressional deadlock was popular sovereignty. As he and many other Democrats reasoned, northerners would get the railroad line and the possibility of excluding slavery with a future popular vote. Southerners would get explicit erasure of the Missouri Compromise line and the possibility of bringing slavery into the north with a future popular vote. Even before the act became law, however, the simmering sectional tensions over

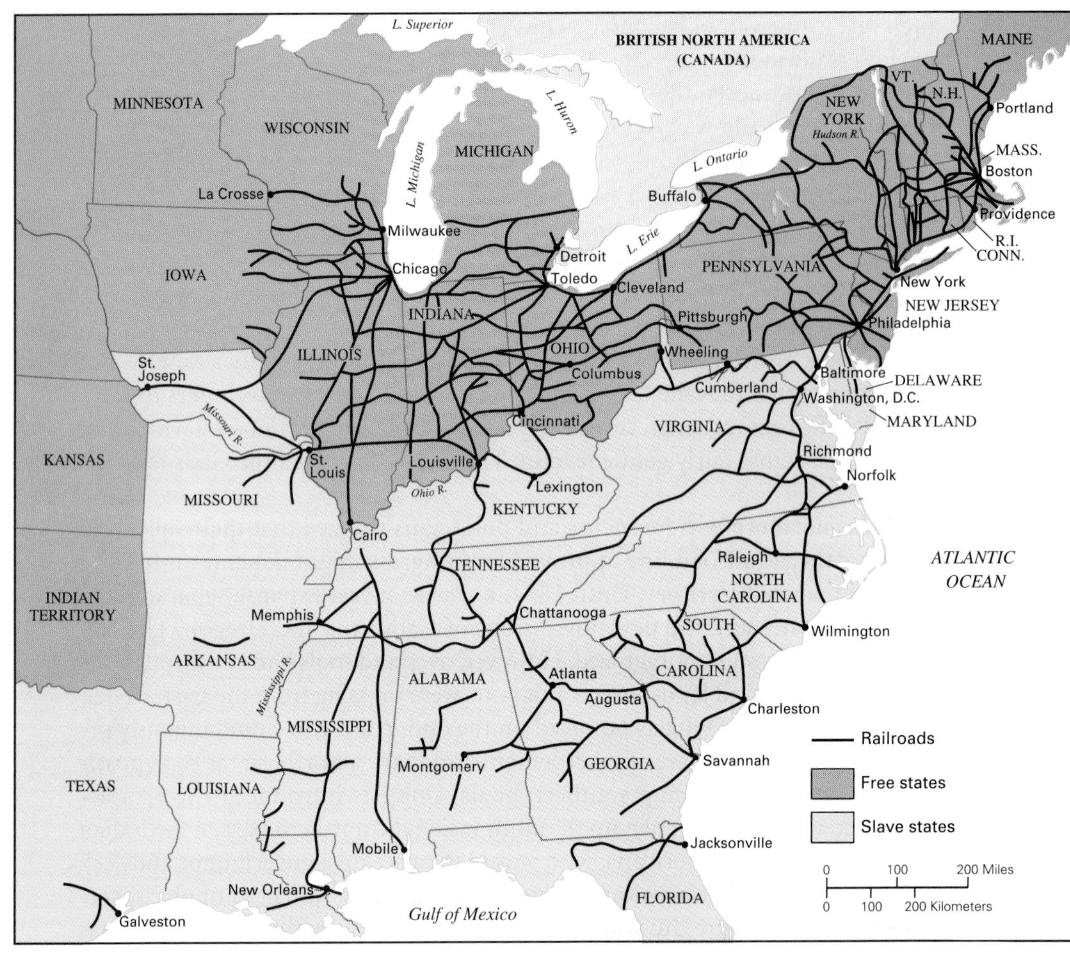

Railroads in the 1850s Only some of the northern and midwestern lines are shown in this map, but those regions constructed a thick network of rail transportation through a combination of private and public funding. Although the South had numerous railroad lines by 1860, many remained unconnected to each other, and in states of incomplete construction and varied track widths.

Kansas-Nebraska began to boil. Southern Democrats and Whigs now joined in support of the act, whereas northern Whigs opposed it loudly as a violation of the free-soil principle. The public debate and congressional vote on the act made clear that the Whigs were now irreconcilably split. Although northern Whigs kept a strong presence in the government, the party could never again run a presidential candidate. As for the Democrats, southern political leaders who supported the act—and slavery's extension—rose on a crest of southern popular acclaim and took many new seats in Congress in the 1854 midterm elections. Northern Democrats, squeezed between their southern party spokesmen and Whig popularity in the North, lost two-thirds of their seats.

Sectional views about railroads, land, and slavery thus played out in the congressional elections. Douglas's dreams of becoming a presidential candidate in 1856 were dashed. Many northern Whigs blamed him for writing "a dastardly plan that fell sweetly into the laps of southern slavers." Rallies in numerous northern cities denounced Douglas and the Democratic Party. In calmer but deeply worried tones, the wealthy bankers, merchants, and manufacturers who were tied to southern cotton, and thus called "Cotton Whigs," feared that the Kansas-Nebraska Act would arouse violent antislavery sentiment and tear the Union apart. Cotton Whigs urged southerners to vote against the act "out of our own mutual self-preservation." But southern Democrats felt too confident about the possibility of extending slavery to heed Whig warnings.

Bleeding Kansas

As soon as Congress passed the Kansas-Nebraska Act in 1854, a rush of events occupied Americans of every political persuasion. Government agents quickly proceeded with extracting treaties from the many Indian tribes in the newly designated territories. The Cheyenne and Sioux moved into the western part of Kansas for a few years. The Kickapoo, Shawnee, Sauk, and Fox agreed to live on reduced reservations. The Wea, Delaware, Iowa, and other small tribes sold their grants to American land companies.

And then the rush of American settlers began. Missourians, led by their own state senator, David Atchison, set up proslavery towns such as Atchison, Leavenworth, and Kickapoo, and staked out the lands around them. When the time came to elect territorial officials, the proslavery settlers not only encouraged people to vote more than once, but brought in a rowdy crew of "border ruffians" to pose as legitimate residents of Kansas. Kansas proslavery agitators dared Missourians to "enter every election district in Kansas . . . and vote at the point of a Bowie knife or revolver." In the coming months and years, the border ruffians also served as willing recruits in an open war to make Kansas a slave state. Identified by their "stinkin', ragged, drunken appearance," they wanted no part of a settled farming or ranching life on the frontier, only the cash bounties their fraudulent votes might bring.

Northerners organized a free-soil response. Right away in 1854, the wealthy Massachusetts manufacturer Amos Lawrence donated large funds to send out antislavery settlers from New England. Their first town, named Lawrence, Kansas, attracted over a thousand people from the summer to winter of 1854. Eli Thayer founded the New England Emigrant Aid Society and continued to channel more free-soilers into Lawrence and Topeka, Kansas. Many of those who agreed to start their lives over in what proved to be a hostile environment were already active in temperance and educational reform organizations, and most had been committed abolitionists back in New England.

Americans soon learned that popular sovereignty would be achieved not by calm deliberation and the ballot, but by bloody conflict. Border ruffians, already supplied with Bowie knives, revolvers, and Kentucky rifles, raided free-soil camps and rustled cattle. Abolitionists happily received crate after crate marked "Bibles" that were actually full of Sharps repeating rifles sent from the East. During 1855 and early 1856, armed slavery defenders arrived from Mississippi and Alabama, and free-soil ranks grew with migrants from Iowa, Illinois, and Indiana.

In the spring of 1856, heavily armed proslavery raiders burned most of Lawrence to the ground, stole their cattle and hogs, and scattered women and children who had watched men slaughter one another. Under cover of night, a small band of abolitionists retaliated by invading five farmsteads on Pottawatomie Creek and murdering the men living there. The murderers were the stalwart, uncompromising abolitionist John Brown, his sons and a son-in-law. But no marshals or sheriffs arrested Brown's bandits. They, and many others, continued to maraud through the countryside in months to come. Few peaceful farming settlers remained on the land by the end of 1856; most fled to military forts for protection. John Brown and his sons tainted the free-soil efforts in Kansas and Nebraska, and proslavery vigilantes in the territories alienated many of their politically active brethren in the southern states. "Kansas bleeds," wrote the northern press. Sectional interests had erupted into a territorial civil war.

The same week that Kansas erupted in violence, Congressman Preston Brooks of South Carolina attacked Senator Charles Sumner as he sat at his desk on the floor of the Senate. Brooks repeatedly struck Sumner, even on the head, with blows so hard that his cane broke. In his speech a few days earlier, "The crime against Kansas," Sumner had insulted Senator Andrew Butler, also of South Carolina and Brooks's uncle, by accusing him of sleeping with "the harlot, slavery." Bound by the traditional southern code of honor, Brooks had no choice but to seek revenge, just as Sumner had felt obliged to express abolitionist principles.

Nativism

Americans' fears of foreign immigrants—their religions, their customs, their need for jobs and material support—was strong by the 1830s and grew in proportion to rising immigration levels. During the 1850s, the American population was still multiplying as rapidly as Benjamin Franklin had noted a century previously, doubling about every twenty-five years. In 1790 only two cities, Philadelphia and New York, had populations over 20,000, but by 1860, forty-three did, and many others approached that size. Each of them experienced the growing pains of providing adequate housing and sanitation services, coping with poverty and ethnic conflict, and meeting the crises of periodic epidemics or shortages. In the countryside, farming populations in midwestern states began to grow rapidly, and family size rose after three decades of steady migration from Chesapeake and northeastern states. By 1840, large numbers of frontier people in the Midwest also were foreign-born.

As in previous eras, more population growth came from natural increase than from immigration. But unprecedented numbers of immigrants did enter America during the 1840s and 1850s. Over 1.7 million people arrived during the 1840s, and over 2.6 million in the 1850s. The immigration rate of about 60,000 per year during the 1830s suddenly tripled in the 1840s, and then quadrupled in the 1850s. Fleeing political and religious intolerance, over a million Germans chose to start over in

Free State Battery, Topeka, 1856 The slave state of Missouri opposed the entry of antislavery advocates for years and, by the 1850s, actively tried to prevent their migration through Missouri on the way to Kansas. "Free-staters" organized migration through Iowa instead, often bringing with them arms. This small cannon, left over from the Mexican War, helped create "Bleeding Kansas." *(Kansas State Historical Society.)*

America. Struggling against famine and utter economic ruin, a million and a half Irish came between 1840 and the Civil War. Both groups of people would continue to stream into America in later decades, too. There were also new immigrant groups, including the nearly 35,500 Chinese who came, primarily to California, by 1860. By that date, more than one-eighth of the U.S. population was foreign-born.

Starving and desperate Irish potato farmers arrived in eastern cities, mainly Boston and New York, with few industrial skills and no cash to move west. In order to make ends meet, everyone in the family worked at something: women washed and cooked in Protestant homes, men heaved loads on city docks or followed construction opportunities with railroads and canals, and children did piecework in sweatshops or scavenged in city alleys for food and fuel. Vibrant and interdependent community relationships developed in the Irish neighborhoods, but beyond the ghetto borders, ethnic and religious prejudice awaited, as did the lowest-paying urban jobs.

Although many Germans came to America for economic opportunity, a significant number of liberal political leaders chose to leave their country when repressive armies defeated the bourgeois revolutions of 1848 and thus ended the experiment in democracy there. Many of the German immigrants carried money and property with them, came in family groups, and brought skills and years of education. And they preferred to move quickly through port cities out to the breadbasket of the Midwest, including Wisconsin, Illinois, and Iowa. Germans usually shunned areas where slavery flourished.

In 1834 Lyman Beecher preached numerous anti-Catholic sermons in Boston, which fueled mob angers and instigated the burning of Ursuline Convent in Charleston, Massachusetts. Samuel F. B. Morse, the inventor of the telegraph, ran for mayor of New York City in 1836 based on his strong anti-immigrant views and fears that "Catholic corruption" would destroy the republican fiber of "true" American culture. And in Philadelphia, Whig reformers and Democratic entrepreneurs and craftsmen heaped scorn on German and Irish newcomers through the 1830s until, in 1844, open religious clashes produced twenty deaths and about a hundred injuries.

Various American interests stigmatized Irish immigrants as poor, Catholic, crammed into urban hovels, and frequent tipplers. Huge numbers of Bostonian Irish were attracted to the political machines that organized party voting and promised charity, drink, and neighborhood development in return for their vote. Despite their unpropertied status, in New York over half of the city's voters were foreign-born in the 1850s, which made them important objects of the emerging political machine at Tammany Hall. Already in the 1780s, the Tammany Society of artisans and mechanics began organizing the working-class vote and cementing neighborhood alliances in New York City. During the 1830s, Tammany was closely affiliated with the Democratic Party and helped sponsor party picnics, parades, publications, and—of course—the vote. During times of economic hardship, ethnic immigrants and American-born workers had few means to correct the capitalist system's inequities. But they did have strength in their numbers and could turn out local and state votes that won important reforms.

While the political machines organized immigrants in their taverns and poor neighborhoods, evangelical and temperance reformers, often Whigs, tried to change immigrants' lives in other ways. Overall, however, they were not as successful. But out of their efforts, a minority of these reformers developed strong nativist, or anti-immigrant, feelings during the 1830s to 1850s. These feelings intensified when Irish immigrants expressed openly their antiblack prejudices and competed violently with free African-Americans for unskilled jobs. In addition, Whigs accused the Irish as a group of being too easily persuaded to vote the way Democratic machine politicians told them to. Immigrants, charged nativists, were responsible for rising levels of urban crime, as well as rising taxes to pay for poor relief.

In 1837 anti-immigrant activists started the Native American Association in Washington, D.C. By 1850, secret societies had formed to oppose "the Catholic presence in our Union" and coalesced as the Order of the Star-Spangled Banner and Native American Clubs. These organizations usually held secret meetings that were open only to Protestants born in America, drawing into their membership white professional and skilled men in northern cities and farmers who feared a declining way of life. In 1851 these nativists formed the American Party, also called the "Know-Nothings" because they refused to divulge information about themselves to the public. Their political program included ending poor relief to noncitizens who did not pay taxes and instituting literacy tests for voting (which they believed would disfranchise many immigrants). They demanded that no foreigners hold offices and called for laws to extend the period before naturalization into citizenship from five to twenty-one years. American Party leaders teamed up with female missionaries and educational reformers to proselytize in immigrant communities about American democracy and the virtues of "women's sphere."

In the 1854 state elections, Know-Nothings won nearly 40 percent of the vote in Pennsylvania and took control of the legislature in Massachusetts. The American Party also garnered large wins in Maryland and New York. Free-soilers with an eye on the West, racists who feared losing jobs and community security as free African-Americans moved nearby, and antislavery advocates who watched the Whig Party decline tended to accept the American Party's nativism. In the eyes of many northerners, the Democratic Party's associations with slavery and Catholic immigrants—"slavery, rum, and Romanism"—were an obvious assault on "freedom, temperance, and Protestantism."

The Republican Party

In 1854 northern Whigs no longer could claim a national party, and many northern Democrats despised Douglas's compromise over Kansas with the South. Many members of these two displaced and disgruntled groups joined with Free-Soilers and the American Party in 1854 to elect many local officials. Within a few months of the election, however, these forces began forming a new political party. Resurrecting the old Jeffersonian term *Republican,* the party's organizers drew together many different strands of the fragmented political culture.

Many political views comfortably coexisted within the Republican Party. Some Republicans were former northern Whig abolitionists; some were former Free-Soil or northern Democratic voters who agreed that slavery should be kept out of the territories but allowed to persist in the South; and some were reformers who focused on temperance, religion, education, and immigration in their home states. Northern and western merchants and manufacturers drifted to the Republican Party, too, because it promised to use a strong national government to promote commerce and internal improvements. Northern and western farmers also liked the Republican Party's commitment to cheap land.

But one demand above all others linked all of these strands to the Republican Party: no slavery in the new territories. Many Republicans loathed and feared the southern way of life. Masters represented force, inhumanity, and absolute power within plantation society, qualities that would be even more dangerous when planters exported them into territories where free white families also lived. Planters, in the minds of many northerners, also deliberately shunned entrepreneurship and hard work, which were qualities valued by Americans who embraced free labor and industrialization. Abraham Lincoln, an early member of the Republican Party, championed northern values of social mobility and a strong work ethic. Like most other Republicans, Lincoln joined in celebrating individualism, even though the

North was, in reality, more class-divided and economically unstable than ever during the mid-1850s.

By 1856, the Republican Party had catapulted to the forefront of national politics. In the presidential election that year, Democrats turned at first to their outstanding national leaders, Stephen A. Douglas and President Franklin Pierce. But both men had promoted the Kansas-Nebraska Act and were identified with the slave South as a result. In 1856, the election of either man would split the party sectionally and cost it the votes of northern Democrats. So the Democratic Party chose to run Pennsylvanian James Buchanan, who had been out of the country during the Kansas-Nebraska deliberations.

The Republicans ran John C. Frémont, the California explorer, for president. But Frémont's name appeared on the ballot in only four southern states, where he won almost no votes anyway. Instead, the southern states really pitted Buchanan against the American Party candidate, former president Millard Fillmore. Fillmore gained strong support from former southern Whigs and took a large percentage of the popular vote in most southern states. But the electoral vote was sectional: Buchanan mopped up the electoral vote of all southern states, while Frémont carried the electoral vote of eleven northern states.

Buchanan gained enough of the popular vote—45.3 percent—to win the election nationally. He had taken hold of the southern vote and scraped together enough support in the North to put a Democrat in the presidential office. But Republicans knew that if they had carried just two more northern states, in particular Pennsylvania and New Jersey, they might have won. Furthermore, Republicans had displaced the American Party as a viable national organization. The election of 1856, sectional as it was, drew out 78.9 percent of eligible voters, one of the highest turnouts in American history. The waning influence of the American Party during the campaign also showed that northerners cared less about the "immigrant problem" than about the extension of slavery into the West. Indeed, a Third Party System had emerged from the contests of 1854 and 1856, one based on deepening sectional differences.

The Slide into War, 1856–1859

The election of 1856 demonstrated many political surprises to wary Americans, but one truth stood out above all the ambiguities: that on the issue of slavery, the North and South had become more entrenched in their positions. Would President Buchanan show the South that his federal office would protect slavery? Or, would he focus on weakening Republicans by negotiating on the matter of free soil?

Southern Stridency

Since the early 1830s, a number of southerners rejected any proposals for gradual emancipation of slaves and turned a deaf ear to northern antislavery appeals. Writers such as Calhoun and Thomas R. Dew (see page 477) were among many who argued for the natural inferiority of African-Americans and the need for slave labor to sustain a southern way of life. By the mid-1840s, in response to the Republican Party's claim on free soil, social mobility, economic advancement, and individualism, southern writers became shrill defenders of the slave system.

By the 1850s, a number of southern writers referred to northern free labor as "wage slavery," including the poet William Grayson from Charleston. Among the most authoritative southern writers, George Fitzhugh codified the southern fears of northern industrialization in two important books: *Sociology for the South; or, The Failure of a Free Society* (1854) and *Cannibals All! or, Slaves Without Masters* (1857). A respected Virginia lawyer and planter, Fitzhugh argued that northern life had succumbed to impersonal market forces. Talk about the freedom of workers was a thin veneer over the reality of treating human laborers as mere commodities, bought and sold according to market values out of any employer's or worker's control. Under the free labor system, profits were the only goal of employers and wages the only goal of workers. Therefore, northerners put almost no focus on personal needs, argued Fitzhugh; they gave each other almost no mutual support and comfort to soften the ambition that drove every individual. The old and weak were unemployable, the very young not yet paid for their work, and all of these northerners together were vulnerable to the "freedom" of poverty, hunger, homelessness, and loneliness.

Fitzhugh insisted that slavery was a more humane kind of labor and more benign social system. Masters were more than employers; they were responsible for housing, medical and old-age care, meals, and most other aspects of slaves' lives. Masters established cultural examples for poor whites and slaves to emulate; they lived a refined life that not only reflected their profits from the labor of slaves but also set a tone of civility and public virtue in the South that slaves grew to respect. Fitzhugh and others writing during the 1840s and 1850s took the southern defense of slavery much further than Jefferson's generation, when many writers still believed in the possibility of "civilizing the dark races" and colonization. By the 1840s writers more frequently justified slavery as a positive good, comparatively more humane and "progressive" than northern industrialization. Slavery, argued Calhoun, made it possible for the master race to perfect itself culturally and intellectually.

Dred Scott

In the mid-1850s, the prevailing view of northerners toward slavery remained rooted in the free-soil position. The prevailing view of southerners was summed up by Calhoun—that the Constitution guaranteed slavery's right to exist in the territories. Time and again, elections and political policies had faced this sectional division. But how would the Supreme Court address it?

The moment to find out came in 1857 when the Court handed down its decision in the famous *Dred Scott* v. *Sandford* case. Dred Scott had been born into slavery and, as an adult, owned by a Missouri army surgeon, John Emerson. Emerson took Scott with him during the 1830s to Illinois, a free state, and then to Wisconsin, a free territory because it lay north of the Missouri Compromise line. While in free land, Scott married another slave, Harriet; their daughter Eliza was born in free territory. In 1846 Emerson returned to Missouri with the Scotts, where Dred Scott sued for his freedom on the grounds of having established residence on free soil.

It took eleven years for the case to climb through the legal system to the Supreme Court. Then, two days after Buchanan assumed office, the Court announced its decision. Northerners had not been hopeful about the pending decision since the Court had been southern-dominated for years and Chief Justice Taney had not given any signs of disappointing the South now. In 1857 northern fears were realized. All of the southern members of the Court supported Taney in a decision that bolstered slavery. The bloc was joined by a northern justice whom Buchanan pressured (all other northern justices dissented).

In the majority opinion, Taney made momentous statements from that exalted bench. He announced that the Missouri Compromise was unconstitutional because the federal government had no right to interfere with the free movement of property throughout the territories, as Calhoun had enunciated for many years. Taney further announced that the entire *Dred Scott* case would be dismissed summarily, on the grounds that only citizens could bring suits in courts of law, and all African-Americans were by birth slaves and not citizens—a pronouncement that threatened the quarter million free African-Americans in the South.

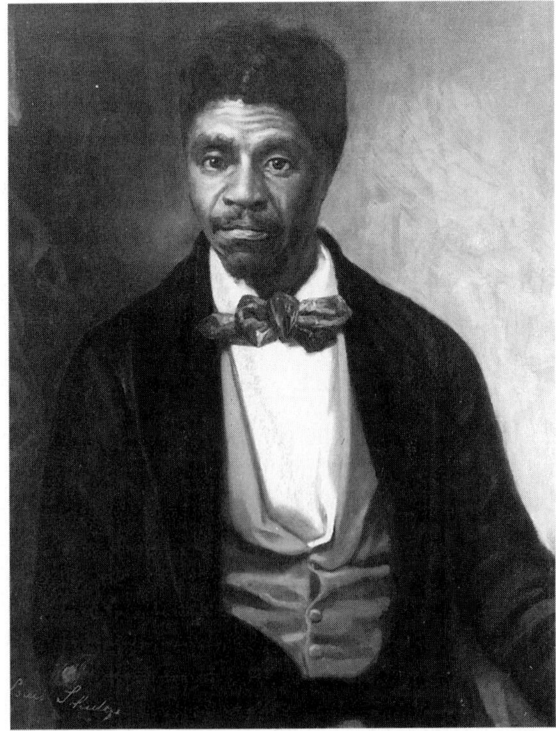

Dred Scott After suing for his liberty in the Missouri courts, Scott found himself caught up in legal and political quarreling that landed his case in the Supreme Court, where justices ruled against him. This painting was done in 1881, years after general slave emancipation had been declared. *(Missouri Historical Society.)*

The northern press denounced *Dred Scott* immediately and loudly. Not only was the Court's decision immoral, wrote many newspaper editorials; justices had also declared their decision "the law of the land," thereby thwarting congressional and state laws. President Buchanan's clear support for the *Dred Scott* decision fanned sectional flames even more. By overturning the Missouri Compromise, the *Dred Scott* decision wiped out one of the cornerstones of the Republican Party's program. Abraham Lincoln grew indignant: he accused Buchanan of conspiring with the southern justices on the Court to tear down the American political system and substitute judge-made law. Lincoln rhetorically, but alarmingly, posed the possibility that the same Court might next try to legalize slavery in the free states.

The Lecompton Constitution

While Taney wrote his *Dred Scott* decision, President Buchanan openly sided with the proslavery settlers in Kansas. Open conflicts between free-soilers and proslave settlers had continued without letup since 1855, and a rigged election that year—huge numbers of Missouri border ruffians voted illegally in the territory—put proslavery forces in charge of the territorial legislature in Lecompton, Kansas. Free-soilers repudiated the Lecompton government as illegitimate and set up their own in Topeka. They also stayed home in June when proslavery leaders called a constitutional convention. The Lecompton Constitution reflected the proslavery majority that did attend and, predictably, endorsed slavery in the future state. Then, despite a clear majority for free-soilers in an October election for new territorial officials, President Buchanan urged Congress to support the Lecompton Constitution and bring Kansas into the Union. If Kansas entered as a slave state, a new parity in the Senate of sixteen free and sixteen slave states would be achieved.

Stephen A. Douglas stepped into the fray once again. Knowing that a proslavery vote on Kansas would alienate the northern Democrats, he separated himself from his party's leader and his president to protest Buchanan's position. Furthermore, Douglas insisted that true popular sovereignty had to be exercised by all the voters in Kansas, and in fair elections. His arguments swayed Congress, which in April 1858 denied Kansas admission to the Union on the basis of the Lecompton Constitution. Back in Kansas a popular referendum also resoundingly rejected the constitution, and in 1859 the territory held a new convention that was dominated this time by Republican Party members. In January 1861, a new proposal—that Kansas come into the Union as a free state—passed in Congress. But by then, many southern representatives were no longer active in national government.

This final vote on Kansas did not resolve deeper tensions. For one thing, the Democratic Party was clearly no longer a united national party. Buchanan and Douglas represented two opposing positions within the same party, each dominated by sectional concerns. Southern Democrats seethed that Douglas had betrayed them, and Buchanan himself had taken a blatantly pro-southern stance. Secondly, Kansas was still bleeding. Daily violence racked the territory, and occasionally mass killings sent new shock waves through the unstable tent towns of the open plains. Constitutions, said one demoralized free-soiler, "are mere parchment with ink, and none wish to take time for reading out here."

Panic and Depression

Americans were familiar with periodic economic crises. Panics in 1792, 1819, and 1837 had started with the ruin of a few financial speculators and turned into full-scale downturns. Years of widespread commercial and manufacturing stalemate, accompanied by unemployment and deepening urban poverty, followed each panic. And in 1857, another panic demonstrated to Americans that they still lacked the institutional and regulatory safeguards to prevent widespread misery. The signs of impending crisis loomed when gold kept pouring in from the West, which inflated currency across the nation. War abroad stimulated the production of grain and flour for export, and westward migration put pressure on banks and creditors to speculate with land and railroad stock.

When exports from the Midwest and South fell off sharply in late 1856 and early 1857, creditors began to call in farmers' loans before cash "dried up." In addition, railroad investors in the Midwest had overextended themselves; in 1857 new construction halted and layoffs began. Soon, credits and debts stopped flowing in other sectors. At first, a relatively small Ohio credit agency and investment firm collapsed in August 1857, and then others followed. Before long, the word was out: newspaper editors rushed to print, and telegraph offices hummed all the way to Wall Street with details about Ohio's misfortunes. Investors on the East Coast rushed to sell stocks and bonds, and to pull assets from banks. Within a month, businesses were failing and thousands of workers lost their jobs. Until 1861, unemployment in the North and along the Ohio River remained at about 10 percent.

Expecting that the depression, like its predecessors, would be long, Republicans in Congress believed that they should raise tariffs to protect manufacturers hurting from the crisis. Many northern Democrats and all southern representatives disagreed and easily outvoted the proposal. Their cotton exports were not suffering and economic dislocation in the South was minimal. Although import-dependent southerners had been opposing tariffs for decades, in 1857 their stance seemed to be still more proof to northerners that the "slave power" intended to divide the Union along sectional lines. Wage workers in the North who lost their jobs in the depression readily believed that stubborn southern sectionalism—rather than excessive midwestern land and railroad speculation—lay at the heart of their misery. As for southerners, continuing relative economic well-being prompted the widespread view that the South was a more stable and prosperous region. This, it turned out, was one of the delusions that made compromise with the North harder in the four years to come.

Depression in the North and Midwest spurred the demand for free land in the national public domain. As a relief to the ruinous poverty of many northern cities, as well as a reward for the risks of migrating, reformers advocated that the government give free 160-acre homesteads to all applicant families. But these hopes met with stiff opposition from two directions. Northern manufacturers believed that free farms would "drain away the best of our hands" for factory work. Southerners feared that small homesteads would fill with free-soilers and deny planters a chance to expand. For two years Congress deliberated on the free land proposal. Only in 1860 did the government finally approve a plan to grant land at 25 cents an acre. President Buchanan, however, vetoed the proposal, and it languished until the Civil War was well under way. Finally in 1863, people everywhere in the existing states applauded the Homestead Act's becoming law.

Southerners also believed they had been successful in lowering tariffs over the early 1850s. In fact, tariffs had been reduced to their lowest point since the War of 1812. Then, when the Panic of 1857 set in, the public coffers emptied quickly and the need for public revenues became acute. Moreover, northern manufacturers clamored for protectionism during the stormy seasons of commercial crisis that followed the panic. Tariffs inched up again, but not as much as these manufacturers wished. By 1859, world prices for cotton rose slowly again, and southern exporters proclaimed the centrality of southern agriculture to the world economy. The South's more rapid recovery seemed to validate Fitzhugh's premise that southern slave plantations were a superior economic form to northern free labor.

Lincoln and the Union, 1856–1860

By 1859, sectionalism had taken a tremendous toll on national political parties and the American political culture. The Whigs had collapsed. The Democrats hovered near break-up. The Republicans were rising but uncertain about how to compromise the strands of difference in the party. Crises in the territories and Border States throughout 1857 and 1858 threatened not to subside, but to spread. More and more Americans began to doubt that there was a political solution to these crises, and to forecast a disastrous social collision of sectional interests.

Lincoln's Rise

Abraham Lincoln's early life and political career were intertwined with the most important cultural and political issues of his generation. Born in 1809 into one of the thousands of farm families moving in a westward direction early in the 1800s, Lincoln was also exposed to the era's fast-paced, ambitious energies of Americans on the make. His family moved from Kentucky, to Indiana, and then to Illinois. Lincoln contributed to the meager family income by ferrying goods on flatboats down the Mississippi River to New Orleans in 1828 and 1831. Then Lincoln decided to leave farming life and became a store clerk in New Salem, in central Illinois.

Lincoln was popular with the rising middle class and the town rowdies alike. His schooling was minimal, except for the kind attentions of a local schoolmaster and a few friends who loaned him books. But he loved to participate in public debates and was a regular client at the local tavern. The first year of his business, local townsmen appointed him to head their company of volunteers for the Black Hawk War.

These experiences shaped Lincoln not for the relative isolation of farm life or the relative calm of an intellectual career. Instead, he threw himself into politics. In 1832 Lincoln ran for the Illinois state legislature with a program Henry Clay would have smiled at, favoring internal improvements and education. Lincoln lost this first race, but he accepted a position as postmaster and deputy county surveyor. And he attached his future to a prominent Whig lawyer and state legislator, and began to study law. In two years, he ran for state office again, and this time he won.

With a panic and depression setting in by mid-1837, Lincoln nevertheless passed his law exams. In 1842 he married Mary Todd, the daughter of a prominent businessman and slave owner from Kentucky. From 1834 through 1840, he continued for four terms in the state legislature's lower house. Here, Lincoln adhered to general Whig measures such as state-chartered banking, more canals and roads, and protectionism. In 1844 he eagerly grabbed at the opportunity to support Henry Clay, the political figure Lincoln admired above all others, in his presidential campaign. By 1846, Lincoln was ready to run for a congressional seat; and he won.

Suddenly, Lincoln was immersed in sectionalism, slavery, and the Mexican-American War, matters that had seemed so remote from his life in Illinois but were consuming the attention of men in Washington. Lincoln had already decided that slavery had caused many injustices in the Midwest. In 1838 he had denounced the mob that attacked and killed the printer Elijah Lovejoy in Alton, Illinois. But Lincoln had just as ardently rejected the violence of abolitionists who tried to deny southern migrants a place in the West. As a midwestern Whig, he knew that abolitionists leaned toward the Liberty Party in 1844, which harmed his hero Henry Clay. And as a student of the Constitution, Lincoln doubted whether the federal government could deprive citizens in the slave states of their property.

These beliefs were not easy to blend and sustain consistently. Lincoln tried to take the high moral road when he went to Congress in 1847. Already the war with Mexico was underway, and when Polk demanded appropriations to support the troops, Lincoln could not in good conscience abandon American men in a foreign war. But he also spoke strongly against Polk's war policies; plainly, he insisted, the war was unconstitutional. Lincoln also voted for the Wilmot Proviso and introduced the first resolution for gradual abolitionism in Washington, D.C.

Thus, Lincoln staked out a moderate position compatible with Whig beliefs and friendly to free-soilers. He opposed slavery's extension, and he supported gradual emancipation and colonization in Africa. But by the end of the 1848 presidential campaign, Lincoln understood that moderation could be costly in the real world of politics. Because of his support for gradualism, northern abolitionists denounced him as a friend to slave owners. Because of his opposition to the immensely popular Mexican-American War, he lost the good will of voters in Illinois. For about five years, Lincoln retreated into his law practice, serving railroad and manufacturing interests in the Midwest, and witnessing the Whig Party crumble in the intensifying sectional controversies of the early 1850s.

Above all, Lincoln feared the demise of moderation in politics. Abolitionists and southern extremists both threatened the Union, he wrote often in the early 1850s. But when Stephen Douglas introduced the Kansas-Nebraska Act and touted its provisions for popular sovereignty, Lincoln decided it was time to return to political life. Popular sovereignty, he believed, was a dangerous opening for the extension of slavery. Denouncing both Douglas and his act as the "gravest mischief to the Union," Lincoln ran for both the state legislature and the national congress in 1854. "Love of justice" required that slavery be confined to the states where it already existed. Already Lincoln was speaking strongly in support of what would become the central planks in the Republican platform later: moral opposition to slavery, the need to use the federal government to keep the territories free, and the hope that the southern slave owners would emancipate their slaves state by state.

Forging Principles

For the next two years, Lincoln worked hard to bring together remnants of the Whigs, free-soilers, abolitionists, Know-Nothings, and Democrats who could be persuaded to reject Douglas's program. By May 1856, he assumed the head of the new Republican Party in Illinois. Following the *Dred Scott* decision, which Lincoln scorned publicly, he ran another vigorous campaign in 1858 against Douglas for the U.S. Senate seat. In that campaign, he iterated some of the most frequently quoted words in American history:

> A house divided against itself cannot stand. . . . I believe this government cannot endure permanently half *slave* and half *free*. I do not expect the Union to be dissolved—I do not expect the house to *fall*—but I do expect it will cease to be divided. It will become *all* one thing, or *all* the other.

The dispute between Douglas and Buchanan over popular sovereignty, Lincoln insisted, paled next to the far greater issue that lay before the nation: slavery or freedom.

As the Senate campaign commenced, Lincoln challenged Douglas to a series of seven debates in Illinois. Thousands of people attended each debate and newspapers buzzed with reports about them. Douglas, long associated with railroad promotion in the state, was a high-profile candidate. Everywhere he went, Douglas raised his proposal for a transcontinental line through Chicago. By then, railroads were booming: the 9,021 miles of rail in 1850 tripled to 30,627 miles in 1860. But the issue of where to put a transcontinental line, and how to fund it, overlapped with the sectionally divisive matters of slavery, free labor, and party politics.

Lincoln was less well known than Douglas in 1858, and had much to prove to his listeners. But at each of the three-hour debates, Lincoln shone as an orator and staked out important ground on which Republicans would stand for years to come (see Competing Voices, page 560). He did not believe that "the various races" in America were socially equal, but he did believe that slavery was a moral wrong. "I, as well as Judge Douglas, am in favor of the race to which I belong, having the superior position." But slavery, he insisted, denied African-Americans the natural rights and liberties outlined in the Declaration of Independence. In so doing, the institution undermined equal opportunity. Black men and white men alike had the right to "labor in the soil" and "eat the bread, without leave of anybody else, which his own hand earns." Time and again, Lincoln also underscored, Democrats had collaborated with the "slave power": in the Kansas-Nebraska Act, in *Dred Scott,* in favoring the Lecompton Constitution, and in defeating improvement and tariff proposals brought to Congress.

Douglas responded with what scholars call the Freeport Doctrine (because he introduced it in Freeport, Illinois), which modified the popular sovereignty position. Settlers, Douglas patiently explained, could keep slavery out of their territories in practice by using their collective local authority against the Supreme Court's decision. In territories that did not prohibit slavery (and thus admitted it), local governing bodies could simply refuse to adopt legislation to protect slavery. By their numbers and their different lifestyles, settlers could, in practice, overwhelm and neutralize efforts to bring in slavery.

Although Douglas narrowly won the Illinois election in 1858, he modified his popular sovereignty position so much that most of his proslavery support evaporated. In response to the Freeport Doctrine, southern Democrats demanded that their party reaffirm its commitment to protecting slavery in the South and permitting its extension. Democrats in the Midwest wished to return to the original popular sovereignty position. But the most brazen spokesmen in the cotton South stepped forward to demand slave codes in the territories, reintroduction of the international slave trade, and meetings to discuss secession from the Union. These "fire-eaters" put fellow party members on notice that not only the defense of slavery where it existed, but its future extension, were nonnegotiable.

The Lincoln-Douglas Debates In their hours-long debates before huge crowds of Illinois voters, Abraham Lincoln and Stephen Douglas took the opportunity to expound not only on state issues but also on the extent of federal authority, definitions of national character, and the blight of slavery. Such open-air speeches, often exercises in eloquent oratory, were crucial vehicles of political opinion-making during the early nineteenth century. *(Corbis-Bettmann.)*

Only a small number of southerners were fire-eaters, and only a small number of northerners were ardent abolitionists. But at certain important moments, each extreme influenced public sentiments beyond the weight of its numbers. John Brown was a violent abolitionist whose actions sent the nation reeling closer to the precipice of national civil war in 1859.

The Election of 1860

By 1859, Republicans were well positioned to win the presidency. William H. Seward of New York, a highly visible senator, wished to be nominated. For years he had been identified as an antislavery spokesman, and some months previously he had warned that an "irrepressible conflict" was building between North and South. But he was not popular among nativists in the North, or among moderate Republicans. The majority of party leaders looked around and found in Abraham Lincoln a more moderate candidate who could surely carry the midwestern states.

The Republican Party had numerous issues inclining in its favor. The Panic of 1857 and ensuing depression gave the party an opportunity to appear the "saving force of the Union's downcast" by promoting free land in the West and protection for ailing craft production. Republicans thus promised a homestead act and a transcontinental railroad. Republicans, by their pledges to raise tariffs, also gained the support of manufacturers. And throughout the Union, voters could choose Lincoln as an opponent of slavery in the territories, but equally an opponent of racial equality.

The election also proved that the Democrats were near break-up. The party held its nominating convention in Charleston, South Carolina, the heart of the "solid south." For days of rancorous discussion, delegates could not decide on a candidate. Stephen A. Douglas could not please enough delegates of both sections to win the necessary two-thirds support for nomination. On the one hand, his long-standing commitment to popular sovereignty made it impossible to accept the southern demand for a slave code that would guarantee slavery's protection in the territories. On the other hand, northerners insisted that support for popular sovereignty was essential for the party candidate's campaign. Deadlocked, the convention adjourned.

When delegates met a second time, in Baltimore, it became clear that the Democratic Party was irrevocably split. Southerners bolted and held their own convention, at which they nominated John C. Breckinridge of Kentucky, a staunch supporter of slavery's extension into the territories. Northern Democrats went ahead and nominated Douglas. Then, with the party split and running two candidates, southern Whigs and Border State nativists formed a third party, the Constitutional Union Party. John Bell of Tennessee represented them at the polls.

A split Democratic Party and a dissenting third party reinforced the near certainty of a Republican Party victory. Breckinridge carried only southern states, and Bell snared some support that might have fallen to Breckinridge and Douglas. Douglas knew he had only a slim chance of winning. In fact, although his popular vote was considerable, he received only twelve electoral votes. Still, he stumped to "save the Union" and traveled through both northern and southern states tirelessly warning against dissolution of the nation.

"Honest Abe," whose name did not even appear on ballots below the southern boundaries of Virginia, Kentucky, and Missouri, ran a race primarily against Douglas in the North. Lincoln and his Republican campaigners buoyed northern optimism for union and "victory against the slave interest." Mass meetings, parades, and nightly speeches absorbed the public in a frenzy of political activity. Meanwhile, the race in deep southern states was primarily between Bell and Breckinridge.

Voter turnout in 1860 was tremendous: a higher percentage of people voted than in any other election to that time and turnout has been topped in American history only once since then, in 1876. But the election was thoroughly sectional in its results. Breckinridge lost southern votes because of Bell's campaign, but Lincoln carried all eighteen of the northern free states (except for a split vote in New Jersey) despite Douglas's energetic stumping. Lincoln's electoral vote overwhelmed the other three candidates combined, and he took 54 percent of the northern states' popular vote. Yet ten southern states did not even put Lincoln's name on their ballots, underscoring even more dramatically the sectional nature of the election.

Disunion

After John Brown's raid, vigilance committees in the interior areas of some southern states kept a watchful eye open for slave revolts. Southerners' fears of growing abolitionist sentiment, and anger about ineffective enforcement of the Fugitive Slave Law, also grew during 1859. Even during the 1860 campaign, some state leaders in the South began to talk of secession. When election results came in, talk turned to shock, and then to horror that the South might forever be overwhelmed

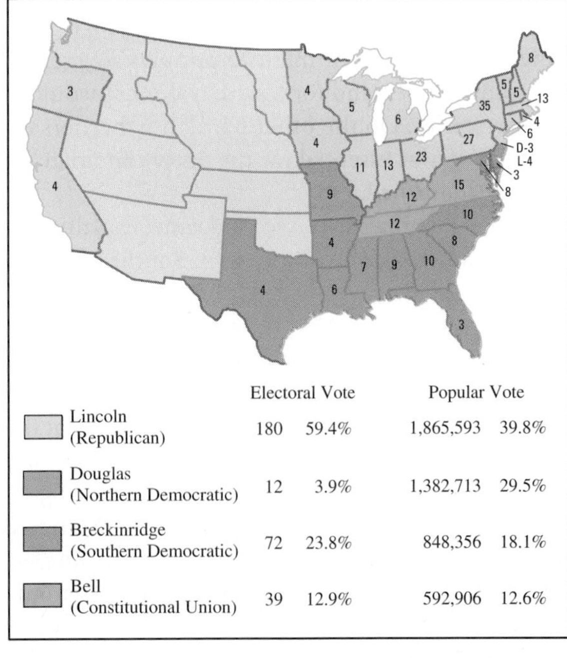

Electoral Vote
Popular Vote
Lincoln (Republican) 180 59.4% 1,865,593 39.8%
Douglas (Northern Democratic) 12 3.9% 1,382,713 29.5%
Breckinridge (Southern Democratic) 72 23.8% 848,356 18.1%
Bell (Constitutional Union) 39 12.9% 592,906 12.6%

The Election of 1860
The division of the existing states proved a deep sectional division in American politics. Lincoln won no electoral votes in the South, Breckenridge won none in the North. States such as California, Illinois, and Pennsylvania shifted to Republican Party support between 1856 and 1860. What this electoral vote map cannot show, however, is the great number of northern Democrats who still opposed Lincoln.

by "free-state enthusiasts." Outspoken planters feared the imminent end of life as they had known it, and Lincoln's election "by and for the north" gave them the opportunity to take some decisive action.

Vigilance committees began to form armed militia units in the Upper South. Alabama, Mississippi, and South Carolina issued calls for special state conventions to discuss their next steps, including secession from the Union. Dissenters who hoped for reconciliation with the North were silenced by proslavery voices, as well as by the rush of events between Lincoln's election and December 20, 1860. On that date, South Carolina seceded from the Union. Buchanan did nothing. Over the next weeks, six more states—Mississippi, Florida, Georgia, Alabama, Louisiana, and Texas—also seceded, with near-unanimous votes in their respective special conventions. Still the president watched and waited.

In South Carolina marching bands and fireworks brought on the dissolution of the Union with grand public excitement. In other seceding states, fanfare also marked declarations of leaving the nation, with little regard for the other eight southern states that had not made any decisions yet. Indeed, southern secessionists believed that their declarations were drastic measures, but ones that would "bring the northern states to their senses" and let "our slavery solution follow its own course." Buchanan's inaction seemed to indicate northern acceptance of the South's peaceful departure from the Union. In fact, this was hardly the case.

Between the fall, when Lincoln was elected, and March, when he took office, proposals for compromise flew about Washington. Most of them involved some concessions to southern interests. But Lincoln refused them all, reaffirming his commitment to no slavery in the territories, and thus alienating potential support for compromise from Border States and southern moderates. Lincoln hoped to prevent the remaining eight southern states from seceding and to promote solutions from within the South itself. For a while this strategy seemed to be working.

But on another matter—whether to let the seceding states remain outside the Union—Lincoln was unyielding. As he put it, no "minority have the right to break up the government whenever they choose." Democracy, he insisted, "would not endure on such a principle." In addition, he could not allow seceded southern states to take over federal military forts and federal customshouses. But should he force seceded states back into the Union with federal troops? Lincoln hesitated, trying to avoid military confrontation.

In February 1861, before Lincoln took the oath of office, the seven seceded states created the Confederate States of America in Montgomery, Alabama. They chose Jefferson Davis as president, and Alexander Stephens of Georgia as vice president. Both men were moderates, not fire-eaters, which offered hope that seceded states might win support from undecided states and convince wavering citizens that secession was peaceful, moral, and legal. After all, argued Davis, if consent of the government is a central principle of American government, and southerners freely consented to leave the Union, then there was no cause for alarm or force to change that decision. The American Revolution itself had been based on the right of the governed to modify their systems of rule when they became outmoded or unjust. But when Confederates also adopted the United States Constitution for their new government, they incorporated two crucial changes: the principles of states' rights rather than federalism, and unambiguous support for slavery's continuation. The Confederacy, then, established the inseparable privilege of white over black, and states over federal authority.

What would Lincoln do once inaugurated? The entire North waited with bated breath to find out. On his ride from Springfield, Illinois, to the White House, Lincoln was careful not to provoke southern sensitivities. Nor did he assuage northern anxieties. His public began to demand some kind of response to the progress of southern events. At his inauguration, March 4, 1861, Lincoln reminded Americans that despite recent events and sectional divisions, they were still one nation of people. "Though passion may have strained, it must not break our bonds of affection. The mystic chords of memory, stretching from every battlefield, and patriot grave, to every living heart and hearthstone, all over this broad land, will yet swell the chorus of the Union, when again touched, as surely they will be, by the better angels of our nature." The crowd murmured, wondering when these "better angels" might appear.

CONCLUSION

After the Mexican-American War, northerners and southerners focused their attention on sectional differences and tied their destinies closely to territorial expansion. In efforts to calm sectional tensions, Congress renegotiated the Missouri Compromise line and framed a Compromise of 1850. Already, shifting interests were reconstituting the political party system. But the violence of the 1850s dashed most hopes that compromises would hold the political party system together.

A number of crises hastened the slide toward the Civil War. The Fugitive Slave Act presented northern antislavery reformers with a direct challenge to their beliefs. "Bleeding Kansas" seemed to prove that popular sovereignty could not peacefully organize the territories. The *Dred Scott* decision drove a deeper wedge between constituencies of the Democratic Party and aligned the Supreme Court with proslavery forces. When President Buchanan offered support for Kansas's Lecompton Constitution, Democrats and Whigs from the North and Midwest flocked to the Republican Party. Southern proslavery voices more stridently defended the "peculiar institution." John Brown's seizure of the Harpers Ferry arsenal was just another step in the escalating tensions.

A number of political and intellectual leaders recalled that in 1858 Senator William H. Seward had called these tensions an "irrepressible conflict." Lincoln's election did nothing to prevent secession of many southern states, and in the months that followed, Lincoln himself could not staunch the flow of blood that soon would flow.

SUGGESTED READINGS

For detailed studies of sectional tensions during the 1850s and the efforts to resolve political differences, start with Michael Holt, *Political Parties and American Political Development from the Age of Jackson to the Age of Lincoln* (1992); Richard H. Abbott, *Cotton and Capital: Boston Businessmen and Antislavery Reform, 1854–1868* (1991); Eric Foner, *Politics and Ideol-*

ogy in the Age of the Civil War (1980) and *Free Soil, Free Labor, Free Men: The Ideology of the Republican Party Before the Civil War* (1970); William E. Gienapp, *The Origins of the Republican Party, 1852–1856* (1987); William Freehling, *The Road to Disunion* (1990); and the older, but very readable, Holman Hamilton, *Prologue to Conflict: The Crisis and Compromise of 1850* (1964). David M. Potter, *The Impending Crisis, 1848–1861* (1976), is the most detailed account of the slide into Civil War, especially the political events. For a more specialized account of politics in the South, see Mark Stegmaier, *Texas, New Mexico, and the Compromise of 1850* (1996).

The reflections of literary circles, both northern and southern, are covered well in Thomas Gossett, *Uncle Tom's Cabin and American Culture* (1985). For the southern attitudes about development and economic competition with the North, see Vicki V. Johnson, *The Men and the Vision of the Southern Commercial Conventions, 1845–1871* (1992), but also see Thomas H. O'Connor, *Lords of the Loom: The Cotton Whigs and the Coming of the Civil War* (1968). The best study of women's roles in the 1850s across the nation is Wendy Hamand Venet, *Neither Ballots nor Bullets: Women Abolitionists and the Civil War* (1991).

Studies that tie the problems of development, slavery, and Native Americans together often focus on the trans-Mississippi West. Among the most helpful are Robert Dykstra, *Bright Radical Start: Black Freedom and White Supremacy on the Hawkeye Frontier* (1993); Joseph Herring, *The Enduring Indians of Kansas: A Century and a Half of Acculturation* (1990); and James A. Rawley, *Race and Politics: "Bleeding Kansas" and the Coming of the Civil War* (1969). Studies that focus on the politics and economics of railroads include Albert Fishlow's *American Railroads and the Transformation of the Ante-Bellum Economy* (1965) and John F. Stover's *The Life and Decline of the American Railroad* (1970) and *Iron Road to the West: American Railroads in the 1850s* (1978). The fine study by James Huston, *The Panic of 1857 and the Coming of the Civil War* (1987), analyzes the economy of the 1850s.

The best overview of the final moments before southern secession is Kenneth Stampp, *American in 1857: A Nation on the Brink* (1990). The increasing extremism of sectional and national politics during the 1850s is covered admirably in Tyler Anbinder, *Nativism and Slavery: The Northern Know Nothings and the Politics of the 1850s* (1991); Stanley Campbell, *The Slave Catchers: Enforcement of the Fugitive Slave Law, 1850–1860* (1970); Thomas P. Slaughter, *Bloody Dawn: The Cristiana Riot and Racial Violence in the Antebellum North* (1991); and Don Fehrenbacher, *The Dred Scott Case: Its Significance in American Law and Politics* (1978). The best collection of scholarly views about the complicated character of John Brown is Paul Finkelman, ed., *His Soul Goes Marching On: Responses to John Brown and the Harpers Ferry Raid* (1995), but see the distinctive view of Stephen B. Oates, *To Purge This Land with Blood: A Biography of John Brown* (1970), as well.

For the Republican Party's rise and growing importance, two works by Don Fehrenbacher—*Prelude to Greatness: Lincoln in the 1850s* (1962) and *The South and Three Sectional Crises* (1980)—are good starting points. See also the 1857 debates covered in Robert Johannsen, *Stephen A. Douglas* (1973) and *The Lincoln-Douglas Debates* (1965). For the Republican Party's national rise and Lincoln's place in the secessionist crisis, see William L. Barney, *The Road to Secession* (1972); Steven A. Channing, *Crisis of Fear: Secession in South Carolina* (1970); and David Herbert Donald, *Lincoln* (1995). Older, but readable and highly informative, is Kenneth Stampp, *And the War Came: The North and the Secession Crisis, 1860–1861* (1960).

Competing Voices

The Lincoln-Douglas Debates

Lincoln Clarifies His Position on the Equality of the Races

Abraham Lincoln, an Illinois lawyer who had served in his state Congress during the 1840s, wished to take a seat in the national Senate in 1858. Boldly, "Honest Abe" challenged his opponent, Stephen A. Douglas of the Democratic Party, to a series of seven debates on current affairs. The first soundoff was on Saturday, August 21, 1858, in Ottawa, Illinois, where nearly twelve thousand people participated in hours-long open-air exchanges. In this excerpt, Lincoln takes up the charge from Douglas that he and his fellow Republicans believed in the perfect natural equality of African-Americans with whites.

My Fellow Citizens: When a man hears himself somewhat misrepresented, it provokes him—at least, I find it so with myself. But when the misrepresentation becomes very gross and palpable, it is more apt to amuse him. (laughter)

. . . Anything that argues me into his [Douglas's] idea of perfect social and political equality with the Negro is but a specious and fantastic arrangement of words, by which a man can prove a horse chestnut to be a chestnut horse. (laughter)

I will say here, while upon this subject, that I have no purpose directly or indirectly to interfere with the institution of slavery in the states where it exists. I believe I have no lawful right to do so, and I have no inclination to do so. I have no purpose to introduce political and social equality between the white and the black races. There is a physical difference between the two, which in my judgment will probably forever forbid their living together upon the footing of perfect equality, and inasmuch as it becomes a necessity that there must be a difference, I, as well as Judge Douglas, am in favor of the race to which I belong having the superior position.

I have never said anything to the contrary, but I hold that, notwithstanding all this, there is no reason in the world why the Negro is not entitled to all the natural rights enumerated in the declaration of Independence, the right to life, liberty, and the pursuit of happiness. (loud cheers) I hold that he is as much entitled to these as the white man. I agree with Judge Douglas he is not my equal in many respects—certainly not in color, perhaps not in moral or intellectual endowment. But in the right to eat the bread, without leave of anybody else, which his own hand earns, *he is my equal and the equal of Judge Douglas, and the equal of every living man.* (great applause)

Douglas Advocates for Popular Sovereignty

Douglas, the incumbent Democratic Party senator from Illinois in 1858, sidestepped the matter of slavery's morality and focused on the more practical political view that no federal court or distant national government should have the final word on the existence of slavery in the territories. In the following passage, Douglas enunciates this reasoning in what has become known as the Freeport Doctrine.

First, he [Lincoln] desires to know if the people of Kansas shall form a constitution by means entirely proper and unobjectionable and ask admission into the Union as a state, before they have the requisite population for a member of Congress, whether I will vote for that admission. . . . I hold it to be a sound rule of universal application to require a territory to contain the requisite population for a member of Congress, before it is admitted as a state into the Union. . . .

The next question propounded to me by Mr. Lincoln is, can the people of a territory in any lawful way against the wishes of any citizen of the United States[,] exclude slavery from their limits prior to the formation of a state constitution? I answer emphatically, as Mr. Lincoln has heard me answer a hundred times from every stump in Illinois, that in my opinion the people of a territory can, by lawful means, exclude slavery from their limits prior to the formation of a state constitution. . . . It matters not what way the Supreme Court may hereafter decide as to the abstract question whether slavery may or may not go into a territory under the Constitution, the people have the lawful means to introduce it or exclude it as they please, for the reason that slavery cannot exist a day or an hour anywhere, unless it is supported by local police regulations. . . . Those police regulations can only be established by the local legislature, and if the people are opposed to slavery they will elect representatives to that body who will by unfriendly legislation effectually prevent the introduction of it into their midst. . . . [T]he right of the people to make a slave territory or a free territory is perfect and complete under the Nebraska Bill. . . .

The third question which Mr. Lincoln presented is, if the Supreme Court of the United States shall decide that a state of this Union cannot exclude slavery from its own limits will I submit to it? I am amazed that Lincoln should ask such a question. . . . He knows that there never was but one man in America [Roger B. Taney, the chief justice], claiming any degree of intelligence or decency, who even for a moment pretended such a thing. . . .

The Black Republican creed lays it down expressly, that under no circumstances shall we acquire any more territory unless slavery is first prohibited in the country. I ask Mr. Lincoln whether he is in favor of that proposition. Are you opposed to the acquisition of any more territory, under any circumstances, unless slavery is prohibited in it? That he does not like to answer. When I ask him whether he stands up to that article in the platform of his party, he turns, Yankee-fashion, and without answering it, asks me whether I am in favor of acquiring territory without regard to how it may affect the Union on the slavery question. . . . I answer that whenever it becomes necessary, in our growth and progress to acquire more territory, that I am in favor of it, without reference to the question of slavery, and when we have acquired it, I will leave the people free to do as they please, either to make it slave or free territory, as they prefer. . . .

Political life during the 1850s was still more local than national in scope, but in the cases of Lincoln and Douglas, the spectacle of their seven debates underscored and furthered their eminent reputations. Douglas had played a prominent role in formulating the Compromise of 1850 and the Kansas-Nebraska Act. Moreover, voters in the Midwest and Northeast identified Douglas as a founding spokesman for popular sovereignty, as well as a foremost advocate of a northern route for a transcontinental railroad. In each role, Douglas seemed to be a moderate politician in a decade of extremes and violence. In light of the *Dred Scott* decision in 1857, in which the Supreme Court made sweeping pronouncements about the nature of the territories and the status of slaves, it became harder to promote the idea that citizens in a given territory might decide for themselves whether to become a slave or free state. But Douglas tried to do just that in his Freeport, Illinois, speech. When he ran for reelection to state office in 1858, he won easily against the newcomer, Abraham Lincoln. For all of these reasons, Douglas also was favored to win the 1860 presidential election.

However, Lincoln's political star was rising. His high-pitched voice held the Ottawa, Illinois, audience in thrall for hours during the first debate with Douglas. At the end of the day, thousands of Republican Party supporters at the debate bore him off in triumph from the platform. In less than two years, Lincoln would accept the Republican Party's nomination for the presidential campaign of 1860. Also known for his moderation, Lincoln never joined the antislavery Liberty or Free-Soil parties, remaining in the Whig Party until it was no longer a viable organization. Although Lincoln believed African-Americans had certain economic rights—to satisfy basic needs and to strive in their labor as whites did—he never wished or assumed that in the free states African-Americans would be socially and culturally the equals of whites. Still, Lincoln's firm moral opposition to slavery in the debates of 1858 made Douglas appear to be a greater defender of slavery than he in fact was. Thus, two prominent men who occupied places toward the center of the intellectual and political spectrum in America in 1858, rather than at either extreme, could articulate deep and consequential differences.

Questions for Analysis

1. What passages demonstrate that Abraham Lincoln was a moderate Republican in 1858?
2. What did Lincoln say that might have angered northern abolitionists? What statements would have been offensive to southerners?
3. Summarize what popular sovereignty means, and compare it with the conditions established by the *Dred Scott* decision.
4. What differences between those two doctrines does Douglas emphasize? How do you think Lincoln would have responded to Douglas?
5. What parts of each speaker's arguments express his core beliefs and party positions, and what parts are just rhetorical flourishes?
6. In an era before radio and television, and in a part of the country not yet saturated by newspapers and telegraph, what do you think was the role of such speeches in molding public opinion? in shaping the views that defined the sections of the country?

15

Transforming the Experiment: The Civil War, 1861–1865

Because of the epic proportions of the Battle of Gettysburg it seemed only fitting that the dead should be honored with a proper ceremony. Officials set aside seventeen acres and announced a date—November 19, 1863. Organizers invited the noted orator Edward Everett to dedicate the new graveyard. As an afterthought, they sent an invitation to President Abraham Lincoln to deliver a "few appropriate remarks." The casual invitation was not meant as an insult: burying war dead was a state responsibility, and no one expected the head of the federal government to play a significant role. Lincoln accepted the invitation, hoping to use the opportunity to mend political fences in Pennsylvania and to redefine the purpose of the war.

It rained in the early morning of the nineteenth, but the sky soon cleared and the sun shone brilliantly on the rolling countryside. Over fifteen thousand people had flooded the small college town bordering the battlefield, most of them relatives of slain soldiers, "who had come from distant parts to look at and weep over the remains of their fallen kindred," a reporter said. Flags flew at half-mast. At ten o'clock, a procession led by Lincoln on horseback crawled to the top of Cemetery Hill, which had anchored the northern end of the Union line. The president, wearing his customary black suit and stovepipe hat, took his seat on the temporary wooden speakers' platform.

From his vantage point on the top of Cemetery Hill, Lincoln had a clear view of the battlefield that had claimed 51,000 casualties in a bloody three-day orgy of violence. Looking to the South, Lincoln could see long rows of coffins waiting for burial—a visual reminder of the cost of civil war—as he sat patiently through Everett's two-hour oration. Near the end of the speech, the president took his manuscript from his coat pocket and put on his steel-rimmed glasses. When Everett sat down, Lincoln stepped to the front of the platform and recited in "a sharp, unmusical treble voice" his hymn to the dead.

"Four score and seven years ago our fathers brought forth on this continent, a new nation, conceived in Liberty, and dedicated to the proposition that all men are created equal." The Civil War, he argued, tested "whether that nation, or any nation so conceived and so dedicated, can long endure." Lincoln called on those gathered to devote themselves to "the unfinished work which they who fought here have thus far so nobly advanced." That work, was nothing short of the preservation of the nation: "That this nation, under God, shall have a new birth of freedom—and that government of the people, by the people, for the people, shall not perish from the earth."

Lincoln's Gettysburg Address took three minutes to deliver, and consisted of only 272 words, but it articulated what the war had come to mean. From the beginning of the Civil War, both North and South fought more over ideas and rights than over land. The Confederates emphasized the founders' commitment to individualism and states' rights. Lincoln at Gettysburg offered a much different view that recognized the power of the national government to define and enforce liberty and that made equality—the "proposition that all men are created equal"—the central concept of American political culture. The conflict was between two societies that had carried the American experiment in different directions. The Gettysburg Address made poignantly clear that the military battles between the Blue and the Grey would also represent a clash between two different ideas of what it meant to be an American.

- How did the Northern and Southern war strategies reflect each society's view of its strength and resources?
- How did culture and institutions influence how each side mobilized for battle?
- What impact did the war have on both societies?
- How did emancipation transform the war?

This chapter will address these questions.

The War Begins, 1861

"War is not merely an act of policy," noted the famous nineteenth-century Prussian military strategist Carl von Clausewitz, "but a true political instrument, a continuation of political intercourse, carried on with other means." Unable to resolve their differences by political compromise, North and South turned to war to achieve their objectives. While battling for control of neutral Border States, Union and Confederate leaders took stock of their assets and liabilities and developed a military strategy

Chronology

1860	Lincoln elected president
	Secession begins
1861	Fort Sumter attacked
	Lincoln institutes martial law in the Border States
	First Battle of Bull Run
	Trent Affair
1862	Peninsular Campaign
	Battle of Shiloh
	Union navy seizes Memphis and New Orleans
	Battle of Antietam
	Battle of Fredricksburg
	Confederate conscription act
	Homestead Act
	Morrill Land Grant Act
1863	Emancipation Proclamation
	Union army enrolls black enlistees
	Federal conscription act
	New York City draft riot
	Battle of Chancellorsville
	Battle of Gettysburg
	Vicksburg falls
1864	Grant made commander of all Union forces
	Grant's Wilderness Campaign
	Lincoln reelected President
	Grant lays siege to Petersburg
	Sherman takes Atlanta and begins his march to the sea
1865	Confederacy enlists black troops
	Petersburg and Richmond fall
	Lee and Johnston surrender

designed to achieve victory. Passions ran high on both sides as North and South defined the purpose of the war.

The Search for Compromise

When Lincoln won election in November 1860, there were thirty-three states in the Union. By the time he took the oath of office in March 1861, only twenty-seven remained. Many secessionists, especially large slave owners, viewed Lincoln and the Republicans as revolutionaries determined to destroy the slaveholding system. Lincoln's election, declared a Southern newspaper, "shows that the North [intends] to free the negroes and force amalgamation between them and the children of the poor men of the South." In fact, Lincoln's approach to the slavery issue was far from revolutionary, and he struggled to reassure the South that he wished only to prevent slavery's spread, not to abolish it. "Do the people of the South really entertain fears that a Republican administration would, directly or indirectly, interfere with their slaves, or with them, about their slaves?" Lincoln asked shortly after his election. "If they do, I wish to assure you . . . that there is no cause for such fears." But even attempts to limit slavery's expansion badly frightened Southern slaveholders, who believed that their peculiar institution needed to grow in order to survive.

While Southern leaders struggled to set up a new government, many moderates in the North searched for compromise. The tired and discredited President Buchanan was in no position to offer decisive leadership, so any resolution of the secession crisis would have to come out of Congress. No compromise could arrest secession unless the Republicans strongly favored it, and initially they showed little interest. But Republican businessmen with close economic ties to the South soon joined Northern Democrats in pressuring congressional Republicans to offer a compromise.

Many moderates rallied around a proposal offered by Kentucky Senator John J. Crittenden. The Crittenden Compromise suggested that Congress extend the Missouri Compromise line of 36°30′ to California as the dividing line between slavery and free soil, forbid federal interference with the internal slave trade, and provide compensation for any slaveholder prevented from recovering escaped slaves in the North.

Abolitionists and free blacks in the North opposed the compromise efforts. Said Frederick Douglass, "If the Union can only be maintained by new concessions to the slaveholders, if it can only be stuck together and held together by a new drain on the negro's blood, then . . . let the Union perish." Lincoln and other party leaders feared that accepting the compromise would doom the Republican Party, which had made opposition to the spread of slavery its core message. Lincoln made it clear that the party had to stand firm. "Entertain no proposition for a compromise in regard to the extension of slavery," he instructed key congressmen. Taking their cue from Lincoln, Republicans in Congress thwarted the Crittenden measures. Compromise was no longer possible.

The Attack on Fort Sumter

In March 1861, an assassination threat forced Lincoln to abandon his plans for a triumphant march into Washington to take the oath of office. Instead, the president, accompanied only by a railroad detective and a close friend, slipped into Washington anonymously on a night train—"like a thief in the night," he said. In a carefully worded inaugural address, delivered on March 4 from the steps of the unfinished Capitol building, the new president was both firm and conciliatory. He promised not to interfere with slavery where it already existed but also denied that any state had the right to secede from the Union and promised to "hold, occupy, and possess" all federal installations in the South. He concluded on a note of reconciliation, reminding white Southerners of the common heritage they shared as Americans. "The mystic chords of memory, stretching from every battlefield, and patriot grave, to every living heart and hearthstone, all over this broad land, will yet swell the chorus of the Union, when again touched, as surely they will be, by the better angels of our nature." The South, however, was in no mood for reconciliation, and profound ideological differences rendered moot Lincoln's eloquent appeal for union.

On setting up their own state governments, the secessionists had seized federal property and installations throughout the Lower South. One of the few still under federal control was a modest garrison of eighty-three men at Fort Sumter in Charleston Harbor, South Carolina. Fort Sumter, under the command of Major Robert Anderson, was no serious military threat to the Confederacy, but Confederate leaders viewed its presence in Charleston, the heart of the secession movement, as an insult to Southern pride. President Jefferson Davis, heeding the calls of his more militant advisers, demanded that the Union withdraw Anderson and his men.

The Confederacy's tough line forced a confrontation with Lincoln. Though he still hoped to avoid war, Lincoln concluded that withdrawal from Fort Sumter would feed Confederate hopes and demoralize the North. On April 6, he decided to send food and other essential nonmilitary supplies to the Fort. Lincoln did not want the North to fire the first shot in the war with the South. His decision forced Davis to choose between war and peace.

Word of Lincoln's decision reached Montgomery on April 8. The next day, the Confederate Congress instructed General P. G. T. Beauregard, the Confederate commander at Charleston, to demand an immediate surrender of Fort Sumter. On April 12, Beauregard, supported by 6,000 eager South Carolina militiamen, sent an ultimatum to Anderson: surrender by 4 A.M. or face attack. Anderson, a career soldier and former slave owner whose devotion to the Union was unshakable, refused to surrender. Confederate artillery shells opened fire on Fort Sumter at 4:30 A.M. For thirty-two hours, Anderson maintained the unequal contest. Then, on the afternoon of Saturday, April 13, with the fort in flames, he surrendered. As he was escorted away, Anderson carried with him the tattered American flag that had flown so proudly over the fort.

The American Civil War had begun. The news of Fort Sumter electrified both the North and the South. Writer Ralph Waldo Emerson noted that "the attack on Fort Sumter crystallized the North into a unit, and the hope of mankind was saved." On the other side, Mary Chesnut, the wife of a former South Carolina senator, observed, "The war spirit is waking us all up." On April 15, Lincoln called on the states

Fort Sumter A Confederate flag waves over the first battleground of the Civil War on April 14, 1861. The Confederate forces under General Beauregard bombarded the fort for two days before Major Robert Anderson surrendered. *(National Archives.)*

for 75,000 militiamen to quell the "insurrection." On May 6, the Confederate Congress countered by formally declaring that a state of war existed.

The Battle for the Border States

The first battles of the Civil War were over control of the Border States. Eight of the fifteen slave states did not send delegates to the Montgomery Convention and hoped to remain neutral in the conflict. Following Fort Sumter, neutrality was no longer possible.

The Union cause had little support in those states that shared close cultural and economic ties to the South. "The militia of Virginia will not be furnished to the powers at Washington," the governor wrote Lincoln. "Your object is to subjugate the Southern States. . . . You have chosen to inaugurate civil war."

When Virginia left the Union, its largest city, Richmond, became the new capital of the Confederacy. The rest of the Upper South quickly followed Virginia out of the Union. Arkansas left on May 6. On May 20, the North Carolina convention, under pressure from pro-Confederate newspapers to withdraw from the "vile, rotten, infidelic, puritanic, negro-worshipping, negro-stealing, negro-equality . . . Yankee-Union," unanimously adopted a secession ordinance. Tennessee seceded on June 8.

The support of the Upper South states was crucial if the South was going to have any chance of winning the war. These states almost doubled the population of the Confederacy, giving it eleven states to stand against the Union's twenty-three. Just as important, they provided the South with natural resources and skilled artisans that it needed to create weapons and feed and clothe an army. Most important of all was the Tredegar Iron Works in Richmond, which provided the Confederacy with its only factory capable of producing heavy ordnance. Virginia put one frontier of the new nation within shouting distance of the Union's capital at Washington. Arkansas and Tennessee extended Confederate control of the vital Mississippi River corridor.

At the same time, the Confederacy struggled to win over the so-called Border States—Delaware, Missouri, Kentucky, and Maryland—whose secession would seriously weaken the Union's military position. While Delaware remained solidly in Union control, the other three states would have increased the South's military manpower by 45 percent and its manufacturing capability by 80 percent. If Maryland seceded, for example, the capital at Washington would have been surrounded by enemy territory. Confederate control of Kentucky would imperil river transportation along the Ohio, which was vital to the Northern economy. The secession of Missouri would further extend Southern control of the Mississippi.

Securing control over Maryland was Lincoln's most pressing strategic goal in late April. Although slavery was of declining importance in Maryland, and Unionist sentiment predominated, Southern sympathizers maintained some strength in Baltimore and along the Eastern Shore. On April 19, a prosecession mob in Baltimore attacked the Sixth Massachusetts Regiment passing through on its way to Washington. Rebel supporters destroyed railroad bridges and telegraph lines north of Baltimore. Since all rail traffic into Washington had to pass through Baltimore, Washington was cut off from communication with the free states.

By the time the Maryland legislature met on April 29 to consider secession, Lincoln was prepared to use whatever means necessary to guarantee a Union victory. He ordered Winfield Scott, the general-in-chief of the Union army, "to adopt the most prompt and efficient means to counteract [secession], even, if necessary, to the bombardment of their cities." Lincoln, instituted martial law in the state, sent federal troops to occupy Baltimore, and suspended the writ of *habeas corpus*, allowing the military to imprison pro-Confederates without formal charges by a grand jury. Union soldiers arrested numerous pro-Southern citizens in Maryland, including the mayor and police chief of Baltimore and thirty-one members of the state legislature, and threw them in prison for months without trial, and in a few cases for more than a year. The intimidation tactics worked. The legislature rejected secession by a vote of 53–13, ending the threat of secession in Maryland.

Lincoln invested an enormous amount of time trying to maintain the neutrality of his home state of Kentucky. While reassuring residents that he "intended to make no attack, direct or indirect, upon the institution or property of any State," Lincoln worked closely with Unionist forces to frustrate Confederate plans to capture the state. Lincoln was not as adroit in his handling of Missouri, where Union rebels—called Jayhawkers—fought a bloody guerrilla war against Confederate agitators—called Bushwhackers. Over the next three years, warfare devastated the countryside and pitted neighbor against neighbor. "The prairies are ablaze," a Kansas paper reported. "There is nothing talked about here except war." In the end, Missouri stayed in the Union.

Divisions in Virginia led to the creation of a new pro-Union border state. Appalachian Virginia, the one-third of the state west of the Allegheny Mountains, and populated overwhelmingly by nonslaveholders and small farmers, was anti-Confederate from the very beginning. After a series of complex, irregular, and probably illegal maneuvers, West Virginia declared its independence and was admitted into the Union in June 1863.

Farther to the west, the Confederate government sent agents to enlist the support of the so-called Five Civilized Tribes (see page 497), which had settled in Indian Country (later to become the state of Oklahoma). The Choctaw and Chickasaw embraced the Confederate cause, but the other tribes split. Many Indian leaders favored neutrality, fearing that the war would aggravate internal tensions and shatter the delicate peace among the tribes. "I am—the Cherokees are—your friends," Principal Chief John Ross told the Confederate representatives, "but we do not wish to be brought into the feuds between yourselves and your northern brethren. Our wish is for peace." But peace and neutrality were no longer possible, and eventually most tribes sided with the Confederacy. Over the next few years, they fought against Union troops in the western theater and against the handful of pro-Union tribes in a bitter internal civil war.

The Balance of Power

Even with alignment of the Border States unsettled, both sides went into the Civil War with considerable advantages and liabilities. The North's chief asset was its enormous size and its thriving industrial economy. There were nearly 21 million people in the North, just 9 million in the Confederacy, 3.5 million of whom were slaves. The North had more than twice as many miles of railroad track as the South. Most of the nation's heavy industry was concentrated in the North. In 1860 Union states produced 97 percent of the nation's firearms, 94 percent of its cloth, and 90 percent of its boots and shoes. One state, New York, produced four times as many manufactured goods as the entire South. The North in 1860 built fourteen out of every fifteen railroad locomotives manufactured in the United States. The Union navy floated ninety ships; the Confederacy had to build a navy from scratch.

Its superior resources and powerful navy shaped the North's military strategy. Five days after the surrender of Fort Sumter, Lincoln announced a blockade of all Confederate ports. "Whereas an insurrection against the Government of the United States has broken out in the States of South Carolina, Georgia, Alabama, Florida, Mississippi, Louisiana, and Texas," he declared, it was "advisable to set on foot a blockade." Lincoln and his generals believed they could achieve victory by squeezing the Confederacy, applying a naval blockade of Southern ports and seizing control of the Mississippi River. The Union reasoned that frustrated Confederates, cut off from essential trade, would gradually lose their will to fight. This so-called Anaconda Plan, named after a giant snake that wraps around and suffocates its prey, assumed a bloodless triumph for the North.

The Rebel states were not intimidated by the Union's advantages in human resources and industrial might. Confederate leaders had the psychological advantage that their people were fighting to preserve their own territory. "Lincoln may bring his 75,000 troops against us," said Vice President Alexander Stephens. "We fight for our homes, our fathers and mothers, our wives, brothers, sisters, sons and daughters!" For decades, Southerners had dominated the nation's military academies and officers' corps, and Confederates could count on experienced military men defecting from the North to lead their army. Also, although the South had only 40 percent as many people as the North, the availability of slaves freed a much larger proportion of whites for military service.

With the obvious example of the American Revolution in mind, Southerners believed that a determined nation could successfully win or maintain its independence against invaders with larger armies and more material resources. George W. Randolph, the Confederate secretary of war in the fall of 1861, confidently stated, "There is no instance in history of a people as numerous as we are inhabiting a country so extensive as ours being subjected if true to themselves." Like George Washington's forces during the American Revolution, Southerners could lose most of the battles and still win the war, but only if they could convince their opponent that victory was too costly. Union armies had to penetrate deep into enemy territory, gain control of it, and eventually break the Confederate will to resist the reestablishment of federal power. This offensive strategy required larger numbers of troops than the defensive operation employed by the Confederacy.

Finally, while drawing parallels between themselves and the American revolutionaries, the Confederates looked for support from an unlikely ally: Great Britain. The Confederacy hoped that Britain, which imported 80 percent of its cotton supply from the South in the 1850s, would rush to its defense once the flow of cotton was cut off by the combined effects of the Union blockade and a voluntary embargo in the South on cotton exports. The North, on the other hand, anticipated that a powerful antislavery sentiment in Britain and France would compel their leaders to oppose the slaveholding South.

Despite their differences, both sides called upon a common history and a shared language to justify the war. People living in the North and South believed they were the true heirs of the American Revolution. The Confederates used the language of individual freedom and liberty to justify their support of slavery and explain their break with the Union. Initially, Lincoln used similar language to explain his hostility toward slavery and his desire to preserve the Union. The contradiction between liberty and slavery built into the foundation of the republic had torn an irreparable breach in the American experiment.

Each side also widely believed that the war would be short and relatively bloodless. Most young men who marched off to battle in early 1861 held a romanticized image of war and glory. The harsh reality of war and death would soon shatter that illusion.

Stalemate on the Battlefield, 1861–1862

The early battles of the war dashed any hope of quick victory for either side. The North scored some victories in the West and gained the upper hand on the sea, but the Army of the Potomac was bogged down in the East, where Confederate forces scored a series of victories in defense of their capital at Richmond. However, when the Confederate army tried to build on their success by invading Maryland, Union forces turned them back in a shockingly bloody battle. Neither side gained a strategic advantage, but both suffered a tremendous loss of human life that was unimaginable when the war began.

The First Battle of Bull Run

While sparring continued for control of the Border States, popular attention in 1861 focused on northern Virginia. Pushed by public pressure for a quick, decisive victory that would demoralize the South, Lincoln ordered Union troops into Virginia. The hundred-mile stretch between the two capitals of Washington and Richmond was destined to become the most bitterly contested military terrain of the war. More than half the Union soldiers who died on the battlefield fell on this bloody ground.

In the summer of 1861, Union General Irvin McDowell had 35,000 troops at Washington. They were disorganized and undisciplined, but their term of enlistment, set for three months, was about to expire. With the public clamoring for a quick end to the war, Lincoln ordered McDowell's "grand army" of recruits to march toward Richmond. It took them two and a half days to march twenty-five miles, a stretch that seasoned troops would have covered in half the time. Newspaper reporters and crowds of spectators accompanied the army. Some brought binoculars, picnic baskets, even bottles of champagne, expecting to see a fight that would crush the rebellion in a single blow.

On July 21, McDowell met General Joseph E. Johnston's Confederate force of 22,000 at Manassas Junction, a little town on a creek called Bull Run, about twenty-five miles southwest of Washington. The North gained the offensive and eager soldiers shouted, "The war is over!" But holding the hill at the center of the Southern line was General Thomas "Stonewall" Jackson, whose troops stood firm long enough for Confederate reinforcements to arrive. The sight of fresh Rebel forces demoralized the Union men, most of whom had now been marching and fighting in brutal heat without food or water for fourteen hours. When the Confederates counterattacked, the Union army retreated.

The Battle of Bull Run gave Americans their first taste of the carnage that lay ahead. Some 4,500 men were killed, wounded, or captured on both sides in the battle that the North, which named battles after the landmark nearest to the fighting, called Bull Run and the South, which chose the town that served as its base, called Manassas (see map).

The defeat at Bull Run sobered the North. "Today will be known as BLACK MONDAY," wrote attorney George Templeton Strong when the bad news reached New York. "We are utterly and disgracefully routed, beaten, whipped by secessionists." Though shaken by the defeat, Lincoln did not panic, and the next day called for the enlistment of 500,000 additional troops to serve for three years. Tens of thousands of volunteers rushed to join the Army of the Potomac, while exhilarated Southerners strengthened fortifications around Richmond.

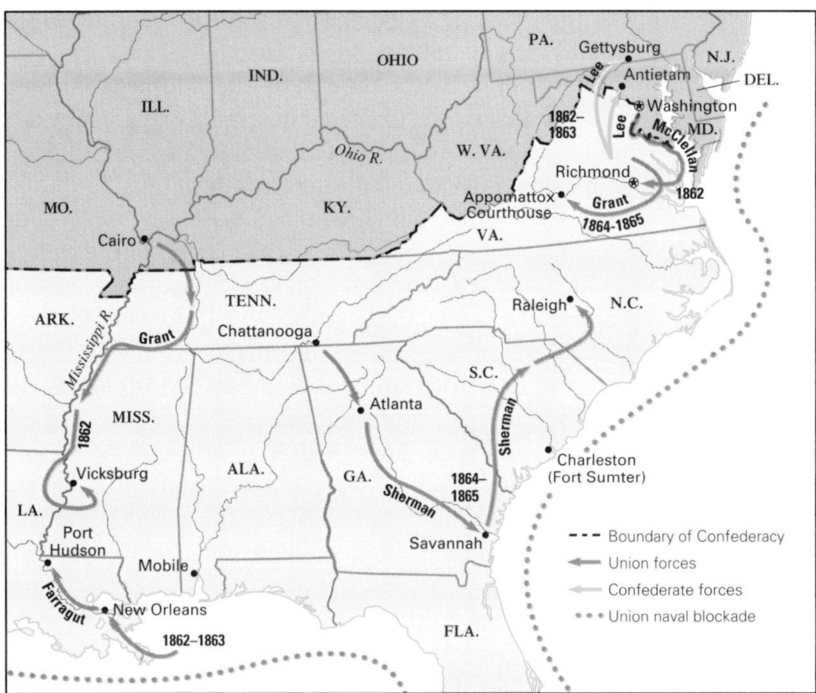

Major Military Offenses of the Civil War While the Confederacy began the war with a strategy of defense, the Union went on the offensive in both the western and eastern theaters in 1862. While Farragut and Grant made slow progress in the West, Confederate forces in the East forced McClellan off the Virginia Peninsula and led the way to Robert E. Lee's first offensive into the North—Antietam. Lee's second offensive into the North at Gettysburg in the summer of 1863 proved to be his last as Grant and Sherman, transferred to the eastern theater, began their attacks on the heart of the South.

The Peninsular Campaign

Following the defeat at Bull Run, Lincoln selected General George McClellan to take charge of the Union forces at Washington. A vain and powerful man who was said to be able to bend a quarter with his fingers and lift a 250-pound man over his head, McClellan was a hero of the Mexican War and the author of manuals on military tactics. "The true course in conducting military operations," McClellan declared, "is to make no movement until the preparations are complete." True to his philosophy, McClellan spent most of the fall and winter in camp, training his new troops for future battles. Congress and the president grew impatient as McClellan delayed. "If General McClellan does not want to use the Army," the frustrated president said, "I would like to borrow it for a time."

In January the president ordered McClellan to move toward Richmond by February 22. Rather than drive through a powerful Confederate force at Manassas Junction, McClellan proposed to circumvent it by floating his vast army to the tip of the York–James Peninsula by sea, then fight west to Richmond. It took three weeks to ferry the Army of the Potomac to Fortress Monroe on the peninsula: 121,500 men, 14,592 horses and mules, 1,150 wagons, 44 batteries of artillery.

Progress up the peninsula was slow, but by the end of May, McClellan's stood poised just five miles outside Richmond. The Confederate capital prepared for disaster. The Confederate Congress fled town. But McClellan hesitated, pleading for reinforcements before beginning the final assault on the city's defenses.

No reinforcements came because Stonewall Jackson had tied down two Federal divisions in a remarkable campaign in Virginia's Shenandoah Valley to the west of Richmond and Washington. In May and June, his 17,000 men had marched 400 miles, inflicted 7,000 Union casualties, seized huge quantities of badly needed supplies, and kept almost 40,000 Federal troops off the peninsula.

Rather than wait for McClellan to attack, Confederate leaders decided to take the offensive. On Friday, May 31, Joseph E. Johnston attacked McClellan's forces in the indecisive battle of Fair Oaks (Seven Pines). The North lost 5,000 men, the South 6,000. After Fair Oaks, Robert E. Lee replaced Johnston in command of the defense of Richmond. "His name might be 'Audacity,'" a Southern officer said of the new commander. "He will take more chances and take them quicker, than any other General in this country, North or South."

Determined not to allow Richmond to fall, Lee attacked McClellan's superior forces on June 26 at Mechanicsville. The attack cost Lee 1,500 men, but he would not let up. He continued forward, determined to drive McClellan off the peninsula. The Union forces won most of the individual battles, but the ever-cautious McClellan fell back steadily. By July 3, McClellan's retreating army had reached the bank of the James River within the protection of Federal gunboats. The Peninsular Campaign was at an end. In just one week, Lee had forced McClellan's huge army to retreat over ground it had spent three months taking, creating fear in Washington and celebrations in Richmond.

Fighting in the West

While most of the nation focused on the battles around Richmond, Union troops were having more success in the West. In 1861 General Ulysses S. Grant seized Paducah, Kentucky, which controlled access to the Tennessee and Cumberland Rivers. In 1862 he led an assault against two Confederate forts protecting the Kentucky–Tennessee border: Fort Henry on the Tennessee River and Fort Donelson on the Cumberland.

Fort Henry quickly fell on February 6, but Fort Donelson resisted longer. In February, with the Union force closing in on the Rebel defenders, the Confederate commander asked for surrender terms. Grant responded: "No terms except an unconditional and immediate surrender can be accepted. I propose to move immediately upon your works." Shortly afterward, the garrison's commander and his 15,000 troops surrendered. The Tennessee and Cumberland Rivers were now in Union hands, and the North celebrated its first major military victory. "Chicago reeled mad with joy," declared the *Chicago Tribune.*

In April, Grant moved south along the Tennessee River to continue his penetration of the Middle South. On a Sunday morning, April 6, 1862, Confederates commanded by Albert Sidney Johnston charged into Grant's camps in a surprise attack that began the bloodiest battle of the war to that point. The fighting, which took place around a small white church called Shiloh, a Hebrew word meaning "place of peace," raged for two days. On the first day, waves of Confederate soldiers pushed the Union army back almost into the river at Pittsburg Landing. However, Union General Don Carlos Buell arrived that night with 25,000 fresh troops, and the next day, the Federal force, now 50,000 strong, counterattacked successfully, forcing the Confederate troops to retreat. When the fighting was over, corpses littered the battlefield so thickly in some places, Grant remembered, that "it would have been possible to walk across the clearing in any direction stepping on dead bodies without a foot touching the ground." One hundred thousand men fought at Shiloh. Nearly one in four was a casualty. Three thousand four hundred and seventy-seven men died in those two days—more than all the Americans who had fallen in the Revolutionary War, the War of 1812, and the Mexican War together.

The Naval War

Grant was working on the Tennessee–Cumberland drainage because it was a link to the Mississippi, but to cut transport and communications more completely, the big river itself had to be controlled. In the spring of 1862, Union fleets attacked Southern strongholds on the river. On June 6, Union ships subdued Memphis. At the same time, another Union fleet of twenty-four ships, commanded by Admiral David G. Farragut, was ordered to sail up the river and seize New Orleans, the South's largest city and busiest port. As they approached New Orleans, a makeshift Confederate squadron of eight ships sailed out to meet them. Farragut sank six of them, and the city surrendered without firing a shot. In what the *New York Tribune* called "A Deluge of Victories," Union forces had conquered 50,000 square miles of land, gained control of 1,000 miles of navigable rivers, and captured the South's prime seaport.

Control of the Mississippi was key to the Union campaign of blockading the South, a strategy made possible because of its superior navy. When the war began, one-quarter of the navy's regular officers had defected to the South. Secretary of the Navy Gideon Welles had just forty-one vessels in commission—half of them officially obsolete. Over the next few years, the Union navy built, bought, or fitted out with guns scores of ships—sailboats, yachts, ferryboats, and tugs. By 1862, Union naval forces had established footholds at key Southern installations, and 427 federal ships rode at anchor off Southern ports to support the blockade. The Union navy controlled or had blocked every major Atlantic Coast harbor, except Charleston and Wilmington, North Carolina.

The Confederacy began the war without a single ship in its navy. Under the innovative leadership of Secretary of the Navy Stephen R. Mallory, the South decided that it could not build a navy as large as the North's. Instead, it would concentrate on a few specialized tasks that would minimize the North's advantage. He authorized the development of mines that were planted at the mouths of harbors and rivers. By the end of the war, mines had sunk or damaged forty-three Union ships. Mallory encouraged the construction of the world's first combat submarine, the C.S.S. *Hunley*. He also built a small number of ironclad ships that could outfight the Union's wooden fleet and punch holes in the blockade. Despite shortages of iron and a lack of rolling mills, the Confederacy developed a surprising number of these vessels. The most famous of the Confederate ironclads was the *Virginia,* originally the United States warship *Merrimack*, which Union forces had intentionally sunk when they abandoned the Norfolk navy yard in Virginia at the beginning of the war.

Raised and refitted, the *Virginia* had its superstructure covered with four-inch iron plate, ten guns, and a cast-iron ram on its bow. On March 8, 1862, just as McClellan began his campaign on the peninsula, the *Virginia* emerged from Norfolk into Hampton Roads and began attacking the wooden vessels of the Union fleet supporting McClellan's forces. The *Virginia* sank the U.S.S. *Cumberland*, the most powerful conventional ship in the Federal navy. In the words of an observer, the *Cumberland*'s cannon fire "struck and glanced off" the iron hull of the *Virginia*, "having no more effect than peas from a pop-gun." The *Virginia*, firing red-hot shot, then set the U.S.S. *Congress* aflame. A low tide forced the *Virginia* to return to her moorings in Norfolk. The worst day in the eighty-six year history of the U.S. Navy had ended, but the *Virginia* planned to return the next day to continue the destruction.

The next morning, however, the *Virginia* was confronted with a new, more powerful, opponent. After learning of the Confederate ironclad's construction, the North had responded by building its own ironclad—the U.S.S. *Monitor*. Armed with two 11-inch guns, the *Monitor* put herself between the *Virginia* and the wooden ships, and a spectacular duel took place. The two ships hammered away at each other, fighting at such close range that five times the vessels collided as the men inside loaded and fired. The battle between the *Virginia* and the *Monitor* ended in a draw, but the Confederate ship had to return to Norfolk to repair its defective engines. Two days later, when forced to abandon Norfolk, the Southerners ran the *Virginia* ashore and burned the vessel to prevent its capture.

Mallory was equally prompt in purchasing or commissioning conventional vessels for the Confederate navy. These ships were designed not to combat Union warships, but rather to harass the United States merchant marine. The most successful of these vessels was the *Alabama*, built in Liverpool, England. Between 1862 and 1864, the *Alabama* patrolled the Atlantic, Indian, and Pacific Oceans, hunting down and destroying sixty-nine Union merchantmen, valued at more than $6 million. Not until nearly the end of the war could the Union navy corner and sink the raider.

The *Trent* Affair and European Neutrality

While waging a battle for control over the seas, both North and South continued to hope for decisive European intervention in the conflict. The British, however, had little desire to get involved in the conflict. "For God's sake," the British foreign minister exclaimed in May 1861, "let us if possible keep out of it." Both sides in the conflict had overestimated their leverage on European decision makers. The South discovered that cotton was *not* king as European manufacturers turned to other suppliers to meet their demands. Antislavery sentiment ran strong in Europe, but the North had not yet made emancipation a war aim. In the end, national self-interest, and the preservation of a delicate balance of power in Europe, dictated a hands-off approach to the American conflict. On May 14, 1861, the British government issued a proclamation of neutrality, which recognized the Confederacy's legal right to engage in war, but also acknowledged the legality of the Union blockade, ensuring that British ships would not challenge it.

Since the South needed British aid more than the North, the neutrality policy favored the Union. Before the end of the year, however, the North had placed its advantage at risk. In November 1861, Union captain Charles Wilkes learned that President Davis was sending permanent envoys to replace the temporary commissioners he had sent to France and Britain. Envoys John Slidell and James M. Mason traveled on a British ship, the *Trent*. On November 8, Wilkes, commanding the U.S.S. *San Jacinto,* stopped the *Trent* on the high seas with two shots across her bow. Then Wilkes forcibly removed Mason and Slidell and brought them back to New York. The two commissioners were later sent as prisoners to Fort Warren in Boston harbor.

Wilkes's action was a clear violation of international law. When news of the incident reached Britain, hostility toward the Union government flared up. "You may stand for this," Prime Minister Lord (Henry) Palmerston told his cabinet, "but damned if I will!" The British foreign minister drafted a stiff letter demanding the immediate release of the envoys. The angry British government at once sent eleven thousand of its best troops to Canada. Largely a symbolic gesture, it was nevertheless a clear warning. After conferring with cabinet members and senators, the president decided on Christmas Day to release the Southern envoys. "One war at a time," Lincoln said, explaining his reasons for backing down to the British threats.

Antietam

As Union advances ground to a halt by midsummer 1862, the Confederates planned a grand offensive of their own. In the West, two Southern armies under Generals Braxton Bragg and Edmund Kirby-Smith swept through eastern Tennessee in August; by September, they were operating in Kentucky. The early phases of their offensive were brilliantly successful, but the campaign as a whole was fruitless because of a lack of coordination between the two Southern armies and because of Bragg's indecisiveness. After a bloody battle at Perryville (October 8), the Confederate forces withdrew toward Chattanooga.

The more daring part of the Confederate offensive unfolded in the East. While McClellan's army was slowly being withdrawn from the peninsula, Lee turned quickly on the Union forces under General John Pope that had remained in Virginia to guard Washington. Concentrating his entire strength on this segment of the Union army, Lee scored a brilliant victory in the Second Battle of Bull Run (August 29–30). In September, with the enemy "weakened and demoralized," Lee led 40,000 soldiers across the Potomac into Maryland. A decisive victory on Union soil, Lee reasoned, would bolster the chances of European intervention, dishearten Northerners, and erode support for the Lincoln administration. He showed little regard for McClellan. "He is a very able general but a very cautious one," Lee told an officer.

On this occasion, however, McClellan had a clear advantage. A Union soldier discovered an envelope containing Lee's orders to his troops. "I have all the plans of

Confederate Dead at Antietam This photograph of corpses awaiting burial was one of ninety-five taken by Matthew Brady and his assistants of the Antietam battlefield, the bloodiest single day of the war. It was the first time Americans had seen war depicted so realistically. When Brady's photographs went on display in New York in 1862, throngs of people waited in line to view their horror. *(Library of Congress.)*

the rebels and will catch them in their own trap if my men are equal to the emergency," McClellan telegraphed Lincoln. On September 15, Lee's army took up positions along the crest of a three-mile ridge just east of the town of Sharpsburg, Maryland. In front ran a little creek called Antietam. By September 16, McClellan had amassed a force of nearly 95,000 men on the other side. Once again McClellan delayed, giving Lee the chance to reinforce his position.

At dawn on September 17, the Union forces attacked. By the end of the day, the armies had suffered more than 25,000 casualties, with at least 5,000 dead. The next day an eyewitness noted "the most appalling sights upon the battlefield . . . the ground strewn with the bodies of the dead and the dying . . . the cries and groans of the wounded . . . the piles of dead men, in attitudes which show the writhing agony in which they died—faces distorted . . . begrimed and covered with clotted blood, arms and legs torn from the body or the body itself torn asunder."

Still, for all the carnage, the Union commander could finally claim a victory. Lee's invasion had been stopped. Lincoln wanted the Union forces to pursue Lee and destroy his outnumbered army. "God bless you and all with you," Lincoln wired his commander. "Destroy the rebel army if possible." But McClellan did not attack, and on the eighteenth, the Confederate army slipped back south across the Potomac, defeated but intact.

Mobilizing for War, 1861–1863

The need to deploy massive armies, raise large sums of money, and produce weapons and material for the war presented both North and South with an unprecedented challenge. Neither side was prepared for the organizational demands imposed by war. As late as 1830, Washington counted only 352 federal employees.

"We have more of the brute force of persistent obstinacy in Northern blood than the South has," Frederick Law Olmstead wrote, "if only we can get it in play. . . ." To get it "in play," Lincoln concentrated an enormous amount of power in the hands of his central government. Davis too was forced to press for government power, but secessionist states' rights ideology hampered his efforts. Lincoln also had to contend with serious opposition but proved more effective in forging consensus, inspiring the people, and, when necessary, using an iron fist to crush dissent. In the end, Lincoln's experiment in centralization marshaled the North's power and contributed to the reach of government after the war.

Raising an Army

By the end of the war, over 2 million men had served in the Union army and 800,000 in the Confederate army. As the war wore on into its second year, the initial zeal for volunteering abated, and both presidents moved, in 1862, to take a more active role in recruiting troops. On April 16, 1862, the Southern Congress passed the first conscription law in American history. The act made every able-bodied white male between the ages of eighteen and thirty-five subject to military service. But the Southern Congress included numerous exemptions, among them a rule allowing people to purchase substitutes and a so-called 20-Negro law, which exempted from service an owner of twenty or more slaves.

Critics condemned the conscription act as a violation of the same states' rights principles that had been invoked to justify secession in the first place. One of the strongest critics, Governor Joseph E. Brown of Georgia, attempted to block implementation of the act. "The Conscription Act, at one fell swoop, strikes down the sovereignty of the States, tramples upon the constitutional rights and personal liberty of the citizens, and arms the President with imperial power." Other critics complained that conscription was class legislation that benefited the educated and the wealthy at the expense of the poor. Opposition to the draft grew rapidly, especially among nonslaveholders, who increasingly described the Civil War as "a rich man's war and a poor man's fight."

In the North, too, conscription evoked bitter criticism. Congress passed the first Northern draft act in March 1863, declaring all able-bodied males between the ages of twenty and forty-five liable for military service. But it promptly contradicted itself by permitting those who could afford to do so to hire substitutes. It also permitted young men to purchase an outright exemption from military service for $300. The fee was too high for most unskilled workers, who were lucky to earn $300 in an entire year. "[This law] is a rich man's bill," Congressman Thaddeus Stevens charged, "made for him who can raise his $300, and against him who cannot raise that sum."

Opposition to the draft was strongest among Irish and German Catholics, and poor midwestern farmers. In Wisconsin, Kentucky, and Pennsylvania, in Troy, Newark, and Albany, there was outright resistance to the enrolling officers, and in several instances federal troops had to be brought in to quell the uprisings. But none of these outbreaks neared the scope or ferocity of the one that rocked New

York City, with its large Irish population and powerful Democratic machine. The drawing of the first draftees' names triggered a three-day riot (July 13–15, 1863) by a mob of predominantly Irish workingmen. The rampaging mob ransacked draft offices, attacked federal buildings, looted stores, and burned homes of the wealthy. Desperately fearful that a Union victory in the war would bring ex-slaves streaming north to take away their jobs, the Irish workers unleashed most of their fury on blacks. After burning the Colored Orphan Asylum, they hunted down any luckless black found on the streets. The violence ended only when troops were rushed back from the front to put down the riot by force.

Financing the War

As in recruiting their massive armies, both sides faced a formidable and unprecedented task in paying for the war. In antebellum America, the national government had only modest responsibilities and limited sources of revenue. This was especially true of the South, which had few public services, no mechanism for levying internal taxes, and no tradition of paying them. The North raised most of its revenue from tariffs and from the sale of public land. As spending on the war increased, both governments needed to look to new ways of raising money.

In the Union, the federal budget mushroomed from $63 million in 1860 to nearly $1.3 billion in 1865. Treasury Secretary Salmon P. Chase used a number of new methods to meet the repeated government shortfalls. First, he sold bonds to the public, which could be redeemed with interest at a later date. Nearly a million Americans, or roughly one in four Northern families, bought the bonds, which funded about two-thirds of the North's military bills.

Taxes were the second weapon in the Union Treasury arsenal to fight the budget gap. In August 1861, Congress passed a 3 percent tax on incomes of more than $800. The following year, Congress passed the Internal Revenue Act, which levied a 3 percent tax on incomes between $600 and $10,000, and 5 percent on incomes over $10,000. Ultimately these taxes brought in about 21 percent of the total wartime expenditures of the Union government.

Finally, the North resorted to printing paper money to finance the war. Early in 1862, Lincoln signed into law the Legal Tender Act, which authorized $150 million in paper money, called greenbacks. Union officials made the greenbacks legal tender, meaning people could use them to pay their bills. But the greenbacks were fiat money—that is, paper money that was not backed by any explicit promise of redemption in gold or silver specie. The move created a storm of protest. Critics denounced it as unsound and immoral. Most Americans believed that gold or silver could provide the only sound currency; thus paper money nonredeemable in specie was inherently dishonest because it represented no real value. Greenbacks also represented the first time the federal government had moved to create a uniform national currency. The Republicans were able to push through the greenback legislation only because of the pressing need to meet the unprecedented costs of the war.

The Confederacy faced a similar financial situation but with far fewer tools. When the war began, the Rebels owned only 30 percent of the nation's wealth and 21 percent of its banking assets. Southern planters found themselves with little money to invest in the war effort, so bond drives raised only 35 to 40 percent of the cost. In 1861 the Southern Congress passed a small tariff and a modest tax on real and personal property. Most states, charged with collecting the revenues, ignored the legislation. In desperation, the Congress adopted a comprehensive tax measure in April 1863 that included an income tax and occupational and license taxes. The law included a "produce loan," which compelled producers of wheat, corn, oats, potatoes, sugar, cotton, tobacco, and other farm products to pay one-tenth of their crop each year to the government. All told, the Confederacy raised only about 5 percent of its income from taxes.

With taxation and bond sales unable to meet the price of the war, the Confederacy came to rely on what Treasury Secretary Christopher Memminger called "the most dangerous of all methods of raising money"—printing paper money. By the end of the war, the Confederate Congress had printed $1.5 billion in notes. These notes financed about 60 percent of the war effort. As Confederate greenbacks flooded the economy, inflation spiraled out of control.

Presidential Leadership

The North had a clear advantage in the leadership of Abraham Lincoln. A masterful politician, sensitive to public opinion, and skilled at balancing competing interests, Lincoln knew when to stand firm and when to compromise. As an admiring Republican noted, "He always moves in conjunction with propitious circumstances, not waiting to be dragged by the force of events or wasting strength in premature struggles with them." The hallmark of Lincoln leadership was the ability to elicit broad public support for his policies. Throughout the war Lincoln generally remained on good terms with his party's vying factions. The most troublesome group were the so-called Radicals, who pushed for Lincoln to prosecute the war more aggressively and to expand Union goals to include emancipation. On the other side were the conservatives, who hoped for the end of slavery but wanted to see it accomplished by voluntary action. Lincoln identified with the moderates, who opposed slavery but feared the consequences of emancipation. By linking the conflict to the deepest values of Northern society, Lincoln managed these internal party differences and inspired popular support for the war. At the outset, he described the war as a struggle that "presents to the whole family of man, the question, whether a constitutional republic, or a democracy" could survive.

A two-party system in the North, which disciplined and channeled political activity, aided Lincoln's effort to maintain public morale. Republicans disagreed among themselves but were united in their opposition to the Democrats, who, though often divided among themselves, opposed the expansion of federal power while clinging to the goal of reunion through peaceful negotiation and opposing any plan to free the slaves. "The Constitution as it is; the Union as it was," they

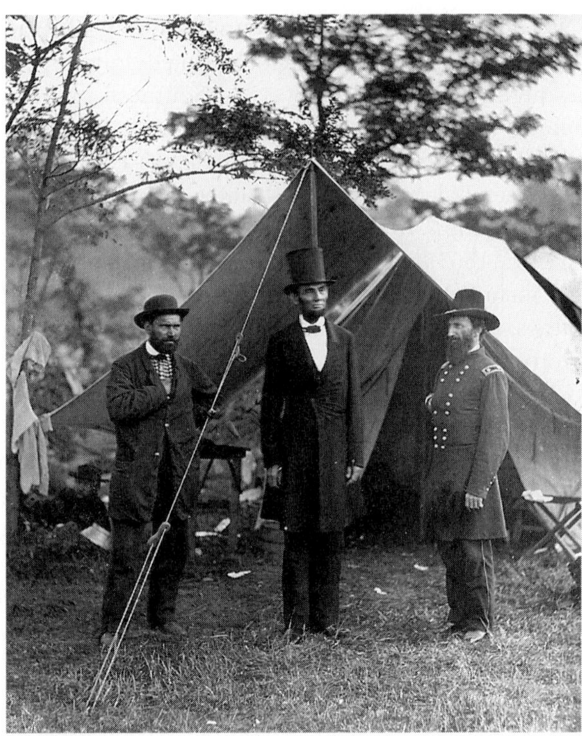

Lincoln at Sharpsburg, October 1862 Very much the commander-in-chief, President Lincoln visited Union forces on the battlefield on several occasions and was deeply involved in every aspect of the war's prosecution. Although his only military experience before taking office consisted of brief service in the Black Hawk War, Lincoln's abilities as a military strategist far exceeded that of most of his generals. Here he stands behind Union lines at Antietam with Allan Pinkerton, the detective who provided the Union army with intelligence information, and General John McClernand, who often accompanied the president in his travels. *(Library of Congress.)*

proclaimed. With the Democrats in opposition, the Republican Party became the means for mobilizing war resources, raising taxes, and enacting conscription. The parties drew clear lines and allowed the public to register their support or disapproval at the polls.

Jefferson Davis had a more difficult time establishing a firm grip on the Confederate government. For one thing, Davis had to struggle with a rift at the heart of the Confederate ideology. He was trying to win a war while forging a nation out of states that were ferociously protective of their prerogatives and deeply suspicious of centralized government. The governor of South Carolina, for example, expressed outrage because officers from outside his state occasionally commanded local troops. The governor of Georgia threatened to secede from the Confederacy. "If the Confederacy falls," Jefferson Davis said, "there should be written on its tombstone: Died of a Theory."

Davis, unlike Lincoln, did not have the advantage of a political party to help forge consensus. As a demonstration of unity, the South rejected rival parties, but the show of solidarity actually encouraged disunity. Without parties to impose discipline on congressmen or governors, Davis's government was plagued by rival, and frequently, personal factions. "They sat with closed doors," Vice President Stephens said of the Confederate Congress. "It was well they did, and so kept from the public some of the most disgraceful scenes ever enacted by a legislative body."

Davis's leadership style compounded his institutional problems. Aloof, stubborn, and humorless, he lacked both Lincoln's common touch and his flexibility and proved far less successful at instilling a sense of unified purpose in his people. "If anyone disagrees with Mr. Davis he resents it and ascribes the difference to the perversity of his opponent," his wife remarked. High turnover plagued the administration. Davis had to contend with three secretaries of state and six secretaries of war. Supremely confident in his own military judgment, Davis frequently quarreled with his commanders. One historian has suggested that the differences between Davis and Lincoln were so great, if the North and South had exchanged presidents, the South would have won the war.

Lincoln and Civil Liberties

Lincoln used tact and skill with rivals in his party but was far less tolerant of dissenters who opposed the war. Lincoln dealt with antiwar obstructionists mainly by military arrest and imprisonment without trial. His early actions in Maryland set the tone. Many critics objected to Lincoln's harsh treatment of dissenters and, in particular, to the suspension of *habeas corpus.* The Constitution (Article I, Section 9) ambiguously declares that *habeas corpus* shall not be suspended "unless when in cases of rebellion or invasion the public safety may require it." But the Constitution does not say who has the power to order such a suspension.

Lincoln eventually extended the military's authority to suspend *habeas corpus* to the whole country. Most of those arrested had in fact engaged in activities with military significance, such as attacking Union soldiers, burning bridges, blowing up supply dumps, and spying. But some men were arrested for merely speaking or writing in favor of peace with the Confederacy or against the war policies of the Union government. No one knows precisely how many Americans were seized and held without trial during the war, but the total was well above 13,500.

One of the most notorious wartime violations of civil liberties occurred in Ohio, where a military court convicted Democratic gubernatorial candidate Clement L. Vallandigham "of having expressed sympathy" for the enemy and having uttered "disloyal sentiments and opinions." The Vallandigham case raised a serious constitutional question: Did the military have the right to impose martial law in an area removed from the battlefield where the civil courts were functioning? Lincoln, who learned of Vallandigham's arrest by reading the papers, attempted to minimize the political damage by commuting his sentence from imprisonment to banishment. In another celebrated case, Lambdin P. Milligan, an Indiana civilian, was convicted of treason by a military court in 1864 for aiding Confederate agents trying to foment an uprising in the North. The Supreme Court, in *Ex parte Milligan* (1866), overturned Milligan's conviction, ruling that civilians cannot be tried by military courts in a region where the regularly established courts of the land are functioning. Constitutional historians consider the Milligan decision to be a landmark in the defense of civil liberties, but the ruling came after the war was over.

War and Society, 1861–1865

"This is essentially a people's contest," Lincoln told Congress in 1861. The Civil War was more than a clash of armies; it was a battle between two societies. No groups escaped the consequences of the war. The millions of men who served as soldiers in the Union and Confederate armies paid the greatest price for the conflict. But their loved ones on the home front also suffered. Women assumed the responsibility for looking after the family, and many found opportunities to help in the war effort. The terrible consequences of war took their toll, especially in the South. "Is anything worth it?" asked Mary Chesnut. "This fearful sacrifice, this awful penalty we pay for war?"

The Soldier's War

The average age of a soldier in either army was twenty-five. Law set the minimum age for enlistment at eighteen, but recruiters frequently ignored it. As many as 800,000 underage soldiers signed up to fight. Charles E. King, believed to be the youngest soldier in the war, was twelve when he enlisted in the Pennsylvania Volunteers. He was barely a teenager when he died at Antietam.

Ordinarily a volunteer enlisted in one of the regiments being raised in his community. In the initial enthusiasm for war, whole towns rushed to sign up. The Tenth Michigan Volunteers was comprised entirely of Flint men; their commander was the mayor. When a regiment had filled its ranks, the town invariably held a farewell ceremony. As they went off to fight, thousands of soldiers posed for *cartes de visite*, small photographic portraits mounted on cards.

The Union army was the best equipped in history to that point. The story was far different in the South where Union invasions, a poor transportation system, the Union blockade, and an economy based on growing cotton and tobacco made it difficult to supply troops with essential supplies. Many solders went into battle in ragged uniforms, even without shoes. A Georgia major reported after Manassas that he "carried into the fight over one hundred men who were barefoot, many of whom left bloody foot-prints among the thorns and briars through which they rushed." Food was often scarce. "I came nearer to starving than I ever did before," noted a Rebel soldier in Virginia.

Even a well-supplied soldier's diet was not very appealing. Union troops were issued beans, bacon, pickled beef—called "salt horse" by the men—"desiccated compressed mixed vegetables," and a dried cake that yielded a thin soup when crumbled into boiling water. But the staple was hardtack—square flour-and-water biscuits so hard, some said, they could stop bullets. In the Southern army, men favored something called "sloosh," cornmeal swirled in bacon grease, then wrapped around a ramrod and cooked over the campfire. Coffee was the preferred drink of both armies. Union troops crushed the beans with their rifle butts, drank four pints of brew a day ("strong enough to float an iron wedge"), and when they could not build a fire, were content to chew the grounds. Southerners often made do with substitutes brewed from peanuts, potatoes, or chicory.

Men of the First Texas Brigade Camp life on both sides of the lines included routine chores, such as washing clothes and cooking. These Confederate troops pose in front of their quarters at Camp Quantico, Virginia, in 1861. Their log cabin was an unusual dwelling for soldiers—most lived in tents during both winter and summer months. Conditions on the field were extremely harsh, and more men died of disease and malnutrition than of battle wounds. *(Austin History Center, Austin Public Library #03674.)*

The Civil War coincided with new technology of warfare that made the battlefield a much more dangerous place. The most important single innovation was a new bullet. For centuries infantry had been equipped with smoothbore muskets that required a solider to ram a bullet down the barrel of the rifle after each firing. In the 1850s, an American adoption of a French invention produced the "minie ball," a bullet sufficiently smaller than the rifle barrel to permit relatively rapid loading and reloading. The new bullet expanded into a gun barrel's rifled grooves and spun at great speed from the muzzle. The minie ball from a rifled barrel could kill at half a mile and was accurate at four hundred yards—five times as far as any earlier one-man weapon.

The traditional infantry charge remained a standard tactic, however. The result was mass slaughter. Frontal assaults in compact formations were suicidal in the face of accurate, long-distance rifle fire. It was not uncommon for regiments to experience battlefield casualties in excess of 50 percent in a single engagement. More than 90 percent of battle wounds came by bullets. Faced with the high probability of death, many soldiers wrote out their own "identification tags" before going into battle, pinning scraps of paper to their uniforms with their names, next of kin, and civilian address. If killed, they hoped to be returned to loved ones for burial near home.

Nevertheless, disease proved a greater adversary than enemy soldiers. "There is more dies by sickness than gets killed," complained a recruit from New York in 1861. His assessment was accurate. Two soldiers died of disease for every one killed in battle. The most common killers were scurvy, dysentery, typhoid, diphtheria, and pneumonia. In one year, 995 of every 1,000 men in the Union army contracted diarrhea and dysentery. Their opponents suffered as badly. "All complainants were asked the same question," a Confederate physician remembered. "How are your bowels? If they were open, I administered a plug of opium; if they were shut, I gave a plug of blue mass."

Medical assistance was usually primitive. One commentator described military hospitals in the war's early years as "dirty dens of butchery and horror." The war was fought, the Union surgeon general remembered, "at the end of the medical middle ages." Physicians knew nothing of what caused the diseases they treated, nor did they understand the need for good sanitation and nutrition. Since scientists were only beginning to comprehend the germ theory of disease, wounds frequently led to gangrene or tetanus. Amputation was the usual remedy. "We operated in old, blood-stained and often pus-stained coats," a surgeon recalled. " . . . We used undisinfected instruments from undisinfected plush-lined cases." Federal medical officials responded to most complaints by handing out generous quantities of opium-based painkillers. By some estimates, they distributed 10 million opium pills and 2.8 million ounces of opium-related medicines, resulting in widespread addiction.

Conditions for troops on the battlefield were horrible, but they were worse for captured soldiers. The Civil War was the first war in which a large number of Americans were held in military prisons. Both sides had more prisoners than they could handle. Nearly 50,000 men died in these prisons, including 13,000 Union soldiers at Andersonville in southwestern Georgia. Opened in 1864 and meant to hold a maximum of 10,000 Federal prisoners, Andersonville held 33,000 by August 1864, more than the fifth-largest city in the Confederacy. In that month, 3,000 prisoners died; on one day, they died at a rate of a man every eleven minutes. At Belle Isle, 90 percent of the survivors weighed less than one hundred pounds. "Can those be men?" asked the poet Walt Whitman.

The imposition of the draft, the realization after Shiloh that the battlefield was a slaughterhouse, wretched provisions, and spreading economic misery on the home front, especially in the South, produced widespread desertions. Union General Joseph Hooker reported that one in four soldiers under his command were absent. The problem was more severe for the South. At Antietam, Lee estimated that one-third to one-half of his soldiers were "straggling"—that is, absent without leave. At the start of 1863, unauthorized absences averaged 30 percent in the Southern armies.

Economic Consequences of the War

Overall, the war produced widespread prosperity in the North. Nourished by government contracts, the profits of industry boomed. Chicago, the country's railroad and livestock capital, experienced unprecedented growth in population, construction, banking, and manufacturing. Coal mining and iron production boomed in

Pennsylvania. Dismal crop harvests in Europe opened up new markets for Northern agriculture, which thrived during the war. Numerous Americans who would take the lead in reshaping the nation's postwar economy created or consolidated their fortunes during the Civil War, among them Andrew Carnegie, John D. Rockefeller, Jay Gould, J. P. Morgan, and Philip Armour. These and other future "captains of industry" managed to escape military service, some by hiring substitutes.

At the same time, Congress adopted policies that promoted further economic expansion. With clear majorities in both Houses, the Republicans in Congress passed the Pacific Railroad Act of 1862, which provided for the development of a transcontinental railroad. The Homestead Act, passed in 1862, granted 160 acres of public land to settlers after five years of residence on the land. By 1865, twenty thousand homesteaders occupied new land in the West under the act. In 1862, Republicans passed the Morrill Land Grant Act to make higher education available to common people. By giving proceeds from the sale of public lands to the states, the act spurred the growth of large state universities, mainly in the Midwest and West.

Perhaps the federal government's most significant long-term contribution to business development was the creation of a national currency and a national banking system. Before the Civil War, private banks (chartered by the states) issued their own banknotes, which were used in most economic transactions; the federal government paid all of its expenses in gold or silver. In 1863, Congress passed the National Bank Act, providing for the chartering of federal banks. This legislation, amended and strengthened in 1864, meant, among other things, that a uniform national currency began to replace the dozens of issues by local banks.

Not all groups in the North benefited from the war. As greenbacks flooded the economy and as consumer goods fell into short supply, prices climbed rapidly—about 20 percent faster than wages. Skilled workers, whose labor was in high demand, might be able to keep up. But unskilled workers were hit hard by inflation. "We are unable to sustain life for the prices offered by contractors, who fatten on their contracts by grinding immense profits out of the labor of their operatives," wrote a group of Cincinnati seamstresses to President Lincoln in 1864.

Inflation, combined with scarcity, crippled the Southern economy and produced widespread suffering. In 1862 prices increased by 300 percent while wages for skilled and unskilled workers grew by only 55 percent. In January 1864, it took twenty-seven Confederate dollars to buy what one dollar had bought in April 1861—an inflation rate of 2,600 percent in less than three years! The average family food bill rose from $6.65 per month before Fort Sumter to $68 by mid-1863. Southern urban workers could not keep up with this kind of inflation. In April 1863, a bread riot broke out in Richmond; over a thousand women, infuriated by soaring prices, stormed through downtown shops, smashing windows and gathering up armfuls of food and clothing. "Bread! Bread!" they shouted. "Our children are starving while the rich roll in wealth." Similar incidents took place in Augusta, Columbus, Milledgeville, Mobile, and a half-dozen other towns. The riots were touched off by working-class housewives protesting not so much food shortages as the exorbitant price of what was available. They simply could not afford to feed their families when industrial wages came nowhere near meeting the tenfold increase in the price of food during the first two years of the war.

State governments experimented with novel ways to address the suffering. As early as the fall of 1861, state governments passed laws preventing the collection of soldiers' debts and providing some financial assistance to the indigent through special county taxes. These measures proved insufficient, and by 1863, the states were distributing food to the poor and spending millions on direct relief. Toward the end of the war, 20 to 40 percent of Confederate white civilians were on some form of public relief. Over half of Georgia's budget in 1864 was devoted to relief, and the funds for this aid to soldiers' families came from stiff progressive taxes that shifted the fiscal burden of the war onto the rich. Ironically, in the battle for individual liberty, many Southern governors presided over a dramatic centralization of the power to collect and distribute revenues in their states.

Women and the War

The writer Louisa May Alcott summarized the feeling of most women on both sides of the conflict when she declared, "As I can't fight, I will content myself with working for those who can." Though officially barred from combat, as many as four hundred women donned men's clothing and volunteered for the armies disguised as men.

Women Volunteer Units The majority of Southern white men served in the Confederate army during the war, leaving their wives and daughters to assume their roles at home. Southern women ran plantations, managed slaves, and even took up arms to defend themselves against any possible danger, such as a slave uprising or the encroaching Union army. The women in this photograph have banded together in a women's defense unit. *(National Archives.)*

Most, however, found other ways to contribute to the war effort. Hundreds of thousands of women took part in organizations that gathered medical and other supplies for soldiers. The largest of these agencies, the U.S. Sanitary Commission, coordinated relief activities throughout the North, shipping large quantities of clothing, food, and medical supplies to troops on the front lines.

Along with aiding the war effort, women filled jobs on the home front left vacant by men gone to war. More than 100,000 jobs opened up during the war. For the first time, the federal government hired women as clerks and copyists. By 1864, women held 33 percent of all manufacturing jobs, up nearly 10 percent since the start of the war. In most cases, companies paid women less than the men they replaced, and they were forced out of their positions once the war ended.

Not all the advances were temporary, however. In some areas, such as the nursing profession, women made permanent inroads. Most army doctors resisted having women in the wards, claiming they were too weak and refined. In addition, they charged that women were incapable of dealing with the bodies of strange men. Women, who stressed their traditional roles as caretakers, won the debate. In 1862 the Confederate Congress passed a law allowing civilian nurses to work in army hospitals, "giving preference in all cases to females where their services may best subserve the purpose." That same year the Union issued an order requiring at least one-third of army nurses to be women. Union nurses were more organized than their Confederate counterparts, thanks to the pioneering work of Dorothea Dix, a fifty-nine-year-old crusader for the mentally ill who assumed the title of Superintendent of Female Nurses in 1861. Referred to as "Dragon Dix" by her fellow nurses because of her autocratic style, Dix barred any applicant she thought interested only in romantic ventures. "All nurses are required to be very plain-looking women. Their dresses must be brown or black, with no bows, no curls, no jewelry and no hoop skirts."

The Decisive Year, 1863

In 1863 a number of decisive moves on the battlefield broke the military stalemate. Lincoln, realizing that bold initiatives were needed to break the logjam, began the year by issuing the Emancipation Proclamation, which redefined the purpose of the war and infused the Union cause with moral purpose. The war, initiated over the issue of limiting the spread of slavery, had been transformed into a moral crusade to free the slaves. The emancipation experiment assigned new power and a new duty to the national government. "The character of the war will be changed," Lincoln observed. "It will be one of subjugation." Later that summer, Union victories at Gettysburg, Vicksburg, and Chattanooga turned the tide of the war.

Emancipation Transforms the War

As the fear of Border State secession receded and Union manpower needs increased, pressure mounted on Lincoln to free the slaves. The very success of Confederate resistance in what Northerners had assumed would be a short, victorious war was converting more and more whites to what had been the abolitionist position from the beginning of the conflict. Containing slavery would never be enough. Northern public opinion was slowly but inexorably turning toward emancipation. Most influential in changing Lincoln's mind was his grim recognition that after eighteen months of combat, the war could not be ended by traditional means. Yet he wanted a victory that would build support at home and abroad for a bold step. Antietam gave him the opportunity for which he had been waiting. On September 22—five days after the battle—the president issued his Emancipation Proclamation, saying it would take effect in one hundred days. On January 1, 1863, Lincoln signed the proclamation. "If my name ever goes into history," he said, "it was for this act."

As of this day, the document declared, the 3 million slaves in the rebellious states "shall be then, henceforth forever free." Lincoln was careful to limit the immediate impact of the proclamation to those slaves living in the rebellious states, or in parts thereof not under Union control. Excluded from the provisions were slaves living in the Border States that remained in the Union—Delaware, Kentucky, Maryland, and Missouri—as well as those living in Union-controlled areas of Tennessee, Louisiana, and Virginia. "The Government liberates the enemy's slaves as it would the enemy's cattle," blustered the *London Spectator,* "simply to weaken them in the coming conflict. . . . The principle asserted is not that a human being cannot justly own another, but that he cannot own him unless he is loyal to the United States."

Despite its limitations, the proclamation set off wild rejoicing among white and black abolitionists. For the first time, the government had committed itself to freeing slaves. Firing the Northern effort with moral purpose, emancipation transformed a war of armies into a conflict over beliefs over what America stood for (see Competing Voices, page 604). "We shout for joy," wrote Frederick Douglass, "that we live to record this righteous decree." In Washington, D.C., a crowd of blacks gathered in front of the White House to cheer the president, who appeared at the window. To Charlotte Forten, a young black woman living in South Carolina, "it all seemed . . . like a brilliant dream." There was even jubilation among the slaves in loyal Border States who were exempted from the proclamation's provisions.

The Emancipation Proclamation officially authorized the enrollment of black troops in the Union army, but in that, it simply recognized changes that were already taking place on the front lines. In 1862 Congress had passed the Militia Act, which called for enrolling blacks in "any military or naval service for which they may be found competent." In areas they controlled, Union forces used blacks labor for physically demanding tasks: chopping wood, hauling supplies, and building fortifications. Congress sanctioned this work by passing confiscation acts declaring that the slaves of any person who supported the rebellion would be free if they fell into Union hands.

Many blacks welcomed the chance to fight for their freedom and for that of their families. As Solomon Bradley of South Carolina put it, "In Such times I used to pray the Lord for this opportunity to be released from bondage and to fight for

African-American Union Soldier Almost 200,000 African-Americans fought for the Union. These soldiers served in racially segregated units under white officers and were assigned the most menial tasks. Nonetheless, they fought bravely when given the chance, helping to elevate the pride of other African-Americans and dispel myths of their inferiority. Their presence also enraged Confederates, who threatened to execute any captured black soldier in Union uniform. *(Chicago Historical Society.)*

my liberty, and I could not feel right so long as I was not in the regiment." Constituting less than 1 percent of the North's population, blacks would make up nearly one-tenth of the Northern army by the end of the war. Although large numbers of free Northern blacks joined the Union army, moie than 80 percent of black soldiers had been recruited in the slave states.

Still, opportunities were limited for African-Americans in the Union army. Union generals used black troops primarily for garrison and rearguard duty, freeing whites for combat service. In many cases, they were stationed in areas where white troops had been decimated by yellow fever and malaria. The combination of poor condition and inferior medical treatment produced a black mortality rate that was 40 percent higher than that of white Union soldiers. Black troops earned $10 a month whereas their white counterparts received $13 plus a clothing allowance of $3.50. If captured by Confederates, blacks ran the risk of being executed under Southern laws for inciting slave insurrections. Realizing that their wartime service gave them a powerful claim to full equality and citizenship at the end of the war, African-Americans endured these indignities and served with distinction.

Gettysburg

The outcome at Antietam gave Lincoln the Northern victory he needed to issue the Emancipation Proclamation and begin the active enlistment of black soldiers. It did not, however, mark an overall change in the North's fortunes on the battlefield. Convinced by Antietam that McClellan was not bold enough to destroy Lee's army, Lincoln replaced him with General Ambrose Burnside. Lee, having regrouped in

Virginia, dug his troops in on the hills overlooking Fredericksburg. In December 1862, Burnside sent his superior force of 120,000 men on a reckless frontal assault of Lee's well-fortified position. A Union officer said the troops seemed to "melt . . . like snow coming down on warm ground." The Rebels beat back fourteen assaults, and over 9,000 Union soldiers died before Burnside decided the hills could not be taken. "It can hardly be in human nature for men to show more valor," a reporter wrote, "or generals to manifest less judgment."

The defeat at Fredericksburg shook Washington. "If there is a worse place than Hell," Lincoln remarked, "I am in it." In March 1863, amid bitter recrimination among congressional Republicans about the faltering war effort, Lincoln replaced Burnside with General Joseph Hooker, a Massachusetts soldier who had demonstrated his tenacious courage on the peninsula and at Antietam. On April 27, Hooker began moving toward Chancellorsville, ten miles west of Fredericksburg. Lee was again outnumbered nearly 2 to 1, but again he scored a decisive victory. On May 6, Hooker retreated, having lost 17,000 men. Chancellorsville was another terrible blow to Northern morale. "My God! My God!" Lincoln cried hearing the news. "What will the country say?" He replaced Hooker with General George G. Meade in late June.

Lee's victories set the stage for another Confederate thrust north, this time reaching into Pennsylvania. Meade shadowed Lee's movements, keeping a defensive wall between the Confederate troops and populated Union cities such as Washington, Baltimore, and Philadelphia. By the morning of July 2, 1863, 150,000 Union and Confederate troops had converged on the tiny town of Gettysburg, Pennsylvania. After chaotic initial clashes, the Southerners occupied a line west along Seminary Ridge. The Union men waited along Cemetery Ridge—a slightly more elevated crest that ran south toward two hills, Big and Little Round Top. In its shape, the Union line resembled the mirror image of a question mark.

For the next two days, the Confederate army assaulted Union positions on a series of hills mostly south of Gettysburg. On July 3, Lee made his last desperate bid for victory by sending three divisions of 15,000 infantrymen, under the leadership of Major General George E. Pickett, across open ground to break the center of the Union line. A Union soldier saw "an overwhelming resistless tide of an ocean of armed men sweeping upon us! . . . on they move, as with one soul, in perfect order. . . ." The battle noise was "strange and terrible, a sound that came from thousands of human throats . . . like a vast mournful roar." Fearsome though the charge was, Union artillery struck with deadly accuracy while a hail of gunfire from the Federal batteries decimated the Confederate troops (see map).

Pickett's charge had failed, and more than 25,000 Confederate soldiers, nearly one-third of Lee's army, had been wounded or had died at Gettysburg, the bloodiest battle of the war. Gettysburg and nearby towns were flooded with the wounded. A Quaker nurse summarized the carnage: "There are no words in the English language to express the sufferings I witnessed today."

The South could not afford such losses. Gettysburg was Lee's last offensive campaign. During a pouring rain on the evening of July 4, the shattered remnant of the Confederate army began its last retreat to the Potomac. Despite Lincoln's pleas to

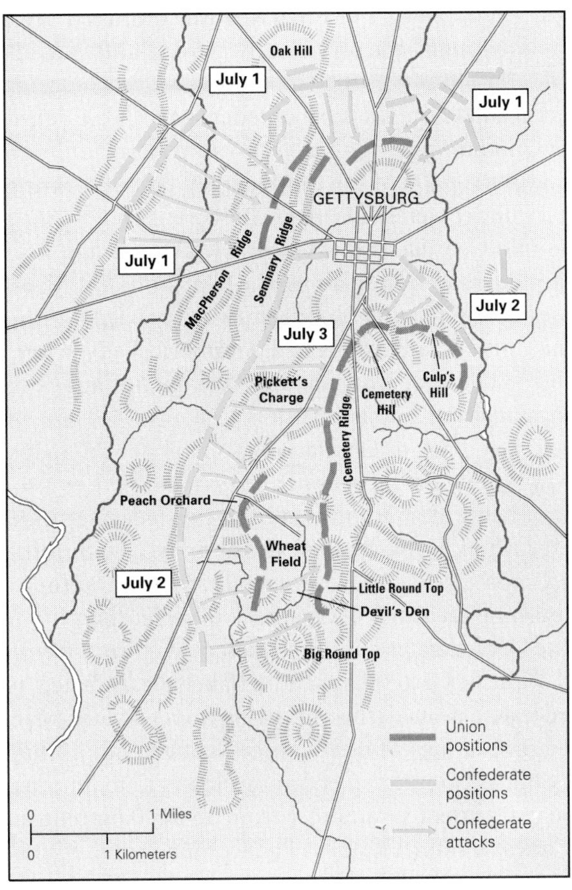

The Battle of Gettysburg Attempting to relieve pressure on Vicksburg, Lee decided to create a diversion by moving his troops northward through Maryland and into southern Pennsylvania. On June 30, a Confederate scavenging party entered the city of Gettysburg looking for shoes and instead found several Union cavalry units. The main forces on both sides quickly converged on the site and on July 1, Confederates attacked the Union position at Seminary Ridge and forced them to pull back south of town to a more defendable position at Cemetery Ridge. For the next two days, Lee was on the offensive, trying to pry the Union army from the ridge—first trying from the flanks (Battle of Little Round Top), and then from the center (Pickett's Charge). Lee's casualties in the three days of battle forced him to retreat south back into Virginia.

follow up victory with an all-out attack that might finish off Lee's army, Meade's forces were too exhausted to pursue the retreating Rebels.

Vicksburg and Chattanooga

On the same day, General John C. Pemberton surrendered the great stronghold of Vicksburg on the Mississippi River to Grant. In May, Grant had moved down the river and crossed into Mississippi to get at Vicksburg from the rear in one of the riskiest military maneuvers of the war. Plunging into enemy territory without any secure base of supplies, Grant surprised the Confederates and laid siege to the city. With the inhabitants on the brink of starvation, Pemberton surrendered. The capture of Vicksburg represented the North's most important strategic victory of the war, justifying Grant's later assertion that "the fate of the Confederacy was sealed when Vicksburg fell." Along with the city, Pemberton gave up 170 cannon, 50,000 small arms, and 30,000 men. Four days later, Port Hudson, Louisiana, fell to a Union expedition led by General Nathaniel P. Banks. Showing boldness and tenacity, Grant had realized one of the key war aims of the Union—control of the

Mississippi. After Grant's triumph at Vicksburg, Lincoln gave him command of all Union armies in the West. "Grant is my man," the president declared, "and I am his the rest of the war."

The year ended on yet another dismal note for the Confederacy with the defeat of Rebel forces poised to retake Chattanooga, Tennessee, an important railroad junction linking the eastern and western parts of the Confederacy. After capturing the city in September, Union forces under General William Rosecrans had pursued the retreating Confederate troops into Georgia. Under General Braxton Bragg, bolstered by reinforcements, the Confederates dug in along the Chickamauga River. On September 19, the two armies clashed in the bloodiest two-day battle of the war—one of the few in which the Confederate troops had a numerical advantage. Casualties totaled over 34,000, and 18,000 were Confederates. Although Bragg won, he had lost 30 percent of the troops he threw into the battle.

The battered Union forces retreated back to Chattanooga. Confederate troops surrounded the city, seizing the hills and cutting off rail and water supply routes. Rosecrans's army was in danger of being starved out, and the Confederates were poised for a much needed victory when, in November, Grant arrived with reinforcements to take charge of the Union forces. On November 24, the Union troops fought their way out of the city, pushing the Confederates back into Georgia.

In a decisive year of battles, the Confederates had surrendered an entire army at Vicksburg, had nearly been bled white at Gettysburg, and had been humiliated at Chattanooga. News of the Confederate defeats dashed lingering hopes of European intervention. "It is now conceded that all idea of intervention is at an end," Henry Adams wrote from London. The South also suffered enormous losses in manpower and morale. In the last half of the year, absentee rates rose from 35 to 40 percent, as families pleaded for their loved ones to return home. "The women write to their husbands to leave the army and come home," Julia Gwyn of North Carolina noted in 1863, "and that's the reason that so many of them are deserting." The end of the war was in sight.

A New Experiment in Warfare, 1864–1865

In 1864, the last full year of the war, Lincoln finally found in Ulysses S. Grant a general who would take advantage of the Union's superior resources. "That man," observed a Confederate officer, "will fight us every day and every hour until the end of this war." Lincoln had transformed the purpose of the war with the Emancipation Proclamation, now it was Grant's turn to mold a new, more aggressive military strategy to achieve victory. While Grant attacked Lee's army in the East, General Sherman invaded Georgia from the West. Amid the changing military fortunes, Lincoln faced an uncertain election in 1864, while Lee and his forces fought on, clinging to life.

Waging Total War

In March 1864, Lincoln appointed Grant to the specially created rank of lieutenant general, last held by George Washington. In that post, Grant held command of all

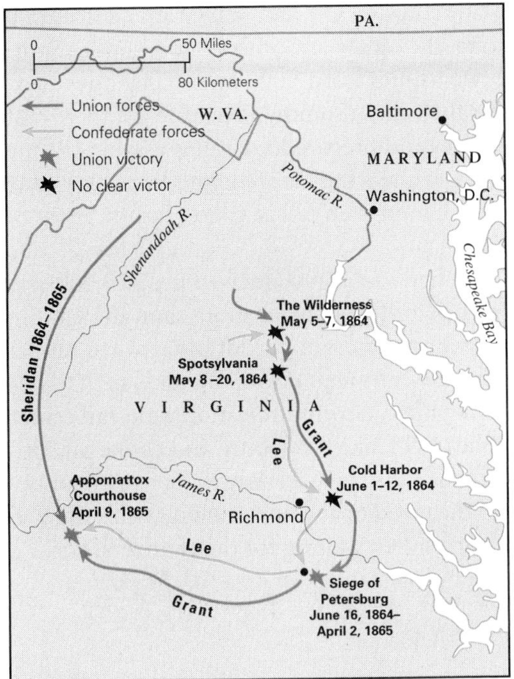

Grant's Campaign in Virginia, 1864–1865 Ulysses S. Grant became general-in-chief of the Union army in March 1864 and by May had begun his campaign in Virginia. Unlike earlier Union generals, Grant did not retreat despite suffering heavy casualties at the Battle of the Wilderness and Cold Harbor. Instead, Grant continued to move his men to the left, advancing slowly southward as Lee, suffering from his own growing casualties and running out of replacements, was forced to follow. Meanwhile, Philip Sheridan's cavalry descended on the Shenandoah Valley, cutting Lee off from his main source of food. Reaching the end of his supplies and manpower, Lee retreated from Petersburg in April 1865 with Grant in hot pursuit. With his escape route blocked by Sheridan, Lee was forced to surrender at Appomattox Courthouse.

the armies of the United States, 533,000 armed men. Grant's all-out and largely successful approach to battle had won the confidence of a president who had been dissatisfied with his more cautious generals. "I wish to express my entire satisfaction with what you have done up to this time," Lincoln said. "The particulars of your plans I neither know nor seek to know."

Grant's strategy was to wage total war. He planned a coordinated movement of federal armies in the East and West so as to apply simultaneous pressure all along the Confederate line. By fighting a coordinated war on all fronts Grant hoped to exploit the North's advantage in numbers and resources. He recognized that victory would result not from winning individual battles but from destroying the resources and morale of the Confederacy. Ultimately, the capacity of Confederate armies to wage war depended on the economic and psychological support they received from the civilian population. To win its war of conquest, the Union under Grant would target civilians as well as Confederate armies. In the East, Grant planned to keep sustained pressure on Lee's army while ordering William T. Sherman to attack the Rebel army in Georgia (see map).

On the night of May 3, 1864, Grant's army crossed the Rapidan River in northern Virginia and began to fight its way through the wilderness west of Fredericksburg. In the first two days of battle, Grant lost 17,000 men. That night in his tent, Grant wept. The next morning, he ordered his men to attack again. "Whatever happens," Grant assured Lincoln, "we will not retreat." Instead, he attempted to move southward around Lee's army, rather than directly toward Richmond. Lee positioned his army to stop him at Spotsylvania Courthouse. On May 12, Grant sent 20,000 men under Winfield Scott Hancock against the center of Confederate troops at Spotsylvania. The Confederates held as the two armies lost 12,000 men. They now raced for a crossroads called Cold Harbor, near the Chickahominy River. Lee got there first and ordered his men to entrench themselves and prepare for Grant's assault. On the morning of June 3, 60,000 Union men assaulted the Confederate lines and were again repulsed. Between 5,600 and 7,000 Union men fell at Cold Harbor, most of them in the first eight minutes.

In thirty days of battle with Lee, Grant had lost 55,000 men to Lee's 30,000, but Grant knew that such losses weakened the Confederacy far more than the Union. Unlike his predecessors, this Union commander did not permit his army to retreat when repulsed, or to rest when victorious. Grant kept going. By now, he had decided to bypass Richmond and target Petersburg, a communications and rail center just south of the Confederate capital. If he could take Petersburg and choke off supplies, Richmond would be forced to surrender, just as Vicksburg had been a year before. In June, Grant dug in for a siege of the city. For the next nine months, the two armies alternately glared at and fought each other, waiting for the chance to strike a decisive blow.

The Election of 1864

Four days after the slaughter at Cold Harbor, Republicans gathered to renominate President Lincoln. "I am going to be beaten," Lincoln said, "and unless some great change takes place, badly beaten." He had reason to feel pessimistic about his chances. Grant was stalled at Petersburg. Sherman was halted near Atlanta. Northern opinion was shocked by the heavy casualties reported from the battlefields. History seemed to be conspiring against Lincoln as well. No other nation had ever held an election during a civil war. Neither party had renominated an incumbent for president since 1840. The last president to win a second term was Andrew Jackson, over three decades earlier.

The Republicans formed a coalition with Democrats supporting the war. The name "Union Party" was substituted for "Republican." To help win the votes of Democrats, party leaders chose the Tennessee war-Democrat, Andrew Johnson, former senator and military governor of his home state, to run for the vice presidency. The Republican platform committed the party to the indivisibility of the Union, the defeat of the rebellion, the avoidance of any compromise with the Confederacy, and the "utter and complete extirpation of slavery" through a constitutional amendment.

Republicans were hardly inspired by Lincoln, and in May a small band of Radical Republicans broke with the president. "Mr. Lincoln is already beaten," cried Horace Greeley, Republican editor of the *New York Tribune*. "He cannot be elected. And we must have another ticket to save *us* from utter overthrow." The Radicals blamed Lincoln for the reverses on the battlefield and feared that he favored a "soft" policy on the South after the war. They selected John C. Frémont, the 1856 Republican nominee, to run for president on a platform that endorsed "the one-term policy for the Presidency." They chose the name Radical Democracy for their party.

The Democratic Party met in Chicago in August, proclaimed the war a failure, demanded an immediate cessation of hostilities, and called for the restoration of the Union by means of a negotiated peace. They nominated the former head of the Army of the Potomac, General George McClellan. Many in the South rejoiced at McClellan's nomination—"the first ray of real light," said Vice President Stephens, "since the war began."

Democrats, early in the campaign at least, hoped to capitalize on the war weariness that was sweeping across the North. They made much of Lincoln's arbitrary use of executive power and the infringement of civil liberties. They objected to the unfairness of the draft. They accused the Republican Congress of rewarding northeastern businessmen at the expense of midwestern farmers by enacting protective tariffs, handing out railroad subsidies, and creating a national banking system. The Democrats endlessly harped on the antiblack theme, protesting that the Lincoln administration had changed the war for union into a war for emancipation. If Lincoln was reelected, they charged, Republicans were planning to amalgamate the black and white races. The word *miscegenation* (race mixing) made its first appearance in an 1864 campaign document.

By the fall, however, the military situation in Georgia had improved, and Republicans united behind Lincoln. On election day, the president scored a decisive victory. Lincoln was reelected in November by a vote of 212 to 21 in the electoral college, carrying all states except New Jersey, Delaware, and Kentucky. His popular vote was less sweeping 2,206,938 (55 percent) to 1,803,787 (45 percent)—400,000 more than McClellan's in a total of 4 million votes cast.

Sherman's March to the Sea

Lincoln's success in the election owed much to Sherman's success in Georgia. While Grant dug in at Petersburg, Sherman was on the move. The first and most important objective was to seize Atlanta, the "Gate City of the South" and the second-most-important manufacturing center in the Confederacy. On September 1, the Confederates evacuated Atlanta. Sherman's troops marched into the city the next day. "Atlanta is gone," wrote Mary Chesnut.

After burning Atlanta, Sherman led his army into the heart of Georgia. On November 16, 1864, he set out with his 62,000 men marching in two vast columns. Their supply train stretched twenty-five miles. A slave watched part of this mighty host stream past and wondered if anybody was left in the north.

Confederate General John Bell Hood promised to fight Sherman to the death. "Better to die a thousand deaths than submit to live under you . . . and your negro allies," he said. The Confederate general's left arm had been crippled at Gettysburg and only a stump remained of his right leg, amputated at Chickamauga. After evacuating Atlanta, Hood, strapped in the saddle, set off to retake Tennessee and his native

Kentucky, hoping Sherman would leave Georgia to chase him. Sherman dispatched a force to follow Hood, but remained with the bulk of his army in Georgia. After a valiant but futile attempt to defeat the Union forces at Franklin, Tennessee, on November 30, Hood's army disintegrated in the battle of Nashville on December 5.

Sherman, meanwhile, swept across Georgia toward Savannah on the coast. He had planned the march with grim determination to make Georgia "an example to rebels": his troops burned public buildings, depots, and machine shops; destroyed stores of cotton; and confiscated ten thousand horses and mules. Grant had ordered Union troops to strip the valley so thoroughly that "crows flying over it for the balance of the season will have to carry their provender." In short, he shattered the military potential of the area and left its civilians struggling to supply their daily needs. Sherman, on Christmas Day, sent a telegram to Lincoln that announced, "as a Christmas gift, the city of Savannah, with 150 heavy guns, plenty of ammunition and about 25,000 bales of cotton." The president was thrilled. "Grant has the bear by the hind leg," he quipped, "while Sherman takes off its hide."

The Collapse of the Confederacy

By early 1865, the Confederacy was desperate. Desertions became even more frequent, food increasingly scarce. A single stick of firewood cost $5 in Richmond. The price of a barrel of flour had risen to $425. "The surgeons and matrons," wrote a hospitalized Confederate soldier, "ate rats and said they were as good as squirrels, but, having seen the rats in the morgue running over the bodies of the dead soldiers, I had no relish for them."

Having seized Savannah, Sherman turned north into South Carolina on January 17. His army laid waste to much of the state where the rebellion began and reached its capital, Columbia, in less than a month. Like Atlanta, Columbia went up in flames. In April Sherman's army, faced by Confederates under the command of Joseph E. Johnston, stood outside the North Carolina capital of Raleigh.

As Union armies moved across the Confederate heartland, President Davis announced his support for proposals calling for the impressment of slaves for service with the army. In February 1865, the scheme received the backing of General Lee, who wrote that employing blacks as soldiers was "not only expedient but necessary" and announced plainly that slaves who served should be given their freedom. The next month, by a very close vote, the Confederate Congress passed an act calling for 300,000 more soldiers, irrespective of color. Promptly the recruiting of black troops began, and some black companies were raised in Richmond and other towns. By this time, however, the end was near, and none of the black Confederate soldiers ever saw military service.

As Sherman continued to advance and Lee remained unable to break the siege at Petersburg, leaders in Richmond increasingly realized that further resistance was useless. A delegation headed by Vice President Stephens met Lincoln onboard a ship at Hampton Roads, Virginia, on February 3, 1865, to discuss terms of surrender. Lincoln insisted on two points: the restoration of the Union and the abolition

Lee After Appomattox
After opposing secession, General Robert E. Lee accepted a commission in the Confederate army and commanded the Army of Northern Virginia for most of the war. Photographer Matthew Brady took this picture of Lee (center), his son Major General G. W. C. Lee (left), and his aide Colonel Walter Taylor (right) eight days after Lee's surrender to General Grant. The forlorn expression on the general's face vividly demonstrates the agony of defeat. *(Library of Congress.)*

of slavery. The Southerners rejected these terms as "unconditional submission to the mercy of conquerors," and the conference broke up. "I can have no common country with the Yankees," declared Davis. Lee also advised continuation of the war, hoping to fight on long enough to win more favorable terms.

The war's last awful battle took place in Virginia. By the spring of 1865, the lines at Petersburg ran for 55 miles. The efficient Union army kept its men fed, supplied, and reinforced. The Confederate army—ill fed, ill clothed, and hopelessly outnumbered—steadily melted away as desertions increased. Lee knew he could no longer defend Richmond. In one of the war's most dramatic moments, seasoned African-American troops under Grant's command led the final assault on the city; black soldiers were among the first Union troops to enter the capital of the Confederacy. They marched in carrying the Stars and Stripes and singing an anthem to John Brown, much to the amazement of Richmond's citizenry, black and white.

Now nearly surrounded, Lee left his trenches at Petersburg on April 2, 1865. He led his army westward in a desperate quest for food and to join forces with Johnston, still fighting Sherman in North Carolina. Grant's huge force eagerly followed and soon blocked Lee's escape route. On April 7, Grant wrote to Lee, "General, the result of the last week must convince you of the hopelessness of further resistance." Seeing no way to save his exhausted and hungry army, Lee consented to discuss Grant's terms of surrender.

The two great generals met in a farmhouse at Appomattox Courthouse on April 9. After a few minutes of friendly conversation, during which they recalled their comradeship in the Mexican War, Grant wrote out the terms of surrender. They were extraordinarily generous. Officers and men could go home without fear of prosecution for treason, and soldiers who owned horses were able to keep them. Lee immediately signed the terms. The agreement served as a model for the surrender of other Confederate armies. Johnston surrendered his army of 37,000 men to Sherman near Durham, North Carolina, on April 26; Generals Richard Taylor in Alabama and Edmund Kirby-Smith in Arkansas surrendered their armies to the Union commanders in the Southwest. All told, some 174,000 Confederate troops laid down their arms. Jefferson Davis was captured on May 10 at Irwinsville, Georgia, and imprisoned for two years. After his release, he lived quietly in the South until his death on December 6, 1889.

CONCLUSION

Both sides approached the war confident of victory. The North planned to use its superior economic resources and powerful navy to strangle the South. Hoping for a decisive victory, Lincoln ordered an assault on Confederate forces in Virginia. The South, confident of its military skill and convinced the North would quickly tire of the conflict, assumed a defensive military posture, forcing the North to secure and control large areas of land. The South also hoped for foreign intervention, believing that a cotton embargo would force the British to support its cause. Leaders on both sides of the conflict expected a short, largely bloodless conflict. The Union defeat at the First Battle of Bull Run shattered that illusion, and the Battle of Shiloh foretold the incredible slaughter that would follow.

The war placed extraordinary demands on both the Union and Confederate governments, leading both to experiment with methods to raise armies and finance the war. Both sides resorted to conscription to recruit soldiers. The North, which had more experience with national government, developed a number of methods to pay for the effort, including higher taxes, bond sales, and the printing of paper money. The Confederacy depended largely on printing paper money, which in turn, produced rampant inflation. On numerous issues related to the war effort, Southern leaders were torn between their ideological commitment to states' rights and their practical need to develop a coordinated national strategy.

The war exacted a terrible toll on the nation. Nearly 3 million men served in the Union and Confederate armies. For many soldiers, new technology and old battlefield strategies were a lethal combination. A new bullet made rifles more accurate from long ranges, but military tactics called for frontal assaults on fortified positions. If not felled by enemy bullets, soldiers often fell victim to poor diet and primitive medical care. Soldiers on the front lines were not the only ones to suffer. In the South, inflation and scarcity produced widespread suffering.

It was a different story in the North, where the war produced a boom in many industries, though most unskilled workers found their wages failed to keep up with inflation. The war also provided new opportunities for women, who filled temporary jobs in wartime industry and created permanent inroads in the nursing profession. At the same time, Republicans used their large majorities in Congress to dramatically increase federal power, creating a national currency and a national banking system.

After eighteen months of indecisive battles, Lincoln altered both the goals and strategy of the war by issuing the Emancipation Proclamation. What began as a conflict over the spread of slavery was now transformed into a war to free the slaves. "This government cannot much longer play a game in which it stakes all, and its enemies stake nothing," Lincoln observed. The president turned to General Ulysses S. Grant to execute the new strategy of "total war" that would defeat and devastate the South. With Lee's surrender at Appomattox, the American experiment entered a new period in a new form.

SUGGESTED READINGS

The best brief treatments of the Civil War can be found in Brooks Simpson, *America's Civil War* (1996); William L. Barney, *Battleground for the Union: The Era of Civil War and Reconstruction, 1848–1877* (1990); and Allen C. Guelzo, *The Crisis of the American Republic: A History of the Civil War and Reconstruction Era* (1995). Geoffrey C. Ward's *The Civil War: An Illustrated History* provides a lucid and colorful account of the war and its consequences. The most comprehensive general treatment of the war is Allan Nevins's four-volume study *The War for the Union* (1959–1971). Other good overviews are two works by James McPherson, *Battle Cry of Freedom: The Civil War Era* (1988) and *Ordeal by Fire: The Civil War and Reconstruction* (1982).

The most thorough military history from the Confederate viewpoint is Shelby Foote's three-volume work *The Civil War: A Narrative* (1958–1974). For a Northern perspective, *How the North Won: A Military History of the Civil War* (1983) by Herman Hattaway and Archer Jones treats all aspects of the Northern war effort. Bruce Catton's three-volume *The Centennial History of the Civil War* (1961–1965) provides a balanced treatment. *Civil War Command and Strategy: The Process of Victory and Defeat* (1992) by Archer Jones is a good overview of Civil War tactics and their place in the larger history of warfare. Charles Royster's *The Destructive War: William Tecumseh Sherman, Stonewall Jackson and the Americans* (1991) explores the relationship between the vicious military tactics used in the war and the American psyche. Howard P. Nash's *A Naval History of the Civil War* (1972) is a good overview of the war on the seas.

Each battle/campaign has its own studies. A few of the best are Joseph Glatthaar, *The March to the Sea and Beyond: Sherman's Troops in the Savannah and Carolinas Campaign* (1985); Stephen W. Sears, *Landscape Turned Red: The Battle of Antietam* (1983); Richard Sommers, *Richmond Redeemed: The Siege of Petersburg* (1981); and James Lee McDonough, *Shiloh: In Hell Before Night* (1977). Michael Shaara's *Killer Angels* (1974) is a brilliant fictionalized account of Gettysburg. Michael Fellman's *Inside War: The Guerilla Conflict in Missouri During the American Civil War* (1989) provides a fascinating look at a lesser-known side of the military war.

The experience of the common soldier is explored in Bell Wiley's classics, *The Life of Johnny Reb* (1943) and *The Life of Billy Yank* (1952). More recent studies include Reid Mitchell, *Civil War Soldiers: Their Expectations and Their Experiences* (1988), James I. Robertson, *Soldiers Blue and Grey* (1988), and Michael Barton, *Goodmen: The Character of Civil War Soldiers* (1981). Each of these works explores the similarities and differences between the cultures, characters, and causes of Northern and Southern troops. Gerald Lindman explores the chasm between the soldier's disillusioning combat experience and the civilian's sustained idealism in *Embattled Courage: The Experience of Combat in the American Civil War* (1988).

Some of the best studies of the war concern the war's impact on Northern and Southern societies. Concerning the North, Philip Shaw Paludan's *"A People's Contest": The Union and Civil War, 1861–1865* (1988) is an excellent examination of how the war fueled the ongoing processes of modernization and industrialization to transform the lives of the American people. George Fredrickson offers a probing look at the war's intellectual impact in *The Inner Civil War: Northern Intellectuals and the Crisis of the Union* (1965). Iver Bernstein's *New York City Draft Riots: Their Significance for American Society and Politics in the Age of the Civil War* (1990) demonstrates how the war magnified and exacerbated the problems of race, class, and power in the rapidly growing American city. In *The Fate of Liberty: Abraham Lincoln and Civil Liberties* (1991), Mark Neely examines Lincoln's ambiguous record on civil liberties through the personal experiences of those arrested by the military during the suspension of the writ of *habeas corpus.* J. Matthew Gallman provides a good overview of the Union home front in *The North Fights the Civil War: The Home Front* (1994).

Several books have been written recently on Southern society, and in particular Southern nationalism during the war. Emory Thomas, in *The Confederate Nation, 1861–1865* (1979), explores the crumbling of Southern identity under the strain of war as it necessitated the abandonment of Southern practices and values, such as decentralized government. Paul Escott examines Jefferson Davis's role in this disintegration in *After Secession: Jefferson Davis and the Failure of Southern Nationalism* (1978), arguing that policies such as the 20-slave law created disunity and hampered the growth of southern nationalism. Wayne Durrill presents a local study of the war's detrimental effect on Southern society in *War of Another Kind: A Southern Community in the Great Rebellion* (1990). Finally, Drew Gilpin Faust looks at failed Southern efforts to create a unified culture through appeals to religion, protest against inflation, and the reform of slavery in *The Creation of Confederate Nationalism: Ideology and Identity in the Civil War South* (1988).

There has recently been an explosion of scholarship on women's war experience. Concerning Southern women, Drew Gilpin Faust's *Mothers of Invention: Women of the Slaveholding South in the American Civil War* (1996) is an engaging look at how elite planter women "invented new selves" in the atmosphere of war and the destruction of slavery. George C. Rable, author of *Civil Wars: Women and the Crisis of Southern Nationalism* (1989), explores Southern women's changing opinions on the war, their loyalty to their class and race, and their participation in the reconstruction of old gender roles at the war's conclusion. A fascinating first-hand account of the war from a Southern woman's perspective is *Mary Chesnut's Civil War,* edited by C. Van Woodward (1981).

Elizabeth Leonard's *Yankee Women: Gender Battles in the Civil War* (1994) offers insight into women's war work, the male opposition they encountered, and the extent to which the Civil War was a watershed in women's progress toward equality. Stephen Oates's excellent biography of Clara Barton, *A Woman of Valor* (1994), is also informative on the subject of women's contribution to the Civil War. Most recently, Jeanie Attie examines the war as a testing ground for women's entrance into the body politic in *Patriotic Toil: Northern Women and the Civil War* (1998). Catherine Clinton and Nina Silber are editors of an impressive collection of essays on the meanings of the war for both men and women, Northern and Southern, *Divided Houses: Gender and the Civil War* (1992).

The politics of the Emancipation Proclamation are addressed in two studies, LaWanda Cox's *Lincoln and Black Freedom: A Study in Presidential Leadership* (1981) and Robert Durden's *The Gray and the Black: The Confederate Debate on Emancipation* (1972). The former dispels the notion on Lincoln as a "reluctant emancipator" and examines the political considerations he was forced to deal with in issuing his proclamation. Durden's book uncovers the surprising support among Southerners, including Jefferson Davis, for some sort of emancipation, but concludes their motives were not humanitarian but strategic.

Several wonderful studies have been done on the black transition from slavery to freedom. Leon Litwack's masterful *Been in the Storm So Long* (1979) is perhaps the most comprehensive. He identifies the ambivalent attitude the former slaves had toward their new situation. Willie Lee Rose's *Rehearsal for Reconstruction* (1964) is a local study of the ex-slaves of the South Sea Islands and the Northern reformers who came down to aid their adjustment. David Blight examines the reaction to emancipation of one of America's greatest black thinkers in *Frederick Douglass's Civil War: Keeping Faith in Jubilee* (1989). Ira Berlin et al. (eds.), *Freedom: A Documentary History* (1982), and C. Peter Ripley (ed.), *Witness for Freedom: African American Voices on Race, Slavery, and Emancipation* (1993), are collections of primary sources documenting the African-American reaction to the war and emancipation.

Dudley Cornish's *The Sable Arm: Black Troops in the Union Army, 1861–1865* (1956) was one of the first studies of black soldiers and is still a useful source. More recently, Joseph T. Glatthaar takes up the subject in *Forged in Battle: The Civil War Alliance of Black Soldiers and White Officers* (1990). Both works account the opposition and discrimination black troops underwent as well as their heroics in battle. Glatthaar's work portrays the complex and evolving relationship they had with their white officers, and the difficult postwar adjustments of both groups. Edwin S. Redkey's (ed.) *A Grand Army of Black Men: Letters from African-American Soldiers in the Union Army, 1861–1865* (1992) presents the black soldier's experience in his own words.

Competing Voices

Civil War Songs

"The Bonnie Blue Flag"

After "Dixie," "The Bonnie Blue Flag" was the most popular Confederate song, both with the army and the public. It was first sung in New Orleans in 1861 by Marion Macarthy, sister of the song's author, Harry Macarthy, a noted Southern author and performer. The words tell the story of secession.

We are a band of brothers, And native to the soil,
Fighting for our Liberty, With treasure, blood, and toil;
And when our rights were threaten'd, The cry rose near and far,
Hurrah for the Bonnie Blue Flag, that bears a Single Star!

Hurrah! Hurrah! For Southern rights hurrah!
Hurrah! Hurrah! For the Bonnie Blue Flag that bears a Single Star.

As long as the Union was faithful to her trust,
Like friends and brethren kind were we, and just;
But now, when Northern treachery attempts our rights to mar,
We hoist on high the Bonnie Blue Flag that bears a single star.

First gallant South Carolina nobly made the stand,
Then came Alabama and took her by the hand;
Next, quickly Mississippi, Georgia, and Florida,
All raised on high the Bonnie Blue Flag that bears a single star.

Ye men of valor gather round the banner of the right,
Texas and fair Louisiana join us in the fight;
With Davis, our loved President, and Stephens, statesmen rare,
We'll rally round the Bonnie Blue Flag that bears the single star.

And here's to brave Virginia, the Old Dominion State,
With the young Confederacy at length has linked her fate;
Impelled by her example, now other States prepare
To hoist on high the Bonnie Blue Flag that bears a single star.

Then cheer, boys, cheer, raise a joyous shout
For Arkansas and North Carolina now have both gone out,
And let another rousing cheer for Tennessee be given,
The single star of the Bonnie Blue Flag has grown to be eleven.

Then here's to our Confederacy, strong we are and brave,
Like patriots of old we'll fight, our heritage to save;
And rather than submit to shame, to die we would prefer,
So cheer for the Bonnie Blue Flag that bears a single star.

"The Stripes and Stars"

Sung to the same tune as the Confederate song, the Union version was written by Colonel J. L. Geddes of the Eighth Iowa Infantry. He wrote it to respond to the "distortions" of the Confederate version.

We're fighting for our Union, we're fighting for our trust,
We're fighting for that happy land where sleeps our Father's dust.
It cannot be dissever'd, tho' it cost us bloody wars.
We never can give up the land where float the Stripes and Stars.

Hurrah! Hurrah! For equal rights hurrah!
Hurrah! For the brave old flag that bears the Stripes and Stars.

We treated you as brothers until you drew the sword,
With impious hands at Sumter you cut the silver cord,
So now you hear our bugles; we come the sons of Mars,
We rally round that brave old flag which bears the Stripes and Stars.

We do not want your cotton, we care not for your slaves,
But rather than divide this land, we'll fill your southern graves.
With Lincoln for our Chieftain, we'll wear our country's scars.
We rally round that brave old flag that bears the Stripes and Stars!

We deem our cause most holy, we know we're in the right,
And twenty millions of freemen stand ready for the fight.
Our bride is fair Columbia, no stain her beauty mars.
O'er her we'll raise that brave old flag which bears the Stripes and Stars.

And when this war is over, we'll each resume our home
And treat you still as brothers where ever you may roam.
We'll pledge the hand of friendship, and think no more of wars,
But dwell in peace beneath the flag that bears the Stripes and Stars!

Although each side shared a commitment to "freedom" and the Constitution, North and South divided over the meaning of those ideals. For the South, freedom was for white men only; Southerners saw no contradiction between their support for individual freedom and their support for the institution of slavery. For white Southerners, freedom meant independence from the national government. The majority of Southerners who did not own slaves supported the war because they believed that encroaching federal power threatened their way of life. They viewed the Constitution as a nonbinding pact between the states and the federal government. If a state did not feel properly represented, or believed the federal government had misused its powers, it could simply withdraw from the Union. "Ours is not a revolution," Jefferson Davis claimed. "Our struggle is for inherited rights. [We seceded] to save ourselves from a revolution" that threatened the cornerstone of the Southern economy and culture—slavery.

At the beginning of the war, most Northerners shared the belief that freedom should be limited to white men. While they did not support the abolition of slavery in the South, most Northerners opposed its expansion into new territories. Freedom meant the chance for the individual to move up in society through hard work. A society that included slaves hampered the freedom of everyone—white and black—by reducing the opportunity for wage labor. In time, many Northerners would expand their definition of freedom to include African-Americans and embrace Lincoln's call for emancipation. Initially, it was the desire to preserve the Union, and not a commitment to expand freedom, that convinced most in the North to take up arms. They viewed the Union as a sacred bond, ordained by God, one that could not be broken at will. Revolution against government was only justified in the case of repressive government, which was certainly not the case in the United States.

These differing motivations of North and South are displayed quite vividly in the music of the era. Southern songs such as "Dixie" and "The Bonnie Blue Flag" usually invoked the defense of home, family, the land, and "Southern rights." Northern songs spoke of liberty and Union and in some cases, as with "The Battle Hymn of the Republic," employed religious imagery to signify the epic proportions of their cause.

Questions for Analysis

1. What lines in "The Bonnie Blue Flag" capture the Southern defense of rebellion?
2. How does the song illustrate the Southern concept of the Union?
3. Why do you think the song does not mention slavery, even though the issue was so central to the war?
4. What lines in "The Stripes and Stars" highlight why Northerners fought?
5. To what concept of rights does the lyric "For equal rights hurrah" refer?
6. What does this song say about the Northern concept of the Union?
7. Contrast the last stanza with the third stanza. What does the change in tone say about the Union attitude toward the South?

16

Reconstruction and the New South, 1864–1900

The opening act of the play *Our American Cousin* had already begun when the president's carriage pulled up on April 14, 1865, to Ford's Theater in Washington. At 8:25 P.M. President Lincoln, accompanied by his wife Mary and a young couple, Major Henry Rathbone and Clara Harris, quietly made his way to the presidential box, which overlooked the stage. But someone in the theater spotted Lincoln, and within minutes the packed crowd of 1,675 were on their feet giving the president an enthusiastic ovation. The actors paused and joined in the demonstration while the band struck up "Hail to the Chief."

Lincoln settled into his black walnut rocking chair; Mrs. Lincoln sat on his right. The guard who had been sitting outside the door leading to the president's box had decided to go across the street to meet some friends. It proved to be a fatal mistake. During the third act, John Wilkes Booth, a deranged actor and Confederate sympathizer, dashed into the president's box, pulled a small pistol from his pocket, and placed it within six inches of Lincoln's head. As he cried out "Sic semper tyrannus!" ("Thus be it ever to tyrants!"), Booth pulled the trigger. The president slumped forward in his chair. Booth jumped out of the haze of blue gun smoke brandishing a dagger. While Mary embraced her husband, Major Rathbone wrestled with the attacker. Booth escaped Rathbone's grasp by slashing his arm to the bone. Then he leaped from the box, only to catch his spur on a flag adorning its rail and crash to the stage.

The president lay mortally wounded. The bullet had struck behind his left ear, tunneled through his brain, and lodged behind his right eye. Four soldiers and two doctors carried him to a small privately owned house across the street. An observer recorded the scene in his diary: "The quaint sufferer lay extended diagonally across the bed, which was not long enough for him. . . . His slow, full respiration lifted the [bed] clothes with each breath he took. His features were calm and striking." The physicians gathered around Lincoln's bed knew that he could not survive his wound. Mary, overcome with grief, refused to accept his fate. "Love, live but one moment to speak to me once—to speak to our children," she cried. Lincoln never spoke again. The following morning, April 15, at 7:22 A.M. Abraham Lincoln, the sixteenth president of the United States, took his last breath. "Now he belongs to the ages," whispered Secretary of War Edwin Stanton.

Union troops engaged in a massive manhunt to find Lincoln's killer. They tracked him down in a barn in Virginia and killed him in a blaze of gunfire. His last words were: "Tell mother I die for my country. I thought I did for the best." Investigators quickly discovered that Booth had not acted alone. On the same night that Booth shot Lincoln, his accomplices planned attacks on Vice President Andrew Johnson and Secretary of State William Seward. Johnson escaped unharmed, but Seward suffered severe stab wounds. A military tribunal convicted eight people of conspiracy to kill the president. Despite often flimsy evidence, four were hanged.

The bullet that killed Lincoln also changed the direction of Reconstruction, the government policy toward the defeated South. Lincoln's death removed from the scene a masterful politician, emboldened those seeking to impose a punitive peace on the South, and elevated to the presidency a man unprepared for the bitter political debates that followed. The experiments of the Reconstruction Era (1863–1877) brought intense struggles between groups with competing notions of government power, individual rights, and race relations. President Johnson, believing he was following Lincoln's plan for a quick "restoration" of the Union, rigidly supported states' rights, leniency toward the former rebels, and noninterference to protect the rights of the freed people. Radical Republicans, who included former abolitionists and freed slaves, challenged Johnson's program and were able to seize control of Reconstruction policy in 1866. Wielding the power of national government, they hoped to punish unrepentant planters, ensure the political and economic rights of the former slaves, and solidify the Republican Party's control of the South.

African-Americans were central players in the Republican effort to "reconstruct" southern society. Freed from the bonds of slavery, they moved to strengthen old institutions such as the family and church, to create new political institutions, and to secure economic independence. Despite important gains, black experiments in freedom were soon frustrated by white Democrats who clamored for the "redemption" of the defeated South. Using violence and intimidation, "Redeemers" successfully fought to recreate the white-dominated social order that had existed before the war. In the face of determined southern Democrats and internal divisions in the North, the Republicans backed away from their commitment to Reconstruction, leaving the experiment incomplete. The "New South" that emerged from war and Reconstruction had changed in significant ways, but for many African-Americans it bore striking similarities to the South of old.

Chronology

1863	Lincoln issues Proclamation of Amnesty and Reconstruction
1864	Radical Republicans pass Wade-Davis Bill
1865	Lincoln assassinated; Johnson becomes president
	Freedmen's Bureau created
	Southern states pass "Black Codes"
	House forms the Joint Committee on Reconstruction
	Thirteenth Amendment passed and ratified; prohibits slavery
1866	Fourteenth Amendment passed; establishes citizenship for blacks
	Fifteenth Amendment passed; gives black males the vote
	Republicans sweep off-year elections
1867	First Reconstruction Act
	Tenure of Office Act
1868	Johnson impeached and acquitted
	Fourteenth Amendment ratified
	Grant elected president
1869	National Woman Suffrage Association and American Woman Suffrage Association founded
1870	Fifteenth Amendment ratified
	Ku Klux Klan launches terrorist campaign
	First Enforcement Act
1871	Last of southern states rejoin the Union
	Ku Klux Klan Act
1872	Liberal Republicans nominate Greeley for president
	Grant reelected president
	Crédit Mobilier, "salary grab," and Whiskey Ring scandals uncovered
	General Amnesty Act
1873	Panic of 1873 begins
	Colfax Massacre
1875	Civil Rights Act of 1875
1876	Presidential election is disputed
1877	Compromise of 1877; Hayes becomes president
1880	Harris publishes *Uncle Remus*
1884	Twains publishes *The Adventures of Huckleberry Finn*
1895	Washington's "Atlanta Compromise"
1896	*Plessy* v. *Ferguson* establishes "separate-but-equal" doctrine

- Why did President Johnson and congressional Republicans divide over Reconstruction policy?
- What did the Radical Republicans hope to accomplish, and what role did government play in their methods?
- How did African-Americans respond to freedom and political participation? How did southern whites react to black participation?
- Why has Reconstruction been called "America's unfinished revolution"?
- How did the New South reflect the failure of Reconstruction? How different was it from the Old South?

This chapter will address these questions.

Presidential Reconstruction: The First Experiment, 1864–1866

The North's victory had ended the Civil War, but the battle for the peace had just begun. The battleground switched to Washington, where congressional Republicans and the White House clashed even before the war ended over a central question: How much authority did the federal government have to impose conditions on the defeated states of the South? Lincoln had experimented with a lenient plan for returning the rebel states to the Union, but his assassination strengthened Republican support for harsher measures. The difficult task of formulating a new policy fell to Vice President Andrew Johnson, a man ill equipped for the difficult challenges ahead.

The Legacy of Battle

The war had devastated southern society. The countryside, said one observer, "looked for many miles like a broad black streak of ruin and desolation." Most major cities were gutted by fire. A northern visitor called Charleston a place of "vacant houses, of widowed women, of rotting wharves, of deserted warehouses, of weed-wild gardens, of miles of grass-grown streets, of acres of pitiful and voiceless barrenness."

More than just razing cities, the Civil War shattered an entire generation of young men in the South. In Alabama, 29 percent of the 122,000 men who bore arms died. One-third of Florida's 15,000 soldiers failed to return. An estimated 23 percent of South Carolina's white male population of arms-bearing age were killed or wounded. Many of those who survived were maimed in battle. In 1866 the state of Mississippi spent a fifth of its revenues on artificial arms and legs for Confederate veterans.

The war ruined the South's economic life. The region's best agricultural lands lay barren. It would take more than a decade for the staples of the southern economy—cotton, tobacco, and sugar—to recover from the wartime devastation. Most factories were dismantled or destroyed, and long stretches of railroad were torn up. According to some estimates, the South's per capita wealth in 1865 was only about half what it had been in 1860. The defeat of the South had also made all Confederate money

The Ruins of Richmond Burned-out shells of buildings were all that remained of the Richmond business district in April 1865. Confederate troops, not wanting supplies to fall into the hands of the Union army, had actually set many of the fires as they fled. The ruins are indicative of the total devastation of the South at the war's end. The massive rebuilding effort was just one of the monumental tasks facing the nation during Reconstruction. *(Library of Congress.)*

worthless. But most unsettling of all the changes the war had brought was the end of slavery. Slave property, which was estimated at over $2 billion in 1860, disappeared.

In contrast, the North emerged from battle with new prosperity and power. The Republicans who dominated the wartime Congress enacted a uniform system of banking and a transcontinental railroad. They also fueled the North's economy through generous appropriations for internal improvements. Railroads thrived by carrying troops and supplies; the meatpacking and textile industries soared in response to demands from troops for food and clothing. The per capita wealth of the North doubled between 1860 and 1870. The number of manufactures increased by 80 percent, and property values increased from $10 billion to over $25 billion. In 1870 the per capita wealth of New York State was more than twice that of all eleven ex-Confederate states.

The war also ravaged the political landscape in America. War-born hostility shaped the competition between the two parties long after the war had ended. Republicans depended on hatred of southern rebels to cement their biracial coalition. "The Democratic party," proclaimed Indiana governor Oliver P. Morton, "may be described as a common sewer and loathsome receptacle, into which is emptied every element of treason, North and South." Democrats appealed to their natural constituency of former slave owners by charging that Republicans were the defenders of economic privilege and political centralization, and a threat to individual liberty. Stressing the potent message of white supremacy also drove an ideological wedge between freed slaves and poor whites.

The war had a long-term impact on the sectional balance of power in the nation. Before 1861, the slave states had achieved an extraordinary degree of power in the national government. In 1861 the United States had lived under the Constitution for seventy-two years. During forty-nine of those years, the country's president had been a southerner—and a slaveholder. After the Civil War, a century passed before another resident of the Deep South was elected president.

The war gave birth to the modern American state, dominated by a national government far more powerful than anything the nation had known previously. The federal budget for 1865 exceeded $1 billion (twenty times the budget for 1860), and with its new army of clerks, tax collectors, and other officials, the federal government became the nation's largest employer. The change in the size and scope of government found expression in language, as northerners replaced references to the country as a "union" of separate states with a new emphasis on a singular, consolidated "nation."

The presence of nearly 3.5 million former slaves represented the most dramatic legacy of the war. The black abolitionist Frederick Douglass observed that the former slave "was turned loose, naked, hungry, and destitute to the open sky." The new challenges that freedom presented forced experimentation by black and white. What labor system would replace slavery? Was freedom enough, or would blacks obtain the right to vote?

Lincoln's Plan for Union

Though not committed to any single plan for Reconstruction, Lincoln favored a lenient and conciliatory policy toward the South, as he made clear in 1863. Lincoln hoped that a charitable approach would produce defections from the southern cause and hasten the war's end. Beyond outlawing slavery, he offered no protection for freed slaves. He also insisted that ultimate authority for Reconstruction of the states rested with the president, not Congress. Since the Union was "constitutionally indestructible," Lincoln argued that the southern states had never officially left the Union but had merely engaged in military rebellion. Therefore, Lincoln's power as commander-in-chief gave him control over the defeated states in the South.

In December 1863, Lincoln issued a Proclamation of Amnesty and Reconstruction declaring that southern states could organize new governments after 10 percent of those who had voted in 1860 declared their loyalty to the Union and accepted the Union's wartime acts outlawing slavery. Each state would then convene a constitutional convention and elect new representatives to Congress. Lincoln offered a general amnesty to all Confederate citizens except high-ranking civil and military officials. His plan did not extend the right to vote to freed people. Carrying out his policy, the president recognized reconstituted civil governments in Louisiana and Arkansas in 1864, and in Tennessee in February 1865.

Many congressional Republicans argued that by declaring war on the Union, the Confederate states had broken their constitutional ties and were "conquered provinces" subject to the authority of Congress. The most strenuous criticism came from a group of Radical Republicans. Most Radicals believed that it was the national government's responsibility to guarantee political rights and economic opportunity to the freed people in the South. Led by Senator Charles Sumner of Massachusetts and Representative Thaddeus Stevens of Pennsylvania, the Radicals wanted the North to impose a more punitive peace settlement. The Radicals planned to reshape southern society by confiscating southern plantations and redistributing the land to freed slaves and white southerners who had remained loyal to the Union. The North must, Stevens contended, "revolutionize Southern institutions, habits, and manners . . . or all our blood and treasure have been spent in vain."

In 1864 the Radicals challenged Lincoln by passing their own, more stringent peace plan. The Wade-Davis Bill, sponsored by Senator Benjamin Wade of Ohio and Representative Henry Winter Davis of Maryland, required that 50 percent of white male citizens had to declare their allegiance before a state could be readmitted to the Union. Moreover, only those southerners who pledged—through the so-called ironclad oath—that they had never voluntarily borne arms against the Union could vote or serve in the state constitutional conventions. The bill required the state conventions to abolish slavery and exclude from political rights high-ranking civil and military officers of the Confederacy.

Lincoln killed the bill with a pocket veto, meaning he "pocketed" it and did not sign it within the required ten days after the adjournment of Congress. The authors of the bill denounced Lincoln's action in the Wade-Davis Manifesto. Lincoln had to understand, they warned, that "the authority of Congress is paramount and must be respected." Flexing its muscle, Congress refused to seat the delegates from states that applied for readmission under Lincoln's plan.

The vast majority of Republicans fell somewhere between Lincoln and the Radicals. Like the president, these so-called moderates wanted a quick end to the war and a speedy restoration of the Union. They showed little interest in the Radical plans for social and economic Reconstruction. Many wanted to keep former Confederate leaders from returning to power and hoped to provide a minimum of political rights for freed people. The former slave, argued Lyman Trumbull, will "be tyrannized over, abused, and virtually reenslaved without some legislation by the nation for his protection." But the critical question was, how much protection? What all Republicans shared was a determination to solidify their party's power in the North and extend their influence in the South. Hostility toward former rebels and political expediency, more than reformist zeal, shaped their approach to the South.

Behind the scenes, Lincoln was working to find common ground among his fellow Republicans. In March 1865, the president and Congress agreed on the creation of the Bureau of Refugees, Freedmen, and Abandoned Lands (Freedmen's Bureau) to provide "such issues of provisions, clothing, and fuel" as might be needed to relieve "destitute and suffering refugees and freedmen and their wives and children." Over the next few years, the bureau built schools, paid teachers, and established a network of courts that allowed freed people to file suit against white people.

Lincoln, a masterful politician, might have maintained a congressional majority behind a fairly moderate program. In the last speech he ever delivered, three days before his death, Lincoln suggested that he might support freedmen's suffrage, beginning with those who had served in the Union army. Whether Lincoln and his party could have forged a unified approach to Reconstruction is one of the great unanswered questions of American history.

Restoration Under Johnson

A few hours after Lincoln's death, Vice President Andrew Johnson of Tennessee was sworn in as president. Johnson rose from humble origins. His father, a porter and janitor, died when Andrew was three. Working as a tailor's apprentice at the age of ten, Johnson taught himself how to read and eventually started his own tailor shop. After prospering in business, he decided to enter politics. A Democrat, Johnson modeled himself after his hero, Andrew Jackson, who had fought for "common people" against powerful interests. "I am for the people," he declared as he rose from state assemblyman to U.S. senator. During the war, Johnson refused to support secession and, after Federal forces captured Nashville, Lincoln appointed him as Tennessee's military governor. Many Republicans believed that Johnson, a southern Democrat who had remained loyal to the Union, could help unify the nation. In 1864 party leaders nominated him to serve as Lincoln's vice president.

Once in office, Johnson tried to continue Lincoln's lenient policy while also appeasing the radicals. Like Lincoln, he insisted that the president held authority over Reconstruction policy, and he was more interested in "restoring" the Union than in "reconstructing" southern society. Unlike Lincoln, however, Johnson was a vain man consumed by deep suspicions and insecurities. He was ill suited for the delicate compromising and negotiating that would be necessary to maintain the Republican coalition. Moreover, Johnson, a states' rights activist, was openly hostile to former slaves and deeply skeptical of Radical plans to provide the freedman with political rights. "This is a country for white men," the president said in 1865, "and by God, as long as I am President, it shall be a government for white men."

Initially, he kept Radicals off balance with his strong denunciations of Confederate leaders. "Treason is a crime and crime must be punished. Treason must be made infamous and traitors must be impoverished," he declared. The president's rhetoric resulted from his populist hostility toward powerful southern planters, but Radicals interpreted it as support for their agenda. "Johnson, we have faith in you," Radical leader Ben Wade of Ohio remarked after visiting the new president. "By the gods, there will be no trouble now in running the government."

During the summer of 1865, Johnson executed his own plan of restoration. He appointed a provisional governor for each of the former Confederate states (except those states that had begun Reconstruction under Lincoln) and instructed the governors to convene constitutional conventions. The president insisted that the new constitutions revoke their ordinances of secession, repudiate the Confederate debt, and ratify the Thirteenth Amendment, which declared that "neither slavery nor involuntary servitude, except as punishment for crime . . . , shall exist within the United States."

Johnson also took a lenient approach to former rebels. He offered "amnesty and pardon, with restoration of all rights of property" to almost all southerners who took an oath of allegiance to the Constitution and the Union. Those ex-Confederates who were excluded from amnesty could petition Johnson personally for a pardon. The president approved nearly 90 percent of the petitions. By October 1865, ten of the eleven rebel states claimed to have passed Johnson's test for readmission to the Union. The Thirteenth Amendment was ratified in December. Satisfied with the South's progress, Johnson told Congress in December that the "restoration" of the Union was virtually complete.

Initially, most Republicans supported the outlines of Johnson's policy. Moderates wanted to strengthen some provisions but agreed that the federal government could not guarantee suffrage or civil rights for African-Americans. Radicals, though calling for stronger protections for blacks, hoped southern leaders would respond favorably to the president's policy and offer the vote to some African-Americans. Over the next few months, however, Republican support for the president's policy faded as evidence mounted of both southern defiance and increasing discrimination against the freed people.

Southern leaders were in no mood for compromise or conciliation; they were committed to restoring the old racial order. The delegates who met to form the new governments in the South showed contempt for northern Reconstruction plans, rejecting even Johnson's benign policy. In fact, the "restoration" government

Taking the Oath of Allegiance President Johnson's Reconstruction plan included amnesty, pardon, and the restoration of property rights to all southerners who would swear allegiance to the Union. The plan, although it expedited the process of readmitting southern states, proved too lenient. The new state constitutions did not protect the freed slaves' civil rights, and southern voters returned several former Confederate leaders, including Confederate Vice President Alexander Stephens, to elected office. (*The South: A Tour of its Battle-Fields and Ruined Cities* by John Trowbridge, 1866.)

looked much like the old Confederate government. Many of the conventions approved of constitutions that limited suffrage to whites. The 1865 Louisiana Democratic platform declared, "There can in no event nor under any circumstances be any equality between the white and other Races." The provisional governor of Alabama declared that "the State affairs of Alabama must be guided and controlled by the superior intelligence of the white man." Southern voters defiantly elected to Congress the former vice president of the Confederacy, Georgia's Alexander Stephens, four Confederate generals, eight colonels, six cabinet members, and a host of other rebels.

All of the newly constituted state governments passed a series of stringent laws, called "Black Codes." The codes varied from state to state, but all were designed to restrict the freedom of the black workers and keep the freed people in a subordinate position. All included economic restrictions that would prevent former slaves from leaving plantations. Some states tried to prevent African-Americans from owning land. Other laws excluded African-Americans from juries and prohibited interracial marriages. Edmund Rhett of South Carolina summed up the purpose of the Black Codes: "The general interest both of the white man and of the negroes requires that he should be kept as near to the condition of slavery as possible, and as far from the condition of the white man as is practicable."

The President versus Congress

Southern resistance angered Radicals and many moderates in Congress. When the Thirty-ninth Congress convened in December 1865, moderates and Radicals refused to allow the newly elected representatives from former Confederate states to take their seats. Immediately after the House of Representatives turned the southerners away, Thaddeus Stevens called for the appointment of a special Joint Committee of Fifteen on Reconstruction "to inquire into the conditions of the States which formed the so-called Confederate States of America." The Joint Committee, consisting of nine House members and six senators, was headed by a moderate, Senator William Pitt Fessenden, but Radicals quickly seized control.

After public hearings that revealed evidence of violence against freed slaves, the committee recommended congressional passage of new legislation to protect them. In January 1866, Congress voted to extend the life of the Freedmen's Bureau and enlarge its powers. In February, Johnson issued a stinging veto message. The following month, Congress passed a civil rights bill that extended the authority of federal courts to protect blacks. Again, Johnson angrily vetoed the measure.

Why did Johnson assume such a confrontational posture? There is no doubt that he sincerely believed both bills to be unconstitutional. The civil rights bill, he declared in his veto message, represented a stride "toward centralization and the concentration of all legislative power in the National Government." Political considerations, however, were just as important. Johnson hoped that by forcing a confrontation he could isolate the Radicals from moderate Republicans. He refused to believe that moderates would break with him over the issue of freed people's rights. Ultimately, he hoped to build a new coalition that would include Democrats in the North and South, and a small number of moderate and conservative Republicans in the North.

But Johnson seriously miscalculated the lines of division within the party. In the words of the *New York Herald*, the president's actions were "a windfall, a godsend. He [Johnson] gave them Johnson to fight instead of fighting among themselves." The Senate vote to override his veto of the Freedmen's Bureau bill should have given him pause. Though the vote fell two votes short, thirty of thirty-eight Republicans voted in favor. In April, moderates joined with the Radicals to override the presidential veto and enacted the Civil Rights Act of 1866. Despite all of their differences, Radicals and moderates now shared a common disdain for the president and his Reconstruction policies, which rewarded rebels and made disaffection respectable in the South. "I have tried hard to save Johnson," observed moderate William Fessenden, "but I am afraid he is beyond hope."

A number of violent incidents in the South strengthened the Radicals' resolve to protect the rights of the freed people. In May, a mob composed of white policemen and firemen invaded a black neighborhood in South Memphis, Tennessee. Before the riot ended, forty-eight people, all but two black, were dead; five black women had been raped; and hundreds of homes, churches, and schools had been torched. Three months later, in New Orleans opponents of Radical Reconstruction went on a violent rampage, killing thirty-four blacks and three white Radicals. "It was not a riot," declared the military commander of the region. "It was an absolute massacre by the police." Radicals blamed Johnson's lenient policies for the outbreak. "Witness Memphis, witness Orleans," cried Sumner. "Who can doubt that the President is the author of these tragedies?"

Most people did not go as far as Sumner in blaming the president for the riots, but the violence undermined Johnson's claim that southern blacks did not need federal protection. In July, Radicals and moderates joined forces again to pass the Freedmen's Bureau bill over a second veto. By overriding two presidential vetoes, Congress asserted its control over Reconstruction.

Congressional Reconstruction: The Radical Experiment, 1866–1870

Commanding a clear majority in Congress, Radicals sent to the states the Fourteenth and Fifteenth Amendments to the Constitution. Believing the federal government should be the protector of individual rights, they designed the amendments to protect the rights of freed people and to strengthen the Republican Party's position in the South. Given the prevailing gender assumptions of the time, Radicals specifically excluded women from the protections of either amendment, angering women's suffrage supporters and creating deep divisions within the movement. Republican efforts to safeguard their gains by limiting the president's power resulted in the nation's first impeachment trial.

Citizenship, Equal Protection, and the Franchise

In June 1866, the coalition of moderates and Radicals passed the Fourteenth Amendment to the Constitution. The amendment was the first national effort to define

American citizenship. It declared that "all persons born or naturalized in the United States" were "citizens of the United States and of the state wherein they reside" and were guaranteed "equal protection" and "due process" under the law. The amendment reflected the growing consensus among Republicans that national legislation was necessary to force the South to deal fairly with blacks. By asserting that the national government played a role in guaranteeing individual rights, the amendment established an important foundation for future challenges to the states' rights doctrine.

The amendment was a compromise measure designed to enhance the Republican Party's power. At the insistence of many moderates, it stopped short of enfranchising black men. But radicals added a provision requiring a reduction in the representation in Congress of any state that denied adult males the vote. Either way the Republicans gained. Southern states would either extend the franchise to black voters, thus increasing the number of likely Republicans, or they would lose seats in Congress. The amendment also included a Radical demand that former Confederate leaders be prevented from holding federal or state offices; but moderates added a clause giving Congress the authority to override the disqualification in individual cases.

To take effect, the amendment had to be ratified by three-quarters of the states, and it became the central campaign issue during the fall 1866 congressional elections. Johnson denounced the amendment and urged southern states not to ratify it. Interpreting the elections as a referendum on the Fourteenth Amendment and his Reconstruction policy, the president planned an unprecedented campaign tour—called "a swing around the circle"—that took him from Washington to Chicago and St. Louis and back. He hoped the trip would exploit public sentiment against extending political rights to blacks and focus anger on Republican leaders. Instead it further eroded support for presidential Reconstruction within his own party. At a number of stops, the president exchanged hot-tempered insults with hecklers. He alienated many moderate Republicans with his description of Radicals as "factious, domineering, tyrannical" men. "Why not hang Thad Stevens and Wendell Phillips?" he shouted to an audience in Cleveland.

Republicans skillfully focused the campaign on Johnson's support for the disloyal South. They successfully employed the tactic of "waving the bloody shirt" to remind northern voters of the thousands of family members and friends who died at the hands of southern armies. Viewing themselves as the defenders of the Union, Republicans held Johnson and the South responsible for thwarting Reconstruction.

On election night the voters appeared to repudiate the president. The Republicans won a three-to-one majority in Congress (margins of 42 to 11 in the Senate, and 143 to 49 in the House) and gained control of the governorship and legislature in every northern state, as well as West Virginia, Missouri, and Tennessee. "This is the most decisive and emphatic victory ever seen in American politics," exclaimed the Radical journal, *The Nation*.

The moderate Republicans interpreted the election results as a clear call for Radical Reconstruction. Congress moved rapidly and, on March 2, 1867, adopted the First Reconstruction Act; supplementary acts followed in 1867 and 1868. These acts reversed presidential restoration and established new requirements for southern states to gain entry into the Union.

The First Reconstruction Act declared that "no legal government" existed in the South. It divided the South (with the exception of Tennessee, which had ratified the Fourteenth Amendment) into five military districts, each under the command of a Union general. To be considered reconstructed, the law required southern states to call new constitutional conventions in which all male citizens were eligible to vote. The convention delegates then had to draft and approve state constitutions that guaranteed black suffrage. Finally, after the newly elected legislatures ratified the Fourteenth Amendment, the states would be accepted into the Union. During 1868, six states—North Carolina, South Carolina, Florida, Alabama, Louisiana, and Arkansas—met the requirements and were readmitted (see map).

The new plan was far tougher than Johnson's policy, but many Radicals wanted to go further. They pressed for federal support for black schools and the disfranchisement of ex-Confederate leaders. A few Radicals called for the distribution of land to former slaves. Thaddeus Stevens advocated confiscating millions of acres of land from the "chief rebels" in the South, and giving forty acres to every adult male freedman. "How can republican institutions, free schools, free churches, free social

Military Reconstruction Districts With the Reconstruction Act of 1867, Congress took control of Reconstruction in the South, dividing the states that had seceded into five military districts. In each district, Union generals assumed control until state constitutional conventions ratified the Fourteenth Amendment and created new constitutions that guaranteed freedmen the right to vote. Only Tennessee was exempt from this Act, having ratified the Fourteenth Amendment in 1866.

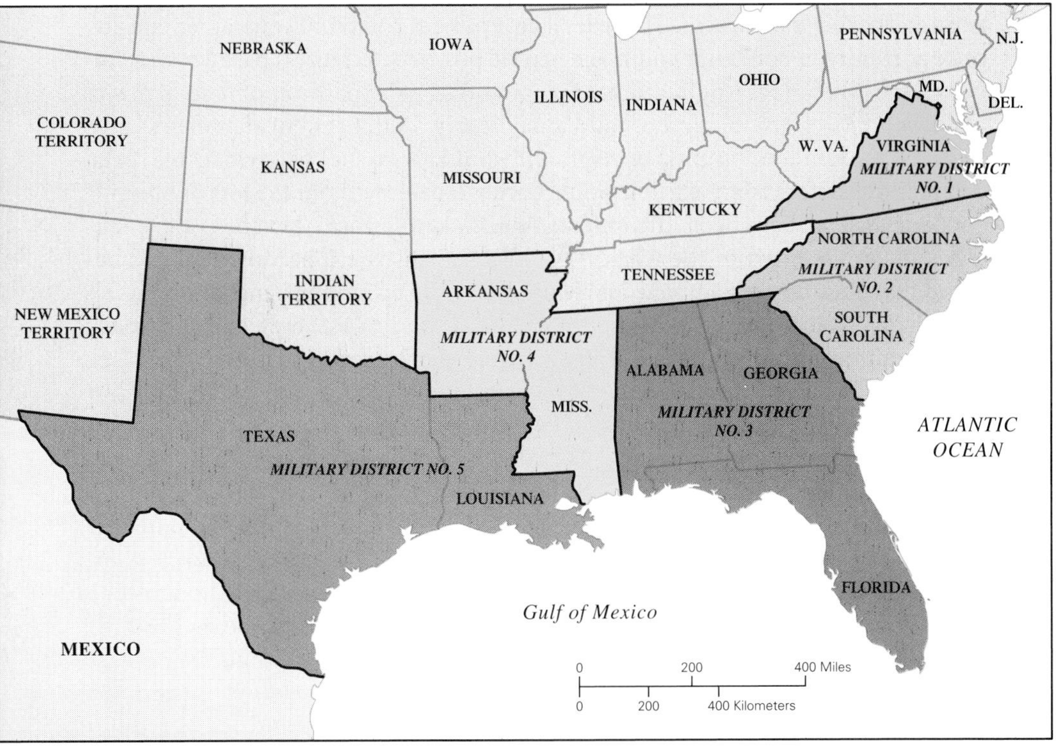

intercourse exist," he asked, in a "community" of wealthy planters and "serfs"? (See Competing Voices, page 650.)

Stevens was right in recognizing that without large-scale redistribution of land, blacks had little hope of achieving economic independence. But the Republicans failed to develop a systematic land distribution program. At the end of the war, as Union armies occupied parts of the South, Union commanders had developed a variety of plans for dealing with confiscated lands. General William T. Sherman set aside the Sea Islands off the Georgia coast and large tracts of land in South Carolina for African-American refugees who burdened his army. Each family received forty acres of land and the loan of army mules. By the summer of 1865, some forty thousand freed people had settled on "Sherman's land." In October, however, Johnson ordered the head of the Freedmen's Bureau to tell Sea Island blacks that they would have to work out arrangements with the legal owners of the land. Angry blacks protested: "Why do you take away our lands? You take them from Us who have always been true, always true to the Government! You give them to our all-time enemies! That is not right!" When some of the Sea Islanders refused to deal with the white owners, Union soldiers forced them to leave or work for their old masters.

In 1866 Republicans tried to address the land problem by passing the Southern Homestead Act, which set aside 44 million acres of land for freedmen and loyal whites. But most freed people, and many whites, lacked the resources to buy the land or purchase the tools needed to work it. For Republicans, even many Radicals, the idea of land reform was too extreme. Despite their support for federally imposed Reconstruction, most Republicans clung to nineteenth-century notions of individualism and limited government. The federal government could only guarantee equality of opportunity; it could not confiscate private property to redress past wrongs. Doing so, most believed, would require an extraordinary expansion of federal power and result in a clear violation of individual liberty. "A division of rich men's lands amongst the landless," argued the *Nation,* "would give a shock to our whole social and political system from which it would hardly recover without the loss of liberty."

Radicals may have been uncomfortable with land reform, but the issue of suffrage was at the heart of the Radical plan for Reconstruction. Most Radicals believed that once blacks had political rights, social and economic benefits would follow. Black enfranchisement would also benefit the party, since grateful black voters in the South could solidify Republican control over the region. To safeguard black votes, Republicans framed the Fifteenth Amendment. Section 1 of the amendment forbade states to deny their citizens the right to vote on the grounds of "race, color, or previous condition of servitude." Section 2 gave Congress power to enforce the amendment by appropriate legislation.

The Republican authors carefully designed the Fifteenth Amendment to further their political ambitions. Like the Fourteenth Amendment, it was the result of compromises between moderates and Radicals. The amendment extended the vote to blacks, but it did not guarantee universal manhood suffrage. Republicans had little to gain from supporting universal male suffrage. Republicans wanted to prevent former Confederates—most of whom were Democrats—from voting. Nor did the amendment, as Radicals proposed, prohibit the use of poll taxes and other methods to restrict black voting. Mainstream Republicans wanted to preserve voting restrictions against immigrants in the North. Massachusetts and Connecticut used literacy tests to deny the vote to recent European immigrants. California used them to prevent Chinese immigrants from voting.

Ratification of the amendment in March 1870 produced widespread Republican jubilation. Frederick Douglass announced that blacks now would "breathe a new atmosphere, have a new earth beneath, and a new sky above." White and black men marched in a large parade through Washington, D.C., waving banners that read "The Nation's second birth" and "the fifteenth amendment, Uncle Sam's bleaching powder."

Reconstruction and Women's Suffrage

The debates over the Fourteenth and Fifteenth Amendments represented a turning point in the struggle for women's suffrage. Nineteenth-century feminists had been closely tied to the antislavery cause, and many male abolitionists had been active in the movement for women's rights. During the war, feminists had put aside the suffrage issue to support the Union cause in abolishing slavery. Once the war ended, however, feminist leaders hoped to refocus public attention on the question of women's suffrage.

Potential allies, however, saw little political reward in extending the franchise to women. Most Republicans believed that black male votes were the key to gaining control of the southern states. Former abolitionists who had supported women's suffrage in the past worried that pushing the issue now would distract attention from the most important question: political and economic rights for former slaves. As Wendell Phillips admonished women leaders, "One question at a time. This hour belongs to the Negro."

Instead of supporting their former suffragist allies, Republicans sanctioned the denial of suffrage. The Fourteenth Amendment, in fact, wrote the term *male* into the Constitution for the first time. Disappointed feminists accepted defeat at the federal level and focused on the reform of state constitutions. In 1866 Elizabeth Cady Stanton, Susan B. Anthony, and Lucy Stone created the Equal Rights Association to lobby and petition for the removal of racial and sexual restrictions on the state level. Not only were their efforts unsuccessful, they also provoked bitter divisions within the suffrage movement, eventually resulting in an open break between Radicals supporting Stanton and Anthony and more moderate followers of Stone. As Republican men withdrew funding and support, many feminist leaders felt betrayed, convinced, as Stanton declared, that woman "must not put her trust in man" in seeking her own rights. "Standing alone, we learned our power," Stanton and Anthony wrote later. "Woman must lead the way to her own enfranchisement and work out her own salvation."

Angry with their former allies, Stanton and Anthony campaigned against ratification of the Fifteenth Amendment. Ratification, Anthony charged, would create an "aristocracy of sex." They employed racist and elitist arguments in opposing the new amendment. Stanton argued that black men should not be elevated over "women of wealth, education, virtue, and refinement." In 1869 she urged her followers to support women's suffrage "if you do not wish the lower orders of Chinese, Africans, Germans and Irish, with the low ideas of womanhood to make laws for you and your daughters." That same year, these radicals formed the all-female National Woman Suffrage Association (NWSA).

Another group of feminists led by Lucy Stone broke with Stanton and supported the amendment, conceding that this was "the Negro's hour." Women, they contended, could afford to wait for the vote. Their goal was to maintain an alliance with Republicans and to support the Fifteenth Amendment. They believed that this was the best way to enlist Republican support for women's suffrage after Reconstruction issues had been settled. To advance their cause, they formed the moderate American Woman Suffrage Association (AWSA), which focused on achieving suffrage at the state level. This disagreement over strategy would divide the women's movement for a generation to come.

The Impeachment of a President

Fearing that Johnson would subvert its plans for the South, Congress passed several laws in March 1867 aimed at limiting his presidential power. The Tenure of Office Act, the most important of the new restrictions, required the president to seek Senate approval before removing any officeholder who had been previously approved by the Senate. In this way, congressional leaders could protect Republican appointees, such as Lincoln appointee Secretary of War Edwin M. Stanton, who opposed the president's Reconstruction policy and was openly collaborating with the Radicals. In August 1867, Johnson suspended Stanton and, as required by the Tenure in Office Act, asked for Senate approval. When the Senate refused, Johnson had Stanton physically expelled from his office and appointed Union General Ulysses S. Grant interim secretary of war.

On February 24, the House of Representatives, seizing on Johnson's violation of the Tenure of Office Act, voted to impeach the president. It charged him with eleven counts of "high crimes and misdemeanors." Of the eleven articles of impeachment, the first eight related to Johnson's attempt to violate the Tenure of Office Act by his "illegal" dismissal of Stanton. Article X accused Johnson of bringing Congress into disgrace by "inflammatory and scandalous harangues" and of degrading his office "to the great scandal of all good citizens."

The trial in the Senate, which the Constitution empowers to act as a court in impeachment cases, opened on March 5, 1868, and continued until May 26, with Chief Justice Salmon P. Chase presiding. To remove the president from office, two-thirds of the Senate, 36 of 54 Senators, needed to vote for impeachment. On the first day of the trial, Radical Benjamin Butler of Massachusetts presented the charges against the president. "This man by murder most foul succeeded to the Presidency, and is the elect of an assassin to that high office, and not of the people," he charged. "We are about to remove him from the office he has disgraced by the sure, safe, and constitutional means of impeachment."

The president's attorney, Henry Stanbery, argued that Stanton was not protected by the Tenure in Office Act because he had been appointed by Lincoln. And in any case, Johnson's removal of Stanton was not a criminal act but a test of the legality of a law that was probably unconstitutional.

As the case came to an end, it was obvious that the vote would be close. "It hangs in almost an even balance," Representative James Garfield wrote two hours before the vote. "There is an intensity of anxiety here, greater than I ever saw during the war." At the last moment, seven moderate Republicans broke ranks, voting for acquittal along with twelve Democrats. The impeachment failed by one vote. The moderates agreed that Johnson had broken the law, but they believed the violation did not warrant removal from office, fearing such a move would establish a dangerous precedent and weaken the presidency.

The Radical Experiment in the South, 1865–1872

With a majority of Democrats and former Confederates prevented from participating in the political life of the South, the Republican Party emerged as the dominant force in southern politics. It controlled the state conventions, wrote the new constitutions, and controlled the new governments. At the same time, millions of African-Americans took advantage of their freedom to strengthen traditional institutions, especially the family and the church. But their hopes for economic independence were frustrated by a new labor system that trapped them between freedom and slavery. Despite political domination, the white South struggled to maintain its own social structure and cultural identity, including distinctions of class and race.

The Southern Republicans

The southern Republican Party was an uneasy coalition of three distinct groups. African-Americans formed the largest group of the Republican rank and file. In five states—Alabama, Florida, South Carolina, Mississippi, and Louisiana—blacks constituted a majority of registered voters. In three others—Georgia, Virginia, and North Carolina—they accounted for nearly half the registered voters. In 1865 and 1866, African-Americans throughout the South organized scores of mass meetings, parades, and petitions that demanded civil equality and the right to vote. Hundreds of African-American delegates, selected by local meetings or churches, attended statewide conventions.

The number of African-Americans who held office during Reconstruction never reflected their share of the electorate. No state elected a black governor; only a few selected black judges. In only one state—South Carolina—did blacks have a majority in the legislature. But blacks did win a number of important political positions throughout the South. Over six hundred blacks, many of them former slaves, served in state legislatures during Republican rule. Sixteen African-Americans served in the

U.S. House of Representatives in the Reconstruction era. In 1870, Mississippi's Hiram Revels became the first African-American member of the United States Senate.

A second group of Republicans were a diverse lot whom critics called "carpetbaggers," suggesting that they came South with all their belongings packed into a single carpet-covered traveling bag. In 1871 a Democratic congressman described a carpetbagger as an "office seeker from the North who came here seeking office by the negroes, by arraying their political passions and prejudices against the white people of the community." In fact, carpetbaggers were a diverse group that included northern businessmen, former Freedmen Bureau agents who had invested money in the region, and Union army veterans who stayed in the South after the war. Most combined a desire for personal gain with a commitment to reform the South by introducing northern ideas and institutions. They made up only a sixth of the delegates to the state conventions, but carpetbaggers held more than half the Republican governorships in the South and almost half its seats in Congress.

The third group consisted of white southerners who resented the planter elite and believed that Republican policies would favor them over the wealthy landowners. They included southern Unionists, small town merchants, and rural farmers. Democrats called them "scalawags," an ancient Scots-Irish term for small, worthless animals. To Democrats, a scalawag was "the local leper of the community," even more hated than the carpetbagger. "We can appreciate a man who lived north, and . . . even fought against us," declared a former North Carolina governor, "but a traitor to his own home cannot be trusted or respected."

It was a fragile coalition. Class differences divided the business-minded carpetbaggers and poor scalawags. With a more limited vision of state power, scalawags opposed high taxes to fund the reformist social programs carpetbaggers endorsed. But race remained the issue with the greatest potential for shattering the Republican coalition in the South. Black demands for political rights and economic independence clashed with the deeply held racial attitudes of most scalawags. "[O]ur people are more radical against rebels than in favor of negroes," declared a scalawag leader.

The Republican Program

Although fragile, this coalition of southern Republicans had a profound impact on public life in the South. Under Republican rule, all the southern states rejoined the Union between 1868 and 1871. In states where the Republican coalition remained unified—South Carolina, Louisiana, and Florida—Reconstruction governments remained in power for as many as nine years. In other states, such as Virginia, they ruled for only a few months. Republicans hoped to remake southern society in the free-labor image of the North.

The new Republican regimes expanded democracy. They repealed Black Codes, modernized state constitutions, extended the right to vote, and made more offices elective. The "fundamental theme" of the South Carolina constitution was "a raceless and classless democracy." Arkansas's document committed the state to "the political and civil equality of all men." Reconstruction administrations guaranteed the political and civil rights of African-American men. They could now serve on juries, school boards, and city councils; hold public office; or work as police officers. To ensure these rights were not violated, many state legislatures passed tough antidiscrimination laws. A South Carolina law, for example, levied a fine of $1,000 or a year's imprisonment for owners of businesses that practiced discrimination.

Believing that education was the foundation for a democracy, many Republican governments established public school systems for the first time. An 1869 Louisiana law prescribed universal free schooling "without distinction of race, color, or previous condition." In theory, public schools were open to both races, but in practice, whites stayed away from schools that admitted blacks. When the Reconstruction government forced the University of South Carolina to admit African-Americans in 1873, nearly all the whites withdrew. Two years later the university was 90 percent black. Few African-Americans objected to the segregation. For now, they agreed with the abolitionist Frederick Douglass, who accepted that separate schools were "infinitely superior" to no schools at all.

African-Americans eagerly embraced the expanded educational opportunities. Throughout the South, African-Americans raised money to build schoolhouses and pay teachers. A Mississippi farmer vowed, "If I never does do nothing more, I shall give my children a chance to go to school, for I consider education next best thing to liberty." By 1869 the Freedmen's Bureau was supervising nearly three thousand schools serving over 150,000 students throughout the South. Over half the roughly 3,300 teachers in these schools were African-Americans. Between 1865 and 1867, northern philanthropists founded Howard, Atlanta, Fisk, Morehouse, and other black universities in the South.

In most cases, however, the efforts to improve education were overwhelmed by crowded facilities and limited resources. Often African-American and poor white children had to skip school so they could help their family by working in the fields. Between 1865 and 1870, only 5 percent of black children in Georgia attended school regularly; for whites, the figure was 20 percent.

The new Republican governments embarked on ambitious programs to rebuild and expand the South's infrastructure, which had been destroyed during the war. They paved new roads and subsidized investment in manufacturing. Believing that transportation was the key to southern industrial development, Republicans poured enormous energy into rebuilding the region's railroad system. Between 1868 and 1872, the South added over three thousand new miles of track. State governments also spent more money than ever before on public institutions such as orphanages and asylums.

Paying for the task of rebuilding the devastated South proved troublesome. Like their northern counterparts, southern states used general property taxes to pay for the expanded services. By levying taxes on personal property as well as real estate, the states hoped to force wealthy planters to bear much of the burden. But despite higher taxes, spending outpaced revenues, producing large deficits. During the 1860s, the southern tax burden rose 400 percent. Between 1868 and 1872, the deficits of Louisiana and South Carolina almost doubled, and between 1868 and 1874, that of Alabama tripled.

Students at Hampton Institute, c. 1870 Education was a top priority for the freed slaves. At first, northern missionary societies funded and staffed most schools and colleges for African-Americans. The American Missionary Association, with the help of the Freedmen's Bureau, founded Hampton Institute in 1868 to provide "industrial training" and teacher training for former slaves. Over time, African-Americans preferred to run their own schools, institutions that became centers of the black community. *(Hampton University Archives.)*

Corruption compounded the revenue problem. In South Carolina, for example, the state maintained a restaurant and barroom for the legislators at a cost of $125,000 for one session. White southerners pounced on the stories of corruption in Republican governments, claiming it proved their charge that blacks were incapable of self-government. Corruption during this period, though widespread, was not limited to one race, one party, or one region. Southern black officials were no more corrupt than their white counterparts, and the Democratic urban machines in the North probably stole more public money than the Republican regimes in the South. Critics ignored the evidence because they were not really concerned with corruption. What they objected to was African-Americans gaining and exercising political power.

The Meaning of Freedom

A black Baptist minister, Henry M. Turner, stressed that freedom meant the enjoyment of "our rights in common with other men." The newly freed slaves sought countless ways to challenge the authority whites had exercised over their lives. Freedmen acquired belongings—dogs, guns, and liquor—that had been forbidden under slavery, and they abandoned the old expressions of humility—tipping a hat, stepping aside, casting eyes low. They dressed as they pleased. As slaves, they often had no surname. Freedom provided them with the opportunity to assume the last name of a prominent person. Free to travel for the first time, many former slaves packed their meager belongings and left the plantation.

For many former slaves, freedom provided the cherished opportunity to reunite with family members. "In their eyes," wrote a Freedmen's Bureau agent, "the work of emancipation was incomplete until the families which had been dispersed by slavery were reunited." Parents reunited with each other and with children who had been taken in by planters and overseers. Thousands of African-American couples who had lived together under slavery flocked to churches to have their relationships sanctioned by marriage. By 1870, the majority of African-Americans lived in two-parent families.

Freedom changed gender relations within the black family. Slavery had imposed a rough equality on men and women: both were forced to work long hours in the fields. But freedom allowed them to define separate spheres. Initially, men continued to work in the fields, while many women wanted to stay at home and attend to the family. Some wives, however, asserted their independence by opening individual bank accounts, refusing to pay off their husbands' debts, and filing complaints of abuse. In most cases, however, economic necessity ended the hopes of independence or domesticity by forcing women back into the fields. According to one former slave, women "do double duty, a man's share in the field, and a woman's part at home. They do any kind of field work, even ploughing, and at home the cooking, washing, milking, and gardening."

African-Americans pooled their resources to buy land and build their own churches. During slavery, southern Protestant churches had relegated blacks to second-class status, forcing them to sit in the back rows and preventing them from participating in many church functions. By 1877, the great majority of black southerners had withdrawn from white-dominated congregations and founded, then filled, their own churches. The new churches, and the ministers who led them, played key roles in the social, political, and religious lives of the parishioners.

Sharecropping

For many African-Americans, economic independence was the most powerful expression of freedom. "All I want is to get to own four or five acres of land, that I can build me a little house on and call my home," a Mississippi black said. Without large-scale redistribution of land, however, few former slaves realized their dream of land ownership. Instead, they were forced to hire out as farm laborers. At first, most freedmen signed contracts with white landowners and worked in gangs, laboring long hours under white supervisors, much as they had in slavery. What the freed people wanted, a Georgia planter observed, was "to get away from all overseers, to hire or purchase land, and work for themselves." The desire to gain a degree of autonomy led many freed people to abandon the contract labor system in favor of tenant farming. As a South Carolina freedman put it, "If a man got to go

Abyssinian Baptist Church
African-Americans demonstrated their preference for autonomy in religious matters by founding their own churches. Their withdrawal from mixed congregations of every denomination was in part a response to the poor treatment they received from white church members. Seating was segregated, and black members were usually barred from church government. Religion had historically been crucial to African-American identity, and these independent churches soon became the most important institutions in their communities. *(Library of Congress.)*

cross the river, and he can't get a boat, he take a log. If I can't own the land, I'll hire or lease land, but I won't contract."

The most widely used form of tenant farming was known as sharecropping. Under this scheme, former plantation owners subdivided their land into farms of 30 to 50 acres, which they leased to workers. The tenants were given seed, fertilizer, farm implements, and food and clothing to take care of their families and grow a cash crop, usually cotton. In return, the landlord took a share of the crop (hence "sharecropping") at harvest time. At first, freed people were enthusiastic about sharecropping. The system provided workers with a sense of freedom and many saw it as a first step toward independence. It allowed families to work the fields together and the reward, usually a half-share of the crop, exceeded the small wages they had received under the old system. While thousands of poor white farmers became sharecroppers, the vast majority were black (see map).

Rather than being a step toward independence, however, sharecropping trapped many African-Americans in a new system of labor that was neither slave nor free. Because of a chronic shortage of capital and banking institutions, sharecroppers turned to local merchants for credit. The merchants, who were often also the landowners, advanced loans to sharecroppers and tenant farmers in exchange for a lien, or claim, on the year's cotton crop. As the only available creditors, merchants and planters could charge usurious interest rates and mark up prices. "It's owed before it's growed," complained many tenant farmers. With half their crop owed to the landowner and half, or often more, owed to the merchant, sharecroppers fell into debt they could not escape.

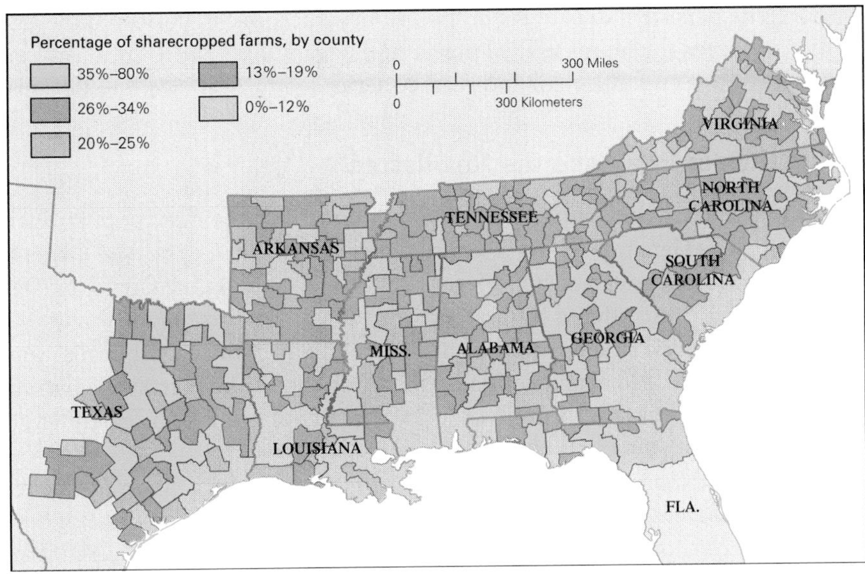

Sharecropping in the South by County, 1880 As a result of the war and the depression of the 1870s, increasing numbers of southerners worked land that they did not own. Without any other economic opportunities, poor whites and blacks alike found themselves tied to the land through sharecropping, an endless cycle of cotton production and perennial debt. The areas with the heaviest concentration of sharecropping were located where cotton remained king—from South Carolina to eastern Texas. (Source: U. S. Census Office, Tenth Census, 1880, *Report of the Production of Agriculture*. Washington, D. C.: Government Printing Office, 1883, Table 5).

In effect, an informal system of debt peonage replaced the formal structure of slavery. A black laborer described his unenviable condition. "I signed a contract—that is, I made my mark for one year. The Captain was to give me $3.50 a week, and furnish me a little house on the plantation. . . ." A year later, he found himself in debt to the planter, and so he signed another contract, this one for ten years. During this time, he was "compelled" to buy his food, clothing, and other supplies from the plantation store." At the end of his contract, he tried to leave the plantation but was told he owed $165 and consequently found himself reduced to a "lifetime slave."

President Grant and the Divided North, 1868–1876

In 1868 Republicans looked to Civil War hero Ulysses Grant to lead the party. But Grant proved a weak leader and soon reports of scandals eroded support for his administration. The revolt of "Liberal Republicans" in 1872 revealed the depth of disaffection with Grant and the growing divisions among Republicans in the North. Concerned by the intrusive federal role in Reconstruction, Northern liberals hoped to end the government's interventionist experiment in the South. The president won reelection, but his second term was dominated by continuing revelations of corruption. The persistent debate about the "money question" underscored the uncertainty Americans felt about federal power and began to set battle lines between the eastern business establishment and rural America.

Ulysses Grant and the "Spoilsmen"

By the time of the Republican national convention in 1868, the most popular man in the country was General Ulysses S. Grant, whose troops had destroyed General Robert E. Lee's Confederate army in Virginia, effectively ending the Civil War. Despite the terrible losses suffered by Grant's army, long lines of veterans formed to shake his hand wherever he went. Months before the election, Republicans were forming Grant clubs. "No man ever had a better chance to be a great magistrate than he," noted an observer. It was no surprise that Republicans nominated Grant on the first ballot at their convention in Chicago.

The campaign exposed the political tensions produced by the Civil War and Reconstruction. The Democrats, who met in New York on July 4, picked Horatio Seymour, former governor of New York, as their candidate. The Democratic platform blasted the Republicans for subjecting the nation, "in time of profound peace, to military despotism and negro supremacy." The Republicans once again reminded voters that they had saved the Union and charged that Democrats were the party of rebellion.

Grant carried the Republicans to victory on election day, winning 214 electoral votes to Seymour's 80 and carrying twenty-six states to Seymour's eight. The popular vote did not match his resounding victory in the electoral college. He won by only 306,592 votes (3,013,421 to 2,706,829). In fact, Grant's victory was made possible by the 450,000 votes cast by the freed people in the southern states under military occupation. In Congress, the Democrats picked up a few seats, but Republicans retained their large majorities in both the House and Senate.

Grant's success on the battlefield did not translate into effectiveness in the White House. The growth in federal power, and the close relationship between government and business, provided elected officials with ample opportunity for personal gain. With a few exceptions, Grant appointed greedy men who could not resist the temptation for personal gain. These "spoilsmen" tainted the Grant administration with scandal. In 1869 the president's brother-in-law gave into the temptation by joining the crafty financier Jay Gould in an effort to corner the gold market. In 1872 a congressional committee confirmed newspaper reports of widespread bribery of high government officials by the Union Pacific Railroad. The railroad promoters created a phony construction company, called Crédit Mobilier, so they could divert profits into their own pockets. While the Union Pacific floundered, the Crédit Mobilier flourished, awarding its stockholders a single-year dividend of 348 percent. Fearful that Congress might intervene and expose the corrupt arrangement, the directors gave stock to a number of prominent Republicans.

In that same year, greedy congressmen pushed through a bill doubling the president's salary and increasing by 50 percent the salary of Congressmen. The congressional increases were made retroactive for two years, thus granting each member $5,000 in back salary. The press vehemently protested the "salary grab," and public indignation forced Congress to repeal the law in 1874.

The most dramatic scandal, which reached into the White House itself, involved the so-called Whiskey Ring, a network of large whiskey distillers and Treasury agents who defrauded the Internal Revenue Service of $4 million in taxes. The ringleader was a former Union general, John A. McDonald, whom Grant had appointed to the post of supervisor of internal revenue in St. Louis. Worst of all, Grant's private secretary, Orville E. Babcock, was involved in the duplicity. There is no evidence that Grant knew about the fraud, but his poor choice of associates earned him widespread public censure.

The Liberal Revolt

As early as 1870, a small but vocal group of distinguished Republicans had become disaffected with Grant's administration. These self-proclaimed "Liberal Republicans" were a mixed lot, though most were educated, middle-class reformers who believed in limited government and rule by an enlightened elite. The Liberals wanted people like themselves to replace the party hacks who dominated the Grant administration. As a result, they made the creation of a civil service system, based on merit rather than political appointments, the centerpiece of their campaign.

In keeping with their belief in limited government, the Liberal Republicans also supported amnesty for all former Confederates and removal of troops from the South. Many saw the "southern question" as a distraction that enabled party spoilsmen to retain the allegiance of voters by "waving the bloody shirt," while avoiding more important issues: civil service reform and effective government. Reconstruction seemed to exemplify the worst consequences of state activism. Reformers had abolished slavery, the Liberals argued; now it was up to African-Americans themselves to make the most of their new opportunities.

In 1872 the Liberal Republicans organized a national convention that produced a platform criticizing the parent party's southern policy and advocating civil service reform. For president they nominated Horace Greeley, the eccentric editor of the *New York Tribune* and a longtime champion of reform. The choice stunned many veteran political observers, who believed that Greeley had little chance of beating Grant. One reporter gibed that there had been "too much brains and not enough whiskey" at the convention.

A month after Greeley's nomination, the regular Republicans met in Philadelphia, choosing Grant for reelection on the first ballot. Despite his declining popularity and new revelations of scandal, Grant was still a powerful political force, enjoying support from southern Republicans, business interests, and Radicals. Above all, he still evoked the glory of his Civil War victory at Appomattox. The Republicans adopted a platform paying lip service to civil service reform and waffling on the tariff issue, but taking a strong stand in favor of political and civil rights for all citizens in every part of the country.

Democrats realized they had a lot to gain by joining forces with the disaffected Liberal Republicans. "Anything to Beat Grant" became their slogan. That meant that Democrats had to support Greeley, who had been a severe critic of the Democratic Party. The choice between Grant and Greeley, moaned Georgia's Alexander Stephens, was a choice between "hemlock and strychnine." At their convention in Baltimore, Democrats overlooked their differences and nominated Greeley.

The campaign degenerated into what the *New York Sun* called "a shower of mud." Greeley campaigned for a "New Departure," declaring that his administration would provide equal rights for black and white, offer universal amnesty to Confederate officers, and establish thrift and honesty in government. Cartoonist Thomas Nast portrayed Greeley as an assassin, shaking hands with John Wilkes Booth over Lincoln's grave.

In the election of 1872, Grant won 56 percent of the popular vote, a larger percentage than in 1868. Grant carried thirty-one states and took 286 of the 349 electoral votes. His popular vote margin (3,596,745 to 2,843,446) was the highest since Andrew Jackson's in 1828. But the election also revealed the extent of southern disaffection with Radical Reconstruction. In the South, the Republicans could muster only 50.1 percent of the popular vote.

The Money Question

Continuing revelations of corruption and persistent arguments about "the money question"—referring to federal monetary policy—dominated Grant's second term in office. To help finance the Civil War, Congress had issued almost $450 million in greenbacks—paper currency that was not backed by either gold or silver. The inflation of the money supply led to a steep increase in prices and shook public faith in the government. When the war ended, the government proposed to call in "greenbacks" for payment in gold or silver.

In general, restricting the money supply hurt debtors and helped creditors. People who had borrowed money when the currency was inflated would have to repay loans when fewer dollars were in circulation. Conversely, creditors who had loaned inflated dollars would receive payment in more valuable currency. The debate, however, was never that simple, since not everyone viewed the issue in terms of economic self-interest. Eastern business interests tended to see the debate over paper currency in religious terms. Government had a moral obligation to back its currency in gold; failure to do so was sinful. In addition to fear over falling farm prices, hatred of the eastern establishment—the "money power"—drove many farmers to favor inflated money.

The conflicting and complicated views on the currency cut across party lines. Despite disagreement within his own party, Grant sided with the advocates of hard money, endorsing payment of the national debt in gold as a point of national honor. The president's support for hard money could not have come at a worse time. In 1873 the bankruptcy of the Northern Pacific Railroad set off the "Panic of 1873"—a steep economic depression that lasted for six years. By 1876, eighteen thousand businesses were bankrupt, and nearly 15 percent of the labor force was unemployed. In 1878 alone, more than ten thousand businesses failed. Those who managed to hold on to their jobs suffered painful wage cuts.

Many people, believing that Grant's tight money policy contributed to the depression, increased their calls to print more greenbacks. In 1874 the Democrats and a handful of Republicans succeeded in passing a bill that increased the number of greenbacks in circulation, but Grant vetoed it. The following year, Republicans passed the Specie Resumption Act, which called for redeeming all greenbacks in circulation by 1879 and replacing them with certificates backed by gold. The legislation satisfied creditors, but it failed to calm the fears of small farmers and debtors who worried that any money standard tied to gold would be too restrictive. As the nation emerged from depression in 1879, the clamor for "easy money" subsided. It would resurface more persistently in the 1890s.

The Failure of Reconstruction, 1870–1877

By the mid-1870s, a number of forces conspired to produce the downfall of Radical Reconstruction. In the South, the persistent tradition of individual rights and local control, combined with a belief in white supremacy, allowed the Democrats to topple a number of Republican state governments. A host of influences—disillusionment with government corruption, fears of a Democratic resurgence, economic strains, and general weariness—convinced northerners it was time to abandon their experiment. In a series of decisions, the Supreme Court signaled the North's retreat. The "Compromise of 1877," which resolved a disputed presidential election, marked the end of Reconstruction.

The South Redeemed

Former large slave owners were the bitterest opponents of the Republican program in the South. The Republican effort to expand political and economic opportunities for African-Americans threatened their vested interest in controlling agricultural labor and their power and status in southern society. In response, they staged a massive counterrevolution to "redeem" the South by regaining control of southern state governments.

Initially, some Democrats tried to woo black voters away from the Republicans with moderate appeals on racial and economic questions. When their appeals fell on deaf ears, they launched an ideological attack designed to unify southern whites and stir up fear and uncertainty among blacks and their allies.

In making their case against Republican rule, the Redeemers tapped into values that had deep roots in American political culture. They claimed that the Republican Party favored centralized power and special privilege over local rule and individual rights. "The principle of the Union is no longer justice, but force," declared a prominent white southerner. Most of all, however, the Redeemer appeal rested on the South's social and cultural foundation of racism and white supremacy. Alabama's State Conservative Committee designated January 30, 1868, a day of fasting and prayer to deliver the people of the state "from the horrors of negro domination." Mississippi Democrats in 1868 condemned the black members of the state's Radical constitutional convention as "destitute alike of the moral and intellectual qualifications required of electors in all civilized communities."

For Democrats, playing "the race card" served two purposes. First, the appeal to racial pride lured poor whites away from the Republicans and prevented the formation of a class-based, biracial coalition. "I may be poor and my manners may be crude, but I am a white man," declared a disgruntled scalawag. "That I am poor is not as important as that I am a white man; and no Negro is ever going to forget that he is not a white man."

Second, Democrats hoped to frighten blacks and Republican whites into avoiding voting and other political action. Throughout the Deep South, planters and their supporters organized secret societies to terrorize blacks and Republicans. The Ku Klux Klan emerged as the most powerful of the new terrorist groups. In 1865 a social circle of young men in Pulaski, Tennessee, organized themselves as the "Invisible Empire of the South." New chapters of the secret lodge quickly formed in other states. Klan members, who included poor farmers as well as middle-class professionals, donned ghostly white robes and indulged in ghoulish rituals. Their intention was to frighten their victims into thinking they were the avenging ghosts of the Confederate dead.

After 1870 the Ku Klux Klan fought an ongoing terrorist campaign against Reconstruction governments and local leaders. Acting as a guerrilla army for those who sought the restoration of white supremacy, Klansmen whipped and killed Republican politicians, burned black schools and churches, and attacked Republican Party gatherings. In some communities, Klan members paraded through the streets carrying coffins bearing the names of prominent Radicals and labeled "Dead, damned and delivered." In the bloodiest episode of violence, Klan members murdered nearly one hundred African-Americans in Colfax, Louisiana, on Easter Sunday 1873.

In response to the racial terrorism, Congress passed three Enforcement Acts in 1870 and 1871. The first act prohibited state officials from interfering with a citizen's right to vote. A second created federal election marshals to oversee congressional elections. In April 1871, Congress passed the Ku Klux Klan Act, which outlawed the Klan and any other conspiratorial group that sought to deprive individuals of their rights under the Constitution. It also empowered the president to suspend *habeas corpus* and to use federal troops to suppress "armed combinations."

The legislation restricted Klan activities, but it could not stem the Democratic resurgence in the South. Democrats redeemed Virginia, North Carolina, and Georgia from Radical rule between 1869 and 1871; Texas followed in 1873, and Arkansas in 1874. In 1875 a notorious campaign of terror and intimidation against black voters allowed the Democrats to seize control of Mississippi. The Democratic slogan became: "Carry the election peaceably if we can, forcibly if we must." Republicans

The Colfax Massacre, 1873 Throughout the Reconstruction period, freed slaves faced the threat of violence from whites who resented any alteration of the social order. The killing of one hundred blacks in Colfax, Louisiana, was the bloodiest incident during Reconstruction. Although three whites were convicted of Colfax crimes by the federal government, the Supreme Court overturned the verdicts in *U.S.* v. *Cruikshank.* The Court argued that under the Fourteenth Amendment, the federal government could prosecute only states, not individuals, for civil rights violations. *(Frank and Marie Therese Wood Print Collections, Alexandria, Va.)*

fearful of violence stayed away from the polls. "The Republicans are paralyzed through fear and will not act," the anguished carpetbag governor of Mississippi wrote to his wife. "Why should I fight a hopeless battle . . . when no possible good to the Negro or anybody else would result?"

The Republican Retreat

At the national level, too, a number of forces were pushing the Republican Party to abandon its Reconstruction experiment. First, the idealism that had once informed Republican efforts had long since faded. The Liberal Republican revolt in the 1872 elections revealed the changing sentiment in the party. Many party leaders felt that "waving the bloody shirt" was counterproductive. Republicans now sought reconciliation, not confrontation, with the South. In May 1872, Congress passed a General Amnesty Act that, with some exceptions, allowed Confederate leaders to vote and to hold public office.

Second, Republicans realized they were paying a heavy political price for their southern policies and receiving little benefit from it. Divided among themselves, Republicans watched their congressional majorities dwindle in the wake of a dramatic Democratic resurgence. In 1874 the Democrats gained a majority in the House of Representatives for the first time since 1856. "The election is not merely a victory but a revolution," declared a New York newspaper.

The Panic of 1873 outweighed Reconstruction as a factor in the Republican defeat, but the election's implications for Reconstruction policy were clear. Northern voters were tired of dealing with the "southern question" and the "Negro question." "The truth is our people are tired out with the worn out cry of 'Southern outrages'!!" a weary Republican cried. "Hard times and heavy taxes make them wish the 'ever lasting nigger' were in hell or Africa."

Third, northerners increasingly accepted the southern view of African-Americans as people inferior in intelligence and morality who required the paternal protection of the superior white race. Negative stereotypes in northern newspapers depicted blacks as ignorant, lazy, and dishonest, incapable of exercising the same rights as whites. "They [blacks] plunder, and glory in it," one northern journalist summed up; "they steal, and defy you to prove it." Even loyal administration supporters were convinced that Reconstruction was organized theft. The *New York Times* called the South Carolina legislature "a gang of thieves," its government "a sort of grand orgie."

Fourth, serious strains emerged within Republican ranks in the South. Race played a central role in fracturing the always fragile southern Republican Party. Poor whites were never willing to concede political equality to blacks. Republicans found it difficult to satisfy their black constituents' demands for equality without alienating whites. White Republicans were also divided among themselves. Scalawags resented carpetbaggers who they believed had seized offices that should have gone to native whites. Meanwhile, in state after state, Democrats skillfully exploited deepening fiscal problems by blaming Republicans for excessive spending and sharp tax increases.

These pressures proved too much for most Republicans. With support for Reconstruction unraveling, Radical pleas for new measures to protect the political and civil rights of African-Americans fell on deaf ears. The one exception was the Civil Rights Act of 1875, passed in the closing hours of the Republican-controlled Congress. The law guaranteed persons of every race "the full and equal treatment" of all public facilities such as hotels, theaters, and railroads.

However, several Supreme Court decisions involving the Fourteenth and Fifteenth Amendments undermined protection of black rights. In the so-called *Slaughterhouse Cases* of 1873, the Court offered a narrow definition of the Fourteenth Amendment by distinguishing between national and state citizenship. The amendment, the justices declared, guaranteed only those rights dependent on national citizenship. What were those rights? Most were of little concern to freed people: access to courts and navigable waterways, the ability to run for federal office, travel to the seat of government, and be protected on the high seas and abroad. By giving the states primary authority over citizens' rights, the courts weakened civil rights enforcement. In 1876 the court decided, in *United States* v. *Cruikshank*, that a mob attack on blacks trying to vote did not violate the Fourteenth Amendment. In 1883 the Court reaffirmed its limited view of the Constitution in *United States* v. *Harris,* which argued that the lynching of four black prisoners did not represent an infringement of their Fourteenth Amendment rights.

The Compromise of 1877

Republican leaders approached the 1876 presidential campaign with foreboding. "My God, it is ruin!" exclaimed Republican James G. Blaine. In an effort to distance themselves from the scandals of the Grant administration, party leaders turned to Ohio governor Rutherford B. Hayes. Not only did Hayes hail from an electoral-vote–rich state, but he had earned a reputation for honesty, possessed an honorable Civil War record, and supported civil service reform. He also had articulated a moderate stance on Reconstruction, which Republicans hoped would appeal to conservative Republicans and moderate Democrats.

Signaling that they planned to make the Grant scandals a central theme of their campaign to gain the presidency, the Democrats nominated Governor Samuel J. Tilden of New York, a well-known fighter of corruption. At their June convention in St. Louis, gleeful Democrats chanted "Tilden and Reform" and passed a platform promising to save the nation from "a corrupt centralism which has honeycombed the offices of the Federal government itself with incapacity, waste, and fraud."

On election night, it appeared that the Democrats had regained the White House for the first time since before the Civil War. Tilden received 51 percent of the popular vote (4,284,020) to Hayes's 48 percent (4,036,572). But Republicans charged that Democrats won the elections in three southern states—Louisiana, South Carolina, and Florida—by fraud and intimidation. Both sides claimed the electoral votes in those states (see map).

When Congress reconvened in January it confronted an unprecedented situation: three states with two different sets of electoral votes. If Congress accepted all the Republican votes, Hayes would have a one-vote electoral majority. The Constitution did not cover such a scenario, and as weeks passed without a solution, people feared that the impasse could escalate into a major national crisis.

On January 29, 1877, Congress set up a Joint Electoral Commission to resolve the dispute. The committee was made up of eight Democrats and eight Republicans, with the swing vote going to an independent member of the Supreme Court, Justice David Davis. But Davis withdrew from the Court and declared himself ineligible for the commission. Since there were no independents or Democrats on the Court, a Republican named Joseph P. Bradley took Davis's seat on the commission. The Republicans now controlled nine seats on the commission, the Democrats eight. Not surprisingly, the commission voted along straight partisan lines and gave the election to Hayes.

But Congress still had to approve the results, and the Democrats were threatening to filibuster. On February 26, 1877, prominent Ohio Republicans and powerful southern Democrats met at the Wormley House hotel in Washington, where they

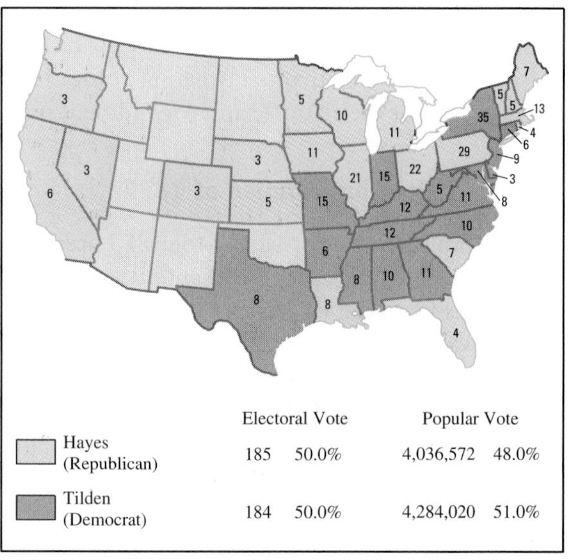

The Election of 1876
Without any clear issues in 1876, Democrats and their presidential nominee Samuel J. Tilden emphasized the corruption that had hampered Grant's administration, while Republican nominee Rutherford B. Hayes linked the Democratic Party to the Confederacy. When the electoral votes were counted, Republicans and Democrats disputed the results in Louisiana, Florida, and South Carolina. Congress made the final decision, selecting Hayes despite the fact that he had trailed Tilden in the uncontested electoral votes.

reached an informal agreement, later called the Compromise of 1877. The Republicans promised that Hayes would withdraw the last federal troops from Louisiana, Florida, and South Carolina, include at least one southerner in his cabinet, and give conservatives control of political patronage. In return, the Democrats promised to support Hayes's election, to accept the Reconstruction amendments, and to refrain from partisan attacks against Republicans in the South. On March 2, 1877, only two days before the scheduled inauguration, the House voted to accept the report and declared Hayes elected by an electoral vote of 185 to 184.

Hayes's election signaled the formal end of the Reconstruction era. In his first month in office, the new president appointed a southern Democrat to his cabinet and withdrew the last of the federal troops from the South. In a speech in Atlanta in the fall of 1877, Hayes told former slaves that their "rights and interests would be safer" if southern whites were "let alone by the general government."

The New South, 1870–1900

At the end of Reconstruction, southern propagandists filled the newspapers with calls for economic experimentation to create a "New South." They wanted the South to abandon its old agrarian ways and transform itself into a bustling center of commerce and industry. Despite the development of new factories and the rise of a few large cities, southern society, steeped in white supremacy, remained economically dependent on cheap labor and king cotton. This burden prevented the South from making major gains. Culturally, southerners remained deeply tied to the past at the same time that they experimented with new forms of artistic expression. For many African-Americans, the New South looked much like the old. Southern leaders developed a number of ingenious methods to limit black voting, and they imposed a rigid system of segregation.

Visions of Industry

In the early 1880s, boosters of the New South told everyone who would listen about the profound changes transforming the region. Led by Henry Grady, editor of the *Atlanta Constitution,* propagandists promised to remake the southern economy in the image of the North, claiming that a society of machines and factories was needed to replace the old agrarian order. Henry Watterson, a Louisville editor and orator, urged that "the ambition of the South is to out-Yankee the Yankee." The first step, however, was to convince southerners of the need for change. "Beyond all question," insisted a Richmond journal, "we have been on the wrong track and should take a new departure."

The clearest evidence of change was the rise of cities. People from every level of rural society left the countryside for towns. "The towns are being recruited by those too poor to be able to live in the country, as well as by those too rich to be willing to live there," observed a reporter. Atlanta, which had only 14,000 residents at the close of the Civil War, had a population close to 40,000 in 1880 and 90,000 two decades later. Birmingham, Alabama, saw its population grow from 3,000 in 1880 to 38,000 in 1900.

The spirit of the New South penetrated the halls of statehouses and governors' mansions. Many state legislatures tried luring northern bankers and capitalists with attractive investment opportunities. William H. Harrison, Jr., a prominent New South spokesman, maintained that no foreign country offered "such tempting inducements to the capitalist for profitable investments" as did the New South. In 1877 five southern states repealed laws reserving land for private homebuilders so that they might entice investors to exploit their coal, iron, and timber resources.

With the aid of new investment, southern industries such as textiles, iron, and lumber experienced a boom. The South's textile mills boasted the latest and most sophisticated machinery. By 1890, textile spindles, which doubled the output per worker, appeared in 90 percent of southern mills compared with only 70 percent of New England mills. Jefferson County, the home of Birmingham, had only twenty-two factories in 1870; thirty years later, it had five hundred. By the late 1880s, southern pig iron production had surpassed the total output of the entire country in 1860. By 1910, the South was producing almost half of all lumber produced in the United States. The lumber industry claimed one in five southern manufacturing workers. "Never before has the lumber business been so active," a paper proudly reported in 1882.

To make their new factories accessible to northern markets, many states built new railroad tracks. Between 1880 and 1890, track mileage more than doubled, from 16,605 to 39,108. The South integrated its railroads with the North by adopting a standard gauge, or track. On May 30, 1886, work crews throughout the South pushed thousands of miles of track three inches closer to create a uniform

Virginia Coalfields After the war, the South lagged far behind the North in economic development. Closing the gap became a major goal of Reconstruction. The discovery of coalfields in Virginia in 1873 provided a major impetus for railroad construction and buoyed the region's economy. Although the South made great strides toward industrialization during Reconstruction, southern industry still accounted for only 10 percent of the United States' industrial capacity by 1900. *(Virginia Historical Society.)*

national railroad system. The change helped railroads to expand the development of land-locked mineral resources of the South, particularly the iron mines of Tennessee, Virginia, and Alabama. By 1898, Birmingham was the largest shipping point for pig iron in the country and the third largest in the world.

King Cotton and the Crop-Lien System

Proponents of the New South exaggerated the amount of change that had actually taken place. Despite the growth of cities and the increase in manufacturing, most people in the South continued to live in rural areas. The 1890 census showed that only 3.9 percent of North Carolinians and 5.9 percent of Alabamans were considered urban. By 1900, the South was still the most rural and agrarian section in the settled portions of the country. Although new industries and signs of progress abounded, the South continued to lag far behind the prosperous North. In 1860 the South housed 17 percent of the country's manufacturing; by 1904 it had only 15 percent.

The economy of the postwar South remained tied to agriculture. The spread of the crop-lien system as the South's main form of agricultural credit forced more and more farmers, both white and black, into growing cash crops—crops that could earn the most money on the open market. Cotton, which yielded more value per acre than any other crop, became the crop of choice. By 1880, nearly three-quarters of the African-American farmers and about one-third of the white farmers in the cotton states were sharecroppers or tenants. The number of cotton mills in the South rose from 161 in 1880 to 400 in 1900. In 1880 there were 45 mills in the United States producing 7 million gallons of cottonseed oil annually for export; by 1900, there were 357, all but 4 in the South.

The South's dependence on a single crop had many unforeseen consequences. For one thing, it made the South less self-sufficient, since many farmers plowed over land that had been used to grow food and replaced it with cotton. By 1880, the South was not growing enough food to feed its people. The near total dominance of "King Cotton" also inhibited economic growth across the region. As more and more farmers turned to cotton growing as the fastest way to obtain credit, expanding production depressed prices. Competition from new cotton centers in the world market, notably Egypt and India, furthered the downward spiral. The decline in cotton prices dragged the rest of the southern economy down with it. By the 1890s, per capita wealth in the South equaled only one-third that of the East, Midwest, or Far West.

Declining cotton prices produced a grim desperation in the South and only increased suspicion and hostility toward the North. In 1879 the *New York Tribune* showed little sympathy: "Fifteen years have gone over the South and she still sits crushed, wretched, busy displaying and bemoaning her wounds."

The Culture of the New South

Paralleling the contrast between industrial boosterism and continued dependence on agriculture, cultural trends pulled the South in different directions. On the one hand, a wave of nostalgia swept across the South as whites honored Civil War soldiers. The movement began as a defense of the "Lost Cause" in the 1860s, then evolved into a nostalgic celebration of old soldiers. Caught up in the "cult of the Confederacy," many white southerners joined the United Confederate Veterans and the United Daughters of the Confederacy, which raised funds for the erection of new monuments. Nine thousand whites of all ages dragged a new statue of Robert E. Lee to its site in Richmond in 1890. Over a hundred thousand people attended the unveiling three weeks later. The region's natives revered Decoration Day, when they carried spring flowers to the graves of the soldiers killed during the war.

At the same time that many white southerners were celebrating the past, southern fiction writers were questioning the relevance of the values and customs that had shaped their society. These writers attempted to explain their region to northern readers at the same time that they challenged prevailing notions of race and gender. In *Uncle Remus: His Songs and Sayings* (1880), Joel Chandler Harris allowed a black slave to tell stories in which the weak could outwit the strong. The success of Harris's book convinced Mark Twain, America's most visible and successful man of letters, to take another look at the South. In 1881 Twain took a boat trip down the Mississippi to reacquaint himself with a region he had explored earlier in his book *Tom Sawyer* (1876). He was shocked by what he witnessed. The New South,

Twain declared, was "a solemn, depressing, pathetic spectacle." His impressions created the backdrop for his greatest work, *The Adventures of Huckleberry Finn*, published in 1884. Among other things, the book explored the enormous distance between the South's perception of itself as a bastion of civilization and its real status as an impoverished and violent place.

Women writers played a prominent role in shaping the literature of the New South. Ruth McEnery Stuart's short stories about white women in fictional "Simpkinsville" portrayed females as active agents and men as ineffectual and absent. Kate Chopin juxtaposed what she saw as more honest and healthier European standards of sexual behavior with the conventions of Protestant America. Her book *The Awakening*, published in 1899, created such an outcry that it was pulled from library and bookstore shelves. The leading woman writer of the New South was Ellen Glasgow. Her most famous novel, *The Deliverance*, became the second best-selling book in America in 1904. It told the story of young people of the South achieving success, but only after overcoming the suffocating burden of southern customs.

Music emerged as the most powerful force for cultural innovation in the New South. Music appealed to people of every description. Musical instruments were among the first mass-produced commodities southerners bought. Cheap banjos were mass-produced in the 1880s, guitars in the 1890s. Students of both races were eager to learn formal music. Instructors taught classical music and voice throughout the towns and cities of the South. Bouncy popular music filled parlors, stages, tents, and streets. Every town of any size had an "opera house" that hosted traveling performers. In 1891 a band tournament in Troy, Alabama, drew four thousand visitors and ten brass bands from nearby towns.

In every other aspect of southern society racial distinctions were hardening, but culturally the line between white and black music was blurring. In southern cities throughout the South, the polyrhythms and improvisation of African music blended with traditional European styles. Much of the experimentation took place in New Orleans, which contained the largest concentration of musicians in the South. The city attracted black and white musicians who trained together, played in the same bands and nightclubs, exchanged ideas, and borrowed styles.

The Triumph of White Supremacy

The Redeemers who gained power in the South ousted, state by state, the carpetbag rule of the Reconstruction era. Some Redeemers gained power by compromising with their opponents; others conquered by brute force. They were a mixed group that included the scions of the old planter class as well as new business leaders. They were united by what they opposed: biracial coalitions and the use of state power as an agent of change.

Free from interference from the North, the Redeemer governments in the South waged an aggressive assault on African-Americans. Democrats regained control of state governments and imposed sweeping changes, slashing social programs, lowering taxes, and placing a premium on restoring social stability. Education programs were especially hard hit. Public schools closed in some parts of Maryland in 1871.

In 1872 only a third of Tennessee's counties levied school taxes; only about 28 percent of the state's children attended school. "Schools are not a necessity," declared the governor of Virginia.

Most important, the Democrats manipulated the law to ensure a stable black work force. Local ordinances in heavily black counties restricted leisure activities—such as hunting, fishing, and gun carrying—that would distract blacks from their work. States passed tough laws against trespassing and theft.

All former Confederate states changed their constitutions to create methods by which they could exclude the black vote. The Mississippi constitution of 1890 set the pattern. It required a poll tax of $2 from prospective voters at registration. Men who intended to vote at elections had to present their receipt at the polls. Anyone who mislaid his receipt forfeited his vote. Other states included literacy tests that required prospective voters to be "able to read the Constitution, or to understand the Constitution when read." Since white Democratic registrars interpreted the ability to read or understand, officials could use these ordinances to discriminate in favor of poor illiterate whites and against black citizens, literate or not. Louisiana adopted the "grandfather clause," which limited the franchise to anyone who had a grandfather on the electoral roll in 1867. Since the grandfathers of most blacks had been slaves, and unable to vote, the measure effectively barred them from voting.

The results of these various efforts to eliminate the black vote were dramatic. Louisiana, for example, contained 130,334 registered black voters in 1896. Eight years later, there were only 1,342. In Alabama 181,000 black voters were registered in 1890; in 1900, 3,000. In the South as a whole, black voter participation fell by 62 percent. In 1900 Ben ("Pitchfork") Tillman of South Carolina boasted on the floor of the Senate, "We have done our best. We have scratched our heads to find out how we could eliminate the last one of them. We stuffed ballot boxes. We shot them. We are not ashamed of it."

Along with disfranchising blacks, southern lawmakers gave informal segregation in public facilities the force of law. Until the 1880s, the South had established a system of segregation by custom. Schools, hospitals, parks, courthouses, hotels, and restaurants were separated by race. Social custom reinforced the distance between the races. Whites never addressed black men they did not know as "mister," but rather as "boy," "Jack," or "George." Black women were never called "Mrs." but rather "aunt" or by their first name. According to custom, the two races did not shake hands, walk together, or fraternize in public. Black men removed their hats in public places reserved for whites, whereas whites did not remove their hats even in black homes.

While some blacks resisted the exclusion from white-owned hotels and restaurants, they could usually find accommodations in black-run businesses. Travel was a different story, for members of both races had no choice but to use the same railroads. When middle-class blacks carrying first-class tickets refused to be consigned to second-class seating, southern whites developed "separate but equal" railcars. These new restrictions—called "Jim Crow laws" after a minstrel song of 1830 that presented blacks as childlike and inferior—made it impossible for blacks and whites to mingle. The laws were soon extended to libraries, hotels, restaurants, hospitals, prisons, theaters, parks, and playgrounds. Blacks and whites used separate bathrooms, separate toilets, and were even buried in separate cemeteries.

The Supreme Court, which had already made discrimination by individuals and businesses legal, now allowed state governments to make segregation a part of the fabric of American life. In *Plessy* v. *Ferguson* (1896), the Court upheld, by a 7 to 1 majority, a Louisiana law that required railroads to provide "equal but separate accommodations for the white and colored races." The Court ruled that the Fourteenth Amendment applied only to political rights and did not extend to "social equality." Legislatures were thus free to pass laws that maintained "the customs and traditions of the people." Justice Henry B. Brown of Michigan, speaking for the majority, ruled with racist candor, "If one race be inferior to the other socially, the Constitution of the United States cannot put them upon the same plane." A year later, the judges endorsed segregated public schools as a means to prevent "commingling of the two races upon terms unsatisfactory to either." The justices also upheld the poll tax and literacy tests, which were used by state officials to disfranchise blacks.

Growing Democratic power emboldened whites to resort to violence, without fear of reprisal. Between 1889 and 1898, blacks suffered 187 lynchings a year in the United States, four-fifths of which were in the South. Lynchings flourished where whites were surrounded by what they called "strange niggers"—blacks who were unknown in the area and had no white person to vouch for them. Most were accused of raping white women. Southern newspapers reported the hangings in graphic detail to stimulate and attract readers and to intimidate blacks.

Democratic restoration also led to the expansion of the convict lease system. In 1876 three Georgia companies contracted to lease the state's convicts for twenty years, in return for a $25,000 annual payment. The convicts were assigned to labor camps in which brutal and degrading conditions prevailed, and overseers forced them to toil from sunrise to sunset, disciplined by the rod and whip.

Southern blacks struggled to persuade whites to stop the persecution. The most prominent voice belonged to Booker T. Washington. Born in 1856 to a slave woman and her white master, whose identity he never knew, Washington later attended the Hampton Institute in Virginia, a black school established and run by northern whites. In 1881 Washington helped organize the Tuskegee Institute, a state vocational school for blacks. He gained national prominence in 1895 when white organizers invited him to speak at Atlanta's Cotton States and International Exposition—the first time in southern history that a black man had been asked to address whites at such an important event.

Washington's speech, which became known as the "Atlanta Compromise," suggested that African-Americans trade political activity and integration for black economic progress. Blacks, he told his segregated audience, should put aside their ambitions for political power and social equality and instead focus on developing useful vocational skills. "It is at the bottom of life we must begin, and not at the top," he said. Political and social equality would proceed naturally once blacks had proven their economic value. "Dignify and glorify common labor," he urged. "Agitation of questions of racial equality is the extremist folly." To both races, he advised cooperation and mutual respect. "In all things that are purely social we can be as separate as the

Lynching Victims After federal troops pulled out of the South in 1876, racial violence gradually reached epidemic proportions, with white southerners lynching thousands of African-Americans before the century's end. The victims, deemed "uppity" by whites, were usually singled out for being too assertive or successful, or for refusing to show the proper deference to whites. These four Kentucky sharecroppers were guilty of being sympathetic toward a black man who had killed his white employer in self-defense. One of the bodies bears the message, "Let white people alone or you will go the same way." *(Gilman Paper Company Collection.)*

fingers, yet one as the hand in all things essential to mutual progress." Washington's message of accommodation was almost universally popular with whites. Blacks were more ambivalent. Southern blacks who favored gradual nonconfrontational change embraced his philosophy, but some northern black leaders complained that Washington had compromised too much.

For the freed people, whose aspirations had been raised by Republican rule, the impact of "redemption" was demoralizing. No one could deny the enormous changes that had transformed American society over the previous two decades: slavery had been abolished and a framework of legal rights had been enshrined in the Constitution. African-Americans created political and social institutions that had not existed before Reconstruction. But as the African-American leader W. E. B. Du Bois observed, "The slave went free; stood a brief moment in the sun; then moved back again toward slavery." Reconstruction had failed to provide blacks with either economic independence or political rights. For many African-Americans, the long road to freedom had just begun.

CONCLUSION

The question of how to deal with the defeated South divided the North at the end of the war. Radicals, who passionately opposed slavery, took an expansive view of federal power, believing that the national government had the right to reshape southern society by breaking up the old plantation system and guaranteeing political and economic rights to the freed people. President Johnson, on the other hand, was a strong supporter of states' rights, opposed the expansion of federal power, and favored a lenient policy toward the former Confederate states. Politics also played a role in the conflicting experiments. Radicals hoped that former slaves would form the foundation of a powerful Republican Party in the South. Johnson, on the other hand, planned to use opposition to Reconstruction to build a new national coalition of moderate Democrats and Republicans.

The president's disdain for compromise and negotiation complicated his relationship with Congress and allowed the Radicals to seize control of Reconstruction policy in 1866. Once in power, the Radicals passed the Fourteenth and Fifteenth Amendments to the Constitution. Republican regimes in the South expanded democracy, built biracial public schools, and embarked on an ambitious public works program. The Radical experiment, however, quickly unraveled, confronted by a rejuvenated Democratic Party in the South that was willing to use violence and intimidation to regain power. At the same time, a steep depression, widespread charges of corruption, and concerns about government power divided the northern Republican Party. The Compromise of 1877 signaled the Republicans' retreat from Reconstruction. The Republicans had destroyed the slave system, but their experiment in securing basic economic and political rights for African-Americans remained incomplete.

African-Americans played a central role in defining the new meaning of freedom in the South. Their experiments cast aside old forms of deference to whites, built up community institutions, and restored ties among family members separated by slavery. Economic independence, however, remained elusive for most African-Americans. By 1880, nearly 75 percent of black southerners were working as sharecroppers.

Propagandists of the New South hoped to remake the southern economy in the image of the North, but southern realities limited economic experimentation. The region remained predominately rural and agricultural, tied to a single crop—cotton. Culturally, many whites celebrated the past at the same time that others questioned the underpinnings of southern society. No ambiguity, however, obscured the way the white South exercised power. The white "Redeemer" governments moved aggressively to limit the rights of African-Americans, prevented them from voting, and imposed a formal system of segregation that would dominate southern life well into the next century.

SUGGESTED READINGS

Eric Foner's *Reconstruction: America's Unfinished Revolution, 1863–1877* (1988) is an impressive synthesis of recent scholarship on all aspects of Reconstruction, with the experience of the freedmen as the central theme. *The Era of Reconstruction, 1865–1877* (1965) by Kenneth Stampp is the classic revisionist work on the period, dismissing the idea of Reconstruction as harsh and corrupt. James McPherson's *Ordeal by Fire: The Civil War and Reconstruction* (1967) includes a basic overview of the events and politics of the time.

Reconstruction under Lincoln's tenure is treated by Peyton McCrary in *Abraham Lincoln and Reconstruction: The Louisiana Experiment* (1978). He argues that Lincoln's primary aim was to restore the South to the Union as expediently as possible. His plan included little in the way of social reform because those in charge erroneously assumed that this would slow down the process. Louis Gerteis demonstrates the haphazard nature of wartime Reconstruction through an examination of the government's dealings with the former slaves in *From Contraband to Freedman: Federal Policy Toward Southern Blacks, 1861–1865* (1973).

Historians generally agree that Lincoln's plan is difficult to assess because it was largely unformed at the time of his death. They therefore have a better grasp on the policies of his successor, Andrew Johnson. Eric McKitrick leads off the barrage of criticism historians have heaped on Johnson with *Andrew Johnson and Reconstruction* (1966). He demonstrates how the president bungled the opportunity to create a moderate coalition through his insistence on a strict interpretation of the Constitution and on personal control. *Andrew Johnson and the Uses of Constitutional Power* (1980) by James Sefton places Johnson's rigid behavior on Reconstruction issues in the larger context of his life and personality. Hans Trefousse examines the impact of Johnson's impeachment on Reconstruction politics in *Impeachment of a President: Andrew Johnson and Reconstruction* (1975). He argues that the failure to remove Johnson forced the president into reckless opposition to Congress, putting limits on congressional attempts at reform.

The rise of the Radical Republicans is discussed by several historians. Edward L. Gambill's *Conservative Ordeal: Northern Democrats and Reconstruction, 1865–1868* (1981) demonstrates how factionalism within the Democratic Party destroyed its chances to mount serious opposition to the Radicals. Michael Les Benedict, in *A Compromise of Principle: Congressional Republicans and Reconstruction* (1974), looks at the inner workings of the Republican Party and finds that the split between moderates and Radicals was not over principles but over their political expediency. In *An American Crisis: Congress and Reconstruction, 1865–1867* (1963), W. R. Brock maintains that Radicals had early and widespread popular support, based primarily on their commitment to economic expansion and equal opportunity.

The collapse of congressional Reconstruction is the subject of William Gillette in *Retreat from Reconstruction, 1869–1879* (1979), a survey of national politics during the time that blames the Republican Party's lack of commitment to racial equality for Reconstruction's short life. In *The Radical Republicans and Reform in New York During Reconstruction* (1973), James Mohr examines Radical Republicans' substantial reform record in New York, which he claims foreshadowed progressivism there, and its destruction in the fight over black suffrage within the Republican Party. David Montgomery, author of *Beyond Equality: Labor and the Radical Republicans, 1862–1872* (1967), argues that the Radicals foundered on the issue of class, not race, dividing over labor policy. Ian Polakoff discusses the official end of Reconstruction in *The Politics of Inertia: The Election of 1876 and the End of Reconstruction* (1973). He argues that the high level of popular participation and factionalism in the parties left them without effective leadership to deal constructively with the disputed election of 1876.

The constitutional aspects of Reconstruction is treated by Harold Hyman in *A More Perfect Union: The Impact of the Civil War and Reconstruction on the Constitution* (1973), in which he demonstrates how the crises of war and reunion transformed the Constitution into a more dynamic document. Stanley Kutler examines the Supreme Court during this period in *The Judicial Power and Reconstruction Politics* (1968), countering the image of the Court as a foe of congressional Reconstruction. In *Emancipation and Equal Rights: Politics and Constitutionalism in the Civil War Era* (1978), Herman Belz evaluates Reconstruction from a constitutional perspective and judges it a success.

For discussion of northern political life in general during congressional Reconstruction, *The Press Gang: Newspapers and Politics, 1865–1878* (1994) by Mark Wahlgren Summers is an entertaining and insightful read. Brooks Simpson examines Grant's stance toward Reconstruction and his transition from soldier to politician in *Let Us Have Peace: Ulysses S. Grant and the Politics of War and Reconstruction, 1861–1868* (1991).

Willie Lee Rose's *Rehearsal for Reconstruction: The Port Royal Experiment* (1964) is perhaps the best examination of wartime Reconstruction in action. She focuses particularly on the experience of blacks and their relationship to white northerners trying to guide them into freedom. Leon Litwack's *Been in the Storm So Long: The Aftermath of Slavery* (1979) and Joel Williamson's *After Slavery: The Negro in South Carolina During Reconstruction* (1966) also discuss the former slaves' response to emancipation.

Examinations of Johnson's plan in the South further a negative view of the president. In *Reunion Without Compromise: The South and Reconstruction, 1865–1868* (1973), Michael Perman contends that Johnson and Congress encouraged southern defiance by giving the South too much choice and that it was this stubbornness that ultimately doomed presidential Reconstruction. Donald Nieman, in *To Set the Law in Motion: The Freedmen's Bureau and the Legal Rights of Blacks, 1865–1868* (1979), examines Johnson's role in the failure of the Freedmen's Bureau to defend adequately the rights of blacks. Dan Carter's *When the War Was Over: The Failure of Self-Reconstruction in the South, 1865–1867* (1985) contrasts with most of these works, portraying the southern white leaders during presidential Reconstruction not as reactionary ardent secessionists but as cautious conservatives.

Numerous studies have been done on the South during congressional Reconstruction. *The Road to Redemption: Southern Politics, 1869–1879* (1984), Michael Perman shows how division within each party in the South led to a merger of moderate factions by the end of Reconstruction. Steven Hahn examines the Reconstruction origins of southern populism in the transition of southern yeomen from subsistence to capitalist farming in *The Roots of Southern Populism: Yeoman Farmers and the Transformation of the Georgia Upcountry, 1850–1890* (1983). James Roark studies the impact of emancipation and Reconstruction on the former slaveholders in *Masters Without Slaves: Southern Planters in the Civil War and Reconstruction* (1977).

The African-American experience during congressional Reconstruction is covered by W. E. B. Du Bois's still classic *Black Reconstruction in America* (1935). More recently, Thomas Holt's *Black Over White: Negro Political Leadership in South Carolina During Reconstruction* (1977) and Edmund L. Drago's *Black Politicians and Reconstruction in Georgia* (1982) examine the experience of blacks in Reconstruction governments.

The role of southern violence in the demise of Reconstruction is discussed in *White Terror: The Ku Klux Klan Conspiracy and Southern Reconstruction* (1967) by Allen Trelease and *But There Was No Peace: The Role of Violence in the Politics of Reconstruction* (1984) by George Rable. Both books argue that the Republican Party died in the South as a result of a vigorous campaign of intimidation and murder on the part of southern whites.

C. Van Woodward's classic *Origins of the New South, 1877–1913* (1951) is still a valuable treatment, focusing on the rise of a business-oriented middle class in the South after the Civil War. Jonathan Weiner offers a different take in *Social Origins of the New South, 1860–1885* (1978). He argues that the New South evolved from the planter elite's rigid control over unskilled labor during the modernization process. Edward Ayers offers an insightful analysis in *The Promise of the New South: Life After Reconstruction* (1992). On the Lost Cause, see Gaines Foster's *The Ghosts of the Confederacy* (1989). Robert Kenzer examines the role of blacks in the economy of the urban South in *Enterprising Southerners* (1997).

The rise of Jim Crow is also discussed by C. Van Woodward in another classic, *The Strange Career of Jim Crow* (1955). He argues that the South only capitulated to racism once the forces of northern liberalism, southern conservatism, and southern radicalism declined in their efficacy in checking racial discrimination. Leon Litwack's *Trouble in Mind: Black Southerners in the Age of Jim Crow* (1998) is a comprehensive and moving account of the trials of African-Americans in the post-Reconstruction South. The perpetuation of black poverty after slavery is the subject of Jay Mandle's *Not Slave, Not Free: The African American Economic Experience Since the Civil War* (1992). He argues that the southern plantation system, responsible for the black economic condition, was simply revised after the war, becoming the equally enslaving sharecropping system.

Competing Voices

The Boundaries of Congressional Reconstruction

A Southern Critique of the Reconstruction Acts

Benjamin H. Hill, a former Confederate senator, gave this speech on July 16, 1867, in Atlanta. He was responding to the passage in March of the Reconstruction Acts, which eliminated the southern governments established under presidential Reconstruction and imposed military rule across the former Confederacy. His seething anger is directed at Congress, which he believed had overstepped its legal boundaries with its ambitious plan for transforming the South.

The people of the North honestly love the Constitution, but the leaders there hate it and intend to destroy it. . . .

By carrying out these measures you disfranchise your own people. Suppose we concede, for argument, that it is right to enfranchise all the negroes; if this be right, by what principle of law or morals do we disfranchise the white people? . . . In the face of the fact that a republican government can rest upon and be perpetuated only by the virtue and intelligence of the people, you propose to exclude the most intelligent from participating in the government forever! . . .

But you say that you are in favor of going into the Union, because if you do not your property will be confiscated. . . . I am ashamed to talk or use arguments about confiscation in time of peace! It is a war power, not known to international law except as a war power, to be used only in time of war, upon an enemy's goods! Confiscation in time of peace is neither more nor less than robbery! . . .

These bills propose at every step to abrogate the Constitution—trample upon the State and its laws—to blot out every hope—to perjure every man who accepts them, with every principle of honor, justice, and safety disregarded, trampled upon, and despised—all to perpetuate the power of their wicked authors. . . . That which is now proposed is *force*. It is proposed by men who do not live in this State, and whose agents do not live here; and it is sought to be accomplished by military power, but under the pretense of your sanction—not to please yourselves, but them. . . .

This whole scheme is in violation of all the issues of the war . . . and all the terms of surrender. More than a hundred thousand men abandoned Lee's army because they were assured that if they laid down their arms they would be in the Union again with all their rights as before. . . . The people—the soldiers of the United States—were then willing to fulfill the obligation; but the politicians intended to deceive you. . . .

My colored friends, will you receive a word of admonition? Of all the people, you will most need the protection of the law. . . . Do you believe that the man who is faithless to the Constitution will be faithful to you? . . . They promise you lands, and teach you to hate the Southern people, whom you have known always and who never deceived you. Are you foolish enough to believe you can get another man's land for nothing, and that the white people will give up their land without resistance?

If you get up strife between your race and the white race, do you not know you must perish? . . . You can have no safety in the Constitution and no peace except by cultivating relations of kindness with those who are fixed here, who need your services, and who are willing to protect you. . . .

Thaddeus Stevens Proposes Land Reform

Pennsylvania congressman Thaddeus Stevens was perhaps the most Radical of the Republicans. In his view, the Reconstruction Acts did not go far enough. He envisioned a complete overhaul of southern institutions and real political and economic opportunity for the freed slaves. In the midst of the debate over the Reconstruction Acts, on March 19, 1867, he introduced a land reform bill that would have given each freedman household forty acres of land. The bill was defeated.

. . . The cause of the war was slavery. We have liberated the slaves. It is our duty to protect them, and provide for them while they are unable to provide for themselves. . . .

Have we not a right, if we chose to go to that extent, to indemnify ourselves for the expenses and damaged caused by the war? We might make the property of the enemy pay the $4,000,000,000 which we have expended, as well as the damages inflicted on loyal men by confiscation and invasion, which might reach $1,000,000,000 more. This bill is merciful, asking less than one tenth of our just claims. . . .

The first section orders the confiscation of all the property belonging to the State governments, and the national government which made war upon us, and which we have conquered. . . .

The fourth section provides first that out of the lands thus confiscated each liberated slave who is a male adult, or the head of a family, shall have assigned to him a homestead of forty acres of land (with $100 to build a dwelling), which shall be held for them by trustees during their pupilage. Let us consider whether this is a just and politic provision.

Whatever may be the fate of the rest of the bill I must earnestly pray that this may not be defeated. On its success, in my judgment, depends not only the happiness and respectability of the colored race, but their very existence. Homesteads to them are far more valuable than the immediate right of suffrage, though both are their due.

Four million persons have just been freed from a condition of dependence, wholly unacquainted with business transactions, kept systematically in ignorance of all their rights and of the common elements of education, without which none of any race are competent to earn an honest living, to guard against the frauds which will always be practiced on the ignorant, or to judge of the most judicious manner of applying their labor. But few of them are mechanics, and none of them skilled manufacturers. They must necessarily, therefore, be the servants and the victims of others unless they are made in some measure independent of their wiser neighbors. . . .

Make them independent of the old masters so that they may not be compelled to work for them upon unfair terms, which can only be done by giving them a small tract of land to cultivate for themselves, and you remove all this danger. You also elevate the character of the freedman. Nothing is so likely to make a man a good citizen as to make him a freeholder. Nothing will so multiply the productions of the South as to divide it into small farms. Nothing will make men so industrious and moral as to let them feel that they are above want and are the owners of the soil which they till. . . .

I do not speak of their fidelity and services in this bloody war. I put it on the mere score of lawful earnings. They and their ancestors have toiled, not for years, but for ages, without one farthing of recompense. They have earned for their masters this very land and much more. . . .

Congress is dictating the terms of peace. . . . This bill is very merciful toward a cruel, outlawed belligerent, who, when their armies were dispersed, would gladly have compromised if their lives were saved. . . . ∎

Thaddeus Stevens, long an advocate for African-American rights, was a leader among both the Radical Republicans and the House of Representatives as a whole, admired even by those who were enraged by his strident style and unorthodox views. He and his fellow Radical Republicans saw in Reconstruction a "golden moment" not only to ensure the equality of blacks under the law, but to foment real change in the South through the destruction of the plantation system and the transformation of the freed slaves into small farmers, self-sufficient and upwardly mobile. On more than one occasion, Stevens introduced plans for the redistribution of southern land, at one time going as far as advocating the seizure of wealthy southerners' property by the federal government. Stevens' plans exemplified innovative social and political thinking, which not only included economic opportunity for the former slaves and the restructuring of southern society, but also envisioned using the federal government in unprecedented ways to accomplish these ends.

Stevens's ambitious ideas challenged existing views of federal power, which suggested that government could ensure legal, but not economic, equality of all its citizens. Even the Reconstruction Acts, which did pass into law, pressed the boundaries of federal power, as southerners were quick to point out. White southerners protested against the federal government's occupation of southern soil, its imposition of martial law, and its insistence on setting the terms of the states' readmission to the Union. After declaring they could secede from the Union, the white South now claimed it had never left and should not be treated as a conquered nation. The South felt it should be able to form new governments quickly, with little federal interference, and with minimal impact on southern institutions and traditions.

Questions for Analysis

1. Why does Hill call congressional Reconstruction unconstitutional? Do his claims have any merit? Explain.
2. Whom does he blame for this alleged assault on the Constitution?
3. What is Hill's advice to the freed slaves? Do you think he is sincere?
4. What are the provisions of Stevens's bill?
5. Why does Stevens believe Congress has the right to pass such a bill?
6. What reasons does he give to support the necessity of land reform?
7. How do you think our society might be different today had Reconstruction gone further? How would it be the same?

Documents

Declaration of Independence in Congress, July 4, 1776

When, in the course of human events, it becomes necessary for one people to dissolve the political bonds which have connected them with another, and to assume, among the powers of the earth, the separate and equal station to which the laws of nature and of nature's God entitle them, a decent respect to the opinions of mankind requires that they should declare the causes which impel them to the separation.

We hold these truths to be self-evident: That all men are created equal; that they are endowed by their Creator with certain unalienable rights; that among these are life, liberty, and the pursuit of happiness; that, to secure these rights, governments are instituted among men, deriving their just powers from the consent of the governed; that whenever any form of government becomes destructive of these ends, it is the right of the people to alter or to abolish it, and to institute new government, laying its foundation on such principles, and organizing its powers in such form, as to them shall seem most likely to effect their safety and happiness. Prudence, indeed, will dictate that governments long established should not be changed for light and transient causes; and accordingly all experience hath shown that mankind are more disposed to suffer, while evils are sufferable, than to right themselves by abolishing the forms to which they are accustomed. But when a long train of abuses and usurpations, pursuing invariably the same object, evinces a design to reduce them under absolute despotism, it is their right, it is their duty, to throw off such government, and to provide new guards for their future security. Such has been the patient sufferance of these colonies; and such is now the necessity which constrains them to alter their former systems of government. The history of the present King of Great Britain is a history of repeated injuries and usurpations, all having in direct object the establishment of an absolute tyranny over these states. To prove this, let facts be submitted to a candid world.

He has refused his assent to laws, the most wholesome and necessary for the public good.

He has forbidden his governors to pass laws of immediate and pressing importance, unless suspended in their operation till his assent should be obtained; and, when so suspended, he has utterly neglected to attend to them.

He has refused to pass other laws for the accommodation of large districts of people, unless those people would relinquish the right of representation in the legislature, a right inestimable to them, and formidable to tyrants only.

He has called together legislative bodies at places unusual, uncomfortable, and distant from the depository of their public records, for the sole purpose of fatiguing them into compliance with his measures.

He has dissolved representative houses repeatedly, for opposing, with manly firmness, his invasions on the rights of the people.

He has refused for a long time, after such dissolutions, to cause others to be elected; whereby the legislative powers, incapable of annihilation, have returned to the people at large for their exercise; the state remaining, in the mean time, exposed to all the dangers of invasions from without and convulsions within.

He has endeavored to prevent the population of these states; for that purpose obstructing the laws for naturalization of foreigners; refusing to pass others to encourage their migration hither, and raising the conditions of new appropriations of lands.

He has obstructed the administration of justice, by refusing his assent to laws for establishing judiciary powers.

He has made judges dependent on his will alone, for the tenure of their offices, and the amount and payment of their salaries.

He has erected a multitude of new offices, and sent hither swarms of officers to harass our people and eat out their substance.

He has kept among us, in times of peace, standing armies, without the consent of our legislatures.

He has affected to render the military independent of, and superior to, the civil power.

He has combined with others to subject us to a jurisdiction foreign to our constitution, and unacknowledged by our laws, giving his assent to their acts of pretended legislation:

For quartering large bodies of armed troops among us;

For protecting them, by a mock trial, from punishment for any murders which they should commit on the inhabitants of these states;

For cutting off our trade with all parts of the world;

For imposing taxes on us without our consent;

For depriving us, in many cases, of the benefits of trial by jury;

For transporting us beyond seas, to be tried for pretended offenses;

For abolishing the free system of English laws in a neighboring province, establishing therein an arbitrary government, and enlarging its boundaries, so as to render it at once an example and fit instrument for introducing the same absolute rule into these colonies;

For taking away our charters, abolishing our most valuable laws, and altering fundamentally the forms of our governments;

For suspending our own legislatures, and declaring themselves invested with power to legislate for us in all cases whatsoever.

He has abdicated government here, by declaring us out of his protection and waging war against us.

He has plundered our seas, ravaged our coasts, burned our towns, and destroyed the lives of our people.

He is at this time transporting large armies of foreign mercenaries to complete the works of death, desolation, and tyranny already begun with circumstances of cruelty and perfidy scarcely paralleled in the most barbarous ages, and totally unworthy the head of a civilized nation.

He has constrained our fellow-citizens, taken captive on the high seas, to bear arms against their country, to become the executioners of their friends and brethren, or to fall themselves by their hands.

He has excited domestic insurrection among us, and has endeavored to bring on the inhabitants of our frontiers the merciless Indian savages, whose known rule of warfare is an undistinguished destruction of all ages, sexes, and conditions.

In every stage of these oppressions we have petitioned for redress in the most humble terms; our repeated petitions have been answered only by repeated injury. A prince, whose character is thus marked by every act which may define a tyrant, is unfit to be the ruler of a free people.

Nor have we been wanting in our attentions to our British brethren. We have warned them, from time to time, of attempts by their legislature to extend an unwarrantable jurisdiction over us. We have reminded them of the circumstances of our emigration and settlement here. We have appealed to their native justice and magnanimity; and we have conjured them, by the ties of our common kindred, to disavow these usurpations, which would inevitably interrupt our connections and correspondence. They, too, have been deaf to the voice of justice and of consanguinity. We must, therefore, acquiesce in the necessity which denounces our separation, and hold them, as we hold the rest of mankind, enemies in war, in peace friends.

We, therefore, the representatives of the United States of America, in General Congress assembled, appealing to the Supreme Judge of the world for the rectitude of our intentions, do, in the name and by the authority of the good people of these colonies, solemnly publish and declare, that these United Colonies are, and of right ought to be, FREE AND INDEPENDENT STATES; that they are absolved from all allegiance to the British crown, and that all political connection between them and the state of Great Britain is, and ought to be, totally dissolved; and that, as free and independent states, they have full power to levy war, conclude peace, contract alliances, establish commerce, and do all other acts and things which independent states may of right do. And for the support of this declaration, with a firm reliance on the protection of Divine Providence, we mutually pledge to each other our lives, our fortunes, and our sacred honor.

Articles of Confederation

(The text of the Articles of Confederation can be found at http://college.hmco.com.)

Constitution of the United States of America and Amendments*

Preamble

We the people of the United States, in order to form a more perfect union, establish justice, insure domestic tranquillity, provide for the common defense, promote the general welfare, and secure the blessings of liberty to ourselves and our posterity, do ordain and establish this Constitution for the United States of America.

Article I

Section 1 All legislative powers herein granted shall be vested in a Congress of the United States, which shall consist of a Senate and a House of Representatives.

Section 2 The House of Representatives shall be composed of members chosen every second year by the people of the several States, and the electors in each State shall have the qualifications requisite for electors of the most numerous branch of the State Legislature.

No person shall be a Representative who shall not have attained to the age of twenty-five years, and been seven years a citizen of the United States, and who shall not, when elected, be an inhabitant of that State in which he shall be chosen.

Representatives and direct taxes shall be apportioned among the several States which may be included within this Union, according to their respective numbers, *which shall be determined by adding to the whole number of free persons, including those bound to service for a term of years and excluding Indians not taxed, three-fifths of all other persons.* The actual enumeration shall be made within three years after the first meeting of the Congress of the United States,

* Passages no longer in effect are printed in italic type.

and within every subsequent term of ten years, in such manner as they shall by law direct. The number of Representatives shall not exceed one for every thirty thousand, but each State shall have at least one Representative; *and until such enumeration shall be made, the State of New Hampshire shall be entitled to choose three, Massachusetts eight, Rhode Island and Providence Plantations one, Connecticut five, New York six, New Jersey four, Pennsylvania eight, Delaware one, Maryland six, Virginia ten, North Carolina five, South Carolina five, and Georgia three.*

When vacancies happen in the representation from any State, the Executive authority thereof shall issue writs of election to fill such vacancies.

The House of Representatives shall choose their Speaker and other officers; and shall have the sole power of impeachment.

Section 3 The Senate of the United States shall be composed of two Senators from each State, *chosen by the legislature thereof,* for six years; and each Senator shall have one vote.

Immediately after they shall be assembled in consequence of the first election, they shall be divided as equally as may be into three classes. The seats of the Senators of the first class shall be vacated at the expiration of the second year, of the second class at the expiration of the fourth year, and of the third class at the expiration of the sixth year, so that one-third may be chosen every second year; *and if vacancies happen by resignation or otherwise, during the recess of the legislature of any State, the Executive thereof may make temporary appointments until the next meeting of the legislature, which shall then fill such vacancies.*

No person shall be a Senator who shall not have attained to the age of thirty years, and been nine years a citizen of the United States, and who shall not, when elected, be an inhabitant of that State for which he shall be chosen.

The Vice-President of the United States shall be President of the Senate, but shall have no vote, unless they be equally divided.

The Senate shall choose their other officers, and also a President *pro tempore,* in the absence of the Vice-President, or when he shall exercise the office of President of the United States.

The Senate shall have the sole power to try all impeachments. When sitting for that purpose, they shall be on oath or affirmation. When the President of the United States is tried, the Chief Justice shall preside: and no person shall be convicted without the concurrence of two-thirds of the members present.

Judgment in cases of impeachment shall not extend further than to removal from the office, and disqualification to hold and enjoy any office of honor, trust or profit under the United States: but the party convicted shall nevertheless be liable and subject to indictment, trial, judgment and punishment, according to law.

Section 4 The times, places and manner of holding elections for Senators and Representatives shall be prescribed in each State by the legislature thereof; but the Congress may at any time by law make or alter such regulations, except as to the places of choosing Senators.

The Congress shall assemble at least once in every year, and such meeting *shall be on the first Monday in December, unless they shall by law appoint a different day.*

Section 5 Each house shall be the judge of the elections, returns and qualifications of its own members, and a majority of each shall constitute a quorum to do business; but a smaller number may adjourn from day to day, and may be authorized to compel the attendance of absent members, in such manner, and under such penalties, as each house may provide.

Each house may determine the rules of its proceedings, punish its members for disorderly behavior, and with the concurrence of two-thirds, expel a member.

Each house shall keep a journal of its proceedings, and from time to time publish the same, excepting such parts as may in their judgment require secrecy; and the yeas and nays of the members of either house on any question shall, at the desire of one-fifth of those present, be entered on the journal.

Neither house, during the session of Congress, shall, without the consent of the other, adjourn for more than three days, nor to any other place than that in which the two houses shall be sitting.

Section 6 The Senators and Representatives shall receive a compensation for their services, to be ascertained by law and paid out of the treasury of the United States. They shall in all cases except treason, felony and breach of the peace, be privileged from arrest during their attendance at the session of their respective houses, and in going to and returning from the same; and for any speech or debate in either house, they shall not be questioned in any other place.

No Senator or Representative shall, during the time for which he was elected, be appointed to any civil office under the authority of the United States, which shall have been created, or the emoluments whereof shall have been increased, during such time; and no person holding any office under the United States shall be a member of either house during his continuance in office.

Section 7 All bills for raising revenue shall originate in the House of Representatives; but the Senate may propose or concur with amendments as on other bills.

Every bill which shall have passed the House of Representatives and the Senate, shall, before it become a law, be presented to the President of the United States; if he approve he shall sign it, but if not he shall return it with objections to that house in which it originated, who shall enter the objections at large on their journal, and proceed to reconsider it. If after such reconsideration two-thirds of that house shall agree to pass the bill, it shall be sent, together with the objections, to the other house, by which it shall likewise be reconsidered, and, if approved by two-thirds of that house, it shall become a law. But in all such cases the votes of both houses shall be determined by yeas and nays, and the names of the persons voting for and against the bill shall be entered on the journal of each house respectively. If any bill shall not be returned by the President within ten days (Sundays excepted) after it shall have been presented to him, the same shall be a law, in like manner as if he had signed it, unless the Congress by their adjournment prevent its return, in which case it shall not be a law.

Every order, resolution, or vote to which the concurrence of the Senate and House of Representatives may be necessary (except on a question of adjournment) shall be presented to the President of the United States; and before the same shall take effect, shall be approved by him, or being disapproved by him, shall be repassed by two-thirds of the Senate and House of Representatives, according to the rules and limitations prescribed in the case of a bill.

Section 8 The Congress shall have power

To lay and collect taxes, duties, imposts, and excises, to pay the debts and provide for the common defense and general welfare of the United States; but all duties, imposts and excises shall be uniform throughout the United States;

To borrow money on the credit of the United States;

To regulate commerce with foreign nations, and among the several States, and with the Indian tribes;

To establish an uniform rule of naturalization, and uniform laws on the subject of bankruptcies throughout the United States;

To coin money, regulate the value thereof, and of foreign coin, and fix the standard of weights and measures;

To provide for the punishment of counterfeiting the securities and current coin of the United States;

To establish post offices and post roads;

To promote the progress of science and useful arts by securing for limited times to authors and inventors the exclusive right to their respective writings and discoveries;

To constitute tribunals inferior to the Supreme Court;

To define and punish piracies and felonies committed on the high seas and offenses against the law of nations;

To declare war, grant letters of marque and reprisal, and make rules concerning captures on land and water;

To raise and support armies, but no appropriation of money to that use shall be for a longer term than two years;

To provide and maintain a navy;

To make rules for the government and regulation of the land and naval forces;

To provide for calling forth the militia to execute the laws of the Union, suppress insurrections, and repel invasions;

To provide for organizing, arming, and disciplining the militia, and for governing such part of them as may be employed in the service of the United States, reserving to the States respectively the appointment of the officers, and the authority of training the militia according to the discipline prescribed by Congress;

To exercise exclusive legislation in all cases whatsoever, over such district (not exceeding ten miles square) as may, by cession of particular States, and the acceptance of Congress, become the seat of government of the United States, and to exercise like authority over all places purchased by the consent of the legislature of the State, in which the same shall be, for erection of forts, magazines, arsenals, dockyards, and other needful buildings; —and

To make all laws which shall be necessary and proper for carrying into execution the foregoing powers, and all other powers vested by this Constitution in the government of the United States, or in any department or officer thereof.

Section 9 *The migration or importation of such persons as any of the States now existing shall think proper to admit shall not be prohibited by the Congress prior to the year 1808; but a tax or duty may be imposed on such importation, not exceeding $10 for each person.*

The privilege of the writ of habeas corpus shall not be suspended, unless when in cases of rebellion or invasion the public safety may require it.

No bill of attainder or ex post facto law shall be passed.

No capitation, or other direct, tax shall be laid, unless in proportion to the census or enumeration herein before directed to be taken.

No tax or duty shall be laid on articles exported from any State.

No preference shall be given by any regulation of commerce or revenue to the ports of one State over those of another; nor shall vessels bound to, or from, one State, be obliged to enter, clear, or pay duties in another.

No money shall be drawn from the treasury, but in consequence of appropriations made by law; and a regular statement and account of the receipts and expenditures of all public money shall be published from time to time.

No title of nobility shall be granted by the United States: and no person holding any office of profit or trust under them, shall, without the consent of the Congress, accept of any present, emolument, office, or title, of any kind whatever, from any king, prince, or foreign state.

Section 10 No State shall enter into any treaty, alliance, or confederation; grant letters of marque and reprisal; coin money; emit bills of credit; make anything but gold and silver coin a tender in payment of debts; pass any bill of attainder, ex post facto law, or law impairing the obligation of contracts, or grant any title of nobility.

No State shall, without the consent of Congress, lay any imposts or duties on imports or exports, except what may be absolutely necessary for executing its inspection laws: and the net produce of all duties and imposts, laid by any State on imports or exports, shall be for the use of the treasury of the United States; and all such laws shall be subject to the revision and control of the Congress.

No State shall, without the consent of Congress, lay any duty of tonnage, keep troops or ships of war in time of peace, enter into any agreement or compact with another State, or with a foreign power, or engage in war, unless actually invaded, or in such imminent danger as will not admit of delay.

Article II

Section 1 The executive power shall be vested in a President of the United States of America. He shall hold his office during the term of four years, and, together with the Vice-President, chosen for the same term, be elected as follows:

Each State shall appoint, in such manner as the legislature thereof may direct, a number of electors, equal to the whole number of Senators and Representatives to which the State may be entitled in the Congress; but no Senator or Representative, or person holding an office of trust or profit under the United States, shall be appointed an elector.

The electors shall meet in their respective States, and vote by ballot for two persons, of whom one at least shall not be an inhabitant of the same State with themselves. And they shall make a list of all the persons voted for, and of the number of votes for each; which list they shall sign and certify, and transmit sealed to the seat of government of the United States, directed to the President of the Senate. The President of the Senate shall, in the presence of the Senate and House of Representatives, open all the certificates, and the votes shall then be counted. The person having the greatest number of votes shall be the President, if such number be a majority of the whole number of electors appointed; and if there be more than one who have such majority, and have an equal number of votes, then the House of Representatives shall immediately choose by ballot one of them for President; and if no person have a majority, then from the five highest on the list said house shall in like manner choose the President. But in choosing the President the votes shall be taken by States, the representation from each State having one vote; a quorum for this purpose shall consist of a member or members from two-thirds of the States, and a majority of all the States shall be necessary to a choice. In every case, after the choice of the President, the person having the greatest number of votes of the electors shall be the Vice-President. But if there should remain two or more who have equal votes, the Senate shall choose from them by ballot the Vice-President.

The Congress may determine the time of choosing the electors and the day on which they shall give their votes; which day shall be the same throughout the United States.

No person except a natural-born citizen, *or a citizen of the United States at the time of the adoption of this Constitution,* shall be eligible to the office of President; neither shall any person be eligible to that office who shall not have attained to the age of thirty-five years, and been fourteen years a resident within the United States.

In cases of the removal of the President from office or of his death, resignation, or inability to discharge the powers and duties of the said office, the same shall devolve on the Vice-President, and the Congress may by law provide for the case of removal, death, resignation, or inability, both of the President and Vice-President, declaring what officer shall then act as President, and such officer shall act accordingly, until the disability be removed, or a President shall be elected.

The President shall, at stated times, receive for his services a compensation, which shall neither be increased nor diminished during the period for which he shall have been elected, and he shall not receive within that period any other emolument from the United States, or any of them.

Before he enter on the execution of his office, he shall take the following oath or affirmation:—"I do solemnly swear (or affirm) that I will faithfully execute the office of the President of the United States, and will to the best of my ability preserve, protect and defend the Constitution of the United States."

Section 2 The President shall be commander in chief of the army and navy of the United States, and of the militia of the several States, when called into the actual service of the United States; he may require the opinion, in writing, of the principal officer in each of the executive departments, upon any subject relating to the duties of their respective offices, and he shall have power to grant reprieves and pardons for offenses against the United States, except in cases of impeachment.

He shall have power, by and with the advice and consent of the Senate, to make treaties, provided two-thirds of the Senators present concur; and he shall nominate, and by and with the advice and consent of the Senate, shall appoint ambassadors, other public ministers and consuls, judges of the Supreme Court, and all other officers of the United States, whose appointments are not herein otherwise provided for, and which shall be established by law: but Congress may by law vest the appointment of such inferior officers, as they think proper, in the President alone, in the courts of law, or in the heads of departments.

The President shall have power to fill up all vacancies that may happen during the recess of the Senate, by granting commissions which shall expire at the end of their next session.

Section 3 He shall from time to time give to the Congress information of the state of the Union, and recommend to their consideration such measures as he shall judge necessary and expedient; he may, on extraordinary occasions, convene both houses, or either of them, and in case of disagreement between them, with respect to the time of adjournment, he may adjourn them to such time as he shall think proper; he shall receive ambassadors and other public ministers; he shall take care that the laws be faithfully executed, and shall commission all the officers of the United States.

Section 4 The President, Vice-President and all civil officers of the United States shall be removed from office on impeachment for, and on conviction of, treason, bribery, or other high crimes and misdemeanors.

Article III

Section 1 The judicial power of the United States shall be vested in one Supreme Court, and in such inferior courts as the Congress may from time to time ordain and establish. The judges, both of the Supreme and inferior courts, shall hold their offices during good behavior, and shall, at stated times, receive for their services a compensation which shall not be diminished during their continuance in office.

Section 2 The judicial power shall extend to all cases, in law and equity, arising under this Constitution, the laws of the United States, and treaties made, or which shall be made, under their authority;—to all cases affecting ambassadors, other public ministers and consuls;—to all cases of admiralty and maritime jurisdiction;—to controversies to which the United States shall be a party;—to controversies between two or more States;—*between a State and citizens of another State;*—between citizens of different States;—between citizens of the same State claiming lands under grants of different States, and between a State, or the citizens thereof, and foreign states, citizens or subjects.

In all cases affecting ambassadors, other public ministers and consuls, and those in which a State shall be party, the Supreme Court shall have original jurisdiction. In all the other cases before mentioned, the Supreme Court shall have appellate jurisdiction, both as to law and fact, with such exceptions, and under such regulations, as the Congress shall make.

The trial of all crimes, except in cases of impeachment, shall be by jury; and such trial shall be held in the State where said crimes shall have been committed; but when not committed within any State, the trial shall be at such place or places as the Congress may by law have directed.

Section 3 Treason against the United States shall consist only in levying war against them, or in adhering to their enemies, giving them aid and comfort. No person shall be convicted of treason unless on the testimony of two witnesses to the same overt act, or on confession in open court.

The Congress shall have power to declare the punishment of treason, but no attainder of treason shall work corruption of blood, or forfeiture except during the life of the person attainted.

Article IV

Section 1 Full faith and credit shall be given in each State to the public acts, records, and judicial proceedings of every other State. And the Congress may by general laws prescribe the manner in which such acts, records, and proceedings shall be proved, and the effect thereof.

Section 2 The citizens of each State shall be entitled to all privileges and immunities of citizens in the several States.

A person charged in any State with treason, felony, or other crime, who shall flee from justice, and be found in another State, shall on demand of the executive authority of the State from which he fled, be delivered up, to be removed to the State having jurisdiction of the crime.

No person held to service or labor in one State, under the laws thereof, escaping into another, shall, in consequence of any law or regulation therein, be discharged from such service or labor, but shall be delivered up on claim of the party to whom such service or labor may be due.

Section 3 New States may be admitted by the Congress into this Union; but no new State shall be formed or erected within the jurisdiction of any other State; nor any State be formed by the junction of two or more States, or parts of States, without the consent of the legislatures of the States concerned as well as of the Congress.

The Congress shall have power to dispose of and make all needful rules and regulations respecting the territory or other property belonging to the United States; and nothing in this Constitution shall be so construed as to prejudice any claims of the United States, or of any particular State.

Section 4 The United States shall guarantee to every State in this Union a republican form of government, and shall protect each of them against invasion; and on application of the legislature, or of the executive (when the legislature cannot be convened), against domestic violence.

Article V

The Congress, whenever two-thirds of both houses shall deem it necessary, shall propose amendments to this Constitution, or, on the application of the legislatures of two-thirds of the several States, shall call a convention for proposing amendments, which, in either case, shall be valid to all intents and purposes, as part of this Constitution, when ratified by the legislatures of three-fourths of the several States, or by conventions in three-fourths thereof, as the one or the other mode of ratification may be proposed by the Congress; provided *that no amendments which may be made prior to the year one thousand eight hundred and eight shall in any manner affect the first and fourth clauses in the ninth section of the first article;* and that no State, without its consent, shall be deprived of its equal suffrage in the Senate.

Article VI

All debts contracted and engagements entered into, before the adoption of this Constitution, shall be as valid against the United States under this Constitution, as under the Confederation.

This Constitution, and the laws of the United States which shall be made in pursuance thereof; and all treaties made, or which shall be made, under the authority of the United States, shall be the supreme law of the land; and the judges in every State shall be bound thereby, anything in the Constitution or laws of any State to the contrary notwithstanding.

The Senators and Representatives before mentioned, and the members of the several State legislatures, and all executive and judicial officers, both of the United States and of the several States, shall be bound by oath or affirmation to support this Constitution; but no religious test shall ever be required as a qualification to any office or public trust under the United States.

Article VII

The ratification of the conventions of nine States shall be sufficient for the establishment of this Constitution between the States so ratifying the same.

Done in Convention by the unanimous consent of the States present, the seventeenth day of September in the year of our Lord one thousand seven hundred and eighty-seven and of the Independence of the United States of America the twelfth. In witness whereof we have hereunto subscribed our names.

Amendments to the Constitution*

Amendment I

Congress shall make no law respecting an establishment of religion, or prohibiting the free exercise thereof; or abridging the freedom of speech, or of the press; or the right of the people peaceably to assemble, and to petition the government for a redress of grievances.

* The first ten Amendments (the Bill of Rights) were adopted in 1791.

Amendment II

A well-regulated militia being necessary to the security of a free State, the right of the people to keep and bear arms shall not be infringed.

Amendment III

No soldier shall, in time of peace, be quartered in any house without the consent of the owner, nor in time of war, but in a manner to be prescribed by law.

Amendment IV

The right of the people to be secure in their persons, houses, papers, and effects, against unreasonable searches and seizures, shall not be violated, and no warrants shall issue but upon probable cause, supported by oath or affirmation, and particularly describing the place to be searched, and the persons or things to be seized.

Amendment V

No person shall be held to answer for a capital, or otherwise infamous crime, unless on a presentment or indictment of a grand jury, except in cases arising in the land or naval forces, or in the militia, when in actual service in time of war or public danger; nor shall any person be subject for the same offense to be twice put in jeopardy of life or limb; nor shall be compelled in any criminal case to be a witness against himself, nor be deprived of life, liberty, or property, without due process of law; nor shall private property be taken for public use without just compensation.

Amendment VI

In all criminal prosecutions, the accused shall enjoy the right to a speedy and public trial, by an impartial jury of the State and district wherein the crime shall have been committed, which district shall have been previously ascertained by law, and to be informed of the nature and cause of the accusation; to be confronted with the witnesses against him; to have compulsory process for obtaining witnesses in his favor, and to have the assistance of counsel for his defense.

Amendment VII

In suits at common law, where the value in controversy shall exceed twenty dollars, the right of trial by jury shall be preserved, and no fact tried by a jury shall be otherwise reexamined in any court of the United States, than according to the rules of the common law.

Amendment VIII

Excessive bail shall not be required, nor excessive fines imposed, nor cruel and unusual punishments inflicted.

Amendment IX

The enumeration in the Constitution, of certain rights, shall not be construed to deny or disparage others retained by the people.

Amendment X

The powers not delegated to the United States by the Constitution, nor prohibited by it to the States, are reserved to the States respectively, or to the people.

Amendment XI

[Adopted 1798]

The judicial power of the United States shall not be construed to extend to any suit in law or equity, commenced or prosecuted against one of the United States by citizens of another State, or by citizens or subjects of any foreign state.

Amendment XII

[Adopted 1804]

The electors shall meet in their respective States, and vote by ballot for President and Vice-President, one of whom, at least, shall not be an inhabitant of the same State with themselves; they shall name in their ballots the person voted for as President, and in distinct ballots the person voted for as Vice-President, and they shall make distinct lists of all persons voted for as President, and of all persons voted for as Vice-President, and of the number of votes for each, which lists they shall sign and certify, and transmit sealed to the seat of government of the United States, directed to the President of the Senate;—the President of the Senate shall, in the presence of the Senate and House of Representatives, open all the certificates and the votes shall then be counted;—the person having the greatest number of votes for President shall be the President, if such number be a majority of the whole number of electors appointed; and if no person have such majority, then from the persons having the highest numbers not exceeding three on the list of those voted for as President, the House of Representatives shall choose immediately, by ballot, the President. But in choosing the President, the votes shall be taken by States, the representation from each State having one vote; a quorum for this purpose shall consist of a member or members from two-thirds of the States, and a majority of all the States shall be necessary to a choice. And if the House of Representatives shall not choose a President whenever the right of choice shall devolve upon them, before *the fourth day of March* next following, then the Vice-President shall act as President, as in the case of the death or other constitutional disability of the President.

The person having the greatest number of votes as Vice-President shall be the Vice-President, if such number be a majority of the whole number of electors appointed; and if no person have a majority, then from the two highest numbers on the list the Senate shall choose the Vice-President; a quorum for the purpose shall consist of two-thirds of the whole number of Senators, and a majority of the whole number shall be necessary to a choice. But no person constitutionally ineligible to the office of President shall be eligible to that of Vice-President of the United States.

Amendment XIII

[Adopted 1865]

Section 1 Neither slavery nor involuntary servitude, except as a punishment for crime whereof the party shall have been duly convicted, shall exist within the United States, or any place subject to their jurisdiction.

Section 2 Congress shall have power to enforce this article by appropriate legislation.

Amendment XIV

[Adopted 1868]

Section 1 All persons born or naturalized in the United States, and subject to the jurisdiction thereof, are citizens of the United States and of the State wherein they reside. No State shall make or enforce any law which shall abridge the privileges or immunities of citizens of the United States; nor shall any State deprive any person of life, liberty, or property, without due process of law; nor deny to any person within its jurisdiction the equal protection of the laws.

Section 2 Representatives shall be apportioned among the several States according to their respective numbers, counting the whole number of persons in each State, excluding Indians not taxed. But when the right to vote at any election for the choice of Electors for President and Vice-President of the United States, Representatives in Congress, the executive and judicial officers of a State, or the members of the legislature thereof, is denied to any of the male inhabitants of such State, being twenty-one years of age and citizens of the United States, or in any way abridged, except for participation in rebellion, or other crime, the basis of representation therein shall be reduced in the proportion which the number of such male citizens shall bear to the whole number of male citizens twenty-one years of age in such State.

Section 3 No person shall be a Senator or Representative in Congress, or Elector of President and Vice-President, or hold any office, civil or military, under the United States, or under any State, who, having previously taken an oath, as a member of Congress, or as an officer of the United States, or as a member of any State legislature, or as an executive or judicial officer of any State, to support the Constitution of the United States, shall have engaged in insurrection or rebellion against the same, or given aid or comfort to the enemies thereof. Congress may, by a vote of two-thirds of each house, remove such disability.

Section 4 The validity of the public debt of the United States, authorized by law, including debts incurred for payment of pensions and bounties for services in suppressing insurrection or rebellion, shall not be questioned. But neither the United States nor any State shall assume or pay any debt or obligation incurred in aid of insurrection or rebellion against the United States, or any claim for the loss of emancipation of any slave; but all such debts, obligations, and claims shall be held illegal and void.

Section 5 The Congress shall have power to enforce, by appropriate legislation, the provisions of this article.

Amendment XV

[Adopted 1870]

Section 1 The right of citizens of the United States to vote shall not be denied or abridged by the United States or by any State on account of race, color, or previous condition of servitude.

Section 2 The Congress shall have power to enforce this article by appropriate legislation.

Amendment XVI

[Adopted 1913]

The Congress shall have power to lay and collect taxes on incomes, from whatever source derived, without apportionment among the several States, and without regard to any census or enumeration.

Amendment XVII

[Adopted 1913]

Section 1 The Senate of the United States shall be composed of two Senators from each State, elected by the people thereof, for six years; and each Senator shall have one vote. The electors in each State shall have the qualifications requisite for electors of [voters for] the most numerous branch of the State legislatures.

Section 2 When vacancies happen in the representation of any State in the Senate, the executive authority of such State shall issue writs of election to fill such vacancies: Provided, that the Legislature of any State may empower the executive thereof to make temporary appointments until the people fill the vacancies by election as the Legislature may direct.

Section 3 This amendment shall not be so construed as to affect the election or term of any Senator chosen before it becomes valid as part of the Constitution.

Amendment XVIII

[Adopted 1919; Repealed 1933]

Section 1 After one year from the ratification of this article the manufacture, sale, or transportation of intoxicating liquors within, the importation thereof into, or the exportation thereof from the United States and all territory subject to the jurisdiction thereof, for beverage purposes, is hereby prohibited.

Section 2 The Congress and the several States shall have concurrent power to enforce this article by appropriate legislation.

Section 3 This article shall be inoperative unless it shall have been ratified as an amendment to the Constitution by the legislatures of the several States, as provided by the Constitution, within seven years from the date of the submission thereof to the States by the Congress.

Amendment XIX

[Adopted 1920]

Section 1 The right of citizens of the United States to vote shall not be denied or abridged by the United States or by any State on account of sex.

Section 2 The Congress shall have power to enforce this article by appropriate legislation.

Amendment XX

[Adopted 1933]

Section 1 The terms of the President and Vice-President shall end at noon on the 20th day of January, and the terms of Senators and Representatives at noon on the 3rd day of January, of the years in which such terms would have ended if this article had not been ratified; and the terms of their successors shall then begin.

Section 2 The Congress shall assemble at least once in every year, and such meeting shall begin at noon on the 3d day of January, unless they shall by law appoint a different day.

Section 3 If, at the time fixed for the beginning of the term of the President, the President-elect shall have died, the Vice-President–elect shall become President. If a President shall not have been chosen before the time fixed for the beginning of his term, or if the President-elect shall have failed to qualify, then the Vice-President–elect shall act as President until a President shall have qualified; and the Congress may by law provide for the case wherein neither a President-elect nor a Vice-President–elect shall have qualified, declaring who shall then act as President, or the manner in which one who is to act shall be selected, and such persons shall act accordingly until a President or Vice-President shall have qualified.

Section 4 The Congress may by law provide for the case of the death of any of the persons from whom the House of Representatives may choose a President whenever the right of choice shall have devolved upon them, and for the case of the death of any of the persons from whom the Senate may choose a Vice-President whenever the right of choice shall have devolved upon them.

Section 5 Sections 1 and 2 shall take effect on the 15th day of October following the ratification of this article.

Section 6 This article shall be inoperative unless it shall have been ratified as an amendment to the Constitution by the Legislatures of three-fourths of the several States within seven years from the date of its submission.

Amendment XXI

[Adopted 1933]

Section 1 The eighteenth article of amendment to the Constitution of the United States is hereby repealed.

Section 2 The transportation or importation into any State, Territory, or Possession of the United States for delivery or use therein of intoxicating liquors, in violation of the laws thereof, is hereby prohibited.

Section 3 This article shall be inoperative unless it shall have been ratified as an amendment to the Constitution by conventions in the several States, as provided in the Constitution, within seven years from the date of submission thereof to the States by the Congress.

Amendment XXII

[Adopted 1951]

Section 1 No person shall be elected to the office of President more than twice, and no person who has held the office of President, or acted as President, for more than two years of a term to which some other person was elected President shall be elected to the office of President more than once. But this article shall not apply to any person holding the office of President when this article was proposed by the Congress, and shall not prevent any person who may be holding the office of President, or acting as President, during the term within which this article becomes operative from holding the office of President or acting as President during the remainder of such term.

Section 2 This article shall be inoperative unless it shall have been ratified as an amendment to the Constitution by the legislatures of three-fourths of the several States within seven years from the date of its submission to the States by the Congress.

Amendment XXIII

[Adopted 1961]

Section 1 The District constituting the seat of Government of the United States shall appoint in such manner as the Congress may direct:

A number of electors of President and Vice-President equal to the whole number of Senators and Representatives in Congress to which the District would be entitled if it were a State, but in no event more than the least populous State; they shall be in addition to those appointed by the States, but they shall be considered for the purposes of the election of President and Vice-President, to be electors appointed by a State; and they shall meet in the District and perform such duties as provided by the twelfth article of amendment.

Section 2 The Congress shall have the power to enforce this article by appropriate legislation.

Amendment XXIV

[Adopted 1964]

Section 1 The right of citizens of the United States to vote in any primary or other election for President or Vice-President, for electors for President or Vice-President, or for Senator or Representative in Congress, shall not be denied or abridged by the United States or any State by reason of failure to pay any poll tax or other tax.

Section 2 The Congress shall have the power to enforce this article by appropriate legislation.

Amendment XXV

[Adopted 1967]

Section 1 In case of the removal of the President from office or of his death or resignation, the Vice-President shall become President.

Section 2 Whenever there is a vacancy in the office of the Vice-President, the President shall nominate a Vice-President who shall take office upon confirmation by a majority vote of both Houses of Congress.

Section 3 Whenever the President transmits to the President pro tempore of the Senate and the Speaker of the House of Representatives his written declaration that he is unable to discharge the powers and duties of his office, and until he transmits to them a written declaration to the contrary, such powers and duties shall be discharged by the Vice-President as Acting President.

Section 4 Whenever the Vice-President and a majority of either the principal officers of the executive departments or of such other body as Congress may by law provide, transmit to the President pro tempore of the Senate and the Speaker of the House of Representatives their written declaration that the President is unable to discharge the powers and duties of his office, the Vice-President shall immediately assume the powers and duties of the office as Acting President.

Thereafter, when the President transmits to the President pro tempore of the Senate and the Speaker of the House of Representatives his written declaration that no inability exists, he shall resume the powers and duties of his office unless the Vice-President and a majority of either the principal officers of the executive department[s] or of such other body as Congress may by law provide, transmit within four days to the President pro tempore of the Senate and the Speaker of the House of Representatives their written declaration that the President is unable to discharge the powers and duties of his office. Thereupon Congress shall decide the issue, assembling within forty-eight hours for that purpose if not in session. If the Congress, within twenty-one days after receipt of the latter written declaration, or, if Congress is not in session, within twenty-one days after Congress is required to assemble, determines by two-thirds vote of both Houses that the President is unable to discharge the powers and duties of his office, the Vice-President shall continue to discharge the same as Acting President; otherwise, the President shall resume the powers and duties of his office.

Amendment XXVI

[Adopted 1971]

Section 1 The right of citizens of the United States, who are eighteen years of age or older, to vote shall not be denied or abridged by the United States or by any State on account of age.

Section 2 The Congress shall have power to enforce this article by appropriate legislation.

Amendment XXVII

[Adopted 1992]

No law, varying the compensation for the services of the Senators and Representatives, shall take effect, until an election of Representatives shall have intervened.

A Statistical Profile of America

POPULATION OF THE UNITED STATES

Year	Number of States	Population	Percent Increase	Population Per Square Mile	Percent Urban/ Rural	Percent Male/ Female	Percent White/ Non-white	Persons Per House-hold	Median Age
1790	13	3,929,214		4.5	5.1/94.9	NA/NA	80.7/19.3	5.79	NA
1800	16	5,308,483	35.1	6.1	6.1/93.9	NA/NA	81.1/18.9	NA	NA
1810	17	7,239,881	36.4	4.3	7.3/92.7	NA/NA	81.0/19.0	NA	NA
1820	23	9,638,453	33.1	5.5	7.2/92.8	50.8/49.2	81.6/18.4	NA	16.7
1830	24	12,866,020	33.5	7.4	8.8/91.2	50.8/49.2	81.9/18.1	NA	17.2
1840	26	17,069,453	32.7	9.8	10.8/89.2	50.9/49.1	83.2/16.8	NA	17.8
1850	31	23,191,876	35.9	7.9	15.3/84.7	51.0/49.0	84.3/15.7	5.55	18.9
1860	33	31,443,321	35.6	10.6	19.8/80.2	51.2/48.8	85.6/14.4	5.28	19.4
1870	37	39,818,449	26.6	13.4	25.7/74.3	50.6/49.4	86.2/13.8	5.09	20.2
1880	38	50,155,783	26.0	16.9	28.2/71.8	50.9/49.1	86.5/13.5	5.04	20.9
1890	44	62,947,714	25.5	21.2	35.1/64.9	51.2/48.8	87.5/12.5	4.93	22.0
1900	45	75,994,575	20.7	25.6	39.6/60.4	51.1/48.9	87.9/12.1	4.76	22.9
1910	46	91,972,266	21.0	31.0	45.6/54.4	51.5/48.5	88.9/11.1	4.54	24.1
1920	48	105,710,620	14.9	35.6	51.2/48.8	51.0/49.0	89.7/10.3	4.34	25.3
1930	48	122,775,046	16.1	41.2	56.1/43.9	50.6/49.4	89.8/10.2	4.11	26.4
1940	48	131,669,275	7.2	44.2	56.5/43.5	50.2/49.8	89.8/10.2	3.67	29.0
1950	48	150,697,361	14.5	50.7	64.0/36.0	49.7/50.3	89.5/10.5	3.37	30.2
1960	50	179,323,175	18.5	50.6	69.9/30.1	49.3/50.7	88.6/11.4	3.33	29.5
1970	50	203,302,031	13.4	57.6	73.6/26.4	48.7/51.3	87.6/12.4	3.14	28.0
1980	50	226,542,199	11.4	64.1	73.7/26.3	48.6/51.4	85.9/14.1	2.75	30.0
1990	50	248,718,301	9.8	70.3	75.2/24.8	48.7/51.3	83.9/16.1	2.63	32.8
1998	50	270,299,000	8.0	76.4	NA	48.9/51.1	82.5/17.5	2.62	35.2

NA = Not available.

IMMIGRANTS TO THE UNITED STATES

Immigration Totals by Decade

Years	Number
1820–1830	151,824
1831–1840	599,125
1841–1850	1,713,251
1851–1860	2,598,214
1861–1870	2,314,824
1871–1880	2,812,191
1881–1890	5,246,613
1891–1900	3,687,546
1901–1910	8,795,386
1911–1920	5,735,811
1921–1930	4,107,209
1931–1940	528,431
1941–1950	1,035,039
1951–1960	2,515,479
1961–1970	3,321,677
1971–1980	4,493,314
1981–1990	7,338,062
1991–1998	7,605,068
Total	64,599,082

THE AMERICAN WORKER

Year	Total Number of Workers	Males as Percent of Total Workers	Females as Percent of Total Workers	Married Women as Percent of Female Workers	Female Workers as Percent of Female Population	Percent of Labor Force Unemployed
1870	12,506,000	85	15	NA	NA	NA
1880	17,392,000	85	15	NA	NA	NA
1890	23,318,000	83	17	14	19	4 (1894 = 18)
1900	29,073,000	82	18	15	21	5
1910	38,167,000	79	21	25	25	6
1920	41,614,000	79	21	23	24	5 (1921 = 12)
1930	48,830,000	78	22	29	25	9 (1933 = 25)
1940	53,011,000	76	24	36	27	15 (1944 = 1)
1950	62,208,000	72	28	52	31	5.3
1960	69,628,000	67	33	55	38	5.5
1970	82,771,000	62	38	59	43	4.9
1980	106,940,000	58	42	55	52	7.1
1990	125,840,000	55	45	54	58	5.6
1998	137,673,000	54	46	53	60	4.5

NA = Not available.

THE AMERICAN ECONOMY

Year	Gross National Product (GNP) and Gross Domestic Product (GDP)[a] (in $ billions)	Steel Production (in tons)	Corn Production (millions of bushels)	Automobiles Registered	New Housing Starts	Foreign Trade (in $ millions)	
						Exports	Imports
1790	NA	NA	NA	NA	NA	20	23
1800	NA	NA	NA	NA	NA	71	91
1810	NA	NA	NA	NA	NA	67	85
1820	NA	NA	NA	NA	NA	70	74
1830	NA	NA	NA	NA	NA	74	71
1840	NA	NA	NA	NA	NA	132	107
1850	NA	NA	592[d]	NA	NA	152	178
1860	NA	13,000	839[e]	NA	NA	400	362
1870	7.4[b]	77,000	1,125	NA	NA	451	462
1880	11.2[c]	1,397,000	1,707	NA	NA	853	761
1890	13.1	4,779,000	1,650	NA	328,000	910	823
1900	18.7	11,227,000	2,662	8,000	189,000	1,499	930
1910	35.3	28,330,000	2,853	458,300	387,000 (1918 = 118,000)	1,919	1,646
1920	91.5	46,183,000	3,071	8,131,500	247,000 (1925 = 937,000)	8,664	5,784
1930	90.7	44,591,000	2,080	23,034,700	330,000 (1933 = 93,000)	4,013	3,500
1940	100.0	66,983,000	2,457	27,465,800	603,000 (1944 = 142,000)	4,030	7,433
1950	286.5	96,836,000	3,075	40,339,000	1,952,000	9,997	8,954
1960	506.5	99,282,000	4,314	61,682,300	1,365,000	19,659	15,093
1970	1,016.0	131,514,000	4,200	89,279,800	1,434,000	42,681	40,356
1980	2,819.5	111,835,000	6,600	121,601,000	1,292,000	220,626	244,871
1990	5,764.9	98,906,000	7,933	143,550,000	1,193,000	394,030	485,453
1998	8,511.0	107,600,000	9,761	129,749,000[f]	1,617,000	682,100	911,900

[a]In December 1991 the Bureau of Economic Analysis of the U.S. government began featuring Gross Domestic Product rather than Gross National Product as the primary measure of U.S. production. [b]Figure is average for 1869–1878. [c]Figure is average for 1879–1888. [d]Figure for 1849. [e]Figure for 1859. [f]Figure for 1997. NA = Not available.

Presidential Elections

Year	Number of States	Candidates	Parties	Popular Vote	% of Popular Vote	Electoral Vote	% Voter Participation[a]
1789	10	**George Washington**	No party			69	
		John Adams	designations			34	
		Other candidates				35	
1792	15	**George Washington**	No party			132	
		John Adams	designations			77	
		George Clinton				50	
		Other candidates				5	
1796	16	**John Adams**	Federalist			71	
		Thomas Jefferson	Democratic-Republican			68	
		Thomas Pinckney	Federalist			59	
		Aaron Burr	Democratic-Republican			30	
		Other candidates				48	
1800	16	**Thomas Jefferson**	Democratic-Republican			73	
		Aaron Burr	Democratic-Republican			73	
		John Adams	Federalist			65	
		Charles C. Pinckney	Federalist			64	
		John Jay	Federalist			1	
1804	17	**Thomas Jefferson**	Democratic-Republican			162	
		Charles C. Pinckney	Federalist			14	
1808	17	**James Madison**	Democratic-Republican			122	
		Charles C. Pinckney	Federalist			47	
		George Clinton	Democratic-Republican			6	
1812	18	**James Madison**	Democratic-Republican			128	
		De Witt Clinton	Federalist			89	
1816	19	**James Monroe**	Democratic-Republican			183	
		Rufus King	Federalist			34	
1820	24	**James Monroe**	Democratic-Republican			231	
		John Quincy Adams	Independent Republican			1	

PRESIDENTIAL ELECTIONS (*Continued*)

Year	Number of States	Candidates	Parties	Popular Vote	% of Popular Vote	Elec-toral Vote	% Voter Partici-pation[a]
1824	24	**John Quincy Adams**	Democratic-Republican	108,740	30.5	84	26.9
		Andrew Jackson	Democratic-Republican	153,544	43.1	99	
		Henry Clay	Democratic-Republican	47,136	13.2	37	
		William H. Crawford	Democratic-Republican	46,618	13.1	41	
1828	24	**Andrew Jackson**	Democratic	647,286	56.0	178	57.6
		John Quincy Adams	National Republican	508,064	44.0	83	
1832	24	**Andrew Jackson**	Democratic	701,780	54.2	219	55.4
		Henry Clay	National Republican	484,205	37.4	49	
		Other candidates		107,988	8.0	18	
1836	26	**Martin Van Buren**	Democratic	764,176	50.8	170	57.8
		William H. Harrison	Whig	550,816	36.6	73	
		Hugh L. White	Whig	146,107	9.7	26	
1840	26	**William H. Harrison**	Whig	1,274,624	53.1	234	80.2
		Martin Van Buren	Democratic	1,127,781	46.9	60	
1844	26	**James K. Polk**	Democratic	1,338,464	49.6	170	78.9
		Henry Clay	Whig	1,300,097	48.1	105	
		James G. Birney	Liberty	62,300	2.3		
1848	30	**Zachary Taylor**	Whig	1,360,967	47.4	163	72.7
		Lewis Cass	Democratic	1,222,342	42.5	127	
		Martin Van Buren	Free Soil	291,263	10.1		
1852	31	**Franklin Pierce**	Democratic	1,601,117	50.9	254	69.6
		Winfield Scott	Whig	1,385,453	44.1	42	
		John P. Hale	Free-Soil	155,825	5.0		
1856	31	**James Buchanan**	Democratic	1,832,955	45.3	174	78.9
		John C. Frémont	Republican	1,339,932	33.1	114	
		Millard Fillmore	American	871,731	21.6	8	
1860	33	**Abraham Lincoln**	Republican	1,865,593	39.8	180	81.2
		Stephen A. Douglas	Democratic	1,382,713	29.5	12	
		John C. Breckinridge	Democratic	848,356	18.1	72	
		John Bell	Constitutional Union	592,906	12.6	39	
1864	36	**Abraham Lincoln**	Republican	2,206,938	55.0	212	73.8
		George B. McClellan	Democratic	1,803,787	45.0	21	
1868	37	**Ulysses S. Grant**	Republican	3,013,421	52.7	214	78.1
		Horatio Seymour	Democratic	2,706,829	47.3	80	

PRESIDENTIAL ELECTIONS (*Continued*)

Year	Number of States	Candidates	Parties	Popular Vote	% of Popular Vote	Electoral Vote	% Voter Participation[a]
1872	37	**Ulysses S. Grant**	Republican	3,596,745	55.6	286	71.3
		Horace Greeley	Democratic	2,843,446	43.9	[b]	
1876	38	**Rutherford B. Hayes**	Republican	4,036,572	48.0	185	81.8
		Samuel J. Tilden	Democratic	4,284,020	51.0	184	
1880	38	**James A. Garfield**	Republican	4,453,295	48.5	214	79.4
		Winfield S. Hancock	Democratic	4,414,082	48.1	155	
		James B. Weaver	Greenback-Labor	308,578	3.4		
1884	38	**Grover Cleveland**	Democratic	4,879,507	48.5	219	77.5
		James G. Blaine	Republican	4,850,293	48.2	182	
		Benjamin F. Butler	Greenback-Labor	175,370	1.8		
		John P. St. John	Prohibition	150,369	1.5		
1888	38	**Benjamin Harrison**	Republican	5,447,129	47.9	233	79.3
		Grover Cleveland	Democratic	5,537,857	48.6	168	
		Clinton B. Fisk	Prohibition	249,506	2.2		
		Anson J. Streeter	Union Labor	146,935	1.3		
1892	44	**Grover Cleveland**	Democratic	5,555,426	46.1	277	74.7
		Benjamin Harrison	Republican	5,182,690	43.0	145	
		James B. Weaver	People's	1,029,846	8.5	22	
		John Bidwell	Prohibition	264,133	2.2		
1896	45	**William McKinley**	Republican	7,102,246	51.1	271	79.3
		William J. Bryan	Democratic	6,492,559	47.7	176	
1900	45	**William McKinley**	Republican	7,218,491	51.7	292	73.2
		William J. Bryan	Democratic; Populist	6,356,734	45.5	155	
		John C. Wooley	Prohibition	208,914	1.5		
1904	45	**Theodore Roosevelt**	Republican	7,628,461	57.4	336	65.2
		Alton B. Parker	Democratic	5,084,223	37.6	140	
		Eugene V. Debs	Socialist	402,283	3.0		
		Silas C. Swallow	Prohibition	258,536	1.9		
1908	46	**William H. Taft**	Republican	7,675,320	51.6	321	65.4
		William J. Bryan	Democratic	6,412,294	43.1	162	
		Eugene V. Debs	Socialist	420,793	2.8		
		Eugene W. Chafin	Prohibition	253,840	1.7		
1912	48	**Woodrow Wilson**	Democratic	6,296,547	41.9	435	58.8
		Theodore Roosevelt	Progressive	4,118,571	27.4	88	
		William H. Taft	Republican	3,486,720	23.2	8	
		Eugene V. Debs	Socialist	900,672	6.0		
		Eugene W. Chafin	Prohibition	206,275	1.4		
1916	48	**Woodrow Wilson**	Democratic	9,127,695	49.4	277	61.6
		Charles E. Hughes	Republican	8,533,507	46.2	254	

PRESIDENTIAL ELECTIONS (*Continued*)

Year	Number of States	Candidates	Parties	Popular Vote	% of Popular Vote	Electoral Vote	% Voter Participation[a]
		A. L. Benson	Socialist	585,113	3.2		
		J. Frank Hanly	Prohibition	220,506	1.2		
1920	48	**Warren G. Harding**	Republican	16,143,407	60.4	404	49.2
		James M. Cox	Democratic	9,130,328	34.2	127	
		Eugene V. Debs	Socialist	919,799	3.4		
		P. P. Christensen	Farmer-Labor	265,411	1.0		
1924	48	**Calvin Coolidge**	Republican	15,718,211	54.0	382	48.9
		John W. Davis	Democratic	8,385,283	28.8	136	
		Robert M. La Follette	Progressive	4,831,289	16.6	13	
1928	48	**Herbert C. Hoover**	Republican	21,391,993	58.2	444	56.9
		Alfred E. Smith	Democratic	15,016,169	40.9	87	
1932	48	**Franklin D. Roosevelt**	Democratic	22,809,638	57.4	472	56.9
		Herbert C. Hoover	Republican	15,758,901	39.7	59	
		Norman Thomas	Socialist	881,951	2.2		
1936	48	**Franklin D. Roosevelt**	Democratic	27,752,869	60.8	523	61.0
		Alfred M. Landon	Republican	16,674,665	36.5	8	
		William Lemke	Union	882,479	1.9		
1940	48	**Franklin D. Roosevelt**	Democratic	27,307,819	54.8	449	62.5
		Wendell L. Wilkie	Republican	22,321,018	44.8	82	
1944	48	**Franklin D. Roosevelt**	Democratic	25,606,585	53.5	432	55.9
		Thomas E. Dewey	Republican	22,014,745	46.0	99	
1948	48	**Harry S Truman**	Democratic	24,179,345	49.6	303	53.0
		Thomas E. Dewey	Republican	21,991,291	45.1	189	
		J. Strom Thurmond	States' Rights	1,176,125	2.4	39	
		Henry A. Wallace	Progressive	1,157,326	2.4		
1952	48	**Dwight D. Eisenhower**	Republican	33,936,234	55.1	442	63.3
		Adlai E. Stevenson	Democratic	27,314,992	44.4	89	
1956	48	**Dwight D. Eisenhower**	Republican	35,590,472	57.6	457	60.6
		Adlai E. Stevenson	Democratic	26,022,752	42.1	73	
1960	50	**John F. Kennedy**	Democratic	34,226,731	49.7	303	62.8
		Richard M. Nixon	Republican	34,108,157	49.5	219	
1964	50	**Lyndon B. Johnson**	Democratic	43,129,566	61.1	486	61.7
		Barry M. Goldwater	Republican	27,178,188	38.5	52	
1968	50	**Richard M. Nixon**	Republican	31,785,480	43.4	301	60.6
		Hubert H. Humphrey	Democratic	31,275,166	42.7	191	
		George C. Wallace	American Independent	9,906,473	13.5	46	
1972	50	**Richard M. Nixon**	Republican	47,169,911	60.7	520	55.2
		George S. McGovern	Democratic	29,170,383	37.5	17	
		John G. Schmitz	American	1,099,482	1.4		

PRESIDENTIAL ELECTIONS (*Continued*)

Year	Number of States	Candidates	Parties	Popular Vote	% of Popular Vote	Electoral Vote	% Voter Participation[a]
1976	50	**James E. Carter**	Democratic	40,830,763	50.1	297	53.5
		Gerald R. Ford	Republican	39,147,793	48.0	240	
1980	50	**Ronald W. Reagan**	Republican	43,904,153	50.7	489	52.6
		James E. Carter	Democratic	35,483,883	41.0	49	
		John B. Anderson	Independent	5,720,060	6.6	0	
		Ed Clark	Libertarian	921,299	1.1	0	
1984	50	**Ronald W. Reagan**	Republican	54,455,075	58.8	525	53.3
		Walter F. Mondale	Democratic	37,577,185	40.6	13	
1988	50	**George H. W. Bush**	Republican	48,886,097	53.4	426	50.1
		Michael S. Dukakis	Democratic	41,809,074	45.6	111[c]	
1992	50	**William J. Clinton**	Democratic	44,909,326	43.0	370	55.2
		George H. W. Bush	Republican	39,103,882	37.4	168	
		H. Ross Perot	Independent	19,741,048	18.9	0	
1996	50	**William J. Clinton**	Democratic	47,402,357	49.2	379	49.1
		Robert J. Dole	Republican	39,196,755	40.7	159	
		H. Ross Perot	Reform	8,085,402	8.4	0	
		Ralph Nader	Green	684,902	0.7	0	
2000	50	**George W. Bush**	Republican	50,456,169	48.0	271	50.7
		Albert Gore	Democratic	50,996,116	49.0	267	
		Ralph Nader	Green	2,783,728	2.7	0	

Candidates receiving less than 1 percent of the popular vote have been omitted. Thus the percentage of popular vote given for any election year may not total 100 percent. Before the passage of the Twelfth Amendment in 1804, the Electoral College voted for two presidential candidates; the runner-up became vice president. Before 1824, most presidential electors were chosen by state legislatures, not by popular vote.

[a]Percent of voting-age population casting ballots. [b]Greeley died shortly after the election; the electors supporting him then divided their votes among minor candidates. [c]One elector from West Virginia cast her Electoral College presidential ballot for Lloyd Bentsen, the Democratic Party's vice-presidential candidate.

Presidents and Vice Presidents

1.	President	**George Washington**	1789–1797
	Vice President	John Adams	1789–1797
2.	President	**John Adams**	1797–1801
	Vice President	Thomas Jefferson	1797–1801
3.	President	**Thomas Jefferson**	1801–1809
	Vice President	Aaron Burr	1801–1805
	Vice President	George Clinton	1805–1809
4.	President	**James Madison**	1809–1817
	Vice President	George Clinton	1809–1813
	Vice President	Elbridge Gerry	1813–1817
5.	President	**James Monroe**	1817–1825
	Vice President	Daniel Tompkins	1817–1825
6.	President	**John Quincy Adams**	1825–1829
	Vice President	John C. Calhoun	1825–1829
7.	President	**Andrew Jackson**	1829–1837
	Vice President	John C. Calhoun	1829–1833
	Vice President	Martin Van Buren	1833–1837
8.	President	**Martin Van Buren**	1837–1841
	Vice President	Richard M. Johnson	1837–1841
9.	President	**William H. Harrison**	1841
	Vice President	John Tyler	1841
10.	President	**John Tyler**	1841–1845
	Vice President	None	
11.	President	**James K. Polk**	1845–1849
	Vice President	George M. Dallas	1845–1849
12.	President	**Zachary Taylor**	1849–1850
	Vice President	Millard Fillmore	1849–1850
13.	President	**Millard Fillmore**	1850–1853
	Vice President	None	
14.	President	**Franklin Pierce**	1853–1857
	Vice President	William R. King	1853–1857
15.	President	**James Buchanan**	1857–1861
	Vice President	John C. Breckinridge	1857–1861
16.	President	**Abraham Lincoln**	1861–1865
	Vice President	Hannibal Hamlin	1861–1865
	Vice President	Andrew Johnson	1865

PRESIDENTS AND VICE PRESIDENTS (*Continued*)		
17. President	**Andrew Johnson**	1865–1869
Vice President	None	
18. President	**Ulysses S. Grant**	1869–1877
Vice President	Schuyler Colfax	1869–1873
Vice President	Henry Wilson	1873–1877
19. President	**Rutherford B. Hayes**	1877–1881
Vice President	William A. Wheeler	1877–1881
20. President	**James A. Garfield**	1881
Vice President	Chester A. Arthur	1881
21. President	**Chester A. Arthur**	1881–1885
Vice President	None	
22. President	**Grover Cleveland**	1885–1889
Vice President	Thomas A. Hendricks	1885–1889
23. President	**Benjamin Harrison**	1889–1893
Vice President	Levi P. Morton	1889–1893
24. President	**Grover Cleveland**	1893–1897
Vice President	Adlai E. Stevenson	1893–1897
25. President	**William McKinley**	1897–1901
Vice President	Garret A. Hobart	1897–1901
Vice President	Theodore Roosevelt	1901
26. President	**Theodore Roosevelt**	1901–1909
Vice President	Charles Fairbanks	1905–1909
27. President	**William H. Taft**	1909–1913
Vice President	James S. Sherman	1909–1913
28. President	**Woodrow Wilson**	1913–1921
Vice President	Thomas R. Marshall	1913–1921
29. President	**Warren G. Harding**	1921–1923
Vice President	Calvin Coolidge	1921–1923
30. President	**Calvin Coolidge**	1923–1929
Vice President	Charles G. Dawes	1925–1929
31. President	**Herbert C. Hoover**	1929–1933
Vice President	Charles Curtis	1929–1933
32. President	**Franklin D. Roosevelt**	1933–1945
Vice President	John N. Garner	1933–1941
Vice President	Henry A. Wallace	1941–1945
Vice President	Harry S Truman	1945
33. President	**Harry S Truman**	1945–1953
Vice President	Alben W. Barkley	1949–1953
34. President	**Dwight D. Eisenhower**	1953–1961
Vice President	Richard M. Nixon	1953–1961

PRESIDENTS AND VICE PRESIDENTS (*Continued*)

35.	President	**John F. Kennedy**	1961–1963
	Vice President	Lyndon B. Johnson	1961–1963
36.	President	**Lyndon B. Johnson**	1963–1969
	Vice President	Hubert H. Humphrey	1965–1969
37.	President	**Richard M. Nixon**	1969–1974
	Vice President	Spiro T. Agnew	1969–1973
	Vice President	Gerald R. Ford	1973–1974
38.	President	**Gerald R. Ford**	1974–1977
	Vice President	Nelson A. Rockefeller	1974–1977
39.	President	**James E. Carter**	1977–1981
	Vice President	Walter F. Mondale	1977–1981
40.	President	**Ronald W. Reagan**	1981–1989
	Vice President	George H. W. Bush	1981–1989
41.	President	**George H. W. Bush**	1989–1993
	Vice President	J. Danforth Quayle	1989–1993
42.	President	**William J. Clinton**	1993–2001
	Vice President	Albert Gore	1993–2001
43.	President	**George W. Bush**	2001–
	Vice President	Richard Cheney	2001–

For a complete list of Presidents, Vice Presidents, and Cabinet Members, go to http://college.hmco.com.

Text Credits

pages 37–39: Samuel Eliot Morison, ed. and trans. *Journals and Other Documents on the Life and Voyages of Christopher Columbus,* Heritage, New York, 1963, pp. 151–155.

pages 79–81: Excerpts from Francis A. McNutt, *Bartholomew De Las Casas: His Life, His Apostolate, and His Writings,* G. P. Putnam's Sons, New York:, 1970, pp. 314–321. Reprinted by permission of Penguin Putnam, Inc.

Index